T0181899

Lecture Notes in Computer Science

Lecture Notes in Artificial Intelligence   14338

Founding Editor

Jörg Siekmann

Series Editors

Randy Goebel, *University of Alberta, Edmonton, Canada*
Wolfgang Wahlster, *DFKI, Berlin, Germany*
Zhi-Hua Zhou, *Nanjing University, Nanjing, China*

The series Lecture Notes in Artificial Intelligence (LNAI) was established in 1988 as a topical subseries of LNCS devoted to artificial intelligence.

The series publishes state-of-the-art research results at a high level. As with the LNCS mother series, the mission of the series is to serve the international R & D community by providing an invaluable service, mainly focused on the publication of conference and workshop proceedings and postproceedings.

Alexey Karpov · K. Samudravijaya ·
K. T. Deepak · Rajesh M. Hegde ·
Shyam S. Agrawal · S. R. Mahadeva Prasanna
Editors

Speech and Computer

25th International Conference, SPECOM 2023
Dharwad, India, November 29 – December 2, 2023
Proceedings, Part I

 Springer

Editors
Alexey Karpov 🆔
St. Petersburg Federal Research Center
of the Russian Academy of Sciences
St. Petersburg, Russia

K. T. Deepak
Indian Institute of Information Technology
Dharwad
Dharwad, India

Shyam S. Agrawal
KIIT Group of Colleges
Gurugram, India

K. Samudravijaya 🆔
Koneru Lakshmaiah Education Foundation
Vaddeswaram, India

Rajesh M. Hegde
Indian Institute of Technology Dharwad
Dharwad, India

S. R. Mahadeva Prasanna 🆔
Indian Institute of Technology Dharwad
Dharwad, India

ISSN 0302-9743   ISSN 1611-3349 (electronic)
Lecture Notes in Artificial Intelligence
ISBN 978-3-031-48308-0   ISBN 978-3-031-48309-7 (eBook)
https://doi.org/10.1007/978-3-031-48309-7

LNCS Sublibrary: SL7 – Artificial Intelligence

This Springer imprint is published by the registered company Springer Nature Switzerland AG
The registered company address is: Gewerbestrasse 11, 6330 Cham, Switzerland

Paper in this product is recyclable.

SPECOM 2023 Preface

The International Conference on Speech and Computer (SPECOM) has become a regular event since the first SPECOM held in St. Petersburg, Russia, in October 1996. The SPECOM conference series was established 27 years ago by the St. Petersburg Institute for Informatics and Automation of the Russian Academy of Sciences (SPIIRAS).

SPECOM is a conference with a long tradition that attracts researchers in the area of speech technology, including automatic speech recognition and understanding, text-to-speech synthesis, and speaker and language recognition, as well as related domains like digital speech processing, natural language processing, text analysis, computational paralinguistics, multi-modal speech, and data processing or human-computer interaction. The SPECOM conference is an ideal platform for know-how exchange – especially for experts working on highly inflectional languages – including both under-resourced and regular well-resourced languages.

In its long history, the SPECOM conference was organized alternately by the St. Petersburg Federal Research Center of the Russian Academy of Sciences (SPC RAS)/SPIIRAS and by the Moscow State Linguistic University (MSLU) in their home towns. Furthermore, in 1997 it was organized by the Cluj-Napoca subsidiary of the Research Institute for Computer Technique (Romania), in 2005 and 2015 by the University of Patras (in Patras and Athens, Greece), in 2011 by the Kazan Federal University (in Kazan, Russia), in 2013 by the University of West Bohemia (in Pilsen, Czech Republic), in 2014 by the University of Novi Sad (in Novi Sad, Serbia), in 2016 by the Budapest University of Technology and Economics (in Budapest, Hungary), in 2017 by the University of Hertfordshire (in Hatfield, UK), in 2018 by the Leipzig University of Telecommunications (in Leipzig, Germany), in 2019 by the Bogaziçi University (in Istanbul, Turkey), in 2020 and 2021 by SPC RAS/SPIIRAS (fully online), in 2022 by the KIIT (in Gurugram, India).

SPECOM 2023 was the twenty-fifth event in the series, this year we celebrated the silver jubilee of the conference. SPECOM 2023 was organized jointly by IIT Dharwad, IIIT Dharwad, NIT Goa, KLE Tech, and KIIT Gurugram. The conference was held during November 29 – December 2, 2023, in a hybrid format, mostly in-person in Hubli-Dharwad, Karnataka, India at Denissons Hotel and online via video conferencing. SPECOM 2023 was sponsored and supported by McAfee, IndSCA, ARM-SOFTECH.AIR, TiHAN, ASM Solutions, the International Speech Communication Association (ISCA) and some other organizations.

This year, beside the regular technical sessions, three special sessions were organized: "Industrial Speech and Language Technology", "Speech Processing and Speech Technology for Under Resourced Languages", and Students Special Session on Speech Analysis. In addition, the one-day Satellite Workshop "Speaker and Language Identification, Verification, and Diarization" was organized by the National Institute of Technology Goa on 2nd December 2023.

During SPECOM 2023, four keynote lectures were given by Bhiksha Raj (Carnegie Mellon University, USA) on "Learning from weak and noisy labels", Visar Berisha (Arizona State University, USA) on "Translating clinical speech analytics from the lab to the clinic: challenges and opportunities", S. Umesh (IIT Madras, India) on "Speech and Language Research For Indian Languages" and Satoshi Nakamura (Nara Institute of Science and Technology, Japan) on "Modeling Simultaneous Speech Translation". In addition, two keynote talks were given at the Satellite Workshop on "Speaker and Language Identification, Verification, and Diarization" by Hema A. Murthy (IIT Madras, India) on "Signal Processing guided Machine Learning" and Oldřich Plchot (Brno University of Technology, Czech Republic) on "Current and emerging trends in extracting speaker embeddings".

This volume contains a collection of submitted papers presented at SPECOM 2023, which were thoroughly reviewed by members of the Program Committee and additional reviewers consisting of more than 120 specialists in the conference topic areas. In total, 94 full papers out of 174 papers submitted for SPECOM 2023 were selected by the Program Committee for presentation at the main conference, the special sessions and the satellite workshop, as well as for inclusion in two volumes of SPECOM 2023 proceedings. Theoretical and more general contributions were presented in common plenary sessions. Problem-oriented sessions as well as panel discussions brought together specialists in niche problem areas with the aim of exchanging knowledge and skills resulting from research projects of all kinds.

We would like to express our gratitude to all authors for providing their papers on time, to the members of the SPECOM 2023 Program Committee for their careful reviews and paper selection, and to the editors and correctors for their hard work in preparing two volumes of the conference proceedings. Special thanks are due to the members of the SPECOM 2023 Organizing Committee for their tireless effort and enthusiasm during the conference organization. We are also grateful to IIT Dharwad, IIIT Dharwad, NIT Goa, KLE Tech, and KIIT Gurugram for organizing and hosting the jubilee 25th International Conference on Speech and Computer SPECOM 2023 in Dharwad, India.

November 2023

Alexey Karpov
K. Samudravijaya
K. T. Deepak
Rajesh M. Hegde
Shyam S. Agrawal
S. R. Mahadeva Prasanna

Organization

The jubilee 25th International Conference on Speech and Computer (SPECOM 2023) was organized by IIT Dharwad, IIIT Dharwad, NIT Goa, KLE Tech, and KIIT Gurugram in Dharwad, Karnataka, India. The conference website is: https://www.iitdh.ac.in/spe com-2023/.

General Chairs

B. Yegnanarayana	IIIT Hyderabad, India
Shyam S. Agrawal	KIIT Group of Colleges, Gurugram, India

Program Committee Chairs

Alexey Karpov	St. Petersburg Federal Research Center of the Russian Academy of Sciences, Russia
K. Samudravijaya	Koneru Lakshmaiah Education Foundation, India
K. T. Deepak	IIIT Dharwad, India
Rajesh M. Hegde	IIT Dharwad, India

Program Committee

Chinmayananda A.	IIIT Dharwad, India
Ajish K. Abraham	All India Institute of Speech and Hearing, India
Nagaraj Adiga	Samsung R&D Bangalore, India
Jahangir Alam	Computer Research Institute of Montreal, Canada
Paavo Alku	Aalto University, Finland
Gerasimos Arvanitis	University of Patras, Greece
Elias Azarov	Belarusian State University of Informatics and Radioelectronics, Belarus
Bharathi B.	SSN College of Engineering, India
Nagaratna B. Chittaragi	Siddaganga Institute of Technology, India
Dinesh Babu Jayagopi	IIIT Bangalore, India
Joyanta Basu	CDAC, Kolkata, India
Milana Bojanić	University of Novi Sad, Serbia
Eric Castelli	International Research Center MICA, Vietnam
Vladimir Chuchupal	Federal Research Center "Computer Science and Control" of the Russian Academy of Sciences, Russia

Liliya Komalova	Moscow State Linguistic University, Russia
Sunil Kumar Kopparapu	Tata Consultancy Services Ltd., India
Evgeny Kostyuchenko	Tomsk State University of Control Systems and Radioelectronics, Russia
Andrew Krizhanovsky	Institute of Applied Mathematical Research of the Karelian Research Centre of the Russian Academy of Sciences, Russia
Mohammad Azharuddin Laskar	Armsoftech Pvt Ltd., India
Benjamin Lecouteux	Université Grenoble Alpes, France
Natalia Loukachevitch	Research Computing Center of Moscow State University, Russia
Elena Lyakso	St. Petersburg State University, Russia
Olesia Makhnytkina	ITMO University, Russia
Maria De Marsico	Sapienza University of Rome, Italy
Yuri Matveev	ITMO University, Russia
Peter Mihajlik	Budapest University of Technology and Economics, Hungary
Nikolay Mikhaylovskiy	Higher IT School of Tomsk State University, Russia
Nobuaki Minematsu	University of Tokyo, Japan
Ganesh S. Mirishkar	IIIT Hyderabad, India
Jagabandhu Mishra	IIT Dharwad, India
Manjunath Mulimani	Tampere University, Finland
Ludek Muller	University of West Bohemia, Czech Republic
Satoshi Nakamura	Nara Institute of Science and Technology, Japan
Géza Németh	Budapest University of Technology and Economics, Hungary
Ruban Nersisson	VIT University, India
Oliver Niebuhr	University of Southern Denmark, Denmark
Dariya Novokhrestova	Tomsk State University of Control Systems and Radioelectronics, Russia
Sergey Novoselov	STC-innovations Ltd., Russia
Stavros Ntalampiras	University of Milan, Italy
Aparna P.	NITK, India
Vasuki P.	SSNCE, India
Win Pa	University of Computer Studies, Yangon, Myanmar
Nick A. Petrovsky	Belarusian State University of Informatics and Radioelectronics, Belarus
Branislav Popović	University of Novi Sad, Serbia
Vsevolod Potapov	Lomonosov Moscow State University, Russia
Rodmonga Potapova	Moscow State Linguistic University, Russia
Saswati Rabha	IIT Guwahati, India

Padmanabhan Rajan	IIT Mandi, India
Kumaraswamy Ramaswamy	Siddaganga Institute of Technology, India
Aleksei Romanenko	STC Ltd., Russia
Sergey Rybin	ITMO University, Russia
Dmitry Ryumin	St. Petersburg Federal Research Center of the Russian Academy of Sciences, Russia
Albert Ali Salah	Utrecht University, The Netherlands
Priyankoo Sarmah	Indian Institute of Technology Guwahati, India
Andrey Savchenko	Sber AI Lab, Russia
Björn Schuller	University of Augsburg, Germany/Imperial College London, UK
Milan Sečujski	University of Novi Sad, Serbia
Guruprasad Seshadri	NXP India Pvt. Ltd., India
Nirmesh Shah	Sony Research India, India
Ajay Kumar Sharma	HCL Technologies Ltd., India
Rajib Sharma	IIIT Dharwad, India
Tatiana Sherstinova	HSE University, St. Petersburg, Russia
Nickolay Shmyrev	Alpha Cephei Inc., Russia
Ingo Siegert	Otto von Guericke University, Germany
Pavel Skrelin	St. Petersburg State University, Russia
Tatiana Sokoreva	Moscow State Linguistic University, Russia
Valery Solovyev	Kazan Federal University, Russia
Victor Sorokin	Institute for Information Transmission Problems of the Russian Academy of Sciences, Russia
Ajay Srinivasamurthy	Amazon Alexa, India
Siniša Suzić	University of Novi Sad, Serbia
Ivan Tashev	Microsoft, USA
Veena Thenkanidiyoor	NIT Goa, India
Laszlo Toth	RGAI, Hungary
Isabel Trancoso	INESC ID Lisboa/IST, Portugal
Jan Trmal	Johns Hopkins University, USA
Moakala Tzudir	IIT Dharwad, India
Vasilisa Verkhodanova	University of Groningen, Campus Fryslan, The Netherlands
Deepu Vijayasenan	NIT-K, India
Anil Kumar Vuppala	IIIT Hyderabad, India
Jainath Yadav	Central University of Bihar, India
Chiranjeevi Yarra	IIITH, India
Zeynep Yucel	Okayama University, Japan
Jerneja Zganec Gros	Alpineon Research and Development Ltd., Slovenia

Organizing Committee

S. R. Mahadeva Prasanna (Chair)	IIT Dharwad, India
Suryakanth V. Gangashetty (Chair)	K L University, India
Ayush Agarwal	McAfee, India
Konjengbam Anand	IIT Dharwad, India
Ananya Angra	IIT Mandi, India
Lalaram Arya	IIT Dharwad, India
Alexander Axyonov	SPC RAS, Russia
Prashanth Bannulmath	IIIT Dharwad, India
Satish Chikkamath	KLE Hubli, India
Amartya R. Chowdhury	IIT Dharwad, India
Dileep A. D.	IIT Mandi, India
Ashwini Dasare	IIIT Dharwad, India
Govind Divakaran	KL University, India
Akilesh Dubay	KL University, India
Amruth Ashok Gadag	IIIT Dharwad, India
Namitha Gokavi	IIIT Dharwad, India
Urvashi Goswami	IIT Mandi, India
Pradyoth Hegde	IIIT Dharwad, India
Denis Ivanko	SPC RAS, Russia
Ildar Kagirov	SPC RAS, Russia
Sishir Kalita	Armsoftech.AIR, India
Alexey Karpov	SPC RAS, Russia
Kanika Kaur	KIIT, Gurugram, India
Kumar Kaustubh	IIT Dharwad, India
Irina Kipyatkova	SPC RAS, Russia
Sujeet Kumar	IIT Mandi, India
Jagabandhu Mishra	IIT Dharwad, India
Sougata Mukherjee	IIT Dharwad, India
Muralikrishna	Manipal Academy of Higher Education, India
Rishith Sadashiv T. N.	IIT Dharwad, India
S. R. Nirmala	KLE Hubli, India
Prakash Pawar	IIIT Dharwad, India
Tonmoy Rajkhowa	IIT Dharwad, India
Dmitry Ryumin	SPC RAS, Russia
Elena Ryumina	SPC RAS, Russia
Sunil Saumya	IIIT Dharwad, India
Kartikay Sharma	KIIT, Gurugram, India
Rajib Sharma	IIIT Dharwad, India
Swapnil Sontakke	IIIT Dharwad, India

Additional Reviewers

Abderrahim Fathan
Jovan Galić
Nikša Jakovljević
Prasanna Kumar
Maxim Markitantov
Rohith Mars
Tijana Nosek

Meghna Pandharipande
Elena Ryumina
Nikola Simić
Pratik Singh
Mikhail Uzdiaev
Alena Velichko
Yang Xiao

Contents – Part I

Automatic Speech Recognition

Extreme Learning Layer: A Boost for Spoken Digit Recognition
with Spiking Neural Networks 3
   Ivan Peralta, Nanci Odetti, and Hugo L. Rufiner

EMO-AVSR: Two-Level Approach for Audio-Visual Emotional Speech
Recognition 18
   Denis Ivanko, Elena Ryumina, Dmitry Ryumin, Alexandr Axyonov,
   Alexey Kashevnik, and Alexey Karpov

Significance of Audio Quality in Speech-to-Text Translation Systems 32
   Tonmoy Rajkhowa, Amartya Roy Chowdhury,
   and S. R. Mahadeva Prasanna

Everyday Conversations: A Comparative Study of Expert Transcriptions
and ASR Outputs at a Lexical Level 43
   Tatiana Sherstinova, Rostislav Kolobov, and Nikolay Mikhaylovskiy

Improving Automatic Speech Recognition with Dialect-Specific Language
Models 57
   Raj Gothi and Preeti Rao

Emotional Speech Recognition of Holocaust Survivors with Deep Neural
Network Models for Russian Language 68
   Liudmila Bukreeva, Daria Guseva, Mikhail Dolgushin,
   Vera Evdokimova, and Vasilisa Obotnina

Computational Paralinguistics

Aggregation Strategies of Wav2vec 2.0 Embeddings for Computational
Paralinguistic Tasks 79
   Mercedes Vetráb and Gábor Gosztolya

Rhythm Formant Analysis for Automatic Depression Classification 94
   Kumar Kaustubh, Parismita Gogoi, and S.R.M Prasanna

Determining Alcohol Intoxication Based on Speech and Neural Networks 107
   Pavel Laptev, Sergey Litovkin, and Evgeny Kostyuchenko

Linear Frequency Residual Cepstral Coefficients for Speech Emotion
Recognition 116
Baveet Singh Hora, S. Uthiraa, and Hemant A. Patil

Enhancing Stutter Detection in Speech Using Zero Time Windowing
Cepstral Coefficients and Phase Information 130
*Narasinga Vamshi Raghu Simha, Mirishkar Sai Ganesh,
and Vuppala Anil Kumar*

Source and System-Based Modulation Approach for Fake Speech Detection ... 142
*Rishith Sadashiv T. N., Devesh Kumar, Ayush Agarwal,
Moakala Tzudir, Jagabandhu Mishra, and S. R. Mahadeva Prasanna*

Digital Signal Processing

Investigation of Different Calibration Methods for Deep Speaker
Embedding Based Verification Systems 159
*Sergey Novoselov, Galina Lavrentyeva, Vladimir Volokhov,
Marina Volkova, Nikita Khmelev, and Artem Akulov*

Learning to Predict Speech Intelligibility from Speech Distortions 169
Punnoose Kuriakose

Sparse Representation Frameworks for Acoustic Scene Classification 177
Akansha Tyagi and Padmanabhan Rajan

Driver Speech Detection in Real Driving Scenario 189
Mrinmoy Bhattacharjee, Shikha Baghel, and S. R. Mahadeva Prasanna

Regularization Based Incremental Learning in TCNN for Robust Speech
Enhancement Targeting Effective Human Machine Interaction 200
Kamini Sabu, Mukesh Sharma, Nitya Tiwari, and M. Shaik

Candidate Speech Extraction from Multi-speaker Single-Channel Audio
Interviews 210
Meghna Pandharipande and Sunil Kumar Kopparapu

Post-processing of Translated Speech by Pole Modification and Residual
Enhancement to Improve Perceptual Quality 222
Lalaram Arya and S. R. Mahadeva Prasanna

Region Normalized Capsule Network Based Generative Adversarial
Network for Non-parallel Voice Conversion 233
*Md. Tousin Akhter, Padmanabha Banerjee, Sandipan Dhar,
Subhayu Ghosh, and Nanda Dulal Jana*

Speech Enhancement Using LinkNet Architecture 245
Anuj Patel, G. Satya Prasad, Sabyasachi Chandra, Puja Bharati,
and Shyamal Kumar Das Mandal

ATT:Adversarial Trained Transformer for Speech Enhancement 258
Aniket Aitawade, Puja Bharati, Sabyasachi Chandra,
G. Satya Prasad, Debolina Pramanik, Parth Sanjay Khadse,
and Shyamal Kumar Das Mandal

Human Identification by Dynamics of Changes in Brain Frequencies
Using Artificial Neural Networks 271
Daniyar Wolf, Yaroslav Turovsky, Roman Meshcheryakov,
and Anastasia Iskhakova

Speech Prosody

Analysis of Formant Trajectories of a Speech Signal for the Purpose
of Forensic Identification of a Foreign Speaker 287
Rodmonga Potapova, Vsevolod Potapov, and Irina Kuryanova

Gestures vs. Prosodic Structure in Laboratory Ironic Speech 301
Polina Vasileva, Uliana Kochetkova, and Pavel Skrelin

Sounds of <sil>ence: Acoustics of Inhalation in Read Speech 314
Priyankoo Sarmah, Wendy Lalhminghlui, and Neeraj Kumar Sharma

Prolongations as Hesitation Phenomena in Spoken Speech in First
and Second Language 322
Natalia Bogdanova-Beglarian, Kristina Zaides, Daria Stoika,
and Xiaoli Sun

Study of Indian English Pronunciation Variabilities Relative to Received
Pronunciation 339
Priyanshi Pal, Shelly Jain, Chiranjeevi Yarra, Prasanta Kumar Ghosh,
and Anil Kumar Vupalla

Multimodal Collaboration in Expository Discourse: Verbal and Nonverbal
Moves Alignment 350
Olga Iriskhanova, Maria Kiose, Anna Leonteva, Olga Agafonova,
and Andrey Petrov

Association of Time Domain Features with Oral Cavity Configuration
During Vowel Production and Its Application in Vowel Recognition 364
Arup Saha, Tulika Basu, and Bhaskar Gupta

Prosodic Interaction Models in a Conversation 380
Anastasia Gorbyleva

Natural Language Processing

Development and Research of Dialogue Agents with Long-Term Memory
and Web Search 391
Kirill Apanasovich, Olesia Makhnytkina, and Yuri Matveev

Pre- and Post-Textual Contexts in Assessment of a Message as Offensive
or Defensive Aggression Verbalization 402
Liliya Komalova

Boosting Rule-Based Grapheme-to-Phoneme Conversion
with Morphological Segmentation and Syllabification in Bengali 415
Krishnendu Ghosh, Sandipan Mandal, and Nilay Roy

Revisiting Assessment of Text Complexity: Lexical and Syntactic
Parameters Fluctuations 430
*Alexandra Vahrusheva, Valery Solovyev, Marina Solnyshkina,
Elzara Gafiaytova, and Svetlana Akhtyamova*

Analysis of Natural Language Understanding Systems with L2 Learner
Specific Synthetic Grammatical Errors Based on Parts-of-Speech 442
Snehal Ranjan, Sai Kalyan Nanduri, Prakul Virdi, and Chiranjeevi Yarra

On the Most Frequent Sequences of Words in Russian Spoken Everyday
Language (Bigrams and Trigrams): An Experience of Classification 455
*Maria V. Khokhlova, Olga V. Blinova, Natalia Bogdanova-Beglarian,
and Tatiana Sherstinova*

Child Speech Processing

Recognition of the Emotional State of Children by Video and Audio
Modalities by Indian and Russian Experts 469
*Elena Lyakso, Olga Frolova, Aleksandr Nikolaev, Egor Kleshnev,
Platon Grave, Abylay Ilyas, Olesia Makhnytkina, Ruban Nersisson,
A. Mary Mekala, and M. Varalakshmi*

Effect of Linear Prediction Order to Modify Formant Locations
for Children Speech Recognition 483
Udara Laxman Kumar, Mikko Kurimo, and Hemant Kumar Kathania

Gammatone-Filterbank Based Pitch-Normalized Cepstral Coefficients
for Zero-Resource Children's ASR 494
    *Syed Shahnawazuddin, Ankita, Avinash Kumar,
    and Hemant Kumar Kathania*

System Assisted Vocal Response Analysis and Assessment of Autism
in Children: A Machine Learning Based Approach 506
    Soma Khan, Tulika Basu, Joyanta Basu, Madhab Pal, and Rajib Roy

Addressing Effects of Formant Dispersion and Pitch Sensitivity
for the Development of Children's KWS System 520
    Jayant Kumar Rout and Gayadhar Pradhan

Emotional State of Children with ASD and Intellectual Disabilities:
Perceptual Experiment and Automatic Recognition by Video, Audio
and Text Modalities 535
    *Elena Lyakso, Olga Frolova, Aleksandr Nikolaev, Severin Grechanyi,
    Anton Matveev, Yuri Matveev, Olesia Makhnytkina, and Ruban Nersisson*

Linear Frequency Residual Features for Infant Cry Classification 550
    S. Uthiraa, Aastha Kachhi, and Hemant A. Patil

Speech Processing for Medicine

Identification of Voice Disorders: A Comparative Study of Machine
Learning Algorithms 565
    Sharal Coelho and Hosahalli Lakshmaiah Shashirekha

Transfer Learning Using Whisper for Dysarthric Automatic Speech
Recognition 579
    Siddharth Rathod, Monil Charola, and Hemant A. Patil

Significance of Duration Modification in Reducing Listening Effort
of Slurred Speech from Patients with Traumatic Brain Injury 590
    *Oindrila Banerjee, D. Govind, Suryakanth V. Gangashetty,
    Akhilesh Kumar Dubey, Rajeev Aravindakshan, Sasikumar Panicker,
    and K. Reshma*

Speech Signal Segmentation into Silence, Unvoiced and Vocalized
Sections in Speech Rehabilitation 601
    *Dariya Novokhrestova, Evgeny Kostyuchenko, Ilya Krivoshein,
    and Lidiya Balatskaya*

Respiratory Sickness Detection from Audio Recordings Using CLIP
Models 611
    Bhuma Chandra Mohan

Investigating the Effect of Data Impurity on the Detection Performances
of Mental Disorders Through Spoken Dialogues 626
    Rohan Kumar Gupta and Rohit Sinha

Author Index 639

Contents – Part II

Industrial Speech and Language Technology

Analysing Breathing Patterns in Reading and Spontaneous Speech 3
Gauri Deshpande, Björn W. Schuller, Pallavi Deshpande,
Anuradha Rajiv Joshi, S. K. Oza, and Sachin Patel

Audio-Visual Speaker Verification via Joint Cross-Attention 18
Gnana Praveen Rajasekhar and Jahangir Alam

A Novel Scheme to Classify Read and Spontaneous Speech 32
Sunil Kumar Kopparapu

Analysis of a Hinglish ASR System's Performance for Fraud Detection 46
Pradeep Rangappa, Aditya Kiran Brahma, Venkatesh Vayyavuru,
Rishi Yadav, Hemant Misra, and Kasturi Karuna

CAPTuring Accents: An Approach to Personalize Pronunciation Training
for Learners with Different L1 Backgrounds 59
Veronica Khaustova, Evgeny Pyshkin, Victor Khaustov, John Blake,
and Natalia Bogach

Speech Technology for Under-Resourced Languages

Improvements in Language Modeling, Voice Activity Detection,
and Lexicon in OpenASR21 Low Resource Languages 73
Vishwa Gupta and Gilles Boulianne

Phone Durations Modeling for Livvi-Karelian ASR 87
Irina Kipyatkova and Ildar Kagirov

Significance of Indic Self-supervised Speech Representations for Indic
Under-Resourced ASR 100
Sougata Mukherjee, Jagabandhu Mishra, and S. R. Mahadeva Prasanna

Study of Various End-to-End Keyword Spotting Systems on the Bengali
Language Under Low-Resource Condition 114
Achintya Kr. Sarkar, Tulika Basu, Rajib Roy, Joyanta Basu,
Michael Tongbram, Yamben Jina Chanu, and Priyanka Dwivedi

Bridging the Gap: Towards Linguistic Resource Development
for the Low-Resource Lambani Language 127
Ashwini Dasare, Amartya Roy Chowdhury, Aditya Srinivas Menon,
Konjengbam Anand, K. T. Deepak, and S. R. M. Prasanna

Studying the Effect of Frame-Level Concatenation of GFCC
and TS-MFCC Features on Zero-Shot Children's ASR 140
Ankita, Shambhavi, and Syed Shahnawazuddin

Code-Mixed Text-to-Speech Synthesis Under Low-Resource Constraints 151
Raviraj Joshi and Nikesh Garera

An End-to-End TTS Model in Chhattisgarhi, a Low-Resource Indian
Language 164
Abhayjeet Singh, Anjali Jayakumar, G. Deekshitha, Hitesh Kumar,
Jesuraja Bandekar, Sandhya Badiger, Sathvik Udupa, Saurabh Kumar,
and Prasanta Kumar Ghosh

An ASR Corpus in Chhattisgarhi, a Low Resource Indian Language 173
Abhayjeet Singh, Arjun Singh Mehta, K. S. Ashish Khuraishi,
G. Deekshitha, Gauri Date, Jai Nanavati, Jesuraja Bandekar,
Karnalius Basumatary, P. Karthika, Sandhya Badiger, Sathvik Udupa,
Saurabh Kumar, Prasanta Kumar Ghosh, V. Prashanthi, Priyanka Pai,
Raoul Nanavati, Sai Praneeth Reddy Mora, and Srinivasa Raghavan

Cross Lingual Style Transfer Using Multiscale Loss Function for Soliga:
A Low Resource Tribal Language 182
Ashwini Dasare, B. Lohith Reddy, A. Sai Chandra Koushik, B. Sai Raj,
V. Krishna Sai Rohith, Satisha Basavaraju, and K. T. Deepak

Preliminary Analysis of Lambani Vowels and Vowel Classification Using
Acoustic Features 195
Leena Dihingia, Prashant Bannulmath, Amartya Roy Chowdhury,
S.R.M Prasanna, K.T Deepak, and Tehreem Sheikh

Curriculum Learning Based Approach for Faster Convergence of TTS
Model 208
Navneet Kaur and Prasanta Kumar Ghosh

Rhythm Measures and Language Endangerment: The Case of Deori 222
Krisangi Saikia and Shakuntala Mahanta

Konkani Phonetic Transcription System 1.0 231
Swapnil Fadte, Edna Vaz Fernandes, Hanumant Redkar,
and Jyoti D. Pawar

Speech Analysis and Synthesis

E-TTS: Expressive Text-to-Speech Synthesis for Hindi Using Data
Augmentation 243
  Ishika Gupta and Hema A. Murthy

Direct Vs Cascaded Speech-to-Speech Translation Using Transformer 258
  Lalaram Arya, Amartya Roy Chowdhury, and S. R. Mahadeva Prasanna

Deep Learning Based Speech Quality Assessment Focusing on Noise
Effects 271
  Rahul Jaiswal and Anu Priya

Quantifying the Emotional Landscape of Music with Three Dimensions 283
  Kirtana Sunil Phatnani and Hemant A. Patil

Analysis of Mandarin *vs* English Language for Emotional Voice Conversion ... 295
  S. Uthiraa and Hemant A. Patil

Audio DeepFake Detection Employing Multiple Parametric Exponential
Linear Units 307
  Md Shahidul Alam, Abderrahim Fathan, and Jahangir Alam

A Comparison of Learned Representations with Jointly Optimized VAE
and DNN for Syllable Stress Detection 322
  Jhansi Mallela, Prasanth Sai Boyina, and Chiranjeevi Yarra

On the Asymptotic Behaviour of the Speech Signal 335
  Priyanka Gupta, Rajul Acharya, Ankur T. Patil, and Hemant A. Patil

Improvement of Audio-Visual Keyword Spotting System Accuracy Using
Excitation Source Feature 344
  Salam Nandakishor and Debadatta Pati

Developing a Question Answering System on the Material of Holocaust
Survivors' Testimonies in Russian 357
  *Liudmila Bukreeva, Daria Guseva, Mikhail Dolgushin,
  Vera Evdokimova, and Vasilisa Obotnina*

Decoding Asian Elephant Vocalisations: Unravelling Call Types,
Context-Specific Behaviors, and Individual Identities 367
  Seema Lokhandwala, Rohit Sinha, Sreeram Ganji, and Balakrishna Pailla

Enhancing Children's Short Utterance Based ASV Using Data
Augmentation Techniques and Feature Concatenation Approach 380
    Shahid Aziz and Syed Shahnawazuddin

Studying the Effectiveness of Data Augmentation and Frequency-Domain
Linear Prediction Coefficients in Children's Speaker Verification Under
Low-Resource Conditions 395
    Shahid Aziz, Shivesh Pushp, and Syed Shahnawazuddin

Constant-Q Based Harmonic and Pitch Features for Normal *vs.*
Pathological Infant Cry Classification 407
    Aditya Pusuluri, Aastha Kachhi, and Hemant A. Patil

Robustness of Whisper Features for Infant Cry Classification 421
    Monil Charola, Siddharth Rathod, and Hemant A. Patil

Speaker and Language Identification, Verification, and Diarization

I-MSV 2022: Indic-Multilingual and Multi-sensor Speaker Verification
Challenge 437
    Jagabandhu Mishra, Mrinmoy Bhattacharjee,
    and S. R. Mahadeva Prasanna

Multi-task Learning over Mixup Variants for the Speaker Verification Task 446
    Abderrahim Fathan, Jahangir Alam, and Xiaolin Zhu

Exploring the Impact of Different Approaches for Spoken Dialect
Identification of Konkani Language 461
    Sean Monteiro, Ananya Angra, Muralikrishna H.,
    Veena Thenkanidiyoor, and A. D. Dileep

Adversarially Trained Hierarchical Attention Network
for Domain-Invariant Spoken Language Identification 475
    Urvashi Goswami, H. Muralikrishna, A. D. Dileep,
    and Veena Thenkanidiyoor

Ensemble of Incremental System Enhancements for Robust Speaker
Diarization in Code-Switched Real-Life Audios 490
    Raj Gohil, Ramya Viswanathan, Saurabh Agrawal, C. M. Vikram,
    Madhu R. Kamble, Kamini Sabu, M. Ali Basha Shaik,
    and Krishna K. S Rajesh

Enhancing Language Identification in Indian Context Through Exploiting
Learned Features with Wav2Vec2.0 503
   Shivang Gupta, Kowshik Siva Sai Motepalli, Ravi Kumar,
   Vamsi Narasinga, Sai Ganesh Mirishkar, and Anil Kumar Vuppala

Design and Development of Voice OTP Authentication System 513
   Pavanitha Manche, Sahaja Nandyala, Jagabandhu Mishra,
   Gayathri Ananthanarayanan, and S. R. Mahadeva Prasanna

End-to-End Native Language Identification Using a Modified Vision
Transformer(ViT) from L2 English Speech 529
   Kishan Pipariya, Debolina Pramanik, Puja Bharati,
   Sabyasachi Chandra, and Shyamal Kumar Das Mandal

Dialect Identification in Ao Using Modulation-Based Representation 539
   Moakala Tzudir, Rishith Sadashiv T.N., Ayush Agarwal,
   and S. R. Mahadeva Prasanna

Self-supervised Speaker Verification Employing Augmentation Mix
and Self-augmented Training-Based Clustering 550
   Abderrahim Fathan and Jahangir Alam

Author Index 565

Automatic Speech Recognition

Extreme Learning Layer: A Boost for Spoken Digit Recognition with Spiking Neural Networks

Ivan Peralta[1], Nanci Odetti[1], and Hugo L. Rufiner[1,2]($\boxtimes$)

^{1} Laboratorio de Cibernética, Facultad de Ingeniería UNER, Oro Verde, Argentina
lrufiner@sinc.unl.edu.ar
^{2} Instituto Señales, Sistemas e Inteligencia Computacional, sinc(i) UNL-CONICET, Santa Fe, Argentina
http://www.sinc.unl.edu.ar

Abstract. The automatic recognition of speaker-independent digits requires high accuracy and robustness to noise and variability. Spiking neural networks (SNNs) are a promising model for this task, as they can mimic the temporal dynamics and energy efficiency of the human auditory system. However, SNNs are difficult to train and often require complex learning algorithms. Spoken digits provide a useful benchmark task to evaluate new SNN architectures. Performance in small vocabulary tasks is an important first step before scaling up to more complex recognition scenarios. In this paper, we propose to use an extreme learning layer (ELL) as a simple and effective way to improve the learning of SNNs for spoken digit recognition. The ELL is a randomly generated layer that maps the input features to the next layer without any further adjustment. The output layer is then trained by entropy minimization. We show that ELL can boost the performance of the SNN on the benchmark data set TIDIGITS. We also compare our approach with some state-of-the-art methods achieving competitive results with less computational cost and complexity. The proposed approach also shows good robustness to additive noise.

Keywords: Spiking neural networks · Extreme learning machines · Automatic speech recognition

1 Introduction

The task of speech recognition has numerous applications in various fields such as education, health, security, and communication. However, despite significant advances, one of the main barriers to speech recognition is the difficulty for current systems to handle noise in the signal, while the human brain is almost immune to it [1]. Therefore, it is important to explore new strategies to address this problem, especially those inspired by the functioning of the auditory system and the human brain.

© The Author(s), under exclusive license to Springer Nature Switzerland AG 2023
A. Karpov et al. (Eds.): SPECOM 2023, LNAI 14338, pp. 3–17, 2023.
https://doi.org/10.1007/978-3-031-48309-7_1

Deep neural networks (DNNs) are the models that currently achieve the best performance in most speech-related tasks. DNNs also have the ability to learn features directly from raw speech samples. However, despite their success, DNNs suffer from some drawbacks such as high computational requirements and high energy consumption [5], which encourages the scientific community to continue looking for alternatives.

One strategy that has generated growing interest in the last years is the use of spiking neural networks (SNNs), a special type of artificial neural network that aims to closely mimic the functioning of biological neurons [10]. This enables event-driven and parallel implementations to improve efficiency [3, 8, 13]. One of the most significant properties of SNNs is their ability to communicate between neurons using pulses that mimic the action potentials of biological neurons. These potentials can be efficiently modelled using binary codes, which facilitates the implementation of SNNs in digital devices [8]. In addition, SNNs mimic the internal potential of the membrane by following a temporal dynamic similar to biological neurons [3], making them suitable for processing temporal signals such as speech [13].

Extreme Learning Machines (ELM) is a learning technique proposed by Huang et al. [7] that allows for fast and efficient training of single hidden layer neural networks. The basic idea behind ELM is to randomly assign the weights of the connections between the input layer and the hidden layer and then calculate the weights of the connections between the hidden layer and the output layer using a closed-form analytical formula. ELMs have several advantages over other neural network training methods. Firstly, it is very fast, as it does not require iterations to adjust the connection weights. Secondly, ELM is very easy to implement, as it does not require the calculation of gradients or the adjustment of hyperparameters such as the learning rate or momentum. Third, ELM has been shown to perform well on various classification tasks, including speech recognition [6].

In this work, we propose a new supervised neural network (DELSNN, Digital Extreme Learning Spiking Neural Network) that is tested on a spoken digit recognition task. The DELSNN was inspired by the classical work presented by Unnikrishnan and Hopfield [14], but we also added an extreme learning layer. Unnikrishnan proposed an analogue network for the recognition of isolated digits using a binary temporal encoding of speech spectral features.

The main contributions are a novel SNN architecture incorporating random projections for feature expansion combined with direct output layer training by entropy minimization, alongside evaluations demonstrating noise robustness for isolated spoken digit recognition. Detailed analysis of the DELSNN training and results is presented for the first time. In a previous work [12], an FPGA implementation and some preliminary results showing real-time capacity were presented.

The rest of the article is organized as follows. Section 2 presents the design and implementation of the proposed DELSNN, as well as the training algorithm and the spike encoding method. Section 3 shows the experimental results obtained in a database of spoken digits in English. Finally, Sect. 4 presents the conclusions and possible lines of future work.

2   Methods

2.1   Proposed DELSNN Model

The SNN proposed in this work is called DELSNN (Digital Extreme Learning Spiking Neural Network), and its goal is to recognize spoken digits in clean or additive noise conditions. The SNN has a feedforward architecture with one input layer and two layers of neurons: the extreme learning layer (ELL) **I** and the output layer **J**. The input layer is not composed of neurons but of a vector **V** that receives a binary encoding of the speech signal as a stimulus, obtained by spectral analysis and mapping to spikes. The neurons of the ELL layer are connected with multiline connections on one side to each coefficient of the input vector, and on the other side to each neuron in the output layer. The output layer has as many neurons as digit classes to recognize (11 in this case), and each one emits a spike when it detects the presence of a specific digit.

The main feature of DELSNN is that it uses temporal delays and random weights in the connections of the neurons for the first layer, allowing for extreme learning without the need to adjust these weights using complex algorithms. Temporal delays introduce temporal diversity in neuron inputs, facilitating class separation. Random weights introduce spatial diversity in neuron inputs, promoting generalization capacity. The only component that requires training are the output layer weights, which are adjusted using a straightforward algorithm based on entropy minimization.

The neuronal model used for SNN neurons is the *spike response model* (SRM), which is one of the models with a good trade-off between realistic and efficient hardware implementation.

A simplified diagram of the DELSNN architecture is shown in Fig. 1, illustrating the flow of data from input spikes to output spikes.

2.2   Speech Signal Encoding

Speech signal encoding is the process of transforming the speech signal into a binary sequence that can be used as a stimulus for SNN. Speech signal encoding consists of two main steps: feature extraction and spike mapping.

In this work feature extraction is based on spectral analysis performed using a Mel scale spectrogram (MSS). This is a widely used and effective psychoacoustic-motivated energy distribution of the speech signal over time and frequency.

The process of spike mapping involves converting the MSS into a binary representation by assigning each value a 0 (no spike) or a 1 (spike). This is accomplished by applying a thresholding function to each frequency band of the spectrogram. If the energy of the band surpasses a certain threshold, a spike is generated. In this study, the thresholding function used for spike mapping differs from [14] as it does not use the lateral inhibition strategy. Instead, an adjustable parameter is used to determine the threshold.

The result of the speech signal encoding is a matrix of spikes, where each row corresponds to a frequency band, and each column to a time window. This

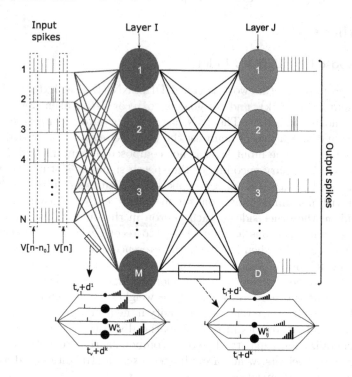

Fig. 1. Simplified diagram of the proposed DELSNN structure.

matrix is used as input for the SNN, where each frequency band corresponds to a coefficient of the vector **V**.

2.3   Neuron Model

The spiking neuron model used for this work is the Spike Response Model (SRM). The SNN operates in a time-driven manner, where the simulation time increments by a constant value, and at each step, the presence of spikes in the input vector **V** is analyzed to update the state of all neurons in the SNN. Below, we describe the operation of a neuron i belonging to the layer **I**. However, this explanation can be applied to any neuron in the SNN.

The state of neuron i is described by the state variable u_i. This neuron fires if u_i reaches the threshold ϑ. At the instant when the threshold is crossed, the discrete firing time $n_i^{(f)}$ is defined, where f indicates the number of firings or spikes emitted by the neuron i. The set of all firing instants of neuron i is defined as:

$$\mathcal{F}_i = \left\{ n_i^{(f)} \right\} = \{ n/u_i[n] > \vartheta \} . \tag{1}$$

The sequence of spikes emitted by a neuron in layer **I** can be written as a sequence of discrete Dirac deltas:

$$S_i[n] = \sum_{n_i^{(f)} \in \mathcal{F}_i} \delta[n - n_i^{(f)}], \quad with \quad \mathcal{F}_i = \left\{ n_i^{(1)}, ..., n_i^{(s)} \right\}. \tag{2}$$

The excitations to the neuron i are given by the spikes coming from each component of the input vector $\mathbf{V}$. Moreover, since the input vector is updated at each simulation instant, the temporal evolution of each component can be described as $V_v[n]$, where n is the simulation time instant, and v (with $1 \le v \le N$) indicates the v-th component of the vector $\mathbf{V}$. A spike that belongs to an element of the input vector is distributed among each of the propagation delays d^k of each connection leaving that component. Once the spikes have been delayed by the propagation delays, they reach the neurons as presynaptic pulses triggering a change in the neuronal state. Each presynaptic spike that excites neuron i increments (or decrements) its variable u_i by an amount $W_{v,i}^k, h[n - d^k]$, where h is the impulse response (spike) of the neuron. The increment or decrease in the variable depends on whether the weight is positive or negative, respectively. The state u_i of neuron i at time n is given by the linear superposition of the contributions from all propagation delays of all components of the input vector. This is described in Eq. 3[1]:

$$u_i[n] = \sum_{\nu=1}^{N} \sum_{k=1}^{K} \sum_{\tau=0}^{\infty} V_\nu[\tau] \, W_{\nu,i}^k \, h[n - \tau - d^k]. \tag{3}$$

If we consider a neuron in the output layer $\mathbf{J}$, the update equation for the state variable u_j of neuron j at time n is given by the linear superposition of the contributions of all spikes coming from neurons in layer $\mathbf{I}$. This is described in Eq. 4:

$$u_j[n] = \sum_{i=1}^{M} \sum_{k=1}^{K} \sum_{\tau=0}^{\infty} S_i[n] \, W_{i,j}^k \, h[n - \tau - d^k]. \tag{4}$$

Similar to Eq. 2, we can represent a sequence of spikes emitted by a neuron in layer $\mathbf{J}$ as a sequence of discrete Dirac deltas:

$$S_j[n] = \sum_{n_j^{(f)} \in \mathcal{F}_j} \delta[n - n_j^{(f)}], \quad \mathcal{F}_j = \left\{ n_j^{(1)}, ..., n_j^{(s)} \right\}, \tag{5}$$

where $n_j^{(f)}$ is the instant of the f-th firing of neuron $j \in \mathbf{J}$.

Considering Eqs. 3 and 4, the internal operation of a neuron, that is, the variation of its state u, can be interpreted as the discrete linear convolution of incoming spike sequences with an impulse response function $h[n]$. This implies that when simulating the operation of the SNN, one can choose an "arbitrary" $h[n]$.

---

[1] The internal summation with the upper limit ∞ indicates that the summation is performed until the entire spike encoding of the digit is completed.

2.4   Output Layer Training Through Entropy Minimization

During each iteration of the process, the SNN is presented with all the training pronunciations encoded in spikes. Projecting these spikes by the fixed random layer ELL enables weight updates of the next layer to be performed through an iterative process. When a pronunciation is presented, it produces a sequence of spikes $(S_i[n])$ at the outputs of neurons in layer **I**. These sequences of spikes $(S_i[n])$ are then distributed in the propagation delays to enter the neurons in the output layer **J**. Equation 4 can be rephrased in the following way:

$$u_j[n] = \sum_{i=1}^{M} \sum_{k=1}^{K} W_{i,j}^k \sum_{\tau=0}^{\infty} S_i[n]h[n - \tau - d^k], \tag{6}$$

$$u_j[n] = \sum_{i=1}^{M} \sum_{k=1}^{K} W_{i,j}^k R_{ik}[n], \tag{7}$$

where $R_{ik}[n] = \sum_{\tau=0}^{\infty} S_i[n]h[n-\tau-d^k]$ is the unweighted response of any neuron belonging to the output layer to the sequence of spikes emitted by the i-th neuron in layer I with the k-th delay. That is, for each digit w in the training word set $\mathbb{W}$, the input data to the second layer consists of $M \times K$ responses $R_{ik}^w[n]$, which will be used to describe the weight update function. In turn, the endpoint n^* is defined as the moment when digit w generated the last spike in layer I. That is:

$$n^* = \max \{n \mid S_i[n] = 1\}. \tag{8}$$

Considering the endpoint n^*, we can define $R_{ik}^w[n^*] = R_{ik}^w$.

Next, we will describe the training considering only the endpoints for each pronunciation of digit w. That is, for each digit, only the $D = 11$ values of the state variables u_j of the output neurons $j = 1, 2, ..., D$ will be used at the endpoint $(u_j[n^*])$. Later, the algorithm will be extended to the rest of the values of n.

The goal is to have the activity of each output neuron represent the membership to a specific digit class. To achieve this, the probability of belonging to a class can be approximated by applying a function to the state variable $u_j[n]$. For this, it is necessary to ensure that the range of this function varies between zero and one. The probability of digit w belonging to the j-th class at instant n^* is defined as $V_j^w[n^*] = V_j^w$. This value is determined by the SNN and is obtained by evaluating $u_j[n^*]$ with a sigmoid function whose range varies between zero and one. Equations 9 and 10 show two possible options for the sigmoid function:

$$V_j^w = \frac{1}{2} \left[1 + \tanh\left(\beta u_j[n^*]\right)\right], \tag{9}$$

$$V_j^w = \frac{1}{1 + e^{-a u_j[n^*]}}. \tag{10}$$

Associated with each digit w in the training set, there are the probabilities $P_{+,j}^w$ that the digit is an instance of category j, and $P_{-,j}^w$ that the digit is not an instance of that category, where $P_{-,j}^w = 1 - P_{+,j}^w$. These probabilities can only take unambiguous values of "1" or "0", given that the class to which each training word belongs is known. The proposed algorithm uses the Kullback-Leibler divergence measure between two probability distributions. In other words, it minimizes the relative entropy between the distribution $P_{+,-,j}^w$ – which represents the desired output values of the SNN – and the distribution $V_{+,-,j}^w$, which is the actual output obtained by the SNN. This is expressed as:

$$\mathcal{D}_{KL}(P\|V) = \sum_W \sum_j \sum_{+,-} P_{+,-,j}^w \ln \left(\frac{P_{-,+,j}^w}{V_{-,+,j}^w} \right), \tag{11}$$

where $V_{+,j}^w = V_j^w = 1 - V_{-,j}^w$. The inclusion of non-membership cases (negative probabilities) is equivalent to what is done when training a multilayer perceptron (MLP). During the training of an MLP, the desired output value of the neuron representing the class of the input pattern is usually set to one, and the outputs of the rest of the neurons in the network are set to zero. This is done because, for a particular word, we only want the SNN output neuron representing the pronounced digit to be active.

To perform the weight adaptation in the last layer, the well-known Newton's method equation can be used:

$$\Delta W_{i,j}^k = -\epsilon \frac{\mathrm{d}\mathcal{D}_{KL}(P\|V)}{\mathrm{d}W_{i,j}^k}. \tag{12}$$

$$\mathcal{D}_{KL}(P\|V) = \sum_W \sum_j \sum_{+,-} P_{+,-,j}^w \left[\ln\left(P_{+,-,j}^w \right) - \ln\left(V_{+,-,j}^w \right) \right] \tag{13}$$

Then, the negative derivative of the divergence is determined as follows:

$$-\frac{\mathrm{d}\mathcal{D}_{KL}(P\|V)}{\mathrm{d}W_{i,j}^k} = \sum_W P_{+,j}^w \frac{V_{+,j}^{w'}}{V_{+,j}^w} - P_{-,j}^w \frac{V_{+,j}^{w'}}{1 - V_{+,j}^w} \tag{14}$$

If we use the sigmoid function described in Eq. 9, we can write:

$$V_j^{w'} = V_j^w \beta R_{i,k}^w \left[1 - \tanh\left(\beta u_j[n^*] \right) \right], \tag{15}$$

$$1 - V_{+,j}^w = \frac{1}{2} \left[1 - \tanh\left(\beta u_j[n^*] \right) \right]. \tag{16}$$

Then, the equation for the weight update becomes:

$$\Delta W_{i,j}^k = \epsilon \sum_W [P_{+,j}^w - V_{+,j}^w] R_{i,k}^w, \tag{17}$$

where the constant ϵ determines the speed at which the algorithm attempts to reach the optimal weight values. If its value is very small, the algorithm will take many iterations to reach the goal. On the other hand, if ϵ is too large, it will not reach an optimal solution. In the experiments conducted in this work, $\epsilon = 0.008$

was used. It can be shown that using the sigmoid function from Eq. 10 leads to the same result. If we calculate the second derivative of the divergence, we get:

$$\frac{d^2 D_{KL}(P||V)}{dW_{i,j}^k} = \sum_W \beta (R_{i,k}^w)^2 V_{+,j}^w [1 - \tanh(\beta u_j[n^*])] \geq 0. \quad (18)$$

Since Eq. 18 is always greater than or equal to zero, the use of Eq. 17 will always lead to the global minimum of the divergence $\mathcal{D}_{KL}(P||V)$.

While the algorithm was described for the endpoint n^*, it can be extended to any temporal point $n \in \mathbb{P}$ of the pronounced word. Simply include the evaluation points described by the set $\mathbb{P}$ in the summation and establish the desired value $(P_{+,j}^w)$ for those points. In the experiments carried out in this work, all points of each pronunciation are used for adaptation. The weight update rule can be expressed by the following equation:

$$\Delta W_{i,j}^k = \epsilon \sum_W \sum_\mathbb{P} \left[P_{+,j}^w - V_{+,j}^w[n] \right] R_{i,k}^{w[n]}, \quad (19)$$

where the desired values are determined by the following rules:

- If the pronounced word belongs to the class of the output neuron
  - $P_{+,j}^w = 1$ if the training point is the endpoint.
  - If the training point does not match the endpoint, $P_{+,j}^w$ is unspecified, and no adaptation is performed.
- If the output neuron does not match the class of the pronounced word, $P_{+,j}^w = 0$ at the endpoint and the other evaluation points.

The choice of the above rules allows training the output neurons to emit spikes in a period of time close to the endpoint of the pronunciation. The algorithm is initialized with all weights set to zero.

3   Results and Discussion

3.1   Database and Experiments

To train and evaluate DELSNN, subsets of the TI-DIGITS database [9] were used. This database comprises isolated English digit pronunciations and digit sequences spoken by various speakers from 21 different dialectal regions in the United States. For this work, only isolated-digit pronunciations were used. The considered digits range from 0 to 9, including both versions of the zero digit commonly used in English speech (zero and oh). The database consists of 326 speakers, including 111 males, 114 females, 50 boys, and 51 girls.

Each speaker produced two pronunciations for each digit, resulting in 22 isolated digit pronunciations per speaker. For the experiments carried out in this work, these speakers were divided into three distinct sets: train, test, and validation.

To train the weights and delay lengths of the final layer, various experiments were performed. The study considered 11 classes (zero, oh, one, two, ..., nine), with 138 pronunciations per class used for the training dataset, 226 pronunciations per class for the evaluation dataset, and 50 pronunciations per class for the validation dataset. As each speaker contributed two pronunciations for each digit, the total number of speakers amounted to 207, with 113 for evaluation (57 females, 56 males), 69 for training (42 females, 27 males), and 25 for validation (15 females, 10 males). These datasets are mutually exclusive, meaning that speakers present in one dataset are not included in the others. Thus, the speech recognition process is independent of the speaker. The partitioning used adheres to the proposals provided in the TIDIGITS database to facilitate comparison with other research.

3.2   Design Decisions and Hyperparameter Tuning

The reproducibility of results is crucial in scientific research. To reproduce an experiment, all relevant parameters must be thoroughly documented. In machine learning, this includes specifying the hyperparameter configuration used to train models, as small variations can greatly impact final performance. A reduced subset of the training partition was used to find suitable values for relevant hyperparameters, such as:

- Number of frequency bands: Values between 16 and 64 were tested. 32 bands were chosen as a good trade-off between resolution and dimensionality.
- Number of neurons M for the ELL layer: Values between 16 and 64 were tested.
- Threshold for spike generation Ψ: Values between 0.25 and 0.75 were evaluated. 0.37 was selected as it provided the best results.
- Sigmoid parameter a (Eq. 10): Values between 0.0001 and 0.1 were tested. $a = 0.001$ provided the fastest convergence.
- Learning rate ϵ: Values between 0.001 and 0.1 were tried. 0.008 resulted in stable learning.

The number of output layer neurons was set to 11, to account for the 1–9 digit classes plus two extra neurons for distinguishing the two "0" versions. The number of training iterations was fixed at 100 based on convergence analysis.

The neuron model parameters were configured as follows: threshold $\theta = 15$ for ELL neurons and $\theta = 1$ for output layer neurons, and impulse response $h[n]$ matching a linearly increasing function. shape. Refractory periods were not taken into account. The weights of the ELL were randomly assigned with a mean $\mu = 0$ and variance $\sigma = 80$. Twenty delays per connection were used, and the duration of the delays starts at zero and increases by a constant value $T_i = 60$ ms. The value T_i also coincides with the duration of the Spike-Response Model (SRM), which only mimics the morphology of a biological response, not its temporal duration. The SNN was configured so that all weights are of integer type to facilitate the transfer to digital design.

Table 1 resumes the main final hyperparameters of the proposed DELSNN model.

Table 1. DELSNN final hyperparameters. See Fig. 1 for notation references.

Stage	Hyperparameter	Value
Spectral Analysis	Sampling frequency (f_m)	8 kHz
	Highest frequency	3785 Hz
	Lowest frequency	227 Hz
	Frequency bands	32
	Window type	Hamming
	Window samples	80
	Overlap	50 %
Spike Encoding	Threshold Ψ	0.37
Neuron model	Firing threshold θ	15 and 1
	Refractory period	0 ms
	Inter-layer delays	0–1200 ms
	SRM T_i	60 ms
	$h[n]$	linearly increasing
SNN Layer **I**	Input neurons N	32
	ELL neurons M	32
	Delays per connection	20
	Weight mean μ	0
	Weight variance σ	80
SNN Layer **J**	Output neurons D	11
	Sigmoid a	0.001
	Learning rate ϵ	0.008

3.3   Performance Metrics

To evaluate the performance of the neural network, various criteria were established to determine the winning neuron when multiple neurons are active in the output layer. The following criteria were used:

- **CMATS (Class with Maximum Accumulated Time of Spikes):** This criterion declares the neuron with the maximum duration of the spike train in its output as the winner.
- **CS (Class with Maximum Number of Spikes):** In this criterion, the neuron that produces the maximum number of spikes in its output is declared the winner, regardless of the time period it took to emit those spikes.
- **DP (First to Discharge Class):** The winner in this criterion is the neuron that fires first and emits a spike.
- **RAND (Random Class):** In this case, the winning neuron is randomly chosen among all the neurons that emitted spikes.

- **HARD (Hard Criterion):** This is the most demanding criterion, as if two neurons emit spikes, the network considers it a failure to determine the class of the input example.

The results obtained with these criteria showed no significant difference in recognition performance, except for the HARD and RAND criteria, which exhibited inferior performance. Consequently, the CMATS criterion was used to measure recognition stability during training. Once stability was achieved, the training process was terminated, and the weights obtained at the last epoch were used to evaluate the network's performance with the evaluation data.

3.4   Effect of Including ELL

The purpose of random weights between the input vector and the first layer is to project signals into a higher-dimensional space, thereby discriminating certain characteristics that could not be separated in the initial representation. The number of neurons in the first layer, which is a key parameter was set to 32, equal to the dimension of the input vector. Although increasing the number of neurons can potentially improve recognition rates, it also significantly increases computational costs. Despite the number of hidden layer neurons equalling the number of dimensions of the input vector, the transformation still increases the dimensionality of internal network representation. This is due to connection delays between the first layer and the input vector. This "expansion" effect in the temporal dimension is analogous to that observed during a convolution with an impulse due to the memory property of linear systems. An example of the response of the first layer of neurons to the presentation of a spike pattern corresponding to a digit at the input of the SNN can be seen in Fig. 2. The above-mentioned expansion of the representation in the time domain can be clearly observed.

The proposed DELSNN was evaluated on clean digits from the TIDIGITS dataset. The training, validation and test partitions described in Sect. 3.1 were used. To assess the benefits of incorporating the extreme learning layer, comparative experiments were conducted training the network with and without the ELL. Without the ELL, the SNN was trained using direct entropy minimization on the output weights. In contrast, the ELL configuration included an additional 20480 randomly initialized input-projection connections.

Figure 3 illustrates the test set accuracy over training iterations for both settings. It can be in observed in Fig. 3(B) that accuracy rapidly increases during the first 10–20 iterations, reaching around 80% (CMATS). After that, more gradual improvements occur until converging at approximately 88% accuracy. After 100 iterations, the ELL network achieves 88.18% accuracy compared to 64.36% for the network without ELL (Fig. 3(A)). So the ELL version converges faster and to a higher level of performance.

The incorporation of randomly projected features provides two key benefits. Firstly, it increases the separation between classes, facilitating the training process. Second, it improves generalisation by improving the variability of internal network representations.

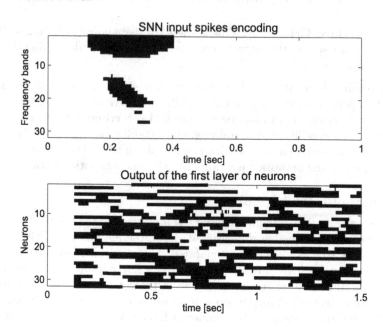

Fig. 2. Response of the first layer of neurons to the presentation of the digit "three". Top: input pattern to the SNN after coding in frequency bands. Bottom: response of the first layer of neurons to the presentation of this spectro-temporal pattern (hidden layer).

Figure 4 shows the accuracy per class after training with and without ELL. As it can be seen, accuracy levels are higher for most digits when using the ELL, especially for challenging cases like 5 and 9. The ELL's ability to better distinguish acoustically similar digits highlights its advantages.

The high deviations in epochs 0–50 may be due to the randomness of the ELL weights and delays, which affect the initial state of the network. Some instabilities in the computation of KL divergence can also contribute to these deviations, as ELL may amplify them. As the training progresses, the output layer weights are adjusted to minimize the entropy, and these deviations decrease.

These results validate the benefits of the proposed extreme learning layer for boosting the training and accuracy of SNN models in speech recognition applications. ELL provides a simple and effective technique to incorporate randomness and improve learning in SNN. This also indicates successful training of the output layer weights through the proposed entropy minimisation algorithm.

3.5 Noise Robustness Evaluation

To evaluate the noise robustness of the proposed DELSNN, experiments were also performed by adding white noise from the NOISEX database [15] to the clean TIDIGITS digits. White noise was chosen to evaluate the noise robustness of the proposed neural network because it contains uniform power at all frequencies of the audible spectrum. This results in a broad spectral mask that obscures a wide variety of critical acoustic cues for discriminating between phonetically similar digits.

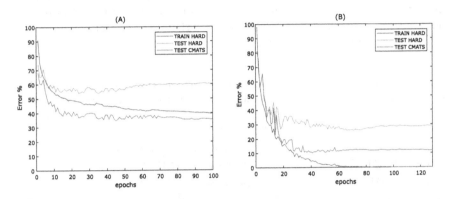

Fig. 3. Overall performance train/test accuracy comparison during training without ELL (A) and with ELL (B) (for clean speech signals).

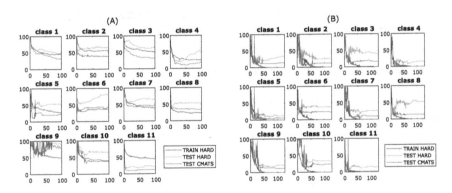

Fig. 4. Per-class performance train/test accuracy comparison during training without ELL (A) and with ELL (B) (for clean speech signals).

The best results obtained for clean and different signal-to-noise ratio (SNR) levels for different threshold Ψ are summarized in Table 2. For $\Psi = 0.370$ it can be observed that accuracy remains relatively stable down to 10 dB SNR, indicating the noise tolerance provided by the SNN encoding and architecture. However, performance degrades more sharply below 10 dB SNR, as noise completely masks discriminative speech characteristics. Nonetheless, the DELSNN can operate at SNR levels where conventional MFCC and HMM-based systems suffer from almost 70% error rates. For larger values of Ψ, stability of accuracy is maintained for higher levels of noise, but speech recognition in clean speech slightly deteriorates.

The increased noise tolerance of the proposed DELSNN compared to conventional speech recognition systems highlights the potential of SNN-based approaches. Further improvements may be achieved by exploring alternative noise-robust spike-coding strategies, such as phase coding [4] or Biologically plausible Auditory Encoding (BAE) [11]. A comparison with deep architectures like CNNs that also use MSE as input feature would be interesting. However, we could not find any published results on the TIDIGITS dataset corrupted with additive noise to include in the comparison.

Table 2. Comparison of different speech recognizers for this task under various levels of white noise. Missing values correspond to values not reported in the bibliography.

Strategy	Threshold Ψ	Clean	20 dB	10 dB	5 dB	0 dB
Lyon ear + LSM [16]	–	97.50%	84.00%	79.50%	–	–
LAM + HMM [2]	–	**98.80%**	**95.75%**	72.79%	–	–
MFCC + HMM [2]	–	**98.80%**	27.50%	12.20%	–	–
BAE + SNN [11]	W/masking	97.40%	91.90%	87.50%	–	**78.20**
MSE+DELSNN	0.785	79.65%	79.44%	79.81%	**80.37%**	58.57%
	0.576	82.58%	82.54%	83.15%	78.76%	18.02%
	0.370	89.14%	89.10%	**88.2%**	43.08%	1.81%

4 Conclusions and Future Work

In this paper, a novel DELSNN incorporating an extreme learning layer for robust spoken digit recognition was proposed and evaluated. The presented results provide initial evidence of the advantages of the EL approach to improving SNN training. Noise robustness experiments also showcase the potential of SNN architectures for speech processing under challenging conditions. Furthermore, as already demonstrated in our previous work, this model can be efficiently implemented on an FPGA platform, providing potential for real-time applications.

For future work, some research directions are identified, like the evaluation of larger vocabulary tasks to assess scalability and the exploration of alternative spike-coding strategies to further improve noise robustness. DELSNN architecture could also be extended to handle connected word recognition by incorporating some mechanisms to deal with coarticulation effects.

Acknowledgements. We would like to express our gratitude to the National University of Entre Ríos UNER for their support and resources provided within the framework of the research and development project PID6187, and to the National University of Litoral with project CAID 50620190100151LI, enabling us to conduct this investigation.

References

1. Bhangale, K.B., Kothandaraman, M.: Survey of deep learning paradigms for speech processing. Wireless Pers. Commun. **125**(2), 1913–1949 (2022)
2. Deng, Y., Chakrabartty, S., Cauwenberghs, G.: Analog auditory perception model for robust speech recognition. In: Proceedings of the 2004 IEEE International Joint Conference on Neural Networks, vol. 3, pp. 1705–1709. IEEE (2004)
3. Gerstner, W., Kistler, W.M.: Spiking Neuron Models: Single Neurons, Populations, Plasticity. Cambridge University Press, Cambridge (2002)
4. Guo, W., Fouda, M.E., Eltawil, A.M., Salama, K.N.: Neural coding in spiking neural networks: a comparative study for robust neuromorphic systems. Front. Neurosci. **15**, 638474 (2021)
5. Gupta, S., Agrawal, A., Pathak, A.: Energy-efficient deep learning: a review. Sustain. Comput.: Inform. Syst. **25**, 100370 (2020). https://doi.org/10.1016/j.suscom.2020.100370
6. Huang, G., Huang, G.B., Song, S., You, K.: Trends in extreme learning machines: a review. Neural Netw. **61**, 32–48 (2015)
7. Huang, G.B., Zhu, Q.Y., Siew, C.K.: Extreme learning machine: theory and applications. Neurocomputing **70**(1), 489–501 (2006)
8. Izhikevich, E.M.: Which model to use for cortical spiking neurons? IEEE Trans. Neural Networks **15**(5), 1063–1070 (2004)
9. Leonard, R.G., Doddington, G.: TIDIGITS. Linguistic Data Consortium, Philadelphia (1993)
10. Maass, W.: Networks of spiking neurons: the third generation of neural network models. Neural Netw. **10**(9), 1659–1671 (1997)
11. Pan, Z., Chua, Y., Wu, J., Zhang, M., Li, H., Ambikairajah, E.: An efficient and perceptually motivated auditory neural encoding and decoding algorithm for spiking neural networks. Front. Neurosci. **13** (2020). https://www.frontiersin.org/articles/10.3389/fnins.2019.01420
12. Peralta, I., Odetti, N., Filomena, E., Rufiner, J., Ricart, N., Rufiner, H.L.: A new spiking neural network with extreme learning for FPGA implementation. In: Proceedings of the 10th Southern Programmable Logic Conference, pp. 49–54 (2019). https://sinc.unl.edu.ar/sinc-publications/2019/POFRRR19
13. Schrauwen, B., Van Campenhout, J.: Parallel hardware implementation of a broad class of spiking neurons using serial arithmetic. In: Proceedings of the 14th European Symposium on Artificial Neural Networks, pp. 623–628. D-Side Publications (2006)
14. Unnikrishnan, K., Hopfield, J.J., Tank, D.W.: Speaker-independent digit recognition using a neural network with time-delayed connections. Neural Comput. **4**(1), 108–119 (1992)
15. Varga, A., Steeneken, H.J.: Assessment for automatic speech recognition: II. NOISEX-92: a database and an experiment to study the effect of additive noise on speech recognition systems. Speech Commun. **12**(3), 247–251 (1993)
16. Verstraeten, D., Schrauwen, B., Stroobandt, D., Van Campenhout, J.: Isolated word recognition with the liquid state machine: a case study. Inf. Process. Lett. **95**(6), 521–528 (2005)

EMO-AVSR: Two-Level Approach for Audio-Visual Emotional Speech Recognition

Denis Ivanko(✉) 📵, Elena Ryumina📵, Dmitry Ryumin📵,
Alexandr Axyonov📵, Alexey Kashevnik📵, and Alexey Karpov📵

St. Petersburg Institute for Informatics and Automation of the Russian Academy of
Sciences, St. Petersburg Federal Research Center of the Russian Academy of Sciences
(SPC RAS), St. Petersburg, Russia
{ivanko.d,ryumina.e,ryumin.d,axyonov.a,
alexey.kashevnik,karpov}@iias.spb.su

Abstract. Emotional speech recognition is a challenging task for modern systems. The presence of emotions significantly changes the characteristics of speech. In this paper, we propose a novel approach for emotional speech recognition (EMO-AVSR). The proposed approach uses visual speech data to detect a person's emotion first, followed by processing of speech by one of the pre-trained emotional audio-visual speech recognition models. We implement these models as a combination of spatio-temporal network for emotion recognition and a cross-modal attention fusion for automatic audio-visual speech recognition. We present experimental investigation that shows how different emotions (happy, anger, disgust, fear, sad, and neutral), valence (positive, neutral, and negative) and binary (emotional and neutral) affect automatic audio-visual speech recognition. The evaluation on CREMA-D data demonstrates up to 7.3% absolute accuracy improvement compared to the classical approaches.

Keywords: Emotional speech recognition · Audio-visual speech recognition · Lip-reading · Affective computing

1 Introduction

Automatic audio-visual speech recognition (AVSR) has recently achieved tremendous success, especially in limited vocabulary tasks by far surpassing human abilities to recognize speech by audio-visual data [3,18,25,26]. However, state-of-the-art (SOTA) video-based speech recognition (VSR) approaches, as well as audio-based speech recognition (ASR) ones still suffer from significant performance degradations in real application scenarios. In particular, their performance degrades drastically when speech recordings are affected by human emotions. In such cases speech signal may not be recognized correctly by modern AVSR systems [16]. In practical scenarios, it is often crucial for applications to understand individuals in an emotional state, where both speech and non-verbal cues like gestures [12,27,37] play vital roles.

A. Karpov et al. (Eds.): SPECOM 2023, LNAI 14338, pp. 18–31, 2023.
https://doi.org/10.1007/978-3-031-48309-7_2

Emotional state recognition in audio-visual data goes beyond speech alone, encompassing emotional cues from facial expressions and gestures. Researchers have also explored gesture recognition to enhance emotional context in communication [7]. Consequently, the pursuit of improving the reliability of AVSR systems in various real-life scenarios has led to a growing emphasis on research in emotional speech and gesture recognition in recent years [1,6,10,35].

Emotions are expressed in a different way in audio and video modalities, and there is no "out of the box" solution for emotion-robust AVSR to date. It changes depending on a speaker's emotional state: timbre, pitch and loudness of the voice, duration of sounds, pauses, and articulation.

This paper presents a novel two-level approach for emotional speech recognition based on audio-visual speech processing (EMO-AVSR). EMO-AVSR is designed for: (1) identifying a class/valence of emotion by face and (2) performing AVSR using pre-trained emotionally-specific models. The presented approach is based on SOTA methodologies for visual emotion recognition (VER) [38], VSR [17,23] and ASR [49], as well as leverages recent advances in deep learning. The main advantage of the proposed approach is in increasing the AVSR accuracy by genuinely tackling the VER at first, followed by the emotionally-specific speech recognition. Until now there is no scientific studies aimed at analyzing an influence of speakers' emotional states on AVSR and lip-reading.

2   Related Work

Despite the recent advances in technology and the publicity of large-scale corpora recorded in real environments, SOTA ASR and VSR approaches still lack a reliable recognition of emotional speech [28,33].

2.1   Emotion Recognition

With the developments of neural network models, and more specifically with the introduction of such deep neural network architectures such as VGG [42], ResNet [14], etc., that are able to consume raw data without a feature extraction phase, modern VER approaches began to develop. For the last five years numerous research works have been published, e.g. [24,41]. There are three common architectures among the SOTA deep learning emotion recognition models: convolutional neural networks (CNN) in combination with recurrent neural networks (RNN) [20,34], 3DCNN [50], and Two-Stream Network [5] for recognizing a spatio-temporal input.

2.2   Audio-Visual Speech Recognition

The general idea of AVSR is to recognize speech based on the processing of both audio and video signals in parallel [17]. Several deep neural network architectures, training strategies and audio-visual fusion techniques have been recently proposed for AVSR [32]. It received a lot of attention due to the availability of large corpora, e.g., LRW [4], LRS [43], etc.

Many deep learning techniques were presented and have replaced the feature extraction step with deep bottleneck architectures [36]. The first CNN based image classifier to discriminate visemes was trained in [21]. In [45], deep bottleneck features were used for word recognition in order to take full advantage of deep convolutional layers and explore high-level features. Similarly, it was applied to every frame of the video in [44]. The authors in [46] proposed to process spatio-temporal information on lips articulation using 3D convolutional filters. Then, researchers in [43] applied an attention mechanism to the mouth region-of-interest (ROI) and Mel-frequency cepstral coefficients. Finally, some end-to-end architectures have been presented recently for AVSR and have attracted a lot of interest. Despite AVSR systems having been developed for many years, they still have a lot of challenges in real-life conditions, such as emotional speech recognition.

2.3   Multimodal Corpora

Nowadays there are a lot of corpora containing emotional speech data [6]. At the same time, there are a lot of corpora aimed for AVSR and lip-reading [19]. However, at the moment there are almost no emotional audio-visual corpora suitable for model training in the scope of deep learning approaches. Despite the variety of existing emotional corpora, there are at least four corpora suitable for automatic AVSR: CREMA-D [2], RAVDESS [22], SAVEE [13], and eNTER-FACE'05 [29]. CREMA-D is the most useful for our research due to the number of speakers and the amount of data available.

3   Proposed Approach

We consider three different AVSR strategies for EMO-AVSR and compare them to the traditional approach (audio-visual model trained on emotionally-neutral phrases). As we mentioned earlier, the CREMA-D corpus [2] is the most suitable for studies of the emotional ASVR among existing ones. Based on conducted analysis, the accuracy of video-based approaches for emotion recognition significantly outperforms audio-based ones on this corpus [2,11]. At the same time, it is well-known that the audio speech-based emotion recognition accuracy is higher in the arousal dimension [15,47], while the visual mimics-based emotions are better recognized in the valence dimension of the emotional space [47]. For the above reasons, we train several VER models and consider three emotional strategies: (1) 6 Emotions, (2) 3-level Valence, and (3) Binary (emotional/neutral data). We do not consider arousal strategies, because there is no annotation for the arousal dimension in CREMA-D.

The proposed two-level EMO-AVSR approach, which includes three emotion recognition strategies, is shown in Fig. 1. We perform audio-visual speech pre-processing followed by emotional class/valence identification based on facial mimics at first. We then applied emotionally-specific models to the AVSR task at the second level.

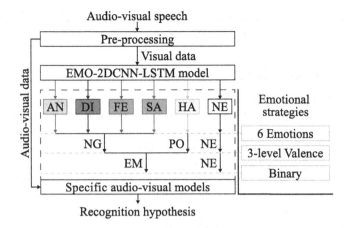

Fig. 1. General methodology of the EMO-AVSR approach for three emotional strategies.

3.1   Data Pre-processing

We divide input audio-visual data into segments of 2-s with a 1-s window step. Then we perform data pre-processing that is different for each modality.

The Face Mesh model from the Google MediaPipe open-source library [9] is used to detect facial and mouth regions on each video frame. We use facial regions for the VER task. Since emotions are stable over some time intervals [8], we downsample video frame rate to the 5 frames per second (FPS), similar to the authors in the work [6,38]. We also resize frames to 224 × 224 pixels and use channel normalization of all the pixels. Thus, we analyze 10 facial ROI in every 2-s segment.

We then analyze the mouth regions for the VSR task. All the images are resized to 88 × 88 × 3 and combined into sequences of 2 s (60 images). In order to maintain the proportions of the lips, we pad the images to the desired size with average pixel values and use a min-max normalization technique. We do not apply any FPS downsampling at this stage.

We apply the Librosa library [30] to extract log-Mel spectrograms with 128 Mel filter-banks at the Short-Time Fourier Transform window lengths of 2048 with a step of 128 for audio speech processing. We also downsample audio signals to 16 kHz. The size of the feature matrix for a 2-s audio segment is 128 × 251. The obtained features are converted into 1D images without resizing and min-max normalization.

3.2   Visual Emotion Recognition Model

We fine-tune a SOTA open-source 2DCNN-LSTM model [6,38] for efficient dynamic VER. It consists of a pre-trained backbone model based on ResNet-50 architecture and a temporal two LSTM layers (with 256 and 512 neurons) to model temporal dependencies across video frames. A fully connected layer of 6 neurons completes the EMO-2DCNN-LSTM model.

3.3   Visual Speech Recognition Model

We use the (2+1)D-based ResNet-18 model architecture [14] and a Bidirectional Long Short-Term Memory (BiLSTM) [31] model to tackle the VSR task. Unlike 3DCNN, (2+1)D processes the input sequence only in the space domain, i.e. by the width and height of the frames. That results in (2+1)D has fewer parameters than 3DCNN and works faster. To analyze the depth of the frame sequence, we use a BiLSTM model. (2+1)D CNN includes twenty 3D convolutional layers. BiLSTM network consists of two BiLSTM layers with 512 consecutive neurons in each layer. A global average pooling layer and a fully connected layer of 12 neurons complete the (2+1)D-BiLSTM network.

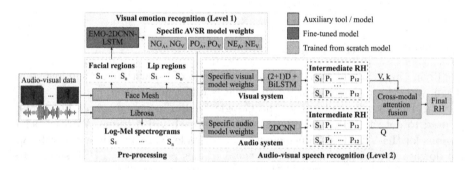

Fig. 2. Pipeline of the proposed EMO-AVSR approach for 3-level Valence strategy. S_i - audio/video segment, $i = 1, ..., n$, RH - recognition hypothesis.

3.4   Audio Speech Recognition Model

We use the 2DCNN-based ResNet-18 model architecture to tackle the ASR task. Log-Mel spectrograms are used as features of an acoustic speech signal. The spectrogram images have the dimension $128 \times 251 \times 1$ that is enable to apply a simple 2DCNN. The ResNet-18 model, together with the log-Mel spectrogram, works well in the ASR task [49]. The 2DCNN model, as well as the (2+1)D model, has twenty convolutional layers, followed by three layers: global average pooling, flatten, and a fully connected layer with 12 neurons.

3.5   Cross-Modal Attention Fusion

Since we are dividing each audio-visual signal into segments of 2 s, our proposed models (VSR and ASR) are to have twelve hypotheses for each segment. We use a cross-model attention network [48, 49] to aggregate hypotheses. Since the length of the audio-visual signal can be different in the CREMA-D corpus, but the average is 2.5 s, we take only the first three vectors with recognition hypotheses. If the audio-visual segment is shorter than 2.5 s, then we add mean values to hypothesis vectors. Thus, the EMO-AVSR approach is the combination of all the proposed models (VER, VSR and ASR). The pipeline of our approach for best emotional strategy is illustrated in Fig. 2.

4   Experimental Evaluation

We used the CREMA-D [2] corpus for experimental evaluation. It contains around 7500 audio-visual clips from 91 speakers. Speakers uttered phrases from a selection of twelve phrases. The number of clips for each phrase is balanced [40]. The phrases were pronounced using one of six different emotions (anger – AN, disgust – DI, fear – FE, happy – HA, neutral – NE, and sad – SA). We divided the data into three subsets taking into account the even distribution by speakers' age and gender, as well as speaker-independence: Train (70%), Validation (10%), and Test (20%).

We used SGD or Adam optimization algorithms with learning rates of (0.01, 0.001, 0.0001 or 0.00001) during the training of all models. The values were selected using the grid search. The models were trained for one hundred epochs. We finish the training process if the performance did not increase on the Validation subset.

First, we fine-tuned open-source VER model [6, 38] to predict six emotions (6 Emotions strategy). Using predictions of the trained model and ground labels, we grouped emotions according to two other strategies. We combined emotions as negative – NG (includes AN, DI, FE, and SA emotions), neutral – NE, positive – PO (includes HA emotion) for 3-level Valence strategy. And NE and emotional EM (all emotions excluding NE) – for Binary one. The confusion matrices of above-mentioned three strategies (see Fig. 3 and Fig. 4) demonstrate that the unweighted average recall (UAR) equals 61.2% for the 6 Emotions strategy, 91.5% – for 3-level Valence, 97.4% – for Binary.

Secondly, we trained emotionally-specific models for ASR, VSR and AVSR tasks. In the process of training emotionally-specific models, we removed phrases that were not spoken with the target emotion from the Train subset. The Validation and Test subsets remained the same for all experiments. For the 6 Emotions strategy, we trained six models based on phrases spoken with one out of six emotions. We provided the results of phrase recognition accuracy (mAcc) obtained by all models in the context of each emotion class separately. We also trained the models based on phrases spoken with all emotion. The first experiment results for AVSR task are presented in Table 1.

Table 1 demonstrates results of the 6 Emotions strategy, as well as the results of classical approach (trained only on emotionally neutral phrases). In case of AVSR approach is trained only on NE phrases (NE TM), the mAcc is equal to 87.7%. For our approach with the 6-Emotions strategy, we trained six different models for every emotion (see values on the diagonal) and the mAcc is equal to 95.1%. Therefore, the usage of six emotionally-specific models for phrase recognition outperforms the model trained on all emotions (All TM) by 2.8% in absolute values. The average values of mAcc (horizontally) show that the NE phrases are recognized better using all trained emotional models. If we train a model only for the FE emotion phrases then we will get the highest value mAcc = 93.9% (vertically) in comparison with other emotional models of our approach.

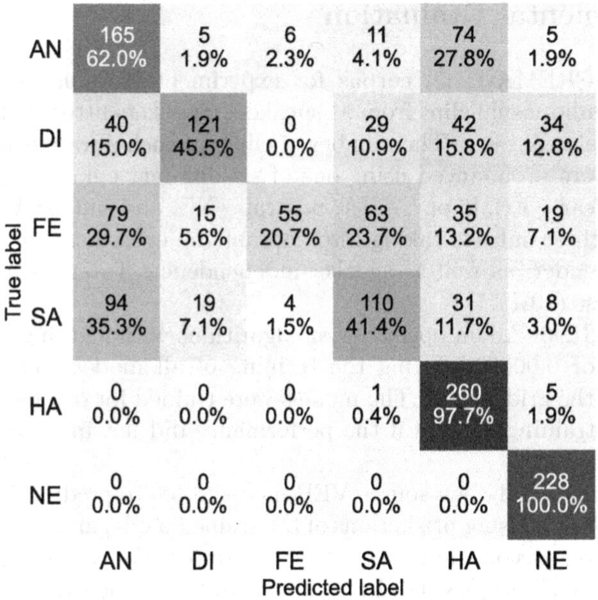

True label
AN
DI
FE
SA
HA
NE
165 62.0%
5 1.9%
6 2.3%
11 4.1%
74 27.8%
5 1.9%
40 15.0%
121 45.5%
0 0.0%
29 10.9%
42 15.8%
34 12.8%
79 29.7%
15 5.6%
55 20.7%
63 23.7%
35 13.2%
19 7.1%
94 35.3%
19 7.1%
4 1.5%
110 41.4%
31 11.7%
8 3.0%
0 0.0%
0 0.0%
0 0.0%
1 0.4%
260 97.7%
5 1.9%
0 0.0%
0 0.0%
0 0.0%
0 0.0%
0 0.0%
228 100.0%
AN DI FE SA HA NE
Predicted label

Fig. 3. Confusion matrices for 6 emotions classification.

True label
NG
PO
NE
816 76.7%
182 17.1%
66 6.2%
1 0.4%
260 97.7%
5 1.9%
0 0.0%
0 0.0%
228 100.0%
NG PO NE
Predicted label
True label
NE
EM
1259 94.7%
71 5.3%
0 0.0%
228 100.0%
NE EM
Predicted label

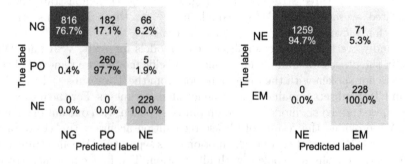

Fig. 4. Confusion matrices for 3 valences and binary classification.

Table 1. Comparison of the phrase recognition accuracy for 6 Emotions strategy by AVSR models. TM is train model.

TM	Recognition accuracy (Acc)						mAcc
	AN	DI	FE	SA	HA	NE	
AN	**98.2**	87.9	81.0	65.6	92.5	86.8	85.4
DI	82.5	**93.6**	84.8	92.5	82.9	93.0	88.2
FE	93.4	89.0	**96.3**	91.8	96.9	96.1	93.9
SA	69.4	87.0	79.4	**87.7**	75.6	88.2	81.2
HA	95.2	90.9	87.1	80.4	**97.2**	94.3	90.9
NE	81.6	89.8	85.4	83.2	88.2	**98.2**	87.7
mAcc	86.7	89.7	85.7	83.5	88.9	92.8	**95.1**
All	93.0	91.2	88.9	90.2	93.9	96.9	92.3

Earlier we obtained the models for NE and PO valence classes within the first experiment. For the second experiment, we only trained the models for the NG valence class. It allowed getting all models for the 3-level Valence strategy. We report the experimental results in Table 2. We present the experimental results for the Binary strategy in Table 3.

Table 2. Comparison of the phrase recognition accuracy for 3-level Valence strategy by AVSR models.

TM	Recognition accuracy			mAcc
	NG	PO	NE	
NG	**96.1**	96.8	98.3	97.1
PO	88.4	**97.2**	94.3	93.3
NE	85.0	88.2	**98.2**	90.5
mAcc	98.8	94.1	96.9	**97.2**

The results presented in Table 2 demonstrate that if emotions are grouped according to 3-level Valence strategy then mAcc = 97.2%. This value exceeds the phrase recognition accuracy using the 6 Emotions strategy by 2.1% (where mAcc = 95.1%, see Table 1). This result shows that all emotions of NG valence have similar voice and facial features that are different from other valence classes.

Table 3 presents that the best way to divide emotions is by valence, because Binary strategy shows worse results. Since NG and PO valence have completely different voice and facial features the fusion of these two valences result to mAcc value drops to 96.2%.

26   D. Ivanko et al.

Table 3. Comparison of the phrase recognition accuracy for Binary strategy by AVSR models.

TM	Recognition accuracy		mAcc
	EM	NE	
EM	**94.1**	96.5	95.3
NE	85.6	**98.2**	91.9
mAcc	89.9	97.4	**96.2**

Thus, we found that for the phrase recognition task, it is better to use a 3-level Valence strategy. Next, we analyze which unimodal approach (ASR or VSR) has a greater contribution to the final prediction for the bimodal approach (AVSR). The experimental results are showed in Table 4.

Table 4. Comparison of the phrase recognition accuracy for 3-level Valence strategy by ASR and VSR models.

TM	ASR				VSR			
	NG	PO	NE	mAcc	NG	PO	NE	mAcc
NG	**93.1**	95.3	96.9	95.1	**90.5**	89.8	90.4	90.2
PO	87.5	**96.9**	89.5	91.3	85.5	**95.5**	78.9	86.7
NE	79.0	82.5	**97.4**	86.3	84.1	73.3	**92.1**	83.2
mAcc	86.5	91.6	94.6	**95.8**	86.7	86.2	87.1	**92.7**

Experimental results (see Table 4) show that the ASR approach outperforms the VSR approaches by 3.1% (95.8% vs. 92.7%). This result allows concluding that when predicting phrases, the audio-visual models more relies on the decision of the audio models.

Thus, we got the following results mAcc = 92.7% (VSR models), 95.8% (ASR model), and 97.2% (AVSR models) using 3-level Valence strategy. These results have been achieved with the assumption that a VER model makes predictions with a high accuracy. We evaluated the trained emotionally-specific models using the emotional labels obtained by our VER model. The results of the experiment are presented in Table 5. The result of recognition of twelve phrases taking into account the distribution to emotions by the EMO-2DCNN-LSTM model and two-level recognition is achieved relative to Baseline (the models trained only on neutral phrases). So, we increase mAcc to 2.6% (VSR models), 5.5% (ASR models), and 7.3% (AVSR models).

Therefore, we proposed an EMO-AVSR approach, which determines the visual emotion using 3-levels Valence strategy at the first-level, followed by emotionally-specific models to get the final AVSR prediction. This approach

Table 5. Comparison of mAcc of our two-level approaches with Baseline (model trained only on NE phrases).

Baseline	ASR	VSR	AVSR
87.7	93.2	90.3	95.6

allowed increasing phrase recognition accuracy by 7.3% relative to the baseline. Moreover, the authors of [39] reported mAcc = 73.3% for the VSR task using a 3DCNN model on the same corpus. We outperform their approach by 19.4% (73.3% vs. 92.7%) using the proposed VSR-based approach with the (2+1)D+BiLSTM.

It should be noted that the proposed approach works in real-time. Processing a 2 s clip on CPU (using Intel i9) takes 1.44 s of which: visual pre-processing – 0.4 s; VER – 0.04 s; ASR – 0.2 s; VSR – 0.8 s. We do not perform any model conversion to speed up data-processing.

5   Conclusion

In this paper, we propose the EMO-AVSR approach for automatic emotional speech recognition. The evaluation on CREMA-D corpus demonstrates that the proposed method achieves up to 7.3% absolute accuracy improvements compared to the classical approach, where the audio-visual model are trained on emotionally-neutral phrases. We demonstrate how different classes of emotions (happy, anger, disgust, fear, sad, and neutral), valence (positive, neutral, and negative) and binary (emotional and neutral) affect automatic audio-visual speech recognition. Source codes and trained models will be available on our GitHub[1].

Our method can be used for recognizing different kinds of emotional speech based on audio-visual data in various scenarios including call centers, health care systems, human-robot interaction, etc. In the future, we aim to annotate the large-scale LRW corpus at the valence states and optimize our approach to the emotion-robust audio-visual 500-word recognition.

Acknowledgments. This research is financially supported by the Russian Science Foundation (project No. 22-11-00321).

References

1. Boháček, M., Hrúz, M.: Sign pose-based transformer for word-level sign language recognition. In: Winter Conference on Applications of Computer Vision (WACV), pp. 182–191 (2022). https://doi.org/10.1109/WACVW54805.2022.00024

---

[1] https://github.com/SMIL-SPCRAS/EMO-AVSR.

2. Cao, H., Cooper, D.G., Keutmann, M.K., Gur, R.C., Nenkova, A., Verma, R.: Crema-D: crowd-sourced emotional multimodal actors dataset. IEEE Trans. Affect. Comput. **5**(4), 377–390 (2014). https://doi.org/10.1109/TAFFC.2014.2336244
3. Chen, C., Hu, Y., Zhang, Q., Zou, H., Zhu, B., Chng, E.S.: Leveraging modality-specific representations for audio-visual speech recognition via reinforcement learning. In: AAAI Conference on Artificial Intelligence, vol. 37, pp. 12607–12615 (2023). https://doi.org/10.48550/arXiv.2212.05301
4. Chung, J.S., Zisserman, A.: Lip reading in the wild. In: Lai, S.-H., Lepetit, V., Nishino, K., Sato, Y. (eds.) ACCV 2016, Part II. LNCS, vol. 10112, pp. 87–103. Springer, Cham (2017). https://doi.org/10.1007/978-3-319-54184-6_6
5. Deng, D., Chen, Z., Zhou, Y., Shi, B.: Mimamo net: integrating micro-and macro-motion for video emotion recognition. In: AAAI Conference on Artificial Intelligence, vol. 34, pp. 2621–2628 (2020). https://doi.org/10.1609/AAAI.V34I03.5646
6. Dresvyanskiy, D., Ryumina, E., Kaya, H., Markitantov, M., Karpov, A., Minker, W.: End-to-end modeling and transfer learning for audiovisual emotion recognition in-the-wild. Multimodal Technol. Interact. **6**(2), 11 (2022). https://doi.org/10.3390/mti6020011
7. Du, Y., Crespo, R.G., Martínez, O.S.: Human emotion recognition for enhanced performance evaluation in E-learning. Progr. Artif. Intell. **12**(2), 199–211 (2023). https://doi.org/10.1007/s13748-022-00278-2
8. Ekman, P., Friesen, W.V.: Nonverbal leakage and clues to deception. Psychiatry **32**(1), 88–106 (1969). https://doi.org/10.1080/00332747.1969.11023575
9. Feng, D., Yang, S., Shan, S.: An efficient software for building lip reading models without pains. In: International Conference on Multimedia & Expo Workshops (ICMEW), pp. 1–2. IEEE (2021). https://doi.org/10.1109/ICMEW53276.2021.9456014
10. Feng, T., Hashemi, H., Annavaram, M., Narayanan, S.S.: Enhancing privacy through domain adaptive noise injection for speech emotion recognition. In: International Conference on Acoustics, Speech and Signal Processing (ICASSP), pp. 7702–7706. IEEE (2022). https://doi.org/10.1109/icassp43922.2022.9747265
11. Ghaleb, E., Popa, M., Asteriadis, S.: Multimodal and temporal perception of audio-visual cues for emotion recognition. In: International Conference on Affective Computing and Intelligent Interaction (ACII), pp. 552–558. IEEE (2019). https://doi.org/10.1109/ACII.2019.8925444
12. Guo, L., Lu, Z., Yao, L.: Human-machine interaction sensing technology based on hand gesture recognition: a review. IEEE Trans. Hum.-Mach. Syst. **51**(4), 300–309 (2021). https://doi.org/10.1109/THMS.2021.3086003
13. Haq, S., Jackson, P.J., Edge, J.: Audio-visual feature selection and reduction for emotion classification. In: Auditory-Visual Speech Processing (AVSP), Tangalooma, Australia (2008)
14. He, K., Zhang, X., Ren, S., Sun, J.: Deep residual learning for image recognition. In: Conference on Computer Vision and Pattern Recognition (CVPR), pp. 770–778 (2016). https://doi.org/10.1109/cvpr.2016.90
15. Ivanko, D., et al.: MIDriveSafely: multimodal interaction for drive safely. In: International Conference on Multimodal Interaction (ICMI), pp. 733–735 (2022). https://doi.org/10.1145/3536221.3557037
16. Ivanko, D., Ryumin, D., Axyonov, A., Kashevnik, A.: Speaker-dependent visual command recognition in vehicle cabin: methodology and evaluation. In: Karpov, A., Potapova, R. (eds.) SPECOM 2021. LNCS (LNAI), vol. 12997, pp. 291–302. Springer, Cham (2021). https://doi.org/10.1007/978-3-030-87802-3_27

17. Ivanko, D., Ryumin, D., Karpov, A.: A review of recent advances on deep learning methods for audio-visual speech recognition. Mathematics **11**(12), 2665 (2023). https://doi.org/10.3390/math11122665
18. Ivanko, D., et al.: DAVIS: driver's audio-visual speech recognition. In: Interspeech, pp. 1141–1142 (2022)
19. Kashevnik, A., et al.: Multimodal corpus design for audio-visual speech recognition in vehicle cabin. IEEE Access **9**, 34986–35003 (2021). https://doi.org/10.1109/ACCESS.2021.3062752
20. Kim, B., Lee, J.: A deep-learning based model for emotional evaluation of video clips. Int. J. Fuzzy Log. Intell. Syst. **18**(4), 245–253 (2018). https://doi.org/10.5391/IJFIS.2018.18.4.245
21. Koller, O., Ney, H., Bowden, R.: Deep learning of mouth shapes for sign language. In: International Conference on Computer Vision Workshops (ICCVW), pp. 85–91 (2015). https://doi.org/10.1109/ICCVW.2015.69
22. Livingstone, S.R., Russo, F.A.: The ryerson audio-visual database of emotional speech and song (RAVDESS): a dynamic, multimodal set of facial and vocal expressions in north American English. PLoS ONE **13**(5), e0196391 (2018). https://doi.org/10.1371/journal.pone.0196391
23. Lu, Y., Li, H.: Automatic lip-reading system based on deep convolutional neural network and attention-based long short-term memory. Appl. Sci. **9**(8), 1599 (2019). https://doi.org/10.3390/APP9081599
24. Luna-Jiménez, C., Kleinlein, R., Griol, D., Callejas, Z., Montero, J.M., Fernández-Martínez, F.: A proposal for multimodal emotion recognition using aural transformers and action units on RAVDESS dataset. Appl. Sci. **12**(1), 327 (2021). https://doi.org/10.3390/app12010327
25. Ma, P., Haliassos, A., Fernandez-Lopez, A., Chen, H., Petridis, S., Pantic, M.: Auto-AVSR: audio-visual speech recognition with automatic labels. In: International Conference on Acoustics, Speech and Signal Processing (ICASSP), pp. 1–5. IEEE (2023). https://doi.org/10.1109/ICASSP49357.2023.10096889
26. Ma, P., Wang, Y., Petridis, S., Shen, J., Pantic, M.: Training strategies for improved lip-reading. In: International Conference on Acoustics, Speech and Signal Processing (ICASSP), pp. 8472–8476. IEEE (2022). https://doi.org/10.1109/ICASSP43922.2022.9746706
27. Mahbub, U., Ahad, M.A.R.: Advances in human action, activity and gesture recognition. Pattern Recogn. Lett. **155**, 186–190 (2022). https://doi.org/10.1016/j.patrec.2021.11.003
28. Makino, T., et al.: Recurrent neural network transducer for audio-visual speech recognition. In: Automatic Speech Recognition and Understanding Workshop (ASRU), pp. 905–912. IEEE (2019). https://doi.org/10.1109/ASRU46091.2019.9004036
29. Martin, O., Kotsia, I., Macq, B., Pitas, I.: The eNTERFACE'05 audio-visual emotion database. In: International Conference on Data Engineering Workshops (ICDEW), pp. 8–8. IEEE (2006)
30. McFee, B., et al.: Librosa: audio and music signal analysis in python. In: Python in Science Conference, vol. 8, pp. 18–25 (2015). https://doi.org/10.25080/MAJORA-7B98E3ED-003
31. Milošević, M., Glavitsch, U.: Combining Gaussian mixture models and segmental feature models for speaker recognition. In: Interspeech, pp. 2042–2043 (2017)
32. Milošević, M., Glavitsch, U.: Robust self-supervised audio-visual speech recognition. In: Interspeech, pp. 2118–2122 (2022). https://doi.org/10.21437/interspeech.2022-99

33. Muppidi, A., Radfar, M.: Speech emotion recognition using quaternion convolutional neural networks. In: International Conference on Acoustics, Speech and Signal Processing (ICASSP), pp. 6309–6313. IEEE (2021). https://doi.org/10.1109/ICASSP39728.2021.9414248

34. Pan, X., Ying, G., Chen, G., Li, H., Li, W.: A deep spatial and temporal aggregation framework for video-based facial expression recognition. IEEE Access **7**, 48807–48815 (2019). https://doi.org/10.1109/ACCESS.2019.2907271

35. Ryumin, D., Ivanko, D., Axyonov, A.: Cross-language transfer learning using visual information for automatic sign gesture recognition. Int. Arch. Photogramm. Remote. Sens. Spat. Inf. Sci. **48**, 209–216 (2023). https://doi.org/10.5194/isprs-archives-xlviii-2-w3-2023-209-2023

36. Ryumin, D., Ivanko, D., Ryumina, E.: Audio-visual speech and gesture recognition by sensors of mobile devices. Sensors **23**(4), 2284 (2023). https://doi.org/10.3390/s23042284

37. Ryumin, D., Karpov, A.A.: Towards automatic recognition of sign language gestures using kinect 2.0. In: Antona, M., Stephanidis, C. (eds.) UAHCI 2017, Part II. LNCS, vol. 10278, pp. 89–101. Springer, Cham (2017). https://doi.org/10.1007/978-3-319-58703-5_7

38. Ryumina, E., Dresvyanskiy, D., Karpov, A.: In search of a robust facial expressions recognition model: a large-scale visual cross-corpus study. Neurocomputing **514**, 435–450 (2022). https://doi.org/10.1016/j.neucom.2022.10.013

39. Ryumina, E., Ivanko, D.: Emotional speech recognition based on lip-reading. In: Prasanna, S.R.M., Karpov, A., Samudravijaya, K., Agrawal, S.S. (eds.) SPECOM 2022. LNCS, vol. 13721, pp. 616–625. Springer, Cham (2022). https://doi.org/10.1007/978-3-031-20980-2_52

40. Ryumina, E., Karpov, A.: Comparative analysis of methods for imbalance elimination of emotion classes in video data of facial expressions. J. Tech. Inf. Technol. Mech. Opt. **129**(5), 683 (2020). https://doi.org/10.17586/2226-1494-2020-20-5-683-691 https://doi.org/10.17586/2226-1494-2020-20-5-683-691

41. Schoneveld, L., Othmani, A., Abdelkawy, H.: Leveraging recent advances in deep learning for audio-visual emotion recognition. Pattern Recogn. Lett. **146**, 1–7 (2021). https://doi.org/10.1016/j.patrec.2021.03.007

42. Simonyan, K., Zisserman, A.: Very deep convolutional networks for large-scale image recognition. arXiv preprint arXiv:1409.1556 (2014)

43. Son Chung, J., Senior, A., Vinyals, O., Zisserman, A.: Lip reading sentences in the wild. In: Conference on Computer Vision and Pattern Recognition (CVPR), pp. 6447–6456 (2017). https://doi.org/10.1109/CVPR.2017.367

44. Takashima, Y., et al.: Audio-visual speech recognition using bimodal-trained bottleneck features for a person with severe hearing loss. In: Interspeech, pp. 277–281 (2016). https://doi.org/10.21437/Interspeech.2016-721

45. Tamura, S., et al.: Audio-visual speech recognition using deep bottleneck features and high-performance lipreading. In: Asia-Pacific Signal and Information Processing Association Annual Summit and Conference (APSIPA), pp. 575–582. IEEE (2015). https://doi.org/10.1109/APSIPA.2015.7415335

46. Tran, D., Bourdev, L., Fergus, R., Torresani, L., Paluri, M.: Learning spatiotemporal features with 3D convolutional networks. In: International Conference on Computer Vision (ICCV), pp. 4489–4497 (2015). https://doi.org/10.1109/ICCV.2015.510

47. Valstar, M., et al.: AVEC 2016: depression, mood, and emotion recognition workshop and challenge. In: International Workshop on Audio/Visual Emotion Challenge, pp. 3–10 (2016). https://doi.org/10.1145/2988257.2988258

48. Vaswani, A., et al.: Attention is all you need. In: Advances in Neural Information Processing Systems (NIPS), vol. 30 (2017)
49. Xu, X., Wang, Y., Jia, J., Chen, B., Li, D.: Improving visual speech enhancement network by learning audio-visual affinity with multi-head attention. arXiv preprint arXiv:2206.14964 (2022). https://doi.org/10.48550/arXiv.2206.14964
50. Yang, J., Wang, K., Peng, X., Qiao, Y.: Deep recurrent multi-instance learning with spatio-temporal features for engagement intensity prediction. In: International Conference on Multimodal Interaction (ICMI), pp. 594–598 (2018). https://doi.org/10.1145/3242969.3264981

Significance of Audio Quality in Speech-to-Text Translation Systems

Tonmoy Rajkhowa[✉], Amartya Roy Chowdhury[✉],
and S. R. Mahadeva Prasanna[✉]

Indian Institute of Technology, Dharwad, Dharwad, India
{pro,212022001,amartya.chowdhury,prasanna}@iitdh.ac.in
http://www.iitdh.ac.in

Abstract. Research on Speech-to-Text Translation systems has shown that their performance is influenced by the size and quality of the training corpus. However, most efforts on corpus creation referred to the size and audio-transcription-translation alignment and text translation as measure of quality of a corpus while not emphasizing much on the audio quality as they are scrapped directly from web-based sources and not recorded in a studio environment. Hence, the absence of higher quality audio may present challenges for these systems in learning the mappings between audio and its corresponding text effectively by the Transformer based encoder-decoder architecture. Even with larger corpora, Direct Speech-to-Text Translation systems have struggled to achieve comparable performance as by their cascaded counterparts, unless they utilize additional external data resources or techniques. A comparative study was conducted on the performance of direct and cascaded speech translation systems without using any external data sources directly or indirectly. This study involved comparing the performance by using both the original and generated high-quality audios generated by a Text-to-Speech Synthesis system from two distinct corpora: Prabhupadavani and MuST-C. The findings revealed that direct Speech-to-Text systems can perform similar to their cascaded counterparts, given that they are trained with a larger corpus that contains high-quality audio. The findings suggest that, when building efficient and robust direct speech-to-text translation systems, it is crucial to consider not only the size and translation quality of the corpus but also the audio quality. By incorporating high-quality audio data into the training process, researchers can enhance the performance of direct Speech-to-Text translation systems forming a viable alternative to cascaded systems.

Keywords: Speech-to-text translation · Direct speech-to-text translation · Text-to-speech synthesis · Transformer

1 Introduction

Speech-to-Text Translation (S2TT) [2,3,7] is the task of translating the speech of one language into the text of another. This task is conventionally achieved

A. Karpov et al. (Eds.): SPECOM 2023, LNAI 14338, pp. 32–42, 2023.
https://doi.org/10.1007/978-3-031-48309-7_3

using a cascaded pipeline of Automatic Speech Recognition (ASR) and Machine Translation (MT) [25]. The ASR system converts speech into its transcription, whereas the MT system translates this transcription to another language. In this cascaded approach, there is the problem of error compounding from the ASR to the MT system, which affects the translation quality of the cascaded system [10,12,27]. In addition, there is a larger inference time owing to the involvement of the two different systems [3,7]. To solve this error propagation effect and larger inference time, efforts were made to translate the speech of the source language directly into the text of the target language without requiring an intermediate source language text [3,7]. However, these Direct Speech-to-Text Translation (DS2TT) systems were unable to outperform or provide similar performance to that of cascaded systems. To explain this performance gap, most of the work in the literature regarded to data scarcity as one of the key challenges, along with improper alignment [8,28] of a corpus. A speech translation corpus normally consists of source language audio along with its transcription and translation into a target language. Hence, most studies have focused on leveraging additional data to address the data scarcity problem and various automatic alignment techniques which may contribute in the improvement of performance of DS2TT systems. This has led to the development of various corpora with increased size, better audio-text alignment, and better translation quality between the source and target language texts. In most of these studies, the quality of a corpus is referred to as the extent of audio-text alignment, along with the translation quality between the source and target language texts. However, to the best of our knowledge, audio quality has not been emphasized as a measure for determining the quality of a corpus. This motivated to study the effect of audio quality on the performance of speech-translation systems. This work will also attempt to investigate if a DS2TT can provide similar performance to that of cascaded systems if large corpora with high-quality audio are available.

The development of a robust Speech-to-Text Translation (S2TT) system presents several challenges. One critical challenge is the availability of high-quality corpora specifically developed for the DS2TT tasks. Because these speech translation systems rely on resource-intensive Deep Learning (DL)-based architectures, they require high-quality data for effective training. Unfortunately, corpora designed for S2TT tasks are relatively scarce compared to those available for Automatic Speech Recognition (ASR) or Machine Translation (MT) tasks. Most S2TT corpora are sourced from diverse web resources, recorded debates during parliamentary proceedings, live lectures, and other real-world scenarios, whereas ASR corpora are often recorded in controlled studio environments, ensuring higher audio quality. Consequently, these audios in S2TT corpora are susceptible to background noise, imperfect alignment, etc., posing challenges for the DS2TT model in capturing contextual understanding and mapping between speech representations and their corresponding translated text. Efforts were made on improving the alignment of audio with its transcription and translation [6,11,21]. However, most corpora developed for S2TT tasks could not ensure the presence of high-quality audios as they were scraped directly from web-based resources. This has led to a challenge in understanding the maximum potential of a speech translation system.

Developmental efforts for a Direct Speech-to-Text Translation (DS2TT) began with an attempt by Bérard et al. (2016) [3] and Duong et al. (2016) [7], where the goal was to directly translate source speech into target text without relying on an intermediate source transcription. Despite significant progress in the field, DS2TT systems continue to face major challenges, with one of the most prominent being the scarcity of suitable datasets for training. While several Speech-to-Text Translation (S2TT) datasets have been introduced, including Fisher-Callhome [19], CoVoST [26], MuST-C [6], mTED-X [21], EuroParl-ST [11], the size of these corpora still lags behind to that of Automatic Speech Recognition (ASR) corpora. Addressing the data scarcity issue, researchers have proposed several methods to augment the available data such as data augmentation, fine-tuning DS2TT using pre-trained ASR and MT models, incorporating mutual learning, curriculum learning, and self-training techniques. Various automatic audio-text alignment techniques were also incorporated while building a corpus. These techniques, collectively, have played a crucial role in augmenting the size of the corpora contributing to notable improvements in the performance of DS2TT systems. However, despite these advancements, the research community has overlooked the role of audio quality in the performance of DS2TT systems. To the best of knowledge, there have been no studies in the literature that specifically highlight the impact of audio quality on the performance of speech translation systems.

The aim of the present work is to study the role of audio quality in the performance of S2TT systems. Additionally, this work is aimed to explore whether Direct Speech-to-Text Translation (DS2TT) systems can provide comparable performance to that of cascaded S2TT systems, particularly when trained with larger corpora containing high-quality audios and without involving any external data sources directly or indirectly. This work may help in setting up guidelines for future corpus creation which may help in building a robust DS2TT system. This paper is organized as follows. Section 2 describes the Experimental Methodology, including the description of datasets, dataset preprocessing techniques, and various tools to develop the ASR, MT, and DS2TT systems and their evaluation methods. Section 3 provides the Results and Analysis, followed by the Summary and Conclusions in Sect. 4.

2   Experimental Methodology

This section describes the details of various corpora used for the study and the architectures of the cascaded and direct speech translation systems.

2.1   Dataset Description and Pre-processing

To begin the work, Prabhupadavani [22] and MuST-C datasets are chosen based on their size and audio quality difference. The Prabhupadavani corpus is a code-mixed multi-domain corpus about Vedic culture and heritage from Indic literature containing 94 h of speech in English language spoken by 130 speakers and the audio was manually aligned with corresponding text in the target languages from five language families. For the experiments, 51,000 English utterances along with its English text transcription and its Hindi text translation are used for training and 1,000 examples are used for testing the system. MuST-C is the benchmark dataset, containing over 400 h of audio. It is a multilingual speech translation corpus which facilitates the building of S2TT systems from English into 8 languages. It contains audio recordings in English collected from TED talks along with its text transcription and translations. For the experiments, the English speech and German text parallel examples are used. There are about 2,50,000 training examples. For the experiments, the English-German pair are taken. These two datasets differ in the quality of audios with MuST-C having better intelligibility than Prabhupadavani, which is prone to higher background noise with lower speech intelligibility. To investigate the maximum potential of both the corpora for S2TT task, high-quality audios were generated using a Text-to-Speech Synthesis (TTS) system which is developed by Ekstep-Vakyansh [5,9] using the Tacotron 2 architecture [23]. This step is done to ensure the minimization of acoustic variability, background noise etc. from the audios.

The 16-bit 16 kHz mono-channel audios are taken as raw inputs. From these raw inputs, 80 dimensional Mel-filterbanks are extracted as features. The texts, both transcriptions and translations, are tokenized using SentencePiece [14] with a vocabulary size set to 2,000 for Hindi text in Prabhupadavani corpus and 10,000 for German text in MuST-C corpus for all ASR, MT and DS2TT tasks.

2.2 Building of Models

This section describes the model settings along with the architectural details and the toolkits used.

Text-to-Speech Synthesis System. Since it is required to generate high quality audios for comparison, the audios were generated using a Text-to-Speech system using the English(male voice) Vakyansh model developed by Open-speech-Ekstep [4]. TTS has achieved a performance comparable to human-level. Further implementation can be found in. The audios are generated for the entire English text sets from both the corpora and the train, dev and test split are kept same as that of the original corpora.

Automatic Speech Recognition and Direct Speech-to-Text System Settings. For building the ASR and DS2TT, the Transformer [24] based encoder-decoder architecture is used. This architecture takes the audio features in sequences as input and outputs the target text as a sequence of characters. For the implementation, the Fairseq toolkit [16] is used. For DS2TT task, the system is trained using text translation of target language, whereas for ASR task, it is trained using its source language transcription. The encoder layer contains 1-dimensional strided convolutional layers [15] to reduce the sequence length of the input sequences before feeding to the Transformer blocks. 6 Transformer blocks were taken in the encoder side and 3 in the decoder side. The final output is the text that is obtained from the character-level embeddings that are generated by the output of the decoder. The block diagram is depicted in Fig. 1.

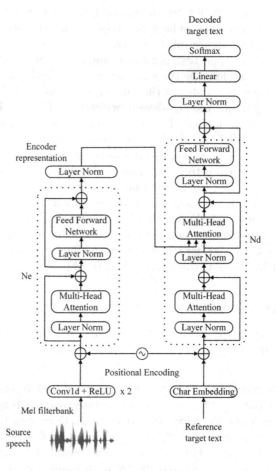

Fig. 1. Block diagram of Transformer based ASR/DS2TT system where N_e refers to encoder block and N_d refers to decoder block.

Machine Translation System Settings. The Machine Translation system is built using the OpeNMT-py [13] toolkit. The Transformer based architecture is used for all MT related task. 6 encoder and 6 decoder layers with an embedding dimension of 512 are used. Both the encoder and decoder has 4 attention heads in each multi-head attention block. For the feed-forward neural network,1024 inner states are kept. A constant dropout of 0.1 is kept for both the attention and feed-forward network.

Cascaded Speech-to-Text Translation System Settings. The cascaded system is the pipeline of ASR and MT system. The decoded text in source language by the ASR is translated using the MT system to generate the text in target language. The final performance is calculated using BLEU metric [17].

2.3 Inference and Evaluation Methods

During inferencing, a beam search with beam size of 5 is used for all the systems. For evaluation, de-tokenized BLEU scores are computed using SacreBLEU for MT [18], DS2TT & cascaded systems. BLEU is the most widely used metrics to evaluate S2TT systems. The ASR systems are evaluated using Word Error Rate (WER) [1].

3 Results and Analysis

The performances of Prabhupadavani and MuST-C corpus, with original and TTS generated audios, using the cascaded S2TT pipeline are given in Table 1. The performances of DS2TT and MT system using MuST-C corpus mentioned in Table 1 & 2 aligns with the performance reported by previous studies. However, this work is the first to report the performance of ASR, MT system, cascaded and direct S2TT systems using Prabhupadavani corpus. The difference in ASR performance between original and TTS generated audios in Prabhupadavani corpus is significant because of the low-quality audios used originally. However, for MuST-C, the corresponding difference is not significant due to the presence of better quality audios with better average PESQ score [20]. However, the text translation quality of Prabhupadavani corpus is better than MuST-C corpus as evident in the difference in BLEU scores from the MT experiments. Overall, the cascaded system performance is seen to be bounded by the MT system. It is evident that despite having inferior grade audio quality, the performance of Prabhupadavani is decent as compared to MuST-C corpus which, despite having better quality audios, the performance is bounded by the lower performance by MT system. This suggests that both audio quality and translation quality plays a role in cascaded S2TT systems.

Table 2 summarizes the performances of DS2TT systems for Prabhupadavani and MuST-C corpus evaluated using BLEU metric. The results from Table 2 demonstrates significant jump in performance when used high-quality audios. Moreover, the DS2TT system built using MuST-C (TTS) corpus achieved comparable performance to its cascaded counterpart. This result suggest that, both, size and audio quality impacts on the performance of direct S2TT systems. MuST-C is about four times the size of Prabhupadavani corpus. This may have contributed sufficient training examples for better learning of audio-text mappings by the encoder-decoder architecture.

Table 1. Performance of cascaded systems for Prabhupadavani and MuST-C corpus with original and TTS generated audios in terms of Word Error Rate (WER) for ASR and Bi-Lingual Evaluation Understudy (BLEU) score for MT and overall S2TT performance (in percentages).

Sl. No	Corpus	ASR (WER)	MT (BLEU)	Cascaded (BLEU)
1	Prabhupadavani (Original)	42.7	41.50	23.93
2	Prabhupadavani (TTS)	5.87	41.50	40.76
3	MuST-C (Original)	11.17	26.40	21.21
4	MuST-C (TTS)	9.77	26.40	23.44

Table 2. Performance of DS2TT systems for Prabhupadavani and MuST-C corpus in terms of BLEU score.

Sl. No	Corpus	DS2TT (BLEU Score)
1	Prabhupadavani (Original)	15.37
2	Prabhupadavani (TTS)	35.90
3	MuST-C (Original)	16.58
4	MuST-C (TTS)	24.33

3.1   Performance Analysis Using High-Quality Audios

The spectrograms of original and TTS generated audios from both the corpus are represented in Fig. 2 & 3. Figure 2 represents spectrograms from MuST-C corpus whereas Fig. 3 represents spectrograms from Prabhupadavani corpus. From the spectrograms, it can be observed that the energies are more prominent in the higher and lower frequency ranges in the TTS generated audios than in the original audios. This results in stronger frequency patterns corresponding to the speech which would help in capturing more speech nuances and also would provide more accurate feature representation. From Fig. 3(a) and Fig. 2(a), we observe that there is a limited frequency representation in the high-frequency range which can lead to information loss. The high-frequency representations are entirely lost for Prabhupadavani original audios than in MuST-C original audios. Also, in the low-frequency range, the representations are not that strong which makes it more challenging to distinguish speech-related representations from noise. Hence, it is evident that the original audios of MuST-C were superior to that of Prabhupadavani corpus which translated to better ASR performance. Thus, owing to the larger size and better quality audios, MuST-C is able to give closer performance with its corresponding models built using TTS generated audios. The performance difference is only 2.23 BLEU score for cascaded systems and 7.75 BLEU score for DS2TT whereas, for Prabhupadavani corpus, the difference is 16.38 BLEU score for cascaded systems and 20.53 BLEU score for DS2TT.

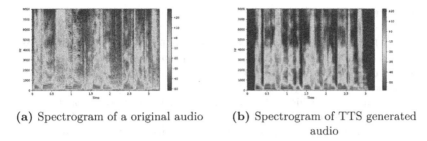

(a) Spectrogram of a original audio

(b) Spectrogram of TTS generated audio

Fig. 2. Spectrograms of an original audio and its corresponding TTS generated audio from MuST-C corpus.

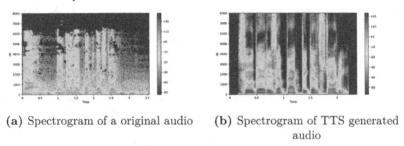

(a) Spectrogram of a original audio

(b) Spectrogram of TTS generated audio

Fig. 3. Spectrograms of an original audio and its corresponding TTS generated audio from Prabhupadavani corpus.

4 Conclusion and Future Work

The aim of this work was to study the effect of audio quality in the performance of direct and cascaded S2TT systems and to investigate if direct systems can provide comparable performance to that of cascaded systems without using any external data sources directly or indirectly in the form of pre-trained models etc. The results from Table 1 and 2 suggests that DS2TT systems can achieve comparable performance to that of cascaded systems if it is trained using larger corpora containing high-quality audio. This study may help to understand the potential of DS2TT over cascaded S2TT systems when high quality corpora is used. In the future, efforts will be directed to explore those attributes of a corpora that are responsible for the preference for building DS2TT over cascaded systems. Additionally, the effect of speech enhancement of audios and its effect on the performance will be studied. Also, methods to extract those training examples that contribute mostly to the performance will be investigated. These understandings may help in building robust Direct Speech-to-Text Translation systems.

References

1. Ali, A., Renals, S.: Word error rate estimation for speech recognition: e-WER. In: Proceedings of the 56th Annual Meeting of the Association for Computational Linguistics (Volume 2: Short Papers), pp. 20–24. Association for Computational Linguistics, Melbourne, Australia (2018)
2. Anastasopoulos, A., Chiang, D., Duong, L.: An unsupervised probability model for speech-to-translation alignment of low-resource languages. In: Proceedings of the 2016 Conference on Empirical Methods in Natural Language Processing, pp. 1255–1263. Association for Computational Linguistics, Austin (2016)
3. Berard, A., Pietquin, O., Servan, C., Besacier, L.: Listen and translate: a proof of concept for end-to-end speech-to-text translation (2016)
4. Chadha, H.S., Gupta, A., Shah, P., Chhimwal, N., Dhuriya, A., Gaur, R.: Vakyansh: TTS Indic languages (2022)
5. Chadha, H.S., et al.: Vakyansh: ASR toolkit for low resource Indic languages. arXiv preprint arXiv:2203.16512 (2022)
6. Di Gangi, M.A., Cattoni, R., Bentivogli, L., Negri, M., Turchi, M.: MuST-C: a multilingual speech translation corpus. In: Proceedings of the 2019 Conference of the North American Chapter of the Association for Computational Linguistics: Human Language Technologies, Volume 1 (Long and Short Papers), pp. 2012–2017. Association for Computational Linguistics, Minneapolis (2019)
7. Duong, L., Anastasopoulos, A., Chiang, D., Bird, S., Cohn, T.: An attentional model for speech translation without transcription. In: Proceedings of the 2016 Conference of the North American Chapter of the Association for Computational Linguistics: Human Language Technologies, pp. 949–959. Association for Computational Linguistics, San Diego (2016). https://doi.org/10.18653/v1/N16-1109, https://aclanthology.org/N16-1109
8. Gaido, M., Negri, M., Cettolo, M., Turchi, M.: Beyond voice activity detection: hybrid audio segmentation for direct speech translation. In: Proceedings of the 4th International Conference on Natural Language and Speech Processing (ICNLSP 2021), pp. 55–62. Association for Computational Linguistics, Trento (2021). http://aclanthology.org/2021.icnlsp-1.7
9. Gupta, A., Chadha, H.S., Shah, P., Chhimwal, N., Dhuriya, A., Gaur, R., Raghavan, V.: CLSRIL-23: cross lingual speech representations for Indic languages. arXiv preprint arXiv:2107.07402 (2021)
10. Indurthi, S., et al.: End-end speech-to-text translation with modality agnostic meta-learning. In: ICASSP 2020 - 2020 IEEE International Conference on Acoustics, Speech and Signal Processing (ICASSP), pp. 7904–7908 (2020). https://doi.org/10.1109/ICASSP40776.2020.9054759
11. Iranzo-Sanchez, J., et al.: Europarl-ST: a multilingual corpus for speech translation of parliamentary debates, pp. 8229–8233 (2020)
12. Jia, Y., et al.: Leveraging weakly supervised data to improve end-to-end speech-to-text translation. In: ICASSP 2019 - 2019 IEEE International Conference on Acoustics, Speech and Signal Processing (ICASSP), pp. 7180–7184 (2019)
13. Klein, G., Kim, Y., Deng, Y., Senellart, J., Rush, A.: OpenNMT: open-source toolkit for neural machine translation. In: Proceedings of ACL 2017, System Demonstrations, pp. 67–72. Association for Computational Linguistics, Vancouver (2017)

14. Kudo, T., Richardson, J.: SentencePiece: a simple and language independent subword tokenizer and detokenizer for neural text processing. In: Proceedings of the 2018 Conference on Empirical Methods in Natural Language Processing: System Demonstrations, pp. 66–71. Association for Computational Linguistics, Brussels (2018). https://doi.org/10.18653/v1/D18-2012, https://aclanthology.org/D18-2012

15. LeCun, Y., Bengio, Y.: Convolutional networks for images, speech, and time series, pp. 255–258. MIT Press, Cambridge (1998)

16. Ott, M., et al.: fairseq: a fast, extensible toolkit for sequence modeling. In: Proceedings of the 2019 Conference of the North American Chapter of the Association for Computational Linguistics (Demonstrations), pp. 48–53. Association for Computational Linguistics, Minneapolis (2019). https://doi.org/10.18653/v1/N19-4009, https://aclanthology.org/N19-4009

17. Papineni, K., Roukos, S., Ward, T., Zhu, W.J.: Bleu: a method for automatic evaluation of machine translation. In: Proceedings of the 40th Annual Meeting of the Association for Computational Linguistics, pp. 311–318. Association for Computational Linguistics, Philadelphia (2002)

18. Post, M.: A call for clarity in reporting BLEU scores. In: Proceedings of the Third Conference on Machine Translation: Research Papers, pp. 186–191. Association for Computational Linguistics, Brussels (2018)

19. Post, M., Kumar, G.S., Lopez, A., Karakos, D.G., Callison-Burch, C., Khudanpur, S.: Improved speech-to-text translation with the fisher and Callhome Spanish-English speech translation corpus. In: International Workshop on Spoken Language Translation (2013)

20. Rix, A., Beerends, J., Hollier, M., Hekstra, A.: Perceptual evaluation of speech quality (PESQ)-a new method for speech quality assessment of telephone networks and codecs. In: 2001 IEEE International Conference on Acoustics, Speech, and Signal Processing. Proceedings (Cat. No.01CH37221), vol. 2, pp. 749–752 (2001)

21. Salesky, E., et al.: The multilingual TEDx corpus for speech recognition and translation, pp. 3655–3659 (2021)

22. Sandhan, J., Daksh, A., Paranjay, O.A., Behera, L., Goyal, P.: Prabhupadavani: a code-mixed speech translation data for 25 languages. arXiv preprint arXiv:2201.11391 (2022)

23. Shen, J., et al.: Natural TTS synthesis by conditioning wavenet on MEL spectrogram predictions. In: 2018 IEEE International Conference on Acoustics, Speech and Signal Processing (ICASSP), pp. 4779–4783 (2018)

24. Vaswani, A., et al.: Attention is all you need. In: Guyon, I., et al. (eds.) Advances in Neural Information Processing Systems, vol. 30. Curran Associates, Inc. (2017)

25. Waibel, A., Fugen, C.: Spoken language translation. IEEE Signal Process. Mag. **25**(3), 70–79 (2008)

26. Wang, C., Pino, J., Wu, A., Gu, J.: CoVoST: a diverse multilingual speech-to-text translation corpus. In: Proceedings of the Twelfth Language Resources and Evaluation Conference, pp. 4197–4203. European Language Resources Association, Marseille (2020)

27. Yang, J., Hussein, A., Wiesner, M., Khudanpur, S.: JHU IWSLT 2022 dialect speech translation system description. In: Proceedings of the 19th International Conference on Spoken Language Translation (IWSLT 2022), pp. 319–326. Association for Computational Linguistics, Dublin (in-person and online) (2022)

28. Zhang, S., Feng, Y.: End-to-end simultaneous speech translation with differentiable segmentation. In: Findings of the Association for Computational Linguistics: ACL 2023, pp. 7659–7680. Association for Computational Linguistics, Toronto (2023). https://doi.org/10.18653/v1/2023.findings-acl.485, https://aclanthology.org/2023.findings-acl.485

Everyday Conversations: A Comparative Study of Expert Transcriptions and ASR Outputs at a Lexical Level

Tatiana Sherstinova[1]([✉]) [iD], Rostislav Kolobov[2] [iD], and Nikolay Mikhaylovskiy[2,3] [iD]

[1] HSE University, Saint Petersburg, Russia 190068
tsherstinova@hse.ru
[2] NTR Labs, Moscow, Russia 129594
{rkolobov,nickm}@ntr.ai
[3] Higher IT School of Tomsk State University, Tomsk, Russia 634050

Abstract. The study examines the outcomes of automatic speech recognition (ASR) applied to field recordings of daily Russian speech. Everyday conversations, captured in real-life communicative scenarios, pose quite a complex subject for ASR. This is due to several factors: they can contain speech from a multitude of speakers, the loudness of the conversation partners' speech signals fluctuates, there's a substantial volume of overlapping speech from two or more speakers, and significant noise interferences can occur periodically. The presented research compares transcripts of these recordings produced by two recognition systems: the NTR Acoustic Model and OpenAI's Whisper. These transcripts are then contrasted with expert transcription of the same recordings. The comparison of three frequency lists (the expert transcription, the acoustic model, and Whisper) reveals that each model has its unique characteristics at the lexical level. At the same time, both models perform worse in recognizing the following groups of words typical for spontaneous unprepared dialogues: discursive words, pragmatic markers, backchannel responses, interjections, conversational reduced word forms, and hesitations. These findings aim to foster improvements in ASR systems designed to transcribe conversational speech, such as work meetings and daily life dialogues.

Keywords: ASR Systems · Acoustic Model · Whisper · Field Recordings · Everyday Conversations · Dialogues · Russian Language · Vocabulary · Word Lists · Backchanneling · Discursive Words · Pragmatic Markers · Interjections · Conversational Word Forms · Hesitations

1 Introduction

Speech recognition technologies are currently advancing at an unprecedented pace. Utilizing neural networks, these systems can produce high-quality transcripts of spoken language in real-time, as exemplified by automatically generated subtitles for YouTube videos. However, challenges persist when dealing with everyday, real-world speech dialogues that encapsulate private interactions among individuals. Unlike curated YouTube

© The Author(s), under exclusive license to Springer Nature Switzerland AG 2023
A. Karpov et al. (Eds.): SPECOM 2023, LNAI 14338, pp. 43–56, 2023.
https://doi.org/10.1007/978-3-031-48309-7_4

recordings intended for mass consumption [15], these sound recordings are derived from authentic communication contexts. Speakers may be at a significant distance from the recording device, the number of interlocutors can greatly fluctuate, and the recordings often contain various background noises reflecting the aural realities of daily life. Frequently, these include unrelated speech elements, such as background television, radio, or simultaneous conversations among other groups of people. The need for collecting this type of field speech data spans both scientific research and practical applications, such as monitoring speech for medical or other specialized purposes. They also serve as invaluable training data for AI systems, enabling them to communicate more authentically or simulate real-world scenarios. The Japanese ESP corpus (from the JST/CREST Expressive Speech Processing project) [6], the BNC [20], and the Russian ORD corpus [3], which forms the basis for this research, are notable examples of databases containing such everyday speech conversations.

The measure of a speech recognition system's quality is its alignment with human auditory perception. Hence, expert human transcription is deemed the "gold standard", providing the reference point for key performance indicators of speech recognition systems, including the Word Error Rate (WER), Character Error Rate (CER), and other associated metrics [1, 16, 23]. In this study, we examine how two modern Automatic Speech Recognition (ASR) models of different types handle these challenges. Our analysis employs a lexical-statistical approach, comparing the frequency lists of words derived from each system.

2 Data and Method

2.1 Data

The study is based on 195 macro-episodes of everyday speech communication taken from the ORD corpus [5, 22], obtained from 104 participants. The data set includes everyday (both casual and institutional) communication dialogues featuring men and women from all age groups (young, middle-aged, and seniors), and across various professional sectors: laborers involved in manufacturing or construction, service industry workers, educators, law enforcement officers, creative professionals, office workers, IT specialists, engineers, humanities scholars, and natural scientists.

The total volume of speech data consists of approximately 300,000 instances of word usage. An anonymized version of this sample is publicly accessible on the ORD corpus website [17]. The macro-episodes used in this study capture the full spectrum of everyday communication—the recordings were made in a variety of settings, such as homes, workplaces (offices and manufacturing sites), universities, medical facilities, shops, cafes, restaurants, and outdoor public spaces [21].

Expert transcription of the recordings was carried out using the ELAN multimedia annotation software [9]. This process involved several iterations where the transcriptions were reviewed and corrected by at least three experts. We employed an "error correction" method, where each expert would correct the errors made by the previous one, retaining the prior transcription for reference if needed. However, ORD expert transcription method does have one minor drawback—the text is presented on a linear scale, which can oversimplify the representation of a multichannel speech signal. Furthermore, not all fragments of the speech signal were decipherable by the experts. In instances where the spoken content was unclear, the experts marked the section with an asterisk followed by the letter H (for "hard to decipher").

2.2 Method

Transcripts were obtained for the same 195 audio recordings of speech episodes using two speech recognition systems: the NTR Acoustic model and the OpenAI Whisper system.

NTR Acoustic Model is a non-autoregressive headless variant of Conformer [8] which uses CTC loss instead of Transducer and is based on NVIDIA NEMO Conformer-CTC large [11]. Conformer-CTC has a similar encoder as the original Conformer but uses CTC loss and decoding instead of RNNT/Transducer loss, which makes it a non-autoregressive model. This model uses the combination of self-attention and convolution modules to achieve the best of the two approaches, the self-attention layers can learn the global interaction while the convolutions efficiently capture the local correlations. The self-attention modules support both regular self-attention with absolute positional encoding, and also Transformer-XL's self-attention with relative positional encodings. Figure 1 presents Conformer-CTC encoder architecture.

In addition to the original NVIDIA NEMO Conformer-CTC training datasets Mozilla Common Voice 10.0 [13] (28 h), Golos-crowd (1070 h) and fairfield (111 h) [14], Russian LibriSpeech (RuLS) [4] (92 h) and SOVA—RuAudiobooksDevices (260 h) [12] and RuDevices (75 h) [12] NTR Acoustic Model is trained on a private Russian part of NTR MediaSpeech dataset (1000 h) [15].

Whisper [19] is an encoder-decoder audio-to-text Transformer [24] that ingests 80-channel logmagnitude mel-spectrogram computed on 25-ms windows with a stride of 10 ms from audio sampled at 16,000 Hz. The encoder processes this input representation with a small stem consisting of two convolution layers with a filter width of 3 and the GELU activation function [10] where the second convolution layer has a stride of two. Sinusoidal position embeddings are then added to the output of the stem after which the encoder Transformer blocks are applied. The transformer uses pre-activation residual blocks [7], and a final layer normalization is applied to the encoder output. The decoder uses learned position embeddings and tied input-output token representations [18]. The encoder and decoder have the same width and number of transformer blocks. Figure 2 summarizes Whisper architecture.

Whisper is trained with multitask approach on a large and diverse dataset [19]. The training tasks included transcription, translation, voice activity detection, alignment, and language identification. The training dataset was constructed from audio that is paired with transcripts on the Internet. Several automated filtering methods were used to improve the transcript quality. These included removing ASR-generated transcripts, ensuring that the spoken language matches the language of the transcript according to CLD2, and removing low-quality data sources based on WER of the initial model.

Thus, for the purpose of this research, two ASR systems of entirely different nature were selected. OpenAI Whisper is essentially a multilingual language model with an acoustic input. It possesses extensive knowledge about languages and written speech and is partly involved in translating spoken language into written form. As such, its

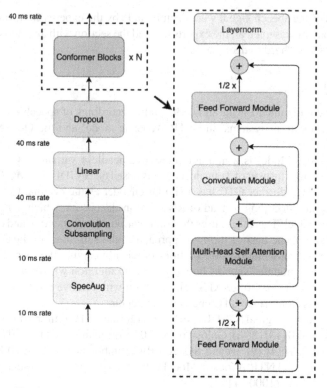

Fig. 1. Overall architecture of the encoder of Conformer-CTC.

errors relative to expert translations are often considered as "excessive literarization" mistakes. In contrast, the NTR Acoustic Model has no understanding of language but acts as a transcription tool. It transcribes exactly "what it hears", without considering the accuracy of spelling. A significant portion of its errors could be classified as "illiterate". Consequently, these two models can be regarded as two opposing poles for ASR, with all other models occupying intermediate positions. Therefore, we can anticipate that the recognition results of the other ASR systems would fall somewhere in the middle of this spectrum. It is for this reason that we decided to use OpenAI Whisper and NTR Acoustic Model these systems for this study.

The models' performance was evaluated based on the Word Error Rate (WER) across 195 speech episodes. The NTR Acoustic Model yielded an average WER of 65%, with a single speech episode achieving the best performance of 30% WER, and the poorest performance reaching 99%. On the other hand, the Whisper system had a lower average WER of 49%, with the best-performing episode yielding a 7% WER and the worst reaching 99%. These numbers are an indication of how complicated the ORD dataset is even for the best contemporary speech recognition systems.

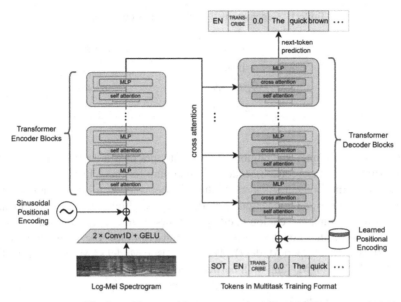

Fig. 2. Whisper architecture overview (from [19]).

To assess the models from a lexical perspective, we employed AntConc [2], a corpus management tool, to create three frequency dictionaries. The referent dictionary represented the transcriptions considered as the "gold standard", which were produced by human experts. The second and third dictionaries comprised the recognition results from the NTR Acoustic Model and the Whisper system, respectively.

One notable aspect of the expert-generated transcriptions is their treatment of overlaid speech. When speakers' volumes were sufficiently loud, the experts discerned multiple speech channels, recording them linearly as a sequence of utterances. Therefore, simultaneous speech from different speakers is transcribed as consecutive utterances. Thus, it becomes inherently impossible to achieve a 100% alignment between the performance of the recognition system and the expert transcription, since the considered recognition systems do not distinguish background speech during overlapping speech.

By comparing the frequency dictionaries, we were able to identify the lexical items that the models recognized more or less effectively.

3   Word Lists Statistics

3.1   Comparison of Frequency Lists

Table 1 presents the primary statistics of the obtained frequency dictionaries. Primarily, we note the distinctly different volumes of transcriptions – the expert transcription contains 302,681 words (tokens), the NTR Acoustic Model (AM) produced 274,305 words, and the OpenAI Whisper Model (WM) transcribed only 236,179 words. The WM contains the fewest words because it appears to clean the text from repetitions, hesitations, and other "garbage" elements of spontaneous speech.

Table 1. General statistics of transcripts obtained.

Transcription	Tokens	Types
Expert transcript	302,681	31,311
AM	274,305	36,846
WM	236,179	28,060

The dictionary volume (the number of different types of words) also varies slightly. It has maximum for the Acoustic Model and minimum for the Whisper Model, which is trained on internet content. As a result, the AM seems to "hear" more variety, while the WM, as a variant of a large language model, only uses high-probability vocabulary.

The Spearman rank correlation coefficient shows high values, indicating a strong agreement between the models and the expert transcriptions. The correlation coefficients are 0.78 for the Expert Model (EM) and Acoustic Model (AM), 0.84 for the EM and Whisper Model (WM), and 0.78 between the AM and WM. This implies that the Whisper system aligns more closely with the expert transcription in terms of ranked word frequencies than the Acoustic Model does.

Table 2 showcases the top 25 words for the generated frequency dictionaries. Normalized frequency is given in ipm (items per million).

The word '*ja*' ('*I*') turned out to be the most frequently used across all models. However, its occurrence is slightly higher in the WM transcriptions, potentially due to the model's propensity to automatically complete incomplete sentences, such as changing '*ushla*' ('*have left*') to '*ja ushla*' ('*I have left*'). The same pattern can be observed in the recognition of the second most frequent personal pronoun '*ty*' ('*you*'), as well as '*on*' ('*he*'), and '*ona*' ('*she*').

Both models have difficulties recognizing the discourse word '*nu*' ('*well*'). This could be attributed to the fact that it commonly occurs at the beginning of sentences and is frequently reduced to the consonant [n]. Since it doesn't carry any lexical meaning, it might be overlooked by the language model. The models also often struggle to identify accurately '*vot*' ('*well*'/'*here you go*'), another commonly used pragmatic marker in everyday spoken Russian. This difficulty could be attributed to the fact that '*vot*' often undergoes phonetic reduction, turning into [ot] or even [ъt]. Moreover, '*vot*' often does not carry a specific lexical meaning, acting instead as a pragmatic marker [25], which could further complicate its recognition by the models.

Both models show a lesser frequency for the particle '*da*' ('*yes*') compared to the expert transcription. This could be because this word is often used as a backchannel response, typically as an agreement during an ongoing conversation. As the models tend to disregard overlapping speech, this discrepancy arises. A similar trend is observed for other forms of backchanneling like '*ugu*' ('*uh-huh*') and '*aga*' ('*aha*'). The particle/conjunction '*a*' is in a similar situation. At the same time, both ASR models provides more occurrences of conjunction '*chto*' ('*what*'), which is more characteristic for written and official language.

Thus, it can be seen that the frequency dictionaries differ significantly not for all words, but only for some, which the models "hear" more or less often compared to the expert transcription. Let's consider the most frequent words of this kind.

Table 2. Top 25 words in transcripts obtained.

Expert transcript			Acoustic Model			Whisper Model		
Rank	Word	Norm.Fr	Rank	Word	Norm.Fr	Rank	Word	Norm.Fr
1	ja	26,999	1	ja	26,372	1	ja (I)	28,212
2	nu	26,946	2	ne	24,294	2	ne	25,366
3	ne	24,527	3	nu	23,889	3	chto	22,297
4	da	23,619	4	chto	22,016	4	nu	21,793
5	a	21,353	5	vot	20,889	5	da	20,057
6	vot	21,353	6	da	19,566	6	v	19,223
7	chto	21,207	7	i	18,308	7	a	18,888
8	i	19,189	8	v	16,985	8	i	17,885
9	v	18,670	9	a	16,886	9	vot	17,203
10	to	16,598	10	to	16,788	10	to	16,360
11	eto	16,503	11	eto	16,336	11	eto	16,051
12	tam	14,348	12	na	13,496	12	tam	13,079
13	u	12,422	13	tam	13,405	13	na	12,673
14	na	12,300	14	u	11,349	14	u	12,643
15	tak	11,140	15	tak	11,053	15	tak	10,335
16	vse	10,566	16	kak	10,368	16	kak	10,136
17	kak	10,354	17	vse	10,302	17	ty	9,815
18	ty	9,773	18	ty	8,585	18	s	7,994
19	s	8,471	19	s	8,046	19	on	7,837
20	on	7,572	20	on	6,854	20	vse	7,350
21	net	6,512	21	net	6,526	21	net	7,283
22	ona	6,168	22	ona	6,070	22	ona	6,982
23	ugu	6,105	23	mne	5,968	23	mne	5,860
24	mne	5,676	24	est'	5,702	24	est'	5,780
25	est'	5,663	25	po	5,282	25	men'a	5,064

3.2 Words that Are Least Recognized

Words that are poorly recognized by the models are intriguing because they are frequently omitted during automatic recognition. Analyzing the lists of the least recognized frequent words showed a significant overlap for both models. The following groups of words were found to be poorly recognized:

1) Discursive words and pragmatic markers, along with their components: "nu" (well), "vot" (well, you know), "govorit" (he/she says), "govorju" (I say), "koroche" (in short/basically), "tipa" (like), "eto samoe" (you know), "v obschem" (in general), etc.
2) Backchannel responses: "ugu" (uh-huh), "aga" (yeah), "da" (yes).
3) Interjections: "oj" (oh), "blin" (damn), "b...d'" (f...k), "akh" (ah), "ekh" (eh), etc.
4) Conversational forms of literary words: "naverno" (probably), "chtob" (in order to), etc.
5) Hesitations and unfinished words: "m" (um), "n" (un), "e" (er), etc.

All these speech elements characterize informal, everyday verbal communication, particularly in a dialogic form. These results for Whisper can likely be attributed to the lack of substantial training data on everyday dialogic speech, resulting in a more formal and "literary" quality of the generated transcriptions. Moreover, for both models, the difficulty in recognizing these words may arise from their occurrence in weak positions— at the beginning or end of phrases, amid the speech of the interlocutor (especially for backchannelling), and when they serve rhythmic functions [26],—leading to their weaker acoustic representation as they lack substantial semantic content. The exclusion of these speech elements by the systems does not have a significant impact on the core content of the utterances but does lead to a loss of the specific colloquial nuances in the transcriptions of oral speech.

Furthermore, consistent differences in the performance of each system are observed. The recognition errors in the Acoustic Model (AM) can be explained by the strong reduction of frequent words in real speech, such as "ty" (you), "on" (he), "tam" (there), "ili" (or), "teb'a" (you), "vidish" (see), and similar words. An interesting characteristic of Whisper is the lack of verbal representation for numerals (represented as numbers) and the limited, albeit irregular, use of the letter "Ё" (jo), which accounts for the reduced occurrence of words like "vsjo" (everything), "jeshche" (still/yet), "jejo" (her).

Table 3 provides two lists of the top 25 words/tokens with the most significant discrepancies in frequency compared to the expert transcription. The lists are ordered by decreasing differences in relative frequency (ipm), and they also include information on differences in rank orders and relative differences expressed in %.

4   Words Not Found in the Expert Transcription

Lastly, the words that were "recognized" by a specific model but are missing in the expert transcription are of special interest. The Table 4 shows the top 25 most frequent words in this category.

The NTR Acoustic Model provides a fairly extensive list of frequent tokens that are not present in the expert transcription. In the vast majority of cases, these are reduced forms of common words, such as "govor(yu)/(it)" (I say/he/she says), "(poni)maesh" (you understand), "ponyat(no)" (I see), "slusha(y)" (listen), "chelove(k)" (man/person), "(nor)mal'no" (normal), etc. For example, "govor" is a shortened form of "govoryu"/'govorit" (I say/he/she says):

– *Kuda on vyshla? (Where did she go?)*
– *Mam, ya govoryu, po delam ochevidno (Mom, I'm speaking to you, obviously, on business).* (ordS72–11[1])

Table 3. Frequent words worst recognized by models.

Acoustic Model					Whisper Model				
#	Word	Rank dif	IPM dif	Relat dif	#	Word	Rank dif	IPM dif	Relat dif
1	a	-4	4466	21	1	nu	-2	5153	19
2	da	-2	4053	17	2	ugu	-51	4382	72
3	nu	-1	3056	11	3	vot	-3	4149	19
4	ugu	-14	2405	39	4	da	-1	3562	15
5	m	-112	1917	73	5	vsjo	-4	3215	30
6	v	1	1685	9	6	a	-2	2464	12
7	ty	0	1187	12	7	m	-206	2244	86
8	u	-1	1074	9	8	jeshche	-9	1347	29
9	tam	-1	944	7	9	i	0	1304	7
10	i	1	880	5	10	tam	0	1269	9
11	k	-22	723	30	11	chego	-46	984	48
12	on	0	719	9	12	zh	-134	902	69
13	n	-1018	671	92	13	tak	0	805	7
14	aga	-30	629	33	14	oy	-37	782	38
15	ya	0	627	2	15	n	-18306	729	99
16	oy	-20	532	26	16	dvadtsat'	-307	695	78
17	vot	1	463	2	17	aga	-34	667	35
18	s	0	425	5	18	govorit	-16	582	22
19	zh	-37	419	32	19	pyat'	-111	565	58
20	fon	-388	414	76	20	veroyatno	-18301	534	99
21	chtoby	-143	380	57	21	chtoby	-448	533	80
22	verojatno	-221	345	64	22	jejo	-29	511	32
23	e	-3047	345	94	23	t	-1508	502	92
24	o	-28	336	23	24	s	1	477	6
25	ili	-10	330	14	25	tri	-61	455	43

---

[1] Hereinafter, the code of the macro-episode of the ORD corpus.

It is worth noting that among the frequent tokens, there are forms that can be traced back not to one but to several completely different words. For instance, "mas" may stand for "maslo" (butter/oil), "master" (master), and even "most" (bridge):

– *Ya, naprimer, sama ne pokupayu natural(noe), ya pokupayu rastitel(noe) mas(lo) (For example, I myself don't buy natural, but vegetable oil) (ordS11–06).*
– *Gde vot eta to ulitsa vykhodit na Liteynyy, kakaya ot tsirka tam cherez mas (=most) pereezzhaesh' (Where is this street connecting to Liteynyy prospect, the one from the circus, where you cross the bridge) (ordS84–22).*

The compiled lists of real words' transcriptions along with their corresponding ortho-graphic representations can serve as a valuable resource for creating a dictionary of reduced forms. This dictionary can showcase the various alterations and distortions that occur in words during spontaneous speech. Such a resource is of great significance for conducting phonetic research on spoken language and for enhancing the training of language models.

Regarding the Whisper model, the frequency list is dominated by words containing the letter "Ё" (yo). As mentioned earlier, this recognition model incorporates this letter, unlike the acoustic model. However, Whisper uses "Ё" irregularly. For example, the word "*jeshcho*" (yet/still) with this letter appeared in the transcriptions only half as often as without it (337 vs. 761). It's worth noting that in the expert transcription used for the study (as well as the version for the ORD website), all instances of "Ё" were replaced with "E" despite the original ORD corpus, which includes it.

Furthermore, Whisper demonstrates good English language comprehension and recognizes the names of many brands and computer terms, such as *Photoshop, USB, Microsoft Office, Wi-Fi*, which were originally written in Russian in the expert transcription. These words have also been included in this list.

From Table 4, it is also evident that among the frequent words recognized by Whisper, there are words that do not actually exist in the language (e.g., "shvejn", "vodonyuchka"). However, upon examining the transcriptions, it becomes apparent that these occurrences should be considered as system glitches—these words are repeatedly present just in a single file, and the transcription of that file has little resemblance to reality.

Let's take, for example, the usage of the word "vodonyuchka". All instances of this word are related to a single episode. This recording represents a noisy speech of a man addressed to his car, which is experiencing some technical issues. In the original file, there were significant pauses between the utterances, which were replaced with 2 ms pause insertions. The system incorrectly recognized two initial words of the recording—"batareechka" and "batareyka" (both meaning "battery")—as "vodonyuchka" (no sense) and then erroneously "recognized" this new word in 22 other places:

Expert transcript:—*Batareechka, batareyka. Ya tebya ponyal. Vse. Tu tu tu. [Pro-fanity]... Nu nakonets-to! (Little battery, battery. I understood you. That's all. Tu tu tu. [Profanity]. Finally!)* (ordS74–02).

Whisper Model transcript:—*Vodonyuchka, vodonyuchka. Ya tebya ponyal. (I under-stood you) Vodonyuchka, vodonyuchka. Vodonyuchka, vodonyuchka. [Profanity]... Vodonyuchka, vodonyuchka* (ordS74–02).

Another glitch in the system was identified during the analysis of the word "shveyn". In this instance, Whisper generated a transcription fragment with a repetitive loop of the

Table 4. Words Not Found in the Expert Transcription.

Acoustic Model				Whisper Model			
#	Word	Frequency	IPM	#	Word	Frequency	IPM
1	b...d'	29	106	1	vs'o	725	3070
2	govor	24	87	2	jeshcho	337	1427
3	mas	21	77	3	jejo	116	491
4	boy	17	62	4	ona	89	377
5	mayesh'	16	58	5	cho (чё)	82	347
6	ponyat	15	55	6	id'ot	67	284
7	mer	14	51	7	shvejn*	61	258
8	uga	12	44	8	ru	41	174
9	slushayu	10	36	9	kub	40	169
10	dtsat'	9	33	10	vodonyuchka*	22	93
11	mala	9	33	11	prishol	22	93
12	stav	9	33	12	chom	22	93
13	glyad'	8	29	13	poyd'om	20	85
14	yer	8	29	14	poyd'ot	19	80
15	sen	8	29	15	dolzhen	19	80
16	khom	8	29	16	prichom	18	76
17	chelovek	8	29	17	ber'ozy	15	64
18	agu	7	26	18	nashol	14	59
19	shay	7	26	19	r	13	55
20	gal	6	22	20	l'ova	13	55
21	ed'e	6	22	21	mojo	13	55
22	krasno	6	22	22	poshel	12	51
23	lega	6	22	23	prid'ot	11	47
24	mali	6	22	24	savushkinu	11	47
25	mal'no	6	22	25	zhivjot	10	42

phrase "ya ponyal, chto dlya shveyn, a v remonte tozhe cherez nikh" (I understood that for shveyn, and in repairs too through them – quite a meaningless phrase), which was repeated 61 times and has nothing to do with the original transcript.

"Vodonyuchka" and "shvejn" repetition cases, along with any other phrase repetitions, represent typical instances of degeneracy observed in texts generated by large language models [27]. If a word appears in the text for any reason, the probability of the model generating it again often increases. This phenomenon explains the repetition of peculiar words in the text. Hence, "vodonyuchka" was an initial recognition error, and then the model degeneratively propagated it through repetition. These examples highlight the need for a preliminary filtering process to exclude files that exhibit such malfunctions, ensuring a more accurate comparison of frequency dictionaries.

Additionally, another distinctive feature of Whisper is its active use of colloquial forms, such as "chyo" (what), while the expert transcription utilizes the word "chto" in the same context. For example:

— Chyo, pryam na Ladogu poedesh'?... Nu chyo tam khoroshego?... Kamney net, ogromnykh etikh valunov, a tak ya ne znayu, chyo tam khoroshego v etoy Ladoge... (What, are you going straight to Ladoga lake?... Well, what's good there?... There are no big rocks, those huge boulders, but I don't know what's good about Ladoga...).
— Chyo ty nesyosh'? (What are you talking about?)
— A chyo? (And what?)
— Chyo ty nesyosh'? (What are you talking about?) (ordS88–03)

Moreover, both ASR models utilize the colloquial form of greeting "zdraste" (hello), which was not employed by the experts in their transcriptions. As a result, some of the discrepancies between the ASR transcripts and the expert model can be attributed not to deficiencies in these systems but rather to the variability in orthographic representation ("zdraste" instead "zdravsvujte"), as well as the usage of the letter "Ё" (yo).

5 Conclusions

The study utilized two ASR systems with distinct characteristics: 1) OpenAI Whisper, a multilingual language model with acoustic input, which exhibits extensive knowledge of languages. Its transcriptions tend to be excessively literary and contain more written language features than the original audio, and 2) NTR Acoustic Model, lacking language understanding but acting as a transcription tool by transcribing exactly "what it hears", without considering spelling accuracy. Other ASR systems for the Russian language would likely yield results falling between those presented.

The research showed that each of the considered systems has its own peculiarities and regular recognition errors. On the lexical level, certain groups of words are poorly recognized by both systems, such as discursive words, pragmatic markers, backchannel responses, interjections, conversational reduced word forms, and hesitations. The challenging recognition of these words can be attributed to various factors, ranging from the lack of sufficiently representative training corpora of spontaneous dialogues to the presence of these words in prosodically weak positions (e.g., used for rhythmic functions). The omission of these speech elements by ASR systems generally does not have a significant impact on the overall comprehension of the message conveyed in the utterance. However, it does lead to the transcripts lacking the specific colloquial nuances of spoken language.

Some differences between ASR transcripts and the expert model are not due to shortcomings in the recognition systems but stem from the variability in the orthographic representation of spoken words and the specific nuances of their pronunciation in each context. Considering this aspect, the WER values mentioned in Sect. 2.2 might be somewhat overstated.

Upon comparing the overall performance of the systems, the Whisper model generally produces more "easily readable" text, resembling written language, and requires less manual correction for most practical purposes (e.g., for publishing interviews recorded on a dictaphone). However, some manual correction remains necessary as the transcripts may contain disruptions like word repetitions and even looped phrases and sentences. Furthermore, when using Whisper, it is important to take into account the likelihood of degeneracy during text generation by large language models. If a word appears in the text for any reason, the probability of the model generating it again is heightened. This phenomenon explains the repetition of peculiar words in the text.

On the other hand, the transcripts generated by the NTR Acoustic Model are less familiar to educated readers, but they more accurately reflect the pronunciation peculiarities of words and phrases. The frequency lists of words obtained with the NTR model, along with references to their orthographic representation, can serve as valuable material for constructing a dictionary of reduced forms, showcasing word distortions in spontaneous speech. This provides essential material for phonetic studies of oral speech and further ASR model training designed for everyday conversations.

Acknowledgements. This article is an output of a research project "Text as Big Data: Modeling Convergent Processes in Language and Speech using Digital Methods" implemented as part of the Basic Research Program at the National Research University Higher School of Economics (HSE University).

References

1. Ali, A., Renals, S.: Word error rate estimation for speech recognition: e-WER. In: Proceedings of the 56th Annual Meeting of the Association for Computational Linguistics. Vol. 2: Short Papers. Melbourne, Australia. Association for Computational Linguistics, pp. 20–24 (2018). https://aclanthology.org/P18-2004.pdf
2. AntConc. http://www.laurenceanthony.net/software.html. Accessed 1 Sept 2023
3. Asinovsky, A., Bogdanova, N., Rusakova, M., Stepanova, S., Ryko, A., Sherstinova, S.: The ORD speech corpus of Russian everyday communication "One Speaker's Day": creation principles and annotation. In: Matoušek, V., Mautner, P. (eds) Text, Speech and Dialogue. TSD 2009. Lecture Notes in Computer Science, vol 5729, pp. 250–257. Springer, Berlin, Heidelberg (2009)
4. Bakhturina, E., Lavrukhin, V., Ginsburg, B.: A toolbox for construction and analysis of speech datasets. Proc. Neural Inf. Process. Syst. Track Datasets Benchmarks, 1 (2021)
5. Bogdanova-Beglarian, N., Sherstinova, T., Blinova, O., Ermolova, O., Baeva, E., Martynenko, G., Ryko, A.: Sociolinguistic extension of the ORD corpus of Russian everyday speech. Ronzhin, A., et al. (eds.), *SPECOM 2016*, Lecture Notes in Artificial Intelligence, LNAI, **9811**, pp. 659–666. Springer, Switzerland (2016)
6. Campbell, N.: Speech & expression; the value of a longitudinal corpus. LREC **2004**, 183–186 (2004)
7. Child, R., Gray, S., Radford, A., Sutskever, I.: Generating long sequences with sparse transformers. arXiv preprint arXiv:1904.10509 (2019)
8. Gulati, A., et al.: Conformer: convolution-augmented transformer for speech recognition. In: Proceedings of the Annual Conference of the International Speech Communication Association, INTERSPEECH, pp. 5036–5040 (2020)

9. Hellwig, B., Van Uytvanck, D., Hulsbosch, M., et al.: ELAN — Linguistic Annotator. Version 4.9.3 [in:] http://tla.mpi.nl/tools/tla-tools/elan/ Linguistic Annotator ELAN. https://tla.mpi.nl/tools/tla-tools/elan/
10. Hendrycks, D., Gimpel, K.: Gaussian Error Linear Units (gelus). arXiv preprint arXiv:1606.08415 (2016)
11. https://catalog.ngc.nvidia.com/orgs/nvidia/teams/nemo/models/stt_ru_conformer_ctc_large
12. https://github.com/sovaai/sova-dataset
13. https://voice.mozilla.org
14. Karpov, N., Denisenko, A., Minkin, F.: Golos: Russian dataset for speech research. Proc. Annu. Conf. Int. Speech Commun. Assoc. INTERSPEECH **2**, 1076–1080 (2021). https://doi.org/10.21437/Interspeech.2021-462
15. Kolobov, R., et al.: Mediaspeech: Multilanguage ASR Benchmark and Dataset. arXiv, arXiv: 2103.16193 (2021)
16. Morris, A.C., Maier, V., Green, P.: From WER and RIL to MER and WIL: improved evaluation measures for connected speech recognition. In: Eighth International Conference on Spoken Language Processing, pp. 2765–2768 (2004). https://www.isca-speech.org/archive_v0/archive_papers/interspeech_2004/i04_2765.pdf?ref=https://githubhelp.com
17. One Speech Day corpus online. https://ord.spbu.ru/
18. Press, O., Wolf, L.: Using the output embedding to improve language models. In: Proceedings of the 15th Conference of the European Chapter of the Association for Computational Linguistics: Volume 2, Short Papers, pp. 157–163, Valencia, Spain, April 2017. Association for Computational Linguistics (2017)
19. Radford, A., Kim, J.W., Xu, T., Brockman, G., McLeavey, C., Sutskever, I.: Robust speech recognition via large-scale weak supervision. Proceedings of the 40th International Conference on Machine Learning, in Proceedings of Machine Learning Research **202**, 28492–28518 (2023)
20. Reference Guide for the British National Corpus. http://www.natcorp.ox.ac.uk/docs/URG.xml
21. Sherstinova, T.: Macro episodes of Russian everyday oral communication: towards pragmatic annotation of the ORD speech corpus. Ronzhin, A., et al. (eds.) SPECOM 2015. Lecture Notes in Artificial Intelligence, LNAI. Vol. 9319. Springer, Switzerland, pp. 268–276 (2015)
22. Sherstinova, T.: The structure of the ORD speech corpus of Russian everyday communication. In: Matoušek, V., Mautner, P. (eds.) TSD 2009. LNCS (LNAI), vol. 5729, pp. 258–265. Springer, Heidelberg (2009). https://doi.org/10.1007/978-3-642-04208-9_37
23. Von Neumann, T., Boeddeker, C., Kinoshita, K., Delcroix, M., Haeb-Umbach, R.: On word error rate definitions and their efficient computation for multi-speaker speech recognition systems. ICASSP 2023 - 2023 IEEE International Conference on Acoustics, Speech and Signal Processing (ICASSP), Rhodes Island, Greece, pp. 1–5 (2023). https://ieeexplore.ieee.org/abstract/document/10094784/
24. Vaswani, A., et al.: Attention is all you need. In: Advances in Neural Information Processing Systems, pp. 5999–6009 (2017)
25. Bogdanova-Beglarian, N., Blinova, O., Sherstinova, T., Troshchenkova, E.: Russian pragmatic markers database: developing speech technologies for everyday spoken discourse. In: 26th Conference of Open Innovations Association FRUCT, FRUCT 2020; Yaroslavl; Russian Federation, pp. 60–66 (2020)
26. Bogdanova-Beglarian, N., Sherstinova, T., Kisloshchuk, A.: On the rhythm-forming function of discursive units. Perm University Herald. Russian and Foreign Philology **2**(22), 7–17 (2013)
27. Holtzman, A., et al.: The curious case of neural text degeneration. In: Proceedings of the 2020 International Conference on Learning Representations, p. 2540 (2020)

Improving Automatic Speech Recognition with Dialect-Specific Language Models

Raj Gothi[(✉)] and Preeti Rao

Centre for Machine Intelligence and Data Science, Indian Institute of Technology
Bombay, Mumbai, India
22m2160@iitb.ac.in, prao@ee.iitb.ac.in

Abstract. We present an end-to-end Automatic Speech Recognition
(ASR) system in the context of the recent challenge tasks for Bhojpuri
and Bengali. Our implementation follows the currently popular wav2vec
models while we investigate ways to leverage the dialect-categorised data
in order to improve ASR performance. We report overall improvements
in word error rate with dialect-specific language models for each of the
languages. We present an analysis that provides insights into some of the
factors underlying the success of dialect-specific language models.

Keywords: Dialects · Language model · Bhojpuri ASR · Bengali ASR

1 Introduction

While ASR systems are typically built for a given language using language-
specific transcribed speech and text resources, a particular challenge is the pervasive phenomenon of the language comprising of multiple dialects. These different forms of the same language, as used across its population of speakers,
arise from variations ranging from geography to socio-cultural characteristics.
Much prior research has addressed the robustness of ASR systems in the face of
multiple dialects by dialect-specific acoustic modeling where the acoustic model
(AM) is trained separately on transcribed speech of each dialect, and then used
with either known or automatically labeled dialect speech [7]. Thus while dialects
have been considered in speech recognition system development mainly for the
accents or word pronunciation variability they introduce in spoken language, it
may be noted that they can actually also encompass significant variations in
grammar and vocabulary [9]. In ASR systems, the syntax and vocabulary constraints that influence the acoustic model predictions are learned via language
modeling from the training data transcripts and possibly also from additional
text resources of the language.

Recently, in the context of Telugu, a language with multiple dialects,
Yadavalli et al. [15] showed that using a dialect-mismatched language model
(LM) significantly degraded ASR performance even when a dialect-specific AM

© The Author(s), under exclusive license to Springer Nature Switzerland AG 2023
A. Karpov et al. (Eds.): SPECOM 2023, LNAI 14338, pp. 57–67, 2023.
https://doi.org/10.1007/978-3-031-48309-7_5

was employed. While they did not register an overall improvement in word-error rate (WER) with dialect-specific LMs, they demonstrated significant differences between matched- and mismatched-LM based ASR for each of three Telugu dialect datasets. By way of analysis, they fine-tuned a BERT-like system (INDIC-BERT [8]) for dialect identification from text to obtain sentence embeddings that exhibited clear clustering based on dialect. No further insights on the relevant dialectical factors was provided. They used the Conformer Model for their Acoustic Model (AM), but training it from scratch, i.e. without any pre-training. Additionally, they employ a separate Transformer LM for their Language Model.

In the present work, we reconsider the question of the role of dialect-specific language modeling for two other Indian languages, namely Bhojpuri (with three dialects) and Bengali (with five dialects). Our ASR system utilizes the wav2vec2 base pre-trained model with fine-tuning on our data for the Acoustic Model (AM), and an n-gram based model for the Language Model (LM). The data is obtained from the recent MADASR challenge [12]. We report improvements in WER on our dataset overall, apart from dialect-specific improvements, with matched LMs. We present an analysis of the datasets in terms of some of the factors that serve to explain the results.

2 Dataset

The dataset used in this research is MADASR[1] (Model ADaptation for ASR in low-resource Indian languages) [12]. MADASR is specifically designed to address the challenges posed by low-resource Indian languages, with a focus on Bengali and Bhojpuri. It provides valuable annotated speech data for these languages, allowing for the development and evaluation of accurate speech recognition systems.

Most Indian languages suffer from limited availability of high-quality data compared to high-resource languages, which hinders research and development efforts. This dataset contains a large amount of labeled speech data in Bengali and Bhojpuri, with 851 hours and 835 hours respectively. To account for the linguistic diversity within each language, the dataset was collected from various dialects representing distinct regions or communities. In Bengali, the dataset comprises speech data from five different dialects (D1, D2, D3, D4, and D5) with statistics as in Table 1. Similarly, the Bhojpuri dataset includes data from three dialects (D1, D2, and D3) as in Table 2. Every utterance in the dataset is also annotated with dialect id, allowing for easy categorization and targeted analysis. This dialect-based data allows the models to better capture and adapt to the specific linguistic characteristics present in each region. Further, this dataset is drawn from diverse domains including Healthcare, Agriculture, Food, Technology, Sports, and others.

The text and transcriptions are in the native script for each of the languages with 72 characters in Bhojpuri and 64 in Bengali. In addition to the word-level

---

[1] MADASR webpage: https://sites.google.com/view/respinasrchallenge2023/home.

Table 1. Training dataset statistics, including audio data hours, speaker count, dialects, total text sentences and unique words of **Bengali** Language, Dialects (D1, D2, D3, D4, D5: Dialect IDs).

Stats	D1	D2	D3	D4	D5	All Dialect
Total Hours	136	191	212	149	163	851
Speakers	379	385	402	402	412	1980
Text sentences	5K	6K	58K	5K	6K	80K
Unique words	9684	7174	47616	8356	10805	58349

Table 2. Training dataset statistics including audio data hours, speaker count, dialects, total text sentences, and unique words of **Bhojpuri** Language, Dialects (D1, D2, D3: Dialect IDs).

Stats	D1	D2	D3	All Dialect
Total Hours	263	316	256	835
Speakers	566	695	665	1926
Text sentences	34K	182K	26K	242K
Unique words	18923	65746	19878	77840

transcription available for each audio utterance, the dataset includes a separate large text corpus for each dialect of both Bengali and Bhojpuri languages. For Bengali, we have filtered out sentences from the text corpus that are not labeled with their corresponding dialect IDs. Consequently, the remaining sentences are annotated with their respective dialect IDs, making this dataset a valuable resource for conducting dialect-aware language modeling experiments. Table 1 and Table 2 list the dataset statistics of train data. We note that the audio data is more or less balanced across the dialects while the text resources are more skewed towards one of the dialects. All our ASR evaluations, of course, utilise audio data. All the results of this paper are based on the Dev dataset (audio + transcription) provided by the Challenge organisers. The ground truth for the Challenge test dataset has not been released. There are no shared speakers or sentences between the train and dev datasets. Furthermore, the Dev dataset is equally distributed across dialects for both the languages.

3 Methodology

In this section, we present the methodology employed in our research to develop an accurate speech recognition system for low-resource Indian languages, specifically Bengali and Bhojpuri. Our approach involves two main components: the Acoustic Model (AM) and the Language Model (LM). End-to-End speech recognition takes audio as input and predicts a character for each frame. By bringing in the Language Model with the E2E Acoustic Model, we rescore the logits predicted by the AM, resulting in meaningful text.

3.1   Acoustic Model

In recent years, self-supervised acoustic models have emerged as a breakthrough approach, showcasing improved results in various speech-related tasks, including speech recognition. The first component of our speech recognition system is the Acoustic Model (AM), which is based on the Wav2vec 2.0 base architecture [1]. It is a cutting-edge self-supervised speech representation learning model. Wav2vec 2.0 pretrained model comprises a CNN based feature encoder, a quantization module, and a transformer-based prediction network. The feature encoder layer processes the raw audio to obtain continuous speech representations, which are then quantized into discrete units by the quantization module. Finally, the transformer-based prediction network predicts the masked speech representation, following a contrastive learning objective.

To leverage the strengths of Wav2vec 2.0, we begin by initializing our AM with the weights of the pre-trained Wav2vec 2.0 base model. Next, we fine-tune the pre-trained Wav2vec 2.0 base model on our specific Bengali and Bhojpuri speech datasets using a transfer learning approach. This involves adding a fully connected layer on top of the transformer block, with the size of the output layer equal to the unique characters of the target languages. During the fine-tuning phase, we employ the Connectionist Temporal Classification (CTC) loss function [4]. CTC is widely used for end-to-end speech recognition tasks as it allows training without requiring explicit alignment between the input speech and the output transcriptions. This makes it suitable for sequence-to-sequence mapping tasks like automatic speech recognition. The initial component of Wav2Vec2 comprises a series of CNN layers responsible for extracting acoustically meaningful yet contextually independent features from the raw speech signal.This layer of the model has already undergone adequate training during the pretraining phase. In line with recommendations from the Wav2vec 2.0 paper [1], we choose to freeze the weights of the feature encoder network during training. All the transformer layers of pre-trained model's weights are updated during fine-tuning on the dataset. By fine-tuning the model on our labeled datasets, it learns to map the speech representations to their corresponding transcriptions.

3.2   Language Model

The Language Model (LM) is an essential component of our speech recognition system that aids in converting the speech representations generated by the Acoustic Model (AM) into meaningful text transcriptions. In our research, we explore and compare two different types of trained language models to enhance the accuracy of speech recognition.

The first language model, denoted as LM-All, is trained on the entire corpus of each language, encompassing all available dialects. This approach aims to create a language model that captures the general linguistic patterns and vocabulary present in Bengali and Bhojpuri without considering the variations due to specific dialects. By training on a diverse dataset, LM-All gains a broad understanding of the overall language characteristics. With our intention to study dialect-specific adaptations, we train separate language models, one for each dialect present in the dataset. We refer to these models as LM-Dialect. Each LM-Dialect is trained using a dialect-specific text corpus, allowing it to capture the unique linguistic variations and nuances associated with that particular dialect. This fine-grained approach can potentially facilitate better recognition of speech from diverse regions and speakers, making it particularly valuable for low-resource languages with multiple dialects like Bengali and Bhojpuri.

For language modeling, we utilize a statistical approach based on KenLM [5]. We conduct experiments with different n-gram LM models to identify the most suitable configuration for our specific datasets. During the speech recognition process, we identify the spoken dialect from the utterance's dialect ID and select the corresponding dialect-based language model (LM-Dialect). The selected LM-Dialect is used to decode the intermediate representations obtained from the AM and convert them into the corresponding text output.

4   Experiments Setup

Wav2vec2 Model Details. We used pre-trained Wav2vec2 [1] base architecture with 90M parameters. The model has 3 modules, feature encoder, transformer block and linear projection. Where feature encoder contains 7 CNN layers each with 512 channels, kernel widths of (10, 3, 3, 3, 3, 2, 2) and strides of (5, 2, 2, 2, 2, 2, 2). There are 12 transformer layers with dimension 768, feed forward network dimension 3072 and 8 attention heads. The convolutional layer used for modeling relative positional embeddings has a kernel size of 128 and 16 groups. The linear projection layer has output dimension given by the size of the set of all characters in the target language and blank symbols.

Fine-Tuning. For our experiments, we fine-tuned a pre-trained wav2vec 2.0 base model checkpoint using the Hugging Face Transformers library [14]. For optimization, we employed the AdamW optimizer [10]. During the fine-tuning process, we set the warmup step to 400. Within these steps, the learning rate increased linearly from 0 to $1e-4$, and after reaching 400 steps, it decreased linearly. To control overfitting, we set the weight decay to 0.005 and dropout rate [13] to 0.1. The model was trained for 3 epochs on each languages. The training was conducted on hardware with an RTX 3060 and RTX 2080 Ti GPUs.

Language Model. In speech recognition, training a model with the CTC loss function enables it to handle variable-length sequences without requiring explicit alignments between input and output. During inference, the model outputs probabilities over characters. The naive greedy decoding approach involves selecting the character with the highest probability at each step, which is the procedure used in the case of acoustic model (AM) alone without a language model (LM). To enhance the model's performance, an n-gram language model can be integrated into the decoding process, replacing the naive greedy decoding with n-gram-boosted beam search decoding [3]. By using pyctcdecode library[2] for the beam search algorithm and leveraging linguistic information from the language model, the system can explore a range of likely word sequences, leading to more accurate and contextually coherent transcriptions in speech recognition tasks.

In our experiments, we utilized KenLM [5] to create a language model trained on the provided speech transcriptions and an additional text corpus provided in the Challenge dataset. During the experiments, we set the beam width to 100. We tested various n-gram configurations, including 3, 4, 5, and 6. We categorized the text corpus data into dialect-specific text using the available dialect IDs.

5 Results

In this section, we present the comparison across the different investigated systems based on the Word Error Rate (WER) metric, where a lower WER indicates better performance. The systems under consideration include:

AM: This represents a decoder with Acoustic model but without the application of any language model.

AM + n-gram LM-All: In this case, the respective n-gram language model (LM) is applied to the AM model outputs. The LM-All is trained on the entire corpus without considering dialects and applied to the recognition of utterances from the corresponding dialect.

AM + n-gram LM-Dialect: Here, the AM model is combined with the n-gram language model specific to each dialect ID. The LM-dialect is trained on separate text data for individual dialects. Finally, the overall performance across the dialect datasets is reported.

Table 3. Comparison of different systems for each of **Bengali** and **Bhojpuri** Languages in terms of Percentage Word Error Rate(WER).

Model	Bengali	Bhojpuri
AM	21.8	21.21
AM + 3 gram LM-All	16.42	17.10
AM + 3 gram LM-Dialect	15.90	16.95
AM + 4 gram LM-All	16.12	16.87
AM + 4 gram LM-Dialect	15.77	16.43
AM + 5 gram LM-All	16.04	16.76
AM + 5 gram LM-Dialect	**15.62**	16.48
AM + 6 gram LM-All	16.06	16.67
AM + 6 gram LM-Dialect	15.68	**16.26**

---

[2] https://github.com/kensho-technologies/pyctcdecode/.

Table 3 shows the WER results obtained from each of these models for Bengali and Bhojpuri languages across different orders of the n-gram. Incorporating language modeling significantly improves the performance of speech recognition for both Bengali and Bhojpuri languages, as expected. The dialect-based language models (LM-Dialect) consistently outperform the whole corpus language models (LM-All) in terms of WER for both Bengali and Bhojpuri. This observation underscores the importance of considering dialect-specific linguistic variations when training language models, at least in Indian language scenarios. The choice of n-gram order has an impact on the performance of language models. We observed that the 5-gram LM-Dialect has achieved better performance in the Bengali language, while the 6-gram LM-Dialect has outperformed in the Bhojpuri language. Although WER improved, we noted that the OOV error rate went up with the shift to dialect-specific LM due to the mismatches between train and dev data that were otherwise compensated for by the much larger all-dialect train and dev datasets.

Table 4. Model Comparison for **Bhojpuri** Dialects in Word Error Rate (WER), Where D1, D2, D3 are dialect IDs.

Dialect model	AM	AM + 6 gram LM-All	AM + 6 gram LM-Dialect
D1	20.56	14.90	**14.70**
D2	20.89	16.00	**15.80**
D3	21.97	18.59	**17.88**
All	21.21	16.67	**16.26**

Table 5. Model Comparison for **Bengali** Dialects in Word Error Rate (WER), Where D1, D2, D3, D4, D5 are dialect IDs.

Dialect model	AM	AM + 5 gram LM-All	AM + 5 gram LM-Dialect
D1	19.76	15.02	**14.02**
D2	21.44	16.08	**15.60**
D3	18.40	14.44	**13.93**
D4	20.71	16.21	**15.73**
D5	27.90	18.19	**18.15**
All	21.21	16.04	**15.62**

Table 4 and 5 present the performance of each model on individual dialects. The results demonstrate that each dialect benefits from the application of Dialect-based Language Model (LM-Dialect) as compared to Whole Corpus Language Model (LM-All) in both Bhojpuri and Bengali languages. The dialect-based language models effectively capture linguistic variations and regional nuances, leading to more accurate transcriptions. These findings underscore the benefit of leveraging dialect-based language models to achieve superior speech recognition results for low-resource languages with multiple dialects.

6   Analysis and Discussion

The variations in performance from language models trained on different dialects, with a fixed acoustic model, point to the influence of the underlying differences in vocabulary and grammar across dialects (rather than accent). We note that there are differences in vocabulary size across our dialect texts but the gains in using dialect-matched LMs leads us to speculate that there are differences also in the distributions of the words that are common across the dialects. We consider words which have a particularly skewed distribution across the dialects of the language, suggesting that the words are more or less unique to one dialect. We expect then that semantically similar but not identical words appear in the other dialects. Semantic similarity can be measured via the similarity of the neighbour-hood context of a word. We use fastText [2] to obtain a semantic score in [0, 1] where 1 indicates matching semantics. As opposed to word2vec, fastText considers subwords (character n-grams) and is therefore capable of providing better embeddings for OOV words. We use the fastText Hindi model for Bhojpuri, and the Bengali model for Bengali.

For our analysis, we select pairs of such semantically similar words after ensuring that at least one of the words in the pair qualifies as a dialect-unique word in terms of at least 80% of the total occurrences lying within a single dialect dataset. For each pair, we compute the orthographic distance between the two words as the edit distance between the grapheme (Unicode) strings [6,11]. The orthographic score is mapped to 0–100% with 100% indicating exact match.

Figure 1a and Fig. 1b show the distribution of the orthographic score for different extents of semantic similarity. We observe that the orthographic score is high (i.e. edit distance is low) for semantically close words. This is an experimental validation of we might expect for dialects of the same language as opposed to the case of distinct languages. Given the high incidence of distinct words across dialects that are semantically and orthographically similar, we expect strong AM-based confusions that can be more effectively resolved with dialect-specific LMs rather than a universal LM.

Figure 2 provides examples of word pairs representing semantically similar words that are orthographically distinct, but very close in orthography (and therefore pronunciation) in the dataset. These closely related words are more likely to confuse the Acoustic Model (AM) during the speech recognition process. Blue-colored words have a higher total count in the entire dataset compared to orange-colored words. As a result, the Whole Corpus Language Model (LM-All) tends to assign higher probabilities to the blue-colored words during the speech recognition process. However, the situation changes when considering specific dialects. In certain dialects, orange-colored words may be more frequent than blue-colored words, contrary to the overall corpus trend. In such

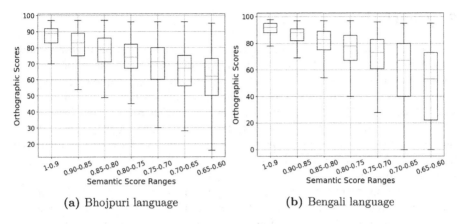

(a) Bhojpuri language   (b) Bengali language

Fig. 1. Box plots of orthographic scores by semantic score ranges for Bengali and Bhojpuri languages. Each plot displays the distribution of orthographic scores for word pairs in different semantic score ranges (1–0.9, 0.90–0.85, 0.85–0.80, 0.80–0.75, 0.75–0.70, 0.70–0.65, 0.65–0.60). The x-axis represents the semantic score ranges, and the y-axis represents the orthographic scores. These plots offer insights into the model's behavior concerning semantic and orthographic similarity in diverse linguistic contexts.

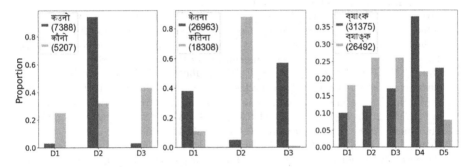

Fig. 2. The distribution across dialects of the two words of a pair where the words are semantically similar and, as a consequence, orthographically close. Bhojpuri (Left and Middle plots) and Bengali (Right plot). Legends within figure shows the words with their counts in the overall dataset. (Color figure online)

cases, the Dialect-based Language Model (LM-Dialect) becomes advantageous as it is tailored to the linguistic characteristics of the specific dialect, capturing the prevalence and nuances of orange-colored words. Consequently, LM-Dialect exhibits better decoding performance than LM-All for these dialects, as it can more accurately reflect the dialect-specific language patterns.

7   Conclusions

Our research targeted a particular aspect of speech recognition in low-resource Indian languages, Bengali and Bhojpuri. We demonstrated the importance of dialect-based language models (LM-Dialect) in capturing unique linguistic variations related to vocabulary. LM-Dialect outperformed the LM applied on the whole language, offering contextually relevant speech recognition. We showed that a particular characteristic of dialects of the same language is the presence of distinct but semantically similar words that are also very close in orthography. This explains, at least partly, the benefits observed with dialect-specific language modeling from dialect specific text resources.

Our findings contribute to improving technology accessibility for diverse linguistic communities, fostering inclusivity and promoting linguistic diversity. Future research in this area can further enhance speech recognition systems for a wide range of languages and dialects.

References

1. Baevski, A., Zhou, H., Rahman Mohamed, A., Auli, M.: wav2vec 2.0: a framework for self-supervised learning of speech representations. ArXiv abs/2006.11477 (2020). https://api.semanticscholar.org/CorpusID:219966759
2. Bojanowski, P., Grave, E., Joulin, A., Mikolov, T.: Enriching word vectors with subword information. Trans. Assoc. Comput. Linguist. **5**, 135–146 (2017)
3. Collobert, R., Puhrsch, C., Synnaeve, G.: Wav2letter: an end-to-end convnet-based speech recognition system. arXiv preprint arXiv:1609.03193 (2016)
4. Graves, A., Fernández, S., Gomez, F., Schmidhuber, J.: Connectionist temporal classification: Labelling unsegmented sequence data with recurrent neural networks. In: Proceedings of the 23rd International Conference on Machine Learning. ICML 2006, New York, NY, USA, pp. 369–376. Association for Computing Machinery (2006). https://doi.org/10.1145/1143844.1143891
5. Heafield, K.: KenLM: faster and smaller language model queries. In: Proceedings of the Sixth Workshop on Statistical Machine Translation, Edinburgh, Scotland, pp. 187–197. Association for Computational Linguistics (2011). https://aclanthology.org/W11-2123
6. Inc, S.: fuzzywuzzy: Fuzzy String Matching in Python (2014). https://github.com/seatgeek/fuzzywuzzy
7. Jain, A., Upreti, M., Jyothi, P.: Improved accented speech recognition using accent embeddings and multi-task learning. In: Interspeech, pp. 2454–2458 (2018). https://doi.org/10.21437/Interspeech.2018-1864
8. Kakwani, D., et al.: IndicNLPSuite: monolingual corpora, evaluation benchmarks and pre-trained multilingual language models for Indian languages. In: Findings of the Association for Computational Linguistics: EMNLP 2020, pp. 4948–4961 (2020)
9. Lei, Y., Hansen, J.H.L.: Dialect classification via text-independent training and testing for Arabic, Spanish, and Chinese. IEEE Trans. Audio Speech Lang. Process. **19**(1), 85–96 (2011). https://doi.org/10.1109/TASL.2010.2045184
10. Loshchilov, I., Hutter, F.: Decoupled weight decay regularization. In: International Conference on Learning Representations (2019). https://openreview.net/forum?id=Bkg6RiCqY7

11. Mouselimis, L.: fuzzywuzzyR: Fuzzy String Matching (2021). r package version 1.0.5, https://CRAN.R-project.org/package=fuzzywuzzyR
12. Singh, A., et al.: Model adaptation for ASR in low-resource Indian languages (2023)
13. Srivastava, N., Hinton, G., Krizhevsky, A., Sutskever, I., Salakhutdinov, R.: Dropout: a simple way to prevent neural networks from overfitting. J. Mach. Learn. Res. **15**(56), 1929–1958 (2014). https://jmlr.org/papers/v15/srivastava14a.html
14. Wolf, T., et al.: Transformers: state-of-the-art natural language processing. In: Proceedings of the 2020 Conference on Empirical Methods in Natural Language Processing: System Demonstrations, pp. 38–45. Association for Computational Linguistics, Online (2020). https://www.aclweb.org/anthology/2020.emnlp-demos.6
15. Yadavalli, A., Mirishkar, G.S., Vuppala, A.: Exploring the effect of dialect mismatched language models in Telugu automatic speech recognition. In: Proceedings of the 2022 Conference of the North American Chapter of the Association for Computational Linguistics: Human Language Technologies: Student Research Workshop, Hybrid: Seattle, Washington, pp. 292–301. Association for Computational Linguistics (2022). https://doi.org/10.18653/v1/2022.naacl-srw.36, https://aclanthology.org/2022.naacl-srw.36

Emotional Speech Recognition of Holocaust Survivors with Deep Neural Network Models for Russian Language

Liudmila Bukreeva👤, Daria Guseva👤, Mikhail Dolgushin(✉)👤,
Vera Evdokimova👤, and Vasilisa Obotnina👤

Saint Petersburg State University, Universitetskaya Emb., 7-9, St. Petersburg 199034, Russia
dolgushin.mikhail@gmail.com, v.evdokimova@spbu.ru

Abstract. Recognition of highly emotional speech remains a challenging case of automatic speech recognition task. The aim of this article is to carry out experiments on highly emotional speech recognition by investigating oral history archives provided by the Yad Vashem foundation. The material consists of elderly peoples' emotional speech full of accents and common language. We analyze and preprocess 26 h of publicly available video interviews with Holocaust survivors. Our objective was to develop a system able to perform emotional speech recognition based on deep neural network models. We present and evaluate the obtained results that contribute to the research field of oral history archives.

Keywords: Question Answering · Corpora · Visual History Archives

1 Introduction

From 2001 to 2006 Czech and American researchers solved the tasks of the Multilingual Access to Large Spoken Archives (MALACH) project [1] in collaboration with the Shoah Visual History Foundation (VHF) [2]. The MALACH project was aimed at developing methods of access to multilingual archives of oral speech collected by VHF. The objective was to find and determine automatic recognition techniques for the spontaneous, emotional, and heavily accented speech of Holocaust survivors. The results of the project were applied later in annotation of the archive materials, keyword extraction, etc. According to the WER (Word Error Rate) metric [3], the overall accuracy of speech recognition for Czech and Russian was 38.57% and 45.75% respectively [4]. It turned out to be sufficient for the keyword extraction and corpus annotation.

Recent success in speech recognition technologies allows to perform this task more productively. Notable progress has been made for English and Czech languages [5, 6] However, there is no similar research made for Russian.

Based on the foregoing, our objective is to automatically recognize emotional, heavily accented speech of Holocaust witnesses in Russian. We are going to use modern neural network technologies for this task in our research.

A. Karpov et al. (Eds.): SPECOM 2023, LNAI 14338, pp. 68–76, 2023.
https://doi.org/10.1007/978-3-031-48309-7_6

Addressing this issue could simplify automatic subtitles generation for available archive recordings containing Holocaust testimonies. Our interest is directed to the technological aspects since we need to take into account various features of elderly interviewees speech, e.g. dialectal expressions.

In Sect. 3, we discuss the data sources of Holocaust survivors' speech in Russian, choose the available ones that might be used to train automatic speech recognition (ASR) systems and check the results obtained. Section 4 gives a brief description of the selected data along with the preprocessing steps. The experiments with the proposed ASR system are presented in Sect. 5.

2 Related Work

The article [7] shows cultural significance of recognizing the highly emotional speech of Holocaust witnesses based on the MALACH corpus data. It presents early attempts to solve this problem along with initial experiments that have been conducted with the latest artificial intelligence methods at the time of writing: from hidden Markov models to LSTM-neural networks. The best result of 21.7% WER gives a powerful boost to the development of ASR systems in comparison to original models in 2006 [4].

The authors of the article [8] follow the practice of the previous article [7] by expanding speech recognition for the Czech part of the MALACH corpus as well as for the English one. In this paper special attention is paid to the preprocessing of the corpus before training, linguistic features of the corpus in both languages and identifying of speakers' metadata to be further used in the test set. As a result, from the estimated overall WER of 38.7% the system achieves 14.65% WER through the development of speech recognition technologies. The advantage of the Czech corpus over the English one arises from the fact that most interviewees speak their native language, therefore, the possibility of interference with other languages is unlikely. On the contrary, in the English part of the dataset native speakers of English could hardly be found, which means that their speech may contain crosslinguistic influence. For that reason, careful selection of a test set for recognizing the English part of the MALACH corpus is crucial to prevent any examples with specific interference from degrading model's performance. This aspect could be relevant to any corpus in another language compiled from the speech of non-native speakers. In addition, the information vector with paralinguistic metadata about speakers (iVector) allows to increase the accuracy of speech recognition significantly.

The study [9] examines aspects of the Russian-Yiddish interference. The Russian language of Yiddish native speakers is characterized by the following interference examples: retention of non-palatalized consonants before front vowels; retention of voiced consonants at the end of words; realization of /i / as [i]; palatalization of sibilants. In terms of prosody, the rise-fall contour can be observed [10].

The article [11] continues the research on the development of a speech recognition system based on the Czech part of the MALACH corpus. It applies End2End [12] approach and describes many experiments with various retraining settings for the monolingual Wav2Vec 2.0 model [13], evaluated on two public datasets (CommonVoice [14] and VoxPopuli [15]) and the dataset from the MALACH project. The results show that monolingual Wav2Vec 2.0 models are stable ASR systems that can take advantage of both large labeled and unlabeled datasets and successfully compete with modern large vocabulary continuous speech recognition (LVCSR) systems. Moreover, the Wav2Vec models demonstrate high recognition accuracy if there is no training data available for the ASR aim. WER for the Czech part of the MALACH corpus without the language model stands at 18.93%, with the language model – 15.31%.

3   Data Overview

In this section, we give an overview of the data that might be selected for the purpose of our research.

The first dataset is an online VHF archive containing 158 video interviews with witnesses of the Holocaust [16]. The average video length in the archive is 20 min. There are two speakers in each video, namely the interviewer and the interviewee. Video recordings may contain noise that complicates the process of the ASR. There is no text transcription for the videos, however, the archive provides keywords highlighted in separate time segments of the recording. Video access is limited.

The second dataset is compiled by the Yad Vashem Foundation [17]. It consists of 24 YouTube video interviews with witnesses of the Holocaust. The length of the videos varies from 40 min to 2 h and 30 min. As in the previous dataset, the interviews have two speakers and noise might occur. Apart from that, speakers may insert words and toponyms in Hebrew. The archive is freely available.

Since access to the VHF archive is limited and there are no datasets in Russian similar to the MALACH project, we decided to form our own dataset based on the video interviews from the Yad Vashem Foundation.

It is possible to use various open source annotated Russian state-of-the-art datasets for training and evaluating a model. For example, the 1240-h dataset Golos developed by SberDevices [18] with the total WER to be about 3.3% and 11.5%, multilingual speech recognition datasets containing a Russian part, such as LibriSpeech [19] with 98 h of Russian speech or abovementioned Common-Voice [14].

4   Data Collection Pipeline

4.1   Data Analysis

In this section, we discuss the features of the dataset based on the video recordings from the Yad Vashem Foundation.

First, we use the approach described in [8] and identify some metadata of the researched archive. We managed to distinguish the following sociolinguistic charac-teristics of speakers from the video recordings: gender, age, region, and native language of the interviewees. Table 1 reveals the age and the number of interviewees for each category. The age group of interviewees comprises the range of almost 20 years with the average age of 88 years old. There are more female speakers, thus, the amount of interview hours counts 13.5 with men and approximately 20 with women.

As shown in Fig. 1, many interviewees come from Russia although their number is less than a half. It is important to note that the vast majority of the narrators did

Table 1. Sociolinguistic characteristics of the interviewees

Age	81 to 98 years old	
Gender	men	9
	women	16
Region	Belarus	5
	Poland	1
	Russia	5
	Ukraine	11
	Romania	3
Native language	Belarussian	2
	Yiddish	7
	Russian	14
	Romanian	1
	Ukrainian	1

not live in Russia whilst they were interviewed. Russian is not the mother tongue for many of them as well, which illustrates Fig. 2. Since Yiddish is the native language for the sufficient number of speakers, their speech is enriched with dialectal expressions (e.g. '*маца*' – '*matzah*' – flatbread; '*идише гельт*' – '*yiddishe gelt*' – money), terms connected with Judaism ('*кашрут*' – '*kashrut*', '*кошер*' – '*kosher*', *Йом-Кипур*' – '*Yom Kippur*', '*Песах*'/'*Пейсах*' – '*Passover*') and toponyms ('*Хайфа*' – '*Haifa*', '*Ашкелон*' – '*Ashkelon*', '*Холопутовка*' – '*Kholoputovka*').

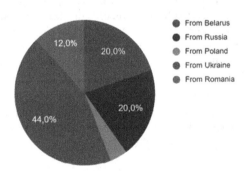

Fig. 1. Interviewees distribution by region.

Along with Yiddish words, dialect expressions from other languages can also be found: e.g. Belarussian '*шмалец*' – '*shmalets*' ('*lard*') originally pronounced as '*смалец*' – '*smalets*' in Russian. For the reasons above, the process of ASR may be complicated in our dataset.

Another reason that makes ASR of our dataset more difficult is variability of the interviewers' speech. Their speech is spontaneous, so the stationary parts are more likely to be absent [20]. The interviewees use formal languages while answering questions initially, but many of them switch to colloquial speech further if they get emotional by telling about severe moments within their stories [21].

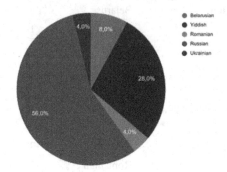

Fig. 2. Interviewees distribution by native language.

4.2 Data Preprocessing

The videos were divided into smaller segments. Parts with the interviewer's speech were removed where possible since both speakers in these segments may say something simultaneously. Segments with empty subtitles were deleted, punctuation marks and extra spaces were removed, and the text was converted to all lower case.

The total set duration amounted to 25.8 h with the average recording time of 5.04 s. Meanwhile, the maximum duration of records was equal to 90.37 s. As a matter of optimization, we have decided to eliminate records that are longer than 10 s. After this removal step the duration of the dataset has been reduced to 17.5 h, where 7.5 h belong to male speakers and 10 h consist of the female speech.

Further, the data was divided into test and train sets, 20% and 80% respectively.

In order to clean texts from rare letters that are not represented in the Russian alphabet, Latin and Hebrew letters have been converted to Cyrillic with the python transliterate module [22]. Numbers were turned to the text form using the num2text module [23].

As a result, we managed to collect the Russian Oral History (ruOH) dataset to be further used for pretraining of the Wav2Vec2 model.

5 Speech Recognition Results

Once we have the ruOH dataset ready, we start the experimental setup. We are going to use the End2End approach [12], namely the Wav2vec2.0 model and convert acoustic segments into a sequence of words.

Since the amount of the dataset counts only 15 h of speech, the training of models from the beginning might be limited. However, additional training of Wav2vec2.0 can show strong performance on that small amount of labeled data.

To evaluate the performance of the models we calculate the word error rate (WER) and character error rate (CER) on the test part of RuOH dataset. We estimate CER along with WER since in our paper we limit ourselves to the acoustic model. We expect that some characters might be incorrectly predicted which may degrade the performance of ASR causing the lower WER score. Thus, we consider both WER and CER metrics in the evaluation of two models.

Firstly, we evaluate the performance of the wav2vec-base pretrained [24] on the Russian part of Common Voice 8.0, Golos, and Multilingual TEDx [25], WER and CER of which equals to 9.82% and 2.30% respectively on Common Voice 8.0. Secondly, we compare the obtained results to the wav2vec-base that has been fine-tuned on our small ruOH dataset. We use the following hyperparameters in our fine-tuning setup:

- Train batch size – 8;
- Validation batch size – 8;
- Number of epochs – 10;
- Learning rate – 1e-4;
- Weight decay – 0.005;
- Warmup steps – 1000.

These parameters were selected empirically. They were largely influenced by the limited computing capacity at our disposal. Table 1 summarizes the obtained results in terms of WER (Table 2).

Table 2. Evaluation of each wav2vec-base performance fine-tuned on the ruOH dataset

	ruOH	
	WER (%)	CER (%)
wav2vec2-xls-r-1b-russian	52.4	31.5
wav2vec2-xls-r-1b-russian + ruOH	35.6	21.5

The model pretrained on ruOH demonstrates significantly better recognition results on ruOH dataset of 0.356 WER and 0.215 CER, consequently outperforms the results achieved for the Russian language previously [4].

The lower result obtained by the model without fine-tuning on the ruOH dataset indicates the complexity of processing the type of speech in this material. However, these results also show the capabilities of end2end models used on rough data without retraining.

6   Conclusion

We have discussed the current state of emotional and accented speech recognition for the Russian language. We have given an overview of theoretical approaches aimed at solving the problem of highly emotional and accented speech recognition.

Our focus has been directed to the Russian speech of Holocaust witnesses extracted from the video interviews archive provided by the Yad Vashem Foundation. We analyzed the sociolinguistic features of the chosen data and optimized the segments of the material in accordance with the computing capacity available at our disposal.

We conducted initial experiments on highly emotional and accented speech recognition with wav2vec-base fine-tuned on Common Voice and Common Voice with ruOH datasets. The model was trained on a smaller part of the filtered data and a relatively small number of training epochs. The better results might be achieved with a greater number of training epochs. Although the hyperparameters were limited, we managed to obtain decent results. Along with the common metric for speech recognition systems WER, we also estimated CER to gain more clarity on our model's performance. Whereas the best WER obtained equals 35% reached by the model pretrained on the ruOH dataset, the best gotten CER turns out to be 21% by the same fine-tuned model.

We emphasize that the metadata we have listed also influences the model's performance. It is relevant for the ruOH dataset because less than a half of speakers come from Russia and not everyone's mother tongue is Russian as well. There is a high chance of the cross-linguistic interference that has an impact on the model's resulting accuracy and probably reduces its performance. Notwithstanding, our experiments show improvements in the emotional and accented speech recognition for Russian.

As a result of our research, a demonstration dataset containing interviews with Holocaust survivors and paralinguistic data about them was processed and published as a HuggingFace Dataset [26]. Inaccuracies in the texts written may occur at times as well as not only a respondent's but an interviewer's speech arises in certain cases. The dataset was not completely fixed in the current version, thus, we plan to correct and improve it in further studies.

References

1. Project MALACH – Multilingual Access to Large Spoken Archives. https://malach.umiacs.umd.edu/
2. USC Shoah Foundation. https://sfi.usc.edu/
3. Word Error Rate. https://en.wikipedia.org/wiki/Word_error_rate
4. Psutka, J., Ircing, P., Psutka, J.V., Hajič, J., Byrne, W., Mírovský, J.: Automatic transcription of Czech, Russian and Slovak spontaneous speech in the MALACH project. In: Eurospeech 2005, pp. 1349–1352. ISCA (2005). https://doi.org/10.21437/Interspeech.2005-489
5. Ramabhadran, B., et al.: USC-SFI MALACH interviews and transcripts english. In: LDC2012S05. Web Download. Philadelphia: Linguistic Data Consortium (2012). https://doi.org/10.35111/7zfn-a492
6. Psutka, J., Radová, V., Ircing, P., Matoušek, J., Müller, L.: USC-SFI MALACH interviews and transcripts Czech. In: LDC2014S04. Web Download. Philadelphia: Linguistic Data Consortium (2014). https://doi.org/10.35111/v2nt-7j09
7. Picheny, M., Tüske, Z., Kingsbury, B., Audhkhasi, K., Cui, X., Saon, G.: Challenging the boundaries of speech recognition: the MALACH corpus. In: Interspeech 2019, pp. 326–330 (2019). https://doi.org/10.21437/Interspeech.2019-1907

8. Psutka, J.V., Pražák, A., Vaněk, J.: Recognition of heavily accented and emotional speech of english and czech holocaust survivors using various DNN Architectures. In: Karpov, A., Potapova, R. (eds) Speech and Computer. SPECOM 2021. Lecture Notes in Computer Science(), vol 12997, pp. 553–564. Springer, Cham (2021). https://doi.org/10.1007/978-3-030-87802-3_50

9. Svetozarova, N., Kleiner, Y., De Graaf, T., Nieuweboer, R.: Russian-Yiddish: Phonetic aspects of language interference. In: Proc. of the XIV International Congress of Phonetic Sciences. San-Francisco, pp. 1397–1400 (1999). https://www.internationalphoneticassociation. org/icphs-proceedings/ICPhS1999/papers/p14_1397.pdf

10. Weinreich, U.: Notes on the Yiddish Rise-Fall Intonation Contour. In: Columbia University (1956)

11. Lehečka, J., Švec, J., Prazak, A., Psutka, J.: Exploring capabilities of monolingual audio transformers using large datasets in automatic speech recognition of Czech. In: Interspeech 2022, 1831–1835 (2022). https://doi.org/10.21437/Interspeech.2022-10439

12. Li, J.: Recent Advances in End-to-End Automatic Speech Recognition. In: APSIPA Transactions on Signal and Information Processing 11(1) (2021). https://doi.org/10.48550/arXiv. 2111.01690

13. Baevski, A., Zhou, H., Mohamed, A., Auli, M.: wav2vec 2.0: A framework for self-supervised learning of speech representation. In: Proceedings of the 34th International Conference on Neural Information Processing Systems, pp. 12449–12460 (2020). https://doi.org/10.48550/ arXiv.2006.11477

14. Ardila, R., et al.: Common Voice: A massively-multilingual speech corpus. In: Proceedings of the 12th Conference on Language Resources and Evaluation (LREC 2020), pp. 4211–4215 (2020). https://doi.org/10.48550/arXiv.1912.06670

15. Wang, C., et al.: VoxPopuli: a large-scale multilingual speech corpus for representation learning, semi-supervised learning and interpretation. In: Proceedings of the 59th Annual Meeting of the Association for Computational Linguistics and the 11th International Joint Conference on Natural Language Processing (Volume 1: Long Papers), pp. 993–1003, Online. Association for Computational Linguistics (2021). https://doi.org/10.18653/v1/2021.acl-long.80

16. USC Shoah Foundation Visual History Archive Online. https://vhaonline.usc.edu/quickS earch/resultList

17. YouTube playlist of Holocaust survivors testimonies by Yad Vashem foundation. https://www. youtube.com/playlist?list=PLanQ0TFmIYBTV8sRAkSDWQLZNhbM-v1xp

18. Karpov, N., Denisenko, A., Minkin, F.: Golos: Russian Dataset for Speech Research. arXiv preprint (2021) https://doi.org/10.48550/arXiv.2106.10161

19. Panayotov, V., Chen, G., Povey, D., Khudanpur, S.: Librispeech: an asr corpus based on public domain audio books. In 2015 IEEE international conference on acoustics, speech and signal processing (ICASSP), pp. 5206–5210 (2015). https://doi.org/10.1109/ICASSP.2015.7178964

20. Bondarko, L., et al.: Phonetic properties of Russian spontaneous speech. In: Proceedings of the 15th International Congress of Phonetic Sciences, Barcelona, pp. 2973–2976 (2003). https:// www.internationalphoneticassociation.org/icphs-proceedings/ICPhS2003/p15_2973.html

21. Lehečka, J., Psutka, J.V., Psutka, J.: Transformer-based automatic speech recognition of formal and colloquial Czech in MALACH Project. In: Sojka, P., Horák, A., Kopeček, I., Pala, K. (eds) Text, Speech, and Dialogue. TSD 2022. Lecture Notes in Computer Science(), vol 13502, pp. 301–312. Springer, Cham (2022). https://doi.org/10.1007/978-3-031-16270-1_25

22. Barseghyan, A.: Transliterate Module Documentation. https://pypi.org/project/transliterate

23. Num2words Module Documentation. https://pypi.org/project/num2words/

24. Grosman, J.: Fine-tuned XLS-R 1B model for speech recognition in Russian. https://huggin gface.co/jonatasgrosman/wav2vec2-xls-r-1b-russian

25. Salesky, E., et al.: The multilingual tedx corpus for speech recognition and translation. In: Proc. Interspeech 2021, pp. 3655–3659 (2021). https://doi.org/10.21437/Interspeech.2021-11
26. RuOH dataset on HuggingFacet. https://huggingface.co/datasets/Mihaj/ruoh_demo

Computational Paralinguistics

Aggregation Strategies of Wav2vec 2.0 Embeddings for Computational Paralinguistic Tasks

Mercedes Vetráb[1]([✉])[ID] and Gábor Gosztolya[1,2][ID]

[1] Institute of Informatics, University of Szeged, Szeged, Hungary
{vetrabm,ggabor}@inf.u-szeged.hu
[2] ELKH-SZTE Research Group on Artificial Intelligence, Szeged, Hungary

Abstract. Throughout the history of computational paralinguistics, numerous feature extraction, preprocessing and classification techniques have been used. One of the important challenges in this subfield of speech technology is handling utterances with different duration. Since standard speech processing features (such as filter banks or DNN embeddings) are typically frame-level ones and we would like to classify whole utterances, a set of frame-level features have to be converted into fixed-sized utterance-level features. The choice of this aggregation method is often overlooked, and simple functions like mean and/or standard deviation are used without solid experimental support. In this study we take wav2vec 2.0 deep embeddings, and aggregate them with 11 different functions. We sought to obtain a subset of potentially optimal aggregation functions, because there are no general rules yet that can be applied universally between subtopics. Besides testing both standard and non-traditional aggregation strategies individually, we also combined them to improve the classification performance. By using multiple aggregation functions, we were able to achieve significant improvements on three public paralinguistic corpora.

Keywords: Paralinguistics · Wav2vec 2.0 · Embeddings · Aggregation

1 Introduction

In the past, the primary focus of automatic speech processing research was generating a transcription for an audio recording (i.e. Automatic Speech Recognition) [14]. From the 1990s to the present, several other topics have received more attention related to phenomena present in human speech, such as speaker recognition and diarisation ("who's speaking when") [13], detecting Parkinson's [15,16,38] or Alzheimer's [3,23,24] disease, assessing the level of depression [6], age and gender recognition [25], emotion recognition [21,41], and estimating the degree of sleepiness [5] or conflict intensity [11]. These subtopics are part of computational paralinguistics, which has recently started to receive more interest.

A. Karpov et al. (Eds.): SPECOM 2023, LNAI 14338, pp. 79–93, 2023.
https://doi.org/10.1007/978-3-031-48309-7_7

In this field, instead of generating transcriptions, we seek to identify non-verbal aspects of human communication such as tone of voice and other vocal cues. Here, we need to associate different lengths of audio recording inputs (i.e. utterances) with a single label output. The final aim is always a classification or a regression at the utterance level. For example, if we have two-minute-long recording, first we have to extract features from it, then classify whether the speaker is angry or not. This means that we have to calculate a fixed-dimensional, classifiable feature vector out of a varying-length recording. A typical strategy for this is to split the input into smaller chunks (i.e. frames) and calculate low-level descriptors (e.g. MFCCs) to get frame-level features. Then we feed them into a neural network to extract frame-level embeddings. Finally we aggregate them into an utterance-level feature and use it to classify the utterance.

Another key technical property of computational paralinguistics is that we typically have small-sized corpora. This usually does not make it suitable for using DNNs as classifiers, and deep learning methods are still in their early stages of development [21,33]. Traditional classification methodologies tend to perform better than end-2-end DNNs [10,29,34]. Nowadays scientists employ DNNs more and more frequently, but mostly for frame-level feature (i.e. embedding) extraction [39]. Deep neural network embeddings can reduce the feature space dimension while preserving important information. It has been effective in capturing complex relationships in the data and outperforming traditional feature extraction methods. The small size of paralinguistical datasets makes it difficult to train a feature extractor DNN from scratch, so usually a standard ASR corpus is used for pretraining. Standard examples are HMM/DNN acoustic models [9], x-vectors [31], ECAPA-TDNN [30] and wav2vec 2.0 [19].

In this study, we focus on the utterance-level aggregation step. Although researchers tend to use task specific aggregations including only the most popular metrics such as mean and standard deviation, our aim is to show that there are other efficient techniques available too. Some of them can handle different paralinguistic subtopics at the same time. With state-of-the-art self-supervised wav2vec 2.0 DNN embeddings, we investigated 11 aggregation strategies including both traditional and less frequently employed ones. We conducted experiments on three different databases to find general trends across various paralinguistic subtopics. We found that certain non-traditional metrics can be highly effective for almost any subtopic, and traditional metrics vary in performance depending on the dataset. We were interested in the classification performance that could be obtained by combining different aggregation functions. By using sequential forward feature selection, we achieved relative error rate improvements of $4 - 10\%$ on the test scores in two datasets. We achieved a slight improvement on the third corpus. Our results, probably indicate that the effective summarisation of frame-level embeddings is a nontrivial task, and classification performance can be improved significantly using multiple aggregation functions, regardless of the actual paralinguistic subtopic. In addition, we present a novel approach rule set for aggregation selection where we identify general patterns using our results and provide guidelines for selecting appropriate aggregation methods for `wav2vec 2.0` embeddings.

2 Proposed Methods

2.1 Wav2vec 2.0 Embeddings

To extract frame-level embeddings, we employed a self-supervised and fine-tuned `wav2vec 2.0` model [12]. The model has two main parts: (1) a Convolutional Neural Network (CNN) block, (2) a BERT-based transformer block. The first part encodes features by transforming the raw input waveform into a sequence of high-level feature representations (i.e. latent speech representation). The CNN has "dilation" between the filter weights, which allows the filter to capture information from a wider range of time steps in the input sequence, without increasing the number of parameters. The second part transforms the CNN output into a sequence of high-level feature vectors, which capture the relationships between the input waveform and the extracted features. It has a contextualised transformer architecture based on the widely used BERT model. The transformer consists of a multi-head self-attention mechanism and a position-wise feed-forward network [4]. The structure of a fine-tuned wav2vec 2.0 model can be seen in Fig. 1.

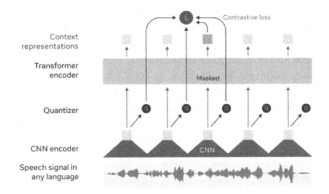

Fig. 1. The fine-tuned wav2vec 2.0 framework structure [1].

The model can be trained with the cross-lingual representation (XLSR) learning approach, which involves two steps: (1) pretraining the model by self-supervised learning on large unlabeled datasets of speech in different languages, (2) fine-tuning this model on a smaller labeled corpus with the target speech language (e.g. German). In this way, the model learns to share discrete tokens across languages. The pretraining step divides the input into small segments while applying random masking. Then it utilises a self-supervised learning (Contrastive Predictive Coding (CPC) approach), where the model encodes the segments into a set of discrete latent variables using two pre-defined codebooks and predicts a future latent variable from the discrete ones. In the fine-tuning step the original output layer is replaced with task-specific layers (typically a recurrent neural network (RNN) and a Softmax layer). Then, the modified network is optimised via Connectionist Temporal Classification (CTC) loss [4].

After the training and the fine-tuning, we can use the network as an embedding extractor by freezing the weights and removing the last few layers. We experiment with two setups, where we extract embeddings from: (1) the last layer of the CNN block, (2) the last layer of the Transformer block. When we feed the paralinguistic utterances into the model, the output of the last remaining layer serves as the embeddings. These feature vectors may contain relevant information about the speaker and other aspects of the speech signal.

2.2 Embedding Aggregation

Since databases contain recordings with different lengths, we have a different number of embedded features for each recording. This means one embedding for each frame window. The aim is to predict one label to one utterance, but we can not simply concatenate these embeddings because traditional classifiers handle only fixed-sized input vector. In order to address this issue, an aggregation step must be employed to transform frame-level embeddings into utterance-level features. The general process of an aggregation is shown in Fig. 2. We had an input recording consisting of y number of frame windows, each containing f number of low-level descriptors. To get an utterance-level feature vector from them, we combine all the y number of vectors by computing a statistical measure such as the mean, variance, or other value for each f features in the time axis. With aggregation we can obtain an utterance-level feature vector that has the same size as an original embedding vector. Since the size of this aggregated vector is independent of the number of the windows (and therefore, of the duration of the utterance), it can be used with any traditional classification method.

3 Databases

We performed our experiments on three public paralinguistic corpora, that covered a variety of topic. However, all three corpora had native German speakers. This allowed us to justifiably employ the same wav2vec 2.0 model for frame-level embeddings extraction, as it was fine-tuned for German speech. All of the databases was used on one of the INTERSPEECH Computational Paralinguistic Challenges [26–28].

3.1 The iHEARu-EAT Database

The Munich University of Technology provided the iHEARu-EAT corpus [18], which includes approximately 2.9 h of close-to-native German speech from 30

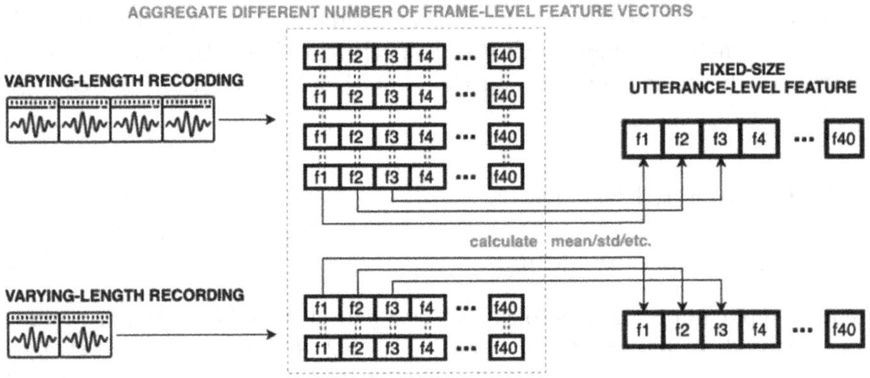

Fig. 2. Creating fixed-sized feature vectors from varying-length utterances.

subjects (15 females, 15 males). It was recorded in a quiet, slightly echoing office room, and the recordings has a sampling rate of 16 kHz. The classification task was to determine the type of food being eaten while speaking: apple, nectarine, banana, crisp, biscuit, gummy bear, and no food. The speakers completed various tasks, such as reading the German version of "The North Wind and the Sun" or providing a spontaneous narrative about their favourite activity. The database was divided into a training set (14 speakers), a development set (6 speakers) and a test set (10 speakers) in a speaker-independent manner.

3.2 The URTIC Database

The Institute of Safety Technology at the University of Wuppertal in Germany provided the Upper Respiratory Tract Infection Corpus (e.g.: URTIC) [18], which contains native German speech from 630 participants (248 females, 382 males). The corpus has a total duration of approximately 45 h. The classification task was to determine whether the speaker had a cold or not. The recordings were downsampled from a sampling rate of 44.1 kHz to 16 kHz. The task assigned to the participants included reading short stories, producing voice commands and speaking spontaneously about a personal experience. The corpus was divided into three sets (train, dev, test), each containing 210 speakers. The training and development sets contained 37 infected and 173 uninfected participants.

3.3 The AIBO Database

The FAU AIBO Emotion Corpus [32] contains recordings of 51 native German children speech, who were playing with a pet robot called AIBO. The recordings were taken from two schools: 9959 recordings from the Ohm school and 8257 from the Mont school, with a total duration of around 9 h. The Ohm subset was divided into a training set (7578 utterances, 20 children) and a development set (2381 utterances, 6 children), while the Mont subset served as the test set (8257 utterances). Classes were merged from the original 11 emotional classes into 5, as Anger (including angry, irritated and reprimanding), Emphatic, Neutral, Positive (motherly and joyful), and the Rest (helpless, surprised, bored, non-neutral other).

4 Experimental Setup

4.1 Wav2vec 2.0 Embeddings

The first step of our method is to extract frame-level embeddings from raw audio data. We used a pretrained and fine-tuned wav2vec 2.0 model and extracted features from two different layers: (1) the last layer of the CNN block and (2) the last layer of the modified Transformer block. These vectors may contain relevant information about the speakers and other aspects of the speech signal. The size of the embeddings was 512 for convolutional and 1 024 for hidden layers.

4.2 Embedding Aggregation

During aggregation, we used 11 different statistical methods to convert frame-level embeddings into an utterance-level feature vector. Besides the traditional approaches of *mean*, *median* and *standard deviation*, we experimented with the *skewness*, the *kurtosis*, the *minimum*, the *maximum* and the 1st, 25th, 75th, 99th *percentiles* (i.e. the value below which a given percentage k of scores falls). Note that median is identical to the 50th percentile. The 1st and 99th percentiles are frequently used as alternatives to minimum and maximum, because they are not that sensitive to outliers [22].

4.3 Classification and Evaluation

We used traditional Support Vector Machines (i.e. SVMs) for classification and utilized the Python port of the LibSVM implementation [2]. Following our previous experiments [7,35,37], we employed the ν-SVM method with a linear kernel. The complexity (C) was determined by testing powers of 10 between 10^{-5} and 10^0. To avoiding peeking and determine the optimal hyperparameter settings, we trained our models on the train set and evaluated them on the development set. In the end, we measured final performance of the best parameter, by training the model on the concatenation of train and dev sets and evaluating it on the test set. To measure the efficiency of an SVM model, we used the Unweighted Average Recall (i.e. UAR) metric [20], corresponding to taking the mean of the class-wise recall scores. This is a widely used metric for these corpora. [27,28,32].

In the case of the AIBO and the URTIC corpora, we always standardized utterance-level features (i.e. converted them so as to have a zero mean and unit variance). Due to the unbalanced class distribution and the relatively large size of these corpora, we also employed downsampling on them (i.e. we discarded training examples from the more frequent classes), as these techniques proved

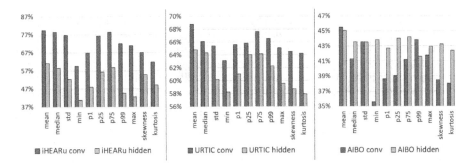

Fig. 3. Development results got from convolutional and transformer (i.e. hidden) layer embeddings while using different aggregation techniques. The x axis represents the aggregation method and the y axis represents the UAR value.

to be beneficial in our previous experiments [8,36]. In the case of iHEARu-EAT, we performed speaker-wise standardization, where the test set speaker IDs were determined by using the single Gaussian-based bottom-up Hierarchical Agglomerative Clustering algorithm [17,40].

5   Experimental Results

First, we compared the performance of the convolutional and the transformer (i.e. hidden) layer embeddings on the development set. Our best results for all 11 aggregation functions are shown in Fig. 3. From our results, convolutional embeddings significantly outperformed the hidden representations on the iHEARu-EAT corpus (79.4%–83.7% and 61.1%–62.9%, convolutional and hidden embeddings, respectively). On the other two corpora, it also had a slight advantage against hidden embeddings (URTIC: 63.3%–68.7% and 64.8%–66.1%, AIBO: 42.7%–45.5% and 43.6%–45.1%, convolutional and hidden embeddings, respectively). Although the hidden layer performed better in percentage terms on the AIBO database, but it varied greatly, proved unreliable and lost robustness. Upon closer inspection, the minimum and maximum aggregations differ from the previous pattern. The reason for the better performance scores with the hidden layer in the case of AIBO might be that emotion recognition requires a higher level analysis than the other two paralinguistic subtask, so the last hidden layer has a better comprehensive overview. A deeper layer, like a convolutional, can analyse smaller details, which is more advantageous in the case of sounds produced by cold or during eating. The other significant difference of the AIBO database compared with the others is that it contains recordings of children's speech. Changes in tones and speech skills can produce slight differences in the analysis results. Due to these observations, we decided to continue our research with convolutional embeddings. Our decision and recommendation is to use the convolutional layer because it behaves more robustly and has the same pattern in all three databases.

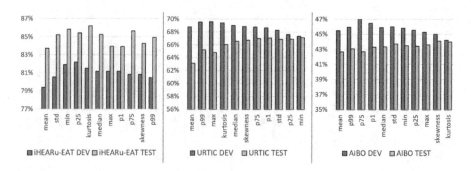

Fig. 4. Development and test results for embeddings got from the convolutional layer, when combining different aggregation strategies with sequential forward selection (SFS). The order of the selected aggregation methods is shown on the x axis.

If we take a closer look at the aggregations, we observe same general trends. The mean aggregation produced the best results on each database, which, as it is perhaps the most frequently used method, is not that surprising. Standard deviation appear to be a promising alternative for a potential combination. Regarding percentiles, the central ones (i.e. 25%, 75%) have competitive performances, so we should pay more attention to these non-traditional aggregations. We would like to recommend their usage more, especially the 75th percentile. The traditional median metric (which is the same as the 50% percentile), had a varying performance depending on the database, while it follows the accuracy curve of the percentiles. This curve shows that if you take all the frame-level vectors of a recording and sort the values for each feature in ascending order, which part of the ordered sequence is the best descriptor of that recording. Last, but not least, for all corpora we obtained very low results with the minimum and maximum aggregations (where minimum is practically the 0th, while the maximum is the 100th percentile). It tells us that wav2vec 2.0 embeddings frequently contain outlier values, which has a significant drawback in classification. Instead of these, the 1st and 99th percentiles are promising alternatives. Although low percentiles may also be minor outliers, but the trend clearly shows that their use is more advisable than the minimum and maximum. Lastly, we tested skewness and kurtosis aggregations, but they gave a significantly lower performance overall.

5.1   Feature Combinations

In the second series of experiments, we wanted to further improve the classification performance, so we used sequential forward selection (SFS) to combine multiple aggregated feature vectors. The basic idea behind SFS is to initialize a subset with only the best method, and then iteratively add one more aggregation to the subset, based on which combination provides the greatest improvement in performance. To combine a subset of aggregations, we took the mean of the corresponding posterior estimates and we measured the efficiency of the averaged posterior by calculating the UAR score. SFS helps to reduce the risk of overfitting, as the selected subset is more likely to be the most relevant and informative for the given prediction task. Our results are shown in Fig. 4.

With the iHEARu-EAT database we were able to improve the development test scores up to the 4th iteration. When adding further aggregation approaches, the development UAR scores naturally decrease. However test set scores behave quite differently as they fluctuate and remain in the 84–86% range.

Table 1. The best development and test results for different aggregation strategies and their combinations for the iHEARu-EAT paralinguistic corpora.

iHEARu-EAT		
Aggregation	Dev	Test
Mean	79.4%	83.7%
Median	78.4%	82.6%
75th percentile	78.4%	81.2%
mean+std+min+p25	**82.2%**	**85.4%**
All	80.5%	85.0%

Table 1 contains an overall statistic about the iHEARu-EAT database. The first three rows show the three best aggregations from the previous experiment of the convolutional layer, which are the mean, the median and the 75th percentile. The penultimate row shows the best result obtained with the combination approaches. This subset of aggregations determined by the development set, contains the mean, standard deviation, minimum and the 25th percentile. Here, we report an 8% relative error rate improvement. The last row shows the UAR scores we obtained when we combined all of the aggregation methods. It has a score close to the best combination, but we noticed that if we include too much unnecessary information, we can lose its ability to generalise.

With the URTIC database, we found that we can improve the development results up to the 3rd iteration. After that, for the development set the UAR scores also naturally decrease, but the test set evaluation scores have further improvements of between 66% and 67%.

Table 2 contains an overall statistic about the database. It has the same pattern as the previous one. The three best simple aggregations from the convolutional layer, were the mean, 75th percentile and 99th percentile, where the percentiles improved the generalisation ability as the higher test results indicate. The best subset of aggregations contains the mean, 99th percentile and the maximum and we report a 1.16% dev, 2.69% test relative error rate improvement against the mean only and 2.81% dev, −2.41% test scores against the 75th percentile. When we combined all of the aggregation methods we got an increase in the test values. In our opinion these results indicate that there is a significant

Table 2. The best development and test scores for different aggregation strategies and their combinations for the URTIC paralinguistic corpora.

URTIC		
Aggregation	Dev	Test
Mean	68.7%	63.1%
75th percentile	67.6%	66.4%
99th percentile	66.5%	66.2%
mean+p99+max	**69.5%**	64.8%
All	67.3%	**67.1%**

difference between the feature distribution of the development and the test sets, because different aggregation types seemed to be important in case of these sets.

Table 3. The best development and test results for different aggregation strategies and combinations for the AIBO paralinguistic corpora.

AIBO		
Aggregation	Dev	Test
Mean	45.5%	42.7%
99th percentile	43.8%	42.9%
Standard dev.	43.5%	43.3%
mean+p99+p75	**47.0%**	42.7%
All	44.2%	**44.0%**

With the AIBO database we found that we could improve development scores up to the 3rd iteration. After that, the development set UAR scores also naturally decrease, but the test set evaluation scores have further improvements between 43% and 44%. Table 3 contains an overall statistic about the database with the same pattern as the previous one. The three best aggregations from the convolutional layer, were the mean, 99th percentile and standard deviation. Here, the second and the third best aggregation also gave slight improvements on the test values. The best subset of aggregations contains the mean, 99th percentile and the 75th percentile. We have relative error rate improvements between 1.41% and 8.05%. When we combined all of the aggregation methods, we observed the same behaviour as that for the URTIC database.

In the view of the three databases, lower than middle percentile values works better for iHEARu-EAT while higher values performs better for URITC and AIBO corpora. Clearly, there is another global tendency about needing 3 or 4 iterations of the SFS to improve the efficiency of our model. As we can see, combinations bring improvements on the test set as well, which means it increases the generalisation ability of the model. These significant improvements represented in relative error reduction values of 8.0–10.4% (iHEARu-EAT), 4.6–10.8% (URTIC) and 0–2.3% (AIBO), and they were obtained using simple, easy-to-implement and quick-to-calculate aggregation techniques. New aggregations can be easily calculated alongside traditional metrics because it can be done in parallel in the stage where all the frame-level features are available for one recording. Each new metric introduces as many new features as we originally had. This leads to an utterance-level feature vector of length 1536–2048, which always contains one or two non-traditional percentile values. This does not drastically increase the dimensionality for a casual set of features extracted from the bottleneck layer (which commonly used in paralinguistics).

6   Conclusion and Future Work

In this study we focused on applying aggregation strategies for deep neural network embeddings in the field of computational paralinguistics.

We performed our experiments on three public paralinguistic corpora, that have a variety of topics, but were uniform in their spoken language. We used a wav2vec 2.0 DNN to extract embeddings and then we investigated 11 more- and less-traditional aggregation strategies for combining frame-level embeddings into utterance-level features. In the second set of experiments, we used sequential forward selection to improve our results and find the overall best aggregation methods and global tendencies across databases.

We found a well-defined general pattern between aggregations. The traditional standard deviation and median aggregations are heavily topic dependent. The mean aggregation is always a good choice, but it is not the only one. Our first results indicate that middle percentile aggregations are competitive techniques. This is true for both the convolutional and hidden layers. Overall, it seems that wav2vec 2.0 embeddings can be expected to contain extreme values, which are not really useful for classification. Owing to this, aggregation methods that are sensitive to outliers might be expected to perform less robust than those that can handle the outlying values better. For the former, the obvious examples are the minimum and maximum, which were clearly outperformed by the first and 99th percentiles. We also found that choosing only one aggregation technique leads to a suboptimal classification performance. In the second phase where we performed SFS initialized with the mean, there was a trend across databases, as the peak of improvement fell on the combination of the first 3–4 techniques. The best combinations typically include the mean, a non-traditional percentile value below and/or above the median. Using multiple aggregations simultaneously, we were able to make improvements on both the development and test sets. Based on all of these, we see a trend in our model. It will have a better generalisation ability if we apply at least the above-mentioned 3 types of aggregations together. This way, we can improve the generalization ability of the model, while keeping the feature space below 2048. The computational demand does not increase drastically due to possible parallelization. Our results suggests that aggregating embedding vectors by just using one function leads to a significant information loss. Quite surprisingly, combining *all* aggregated feature sets led to significant improvements on the test set, which could indicate that there is a big stochastic difference between the development and test data.

This, in our opinion, indicates that aggregating the frame-level embeddings is a task which is far from trivial, and that significant improvements can be obtained in the classification performance using other techniques instead of the traditional mean and/or standard deviations. In the case of SFS, working with posteriors is a more time and memory consuming choice, but because of the possible differences, in the near future we plan to retrain our models with the concatenated feature sets. Another possible future direction is to gain more insights using other aggregation methods and datasets, and systematically explore them. Additional research opportunity is to give more emphasis on the important vectors with weighted aggregation, where weights can be learned.

Acknowledgements. This research was supported by the NRDI Office of the Hungarian Ministry of Innovation and Technology (grant no. TKP2021-NVA-09), and within the framework of the Artificial Intelligence National Laboratory Program (RRF-2.3.1-21-2022-00004).

References

1. Baevski, A., Auli, M., Conneau, A.: Wav2vec 2.0: learning the structure of speech from raw audio (2020). https://ai.meta.com/blog/wav2vec-20-learning-the-structure-of-speech-from-raw-audio/
2. Chang, C.C., Lin, C.J.: LIBSVM: a library for support vector machines. ACM Trans. Intell. Syst. Technol. **2**, 1–27 (2011). https://doi.org/10.1145/1961189.1961199
3. Chen, J., Ye, J., Tang, F., Zhou, J.: Automatic detection of Alzheimer's Disease using spontaneous speech only. In: Proceedings of the Interspeech 2021, pp. 3830–3834 (2021). https://doi.org/10.21437/Interspeech.2021-2002
4. Conneau, A., Baevski, A., Collobert, R., Mohamed, A., Auli, M.: Unsupervised Cross-lingual Representation Learning for Speech Recognition (2020). https://doi.org/10.48550/ARXIV.2006.13979
5. Egas-López, J.V., Gosztolya, G.: Deep Neural Network Embeddings for the estimation of the degree of sleepiness. In: IEEE International Conference on Acoustics, Speech and Signal Processing, ICASSP, pp. 7288–7292 (2021). https://doi.org/10.1109/ICASSP39728.2021.9413589
6. Egas-López, J.V., Kiss, G., Sztahó, D., Gosztolya, G.: Automatic assessment of the degree of clinical depression from speech using X-Vectors. In: ICASSP 2022–2022 IEEE International Conference on Acoustics, Speech and Signal Processing (ICASSP), pp. 8502–8506 (2022). https://doi.org/10.1109/ICASSP43922.2022.9746068
7. Egas-López, J.V., Vetráb, M., Tóth, L., Gosztolya, G.: identifying conflict escalation and primates by using ensemble x-vectors and fisher vector features. In: Proceedings of the Interspeech 2021, pp. 476–480 (2021). https://doi.org/10.21437/Interspeech.2021-1173

8. Gosztolya, G.: Using the Fisher vector representation for audio-based emotion recognition. Acta Polytechnica Hungarica **17**, 7–23 (2020)
9. Gosztolya, G., Tóth, L., Svindt, V., Bóna, J., Hoffmann, I.: Using acoustic deep neural network embeddings to detect multiple sclerosis from speech. In: Proceedings of ICASSP, pp. 6927–6931 (2022)
10. Gosztolya, G., Beke, A., Neuberger, T.: Differentiating laughter types via HMM/DNN and probabilistic sampling. In: Speech and Computer, SPECOM 2019. vol. 11658, pp. 122–132 (2019)
11. Grezes, F., Richards, J., Rosenberg, A.: Let me finish: automatic conflict detection using speaker overlap. In: Proceedings of the Interspeech 2013, pp. 200–204 (2013). https://doi.org/10.21437/Interspeech.2013-67
12. Grosman, J.: Fine-tuned XLSR-53 large model for speech recognition in German (2021). https://huggingface.co/jonatasgrosman/wav2vec2-large-xlsr-53-german
13. Han, K.J., Kim, S., Narayanan, S.S.: Strategies to improve the robustness of Agglomerative Hierarchical Clustering under data source variation for speaker diarization. IEEE Trans. Audio Speech Lang. Process. **16**, 1590–1601 (2008). https://doi.org/10.1109/TASL.2008.2002085
14. Hinton, G., et al.: Deep Neural Networks for Acoustic Modeling in Speech Recognition: the shared views of four research groups. IEEE Signal Process. Mag. **29**, 82–97 (2012). https://doi.org/10.1109/MSP.2012.2205597
15. Jeancolas, L., et al.: X-Vectors: new quantitative biomarkers for early Parkinson's Disease detection from speech. Front. Neuroinform. **15**, 1–18 (2021). https://doi.org/10.3389/fninf.2021.578369
16. Kadiri, S., Kethireddy, R., Alku, P.: Parkinson's Disease detection from speech using Single Frequency Filtering Cepstral Coefficients. In: Proceedings of the Interspeech 2020, pp. 4971–4975 (2020). https://doi.org/10.21437/Interspeech.2020-3197
17. Kaya, H., Karpov, A., Salah, A.: Fisher vectors with cascaded normalization for paralinguistic analysis. In: Proceedings of the Interspeech 2015, pp. 909–913 (2015). https://doi.org/10.21437/Interspeech.2015-193
18. Krajewski, J., Schieder, S., Batliner, A.: Description of the upper respiratory tract infection corpus (urtic). In: Proceedings of the Interspeech 2017 (2017)
19. Lin, W.W., Mak, M.W.: Wav2spk: a simple DNN architecture for learning speaker embeddings from waveforms. In: Proceedings of Interspeech, pp. 3211–3215 (2020)
20. Metze, F., Batliner, A., Eyben, F., Polzehl, T., Schuller, B., Steidl, S.: Emotion recognition using imperfect speech recognition. In: Proceedings of the Interspeech 2010, pp. 478–481 (2010). https://doi.org/10.21437/Interspeech.2010-202
21. Mustaqeem, Kwon, S.: CLSTM: deep feature-based speech emotion recognition using the hierarchical ConvLSTM network. Mathematics **8**, 1–19 (2020). https://doi.org/10.3390/math8122133
22. Oflazoglu, C., Yildirim, S.: Recognizing emotion from Turkish speech using acoustic features. In: EURASIP Journal on Audio Speech and Music Processing 2013 (2013). https://doi.org/10.1186/1687-4722-2013-26
23. Pappagari, R., et al.: Automatic detection and assessment of Alzheimer Disease using speech and language technologies in low-resource scenarios. In: Proceedings of the Interspeech 2021, pp. 3825–3829 (2021). https://doi.org/10.21437/Interspeech.2021-1850
24. Pérez-Toro, P., et al.: Alzheimer's detection from English to Spanish using acoustic and linguistic embeddings. In: Proceedings of Interspeech 2022, pp. 2483–2487 (2022). https://doi.org/10.21437/Interspeech.2022-10883

25. Přibil, J., Přibilová, A., Matoušek, J.: GMM-based speaker age and gender classification in Czech and Slovak. J. Electr. Eng. **68**, 3–12 (2017). https://doi.org/10.1515/jee-2017-0001

26. Schuller, B., Steidl, S., Batliner, A.: The INTERSPEECH 2009 emotion challenge. In: Proceedings of the Interspeech 2009, pp. 312–315 (2009). https://doi.org/10.21437/Interspeech. 2009–103

27. Schuller, B., et al.: The INTERSPEECH 2017 computational paralinguistics challenge: addressee, cold & snoring. In: Proceedings of the Interspeech 2017, pp. 3442–3446 (2017). https://doi.org/10.21437/Interspeech.2017-43

28. Schuller, B., et al.: The INTERSPEECH 2015 computational paralinguistics challenge: Nativeness, Parkinson's & eating condition. In: Proceedings of the Interspeech 2015, pp. 478–482 (2015). https://doi.org/10.21437/Interspeech.2015-179

29. Schuller, B.W., et al.: The INTERSPEECH 2019 computational paralinguistics challenge: Styrian dialects, continuous sleepiness, baby sounds & orca activity. In: Proceedings of the Interspeech 2019, pp. 2378–2382 (2019). https://doi.org/10.21437/Interspeech.2019-1122

30. Sheikh, S.A., Sahidullah, M., Hirsch, F., Ouni, S.: Introducing ECAPA-TDNN and Wav2Vec2.0 Embeddings to Stuttering Detection (2022). https://doi.org/10.48550/ARXIV.2204.01564

31. Snyder, D., Garcia-Romero, D., Sell, G., Povey, D., Khudanpur, S.: X-Vectors: robust DNN embeddings for speaker verification. In: IEEE International Conference on Acoustics, Speech and Signal Processing, ICASSP, pp. 5329–5333 (2018). https://doi.org/10.1109/ICASSP.2018.8461375

32. Steidl, S.: Automatic classification of emotion related user states in spontaneous children's speech. Logos-Verlag Berlin, Germany (2009). https://d-nb.info/992551641

33. Tzirakis, P., Zhang, J., Schuller, B.W.: End-to-end speech emotion recognition using deep neural networks. In: 2018 IEEE international Conference on Acoustics, Speech and Signal Processing (ICASSP), pp. 5089–5093 (2018)

34. Van Segbroeck, M., et al.: Classification of cognitive load from speech using an i-vector framework. In: Proceedings of the Interspeech 2014, pp. 751–755 (2014). https://doi.org/10.21437/Interspeech.2014-114

35. Vetráb, M., Gosztolya, G.: Speech emotion detection form a Hungarian database with the Bag-of-Audi-Words technique (in Hungarian). In: Proceedings of MSZNY, pp. 265–274. Szeged (2019)

36. Vetráb, M., Gosztolya, G.: Using hybrid HMM/DNN embedding extractor models in computational paralinguistic tasks. Sensors **23**, 5208 (2023)

37. Vetráb, M., et al.: Using spectral sequence-to-sequence autoencoders to assess mild cognitive impairment. In: IEEE International Conference on Acoustics, Speech and Signal Processing, ICASSP, pp. 6467–6471 (2022). https://doi.org/10.1109/ICASSP43922.2022.9746148

38. Vásquez-Correa, J., Orozco-Arroyave, J.R., Nöth, E.: Convolutional Neural Network to model articulation impairments in patients with Parkinson's Disease. In: Proceedings of the Interspeech 2017, pp. 314–318 (2017). https://doi.org/10.21437/Interspeech.2017-1078

39. Wagner, J., Schiller, D., Seiderer, A., Andre, E.: Deep learning in paralinguistic recognition tasks: are hand-crafted features still relevant? In: Interspeech, pp. 147–151 (2018). https://doi.org/10.21437/Interspeech.2018-1238

40. Wang, W., Lu, P., Yan, Y.: An improved hierarchical speaker clustering. Acta Acustica **33**, 9–14 (2008)
41. Zhao, Z., Bao, Z., Zhang, Z., Cummins, N., Wang, H., Schuller, B.: Attention-enhanced connectionist temporal classification for discrete speech emotion recognition. In: Proceedings of the Interspeech 2019, pp. 206–210 (2019). https://doi.org/10.21437/Interspeech.2019-1649

Rhythm Formant Analysis for Automatic Depression Classification

Kumar Kaustubh[1]([✉]), Parismita Gogoi[2,3], and S.R.M Prasanna[1]

[1] Indian Institute of Technology, Dharwad, India
{221022003,prasanna}@iitdh.ac.in
[2] Indian Institute of Technology, Guwahati, India
parismitagogoi@iitg.ac.in
[3] DUIET, Dibrugarh University, Dibrugarh, India

Abstract. This paper presents a study on the application of Rhythm Formant Analysis (RFA) for automatic depression classification in speech signals. The research utilizes the EATD-corpus, a dataset specifically designed for studying depression in speech. The goal is to develop an effective classification system capable of distinguishing between depressed and non-depressed speech based on Rhythm Formant (RF) features. The proposed methodology involves extracting RFs from the speech signals using signal processing techniques. Two kinds of RFs, namely Amplitude Modulation (AM) and Frequency Modulation (FM) RFs and their combinations are analyzed and used as features for classification. These features provide valuable information about the temporal and spectral characteristics of the speech. The classification system is built using a Decision Tree (DT) classifier and its results are compared with logistic regression and random forest. The model's performance is evaluated using the accuracy, F1 scores for each class and their macro and weighted averages. Experimental results demonstrate promising outcomes, with the DT classifier achieving an accuracy of 70%, a weighted average F1 score of 0.73 and a macro average F1 score of 0.53 when using FM RFs as feature, showing much better performance compared to other features and classifiers. These results indicate that the proposed approach effectively captures discriminative features related to depression in the speech signals. The findings suggest that RFs have the potential to serve as a valuable tool for building automatic depression classification systems.

Keywords: Rhythm Formant Analysis · Depression Classification · EATD-corpus

1 Introduction

Depression, a mental health disorder affecting millions worldwide, poses a significant challenge to clinicians and researchers alike due to its complex nature and varying symptoms. Accurate and timely diagnosis of depression is crucial

A. Karpov et al. (Eds.): SPECOM 2023, LNAI 14338, pp. 94–106, 2023.
https://doi.org/10.1007/978-3-031-48309-7_8

for effective treatment and intervention. Depression is characterized by persistent feelings of sadness, hopelessness, and a loss of interest in daily activities. Clinicians currently rely on a variety of methods to diagnose depression, including interviews, self-report questionnaires, and psychiatric assessments [3]. While these approaches have proven valuable in many cases, they are subjective and prone to biases. The interpretation of interview responses and questionnaire results can vary based on the clinician's experience, cultural background, and personal biases, subsequently leading to misdiagnosis or delayed treatment. Speech, as a potential candidate for depression detection, offers several advantages over traditional diagnostic methods. Speech is a fundamental aspect of human communication and reflects various emotional and cognitive states [4]. In the past, researchers have come up with many acoustic features which were capable of capturing the patterns in the speech of a depressed individual, including Low-Level-Descriptors (LLDs) [12]. One such study involves the analysis of GMM based features along with power spectral densities within multiple subbands which turned out to be effective in addressing patterns associated with depressed and non-depressed speech samples [13]. While these features have been helpful in such tasks, deep neural networks in combination with handcrafted features have also been utilized in order to achieve better performance [8]. Using deep learning, attempts have been made to develop systems for measuring depression severity by combining transfer learning, attention based learning and unsupervised learning [14]. Researchers have also implemented deep learning architectures involving convolutional and recurrent neural networks using spectrograms for similar emotion recognition tasks [10]. LSTM, a variant of RNN which is effective in handling long time series data, has also been effective in detecting depression from speech [1].

In this paper, we aim to explore the potential of Rhythm Formant Analysis (RFA) as a novel approach for automatic depression classification. By investigating the relationship between speech rhythm patterns and depressive states, we seek to contribute to the ongoing efforts in developing objective and reliable tools for depression assessment. One of the relevant features used for classifying speeches of depressed and non-depressed subjects are Mel Frequency Cepstral Coefficients (MFCCs) [2], which provide compact representation of the speech signals and are effective in capturing important characteristics of speech. Rhythm Formants (RFs), on the other hand, have been employed by researchers in machine learning to classify different speaking styles in speech-related classification tasks [5]. This serves as one of the motivations to investigate the distinctive rhythm patterns that might be associated with speeches of depressed and non-depressed individuals. Based on our initial investigation, we have observed notable variations in the arrangement of t-SNE plots for MFCCs, Amplitude Modulation (AM), Frequency Modulations (FM) RFs and their combination, as shown in Fig. 1 below. Figure 1 (a) is the 2-dimensional t-SNE representation of 13-dimensional MFCCs, Fig. 1 (b) shows the 2-dimensional t-SNE representation after concatenation of 6-dimensional AM RFs and 6-dimensional FM RFs to create a 12-dimensional feature space. Figure 1 (c) and Fig. 1 (d) presents the 2-

dimensional t-SNE plots for 6-dimensional AM and FM RFs, respectively. These variations indicate that these features capture different informations which further motivates the usage of RFs for carrying out this classification task. From the t-SNE plots in Fig. 1, we can observe that MFCCs are much more confined in the feature space compared to other features.

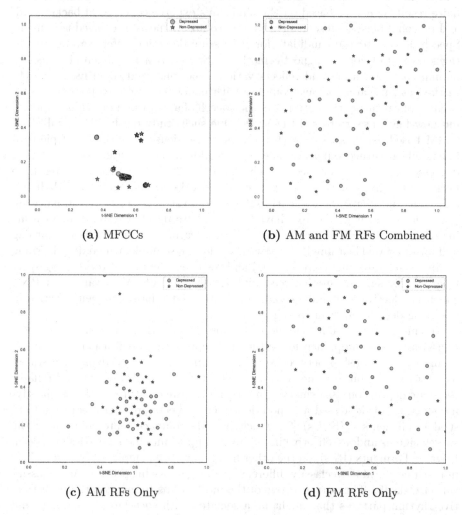

(a) MFCCs

(b) AM and FM RFs Combined

(c) AM RFs Only

(d) FM RFs Only

Fig. 1. 2-dimensional t-SNE visualization for (a) 13-dimensional MFCCs, (b) 12-dimensional RFs after concatenating 6-dimensional AM and FM RFs, (c) 6-dimensional AM RFs and (d) 6-dimensional FM RFs.

The paper is arranged in the following sections: In Sect. 2, AM and FM RFs and their potential use in depression classification have been discussed along with the signal processing steps involved in their extraction. Section 3 presents the classification system built using FM RFs as features with a Decision Tree (DT) classifier. Section 4 describes the dataset and the experiments performed, followed by Sect. 5 where the evaluation metrics and classification results are discussed. Finally, in Sect. 6, the paper is concluded with possible future work directions.

2   Rhythm Formant Analysis

Four assertions in RFA including speech modulation knowledge, simultaneous RFs, serial RFs and asymmetrical rhythms are put forward by Gibbon in his exploratory paper on RFA [6]. The key feature of RFA is the concept of spectral peak values in Low-Frequency (LF) spectrum which are coined as LF rhythm formants. RFA approach explicitly relates to the time-stamps of linguistic categories (e.g. syllable, foot) for each language. Speech rhythms are described as waves with frequencies below 10 Hz [6]. This rhythm can be found by analyzing the changes in loudness and pitch of speech at these LFs. RFA involves looking at the variations in pitch (FM) and loudness (AM) across the whole sample. In our study, we employ a method called RF detection, which involves analyzing the spectral peaks of demodulated AM and FM signal envelopes in the frequency domain [7]. This approach allows us to identify and characterize rhythmic patterns present in the speech signals. For extracting the FM RFs, we first normalize the speech signal between -1 and 1. Next, we obtain the pitch contour and transform it into the frequency domain using Fourier transform. Then, we extract the LF segments (0 Hz to 10 Hz) from the magnitude of the Fourier transform and normalize it to have a value between 0 and 1. Finally, we pass it through a peak-picking algorithm to obtain the FM RFs [7]. Figure 2 illustrates these steps using a block diagram.

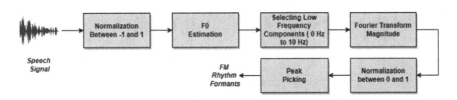

Fig. 2. Block diagram showing signal processing steps for extraction of FM rhythm formants.

Extraction of AM RFs involves a similar approach where we first normalize the speech signal between -1 and 1 and obtain the amplitude envelop using the absolute value of Hilbert transform. After passing the amplitude envelope through a median filter, we then transform the resulting signal into frequency domain using Fourier transform. Again, we extract the LF components (0 Hz to 10 Hz) from the magnitude of the Fourier transform and normalize it between 0

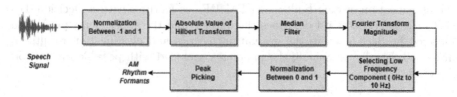

Fig. 3. Block diagram showing signal processing steps for extraction of AM rhythm formants.

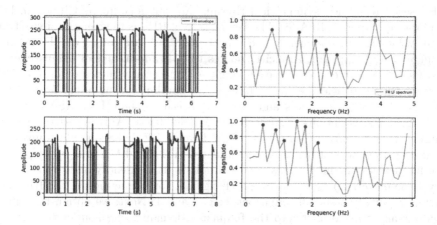

Fig. 4. FM envelope and LF spectrum of a non-depressed (top panel) and depressed speech sample (bottom panel). The peaks in the LF spectrum are representing FM RFs.

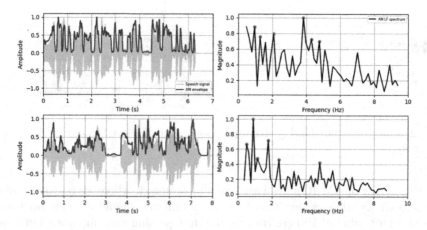

Fig. 5. AM envelope and LF spectrum of a non-depressed (top panel) and a depressed speech sample (bottom panel). The peaks in the LF spectrum are representing AM RFs.

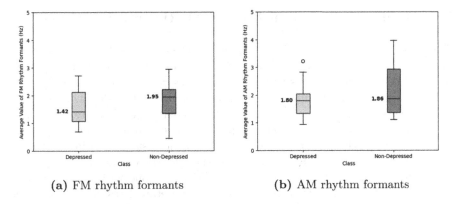

(a) FM rhythm formants   (b) AM rhythm formants

Fig. 6. Box plot showing median values of (a) FM RFs and (b) AM RFs averaged across each of the selected speech samples for depressed and non-depressed class.

and 1. Finally, we use a peak picking algorithm to obtain the AM RFs [7]. The same is illustrated in the block diagram shown in Fig. 3.

Using the FM RF extraction steps, the generated FM envelope and peaks in the LF spectrum, which represent the FM RFs, are shown in the Fig. 4 for a depressed and a non-depressed speech sample. Similarly, using AM RF extraction steps, the generated AM envelope and peaks in the LF spectrum, which represent the AM RFs are shown in Fig. 5 for the same depressed and non-depressed speech samples as used in FM RFs. It can be observed from Fig. 4 and Fig. 5 that, on average, RFs in case of depressed speech samples are at lower frequencies compared to non-depressed speech samples. The average of FM RFs comes out to be 1.34 Hz and 2.24 Hz for depressed and non-depressed speech samples, respectively, used in the illustration whereas the average in case of AM RFs comes out to be 1.93 Hz and 2.87 Hz for depressed and non-depressed speech samples, respectively.

Strengthening the case for the potential of AM and FM RFs in the classification task, we present a box plot in Fig.6. For this plot, we randomly selected 15 speech samples from each class and extracted the first 6 AM and FM RFs. Next, we calculated the average value for each speech sample across the first 6 AM and FM RFs. After calculating this average, the median values of FM RFs for the depressed and non-depressed class for the selected samples are calculated as 1.42 Hz and 1.95 Hz, respectively as shown in Fig. 6 (a). Similarly, the median value of depressed and non-depressed class for these selected samples comes out to be 1.80 Hz and 1.86 Hz respectively for average value of AM RFs across each sample as shown in Fig. 6 (b). The lower median value for the depressed class in both the cases suggests that, on average, the AM and FM RFs tend to be lower in individuals classified as depressed. This implies a potential characteristic or trend in the speech patterns of individuals with depression, as compared to those without.

3   Classification System Using FM Rhythm Formants

The paper presents a system for depression classification based on the FM RF feature extraction method. The system utilizes the top 6 FM RF features extracted using signal processing techniques as described in the previous section and uses them as the 6-dimensional feature vector for the classification task. The system employs a standard decision tree classifier which takes in the feature vector to classify the speech samples into two categories: depressed and non-depressed. Although we attempted to build the system by utilizing a combination of AM and FM RFs along with the 13 MFCCs and explored other classifiers as well, it turns out that using FM RFs alone with a decision tree outperforms the combination. The experiments, detailed results and possible explanations are discussed in the subsequent sections. This system holds the potential to assist mental health professionals in detecting and intervening with individuals at risk of depression, complementing their expertise.

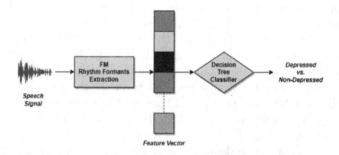

Fig. 7. Classification system built after extracting FM rhythm formants, using them for creating a 6-dimensional feature vector and passing it through a decision tree classifier to obtain a label either as depressed or non-depressed.

4   Dataset and Experimental Description

The study employed a Chinese dataset known as Emotional Audio-Textual Depression corpus (EATD-corpus), which consists of speech recordings from individuals classified as either depressed or non-depressed [11]. The dataset includes a total of 162 different speakers, with 30 classified as depressed and 132 as non-depressed. The categorization is based on the indexed Self-Rating Depression Scale (SDS) score (Raw SDS score multiplied by 1.25), where a score of 53 or higher signifies depressed, while a score below 53 indicates non-depressed. The SDS questionnaire comprises 20 items designed to evaluate four key attributes often associated with depression: its pervasive influence, physiological signs, additional disturbances, and changes in psychomotor activities. This questionnaire is commonly employed by psychologists as a screening tool to identify individuals who may be suffering from depression in clinical practice, making the dataset suitable for this study. The total duration of the dataset is around 2.26 h. The training dataset consists of 83 speakers, with 19 categorized as depressed and 64 as non-depressed. Each individual provided three responses, leading to a total of 57 depressed samples and 192 non-depressed samples. Likewise, the testing dataset comprises 79 speakers, with 11 identified as depressed and 68 as non-depressed. Each individual in the testing set also provided three responses, resulting in a total of 33 depressed samples and 204 non-depressed samples. Table 1 below shows exact distribution of the dataset.

Table 1. Distribution of the dataset.

	Depressed	Non-Depressed	Total Data
Train	57 samples (14 min 06 s)	191 samples (56 min 07 s)	70 min 13 s
Test	33 samples (7 min 48 s)	204 samples (50 min 28 s)	58 min 16 s

In our study, we have conducted a detailed experiment that looks into the process of analyzing depressed and non-depressed speech signals. The main goal of this analysis is to extract and examine RFs from the speech signals. Initially, each of the audio files, which are present in WAV format, are loaded using the default sampling rate of 16000 Hz. After the successful import of audio data, signal normalization is performed to ensure that the audio signal fits within a standardized range of -1 to 1, achieved by dividing the signal by its maximum value. For the extraction of FM RF features, the fundamental frequency (F0) is estimated using the AMDF (Absolute Magnitude Difference Function) algorithm, which calculates the difference between a particular frame of a signal and its delayed version which results in smallest sum of absolute difference. After F0 estimation, we select the LF components between 0 Hz to 10 Hz, and a Fourier transform is computed. The magnitude of the Fourier transform is then normalized between 0 and 1. Finally, this normalized magnitude is passed through a peak picking algorithm to detect the top 6 peaks, which are the FM RFs. For the calculation of AM RFs, a similar procedure is followed. After normalizing the speech sample, the envelope for AM signal is calculated. The Hilbert transform of the signal is computed to gain the instantaneous phase and amplitude, and then the absolute value of the Hilbert transform is derived to ascertain the envelope. To get a smoother signal, a median filter, with a window size of 501, is applied to the envelope, which is then normalized by dividing it by its maximum value. Subsequently, a spectral analysis is performed on the normalized envelope, and the LF segment of 0 Hz to 10 Hz is extracted from the magnitude component of the Fourier transform of the envelope. After extraction, the magnitude components are normalized between 0 and 1. Finally, this normalized magnitude is passed through a peak picking algorithm to detect the top 6 peaks, which are the AM RFs. We have also extracted 13 MFCCs and used them as feature vector with different classifiers for comparing with the RF results.

After extracting these features, they form the basis of the four separate experiments conducted in this study. In the first experiment, we utilize only the 13 MFCCs as the 13-dimensional feature vector. The second and third experiment focuses solely on AM and FM RFs. Using both AM and FM RFs separately, we generate 6-dimensional feature vector for each case. In the fourth and final experiment, a combination of AM and FM RFs is used by concatenating them and creating a 12-dimensional feature vector. All the four feature vectors are then used in three different machine learning algorithms: DT classifier, random forest and Logistic Regression (LR) to carry out the binary classification task, which finally provides us with the label either as depressed or non-depressed. All the classifiers' parameters were kept as default for conducting each of these experiments. Since the classifiers used are relatively simple and interpretable, we refrained from using cross-validation to expedite the training and evaluation process. The results of these experiments along with the evaluation metrics are described in the next section.

5   Evaluation Metrics and Results

In the conducted study, we aimed to evaluate the performance of various machine learning classifiers for detecting depression based on the experiments conducted. Following key evaluation metrics were used to assess the performance of the models: accuracy, F1 scores of each class, Macro Average (MA) F1 score, and Weighted Average (WA) F1 score. We have also tabulated the values of Precision (P) and Recall (R) for each class as well as their MA and WA. Accuracy (A) measures the percentage of correct predictions made by the model [9]. It is given by the formula:

$$A = \frac{TP + TN}{TP + TN + FP + FN} \tag{1}$$

where TP, TN, FP, FN represents the True Positive, True Negative, False Positive and False Negative, respectively. Precision (P) focuses on the correctness of positive predictions [9] and is given by the following formula:

$$P = \frac{TP}{TP + FP} \tag{2}$$

Recall emphasizes the completeness of positive predictions and provides insights into the system's ability to minimize FNs [9]. Recall (R) can be calculated as follows:

$$R = \frac{TP}{TP + FN} \tag{3}$$

The F-Measure or F1 score is the harmonic mean of P and R [9], where P and R are precision and recall as described above. The F1 score is given by the formula:

$$F1 = 2 * \frac{P * R}{P + R} \tag{4}$$

In Table 2 below, the classification results for LR is presented for each of the four features. The model is able to achieve an accuracy of 66% when MFCCs are used as features and an F1 score of 0.15 and 0.79 for Depressed (D) and Non-Depressed (ND) class. It achieves a precision value of 0.12, 0.85 and a recall value of 0.21, 0.74 for depressed and non-depressed class respectively. The other three features are showing highly biased results. Even though they are showing a better accuracy compared to MFCCs, the F1 scores indicates their bias towards the non-depressed class. Since, LR assumes a linear boundary between the features and target class it may not be effective in capturing the complex decision boundaries, limiting its performance on complex relationships present in the AM and FM RFs.

Table 2. Classification results for LR.

Features	Accuracy	F1 Score		F1 Score (MA)	F1 Score (WA)	Precision		Precision (MA)	Precision (WA)	Recall		Recall (MA)	Recall (WA)
		D	ND			D	ND			D	ND		
MFCCs	66%	0.15	0.79	0.47	0.70	0.12	0.85	0.48	0.75	0.21	0.74	0.48	0.67
FM RFs	86%	0.06	0.93	0.49	0.80	1.00	0.86	0.93	0.88	0.03	1.00	0.52	0.86
AM RFs	85%	0.00	0.92	0.46	0.79	0.00	0.86	0.43	0.74	0.00	1.00	0.50	0.86
AM+FM RFs	81%	0.04	0.92	0.47	0.78	0.08	0.86	0.47	0.75	0.03	0.94	0.49	0.82

In Table 3, we have tabulated the classification results for random forest classifier for all the four feature vectors. The random forest achieves an accuracy of 85%, 83%, 80% and 83% for MFCCs, FM RFs, AM RFs and the combination of AM and FM RFs, respectively. Similar to LR, random forest also turns out to be biased towards the non-depressed class as can be observed from the F1 scores of both the classes which are 0.00 in case of MFCCs and the combination of AM and FM RFs and 0.09 and 0.08 for FM RFs and AM RFs, respectively for the depressed class. Random forest is capable of modeling non-linear relationship by combining multiple DTs, however it introduces complexity and hence, no substantial improvements in F1 score is achieved as can be noticed from the results in Table 3.

Table 3. Classification results for random forest.

Features	Accuracy	F1 Score		F1 Score (MA)	F1 Score (WA)	Precision		Precision (MA)	Precision (WA)	Recall		Recall (MA)	Recall (WA)
		D	ND			D	ND			D	ND		
MFCCs	85%	0.00	0.92	0.46	0.79	0.00	0.86	0.43	0.74	0.00	0.99	0.50	0.85
FM RFs	83%	0.09	0.91	0.50	0.79	0.20	0.86	0.53	0.77	0.06	0.96	0.51	0.83
AM RFs	80%	0.08	0.89	0.48	0.77	0.12	0.86	0.49	0.75	0.06	0.93	0.49	0.80
AM+FM RFs	83%	0.00	0.91	0.45	0.78	0.00	0.85	0.43	0.73	0.00	0.97	0.48	0.83

Table 4 below shows the classification results for the DT model corresponding to all the features. The DT turns out to be most effective among all the classifiers used. The DT achieves an accuracy of 60%, 70%, 66%, 68% for MFCCs, FM RFs, AM RFs and the combination of AM and FM RFs, respectively. The model also achieves an improved F1 score for each of the features out of which the FM RF shows the most improved results with an F1 score of 0.24 and 0.82 for Depressed (D) and Non-Depressed (ND) classes, respectively. The confusion matrix shown in Fig. 8 (d) below suggests that in case of FM RFs, the DT classifier is able to predict the highest number of samples correctly compared to other features. Out of 200 non-depressed speech samples used for testing, it has correctly predicted 153 and out of 33 depressed speech samples, it is able to predicted 11 of them correctly. The confusion matrices for other feature are also presented in Fig. 8 for the purpose of comparison. Since, the DT model is least biased and performing best with FM RFs, the classification system has been built using them.

Table 4. Classification results for DT.

Features	Accuracy	F1 Score		F1 Score (MA)	F1 Score (WA)	Precision		Precision (MA)	Precision (WA)	**Recall**		Recall (MA)	Recall (WA)
		D	ND			D	ND			D	ND		
MFCCs	60%	0.18	0.74	0.46	0.66	0.13	0.85	0.49	0.75	0.30	0.66	0.48	0.61
FM RFs	70%	**0.24**	**0.82**	**0.53**	**0.73**	**0.19**	**0.87**	**0.53**	**0.78**	**0.33**	**0.77**	**0.55**	**0.70**
AM RFs	66%	0.13	0.79	0.46	0.70	0.11	0.85	0.48	0.74	0.18	0.74	0.46	0.67
AM+FM RFs	68%	0.23	0.80	0.52	0.72	0.18	0.87	0.52	0.77	0.33	0.74	0.54	0.69

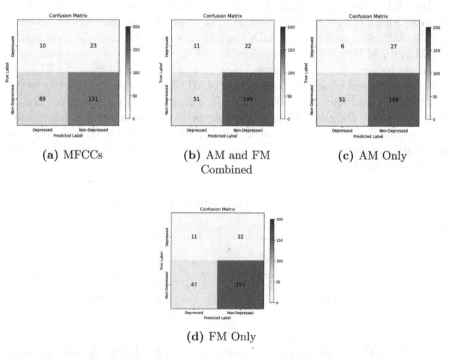

(a) MFCCs   (b) AM and FM   (c) AM Only
                       Combined

(d) FM Only

Fig. 8. Confusion matrices showing the number of true and false prediction made by the decision tree classifier for (a) MFCCs, (b) A combination of AM and FM RFs, (c) AM RFs and (d) FM RFs for the test data.

The improvement in the DT model can be explained based on its working principle. DTs have high decision boundary flexibility, allowing them to capture non-linear decision boundaries in the feature space in a much better way. By creating hierarchical decision rules, they are capable of handling the sequential data like AM and FM RFs which contains important time-frequency patterns.

6   Conclusion and Future Work

In this paper, AM and FM RFs and their combination have been studied for automatic classification of depression using speech data. Three different classifiers, i.e. LR, random forest and DT were trained for each of the feature vectors and their performance was compared against MFCCs. FM RFs, when used as the feature vector for the DT classifier performed the best. By best, we mean that this system was least biased among the systems discussed in this paper in performing the classification task. In conclusion, RFs have the potential to capture the essential patterns from the speech data which may be indicative of depression. Experimentation on larger and balanced datasets could help establish its real-world applicability and reliability in aiding mental health assessments. Furthermore, using other relevant features along with the RFs may also have the potential to improve the system's performance. While the dataset used in this study serves its purpose, further studies can be conducted using other existing datasets to improve the generalizability of the model.

References

1. Al Hanai, T., Ghassemi, M.M., Glass, J.R.: Detecting depression with audio/text sequence modeling of interviews. In: Interspeech, pp. 1716–1720 (2018)
2. Alghowinem, S., Goecke, R., Wagner, M., Epps, J., Breakspear, M., Parker, G., et al.: From joyous to clinically depressed: Mood detection using spontaneous speech. In: FLAIRS Conference, vol. 19 (2012)
3. Cummins, N., Scherer, S., Krajewski, J., Schnieder, S., Epps, J., Quatieri, T.F.: A review of depression and suicide risk assessment using speech analysis. Speech Commun. **71**, 10–49 (2015)
4. France, D.J., Shiavi, R.G., Silverman, S., Silverman, M., Wilkes, M.: Acoustical properties of speech as indicators of depression and suicidal risk. IEEE Trans. Biomed. Eng. **47**(7), 829–837 (2000)
5. Gibbon, D.: Speech rhythms: learning to discriminate speech styles. Proc. Speech Prosody **2022**, 302–306 (2022)
6. Gibbon, D.: The rhythms of rhythm. J. Int. Phon. Assoc. **53**(1), 233–265 (2023)
7. Gibbon, D., Li, P.: Quantifying and correlating rhythm formants in speech. arXiv preprint arXiv:1909.05639 (2019)
8. He, L., Cao, C.: Automated depression analysis using convolutional neural networks from speech. J. Biomed. Inform. **83**, 103–111 (2018)
9. Hossin, M., Sulaiman, M.N.: A review on evaluation metrics for data classification evaluations. Inter. J. Data Mining Knowl. Manag. Process **5**(2), 1 (2015)
10. Satt, A., Rozenberg, S., Hoory, R., et al.: Efficient emotion recognition from speech using deep learning on spectrograms. In: Interspeech, pp. 1089–1093 (2017)

11. Shen, Y., Yang, H., Lin, L.: Automatic depression detection: an emotional audio-textual corpus and a gru/bilstm-based model. In: ICASSP 2022–2022 IEEE International Conference on Acoustics, Speech and Signal Processing (ICASSP), pp. 6247–6251. IEEE (2022)
12. Wu, P., Wang, R., Lin, H., Zhang, F., Tu, J., Sun, M.: Automatic depression recognition by intelligent speech signal processing: a systematic survey. CAAI Trans. Intell. Technol. **8**(3), 701–711 (2023)
13. Yingthawornsuk, T., Keskinpala, H.K., Wilkes, D.M., Shiavi, R.G., Salomon, R.M.: Direct acoustic feature using iterative em algorithm and spectral energy for classifying suicidal speech. In: Eighth Annual Conference of the International Speech Communication Association (2007)
14. Zhao, Z., et al.: Automatic assessment of depression from speech via a hierarchical attention transfer network and attention autoencoders. IEEE J. Selected Topics Signal Process. **14**(2), 423–434 (2019)

Determining Alcohol Intoxication Based on Speech and Neural Networks

Pavel Laptev$^{(\boxtimes)}$, Sergey Litovkin , and Evgeny Kostyuchenko

Tomsk State University of Control Systems and Radioelectronics, 634050 Tomsk, Russia
`laptev.p.738-1@e.tusur.ru`

Abstract. This study considers an approach to the analysis of human speech using neural networks to perform the task of determining the state of alcahol intoxication. In the course of the study, a personal data set was created, consisting of 340 audio files, and increased to the size of 1020 audio files, using augmentation methods, namely slowing down and speeding up audio files. As input data for neural networks, spectrograms and MFCC visualization with size of 256×256 and 512×512 pixels were considered, thanks to which four VGG16 models were trained. As a result of the study, the best model was identified, namely, trained on spectrograms of size 512×512, having F-score and UAR values of 0.73 and 0.77 for the test samples, and 0.82 and 0.83 in the form of averages of 10-fold cross-validation.

Keywords: Neural Networks · VGG16 · Spectrogram · Speech Analysis · Alcohol Intoxication

1 Introduction

In the modern world, the problem of alcohol consumption is still relevant. Its leads to a slow reaction, cloudy thinking, deviation from accepted norms of behavior, and other consequences [1–4]. Also, drinking alcohol can lead to terrible consequences in areas such as traffic, construction, and cases of injuries due to alcohol consumption in general only increase every year. According to the World Health Organization (WHO), about 3 million people die every year due to alcohol consumption, which is about 5% of the total number of deaths. At the same time, if we consider deaths between the ages of 20 and 39, then deaths due to alcohol consumption amount to 13.5%. These statistics are taken from the official website of the WHO [5].

To prevent such situations, it is necessary to introduce restrictions on the use of alcohol and conduct periodic checks. The checks are usually done in two ways: physical coordination exercises, or measurement of blood alcohol content by breath or blood test. However, both of these methods require either a medical education or expensive equipment. Moreover, only blood-alcohol analyzers are truly accurate, as changes in coordination may vary from individual to individual.

As a result, it is necessary to develop a new simple and convenient way to test the alcohol intoxication of a person, which would be quite cheap for the average user, but at the same time possess high accuracy.

© The Author(s), under exclusive license to Springer Nature Switzerland AG 2023
A. Karpov et al. (Eds.): SPECOM 2023, LNAI 14338, pp. 107–115, 2023.
https://doi.org/10.1007/978-3-031-48309-7_9

Due to the relevance of the problem and the lack of a generally accepted solution, the goal of future research is to develop a system for analyzing human speech using machine learning methods and neural networks to determine the state of alcohol intoxication.

2 Related Works

Drinking alcohol has a negative effect on human attention, reaction, and also on his thinking. In turn, changes in thinking lead to a change in human speech, for example, an increase in pauses, stretching, or changes in sounds. At the same time, since the physiological characteristics of a person themselves remain unchanged, the influence of alcohol becomes an indisputable fact.

For example, it has been proven that when alcohol is consumed, the pronunciation of sonorous sounds changes [9, 10], in particular the sound "s" [11]. At the same time, it is worth noting that the changes themselves affect with different strengths with different intoxication. Thus, when the level of intoxication is above 1.5‰, speech changes become noticeable by ear [10]. However, do not forget that alcohol affects each person in different ways, depending on his physiological characteristics: weight, height, age, etc. [12]. The effect of alcohol on the duration of pauses and pronunciation of sounds was proved in the article [13].

Research on the use of human speech as the basis for the analysis of intoxication [6, 7] has been going on for quite a long time, but for all the time not a single finished product has been released that would fulfill the task. For example, in the article [8], the authors consider four approaches to the identification of speech in telephone conversations. They found that the best among those considered was parallel PRLM, which reached the minimum error rate of 2%.

There are several approaches to consider the influence of alcohol. One of them is considering intoxication as one of the types of speech state (joy, anger, sadness, etc.), which can change the intonation of speech. This approach was used by the authors of the article [14]. More about the methods and methodology for recognizing and analyzing emotions is described in the article [15].

The second possible approach is to consider speech after alcohol consumption as an accent or dialect for a particular language. This is based on a change in the pronunciation of sounds, which is precisely the feature of accents. This approach was also considered in the article [14].

In general, it is also possible to consider the speech of a drunk person as the speech of a person who has experienced or is experiencing certain illnesses. So, for example, due to a stroke, the patient may suffer from aphasia, i.e. disorder, expressed in violation of the pronunciation of words. A more detailed consideration of the effect of stroke on human pronunciation is considered in the article [16].

In addition to stroke, a person's speech can also be affected by Parkinson's disease. A more detailed explanation of the causes and impact of Parkinson's disease on speech is shown in the article [17], which discusses the restoration of speech using electromyography.

3   Materials and Methods

3.1   Creation of Dataset

Data collection was carried out using our own client-server application and a Samsung Galaxy S21 smartphone to guarantee the uniformity of the sound parameters of the recording.

As a basis for recording audio files, it was decided to use tongue twisters. In total, 20 tongue twisters were prepared, aimed at the pronunciation of vowels and sonorous sounds, since they are the ones that are subject to the greatest change when intoxicated [9–11].

The recording of the subjects was made in two states – Sober and Drunk, in order to guarantee the recording of changes in the speech of the subjects. At the same time, it was decided to set the minimum limit of intoxication of the subjects to 1.5‰, since it is precisely this value that makes it possible to reliably establish intoxication relying on human hearing [10]. The determination of the required amount of alcohol to achieve the minimum mark of intoxication was carried out on the basis of the Widmark formula [18]. Since this formula has an error associated with the physiological characteristics of a person, it was decided to increase the mass of pure alcohol in the drink by 5 g in order to guarantee the required degree of intoxication.

The order in which subjects were recorded was as follows:

1. The subject recorded 20 audio recordings of tongue twisters in a Sober state;
2. The required amount of alcohol was calculated to achieve the required state of intoxication;
3. Within an hour, the subject consumed the required amount of alcohol;
4. After 30 – 60 min after drinking alcohol (depending on the physiological characteristics and condition of the subject), the subject recorded 20 audio recordings of tongue twisters while Drunk.

A pause of 30–60 min after drinking is done so that the consumed alcohol has time to be absorbed by the body. Drinks without carbon dioxide content and an alcohol content of at least 20% were also used to accelerate the effect of alcohol on the body and level the influence of undesirable effects of carbon dioxide: acceleration of intoxication, at lower ppm rates.

As a result, 340 recordings of 10 different people were collected. Since this value is quite small from the point of view of training neural networks, it was decided to use the data set augmentation method based on the speeding up and slowing down of audio recordings. Recordings were slowed down and accelerated by factors of 0.9 and 1.1, respectively. This made it possible to increase the number of recordings by 3 times to a value of 1020 audio recordings.

The created dataset consists of audio recordings with the following parameters:

1. recording format – "wav";
2. sampling frequency – 44100 Hz;
3. bitrate – 16 kb/s;
4. number of audio channels – 2;
5. minimum recording duration (excluding augmentation) – 2 s;

6. maximum recording duration (excluding augmentation) – 15 s;
7. average duration (excluding augmentation) – 4.24 s;
8. minimum recording duration (including augmentation) – 1 s;
9. maximum recording duration (including augmentation) – 16 s;
10. average duration (including augmentation) – 4.25 s.

The static parameters of the created data set without augmentation and with it are shown in Table 1, from which you can see that during the augmentation of the data set, the static parameters did not change critically, which allows us to declare the validity of the augmentation.

Table 1. Dataset statistics.

Number of recordings	Range of duration, sec	Average duration, sec	MSE of average duration	Deviation of drunken speech from sober
Non augmented				
Sober				
200	2–8	3.8	1.77	-
Drunk				
140	2–15	4.87	4.51	2.74
Augmented				
Sober				
600	1–9	3.85	1.79	-
Drunk				
420	1–16	4.83	4.52	2.7

Figure 1 shows the ratio of genders and ages of the subjects.

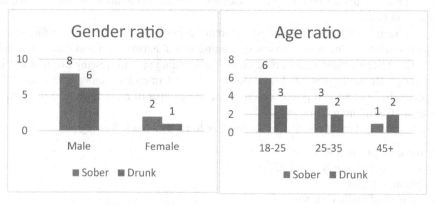

Fig. 1. Gender and age ratio in different states.

Also, in addition to the augmentation, additional test recordings were created by raising the tone of the recording using the Audacity program. In total, 60 additional entries were made – 30 for each state, including different speakers.

3.2 Creating Input Data for the Neural Network

It was decided to use the spectrograms of audio files and the Mel-frequency cepstral coefficients (MFCC) visualization, with the dimensionality of 20, of the same files as input data for the neural network in order to choose the optimal solution. The use of such input data will allow the use of convolutional neural networks, which often perform better in the problem of extracting parameters. It will also allow us to normalize the input data and use audio files of different lengths. This is achieved by fixing the size of the output images. Thus, the final images can be slightly compressed in width, but the information content remains almost unchanged.

Figure 2 shows examples of input data for one audio file.

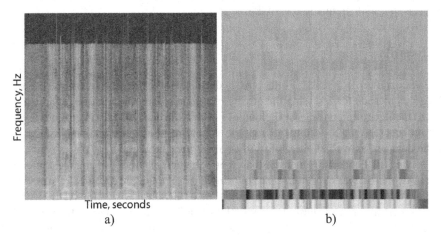

Fig. 2. Example of input data: a) spectrogram; b) MFCC.

3.3 Neural Network Training

As a neural network for the analyzer, it was decided to use the VGG16 convolutional neural network, the architecture of which is shown in Fig. 3. This architecture was presented by K. Simonyan and A. Zisserman [19, 20] and showed impressive results when trained on ImageNet. Also, this model was originally created for the task of classifying objects, to which, in essence, which is what the determination of alcohol intoxication is.

The network was trained with the following parameters:

1. batch size – 5;
2. optimizer – Adagrad with a learning rate equal to 0.001;
3. loss function – mean squared error (MSE);

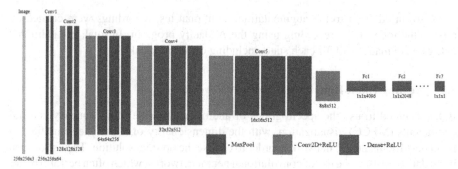

Fig. 3. VGG16 architecture.

4. number of epochs – 200.

At the same time, the network was trained with different input data of each type, namely: on an augmented data set with an image size of 512 × 512, as well as the same data sets, but with an image size of 256 × 256.

4   Results

Mean squared error (MSE), F-measure, and Unweighted average recall (UAR) were chosen as metrics for assessing the quality of training. The choice of the first metric is due to the desire to consider at the output not just the class of the record, but a value that reflects the degree of intoxication, the second metric is due to a small imbalance in the data set, as well as the ability to estimate the probabilities of errors of the first and second kind, since this metric is based on calculations precision and recall metrics. The UAR metric was chosen in order to be able to compare the obtained results with a similar study in the field of determining the state of alcohol intoxication ADLAIA [21].

The performance of these metrics is shown in Table 2. All the results was In this table "Orig" means original test recordings, "Pitch" – additional test recordings created with Audacity, "GT" – reference values of intoxication states. All results were obtained based on a test sample and additional test sample ("Pitch") which contains 60 recordings from different people in both states. Also all the recordings in test sample were. Also, all recordings in the test sample were original, i.e. recordings obtained during augmentation were not used.

Models trained on spectrograms of audio recordings have the highest performance, especially the model trained on spectrograms of 512 × 512 pixels. Compared to ADLAIA scores, the resulting model outperforms it by 9% and 15% when considering the results of the test set and the average of 10-fold cross-validation. Also, this model shows the best performance among other models in terms of MSE metrics based on the determining of drunk recordings, which is more critical, since it is the recognition of intoxication that is the initial task, which means that errors among these recordings are more significant. A low MSE, on the other hand, indicates the unlikely occurrence of errors in determining exactly drunk users.

Table 2. Metrics of trained models.

Metrics			Spectrograms		MFCC	
			256 × 256	512 × 512	256 × 256	512 × 512
MSE	Sober	Orig-GT	0.0345	0.1639	0.0269	0.0245
		Pitch-GT	0.0312	0.1728	0.0708	0.0502
		Orig-Pitch	0.0072	0.0304	0.0340	0.0092
	Drunk	Orig-GT	0.6030	0.1734	0.5195	0.6021
		Pitch-GT	0.7631	0.1847	0.4761	0.5320
		Orig-Pitch	0.0887	0.0333	0.0404	0.0108
F-score	Test split		0.5	0.73	0.67	0.65
	Cross-validation		0.81	0.82	0.76	0.74
UAR	Test split		0.64	0.77	0.68	0.62
	Cross-validation		0.82	0.83	0.77	0.75

5 Conclusion

In this study, we collected a data set for the task of determining the state of alcoholic intoxication of a person based on his speech, and also trained neural networks on different variations of the input data, for a detailed comparison of their indicators.

A total of 340 audio recordings of subjects were collected, with a ratio of 200:140 of sober and drunk recordings, respectively. After applying augmentation methods, namely slowing down and speeding up audio recordings, the final data set contains 1020 recordings of subjects, in the same ratio of sober recordings to drunk ones.

Spectrograms of audio recordings and MFCC visualization of 256 × 256 and 512 × 512 sizes were considered as input data, due to which 4 VGG16 models were trained in total. The trained models were also run through cross-validation to get a more detailed picture of the quality of intoxication detection.

The best model turned out to be VGG16 trained on 512 × 512 pixel spectrograms. It has F-score and UARs of 0.73 and 0.77 for the test set, and 0.82 and 0.83 for 10-fold cross-validation averages. Based on the results obtained, we can conclude that this model performs better than a similar model from the ADLAIA study, being ahead of it by 9% according to the results of the UAR metric on the test set, and by 15% according to the results of the same metric, but on cross-validation. However, it is worth noting that these results were obtained by analyzing a fairly small data set, and when conducting training and comparison based on a larger data set, the final results may be affected.

Also, based on the results of the study, a public client-server application "Gradus" was implemented, the purpose of which is to increase the data set, due to user recordings, as well as testing the model in real conditions. At the moment, the application is available for download in Rustore [22] and Google Play [23].

Acknowledgments. This research was funded by the Ministry of Science and Higher Education of the Russian Federation within the framework of scientific projects carried out by teams of research laboratories of educational institutions of higher education subordinate to the Ministry of Science and Higher Education of the Russian Federation, project number FEWM-2020–0042. The authors would like to thank the Irkutsk Supercomputer Center of SB RAS for providing access to the HPC-cluster «Akademik V.M. Matrosov» [24].

References

1. Andrews, M.L., Cox, W.M., Smith, R.G.: Effects of alcohol on the speech of non alcoholics. Central States Speech J. **28**(2), 140-143 (1977). https://doi.org/10.1080/10510977709367933
2. Beam, S.L., Gant, R.W., Mecham, M.J.: Communication deviations in alcoholics; a pilot study. J. Stud. Alcohol **39**(3), 548–551 (1978)
3. Sobell, L.C., Sobell, M.B.: Effects of alcohol on the speech of alcoholics. J. Speech Hear. Res. **15**(4), 861–868 (1972)
4. Chin, S., Pisoni, D.: Alcohol and Speech. Brill (1997)
5. World Helth Organization: Alcohol. https://www.who.int/news-room/fact-sheets/detail/alcohol. Accessed 20 June 2023
6. Brenner, M., Cash, J.R.: Speech analysis as an index of alcohol intoxication–the Exxon Valdez accident. Aviat. Space Environ. Med. **62**(9 Pt 1), 893–898 (1991)
7. Klingholz, F., Penning, R., Liebhardt, E.: Recognition of low-level alcohol intoxication from speech signal. J. Acoustical Society of America **84**(3), 929–935 (1988)
8. Zissman, M.A.: Comparison of four approaches to automatic language identification of telephone speech. IEEE Trans. Speech and Audio Processing **4**(1), 31 (1996)
9. Pisoni, D.B., Martin, C.S.: Effects of alcohol on the acoustic-phonetic properties of speech: perceptual and acoustic analyses. Alcoholism: Clinical and Experimental Res. **13**(4), 577–587 (1989)
10. Sigmund, M., Zelinka, P.: Analysis of voiced speech excitation due to alcohol intoxication. Information Technology and Control **40**(2), 143–150 (2011)
11. Johnson, K., Pisoni, D.B., Bernacki, R.H.: Do voice recordings reveal whether a person is intoxicated? A Case Study. Phonetica **47**(3–4), 215–237 (1990)
12. Crow, K.E., Batt, R.D.: Human Metabolism of Alcohol (1989)
13. Lester, L., Skousen, R.: The Phonology of Drunkenness. Papers from the parasession on natural phonology, pp. 233–239 (1974)
14. Biadsy, F., Wang, W.Y., Rosenberg, A., Hirschberg, J.B.: Intoxication detection using phonetic, phonotactic and prosodic cues. Proceedings of the Annual Conference of the International Speech Communication Association, INTERSPEECH, pp. 3209–3212 (2011). https://doi.org/10.21437/Interspeech.2011-803
15. Bojanić, M., Delić, V., Karpov, A.: Call redistribution for a call center based on speech emotion recognition. Appl. Sci. **10**(13), 4653 (2020)
16. Lincoln, N.B., Mulley, G.P., Jones, A.C., McGuirk, E., Lendrem, W., Mitchell, J.R.A.: Effectiveness of speech therapy for aphasic stroke patients: a randomised controlled trial. The Lancet **323**(8388), 1197–1200 (1984)
17. Leanderson, R., Meyerson, B.A., Persson, A.: Effect of L-dopa on speech in Parkinsonism: an EMG study of labial articulatory function. J. Neurol. Neurosurg. Psychiatry **34**(6), 679–681 (1971)
18. Watson, P.E., Watson, I.D., Batt, R.D.: Prediction of blood alcohol concentrations in human subjects. updating the widmark equation. Journal of Studies on Alcohol **42**(7), 547–556 (1981)

19. Simonyan, K., Zisserman, A.: Very Deep Convolutional Networks for Large-Scale Image Recognition. arXiv, arXiv:1409.1556 (2014)
20. Ferguson, M., Ak, R., Lee, Y.T.T., Law, K.H.: Automatic localization of casting defects with convolutional neural networks. In: 2017 IEEE International Conference on Big Data, Boston, MA, USA, pp. 1726–1735 (2017)
21. Bonela, A.A., He, Z., Nibali, A., Norman, T., Miller, P.G., Kuntsche, E.: Audio-based deep learning algorithm to identify alcohol inebriation (ADLAIA). Alcohol **109**, 49–54 (2023)
22. Rustore: Gradus. https://apps.rustore.ru/app/ru.gradus.app. Accessed 13 Sep 2023
23. Google Play: Gradus. https://play.google.com/store/apps/details?id=ru.gradus.app. Accessed 13 Sep 2023
24. Irkutsk Supercomputer Center SB RAS. http://hpc.icc.ru/. Accessed 12 July 2023

Linear Frequency Residual Cepstral Coefficients for Speech Emotion Recognition

Baveet Singh Hora$^{(\boxtimes)}$, S. Uthiraa, and Hemant A. Patil

Speech Research Lab, DA-IICT, Gandhinagar, Gujarat, India
{201901256,uthiraa_s,hemant_patil}@daiict.ac.in

Abstract. As technology advances, our reliance on machines grows, necessitating the development of effective approaches for Speech Emotion Recognition (SER) to enhance human-machine interaction. This paper introduces a novel feature extraction technique called Linear Frequency Residual Cepstral Coefficients (LFRCC) for the SER task. To the best of our knowledge and belief, this is the first attempt to employ LFRCC for SER. Experimental evaluations were conducted on the widely used EmoDB dataset, focusing on four emotions: anger, happiness, neutrality, and sadness. Results demonstrated that the proposed LFRCC features outperform state-of-the-art Mel Frequency Cepstral Coefficients (MFCC) and Linear Frequency Cepstral Coefficients (LFCC) relatively by a significant margin: **25.64 %** and **10.26 %**, respectively, when using a residual neural network (ResNet); and **12.37 %** and **4.67 %**, respectively when combined with the Time-Delay Neural Network (TDNN) as classifier. Furthermore, the proposed LFRCC features exhibit a better Equal Error Rate (EER) than the other two baseline methods. Additionally, classifier-level and score-level fusion techniques were employed, and the combination of MFCC and LFRCC at the score-level achieved the highest accuracy of **94.87 %** and the lowest EER of **3.625%**. The better performance of the proposed feature set may be due to its capability to capture excitation source information via linearly-spaced subbands in the cepstral domain.

Keywords: Speech emotion recognition · Narrowband spectrogram · Linear frequency residual cepstral coefficients (LFRCC) · EmoDB · LP residual · Excitation source

1 Introduction

It is well known that our emotional state has a significant influence on our speech patterns, such that identical utterances may be perceived differently based on the associated emotion. With the development of technology and man's reliance on machines, reliable emotion detection is crucial for successful human-computer interaction. This has led to the development of a new research field, namely,

A. Karpov et al. (Eds.): SPECOM 2023, LNAI 14338, pp. 116–129, 2023.
https://doi.org/10.1007/978-3-031-48309-7_10

Speech Emotion Recognition (SER). Its applications include driver's behavior monitoring during autonomous driving, call center services, monitoring patients, mental health issues detection, and better human-machine interaction.

A speech signal comprises two essential components with respect to its production: the source, known as the excitation source, and the system, which represents the vocal tract system. In particular, the vocal tract is a natural physical system with the attribute of inertia for being unable to change its state unless an external source is applied. In practice, its primary excitation source is a glottal activity & glottal vibration, but no vibration can also act as the driving force to excite the vocal tract system to produce intelligible speech.

Various features, namely prosodic, source, and system features, have been employed for SER in the existing literature. Notably, the prosodic and system-based features have received the most attention in research studies. However, exploring excitation source information in speech for SER is relatively limited, as highlighted in [8]. This limitation serves as a motivation for the adoption of Linear Frequency Residual Cepstral Coefficients (LFRCC) in this study.

In earlier studies, traditional machine learning algorithms, such as Gaussian Mixture Models (GMMs) or Support Vector Machines (SVMs), were commonly employed in SER [15]. GMMs effectively modeled speech feature distributions and captured variations among different emotion classes, while SVMs were utilized for their capacity to learn decision boundaries that can distinguish between emotions [2].

As research progressed, more advanced classifiers, particularly neural network-based models, gained popularity and became prominent due to their ability to learn hierarchical and temporal representations from speech data automatically [1,3]. In this study, we leverage the advantages of Residual Neural Networks (ResNet) and Time Delay Neural Networks (TDNN) for SER tasks. ResNet's skip connections address the vanishing gradient problem, enabling deeper networks, feature reuse, and efficient training with a reduced risk of overfitting [5]. TDNN, on the other hand, excels at modeling temporal dependencies, handling variable-length inputs, offering efficiency and parallelization [12], and exhibiting shift-invariance. These qualities motivated their selection for this work.

In this work, we investigate the LFRCC features, which already had proved effective for anti-spoofing [16] for speaker verification, i.e., to capture the characteristics of natural vs. spoofed speech. Given the success of LFRCC in capturing the acoustic characteristics of natural speech signals, this study investigates its possible potential for SER tasks. We compare the proposed features with the state-of-the-art Mel Frequency Cepstral Coefficients (MFCC) and Linear Frequency Cepstral Coefficients (LFCC) features using deep learning models, namely, ResNet and TDNN with Attention Statistics Pooling.

The rest of the paper is organized as follows: Sect. 2 presents details of Linear Prediction. Section 3 provides the information for the extraction of the features. Section 4 shows the experimental setup used for the study. Section 5 presents the experimental results and analysis. Finally, Sect. 6 concludes the paper along with the potential future of research directions.

2   Linear Prediction

The initial application of the Linear Prediction (LP) method can be traced back to speech coding applications, drawing inspiration from the fields of system identification and control [10]. In LP analysis, the representation of each speech sample involves a linear combination of past 'p' speech samples. Here, 'p' denotes the order of linear prediction, and the weights associated with the combination are referred to as Linear Prediction Coefficients (LPCs) [10]. Given the current speech sample as s(n), the predicted sample can be expressed as follows:

$$\hat{s}(n) = -\sum_{k=1}^{p} a_k s(n-k), \tag{1}$$

a_k is the Linear Prediction Coefficient (LPC) coefficient. The LPCs (i.e., a_k) are utilized to predict the speech samples $s(n)$ by $\hat{s}(n)$, and the discrepancy between the actual speech sample $s(n)$ and the predicted sample $\hat{s}(n)$ is termed as the LP residual $r(n)$, which can be expressed as follows:

$$r(n) = s(n) - \hat{s}(n) = s(n) + \sum_{k=1}^{p} a_k s(n-k). \tag{2}$$

Specifically, our method applies all-pole inverse filtering to the speech signal with the LP analysis. We have

$$A(z) = 1 + \sum_{k=1}^{p} a_k z^{-k}, \tag{3}$$

$$H(z) = \frac{G}{1 + \sum_{k=1}^{p} a_k z^{-k}}. \tag{4}$$

In this context, the variable $A(z)$ denotes an inverse filter associated with an all-pole Linear Prediction (LP) filter $H(z)$. This filter represents the system information related to the vocal tract, while the term G is referred to as the gain term in the LP model. It is worth noting that the system information is combined with the excitation source information, and the LP residual effectively captures this source information. In particular, it is known in the speech literature that LP residual attains a peak at every Glottal Closure Instant (GCI). The LP residual is subjected to cepstral-domain processing to extract the desired information. This process enables the spectral envelope representation of the excitation source signal, which is discussed in the next section.

3   Linear Frequency Residual Cepstral Coefficients

Figure 1 illustrates the functional block diagram of the proposed feature set. The input speech signal undergoes pre-emphasis filtering to balance the lower and higher frequency components [16]. Subsequently, the signal is processed with the steps mentioned in the LP block, resulting in the LP residual waveform, denoted as $r(n)$. The LP residual waveform is then divided into frames and subjected to windowing, with a duration of 25 ms and a frame shift of 15 ms. In the next step, the power spectrum is estimated for each frame of the LP residual and passed through a filterbank consisting of 40 linearly-spaced triangular subband filters. To obtain the desired LFRCC features with minimal distortion, the Discrete Cosine Transform (DCT) and Cepstral Mean Normalization (CMN) techniques are applied to the power spectrum. This sequence of operations yields the final LFRCC features that capture relevant speech signal characteristics.

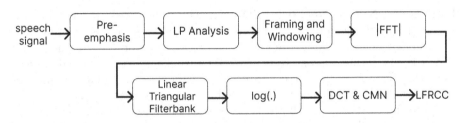

Fig. 1. Schematic block diagram of LFRCC feature extraction. After [16].

4   Experimental Setup

4.1   Dataset Used

To evaluate the effectiveness of excitation source-based features for SER, the present research utilized the EmoDB dataset developed in 2005. EmoDB is a German speech corpus comprising recordings from ten actors, comprising an equal distribution of five male and five female speakers. These speakers were asked to utter ten German phrases while being recorded under favorable conditions. The dataset encompasses seven distinct emotions: anger, joy, neutral, sadness, disgust, boredom, and fear [4] as shown in Table 1. The current study narrowed the focus to four specific emotions: anger, happiness, neutrality, and sadness. Additionally, one male speaker was reserved for the purpose of testing in this investigation as per Leave One Speaker Out (LOSO) method.

Table 1. Main Properties of the Speech Corpus in the Experiments (F - Female, M - Male).

Database	Speakers	Emotions
German Emotional Database (EmoDB)	10 (5M, 5F)	7 (anger, joy, disgust, neutral, sadness, boredom, and fear)

4.2 Classifiers Used

In SER, neural network (NN) models are used extensively for their ability to capture the non-linear relation present among speech signal samples [9]. This work implements two deep learning models to classify emotions, whose details are below.

Time Delay Neural Network (TDNN): The state-of-the-art TDNN architecture [12] has been chosen for experimentation. Table 2 provides a comprehensive overview of this architecture's layers. A dropout rate of 0.2 is applied at all TDNN layers during training to enhance the model's performance and prevent overfitting. The *categorical cross-entropy* loss function is utilized for classification tasks for training. Additionally, we used the *attentive statistics pooling* mechanism, which incorporates both higher-order statistics and attention mechanisms and has proven effective in capturing speaker-related information [11]. However, its potential for capturing emotional information is also noteworthy. Considering the standard deviation vector, this pooling method can capture long-term variability and the dynamic nature of emotions expressed over an utterance.

Furthermore, the attention mechanism enables the identification of speech frames that are more important and informative for discriminating emotions. This selective frame weighting and non-linear activation functions allow the pooling method to capture the complex patterns and variations inherent in emotional expressions. Ultimately, by aggregating frame-level features with higher weights, the attentive statistics pooling method can create an utterance-level representation that emphasizes emotional cues, making it a promising approach for extracting and understanding emotional information from speech signals.

Residual Neural Network (ResNet): The ResNet model has already been adopted for emotion recognition tasks [17]. The ResNet architecture used for this experiment is shown in Table 3. The loss function we used during training was *categorical cross-entropy*. The Resblock consists of two Conv1D layers; Batch Normalization and ReLU activation follow each layer. The residual connections in ResNet alleviate the vanishing gradient problem and improve the flow of gradient information during training [5]. This enables the network to learn emotional cues more effectively and capture subtle patterns associated with different emotions, thereby enhancing the network's ability to discriminate between emotional states.

Table 2. TDNN Architecture.

Layer	Kernel size	Filter size	Stride	Output shapes
TDNN	5	64	1	(batch_size, 64, 1)
TDNN	5	128	1	(batch_size, 128, 1)
TDNN	7	128	1	(batch_size, 128, 1)
TDNN	1	64	1	(batch_size, 64, 1)
TDNN	1	64	1	(batch_size, 64, 1)
Classic Attention	–	64	–	(batch_size, 64, 1)
Linear	128	128	1	(batch_size, 128)
Statistics pooling here				
Linear	64	64	1	(batch_size, 64)
Output	–	4	–	(batch_size, number of classes = 4)

Table 3. ResNet Architecture.

Layer	Details
Conv1	Input Channels: *in_channels* Output Channels: *out_channels* Kernel Size: 3 Stride: *1* Padding: 1
BN1	Type: BatchNorm1d
Res_Block1	Input Channels: *64* Output Channels: *32*
Res_Block2	Input Channels: *32* Output Channels: *16*
Res_Block3	Input Channels: *16* Output Channels: *16*
Avg_Pool	AdaptiveAvgPool1d
FC	Input Channels: *16* Output: num_of_classes = *4*

4.3   Baseline Considered

The state-of-the-art MFCC and LFCC features are used for comparing the proposed features. Then *39*-D feature vector was formulated containing static, delta, and double-delta parameters. The window length used was 25 ms, the number of subband filters was 40, and the number of points used in the Fast Fourier Transform (NFFT) was 512.

5   Experimental Results

5.1   Spectrographic Analysis

Figures 3 and 4 present the spectrograms of the original signal and the LP residual signal for both a female and a male speaker uttering the same sentence. In comparison to the spectrogram of the original signal, the LP residual spectrogram preserves certain details, such as the explicit representation of formants, pitch harmonics (horizontal pitch striations in a narrowband spectrogram), and overall spectral energy distribution. Further, since the LP residual is known to be intelligible, we also expect to see formant structures in the LP residual spectrogram. A notable observation shared across all emotions is the prominent energy presence at higher frequencies in the LP residual spectrograms, as highlighted by the black boxes in Fig. 3 and Fig. 4. Moreover, the width between the horizontal striations is found to be more significant for females due to their higher fundamental frequency (F_0) compared to males. Notably, anger exhibits short pauses caused by irregular breathing (puffs) in contrast to neutral and sad emotions, which feature longer pauses and low formant fluctuation due to deeper breathing. A significant distinction between happy and angry emotions lies in the distribution of high-energy content. In the case of happy emotions, the large energy density is evenly spread throughout the utterance, gradually diminishing towards the end. Conversely, anger emotions concentrate the large energy density at higher frequencies, maintaining it consistently throughout the utterance, as clearly depicted in the LP residual spectrogram. These observations were made by analyzing multiple sentences, one of which is represented in Fig. 3 and Fig. 4.

5.2   Impact of LP Order

In the proposed method, the LFRCC feature set is obtained by varying the prediction order (p) from 4 to 25 for a sampling frequency of 16 KHz, as depicted in Fig. 5. The results indicate that the highest classification accuracy is achieved using an LP order of *20*. Remarkably, this optimal LP order remains consistent regardless of the classifier employed. For both TDNN and ResNet, an LP order of *20* yields relatively highest accuracy rates of **89.29 %** and **87.17 %**, respectively (as illustrated in Fig. 5). Additionally, it is worth noting that the accuracy of emotion classification tends to be higher for higher LP orders (16–25) than for lower LP orders (4–15). This observation can be attributed to the fact that higher LP orders allow for better capture of contextual information of emotional aspects, especially concerning speech prosody, which is predominantly *supraseg-mental* in nature and, thus, requires a longer duration of the speech signal.

5.3   Significance of Pitch Contour

Speech is a powerful form for expressing emotions, and the pitch or fundamental frequency (F_0) contour plays a crucial role in conveying emotional information [14]. It encompasses variations and patterns in pitch that provide valuable

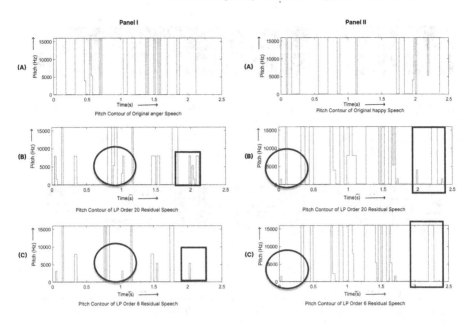

Fig. 2. Panel-I (a) pitch contour of original anger speech sample; Panel-II (a) pitch contour of original happy speech sample; Panel-I (b) and Panel-II (b) shows pitch contour of the LP residual for $p=20$; Panel-I (c) and Panel-II (c) shows pitch contour of the LP residual for $p=6$.

cues about the speaker's emotional state. We can gain initial insights into the speaker's emotional expression by analyzing the pitch level. Higher pitch levels may indicate excitement or anger, while lower levels can suggest sadness or calmness. It's crucial to acknowledge that speaker-dependent variations exist, owing to individual vocal characteristics and cultural influences that can give rise to distinct emotional pitch patterns. Understanding the pitch contour allows us to discern the emotional nuances present in speech signals. Our experiment employed the *YIN* algorithm for pitch contour plotting. Notably, we opted not to utilize overlapping frames in our analysis, considering that overlapping might introduce complexity and potentially obscure the specific effects of LP orders on pitch information. Figure 5 depicts the impact of LP order on speech and compares the pitch contour plots of LP order 6 (lowest accuracy in Fig. 5) and LP order 20 (highest accuracy in Fig. 5) for *anger and happy emotion* samples. The encircled areas in Fig. 2 depict the differences in pitch information for the two LP orders.

The pitch contour of the original emotional signals suggests significant pitch variations, possibly due to changes in speech style and prosody. In contrast, the pitch contour in the residual signal suggests that the LPC modeling successfully captures and decreases the pitch-related variations compared to the original speech signal, resulting in a more consistent and uniform plot. The increased

Fig. 3. Spectrographic analysis for (a) original speech signal, and (b) the corresponding LP residual. Panel I, Panel II, Panel III, and Panel IV represent the spectrograms of a female speaker for the emotions anger, happy, sad, and neutral, respectively, for the sentence *"Das will sie am Mittwoch abgeben (She will hand it in on Wednesday)"*.

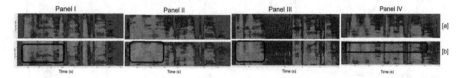

Fig. 4. Spectrographic analysis for (a) original speech signal, and (b) the corresponding LP residual. Panel I, Panel II, Panel III, and Panel IV represent the spectrograms of a male speaker for the emotions anger, happy, sad, and neutral, respectively, for the sentence *"Das will sie am Mittwoch abgeben (She will hand it in on Wednesday)"*.

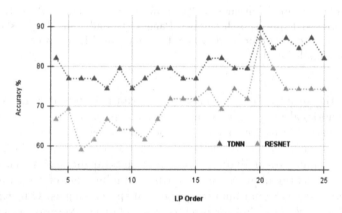

Fig. 5. Effect of LP orders for LFRCC using TDNN and ResNet Classifiers.

number of peaks (encircled areas) in the pitch contour plot for LP order 20, compared to LP order 6, indicates that the higher order LP model more accurately captures finer pitch details. This finding enhances the credibility of the results in Fig. 5. LP order 20 outperforms LP order 6 in accuracy, suggesting the presence of more relevant and steadfast pitch information that contributes to its superior performance.

5.4   Results with Score-Level Fusion

To understand the complementary information captured by different features, score-level fusion is performed using the following data fusion strategy. We will try different α values between 0.0 and 1.0 with a step size of 0.1

$$L_{Score\_fused} = \alpha L(classifier)_{feature1} + (1 - \alpha)L(classifier)_{feature2}, \quad (5)$$

In the equation, $L_{feature1}$ is the raw score from the classifier of either MFCC or LFCC given as input feature, while $L_{feature2}$ represents the classifier raw score for LFRCC. Figure 6 and Fig. 7 illustrate the accuracy, and Fig. 9 and Fig. 10 show the Equal Error Rate (EER) of the score-level fusion on ResNet and TDNN, respectively. It is observed that MFCC and LFRCC give the best classification accuracy of **94.87%** and *87.18%*, and the feature pair gives the lowest EER for TDNN and ResNet classifiers, respectively, as observed in Fig. 9 and 10. MFCC and LFRCC achieve the highest classification results because, in our opinion, MFCC effectively captures spectral information in the lower frequency regions of speech, while LFRCC captures excitation information in the higher frequency regions. By combining these two feature sets, the major emotional content in speech signals can be captured comprehensively.

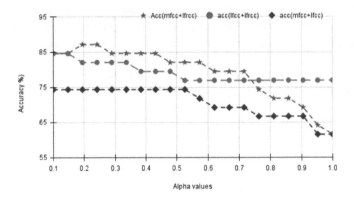

Fig. 6. Score-level fusion of features using the ResNet classifier.

5.5   Results with Classifier-Level Fusion

$$L_{Classifier\_fused} = \alpha L(feature)_{Classifier1} + (1 - \alpha)L(feature)_{Classifier2}, \quad (6)$$

Figure 8 depicts the classifier-level fusion. In this, raw scores from each classifier (TDNN and ResNet) are multiplied by the weight α, and then all the weighted outputs are added together to obtain the final output, as shown in the

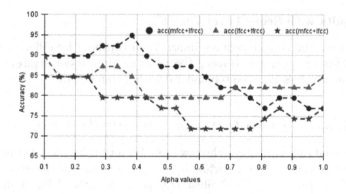

Fig. 7. Score-level fusion of features using the TDNN classifier.

above equation (6). The final score is then used to determine the accuracy of the classification. In short, we use the same feature as input to both classifiers and combine their outputs to obtain a final score in classifier-level fusion, whereas, in score-level fusion, classifiers remain the same while raw scores from different feature sets are used. It is observed that the highest classification accuracy obtained for MFCC is **76.92 %**, LFCC is **84.62 %**, and LFRCC is **87.18 %**, at the α values shown in Fig. 8, these are close to the outcomes of the single TDNN classifier as visible in Table 4. This suggests that classifier characteristics did not significantly enhance accuracy compared to score-level fusion, where a substantial improvement was observed from the combination of MFCC and LFRCC feature sets. This proves that the results obtained are not significantly dependent on the classifier, thereby proving that the proposed LFRCC feature set captures emotional information, at least not worse than MFCC or LFCC.

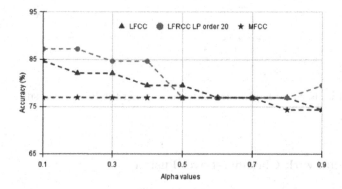

Fig. 8. Classifier-level fusion for single feature sets using the TDNN and the ResNet classifiers.

5.6   Performance of LFRCC on SER

Table 4 shows that the cepstral coefficients with linear filterbanks (i.e., LFCC) result in better classification than the Mel filterbanks (i.e., MFCC), irrespective of the classifiers used for SER. This suggests that LFCC can potentially capture emotional information well in higher frequency regions compared to the MFCC as the width of the triangular filters in MFCC increases with frequency, thus ignoring fine spectral details. In particular, anger and happiness operate in higher frequency regions (Sect. 5.1), which is captured better by LFCC due to the constant difference between the width of subband filters in the filterbank.

The LFRCC feature set demonstrates superior performance compared to the baseline MFCC and LFCC features, achieving a **25.64%** and **10.26%** absolute improvement, respectively, with the ResNet and a **12.37 %** and **4.67 %** improvement, in the case of TDNN (as shown in Table 4). Also, this improved performance can be seen from lower EER for the case of LFRCC, obtaining **10.56%**, **7.19%** for ResNet and TDNN, respectively, as can be observed from Table 4.

It is widely acknowledged that the lungs are crucial in providing the necessary airflow, which acts as a power supply for speech production. Consequently, changes in respiratory patterns directly impact the timing, duration, and overall rhythm of speech. As a result, respiratory patterns can influence emotional expression in speech signals [6,7]. The LFRCC feature set effectively captures this excitation source information (as discussed in Sect. 5.1). Specifically, the section around the Glottal Closure Instants (GCI) in the LP residual signal exhibits a high signal-to-noise ratio (SNR) due to periodic excitation. During the Glottal Closure (GC) phase, the excitation source is completely isolated from the vocal tract [9]. This region contains valuable information that cannot be adequately captured by MFCC and LFCC, making LFRCC a compelling choice for representing these features.

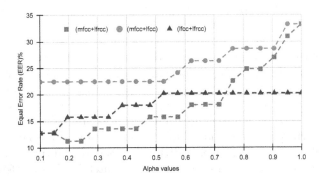

Fig. 9. EER values for score level fusion on Resnet.

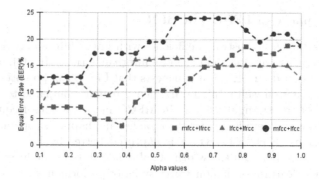

Fig. 10. EER values for score-level fusion on TDNN.

Table 4. Classification Accuracy and EER.

Classifier	Feature	Accuracy (%)	EER (%)
ResNet	**MFCC**	61.54	33.32
	LFCC	76.92	20.25
	LFRCC	**87.18**	*10.56*
TDNN	**MFCC**	76.92	18.84
	LFCC	84.62	12.74
	LFRCC	**89.29**	**7.19**

6   Summary and Conclusion

This study proposed an excitation source-based LFRCC feature set for emotion recognition. The vocal tract system features, such as MFCC and LFCC, were used for performance comparison. The objective was to exploit the complementary information in LP residual-based features, and they proved to perform much better than the state-of-the-art spectral features, indicating that the proposed features contain specific discriminative power to classify emotions. The significance of using a linear filterbank over Mel filterbank was also observed. Pitch contour and spectrogram analysis provide cues regarding optimal LP order selection and relevant emotion-based information. Moreover, the results from classifier-level fusion proved the efficiency of the proposed feature regardless of the classifier used. It is also known that breathing patterns are different for normal *vs.* mentally disturbed patients and indicates the possible potential of emotional recognition of mentally challenged individuals. As part of future research directions, exploring the incorporation of an average pitch level as a reference point holds the potential to mitigate speaker-dependent variations and can improve inferences from contour plots. Additionally, investigating the integration of this feature set with advanced neural network architectures, such as DCNNs [3] and autoencoders [13], presents a promising avenue for further research.

References

1. Akçay, M.B., Oğuz, K.: Speech emotion recognition: emotional models, databases, features, preprocessing methods, supporting modalities, and classifiers. Speech Commun. **116**, 56–76 (2020)
2. Anagnostopoulos, C.N., Iliou, T., Giannoukos, I.: Features and classifiers for emotion recognition from speech: a survey from 2000 to 2011. Artif. Intell. Rev. **43**, 155–177 (2015)
3. Bhangale, K., Kothandaraman, M.: Speech emotion recognition based on multiple acoustic features and deep convolutional neural network. Electronics **12**(4), 839 (2023)
4. Burkhardt, F., Paeschke, A., Rolfes, M., Sendlmeier, W.F., Weiss, B., et al.: A database of german emotional speech. In: Interspeech, Lisbon, Portugal, vol. 5, pp. 1517–1520 (2005)
5. He, K., Zhang, X., Ren, S., Sun, J.: Deep residual learning for image recognition. In: Proceedings of the IEEE Conference on Computer Vision and Pattern Recognition (CVPR), Las Vegas, NV, USA, pp. 770–778 (2016)
6. Homma, I., Masaoka, Y.: Breathing rhythms and emotions. Exp. Physiol. **93**(9), 1011–1021 (2008)
7. Jerath, R., Beveridge, C.: Respiratory rhythm, autonomic modulation, and the spectrum of emotions: the future of emotion recognition and modulation. Front. Psychol. **11**, 1980 (2020)
8. Koolagudi, S.G., Reddy, R., Rao, K.S.: Emotion recognition from speech signal using epoch parameters. In: International Conference on Signal Processing and Communications (SPCOM), pp. 1–5. IISc Bangalore, India (2010)
9. Krothapalli, S.R., Koolagudi, S.G.: Characterization and recognition of emotions from speech using excitation source information. Int. J. Speech Technol. **16**, 181–201 (2013)
10. Makhoul, J.: Linear prediction: a tutorial review. Proc. IEEE **63**(4), 561–580 (1975)
11. Okabe, K., Koshinaka, T., Shinoda, K.: Attentive statistics pooling for deep speaker embedding. In: Interspeech, Hyderabad, India, pp. 2252–2256 (2018)
12. Peddinti, V., Povey, D., Khudanpur, S.: A time delay neural network architecture for efficient modeling of long temporal contexts. In: Interspeech, Dresden, Germany, pp. 3214–3218 (2015)
13. Sadok, S., Leglaive, S., Séguier, R.: A vector quantized masked autoencoder for speech emotion recognition. In: 2023 IEEE International Conference on Acoustics, Speech, and Signal Processing Workshops (ICASSPW), pp. 1–5 (2023)
14. Scherer, K.R.: Vocal communication of emotion: a review of research paradigms. Speech Commun. **40**(1–2), 227–256 (2003)
15. Swain, M., Routray, A., Kabisatpathy, P.: Databases, features and classifiers for speech emotion recognition: a review. Int. J. Speech Technol. **21**(1), 93–120 (2018). https://doi.org/10.1007/s10772-018-9491-z
16. Tak, H., Patil, H.A.: Novel linear frequency residual cepstral features for replay attack detection. In: Interspeech, Hyderabad, India, pp. 726–730 (2018)
17. Tripathi, S., Kumar, A., Ramesh, A., Singh, C., Yenigalla, P.: Focal loss based residual convolutional neural network for speech emotion recognition. arXiv preprint arXiv:1906.05682 (2019)

Enhancing Stutter Detection in Speech Using Zero Time Windowing Cepstral Coefficients and Phase Information

Narasinga Vamshi Raghu Simha$^{(\boxtimes)}$(ID), Mirishkar Sai Ganesh(ID), and Vuppala Anil Kumar(ID)

International Institute of Information Technology Hyderabad, Hyderabad, India
{narasinga.vamshi,mirishkar.ganesh}@research.iiit.ac.in,
anil.vuppala@iiit.ac.in

Abstract. Stuttering is a speech disorder that affects speech fluency and rhythm, with millions worldwide experiencing it. Early diagnosis and treatment can significantly improve speech fluency and the quality of life for individuals who stutter. Automatic detection of stuttering events can help diagnose, monitor, and develop effective interventions. Therefore, this paper aims to propose a feature space-based classifier for detecting stuttering events in speech. To achieve this, we have investigated Zero Time Windowing Cepstral Coefficients (ZTWCC) as a feature set for stutter detection using classifiers such as SVM, LSTM, and Bidirectional LSTM. We compared the performance of ZTWCC with the standard handcrafted features, such as MFCC, CQCC, and SFFCC, on the SEP-28K dataset with and without including phase information. The results in both cases indicate that ZTWCC is giving a higher F-1 score than baseline MFCC features.

Keywords: Stutter detection · Zero time windowing · Zero time windowing cepstral coefficients · Phase information

1 Introduction

Communication is an act of exchange of information either through any media or symbols, or signs. In Humans, a common way of expressing opinions is through text, facial expressions, or speech. Speech is a natural mode of communication where we can express our opinions or feelings. However, certain individuals may experience difficulty with speech production due to a speech disorder. Speech disorders are communication disorders that manifest in various ways, including the inability to speak fluently, problems with articulation, and difficulty forming connections between words [8,9]. Stuttering is one such problem where a person with stuttering (pws) experiences interruptions during the flow of speech by repetitions, pauses, or prolongations of sounds [9]. Stuttering, also called Stammering, is a neural speech disorder caused by any brain injury or quick changing of the neural connections that support emotional and speech functions [8, 28, 29].

A. Karpov et al. (Eds.): SPECOM 2023, LNAI 14338, pp. 130–141, 2023.
https://doi.org/10.1007/978-3-031-48309-7_11

Stuttering can be characterized as periods of abnormal and continuous pauses in the normal flow of speech. And these speech abnormalities are usually accompanied by abnormal behaviours such as head shaking, lip tremors, rapid eye movements, and abnormal lip shapes [23]. Stuttering can be broadly categorized into disfluencies such as 1) Blocks, 2) Prolongations, 3) Part-Word repetitions, 4) Word repetitions, 5) Phrase repetitions, 6) Mono syllabic-word repetitions, 7) Filled pauses or Interjections. Identifying and classifying stuttering is an exciting research problem that falls into an interdisciplinary domain involving pathology, signal processing, and acoustics, making it difficult to detect.

In the process of speech production, it is imperative to acknowledge that the excitation source and the configuration of the vocal tract undergo continuous temporal variations, characterized by substantial mutual influence between these two components. This dynamic nature of the speech production system presents a formidable signal processing conundrum, necessitating the extraction of pertinent features pertaining to the evolving vocal tract system from the speech signal. It is noteworthy that conventional short-time spectrum analysis techniques encounter challenges in preserving the fidelity of information pertaining to the vocal tract system. This limitation manifests in two distinct domains: temporally, as observed in the narrowband (NB) spectrogram, and spectrally, as evident in the wideband (WB) spectrogram. The utilization of these spectrographic representations can inadvertently result in information degradation, a phenomenon inherent to their respective domain constraints. Furthermore, it is important to consider the temporal averaging effect present in the narrowband (NB) spectrogram, which has the potential to compromise valuable and essential information pertaining to the vocal tract system. This critical information is typically captured within the signal shortly after the occurrence of the impulse-like excitation, a phenomenon that consistently transpires in the vicinity of the glottal closure instant (GCI) during each glottal cycle. For this purpose, in this study, we have used the Zero Time Window (ZTW) method, which operates at a very short (smaller than 5ms) segment of speech where it provides better resolution in both the time and frequency domain. In addition, we even explored the use of phase information among the frames for the classification of Stuttering, as stuttering cannot be captured in a frame-by-frame manner.

Speech Pathologists and Speech Therapists play a critical role in assessing individuals with stuttering, which is typically accomplished through manual analysis of speech recordings, as documented in several studies [9,17]. Stuttering severity is commonly evaluated by computing the ratio of stuttered words or syllables to the total number of words or syllables in the speech sample. Despite the effectiveness of manual assessment methods, they are associated with several limitations, including high costs, time-consuming processes, and laborious procedures.

In recent years, there have been significant advancements in machine learning and deep learning technologies, which have revolutionized the field of speech analysis. These approaches have demonstrated the potential for automated detection and classification of stuttering. A growing body of research has explored the application of these methods to automatically detect and classify stuttering [3,13,24,26]. While these automated approaches hold promise for streamlining the assessment process and reducing costs, there are still several challenges that must be addressed, including the need for large datasets and the potential for false positives or false negatives. Nonetheless, ongoing research continues to develop and validate automated methods for detecting and classifying stuttering. Previous research efforts in this area have focused mainly on publicly available datasets such as UCLASS [10], LibriStutter [13], SEP-28K [16], Fluency Bank [22], and KSoF [1] datasets. For the purposes of this study, we utilized the SEP-28K dataset as a basis for our experimental evaluation. In earlier works, a variety of features, such as Mel-Frequency Cepstral Coefficients (MFCC), Linear Predictive Coding Coefficients (LPCC), and Perceptual Linear Prediction (PLP), were frequently used for stuttering detection and classification.

Classifiers such as SVM, LSTM, and Bi-LSTM have been used for the classification task. Apart from the proposed feature Zero Time Windowing Cepstral Coefficients (ZTWCC), experiments were conducted on standard handcrafted features such as Mel-Frequency Cepstral Coefficients (MFCC), Constant Q Cepstral Coefficients (CQCC), Single Frequency Filtering Cepstral Coefficients (SFFCC) for comparison purpose. Experiments are performed on the feature sets in 2 ways. One includes phase information to the cepstral coefficients, and the other with only cepstral coefficients. We found that the proposed ZTWCC gives better results than MFCC, CQCC, and SFFCC in both scenarios.

The rest of the paper is organized as follows: Sect. 2 describes the previous works that have been taken in Stutter detection and classification. Section 3 briefly explains the computation process of zero time windowing and extraction of ZTWCC and Phase information. The proposed system for classification followed by experimental setup was explained in Sects. 4 and 5. At last, Results are discussed in Sect. 6, followed by providing a Conclusion in Sect. 7.

2 Related Work

Most of the studies in the past that worked on Stutter detection tasks explored traditional classifiers on hand-picked features such as MFCCs [25]. Recently, the focus has shifted to Deep learning due to increased computational efficiencies. In [17], the authors used a hidden Markov model for stutter detection, taking input features for speaking rate, duration, and disfluent frequency. [30] used MFCCs for training an HMM for stutter detection. In [6], MFCCs were used for recognizing repetitions and prolongations using K-NN and LDA. The authors of [5] used LPCC features for classifying prolongations and repetitions. In [14], a deep neural architecture was proposed for classifying stutter events using spectrograms as input. In [26], the detection of stuttering events is proposed for labelled dysfluency data using the metric average duration of phonemes. [3] used Support Vector Machines (SVM) for detecting prolongations by taking PLPs as a feature set. In [13], a ResidualNeurlNetwork (ResNet) in combination with bidirectional long short-term memory networks (Bi-LSTM) is used to classify the stuttering events by assuming each stuttering event as a binary classification problem. [24] used time-delay neural networks (TDNN) to classify the different stuttering types on the UCLASS dataset. [26] used multi-task learning with LSTM to detect stuttering and adversarial learning to learn the robust representation of stuttering for the podcast dataset. In recent times, [2] used the wav2vec2.0 model as a feature extractor to leverage the benefits of the self-supervised pre-trained model, which is trained on a huge amount of data for stutter detection. [27] examined the emphasized channel attention, propagation, and aggregation-time-delay neural network (ECAPA-TDNN) embeddings for the stutter detection tasks. MFCC, PLP, spectrograms, etc., have been used as features for detecting stutters in most of the works stated above. And used UCLASS, Podcast 28k, Fluency Bank, and KSoF datasets for the stutter detection tasks. In [12], ZTWCC was employed for dialect classification. For discriminating the breathy voice from the tense voice, [11] used ZTWCC features.

The present study's findings highlight the exigency for enhanced features in the realm of Stutter event detection, particularly in discerning and distinguishing distinct speech sound characteristics. The present research investigates the efficacy of the Zero-Time Windowing (ZTW) technique in providing high-resolution spectra that can effectively differentiate various speech sound characteristics compared to the commonly used discrete Fourier transform (DFT) spectra. To capture the nuances of articulation/sound characteristic variations, this study proposes utilizing cepstral coefficients derived from the ZTW spectra, which shall henceforth be referred to as ZTWCC. In this study, our research endeavours extend beyond ZTWCC and explore the efficacy of handcrafted features such as MFCC, CQCC, and SFFCC for the task of stutter event detection. Additionally, we investigate the impact of incorporating phase information upon concatenating the extracted features on the performance of the classifier model developed for the stutter event detection task. From here on, we can use Stutter detection and classification interchangeably.

3   Methods

3.1   ZTW

The ZTW technique was first introduced in [4] to derive instantaneous spectral characteristics, thereby enabling the capture of time-varying features of the speech production mechanism. In contrast to conventional windows such as Hamming windows, the ZTW method utilizes a heavily decaying window, emphasizing samples located near the zeroth time instant. This unique feature of the ZTW method confers higher temporal resolution as the window is shifted for each time instant. Furthermore, the spectrum estimation uses group delay, which has been demonstrated to yield a superior spectral resolution. Consequently, the ZTW method offers the advantages of both higher temporal resolution and good spectral resolution simultaneously. The procedural steps involved in extracting instantaneous spectral characteristics using the ZTW method which is delineated below:

1. To eliminate the impact of low-frequency trends present in the speech signal (s[n]), a pre-emphasis technique is employed.
2. A speech segment of duration L ms is considered at each instant. Specifically, $s[n]$ is defined for $n = 0, 1, ..., M - 1$, where the number of samples M is given by $M = L \times \frac{fs}{1000}$, and fs denotes the sampling frequency.
3. Apply a heavily decaying window $w_1^2[n]$ to the segment under consideration. The window is defined as:

$$w_1[n] = \left\{ 0, for \quad n = 0, \frac{1}{4\sin^2\left(\frac{\pi n}{2N}\right)}, for \quad n = 1, \ldots, N - 1. \right. \tag{1}$$

We consider a discrete Fourier transform (DFT) of a signal $s[n]$ with N samples, where $N \gg M$. Multiplying $s[n]$ by a window $w_1^2[n]$ is equivalent to four times integration in the frequency domain. However, truncating the signal at the instant $n = M - 1$ may result in a ripple effect in the frequency domain. To mitigate this effect, we use a window $w_2[n]$, the square of a half-cosine window. Using $w_2[n]$ reduces the ripple effect and improves the spectral estimation of the signal.

$$w_2[n] = 4\cos^2\left(\frac{\pi n}{2M}\right) where \quad n = 0, 1, \ldots, M - 1. \tag{2}$$

4. Estimation of the spectrum is done by the numerator of group delay(NGD) function $(g[k])$, which is applied to the windowed signal (i.e., $x[n]=w_1^2[n]w_2[n]s[n]$) is represented as

$$g[k] = X_R[k]Y_R[k] + X_I[k]Y_I[k], \quad k = 0, 1, ..., N - 1 \tag{3}$$

$X_R[k], X_I[k]$ are real and imaginary parts of N-point DFT $X[k]$ of $x[n]$ and $Y_R[k], Y_I[k]$ are real and imaginary parts of N-point DFT $Y[k]$ of $y[n] = nx[n]$
5. Double differentiation of the numerator of Group Delay(NGD) function is carried down to highlight a sharper representation of peaks in the spectrum corresponding to formants of the vocal tract system. The Hilbert envelope of the double-differenced NGD function is then computed, giving rise to the HNGD/ZTW spectrum, denoted as $X[n, k]$. The same has been depicted in Fig. 1.

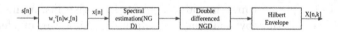

Fig. 1. Schematic block diagram of ZTW computation.

3.2 ZTWCC

In this work, we compute the ZTWCC features from the cepstrum of the ZTW spectrum. Cepstrum c[n,k] is computed by

$$c[n, k] = IFFT(log(X[n, k])) \tag{4}$$

Of the entire c[n,k], only the first 14 cepstral coefficients are considered, including 0th coefficient, which is named as zero time windowing cepstral coefficients(ZTWCCs). Figure 2 shows the schematic diagram of extracting ZTWCC from the ZTW spectrum.

Fig. 2. Block diagram of ZTWCC feature extraction

3.3 Phase Information

Previous research on phase in speech has suggested that phase information is not perceptually significant and that the human auditory system is insensitive to changes in phase. These conclusions were drawn from a range of studies examining the effects of phase manipulation on speech perception and have been widely accepted in speech and audio processing. While amplitude information has been shown to play a critical role in speech perception, the contribution of phase information to speech perception has been the subject of ongoing debate. Despite the previous findings, recent research has begun to challenge the notion that phase information is irrelevant for speech perception, suggesting that further investigation is needed to fully understand the role of phase in the auditory perception of speech. Contrary to earlier research, [18,19,21] have demonstrated the perceptual significance of the phase component in speech through a series of experiments involving modified phase information for signal reconstruction. These findings indicate that phase-based features complement magnitude spectral features [20]. Other studies have also highlighted the importance of phase information in speech processing. For instance, [7] utilized Fourier phase information for pathological voice detection, while [15] studied the correlation between phase distortion and the shape of the periodic pulse in the glottal source, which is connected to voice quality. These studies demonstrate the potential of the Fourier phase for voice quality assessment. In the case of stuttering, poor phonation and respiration can lead to reduced voice quality. Therefore, it is hypothesized that including phase features alongside magnitude features can enhance the performance of stuttering detection systems. This study investigates the relevance of the analytic phase in stuttering speech processing.

Phase Detection. Phase detection is the process of extracting the phase information of a speech signal. Hilbert transform was used to obtain the analytic signal of a speech signal, which is a complex signal that contains both the original signal and its Hilbert transform.

$$A(t) = x(t) + jH(x(t)) \tag{5}$$

where $x(t)$ is the original speech signal, $H(x(t))$ is the Hilbert transform of $x(t)$, and j is the imaginary unit. The phase information of the analytic signal can be obtained by taking the arc tangent of the ratio of the imaginary part to the real part.

$$\phi(t) = \tan^{-1}(H(x(t)/x(t))) \qquad (6)$$

where $\phi(t)$ contains the phase information.

4 Proposed Work

This section delineates the comprehensive details of the proposed system for detecting stutter events in the podcast SEP-28K dataset. Figure 3 shows a schematic diagram of the proposed architecture for the stutter classification.

As most of the work is going on in model space from the literature, in this, we are working on feature space where we are proposing a feature that has both high temporal and spectral resolution, which will be helpful in stutter detection problems. The proposed feature is Zero Time windowing Cepstral Coefficients(ZTWCC) extracted from the ZTW cepstrum. In addition, we even examined the effect of adding phase information to cepstral coefficients for stutter detection. The process of extracting ZTWCC and Phase information is briefly explained in Sect. 3.

In this work, we have conducted two types of experiments. One with the cepstral features and the other with adding the phase information to the cepstral features. Cepstral features such as MFCC, CQCC, and SFFCC were compared with the proposed ZTWCC feature. While extracting the ZTWCC features for each audio sample, we tried with different nFFT points(128,256,512). But the results were tabulated for only ZTWCC with 128 nFFT points as it gives better results than nFFT with 256 and 512.

We have explored the existing classifiers like SVM, LSTM, and Bi-LSTM for the classification task and reported the results. The most common handcrafted features MFCCs are considered baseline features in this work for both experimental studies. All the classifiers were trained in one-vs-one fashion, i.e., clean vs. stutter type classification.

5 Experimental Setup

This section presents a detailed description of the database employed in our study, the evaluation metrics for assessing the system's performance, and the systems we adopted for comparison.

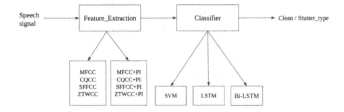

Fig. 3. Proposed architecture for the classification of stuttering events.

5.1 Database

Both experiments were performed on the Podcast SEP-28K dataset. The dataset comprises over 28177 audio samples, each comprising about 3 sec making over approximately 23 h. The dataset is prepared so that each sample should contain at least one stutter type. In this work, first, we have segregated the audio samples into different folders depending on the labels provided in the dataset. Samples were separated depending on the label count in the CSV file. After separating the samples into each stuttering type, we found that samples for each type are very low in number compared to the clean samples. So, we have used the Python SMOTE library to balance the dataset for the classification task. Then we resampled the audio samples into 8kz for the experimental purpose. The dataset is divided into a train set and a test set depending on the split ratio of 0.33 and then given to classifiers for training and testing. All the features were first extracted in Matlab, and the classifiers were trained on these extracted features in Python.

5.2 Metrics

All the experimental classifiers were evaluated on an F-1 score basis as a metric. The F1-score is a widely adopted performance metric that balances false positives and negatives, making it unbiased to the majority class. This characteristic is particularly crucial in scenarios where the dataset exhibits class imbalance, ensuring that the evaluation metric is not skewed toward the dominant class.

We have performed experiments with three different classifiers for each feature type over all the stutter types and tabulated the results. Classifiers such as Support vector Machine (SVM), Long Short Term Memory (LSTM), and Bidirectional LSTM (Bi-LSTM) are explored. "rbf" kernel was used while training SVM. Binary cross-entropy loss function, Adam optimizer, and sigmoid activation function were used while training LSTM and Bi-LSTM with a learning rate of 0.01.

6 Results and Discussions

The Tables 1 and 2 represent the F-1 score for different stuttering types. B: Blocks, I: Interjections, S: Sound repetitions, W: Word repetitions, P: Prolongation on the SEP-28k dataset for each classifier SVM, LSTM, and Bi-LSTM on different feature types MFCC, CQCC, SFFCC, and ZTWCC.

Table 1 shows the performance of each classifier on each stutter type with different cepstral features, whereas Table 2 shows results with cepstral features that are concatenated with phase information.

Table 1. F-1 Score for all stuttering types of each classifier on just cepstral features.

Classifier	Feature_Type	Stutter_Type				
		B	I	S	W	P
SVM	MFCC	0.6210	0.6025	0.6246	0.6126	0.6514
	CQCC	0.6011	0.5848	0.6113	0.5663	0.6150
	SFFCC	0.5438	0.5698	0.5699	0.6590	0.4718
	ZTWCC	0.6008	0.6074	0.5626	0.5783	0.6261
LSTM	MFCC	0.5585	0.6805	0.6427	0.6929	0.7307
	CQCC	0.7124	0.6820	0.7045	0.7000	0.7252
	SFFCC	0.6743	0.5763	0.6986	0.5001	0.6669
	ZTWCC	0.6896	0.7020	0.7064	0.7061	0.7375
Bi-LSTM	MFCC	0.7129	0.7109	0.7285	0.6977	0.7242
	CQCC	0.7038	0.6952	0.7083	0.6963	0.7066
	SFFCC	0.6899	0.6564	0.6795	0.6305	0.6630
	ZTWCC	**0.7223**	**0.7216**	**0.7328**	**0.7045**	**0.7359**

In both experiments, our proposed feature ZTWCC gave a better F-1 score than the baseline MFCC feature when trained on the Bi-LSTM classifier.

From Table 1, we can observe that LSTM and Bi-LSTM are performing better than SVM across most types of stuttering events. For SVM, the best performance was observed on the P-type stuttering with MFCC feature type with an F-1 score of 0.6514, while the worst performance was seen for the S-type stuttering with SFFCC feature type, with an F-1 score of 0.5438. In the case of the SVM classifier, MFCC features gave better F-1 scores than all other features. For the LSTM classifier, the CQCC and ZTWCC feature types performed the best across most stuttering types. Compared to MFCC, both CQCC and ZTWCC performed better for all the stuttering types except for P, where MFCC is slightly better than CQCC, but the proposed feature ZTWCC gave better performance for all the stuttering types. The CQCC feature gave better results than all other features, even outperforming the proposed ZTWCC for the B stuttering type with an F-1 score of 0.7124. For the Bi-LSTM classifier, the MFCC and ZTWCC feature types generally performed the best across most stuttering types. However, ZTWCC gave a better F-1 score than the baseline MFCC feature for all stuttering types. CQCC is the next feature that performed well. Out of all the feature types in all the stuttering types for each classifier, SFFCC has the lowest F-1 scores, and ZTWCC, when trained on Bi-LSTM, has the highest F-1 score values among all the stuttering types and classifiers. From Table 1, we can observe an absolute improvement of over 0.5–2% of F-1 score for ZTWCC when compared with baseline MFCC. However, the LSTM classifier shows an absolute improvement of about 0.5–6% in the F-1 score for almost every stuttering type. Overall, when cepstral features are considered, ZTWCC performs better when trained on Bi-LSTM.

Table 2. F-1 Score for all stuttering types of each classifier on cepstral features and phase information.

Classifier	Feature_Type	Stutter_Type				
		B	I	S	W	P
SVM	MFCC	0.6251	0.6292	0.6224	0.6480	0.6615
	CQCC	0.5896	0.5877	0.6158	0.5657	0.5982
	SFFCC	0.5743	0.6180	0.5852	0.6444	0.5391
	ZTWCC	0.5816	0.5842	0.6210	0.5932	0.6246
LSTM	MFCC	0.7100	0.6741	0.7674	0.7452	0.7562
	CQCC	0.7290	0.6997	0.7709	0.7416	0.7261
	SFFCC	0.7177	0.6696	0.7417	0.7233	0.7104
	ZTWCC	0.7228	0.7100	0.7790	0.7553	0.7492
Bi-LSTM	MFCC	0.7342	0.7511	0.7812	0.7457	0.7402
	CQCC	0.7253	0.7341	0.7537	0.7341	0.7347
	SFFCC	0.6695	0.6806	0.7266	0.6963	0.7129
	ZTWCC	**0.7384**	**0.7537**	**0.7913**	**0.7588**	**0.7468**

Compared with Table 1, in Table 2, a 2–6% improvement in the F-1 score can be seen for all stuttering types when compared with cepstral features and the combination of phase information and cepstral features. In this experiment, too, in the case of the SVM classifier, the MFCC feature gave better results compared to all other features where the best F-1 score was with Prolongation of 0.6615 and the worst F-1 score was with SFFCC for prolongation having an F-1 score of 0.5391. In the case of LSTM, CQCC and ZTWCC performed better than MFCC. CQCC outperformed MFCC in Block, Interjection, and Sound repetition stuttering types, whereas ZTWCC gave better results for all the stuttering types. For Bi-LSTM, ZTWCC gave a better F-1 score than all other features. Even MFCC gave good results but not as much as ZTWCC. In Bi-LSTM, SFFCC has the worst F-1 score of 0.6695 for B and the highest F-1 score of 0.7913 for S.

Comparing both results, we can observe that the proposed feature ZTWCC performs well for classifying stuttering events. On comparing the results with the experiment conducted on cepstral features, We can see an absolute improvement of about 0.5–4% for all the stuttering types for Bi-LSTM when trained on the cepstral features combined with phase information for the ZTWCC feature set.

7   Conclusion

In this work, we proposed a ZTWCC (a high temporal and spectral resolution) feature for the classification of stuttering on the SEP-28K dataset. Experimental results showed an improvement of 0.5–4% in F-1 score comparing among cepstral coefficients and an improvement of about 2-6% of F-1 score comparing (Phase information + cepstral coefficients) and cepstral coefficients. Classifiers such as SVM, LSTM, and Bi-LSTM are trained and tested. In both scenarios, the proposed feature ZTWCC has outperformed the baseline standard MFCC features in the stutter detection task when trained on the Bi-LSTM classifier.

References

1. Bayerl, S., Wolff von Gudenberg, A., Hönig, F., Noeth, E., Riedhammer, K.: Ksof: the kassel state of fluency dataset - a therapy centered dataset of stuttering. In: Proceedings of the Language Resources and Evaluation Conference, pp. 1780–1787. European Language Resources Association, Marseille, France (Jun 2022)
2. Bayerl, S.P., Wagner, D., Nöth, E., Riedhammer, K.: Detecting dysfluencies in stuttering therapy using wav2vec 2.0. arXiv preprint arXiv:2204.03417 (2022)
3. Bayerl, S.P., Wagner, D., Noeth, E., Riedhammer, K.: Detecting dysfluencies in stuttering therapy using wav2vec 2.0. In: Proceedings of Interspeech 2022, pp. 2868–2872 (2022). https://doi.org/10.21437/Interspeech. 2022–10908
4. Bayya, Y., Gowda, D.N.: Spectro-temporal analysis of speech signals using zero-time windowing and group delay function. Speech Commun. 55(6), 782–795 (2013)
5. Chee, L.S., Ai, O.C., Hariharan, M., Yaacob, S.: Automatic detection of prolongations and repetitions using lpcc. In: 2009 International Conference for Technical Postgraduates (TECHPOS), pp. 1–4. IEEE (2009)
6. Chee, L.S., Ai, O.C., Hariharan, M., Yaacob, S.: Mfcc based recognition of repetitions and prolongations in stuttered speech using k-nn and lda. In: 2009 IEEE Student Conference on Research and Development (SCOReD), pp. 146–149. IEEE (2009)
7. Drugman, T., Dubuisson, T., Dutoit, T.: Phase-based information for voice pathology detection. In: 2011 IEEE International Conference on Acoustics, Speech and Signal Processing (ICASSP), pp. 4612–4615. IEEE (2011)
8. Duffy, J.R.: Motor speech disorders e-book: substrates, differential diagnosis, and management. Elsevier Health Sciences (2019)
9. Guitar, B.: Stuttering: an integrated approach to its nature and treatment. Lippincott Williams & Wilkins (2013)
10. Howell, P., Davis, S., Bartrip, J.: The university college london archive of stuttered speech (uclass) (2009)
11. Kadiri, S.R., Yegnanarayana, B.: Breathy to tense voice discrimination using zero-time windowing cepstral coefficients (ZTWCCs). In: Proceedings of Interspeech 2018, pp. 232–236 (2018). https://doi.org/10.21437/Interspeech. 2018–2498
12. Kethireddy, R., Kadiri, S.R., Kesiraju, S., Gangashetty, S.V., et al.: Zero-time windowing cepstral coefficients for dialect classification. In: Odyssey, pp. 32–38 (2020)
13. Kourkounakis, T., Hajavi, A., Etemad, A.: Detecting multiple speech disfluencies using a deep residual network with bidirectional long short-term memory. In: ICASSP 2020-2020 IEEE International Conference on Acoustics, Speech and Signal Processing (ICASSP), pp. 6089–6093. IEEE (2020)

14. Kourkounakis, T., Hajavi, A., Etemad, A.: Fluentnet: end-to-end detection of stuttered speech disfluencies with deep learning. IEEE/ACM Trans. Audio Speech Lang. Process. **29**, 2986–2999 (2021)
15. Koutsogiannaki, M., Simantiraki, O., Degottex, G., Stylianou, Y.: The importance of phase on voice quality assessment. In: Fifteenth Annual Conference of the International Speech Communication Association (2014)
16. Lea, C., Mitra, V., Joshi, A., Kajarekar, S., Bigham, J.P.: Sep-28k: a dataset for stuttering event detection from podcasts with people who stutter. In: ICASSP 2021–2021 IEEE International Conference on Acoustics, Speech and Signal Processing (ICASSP), pp. 6798–6802. IEEE (2021)
17. Nöth, E., et al.: Automatic stuttering recognition using hidden Markov models. In: Proceedings of 6th International Conference on Spoken Language Processing (ICSLP 2000), pp. vol. 4, 65–68 (2000). https://doi.org/10.21437/ICSLP.2000-752
18. Oppenheim, A.V., Lim, J.S.: The importance of phase in signals. Proc. IEEE **69**(5), 529–541 (1981)
19. Oppenheim, A.V., Lim, J.S., Curtis, S.R.: Signal synthesis and reconstruction from partial fourier-domain information. JOSA **73**(11), 1413–1420 (1983)
20. Paliwal, K., Wójcicki, K., Shannon, B.: The importance of phase in speech enhancement. Speech Commun. **53**(4), 465–494 (2011)
21. Paliwal, K.K., Alsteris, L.: Usefulness of phase spectrum in human speech perception. In: Eighth European Conference on Speech Communication and Technology (2003)
22. Ratner, N.B., MacWhinney, B.: Fluency bank: a new resource for fluency research and practice. J. Fluency Disord. **56**, 69–80 (2018)
23. Riva-Posse, P., Busto-Marolt, L., Schteinschnaider, Á., Martinez-Echenique, L., Cammarota, Á., Merello, M.: Phenomenology of abnormal movements in stuttering. Parkinsonism Related Disorders **14**(5), 415–419 (2008)
24. Sheikh, S.A., Sahidullah, M., Hirsch, F., Ouni, S.: Stutternet: stuttering detection using time delay neural network. In: 2021 29th European Signal Processing Conference (EUSIPCO), pp. 426–430. IEEE (2021)
25. Sheikh, S.A., Sahidullah, M., Hirsch, F., Ouni, S.: Machine learning for stuttering identification: review, challenges and future directions. Neurocomputing (2022)
26. Sheikh, S.A., Sahidullah, M., Hirsch, F., Ouni, S.: Robust stuttering detection via multi-task and adversarial learning. In: 2022 30th European Signal Processing Conference (EUSIPCO), pp. 190–194. IEEE (2022)
27. Sheikh, S.A., Sahidullah, M., Hirsch, F., Ouni, S.: Introducing ecapa-tdnn and wav2vec2. 0 embeddings to stuttering detection. arXiv preprint arXiv:2204.01564 (2022)
28. Smith, A., Weber, C.: How stuttering develops: the multifactorial dynamic pathways theory. J. Speech Lang. Hear. Res. **60**(9), 2483–2505 (2017)
29. Ward, D.: Stuttering and cluttering: frameworks for understanding and treatment. Psychology Press (2017)
30. Wiśniewski, M., Kuniszyk-Jóźkowiak, W., Smołka, E., Suszyński, W.: Automatic detection of disorders in a continuous speech with the hidden markov models approach. In: Computer Recognition Systems, vol. 2, pp. 445–453. Springer (2007). https://doi.org/10.1007/978-3-540-75175-5_56

Source and System-Based Modulation Approach for Fake Speech Detection

Rishith Sadashiv T. N.[1]([✉]), Devesh Kumar[1], Ayush Agarwal[2],
Moakala Tzudir[1], Jagabandhu Mishra[1], and S. R. Mahadeva Prasanna[1]

[1] Indian Institute of Technology Dharwad, Dharwad 580011, India
{221022005,200030017,moakala.tzudir,jagabandhu.mishra.18,
prasanna}@iitdh.ac.in
[2] McAfee, Bengaluru, India
ayush_agarwal@mcafee.com

Abstract. The advancement of deep learning technology in speech generation has made fake speech almost perceptually indistinguishable from real speech. Most of the attempts in literature are dataset dependent and fail to detect fake speech in domain variability or cross-dataset scenarios. This study explores the potential of excitation source features to detect fake speech in domain variable conditions. Motivated by the distinction observed using excitation source information, this work proposes a new feature called residual modulation spectrogram for fake speech detection. ResNet-34 is used for the binary classification task to distinguish between fake and real speech. The modulation spectrogram is used as the baseline feature. The proposed approach performs well in domain variability in most cases and shows generalizability across different datasets. Additionally, the score-level combination of residual modulation spectrogram and modulation spectrogram shows enhanced performance. This justifies the efficacy of source and system information in domain variability scenarios.

Keywords: Fake speech detection · Domain variability · Fake vs real speech · source and system information · Residual modulation spectrogram

1 Introduction

Fake speech samples have become perceptually indistinguishable from human-generated speech with the rise of technological developments in deep learning [23]. As a result, differentiating between fake and real speech has become even more challenging. These samples could be used maliciously to imitate and impersonate an individual/organization or obtain unauthorized access by spoofing systems like Automatic Speaker Verification (ASV). Enormous volumes of voice recordings are broadcast online daily, making it difficult to identify which ones are fake [3]. For instance, scammers impersonated a chief executive's voice of a German-based firm to defraud funds from a UK-based firm over a phone call [1].

A. Karpov et al. (Eds.): SPECOM 2023, LNAI 14338, pp. 142–155, 2023.
https://doi.org/10.1007/978-3-031-48309-7_12

As a consequence, there are now widespread public concerns about cyber security related to the downsides of technological advancement. Therefore, designing an effective system to detect fake speech is extremely essential.

Fake Speech Detection (FSD) is one of the emerging research areas in speech. Fake speech is any speech sample that is synthetically generated using different Text-to-Speech (TTS) models [19] and Voice Conversion (VC) techniques [27], which is indistinguishable from real speech. The waveform and spectrogram of a real speech sample and its corresponding fake speech sample are plotted in Fig. 1. The fake speech sample is generated using the parallel WaveGAN technique. It can be observed that in either of the plots, there are no clear artifacts that could distinguish between real and fake speech. Several fake speech datasets are publicly available to the research community that contains fake speech samples generated from different synthesis and conversion techniques. Some of the widely used datasets in FSD are ASVspoof 2015 [26], ASVspoof 2019 [23], Fake-or-Real (FoR) [21], and ADD 2022 [28].

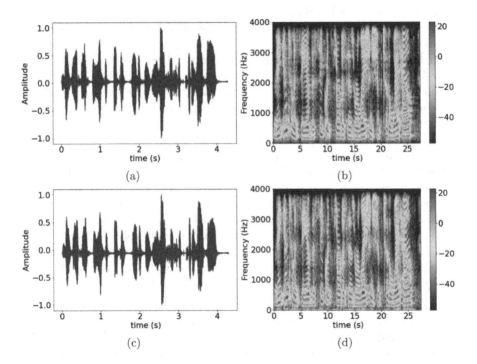

Fig. 1. Time-domain representation and Spectrogram of real and fake speech. (a) is the time-domain representation of real speech, and (b) is the spectrogram of real speech. (c) is the time-domain representation of fake speech, and (d) is the spectrogram of fake speech.

Numerous works in the literature have attempted FSD tasks using the aforementioned datasets. Several studies are explored in FSD with hand-crafted features such as Mel Frequency Cepstral Coefficient (MFCC), Constant Q Cepstral Coefficients (CQCC), Linear Frequency Cepstral Coefficient (LFCC), Gammatone Frequency Cepstral Coefficient (GFCC), chroma features, OpenSMILE features using different Machine Learning (ML) and Deep Learning (DL) models [2,6,11–13]. There are a number of research works in FSD that exploits the time-frequency representation of speech. Some of the image-based features used in FSD system are spectrogram, Mel-spectrogram and modulation spectrogram using DL models [11,14,25]. Recently, various studies have conducted FSD tasks using end-to-end DL models, where the raw waveform is fed directly to classify fake and real speech [7,24]. In recent studies [12,14], it has been shown that models trained on one dataset fail to detect fake speech in domain variability. Domain variability is a condition in which a dataset contains speech samples that are recorded in different environments, background noise and sensors. In most approaches, the models are trained on one dataset. Such models might be tuned to the acoustic conditions of that dataset and fail to detect fake speech when tested on samples from another dataset. Cross-dataset testing is a way of testing a trained model in domain variability.

Based on the literature, it is observed that most of the existing works explored various aspects of vocal tract information to identify fake speech. To the best of our knowledge, the source information has not been explored in FSD systems. As such, we believe that the impulse like periodic excitation source information (ranges throughout the spectrum), may carry some artifacts to distinguish between fake and real speech [17,18]. An automatic FSD system has been attempted in our previous work using a modulation spectrogram where it outperforms the conventional time-frequency spectrogram [14]. Hence, in continuation of our previous work [14], this paper proposes the modulation-based representation of the Linear Prediction (LP) residual signal to capture source information for FSD. In regard to the source characteristics, LP residual is used as the input signal to generate modulation spectrogram, represented as residual modulation spectrogram. The modulation spectrogram, representing the system is used as the baseline feature. Three different datasets are used for cross-dataset experiments. Additionally, the residual modulation spectrogram is fused with the modulation spectrogram to obtain additional information for FSD tasks.

The contributions of the present work are as follows:

1. Residual modulation spectrogram, a representation of the source signal, is proposed. Frequency vs modulation frequency representation is used to classify fake and real speech.
2. Performances on cross-domain datasets are evaluated to build a generalized FSD system.
3. Score combination of the source and system-based modulation spectrogram is performed to show the efficacy for a more robust system.

The remainder of this paper is arranged as follows: The motivation of this work is presented in Sect. 2. The proposed FSD system is described in Sect. 3. Section 4 reports the results of the experiments and these results are discussed in Sect. 5. Finally, the paper is concluded in Sect. 6 with possible future directions.

2   Motivation

From our previous study [14], it has been seen that the modulation spectrogram method works well in speaker, session, and gender variabilities, but it fails to detect fake speech in domain variability. Further, due to the energy-carrying nature of vocal tract resonances, the modulation spectrogram mainly emphasizes vocal tract information, and the excitation source information is suppressed [16,18,22]. The hypothesis is that the hidden excitation source information might have additional artifacts that could aid the performance in domain variability. The main task of any spoofing attack is to replicate the high-intensity regions of the spectrogram of speech to make the synthesized speech more natural. The high-intensity formants are responsible for clarity in speech. Also, most of the features are extracted from the high-intensity regions for any analysis of speech signals. So, speech synthesis techniques might not give much priority to reconstructing the low-intensity regions of the spectrogram. As a result, it is assumed that the artifacts for distinguishing fake speech from real speech might be present in the low-intensity regions of the spectrum. The excitation information is spread out throughout the spectrum, with comparatively lower intensity than the vocal tract resonances [18]. Hence, the excitation source information can be explored as alternative information to discriminate between real and fake speech. The LP residual signal is therefore extracted from the speech signal and the modulation spectrum of the same is used as a representation of excitation source information. The same is termed as residual modulation spectrogram. Further, it is hypothesized that a combination of the modulation spectrogram and residual modulation spectrogram (as it represents different information) may yield better results in domain variability compared to the standalone performance achieved using either modulation or residual modulation spectrum.

To show the distinction capability of the residual modulation spectrogram, the t-SNE plot is computed for the datasets used in *Magazine et al.* [14]. The obtained t-SNE plots from the three datasets are shown in Fig. 2. The embeddings obtained from the learned model of each dataset of the residual modulation spectrogram are used to generate the t-SNE plot. The t-SNE plot for each learned model is plotted using the test samples of all three datasets. The figure shows good separability across fake and real speech (except for the CMU Arctic dataset). As a result, the t-SNE plot motivated us to build an FSD system using residual modulation spectrogram to classify fake and real speech.

Additionally, Structural Similarity Index Measure (SSIM) is computed to check the similarity between corresponding fake and real speech, since the modulation spectrogram and residual modulation spectrogram features are images. SSIM is a measure that determines the differences between two images at pixel level [9]. The score of SSIM varies from zero to one. A higher score of SSIM means higher similarity between two images. The SSIM scores are computed on real-fake speech pairs of all the datasets used in *Magazine et al.* [14] using modulation spectrogram and residual modulation spectrogram features. Box plots are generated using these scores. In Fig. 3, in each plot, the left box represents scores obtained using the modulation spectrogram, and the box on the right rep-

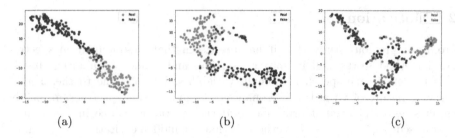

Fig. 2. t-SNE representation of real and fake speech using residual modulation spectrogram on (a) LibriTTS dataset (b) LJ Speech dataset (c) CMU Arctic dataset

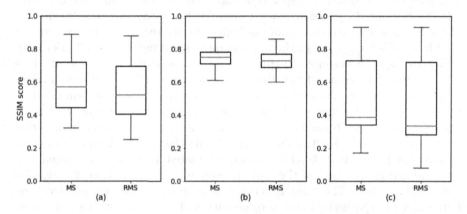

Fig. 3. Box plot of SSIM scores for (a) LJ Speech dataset, (b) CMU Arctic dataset, and (c) LibriTTS dataset.

resents the scores obtained using the residual modulation spectrogram. It can be observed from the plot that both features have similar SSIM score distributions on all the datasets. However, the SSIM scores corresponding to the residual spectrogram show slightly better evidence. Hence, the assumption is that both features are at par with each other in terms of discrimination capability carrying different information. These observations motivate the building of the FSD system using both modulation and residual modulation spectrum.

3   Proposed FSD System

This section describes the proposed FSD system as illustrated in Fig. 4, where the LP residual signal is used as the input signal to extract the residual modulation spectrogram. The extracted spectrogram-based features are then fed to the ResNet-34 classifier for the two-class classification task. The description of the residual modulation spectrogram and ResNet-34 classifier are presented in the following subsections.

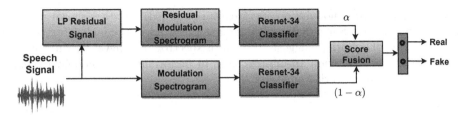

Fig. 4. Block diagram of the proposed FSD system

3.1   Residual Modulation Spectrogram

The residual modulation spectrogram is extracted from the speech signal by obtaining the modulation spectrogram of its LP residual signal. The LP residual signal $r(n)$ is first extracted from the signal speech $s(n)$. In LP analysis, the time-varying vocal tract information is represented by the LP Coefficients (LPC), while the LP residual represents the excitation source [15,20]. The representation of LP residual signal is given in Eq. 1, where p is the number of poles and a_k values are the LPCs. The LP residual signal is obtained by following the inverse filtering approach [15,20].

$$r(n) = s(n) - \sum_{k=1}^{p} a_k s(n - k) \tag{1}$$

The modulation spectrogram is a two-dimensional representation of a speech signal in terms of conventional frequency and modulation frequency. The modulation spectrogram $R(f, f_{mod})$ of the LP residual signal $r(n)$ is obtained by performing two transformations on the signal. Initially, frequency transformation is done on $r(n)$ to obtain its spectrogram $R(n, f)$. Next, frequency transformation is performed for all frequency components of $|R(n, f)|$. A more detailed explanation of the modulation spectrogram extraction can be found in [5]. The modulation spectrogram is obtained using Eq. 2, where F represents the Fourier transform operator.

$$R(f, f_{mod}) = F|R(n, f)| \tag{2}$$

Figure 5 makes a comparison between a real and fake speech pair using different features. The subplots in the first row ((a), (b), (c), and (d)) are the features extracted from real speech, and the subplots in the second row ((e), (f), (g) and (h)) are the features extracted from fake speech. The time-domain plots of the real and fake speech are shown in the first column ((a) and (e)). By mere visual inspection, it is difficult to make out any distinction between time-domain plots of real and fake speech. This is true for the LP residual plots shown in column three ((c) and (g)) as well. This shows that fake speech samples are indeed indistinguishable from real speech samples. However, it can be seen that the corresponding modulation spectrogram plots ((b) and (f)) shown in the second column and residual modulation spectrogram plots ((d) and (h)) shown in the last column display a few distinguishing characteristics in the higher frequency regions. This observation suggests that both spectrograms have discriminative evidence and may provide an improvement in performance by modeling them through a neural network framework.

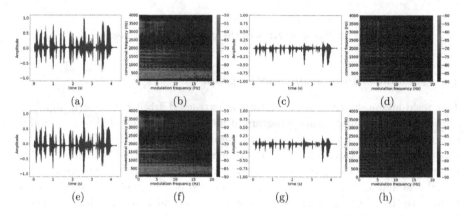

Fig. 5. Comparison among different features. Plots (a), (b), (c) and (d) are the time-domain representation, modulation spectrogram, LP residual signal and residual modulation spectrogram of real speech, respectively. Plots (e), (f), (g) and (h) are the time-domain representation, modulation spectrogram, LP residual signal and residual modulation spectrogram of fake speech, respectively.

3.2 ResNet-[34] Classifier

This work uses ResNet-34 [8] model as the classifier. It is a convolutional neural network consisting of residual blocks. Each block consists of two convolutional layers with shortcut connections from the input of the first convolutional layer to the output of the second convolutional layer. These shortcut connections perform identity mapping. Both the convolution layers in the residual blocks have 3×3 kernels and ReLU activation is used. The ResNet-34 model is divided into 5 layers namely, conv1, conv2_x, conv3_x, conv4_x and conv5_x. The first layer conv1 contains 64 filters of kernel size 7×7. It applies convolution with stride 2. The output of conv1 is passed through a 3×3 max pooling layer with stride 2 and fed to the next layer. The second layer conv2_x consists of three residual blocks with convolution layers having 64 filters. The output of this layer is passed to the conv3_x layer, which contains four residual blocks having convolutional layers with 128 filters. This layer is followed by conv4_x and conv5_x consisting of six residual blocks with filter size 256 and three residual blocks with filter size 512, respectively. Downsampling is performed with the first convolutional operation of each layer using stride 2. The dimensionality changes in every layer because of

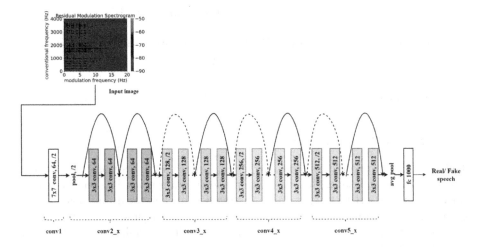

Fig. 6. ResNet-34 model used for real and fake speech classification

downsampling. In such cases, the dimensionality of the inputs coming from the shortcut connections is also changed. The output of the conv5_x layer is passed through a global average pooling layer followed by a fully connected layer with softmax activation function. The block diagram of the ResNet-34 model used for classification is shown in Fig. 6.

4 Experiments and Results

This section describes the experiments and results obtained using the proposed method. Initially, a brief description of the datasets used to conduct the experiment is explained. Following that, the baseline method and its limitations are described. Next, the results obtained using the proposed method are compared with the baseline method. Finally, the scores from the baseline and the proposed method are combined to further improve the performance.

4.1 Database Description

The same datasets used in *Magazine et al.* [14] are considered in this paper. Three datasets are formed using CMU Arctic [4], LJ Speech [10], and LibriTTS [29] datasets, respectively. A subset of these aforestated datasets is taken as real speech. The corresponding fake speech samples for each dataset are generated using the Parallel WaveGAN system. All three datasets are partitioned into train, development, and test sets resulting in an equal number of real and fake speech samples across all sets. Table 1 shows the composition of the three datasets.

Table 1. Composition of the three datasets used.

Database	Train samples	Development samples	Test samples
CMU Arctic	832	278	90
LJ Speech	676	226	98
LibriTTS	568	190	84

4.2 Baseline Method

The approach proposed in *Magazine et al.* [14] is used here as the baseline system. In this approach, the modulation spectrogram is used as the front end since it captures artifacts that could distinguish between real and fake speech better than the conventional spectrogram. It has been shown that the SSIM [9] score between real and fake speech is lesser with modulation spectrogram than with spectrogram. Also, the modulation spectrogram captures the long-term temporal information in fake speech that helps in the classification process. Along with this feature, the ResNet-34 [8] classifier is used as the back end. It takes in the modulation spectrogram image as a feature and performs the binary classification tasks. This approach has been tested on various diverse conditions of the dataset, such as session variability, speaker variability, gender variability, synthesizer variability, and domain variability. The study has shown that this approach is able to classify real and fake speech in all of these variability scenarios except for the domain variability scenario.

4.3 ResNet-[34] Classification Result

The results obtained using the baseline system in the cross-dataset setting are shown in Table 2. From these results, it can be observed that the baseline provides promising performance when the training and testing sets belong to the same domain. However, it gives a degraded performance in the domain variability scenario. This shows that the modulation spectrogram feature cannot generalize between real and fake speech over different domains. The same cross-dataset experiments are conducted with the proposed feature. The performances are reported in terms of accuracy and Equal Error Rate (EER) tabulated in Table 3. Here, the performances in the same domain cases are comparable with the results reported in Table 2, barring a couple of exceptions with the CMU test dataset. However, the domain variability framework performances are better than the baseline results for most cases (highlighted in bold in Table 3). This shows that the residual modulation spectrogram has better generalization capability than the modulation spectrogram.

The decent classification accuracy of the residual modulation spectrogram encouraged us to explore them further in combination. Considering this, it is observed that the model trained on residual modulation spectrogram performs well in cross-dataset cases, while the model trained on modulation spectrogram performs well in the same domain cases. Therefore, the score-level combination is

Table 2. Accuracy results using the baseline model

Test Train	CMU Arctic	LibriTTS	LJ Speech
CMU Arctic	90	53	50
LibriTTS	83	100	72
LJ Speech	56	67	100

Table 3. Accuracy and EER Results for Residual Modulation Spectrogram

Test Train	CMU Arctic		LibriTTS		LJ Speech	
	Accuracy (%)	EER(%)	Accuracy (%)	EER(%)	Accuracy (%)	EER(%)
CMU Arctic	80	20	**60.7**	26.19	**54**	18.36
LibriTTS	60	20	98.9	2.38	**96.9**	0
LJ Speech	**57.7**	33.33	**96.4**	2.38	97.9	0

computed to improve the classification performance by considering the trained models of the residual modulation spectrogram and modulation spectrogram. The combination score is evaluated using Eq. 3.

$$S_{comb} = \alpha S_{RMS} + (1 - \alpha)S_{MS} \qquad (3)$$

In Eq. 3, S_{comb} represents the combined score, and S_{RMS}, S_{MS} represents the scores of the residual modulation spectrogram model and modulation spectrogram model, respectively. α and $1 - \alpha$ are the weights used for the score-level combination. The value of α varies from zero to one. The weight values are selected based on the best-performing weights on the development set. The models trained on the LibriTTS dataset are combined with α equal to 0.4, and the models trained on CMU Arctic and LJ Speech datasets are combined using α equal to 0.2. Figure 7 shows the t-SNE distribution of real and fake speech using the combined embeddings of the trained models. The t-SNE plots for each combined model are generated using the fake and real samples from the test set of all three datasets. A good separation between fake and real speech can be seen for all three combined models.

The classification results obtained from the score-level combination are tabulated in Table 4. It can be seen from the table that there is a significant increase in the performance in most cases when compared to the baseline system (highlighted in bold in Table 4). This observation signifies the effectiveness of source information by capturing discriminating artifacts for better classification of fake and real speech.

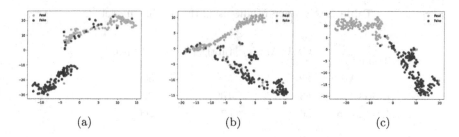

(a)   (b)   (c)

Fig. 7. t-SNE distribution of real and fake speech using score-level combination models trained with (a) CMU Arctic dataset, (b) LJ Speech dataset and (c) LibriTTS dataset.

Table 4. Accuracy and EER for Score-Level Combination

Test Train	CMU Arctic		LibriTTS		LJ Speech	
	Accuracy (%)	EER (%)	Accuracy (%)	EER (%)	Accuracy (%)	EER (%)
CMU Arctic	**96.67**	2.22	**83**	11.90	**54.08**	44.90
LibriTTS	**90**	11.11	98.8	2.38	63.26	0
LJ Speech	**56.67**	24.44	**97.6**	4.76	100	0

5   Discussion

It can be seen from the results that the residual modulation spectrogram provides better performance in domain variability cases than the modulation spectrogram. In contrast, the modulation spectrogram feature works well in the same domain. This result goes along with our hypothesis that the modulation spectrogram and residual modulation spectrogram contain different information that is relevant to the classification task. It can be observed that the residual modulation spectrogram shows a slight degradation in results for the same domain cases. Despite this, the score-level combination of the two approaches shows improvement in most cases. However, it is seen that there is a degradation in the performance of the model trained on the LibriTTS dataset, although the initial t-SNE plot obtained from the said model (see Fig. 7 (c)) showed good separation. This degradation in performance could be attributed to the selection of weights for the score-level combination. Further studies have to be made in this regard.

6   Conclusion and Future Work

This work introduces a new feature, residual modulation spectrogram for the fake speech detection task. It emphasizes the excitation source information and performs well in domain variability cases. This feature shows good capability and generalizability to detect fake speech across different datasets. Further, the score-level combination of residual modulation spectrogram and modulation spectrogram based systems provides improved performance in most cases.

Future work includes addressing the degradation in the performance of the LibriTTS case. In addition, the robustness of this approach has to be validated on a larger standard dataset. Another potential extension would be to use self-supervised models for the classification task.

Acknowledgement. The authors would like to acknowledge the Ministry of Electronics and Information Technology (MeitY), Government of India for funding this research work and "Anantganak", the high performance computation (HPC) facility, IIT Dharwad, for enabling us to perform our experiments.

Disclaimer

References

1. Fraudsters Used AI to Mimic CEO's Voice in Unusual Cybercrime Case. https://www.wsj.com/articles/fraudsters-use-ai-to-mimic-ceos-voice-in-unusual-cybercrime-case-11567157402
2. Alzantot, M., Wang, Z., Srivastava, M.B.: Deep residual neural networks for audio spoofing detection. arXiv preprint arXiv:1907.00501 (2019)
3. Ballesteros, D.M., Rodriguez-Ortega, Y., Renza, D., Arce, G.: Deep4snet: deep learning for fake speech classification. Expert Syst. Appl. **184**, 115465 (2021)
4. Black, A.W.: CMU wilderness multilingual speech dataset. In: ICASSP 2019–2019 IEEE International Conference on Acoustics, Speech and Signal Processing (ICASSP), pp. 5971–5975. IEEE (2019)
5. Cassani, R., Albuquerque, I., Monteiro, J., Falk, T.H.: AMA: an open-source amplitude modulation analysis toolkit for signal processing applications. In: 2019 IEEE Global Conference on Signal and Information Processing (GlobalSIP), pp. 1–4 (2019). https://doi.org/10.1109/GlobalSIP45357.2019.8969210
6. Chintha, A., et al.: Recurrent convolutional structures for audio spoof and video deepfake detection. IEEE J. Selected Topics Signal Process. **14**(5), 1024–1037 (2020)
7. Fang, X., et al.: Semi-supervised end-to-end fake speech detection method based on time-domain waveforms. J. Comput. Appl. **43**(1), 227 (2023)
8. He, K., Zhang, X., Ren, S., Sun, J.: Deep residual learning for image recognition. In: Proceedings of the IEEE Conference on Computer Vision and Pattern Recognition, pp. 770–778 (2016)
9. Hore, A., Ziou, D.: Image quality metrics: PSNR vs. SSIM. In: 2010 20th International Conference on Pattern Recognition, pp. 2366–2369. IEEE (2010)
10. Ito, K., Johnson, L.: The LJ speech dataset. https://keithito.com/LJ-Speech-Dataset/ (2017)

11. Khochare, J., Joshi, C., Yenarkar, B., Suratkar, S., Kazi, F.: A deep learning framework for audio deepfake detection. Arab. J. Sci. Eng. **47**(3), 3447–3458 (2021). https://doi.org/10.1007/s13369-021-06297-w
12. Kumar, D., Patil, P.K.V., Agarwal, A., Prasanna, S.R.M.: Fake speech detection using OpenSMILE features. In: Prasanna, S.R.M., Karpov, A., Samudravijaya, K., Agrawal, S.S. (eds.) Speech and Computer: 24th International Conference, SPECOM 2022, Gurugram, India, November 14–16, 2022, Proceedings, pp. 404–415. Springer International Publishing, Cham (2022). https://doi.org/10.1007/978-3-031-20980-2_35
13. Lei, Z., Yang, Y., Liu, C., Ye, J.: Siamese convolutional neural network using gaussian probability feature for spoofing speech detection. In: INTERSPEECH, pp. 1116–1120 (2020)
14. Magazine, R., Agarwal, A., Hedge, A., Prasanna, S.M.: Fake speech detection using modulation spectrogram. In: Speech and Computer: 24th International Conference, SPECOM 2022, Gurugram, India, November 14–16, 2022, Proceedings. pp. 451–463. Springer (2022). https://doi.org/10.1007/978-3-031-20980-2_39
15. Makhoul, J.: Linear prediction: a tutorial review. Proc. IEEE **63**(4), 561–580 (1975)
16. Mishra, J., Pati, D., Prasanna, S.M.: Modelling glottal flow derivative signal for detection of replay speech samples. In: 2019 National Conference on Communications (NCC), pp. 1–5. IEEE (2019)
17. Mishra, J., Singh, M., Pati, D.: LP residual features to counter replay attacks. In: 2018 International Conference on Signals and Systems (ICSigSys), pp. 261–266. IEEE (2018)
18. Mishra, J., Singh, M., Pati, D.: Processing linear prediction residual signal to counter replay attacks. In: 2018 International Conference on Signal Processing and Communications (SPCOM), pp. 95–99. IEEE (2018)
19. Ning, Y., He, S., Wu, Z., Xing, C., Zhang, L.J.: A review of deep learning based speech synthesis. Appl. Sci. **9**(19), 4050 (2019)
20. Prasanna, S.M., Gupta, C.S., Yegnanarayana, B.: Extraction of speaker-specific excitation information from linear prediction residual of speech. Speech Commun. **48**(10), 1243–1261 (2006)
21. Reimao, R., Tzerpos, V.: For: a dataset for synthetic speech detection. In: 2019 International Conference on Speech Technology and Human-Computer Dialogue (SpeD), pp. 1–10. IEEE (2019)
22. Siddhartha, S., Mishra, J., Prasanna, S.M.: Language specific information from LP residual signal using linear sub band filters. In: 2020 National Conference on Communications (NCC), pp. 1–5. IEEE (2020)
23. Todisco, M., et al.: Asvspoof 2019: future horizons in spoofed and fake audio detection. arXiv preprint arXiv:1904.05441 (2019)
24. Wang, C., et al.: Fully automated end-to-end fake audio detection. In: Proceedings of the 1st International Workshop on Deepfake Detection for Audio Multimedia, pp. 27–33 (2022)
25. Wijethunga, R., Matheesha, D., Al Noman, A., De Silva, K., Tissera, M., Rupasinghe, L.: Deepfake audio detection: a deep learning based solution for group conversations. In: 2020 2nd International Conference on Advancements in Computing (ICAC). vol. 1, pp. 192–197. IEEE (2020)
26. Wu, Z., et al.: ASVspoof 2015: the first automatic speaker verification spoofing and countermeasures challenge. In: INTERSPEECH, pp. 2037–2041 (2015)

27. Yamamoto, R., Song, E., Kim, J.M.: Parallel wavegan: a fast waveform generation model based on generative adversarial networks with multi-resolution spectrogram. In: ICASSP 2020–2020 IEEE International Conference on Acoustics, Speech and Signal Processing (ICASSP), pp. 6199–6203. IEEE (2020)
28. Yi, J., et al.: Add 2022: the first audio deep synthesis detection challenge. In: ICASSP 2022–2022 IEEE International Conference on Acoustics, Speech and Signal Processing (ICASSP), pp. 9216–9220. IEEE (2022)
29. Zen, H., et al.: Libritts: a corpus derived from librispeech for text-to-speech. arXiv preprint arXiv:1904.02882 (2019)

Digital Signal Processing

Investigation of Different Calibration Methods for Deep Speaker Embedding Based Verification Systems

Sergey Novoselov[1], Galina Lavrentyeva[1], Vladimir Volokhov[1,2],
Marina Volkova[1,2], Nikita Khmelev[1,2(✉)], and Artem Akulov[1,2]

[1] ITMO University, St.Petersburg, Russia
{novoselov,lavrentyeva,volokhov,mvvolkova,khmelev,akulov}@speechpro.com
[2] STC Ltd., St.Petersburg, Russia

Abstract. Deep speaker embedding extractors have already become new state-of-the-art systems in the speaker verification field. However, the problem of verification score calibration for such systems often remains out of focus. An irrelevant score calibration leads to serious issues, especially in the case of unknown acoustic conditions, even if we use a strong speaker verification system in terms of threshold-free metrics. This paper presents an investigation over several methods of score calibration: a classical approach based on the logistic regression model; the recently presented magnitude estimation network MagNetO that uses activations from the pooling layer of the trained deep speaker extractor and generalization of such approach based on separate scale and offset prediction neural networks. An additional focus of this research is to estimate the impact of score normalization on the calibration performance of the system. The obtained results demonstrate that there are no serious problems if in-domain development data are used for calibration tuning. Otherwise, a trade-off between good calibration performance and threshold-free system quality arises. In most cases using adaptive s-norm helps to stabilize score distributions and to improve system performance.

Keywords: Speaker verification · Calibration · MagNetO

1 Introduction

The current state-of-the-art systems in the speaker recognition (SR) task are completely guided by the deep learning paradigm and are based on deep neural network speaker embeddings extractors. Previously frame level part of these extractors was based on TDNN (time delay neural network) blocks that contain only 5 convolutional layers with temporal context. Nowadays they use deeper ResNet architectures [8,18]. The trend towards increasingly deep neural networks in image classification is also reflected in speaker recognition task [1,12]. Moreover, these networks are trained using angular losses [15,18], thus resulting in speaker embeddings that can be compared with cosine distance without the use of any trainable backend scoring model.

Raw scores obtained both from the back-end model and by the cosine metric can be effectively utilized for solving speaker recognition tasks in the concrete acoustic domain by adjusting the decision threshold. However, in most cases, the mismatches in training and testing conditions lead to scores distributions scaling and shifting for different domains and signal quality (SNR, duration). Such scores instability impairs SR systems in real applications. In order to deal with this problem different calibration strategies [6,17] and compensation techniques [7, 10] were implemented.

This paper presents an investigation over several methods of score calibration: from the classical approaches to recently proposed neural network based.

The contributions of our paper are as follows:

- We experimented with a range of score calibration procedures, including a classical approach based on the logistic regression model and recently presented magnitude estimation network MagNetO [7].
- We considered the generalization of such approach based on separate scale and offset prediction neural networks developed during the study.
- We investigated the the importance of score normalization in all of these approaches and considered the use of adapted s-normalization [5] after the calibration to analyze its effectiveness.
- We explored the regularisation technique during training neural network based calibration approaches in order to improve the final performance of the SR system.

2   Problem Overview

The mismatches in training, testing, and enrollment conditions can lead to scores distributions scaling and shifting. Thus the scores produced by the model, no matter if PLDA backend or cosine metric is used, are not well calibrated or not calibrated at all. Additional calibration step that transforms the scores to proper log-likelihood ratios is demanded.

The standard calibration recipe supposes to apply an affine transformation to the raw scores to compensate its shift and scale for mismatched data conditions. The classical approach implies using linear logistic regression to train the parameters of this affine transformation, using binary cross-entropy [3]. Let $s_{i,j}$ and $l_{i,j}$ be the raw and calibrated scores for i and j utterances comparison, then calibration can be processed by $l_{i,j} = \alpha s_{i,j} + \beta$

where α, β are scaling and offset calibration parameters. These parameters are usually trained on a calibration training database using prior-weighted binary cross entropy loss.

$$C_\pi = \frac{\pi}{|T|} \sum_{i,j \in T} \log(1 + e^{-p_{i,j}}) + \frac{1-\pi}{|N|} \sum_{i,j \in N} \log(1 + e^{p_{i,j}}) \qquad (1)$$

where π is the prior probability for a target trial (operating point), T is a set of target trials and N is a set of non-target trials and $p_{i,j} = l_{i,j} + \log(\pi/1 - \pi)$. Another option is to use more general version of this loss with operating point being integrated out. It is called cost of the likelihood ratio (CLLR) and indicates score calibration across all operating points along a detection error tradeoff (DET) curve [2]. This metric is usually used for calibration performance measurements. According to our observations there is no big difference in performance of the systems trained with these losses. Many papers proposed to use duration, domain labels or other additional information to improve calibration capability [14].

2.1 Condition-Aware Calibration

Our work about the blind quality estimation of the speech signal [10] confirms that additional information about enrollment and test conditions can compensate speech condition scores shifting in speaker verification task. According to [10] Quality Measure Functions based on signal-to-noise-ratio and reverberation time allow to improve the SR system performance on VOiCES eval protocol, where SR systems demonstrated performance degradation compared to results obtained on the development protocol [8].

Our additional experiments confirm that statistic pooling layer of the deep speaker embedding extractor also contains information about acoustic conditions. In these experiments, the fixed ResNet system trained for speaker recognition task was used to extract the activations of its pooling layer. These values were then used as an input to train simple neural network model with several fully connected layers to predict SNR and RT60 of the audio samples. This model was successfully trained using the Quality Estimation (QE) network from [10] as a teacher.

Results from these experiments in addition to the impressive results of the mentioned above papers lead us to a conclusion that post-pooling activations contain specific information for the calibration process and can be used for condition-aware calibration.

MagNetO. The above conclusions correspond to the results of [7] where authors proposed a magnitude estimation network that uses extracted x-vectors (statistic pooling activations of the TDNN system preliminary trained with angular softmax) to predict calibrated scores. This network maps speaker embedding to its magnitude, which plays the role of a scale factor in a classic calibration approach based on the linear regression model. It is trained using pairs of target and impostor trials with prior-weighted binary cross-entropy loss.

Since this approach is not a linear transformation of the scores it was mainly proposed by the authors to improve the discriminating ability of the system.

Generalized model. Inspired by the results obtained in [7] we consider a generalized neural network based approach for condition-aware speaker embeddings calibration. The calibration neural network is trained directly for the speaker verification task, using binary classification for target and non-target trials. Similar to the work mentioned above, this approach uses post-pooling activation to predict the scale and offset parameters used to present scores as log-likelihood-ratios. However, it can be considered as a more general approach as it does not map its input to the magnitude for each embedding but produces scale and off-set parameters for each trial. This approach allows to use the enrollment and test utterances duration (or any other specific information) as an additional input and forces the neural network to take into account the differences in its conditions. Moreover, we use two different neural networks for scale and offset parameters.

In our experiments, we fixed one of our ResNet-based embedding extractors and compare several approaches for its scores calibration. We consider standard calibration via linear logistic regression as a baseline system. We also investigate MagNetO approach with our embedding extractor and compare it with our modifications on the public datasets from NIST SREs (NIST 2016, NIST 2019), VOiCES Challenge, and our private dataset STC_calls for cross channel test.

3 Embedding Extractor

During our experiments, we used a deep speaker embedding extractor with residual network architecture named ResNet-101 [9].

This extractor was trained on 64 Mel filter bank log-energies with U-net VAD from [8].

This neural network was firstly pre-trained on the train dataset with 4.5-sec utterance duration and after that fine-tuned on utterances with a longer duration (12 sec). In both cases, the training process was performed with additive angular margin softmax loss. The described network was fixed and used further in all conducted experiments for embedding extraction from the second from the last dense layer (Dense1).

4 Calibration

Extracted embeddings are further used for score estimation for each trial. Current state-of-the-art models trained with angular losses mostly use the cosine similarity metric since it shows comparable performance to PLDA backends. That is the reason it was used in our experiments as well.

As a baseline we use a standard approach with logistic regression described earlier. The baseline was trained using CLLR loss on NIST SRE 2018 dev dataset only.

In the second step, the aim was to reproduce the MagNetO approach with our ResNet-101 extractor. Speaker embeddings are used here as an input to the neural network with MagNetO-2-like topology. It consists of 3 affine layers, 2.8M parameters in total. We changed ReLU to PReLU activations as it demonstrated better performance and we did not use any data augmentation in order to speed up the experiment.

MagNetO network is trained on pairs of target and impostor trials with prior-weighted binary cross-entropy loss. However, this approach estimates the magnitude of each embedding independently and does not consider the embedding of the other trial used in the scoring procedure. This lead us to a more general approach we called SONet (Scale and Offset networks) by analogy with MagNetO. Firstly, unlike MagNetO, SONet takes as an input both enrollment and test statistics pooling outputs concatenated into one. This allows training calibration more accurately with respect to possible mismatches in acoustic conditions. Secondly, Offset is predicted by a different neural network. We consider it as a generalization of the previous approach. In our experiments, MagNetO and SONet were trained with CLLR loss, since it shows similar results to prior-weighted binary cross-entropy loss used in the original paper.

Since the main goal was to evaluate how well the systems can be calibrated for all acoustic conditions. To perform an accurate comparison for all the considered systems we have to put them in the same circumstances. This means that their decision thresholds have to be tuned on the same calibration set. For this purpose in our experiments, all MagNetO and SONet based systems were additionally tuned on NIST2018 dev dataset using the classical calibration approach.

4.1 Modifications

Duration. First of all, we propose that adding information about the duration of the utterances as an input to the deep neural network should help to improve the calibration. According to [17] we used the logarithm of duration.

Score Normalization is usually used to reduce the variability of trial scores. As a result, it leads to better calibration and improves system performance. In the proposed systems we apply the adaptive symmetric normalization technique (S-norm) as presented in [11]. This approach implies using an adaptive cohort for each trial, selected from normalization dataset as the X utterances closest to the test t and enrollment e.

To perform the adapted s-normalization in our experiments we used multilingual BABEL speech dataset as a normalization set. We selected 200 top closest scores as described above for each trial to get a normalized score.

Regularization. According to the [7] neural network based calibration trained with prior-weighted binary cross-entropy loss presents "non-monotonic mapping of the scores, and therefore, it can improve the speaker discrimination". In other words, a calibration neural network is partially trained to solve speaker recognition tasks. During our investigation, we explored the training loss improvement by enforcing the "calibration" properties of the system. The main purpose was to make scale and offset factors speaker-independent but remain acoustic dependent. This can be achieved by acoustic domain-dependent batch training procedure with standard deviation loss regularization of the scale and offset factors within the batch. This std loss regularization is used in combination with CLLR loss.

5 Experimental Setup

5.1 Training Dataset

In all our experiments we used one fixed training dataset consisting of telephone and microphone data from various public and private datasets. It includes Switchboard2 Phases 1, 2, and 3, Switchboard Cellular, data from NIST SREs from 2004 through 2010 and 2019, VoxCeleb 1,2 [4, 13] and an extended version of Russian speech subcorpus named RusTelecom v2. RusTelecom is a private Russian speech corpus of telephone speech, collected by call-centers in Russia. We used standard Kaldi augmentation recipe to increase the amount and diversity of the training data.

5.2 Test Datasets and Metrics

Our experimental setup includes evaluation on the most popular datasets NIST2016 eval, NIST2019 eval, VOiCES eval, and private STC_calls subset, mainly used to estimate calibration performance in the challenging scenario with different domains of enrollment and test.

The base STC_calls contains voices of 1000 speakers, collected in various noise conditions simultaneously on the telephone and several microphone devices. It contains both text-dependent and text-independent scenarios. In our experiments, we used cross-channel protocol with 30-sec telephone enrolment and 5-sec microphone test, collected on a far-field microphone array. Since the final systems tuning of scale and offset for all the systems was performed using NIST2018 dev set, here only for NIST2019 eval the development set contains in-domain data, other test sets represent mismatched dev-test acoustic conditions: NIST2016 eval set contains utterances of different language, VOiCES eval set represents a different channel, and STC_calls cc includes both different language and channel.

We evaluate speaker recognition system performance in terms of Equal Error Rates (EER) and minimum detection cost functions with $P_{tar} = 0.05$: $C_{min}^{0.05}$ [16,17]. To estimate calibration performance of the systems at this point we use conventional actual detection cost function $C_{act}^{0.05}$ [16].

6 Experimental Results and Discussions

According to the results, presented in Table 1 and 2, baseline system demonstrates good calibration for in-domain data (NIST2019 eval) and bad calibration for other conditions. MagnetO allows increasing the quality of SR system in terms of EER, while SONet provides an additional performance gap, achieving 4.5% EER on the VOiCES eval set. On the one hand, it should be noted that these are impressive results compared to top task-oriented systems from [8]. On the other hand, the original MagNeto without any modifications has its limits in terms of its calibration ability for varying acoustic conditions. Being its generalization, SONet seems to have the same problems, even though it can achieve better performance, for example on VOiCES eval set.

Table 1. Performance of the considered calibration approaches in terms of EER, minDCF and actDCF for $P_{tar} = 0.05$.

Systems	Matched dev-test conditions		
	NIST2019 eval		
	EER	$C_{min}^{0.05}$	$C_{act}^{0.05}$
Baseline	2.779	0.162	0.185
Baseline + snorm	2.931	0.169	0.195
MagNetO	2.648	0.16	0.165
MagNetO + dur	2.704	0.158	0.165
MagNetO + dur + snorm	2.681	0.157	**0.161**
MagNetO + dur + stdloss	2.802	0.163	0.167
MagNetO + dur + snorm + stdloss	2.931	0.169	0.193
SONet	2.891	0.165	0.168
SONet + dur	2.697	0.158	0.168
SONet + dur + snorm	**2.647**	**0.154**	0.167
SONet + dur + stdloss	2.795	0.163	0.181
SONet + dur + snorm + stdloss	2.938	0.169	0.182

Table 2. Performance of the considered calibration approaches in terms of EER, minDCF and actDCF for $P_{tar} = 0.05$.

Systems	Mismatched dev-test conditions								
	NIST2016 eval			VOiCES eval			STC_calls cc		
	EER	$C_{min}^{0.05}$	$C_{act}^{0.05}$	EER	$C_{min}^{0.05}$	$C_{act}^{0.05}$	EER	$C_{min}^{0.05}$	$C_{act}^{0.05}$
Baseline	6.844	0.408	0.577	5.933	0.219	0.54	12.478	**0.604**	0.975
Baseline + snorm	5.668	**0.256**	**0.257**	6.331	0.229	0.245	12.907	0.609	0.737
MagNetO	6.672	0.447	2.418	5.44	0.21	0.242	11.957	0.631	0.723
MagNetO + dur	6.478	0.402	2.114	5.607	0.216	0.256	12.067	0.631	0.743
MagNetO + dur + snorm	5.475	0.332	0.512	6.52	0.236	0.363	12.89	0.617	0.795
MagNetO + dur + stdloss	6.865	0.406	0.944	5.962	0.22	0.424	12.51	0.607	0.935
MagNetO + dur + snorm + stdloss	5.668	**0.256**	**0.257**	6.331	0.229	0.244	12.907	0.609	0.74
SONet	6.588	0.399	2.042	4.512	0.196	0.261	**11.5**	0.609	0.746
SONet + dur	6.568	0.387	1.699	**4.383**	**0.193**	0.295	11.787	0.638	0.782
SONet + dur + snorm	**5.466**	0.292	0.883	4.517	0.199	0.236	11.582	0.623	**0.713**
SONet + dur + stdloss	6.813	0.399	1.132	5.918	0.219	0.381	12.494	0.606	0.91
SONet + dur + snorm + stdloss	5.676	**0.256**	**0.257**	6.344	0.23	**0.234**	12.927	0.609	0.767

In case the development dataset acoustic conditions match those of the test set, MagNetO and SONet based approaches can help to improve both the quality of the final systems in terms of EER and its calibration ability. Which means that there is no problem with the in-domain calibration task. And results for NIST2019 prove that.

Score normalization brings a stable gain in terms of both SR and calibration quality, even with out-of-domain s-norm cohort (VOiCES, STC_calls cc). The baseline system with this modification show extremely good minDCF results.

Duration-aware versions of MagNetO and SONet demonstrate benefits in some cases (NIST2016, VOiCES) compared to their original versions, however, it does not seems to be a common solution for all tests with mismatches conditions.

An interesting observation is that weighted cross-entropy and CLLR loss used for training here have complex properties. There are two options to decrease calibration training losses. One of them is to directly improve speaker discrimination properties of the verification system. From this point of view, the calibration operation can be considered as a "fusion" model of origin raw score and offset "score". The weights of this fusion are determined by scale factor α. Since the stat-pooling layer output is rich in speaker information, scale and offset factors in this scenario should be considered to be speaker-dependent. Our experiments show that training the system with CLLR or weighted cross-entropy loss without any regularization components leads to better discriminative properties of the SONet system compared to the baseline system. And as an opposite, it has not so good calibration or stabilization characteristics.

Experimental results, presented in Table 1, confirms that proposed std loss regularization combined with score normalization allows to achieve low actual costs for both MagNetO and SONet based systems on all considered test benchmarks and at the same time it slightly degrades the quality of these systems in terms of EER.

7   Conclusions

The comparative analysis of classical and recently proposed solutions for score calibration was carried out in this paper. A generalized score calibration model was described with several modification ideas, that can help to improve the final system performance and/or its robustness on out-of-domain data. Experimental results, obtained here confirm that the statistic pooling layer of deep speaker embeddings extractor provides useful information to perform SR system calibration for a variety of acoustic conditions. We verified that such calibration systems could be trained using the benefits of adaptive s-norm scores normalization. The duration-aware calibration systems could be slightly better than the systems without duration inputs. Such "tricks" improve scores stabilization and enforce the robustness of the verification system to different acoustics conditions. For strong calibration performance, regularization techniques like offered std loss component can be used.

An overall recommendation, based on the obtained experimental results, is that if a system robust to varying acoustic conditions is required it is better to use the classical calibration approach for raw scores after score normalization. However, if there are in-domain data and the system needs to be tuned for these specific conditions, SONet based approach with the proposed modifications can help and calibration of the final system will not degrade.

Acknowledgements. This work was supported by the Analytical Center for the Government of the Russian Federation (IGK 000000D730321P5Q0002), agreement No. 70-2021-00141.

References

1. Alam, J., et al.: Analysis of ABC submission to NIST SRE 2019 CMN and VAST challenge (January 2021), 289–295 (2020). https://doi.org/10.21437/odyssey.2020-41
2. Brümmer, N., Swart, A., van Leeuwen, D.: A comparison of linear and non-linear calibrations for speaker recognition (2014). http://arxiv.org/abs/1402.2447
3. Brümmer, N., et al.: Likelihood-ratio calibration using prior-weighted proper scoring rules. Proceedings of the Annual Conference of the International Speech Communication Association, INTERSPEECH, pp. 1976–1980 (2013), http://arxiv.org/abs/1307.7981
4. Chung, J.S., et al.: VoxCeleb2: deep speaker recognition. In: Proceedings of the Annual Conference of the International Speech Communication Association, INTERSPEECH **2018**, 1086–1090 (2018). https://doi.org/10.21437/Interspeech.2018-1929, http://arxiv.org/abs/1806.05622http://dx.doi.org/10.21437/Interspeech.2018-1929
5. Colibro, D., et al.: Nuance-politecnico di torino's 2016 NIST speaker recognition evaluation system. In: INTERSPEECH 2017, pp. 1338–1342. Stockholm, Sweden (2017)
6. Ferrer, L., et al.: A discriminative condition-aware backend for speaker verification. In: ICASSP, IEEE International Conference on Acoustics, Speech and Signal Processing - Proceedings (2020). https://doi.org/10.1109/ICASSP40776.2020.9053485
7. Garcia-Romero, et al.: MagNetO: X-vector magnitude estimation network plus offset for improved Speaker Recognition, pp. 1–8 (2020). https://doi.org/10.21437/odyssey.2020-1
8. Gusev, A., et al.: Deep speaker embeddings for far-field speaker recognition on short utterances. Tech. rep
9. He, K., et al.: Deep residual learning for image recognition. In: Proceedings of the IEEE Computer Society Conference on Computer Vision and Pattern Recognition. vol. 2016-December, pp. 770–778. IEEE Computer Society (2016). https://doi.org/10.1109/CVPR.2016.90, http://image-net.org/challenges/LSVRC/2015/
10. Lavrentyeva, G., et al.: Blind speech signal quality estimation for speaker verification systems. In: Proceedings of the Annual Conference of the International Speech Communication Association, INTERSPEECH. vol. 2020-Octob, pp. 1535–1539 (2020). https://doi.org/10.21437/Interspeech.2020-1826, http://dx.doi.org/10.21437/Interspeech.2020-1826
11. Matějka, P., et al.: Analysis of score normalization in multilingual speaker recognition. In: Proceedings of Interspeech 2017. pp. 1567–1571 (2017). https://doi.org/10.21437/Interspeech.2017-803, http://dx.doi.org/10.21437/Interspeech.2017-803

12. Nagrani, A., et al.: VoxSRC 2020: The second VoxCeleb speaker recognition challenge. Tech. rep., http://www.robots.ox.ac.uk/~vgg/data/voxceleb/competition2020.html
13. Nagrani, A., et al.: Voxceleb: large-scale speaker verification in the wild. Comput. Speech Lang. **60**, 101027 (2020). https://doi.org/10.1016/j.csl.2019.101027
14. Nautsch, A., et al.: Robustness of quality-based score calibration of speaker recognition systems with respect to low-SNR and short-duration conditions. Tech. rep
15. Novoselov, S., et al.: On deep speaker embeddings for text-independent speaker recognition. arXiv preprint arXiv:1804.10080 (2018)
16. Sadjadi, O., et al.: NIST 2021 speaker recognition evaluation plan (2021)
17. Shulipa, A., et al.: Scores calibration in speaker recognition systems, pp. 596–603 (2016). https://doi.org/10.1007/978-3-319-43958-7_72
18. Zeinali, H., et al.: BUT system description to VoxCeleb speaker recognition challenge 2019. Tech. rep. (2019). http://www.openslr.org/17/

Learning to Predict Speech Intelligibility from Speech Distortions

Punnoose Kuriakose[✉]

Flare Speech Systems, Bangalore, India
punnoose@flarespeech.com

Abstract. This paper discusses a learning approach to predict speech intelligibility in a non-intrusive manner. The difference in the objective intelligibility of a speech signal and its distorted versions, as a function of the signal-to-noise ratio (SNR) of the speech signal is explored in detail. The speech signal and the distorted version are used as input to directly learn the intelligibility score. Multiple distortion-based models to learn speech intelligibility are explored. The proposed approach is compared to non-matching reference based speech intelligibility prediction. We report that, on unseen data, the learned speech intelligibility outperforms the benchmark by a good margin in terms of correlation with extended short term objective intelligibility (ESTOI).

Keywords: STOI · ESTOI · Speech intelligibility

1 Introduction

Speech intelligibility refers to the percentage of words that can be identified in a noisy utterance. Articulation Index (AI) is one of the earliest speech intelligibility measures, which is set as a function of speech and the noise intensities in the different frequency ranges of speech [7]. Objective speech intelligibility measures like speech intelligibility index (SII) [20] and speech transmission index (STI) [28] have been the defacto speech intelligibility measures that were developed in conjunction with the transmission of speech through telephone channels. SII assesses the intelligibility measure as an estimate of SNR in psychoacoustically motivated frequency bands. STI works by dividing the speech frequency into different octave bands and each band is coded by a set of modulating frequencies. Before a speech signal is transmitted, an estimate of modulations is computed. After the speech transmission, the same modulations are computed and compared to get an estimate of how much speech intelligibility is lost. The basic STI is improved by estimating the speech-to-noise envelope power ratio at the output of a modulation filterbank and relating this metric to speech intelligibility [13].

Both SII and STI derivatives are unsuitable to reliably compute the intelligibility index for speech corrupted by non-linear processing, especially spectral subtraction, and other speech enhancement algorithms. Perceptually motivated intelligibility measures like Perceptual Evaluation of Speech Quality (PESQ) [22], Perceptual Objective Listening Quality Analysis (POLQA) [4] and VisQOL [9] are extensively used for speech quality assessment. Recently, new intelligibility measures like STOI [30] and ESTOI [10] have been developed to address the effects of the non-linear processing of speech. STOI is fundamentally based on the correlation between one-third octave bands of the test speech and the reference speech. Although STOI performs well for many acoustic scenarios, it is not well suited for distorted speech with modulated noise sources. ESTOI is based on the correlation between the clean and the distorted spectra so that the traces of the clean speech can be detected. Signal-to-distortion ratio (SDR) [31] and scale-invariant signal-to-distortion ratio (SI-SDR) [24] have been also used extensively as generic speech intelligibility metrics.

These intelligibility measures are intrusive in the sense that the ground truth reference recording is required to compute the intelligibility score. In most cases, the reference speech is simply unavailable. On the other hand, non-intrusive approaches compute the speech intelligibility score without any reference recording. Automatic speech recognition (ASR) related measures like degree of uncertainty in the ASR decoding process, log-likelihood ratio, etc. have been used for non-intrusive speech intelligibility assessment [23]. Importantly, the correlation between speech reception threshold (SRT) and various ASR-derived measures has been demonstrated, which allows ASR-derived measures to be used for speech intelligibility assessment [25]. Phoneme detection probabilities from phoneme classification have been used for non-intrusive speech intelligibility estimation [15].

Rather than predicting the intelligibility of a whole utterance, intelligibility at the phoneme level or word level can be predicted by taking advantage of the knowledge of the human auditory process and can be combined to score the utterance level intelligibility [11,12]. ASR-based speech intelligibility is heavily model intensive and may not be suitable for real-time operation. The context of the utterance also affects the speech reception thresholds and can be used for speech intelligibility prediction. In [14], authors use the transcript and the distorted speech to synthesize an estimated clean reference speech using the twin hidden Markov model (THMM). Eventually, the existing intrusive measures like STOI are used to predict speech intelligibility from the reference speech.

The majority of non-intrusive speech quality assessment uses various deep neural network architectures [2,3,6,8,18,18,27,32]. Most of these neural networks are trained to predict objective speech quality measures. Recently, there have been neural network architectures directly aimed at predicting subjective mean opinion scores (MOS) [16,19,21]. Getting subjective opinions on speech quality for training the models severely limits this approach. Additionally, honoring subjective scores on speech quality necessitates metric like properties to the intelligibility score. Serra et al. [26] proposed a semi-supervised approach SESQUA, to learn the speech quality by optimizing MOS and other complementary scores derived from pairwise speech signal ranking, speech degradation type, speech degradation strength, etc. An encoder converts the input speech into a latent representation and multiple heads convert the representation to a speech quality score based on multiple optimization criteria. The requirement of noisy and clean speech parallel corpus, as well as subjective speech quality scores limits the scope of the approach.

Recently, there have been attempts to utilize some form of reference in the non-intrusive approaches to predict the speech quality score. Manocha et al. [17] introduced an approach NORESQA which uses non-matching references to predict a speech signal's quality. A speech signal is concatenated with a non-matching reference signal and fed to a neural network which is trained to predict the difference in speech quality scores between the input signals. During testing, the test speech signal is coupled with any clean reference signal to get the predicted speech quality difference between the signals. With a clean reference signal, the quality of the actual speech signal is easily computable.

In this paper, we use NORESQA as a baseline and instead of using multiple reference signals for training, we use a distorted version of the same input signal as an additional input. The rest of the paper is organized as follows. First, different distortions and their effect on the intelligibility of the original noisy speech signal are examined across different noise levels. Then, multiple intelligibility learning models are learned and evaluated on standard speech datasets. Section 4 concludes the paper.

2   Our Approach

In the NORESQA setting, the learned intelligibility is based on the input and reference, with the target being the difference in objective intelligibility between the input and the reference. In such a setting, the difference in phonetic features contributes heavily to learning the difference in speech intelligibility. In other words, it is difficult to disassociate the learning from the phonetic difference between the inputs and base it on the speech quality difference between the inputs. This is because phonetic difference dominates the speech quality difference, especially in a high SNR setting. On the other hand, while using a distorted version of the same input signal as the reference, intelligibility is learned as a function of the noise-induced speech quality difference between the input signal and the distorted signal.

2.1   SNR vs ESTOI for Various Distortions

The intelligibility of distorted noisy speech primarily depends on the amount of noise and the type of distortion. Figure 1 shows the mean of difference in ESTOI between noisy speech and its distorted versions at various noise levels computed on 1000 recordings of TIMIT train dataset. Three distortions, namely, tanh distortion, clipping, and pitch shift are applied on the noisy speech using Audiomentation library [1]. Tanh distortion adds harmonics to the signal and changes the timbre of the signal. Pitch shift distortion shifts the pitch up or down by the specified number of semitones. In clipping distortion, the specified

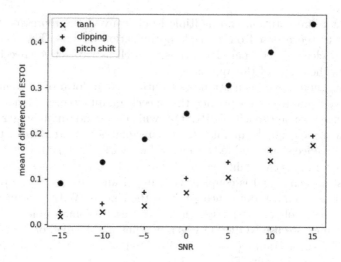

Fig. 1. Mean of difference in ESTOI between noisy speech and its distorted versions, at various noise levels.

percentage of samples are clipped if they are below the 15th or above the 85th percentile. All the distortions are applied with the default values, except the probability of the distortion being applied set to 1. It is evident from the figure that, as the signal quality improves, the difference between the ESTOI of the speech and its distorted versions increases. As the speech quality deteriorates, any distortion won't reduce the intelligibility further.

2.2 Models

The inception architecture [29] in the feature extraction stage of NORESQA is used for all the models. We skip the temporal learning block and the head for preference loss in the original setting. The models used are

1. model_NORESQA: $f(X, Y) \rightarrow (s_x - s_y)$. The target is the difference in ESTOI between the input speech and the reference. The reference Y can be any recording with a known ESTOI.
2. model_distortion: $f(X, X') \rightarrow s_x$. The input to the network is the input speech X and a distorted version X'. The target is the ESTOI of the input speech X. The learning process associates the input speech and the distorted version, with the quality of the input speech.

For all models, the input speech files are trimmed to 2 and 3-second recordings. For each input recording, 512 point STFT is computed on 25ms frames with a 10ms shift. The STFT of the input recording is concatenated with the STFT of the reference recording to form a combined STFT where magnitude and phase spectrograms are treated as separate channels. The combined STFT of the dimension $2 \times T \times 512$, where T is the number of frames, is fed to a series of 4 inception blocks sequentially. Each inception block contains 24 1×1 filters, 32 3×3 filters, and 8 5×5 filters, thus outputting a total of 64 feature maps. These feature maps are concatenated at the depth axis and passed through a 1×4 maxpool block with default stride and passed as input to the next inception block. The feature map from the fourth inception block is of dimension $64 \times T \times 2$. ReLU is used as the activation function after every convolution. The final feature map is flattened and run through a fully connected network of the architecture $N \times 500 \times 400 \times 1$, where N is the size of the latent vector depending on the input signal duration. ReLU is used as the activation function for all the intermediate layers of the fully connected network, except for the last layer which doesn't use any activation function. For model_NORESQA, the target is the ESTOI difference between the input and the reference signal. For the model_distortion, the target is the corresponding ESTOI of the input recording. Backpropagation is performed with a minibatch size of 16 with mean square error as loss for all experiments.

3 Experimental Details and Results

We primarily conduct 2 sets of experiments on 2-s as well as 3-s recordings. For 2-s recordings, for the first set of experiments, a subset of TIMIT train dataset is used along with the QUT background noise [5] as the training dataset. A minibatch from the training dataset is randomly selected and the noise is added at a randomly selected SNR between $-15\,\mathrm{dB}$ and $15\,\mathrm{dB}$ to each speech recording in the minibatch. 600 epochs of minibatches are trained for all the models. For testing, the TIMIT test dataset is mixed with QUT background noise at randomly selected SNR. For the second set of experiments, a small development subset (1300 clean recordings) of LibriSpeech is mixed with QUT background noise for testing, while training remains the same. Similarly, 3-second recording experiments follow the same process except for the number of random minibatches set as 1500. We report the Pearson correlation coefficient ρ between the predicted intelligibility and the original ESTOI of the testing data (Tables 1 and 2).

Table 1. Pearson correlation coefficient between the predicted speech intelligibility and ESTOI on 2-second recordings.

Model	Experiment 1	Experiment 2
model_NORESQA	0.77	0.70
model_tanh	0.82	0.61
model_clipping	0.83	0.75
model_pitchshift	0.84	0.73

Table 2. Pearson correlation coefficient between the predicted speech intelligibility and ESTOI on 3-second recordings.

Model	Experiment 1	Experiment 2
model_NORESQA	0.65	0.63
model_tanh	0.80	0.68
model_clipping	0.83	0.73
model_pitchshift	0.85	0.69

For the 2 and 3-s recordings, for Experiment 1 and Experiment 2, model_distortion perform better than model_NORESQA in terms of correlation with ESTOI. For longer time durations, the difference in speech quality between the input and the distorted signal seems to capture the objective intelligibility better than that captured by phonetic differences. Overall, distortion based on clipping generalizes better compared to other distortions.

4   Conclusion and Future Work

This paper proposes a new approach to non-intrusive speech intelligibility prediction using the input and a distorted version of the input as the reference. The change in objective intelligibility of a speech recording by distortion, as a function of the speech quality is explored in detail. The proposed approach is benchmarked against NORESQA architecture with varying references, and we report that the proposed approach outperforms the benchmark NORESQA by a good margin on unseen test data distributions.

In the future we plan to experiment with other distortions like time stretch, reversing, tinkering with the volume of different bands, etc. Rather than distorting the whole recording, distortions can be applied at a shorter frame level or phoneme level and the corresponding change in the objective intelligibility measure can be quantified and subsequently used to predict speech intelligibility.

References

1. audiomentations: A Python library for audio data augmentation. https://github.com/iver56/audiomentations
2. Andersen, A.H., de Haan, J.M., Tan, Z.H., Jensen, J.: Nonintrusive speech intelligibility prediction using convolutional neural networks. IEEE/ACM Trans. Audio Speech Lang. Process. **26**(10), 1925–1939 (2018). https://doi.org/10.1109/TASLP.2018.2847459
3. Avila, A.R., Gamper, H., Reddy, C., Cutler, R., Tashev, I., Gehrke, J.: Nonintrusive speech quality assessment using neural networks. arXiv (2019)
4. Beerends, J., et al.: Perceptual objective listening quality assessment (polqa), the third generation itu-t standard for end-to-end speech quality measurement part i-temporal alignment. AES: J. Audio Eng. Soc. **61**, 366–384 (2013)

5. Dean, D., Sridharan, S., Vogt, R., Mason, M.: The qut-noise-timit corpus for evaluation of voice activity detection algorithms. In: Hirose, K., Nakamura, S., Kaboyashi, T. (eds.) Proceedings of the 11th Annual Conference of the International Speech Communication Association, pp. 3110–3113. International Speech Communication Association, CD Rom (2010)
6. Dong, X., Williamson, D.S.: An attention enhanced multi-task model for objective speech assessment in real-world environments. In: ICASSP 2020–2020 IEEE International Conference on Acoustics, Speech and Signal Processing (ICASSP), pp. 911–915 (2020). https://doi.org/10.1109/ICASSP40776.2020.9053366
7. French, N.R., Steinberg, J.C.: Factors governing the intelligibility of speech sounds. J. Acoust. Soc. Am. **19**, 90–119 (1945)
8. Fu, S.W., Tsao, Y., Hwang, H.T., Wang, H.: Quality-net: an end-to-end non-intrusive speech quality assessment model based on BLSTM. ArXiv abs/1808.05344 (2018)
9. Hines, A., Skoglund, J., Kokaram, A., Harte, N.: Visqol: an objective speech quality model. EURASIP J. Audio Speech Music Process. **2015**(13), 1–18 (2015)
10. Jensen, J., Taal, C.H.: An algorithm for predicting the intelligibility of speech masked by modulated noise maskers. IEEE/ACM Trans. Audio Speech Lang. Process. **24**(11), 2009–2022 (2016). https://doi.org/10.1109/TASLP.2016.2585878
11. Jürgens, T., Brand, T.: Microscopic prediction of speech recognition for listeners with normal hearing in noise using an auditory modela). J. Acoust. Soc. Am. **126**(5), 2635–2648 (2009). https://doi.org/10.1121/1.3224721
12. Jürgens, T., Fredelake, S., Meyer, R., Kollmeier, B., Brand, T.: Challenging the speech intelligibility index: macroscopic vs. microscopic prediction of sentence recognition in normal and hearing-impaired listeners, pp. 2478–2481 (2010). https://doi.org/10.21437/Interspeech.2010--666
13. Jürgensen, S., Dau, T.: Predicting speech intelligibility based on the signal-to-noise envelope power ratio after modulation-frequency selective processing. J. Acoust. Soc. Am. **130**(3), 1475–1487 (2011). https://doi.org/10.1121/1.3621502
14. Karbasi, M., Abdelaziz, A.H., Kolossa, D.: Twin-hmm-based non-intrusive speech intelligibility prediction. In: 2016 IEEE International Conference on Acoustics, Speech and Signal Processing (ICASSP), pp. 624–628 (2016). https://doi.org/10.1109/ICASSP.2016.7471750
15. Karbasi, M., Bleeck, S., Kolossa, D.: Non-intrusive speech intelligibility prediction using automatic speech recognition derived measures. arXiv: Audio and Speech Processing (2020)
16. Lo, C., et al.: Mosnet: deep learning based objective assessment for voice conversion. CoRR **abs/1904.08352** (2019). http://arxiv.org/abs/1904.08352
17. Manocha, P., Xu, B., Kumar, A.: Noresqa - a framework for speech quality assessment using non-matching references. In: Neural Information Processing Systems (2021)
18. Martinez, A.M.C., Spille, C., Roßbach, J., Kollmeier, B., Meyer, B.T.: Prediction of speech intelligibility with DNN-based performance measures. Comput. Speech Lang. **74**, 101329 (2022). https://doi.org/10.1016/j.csl.2021.101329
19. Patton, B., Agiomyrgiannakis, Y., Terry, M., Wilson, K.W., Saurous, R.A., Sculley, D.: Automos: Learning a non-intrusive assessor of naturalness-of-speech. CoRR abs/1611.09207 (2016). http://arxiv.org/abs/1611.09207
20. Pavlovic, C.: Sii–speech intelligibility index standard: Ansi s3.5 1997. J. Acoust. Soc. Am. **143**(3_Supplement), 1906–1906 (2018). https://doi.org/10.1121/1.5036206

21. Reddy, C.K.A., Gopal, V., Cutler, R.: Dnsmos p. 835: a non-intrusive perceptual objective speech quality metric to evaluate noise suppressors. In: ICASSP 2022– 2022 IEEE International Conference on Acoustics, Speech and Signal Processing (ICASSP), pp. 886–890 (2022). https://doi.org/10.1109/ICASSP43922.2022. 9746108

22. Rix, A., Beerends, J., Hollier, M., Hekstra, A.: Perceptual evaluation of speech quality (pesq)-a new method for speech quality assessment of telephone networks and codecs. In: 2001 IEEE International Conference on Acoustics, Speech, and Signal Processing. Proceedings (Cat. No.01CH37221), vol. 2, pp. 749–752 (2001). https://doi.org/10.1109/ICASSP.2001.941023

23. Roßbach, J., Röttges, S., Hauth, C.F., Brand, T., Meyer, B.T.: Non-intrusive binaural prediction of speech intelligibility based on phoneme classification. In: ICASSP 2021–2021 IEEE International Conference on Acoustics, Speech and Signal Processing (ICASSP), pp. 396–400 (2021)

24. Roux, J.L., Wisdom, S., Erdogan, H., Hershey, J.R.: SDR - half-baked or well done? ICASSP 2019–2019 IEEE International Conference on Acoustics, Speech and Signal Processing (ICASSP), pp. 626–630 (2018)

25. Schädler, M., Warzybok, A., Hochmuth, S., Kollmeier, B.: Matrix sentence intelligibility prediction using an automatic speech recognition system. Int. J. Audiol. **54**, 1–8 (2015)

26. Serrà, J., Pons, J., Pascual, S.: SESQA: semi-supervised learning for speech quality assessment. In: ICASSP 2021–2021 IEEE International Conference on Acoustics, Speech and Signal Processing (ICASSP), pp. 381–385 (2021)

27. Soni, M.H., Patil, H.A.: Novel deep autoencoder features for non-intrusive speech quality assessment. In: 2016 24th European Signal Processing Conference (EUSIPCO), pp. 2315–2319 (2016). https://doi.org/10.1109/EUSIPCO.2016. 7760662

28. Steeneken, H.J.M., Houtgast, T.: A physical method for measuring speech-transmission quality. J. Acoust. Soc. Am. **67**(1), 318–26 (1980)

29. Szegedy, C., et al.: Going deeper with convolutions. In: 2015 IEEE Conference on Computer Vision and Pattern Recognition (CVPR), pp. 1–9 (2015). https://doi. org/10.1109/CVPR.2015.7298594

30. Taal, C.H., Hendriks, R.C., Heusdens, R., Jensen, J.: A short-time objective intelligibility measure for time-frequency weighted noisy speech. In: 2010 IEEE International Conference on Acoustics, Speech and Signal Processing, pp. 4214–4217 (2010). https://doi.org/10.1109/ICASSP.2010.5495701

31. Vincent, E., Gribonval, R., Fevotte, C.: Performance measurement in blind audio source separation. IEEE Trans. Audio Speech Lang. Process. **14**(4), 1462–1469 (2006). https://doi.org/10.1109/TSA.2005.858005

32. Zhang, Z., Vyas, P., Dong, X., Williamson, D.S.: An end-to-end non-intrusive model for subjective and objective real-world speech assessment using a multi-task framework. In: ICASSP 2021–2021 IEEE International Conference on Acoustics, Speech and Signal Processing (ICASSP), pp. 316–320 (2021). https://doi.org/10. 1109/ICASSP39728.2021.9414182

Sparse Representation Frameworks for Acoustic Scene Classification

Akansha Tyagi$^{(\boxtimes)}$ and Padmanabhan Rajan

School of Computing and Electrical Engineering, Indian Institute of Technology, Mandi, India
d19030@students.iitmandi.ac.in, padman@iitmandi.ac.in

Abstract. This work addresses the task of acoustic scene classification (ASC) by using sparse representation frameworks, motivated by the inherent sparseness of audio data. We explore three different sparse representation classification (SRC) frameworks, generating sparse acoustic scene representations. The first two frameworks focus on producing linear and non-linear features respectively. On the other hand, the third framework presents a novel approach-a two-branch deep sparse auto-encoder (DSAE) representation framework that generates non-linear and discriminative features. In the proposed framework, the first branch induces sparsity, while the second focuses on enforcing discrimination within the learned sparse acoustic scene representations. These representations are later used to classify the acoustic scene data into different acoustic scene classes. We also compare the performance of the three sparse frameworks by evaluating them on three ASC datasets. Our results indicate that acoustic scene representations based on DSAE outperform the sparse representations obtained from the other two frameworks. This results in an average performance gain of approximately 8% across all the ASC datasets.

Keywords: Acoustic Scene Classification · Sparse Representation Classification · Sparse Auto-Encoder · Sparse Representation

1 Introduction

Acoustic scene classification (ASC) [3] is a task that involves categorizing environmental audio recordings to their respective acoustic scenes or environmental categories, such as 'park', 'airport', 'bus' etc. ASC is an important aspect of computational auditory scene analysis (CASA), which uses computational methods for analyzing audio scenes [16]. It has applications in location-aware services, smart mobile devices, audio information retrieval, surveillance, audio event detection, and multimedia content analysis. The task of ASC encounters several challenges including variability in different acoustic environments, limited availability of training data, co-occurring sound events, location-variation and device-variation. In many cases, the time frequency representation (spectrograms) of environmental sounds are sparse, which means only a few time-frequency bins are occupied. By using sparse representations, we can focus on

A. Karpov et al. (Eds.): SPECOM 2023, LNAI 14338, pp. 177–188, 2023.
https://doi.org/10.1007/978-3-031-48309-7_15

the informative features of an audio recording while filtering out noise and non-relevant information.

Established sparse representation frameworks such as sparse representation classification (SRC) [17], have proven to be effective in addressing the challenges posed by unwanted variations like diverse expressions, illumination, and noise in the domain of face recognition. SRC framework has also been applied for the task of speaker verification in the audio domain, as demonstrated by [9] and for the task of phoneme classification, as mentioned in [14]. In addition, the introduction of deep learning has resulted in the incorporation of deep learning architectures into sparse frameworks. For instance, the deep sparse representation classification (DSRC) framework [1] is an auto-encoder based method for the SRC approach, which introduces sparsity in the features obtained from the encoder network, and later utilizes them for classification. The authors' primary focus was on two tasks: handwritten digit recognition and face recognition.

The objective of our work is to investigate the efficacy of SRC frameworks in categorizing different acoustic scenes and also provide a comparative analysis of the performance of non-deep learning and deep learning SRC frameworks. In addition, we also propose a novel sparse auto-encoder-based sparse representation classification method. This new method aims to enhance the classification process further by ensuring discrimination in the learned sparse features.

The manuscript's primary contributions are:

1. An evaluation of the effectiveness of sparse representation frameworks for classifying different acoustic scene classes.
2. A novel two-branch deep sparse auto-encoder (DSAE) framework for learning sparse and discriminative acoustic scene representations using a margin-based loss function.
3. A comparative analysis of the performance of different sparse representation frameworks on three ASC datasets.

2   Sparse Representation Frameworks for ASC

This section provides an overview of two sparse representation frameworks: sparse representation classification (SRC) [17] and deep sparse representation classification (DSRC) [1]. SRC is a conventional sparse framework that employs linear transformations to learn sparse features. On the other hand, DSRC is a non-linear variant of SRC that utilizes an auto-encoder framework to learn non-linear sparse features. For both frameworks, we first present a concise description of their main methodology and explore their respective applications in the context of ASC.

2.1   Sparse Representation Classification (SRC)

The authors in [17] proposed, the now well-established sparse representation classification method for face recognition. The method models each test example as a linear combination of the basis elements of an overcomplete dictionary. The overcomplete dictionary consists of the training examples arranged class-wise.

We aim to use this framework for classifying different acoustic scene classes. The overall framework consists of three main components, presented in Fig. 1, and are as follows:

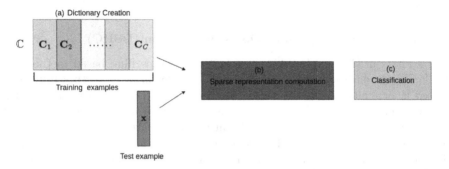

Fig. 1. Pictorial representation of the main steps in SRC. (a) Creation of a dictionary in which the training examples from different acoustic scene classes are arranged class-wise. (b) Compute the sparse representation, including the sparse coefficient vector. (c) Classification, which involves assigning an acoustic scene class to a test example.

1. **Dictionary creation** : In this step, an overcomplete dictionary denoted by $\mathbb{C} \in \mathbb{R}^{d \times n}$ is created, where $\mathbb{C} = [\mathbf{C}_1 \ \mathbf{C}_2 \ \cdots \ \mathbf{C}_C]$. The dictionary comprises of training examples from all the C acoustic scene classes arranged classwise, forming the basis elements. Each $\mathbf{C}_i = [\mathbf{e}_{i,1} \ \mathbf{e}_{i,2} \ \cdots \ \mathbf{e}_{i,n_i}]$, where $\mathbf{e}_{ij} \in \mathbb{R}^d$ and $j \in [1 \cdots n_i]$, with n_i representing the number of training examples for i^{th} acoustic scene and $i \in [1 \cdots C]$.

2. **Sparse representation computation** : In this step the sparse representation is computed corresponding to the test examples. Each test example $\mathbf{x} \in \mathbb{R}^d$ is represented as a linear combination of the basis elements of the overcomplete dictionary, expressed in matrix notation as:

$$\mathbf{x} = \mathbb{C}\,\mathbf{a} \qquad (1)$$

where $\mathbf{a} \in \mathbb{R}^n$ represents the sparse coefficient vector and n is the total number of training examples. Ideally, the test example's true class's basis elements should be sufficient for its representation, resulting in a sparsity of $\mathbf{a}$. This sparse representation retains the class information and is determined by solving the following l_1 minimization problem:

$$\hat{\mathbf{a}} = \arg\min \|\mathbf{a}\|_1 \ \text{ s.t } \ \mathbb{C}\,\mathbf{a} = \mathbf{x} \qquad (2)$$

3. **Classification** : Once the sparse coefficient vector $\hat{\mathbf{a}}$ is determined using Eq. 2, the class of $\mathbf{x}$ is determined by solving the following equation:

$$\text{class}(\mathbf{x}) = \underset{i}{\arg\min} \, \|\mathbf{x} - \mathbf{C}\delta_i(\hat{\mathbf{a}})\|_2^2 \tag{3}$$

where δ_i selects the coefficients corresponding to i^{th} acoustic scene.

For further insights into the above-mentioned algorithm, the readers are referred to [17].

2.2   Deep Sparse Representation Classification (DSRC)

The authors in [1] introduced a transductive deep learning based method for SRC. The system uses a convolutional auto-encoder network, with a fully connected layer (called as sparse coding layer) positioned in between the encoder and decoder networks to learn the deep and sparse features. The sparse coding layer induces sparsity in the learned features which are later used to predict the class labels of test examples. While the original method focuses on using the estimated sparse representations for image classification, our work aims to employ them for classifying different acoustic scene classes.

Being a transductive learning based model, it is required that both the train and test examples are jointly provided as input to the network, represented as:

$$\mathbf{X} = [\mathbf{X}_{tr} \, \mathbf{X}_{te}] \tag{4}$$

where $\mathbf{X}_{tr} \in \mathbb{R}^{d \times n}$ represents d-dimensional n train examples organized classwise and $\mathbf{X}_{te} \in \mathbb{R}^{d \times m}$ represents d-dimensional m test examples. The output of the network is represented as:

$$\hat{\mathbf{X}} = [\hat{\mathbf{X}}_{tr} \, \hat{\mathbf{X}}_{te}] \tag{5}$$

where $\hat{\mathbf{X}}_{tr}$ and $\hat{\mathbf{X}}_{te}$ are the estimated outputs of $\mathbf{X}_{tr}$ and $\mathbf{X}_{te}$ respectively.

The DSRC network consists of three primary components, as presented in Fig. 2 and mentioned as follows:

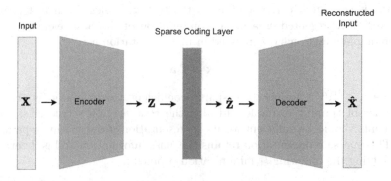

Fig. 2. Schematic diagram of DSRC system consisting of the encoder, sparse coding layer, and decoder.

1. **Encoder:** It comprises of fully connected layers that transform $\mathbf{X}$ into an encoded representation. The last fully connected layer outputs $\mathbf{Z}$, which contains encoded representations for both train and test examples, represented as:

$$\mathbf{Z} = [\mathbf{Z}_{tr}\,\mathbf{Z}_{te}] \tag{6}$$

where $\mathbf{Z}_{tr} \in \mathbb{R}^{\hat{d}\times n}$ and $\mathbf{Z}_{te} \in \mathbb{R}^{\hat{d}\times m}$ corresponds to $\hat{d}$-dimensional encoded representation of train and test examples.

2. **Sparse coding layer:** It takes the encoder's output $\mathbf{Z}$ as input and generates $\hat{\mathbf{Z}}$, represented as:

$$\hat{\mathbf{Z}} = [\hat{\mathbf{Z}}_{tr}\,\hat{\mathbf{Z}}_{te}]$$

$$\text{where} \quad \hat{\mathbf{Z}}_{tr} = \mathbf{Z}_{tr} \quad \text{and} \quad \hat{\mathbf{Z}}_{te} = \mathbf{Z}_{tr}\mathbf{A} \tag{7}$$

Here, $\mathbf{A} \in \mathbb{R}^{m\times n}$ is the sparse coefficient matrix and each column $\mathbf{a}$ of $\mathbf{A}$ represents the sparse code corresponding to a test example, obtained similar to Eq. 2 by solving the optimization function:

$$\hat{\mathbf{a}} = \arg\min \|\mathbf{a}\|_1 \quad \text{s.t} \quad \mathbf{Z}_{tr}\,\mathbf{a} = \mathbf{z}_{te} \tag{8}$$

where $\mathbf{z}_{tr}$ and $\mathbf{z}_{te}$ form the columns of $\mathbf{Z}_{tr}$ and $\mathbf{Z}_{te}$ respectively. The class of a test example is estimated similar to Eq. 3, by solving the following optimization function:

$$\text{class}(\mathbf{x}_{te}) = \arg\min_i \|\mathbf{z}_{te} - \mathbf{Z}_{tr}\delta_i(\hat{\mathbf{a}})\|_2^2 \tag{9}$$

where $\hat{\mathbf{a}}$ is the estimated sparse representation corresponding to $\mathbf{z}_{te}$ and i represents the acoustic scene index.

3. **Decoder:** The decoder network consists of fully connected layers akin to the encoder network and accepts $\hat{\mathbf{Z}}$ from the sparse coding layer. Each layer in the decoder network maps the estimated sparse representation back to the original input space, generating a transformed output denoted as $\hat{\mathbf{X}}$, which represents the reconstructed form of the encoder's input.

For training the auto-encoder network to learn both feature embeddings and sparse representations for test examples, a loss function that includes Eq. 8 and mean squared error $\left\|\mathbf{X} - \hat{\mathbf{X}}\right\|_F^2$ is employed in an end-to-end fashion. Finally, the process of classification involves the utilization of Eq. 9. More details about the architecture can be referred from Sect. 4.3. In the next section, we describe the proposed DSAE framework.

3   Discriminative Sparse Auto-Encoder (DSAE) Framework

The auto-encoder based representations lack the desired discriminative content required for optimal classification performance. To address the same, we propose

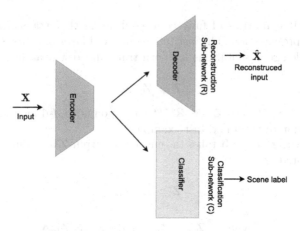

Fig. 3. A schematic diagram of discriminative sparse auto-encoder (DSAE) framework, composed of two branches.

a deep sparse auto-encoder (DSAE) system which is a two branch deep learning network that incorporates both sparsity and discriminative content in its learnt representations. The proposed system's architecture is illustrated in Fig. 3 which comprises of two sub-networks, namely the reconstruction sub-network 'R' and the classification sub-network 'C'. Both of them are connected at the bottle-neck layer of the encoder. The sub-network 'R' consists of the encoder and a decoder, while 'C' consists of the encoder and a deep neural network classifier. The reconstruction sub-network learns the representation of the input data $\mathbf{X}$ by minimizing the reconstruction loss $\mathrm{L_R}$ between $\mathbf{X}$ and its reconstructed representation $\hat{\mathbf{X}}$. On the other hand, the classification sub-network classifies the input data $\mathbf{X}$ and uses the classification loss $\mathrm{L_C}$. The entire network, including both sub-networks, is trained on an end-to-end basis. The overall loss function is a combination both the loss functions. We use arcface [5] as the classification loss corresponding to 'C' and mean squared error (MSE) as the reconstruction loss corresponding to 'R'. Overall, the total loss function can be written as

$$\mathrm{L} = \lambda_1 \mathrm{L_R} + \lambda_2 \mathrm{L_C} \tag{10}$$

where

$$\mathrm{L_R} = \left\| \mathbf{X} - \hat{\mathbf{X}} \right\|_F^2$$

$$\mathrm{L_C} = \frac{e^{s \cdot cos(\theta_y + m')}}{e^{s \cdot cos(\theta_y + m')} + \sum_{j=1, j \neq y}^{C} e^{s \cdot cos\theta_j}}$$

and

$$cos(\theta_y) = \frac{\mathbf{w}_y^T \mathbf{x}}{\|\mathbf{w}_y\|_2^2 \|\mathbf{x}\|_2^2}$$

The true class of an example is denoted by y. The angle θ_y (measured in radians) represents the angle between the feature vector $\mathbf{x}$ and weight vector $\mathbf{w}_y$, which corresponds to the true class column in the weight matrix $\mathbf{W} \in \mathbb{R}^{\hat{d} \times C}$, where $\hat{d}$ represents the encoded representation dimension corresponding to $\mathbf{x}$. The scaling factor and margin value are denoted by s and m' respectively. For more details on the loss function, we encourage the readers to refer to [5].

The inclusion of the arcface loss in the classification sub-network incorporates both between-class separation and within-class compactness in addition to enhancing the discrimination capacity of the overall framework. More details about the architecture and parameters of the proposed system can be referred from Sect. 4.3.

The advantages of the proposed framework over the other two sparse representation frameworks are two fold :

1. In contrast to the other two methods which only ensure sparsity, DSAE learns discriminative sparse representations.
2. The DSAE network can be trained batch-wise instead of requiring all the training examples to be provided simultaneously as it is not based on transductive learning.

4   Experimental Evaluation

In this section, we present the details of the experiments performed using three different sparse representation classification frameworks for acoustic scene classification. We commence by offering a concise overview of the used datasets. Subsequently, we delve into details of the feature extraction process. Following that, we provide description of the two baseline systems (SRC, DSRC), DCASE baseline systems and the proposed system (DSAE). Next, we present the classification results and finally provide conclusion by summarizing our findings.

4.1   Dataset Description

We have used three detection and classification of acoustic scenes and events (DCASE) task 1A ASC development datasets of years 2018[1], 2019[2] and 2020[3] for conducting experiments. All datasets contain data from the following ten acoustic scene classes namely : 'airport', 'metro', 'metro-station', 'bus', 'park', 'public square', 'shopping mall', 'street pedestrian', 'tram' and 'street traffic'. Datasets of the years 2019 and 2020 consist of data from ten European cities namely : 'barcelona', 'helsinki', 'london', 'stockholm', 'vienna', 'lyon', 'milan', 'paris' and 'prague' but the 2018 dataset excludes data from the last four cities. In addition to the data collected from different recording cities, the 2020 dataset comprises of audio recordings captured using multiple recording devices as well [7].

---

[1] https://dcase.community/challenge2018/index.
[2] https://dcase.community/challenge2019/index.
[3] https://dcase.community/challenge2020/index.

4.2   Feature Extraction

We used the open-source OpenL3 Python library[4], to obtain feature representations corresponding to the audio recordings of the DCASE datasets. This library includes the L^3-Net [4] network, which was trained on the Audioset dataset [6]. Out of the two pre-trained L^3-Net network versions namely 'music' (model trained on music data) and 'env' (model trained on environment data), we opted to use 'env' as acoustic scene recordings consist of environmental sounds. The network accepts a raw audio signal as input and outputs a 512×97 embedding corresponding to the same. We compute the average across the time axis to get a column vector of dimension $d = 512$ and use it as the feature representation corresponding to an audio signal.

4.3   Results and Discussion

As we move forward, we will discuss the two baselines: DSRC and SRC, as well as the proposed DSAE system in more detail. Furthermore, we present the architecture details of the deep sparse frameworks, DSRC and DSAE. Finally, we provide the classification results and compare the performance of all the sparse frameworks.

4.3.1 Baseline Systems

SRC follows a traditional approach for computing sparse representations, while the DSRC leverages deep learning to compute nonlinear sparse representations. SRC being a linear method, expresses a test example $\mathbf{x}$ as a linear combination of training examples ordered class-wise in the form of a dictionary $\mathbb{C}$. Using $\mathbb{C}$, a sparse coefficient vector $\mathbf{a}$ is constructed, which forms the sparse representation for $\mathbf{x}$. DSRC is an auto-encoder-based approach comprising of an encoder with three dense layers, a decoder with an equal number of layers, and a sparse coding layer (dense layer) situated between the encoder and decoder networks. The overall network employs mean squared error (MSE) as part of the loss function and uses ADAM as the optimizer. The remaining training procedures adhere to standard practices. Due to its transductive learning nature, DSRC processes all training and testing examples as a single large batch. Both SRC and DSRC employ L^3-Net features with a dimensionality of $d = 512$ and adhere to the standard DCASE protocols for the train-test split.

In addition, there are three DCASE baseline systems for the years 2018, 2019, and 2020 respectively. The baseline systems for 2018 and 2019 utilize log mel spectrogram as the feature representation and employ a CNN as the classifier. On the other hand, the baseline system for DCASE 2020 makes use of L^3-Net features and employs a DNN as the classifier.

---

[4] https://github.com/marl/openl3.

4.3.2 Proposed System

DSAE uses a sparse auto-encoder [12] based framework with the overall network consisting of two sub-networks. The first sub-network consists of a sparse auto-encoder with two dense layers in both the encoder and decoder networks. In order to induce sparsity within this subnetwork, l_1 regularizer is applied to the dense layer located between the encoder and decoder networks, functioning as an activity regularizer. The classification sub-network is constructed using two dense layers, along with the final classification layer including the margin-based loss function arcface [5].

In addition to the aforementioned architecture details, the DSAE framework uses standard training procedures like ADAM optimizer, rectified linear unit (ReLU) activation function, and a batch size of 100. The total loss of the network is a combination of two components: mean squared error (MSE) and arcface. Similar to the baseline systems, the input features used have a dimensionality of 512. The empirically obtained values for m' and s are 0.20 and 3, respectively. Furthermore, the train-test split adheres to the standard protocols established by DCASE.

4.3.3 Classification

Figure 4 illustrates the classification results for various acoustic scene classes across three DCASE datasets (DCASE 2018, 2019, and 2020), utilizing the sparse representation frameworks SRC, DSRC, and DSAE. In comparison to SRC, DSRC exhibits an improvement of approximately 8% in the classification performance for all the datasets. However, DSAE surpasses both SRC and DSRC, providing superior results with a performance gain of around 4% compared to DSRC and nearly 13% compared to SRC across all the datasets.

This performance gain by DSAE can be primarily attributed to the incorporation of classification sub-network and the utilization of arcface loss. The introduction of the arcface loss function promotes compactness within the different clusters corresponding to different acoustic scene classes, as observed in Fig. 5. While the usage of categorical cross-entropy alone ensures discrimination between different acoustic scene classes, the inclusion of arcface enhances the compactness within these clusters.

Furthermore, the proposed system demonstrated comparable performance to other systems of similar complexity. For DCASE 2018, the proposed system was compared to Wang et al. [8] and Ren et al. [13], both utilizing a CNN-based classifier. Similarly, for DCASE 2019, comparisons were made with Salvati et al. [15] and Lian et al. [10], systems of similar complexity without data augmentation. Additionally, in DCASE 2020, the proposed system's performance was compared to Zhang et al. [18] and Aryal et al. [2], both using L^3-Net features and a CNN-based classifier.

Comparison of different methods for ASC for DCASE 2018

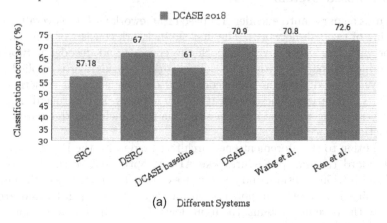

(a)   Different Systems

Comparison of different methods for ASC for DCASE 2019

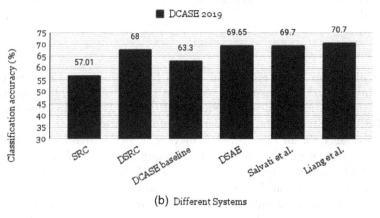

(b) Different Systems

Comparison of different methods for ASC for DCASE 2020

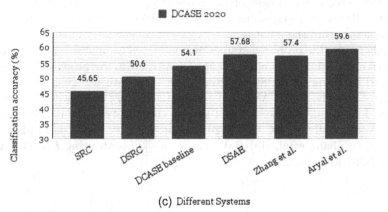

(c) Different Systems

Fig. 4. Acoustic scene classification performance of different sparse and other comparable systems for DCASE 2018, 2019 and 2020 datasets.

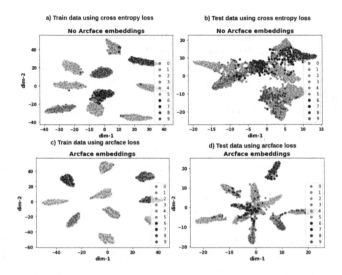

Fig. 5. Comparison of t-SNE [11] plots demonstrating the compactness achieved within different clusters corresponding to different acoustic scenes using arcface and categorical cross-entropy (No arcface) for the DCASE 2018 dataset. The plots show: a) Training data using categorical cross-entropy, b) Testing data using categorical cross-entropy, c) Training data using arcface, and d) Testing data using arcface.

5   Conclusion

In this work, we analyzed the performance of three different sparse representation frameworks for ASC. Additionally, we proposed a novel sparse auto-encoder-based system DSAE that not only learns sparse but also discriminative and compact representations. One significant advantage of the proposed system over the DSRC baseline is the utilization of a loss function that incorporates both reconstruction and classification objectives. By integrating a margin-based loss function (arcface) into the classification process, our proposed system achieves compactness in the learned discriminative and sparse representations. The compactness attained among the various acoustic scenes facilitates open-set acoustic scene classification as well.

References

1. Abavisani, M., Patel, V.M.: Deep sparse representation-based classification. IEEE Signal Process. Lett. **26**(6), 948–952 (2019). https://doi.org/10.1109/LSP.2019.2913022

2. Aryal, N., Lee, S.W.: Attention-based resnet-18 model for acoustic scene classification. Detection and Classification of Acoustic Scenes and Events (DCASE) Challenge (2020)

3. Barchiesi, D., Giannoulis, D., Stowell, D., Plumbley, M.D.: Acoustic scene classification: classifying environments from the sounds they produce. IEEE Signal Process. Mag. **32**(3), 16–34 (2015)

4. Cramer, J., Wu, H.H., Salamon, J., Bello, J.P.: Look, listen, and learn more: design choices for deep audio embeddings. In: IEEE International Conference on Acoustics, Speech and Signal Processing (ICASSP) (2019)
5. Deng, J., Guo, J., Xue, N., Zafeiriou, S.: ArcFace: additive angular margin loss for deep face recognition. In: IEEE/CVF Conference on Computer Vision and Pattern Recognition (CVPR) (2019)
6. Gemmeke, J.F., et al.: Audio set: an ontology and human-labeled dataset for audio events. In: IEEE International Conference on Acoustics, Speech and Signal Processing (ICASSP) (2017)
7. Heittola, T., Mesaros, A., Virtanen, T.: Acoustic scene classification in DCASE 2020 challenge: generalization across devices and low complexity solutions. arXiv preprint arXiv:2005.14623 (2020)
8. Jun, W., Shengchen, L.: Self-attention mechanism based system for dcase2018 challenge task1 and task4. Detection and Classification of Acoustic Scenes and Events (DCASE) Challenge (2018)
9. Kua, J.M.K., Ambikairajah, E., Epps, J., Togneri, R.: Speaker verification using sparse representation classification. In: 2011 IEEE International Conference on Acoustics, Speech and Signal Processing (ICASSP), pp. 4548–4551. IEEE (2011)
10. Liang, H., Ma, Y.: Acoustic scene classification using attention-based convolutional neural network. Detection and Classification of Acoustic Scenes and Events (DCASE) Challenge (2019)
11. Van der Maaten, L., Hinton, G.: Visualizing data using t-sne. J. Mach. Learn. Res. 9(11) (2008)
12. Ng, A., et al.: Sparse autoencoder. CS294A Lect. notes 72(2011), 1–19 (2011)
13. Ren, Z., Kong, Q., Qian, K., Plumbley, M., Schuller, B.: Attention-based convolutional neural networks for acoustic scene classification. Detection and Classification of Acoustic Scenes and Events (DCASE) Challenge (2018)
14. Sainath, T.N., Carmi, A., Kanevsky, D., Ramabhadran, B.: Bayesian compressive sensing for phonetic classification. In: 2010 IEEE International Conference on Acoustics, Speech and Signal Processing, pp. 4370–4373 (2010). https://doi.org/10.1109/ICASSP.2010.5495638
15. Salvati, D., Drioli, C., Foresti, G.L.: Urban acoustic scene classification using raw waveform convolutional neural networks. Detection and Classification of Acoustic Scenes and Events (DCASE) Challenge (2019)
16. Virtanen, T., Plumbley, M.D., Ellis, D. (eds.): Computational Analysis of Sound Scenes and Events. Springer, Cham (2018). https://doi.org/10.1007/978-3-319-63450-0
17. Wright, J., Yang, A.Y., Ganesh, A., Sastry, S.S., Ma, Y.: Robust face recognition via sparse representation. IEEE Trans. Pattern Anal. Mach. Intell. 31(2), 210–227 (2009). https://doi.org/10.1109/TPAMI.2008.79
18. Zhang, C., Zhu, H., Ting, C.: Simple convolutional networks attempting acoustic scene classification cross devices. Detection and Classification of Acoustic Scenes and Events (DCASE) Challenge (2020)

Driver Speech Detection in Real Driving Scenario

Mrinmoy Bhattacharjee[1] , Shikha Baghel[2]([✉]) ,
and S. R. Mahadeva Prasanna[1]

[1] Department of EE, Indian Institute of Technology Dharwad, Dharwad, Karnataka,
India
{mrinmoy.b,prasanna}@iitdh.ac.in
[2] Department of EE, Indian Institute of Science Bengaluru, Bengaluru, Karnataka,
India
shikhabaghel@iisc.ac.in

Abstract. Developing high-quality artificial intelligence based driver
assistance systems is an active research area. One critical challenge is
developing efficient methods to detect a driver speaking while driving.
The availability of such methods would be vital in implementing safety
features like blocking phone calls during driving, stress management of
drivers, and other voice-based assistance applications. The present work
tackles the While-Driving Speech (WDS) detection problem and makes
three principal contributions. The first contribution is the creation of a
manually annotated speech dataset curated from car review videos that
consist of actual (non-acted) WDS data. Secondly, this work analyzes
the effect of cognitively overloaded situations like driving on the prosodic
characteristics of speech. Lastly, benchmark performances on the newly
created dataset using standard speech classification approaches in detecting WDS are reported. This work is expected to spark interest in the
community to explore this problem and develop more creative solutions.

Keywords: Driver assistance · Driving speech · Cognitive overload ·
Computational para-linguistics

1 Introduction

The advancement of digital technology has made a lot of content, like entertainment, easily accessible and has been a helpful addition to the daily lives of
people. However, such progress comes with its drawbacks. For instance, reports
suggest that using mobile phones or gadgets while driving increases the risk
of accidents [5]. Involvement of a driver (while driving) in secondary cognitive
tasks impairs her/his driving performance. In recent years, significant efforts
have been made to develop intelligent cars capable of semi or fully autonomous
driving. Cars now come equipped with intelligent in-car systems [10] that can
be used to give feedback or instructions to the driver. In this direction, extensive research and development are underway in many countries [10]. Some signal

A. Karpov et al. (Eds.): SPECOM 2023, LNAI 14338, pp. 189–199, 2023.
https://doi.org/10.1007/978-3-031-48309-7_16

processing research areas in smart vehicle technologies include modeling driver behavior, driver monitoring, in-vehicle interactive dialog system, noise control, etc. [10]. For these applications, the automatic detection of the While-Driving Speech (WDS) of the driver is an essential pre-processing task. Detecting WDS is very challenging due to the presence of high-intensity background noises like street noise, car engine noise, vibration noises, bubble noise, etc. [11,16]. This paper attempts to detect WDS in a continuous audio signal recorded in natural driving scenarios.

1.1 Related Works

Researchers have shown interest in investigating various aspects of a driver's speech. In a study by Wood et al. (2004), they utilized data from a DriveSafety simulator to identify cognitive workload in drivers. Drivers were asked to have four conversational interactions ($\approx$3 min each) in intense and neutral modes. Different speech features, such as average and standard deviation of F_0, pause, and speech segment durations, were used to analyze and differentiate neutral conversations from intense conversations [26]. Bořil et al. [5] studied frustration and cognitive overload in driver's speech, collected from a set of 68 subjects (33 females and 35 males) from UTDrive database [2]. UTDrive corpus contains speech signals recorded from real driving sessions. Bořil et al. [5] conducted a study on the emotional states of drivers, focusing on neutral and negative emotions only. Bořil et al. [5] also examined the drivers' interactions with their co-driver, analyzing changes in speech production features. These features included fundamental frequency (F_0), the first four formant frequencies in voiced speech segments, spectral energy spread, spectral center of gravity, spectral slope, and duration of the voiced segment. These speech features were considered as indicators of cognitive load tasks. Bořil et al. [5] also attempted two classification tasks: distinguishing between neutral and negative emotions, and differentiating between interactions with a co-driver and interactions with an automated dialog system.

Sathyanarayana et al. [22] studied the effect of in-vehicle speech on driver's distraction. Also, an active-speech segment detection approach was proposed to identify in-vehicle speech activity. The in-vehicle speech represents any speech generated inside the vehicle, such as driver or passengers interacting with each other or over the phone, GPS instruction, radio, etc. A statistical voice activity detector was used in combination with a pitch tracker. The pitch tracker used the average magnitude difference function (AMDF). A combination of Gaussian mixture models (GMM) and Hidden Markov Models (HMM) was used for modeling the system. Sathyanarayana et al. [22] conducted a study on the impact of in-vehicle speech on driver distraction. They also proposed an approach for detecting active-speech segments to identify instances of in-vehicle speech activity. In-vehicle speech referred to any speech produced inside the vehicle, including interactions between the driver and passengers, phone conversations, GPS instructions, radio communications, and more. Sathyanarayana et al. [22] employed a statistical voice activity detector along with a pitch tracker that utilized the average magnitude difference function (AMDF). To model the system, a combination of Gaussian mixture models (GMM) and Hidden Markov Models (HMM) was utilized. Sathyanarayana et al. [22] observed that in-vehicle speech increases driver distraction when the driver is already occupied with a secondary task. The same research group [23] extended their previous work [22] by studying driver involvement in in-vehicle speech activities. They considered overlapped speech to represent competitive interactions in which the driver is also a participant. To detect overlapped speech, Shokouhi et al. [23] employed various features, including Average Spectral Aperiodicity, Kurtosis, Spectral Flatness Measure, and Mel Frequency Cepstral Coefficients (MFCC). These features were used in conjunction with GMM-based modeling to identify instances of overlapped speech during driving situations. Shokouhi et al. [23] identified a connection between the amount of overlapped speech regions and driver performance. Additionally, Some works have also investigated and employed driver's emotion recognition in analyzing driver performance [14]. Martelaro et al. [15] shared their experiences with a speech-based in-car assistant designed to assist drivers in completing complex tasks. Martelaro et al. [15] utilized data recorded in a STISIM simulator equipped with a large LCD screen as part of the experimental setup.

1.2 Motivation

The majority of previous research utilized data recorded in simulated driving conditions [5,10,15]. However, only a few studies employed data recorded from real driving scenarios, such as the UTDrive database [2]. The few existing corpora collected in real scenarios required multiple costly devices (or sensors), which are generally not installed into vehicles [14]. Additionally, such datasets are recorded with a specific task in mind, leading to a constrained scope. Therefore, there is a lacuna of freely available, natural, and free-style driver's speech datasets for research purposes [10].

Additionally, automatic detection of the driver's speech in real driving scenarios becomes a crucial prepossessing task for many applications such as driver's stress, cognitive load, and distraction detection. Before delving into the analysis and processing of extensive real driving data, it is essential to examine the data at a detailed and micro level [10]. To address these limitations, this study makes the following contributions:

1. The present work introduces a corpus of Natural and Real Driving Speech, which consists of speech signals recorded during real driving scenarios.
2. An analysis for while-driving speech (WDS) vs. non-driving speech (NDS) is presented using speech features, namely, F_0, ratio of mean and standard deviation of auto-correlation of onset strength envelope, spectral bandwidth, and spectral roll-off.
3. Further, a classification of WDS vs. NDS is attempted using MFCC, openS-MILE feature set, X-vectors, and Wav2vec 2.0 embeddings, using Random Forest (RF), Support Vector Machines (SVM) and Deep Neural Network (DNN) classifiers.

2   Natural and Real Driving Speech Corpus

This work contributes a manually annotated driver's speech corpus named Natural and Real Driving (NRD)-Speech Corpus. This work attempts to circumvent the challenges and costs involved in collecting driver's speech as experienced by previous researchers. Recruiting volunteers to record their speech while driving in a simulated or real environment might compromise the quality of the signal captured. Such simulated situations may not represent real scenarios when drivers speak without hesitation. This work proposes a way of obtaining real driver's speech in a surrogate manner, as described next.

There is an under-utilized resource available that can be mined to obtain real driver's speech without any simulation involved. Many car review platforms hire media presenters to review newly launched car models. The presenters provide a detailed review of the car specifications, including the driving experience in those cars. In such videos, the presenter's voice is recorded in driving mode without any instructions relating to data collection. Hence, such data may contain real characteristics of the driver's speech. In this work, such car review videos are collected and manually annotated into WDS and NDS. Audio data is extracted from the car review videos downloaded from YouTube. The audio contains the driver's speech while driving in a real environment and voice-over speech recorded in a clean ambiance. The speech while driving is considered as *WDS* category. The rest of the speech in the dataset is referred to as *NDS* category in this paper. The NRD-Speech Corpus is created from 12 car review videos of two male presenters and one female presenter (4 videos each). The dataset size is approximately 2 h and 7 min, with the amount of WDS being about 35 min. This study is in its early stages, aiming to conduct an initial investigation into the relationship between cognitive load and driving. Therefore, we can presume that the dataset size is satisfactory for the present scope of the research. The link to access the dataset will be shared upon acceptance of the paper.

3   Characteristics of Driver's Speech

When a person drives a car and simultaneously engages in speech-related tasks like talking on the phone or conversing with a passenger, their speech is referred to as a While-Driving Speech (WDS). In such situations, the driver's attention is divided between recognizing obstacles on the road and comprehending the ongoing conversation. Consequently, it can be reasonably assumed that the speech produced by the driver in such a context will differ from their regular speech. This section examines these differences by analyzing speech signal characteristics, namely pitch, tempo, spectral spread, and roll-off.

The first characteristic used to analyze the difference between WDS and normal speech is pitch. The histograms of different pitch frequencies (F_0) obtained from WDS and normal speech are illustrated in Fig. 1(a). It may be noted that since the dataset consists of both male and female speakers, F_0 values range from $[\approx 50 \ldots \approx 200]$ Hz. As the signals being analyzed cover diverse noise conditions,

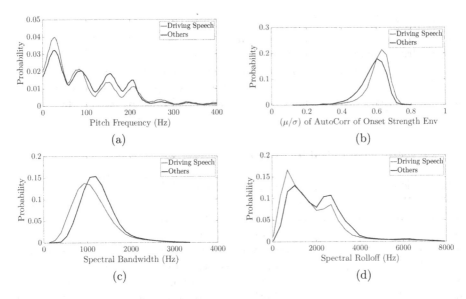

Fig. 1. Histogram plots of various prosodic and spectral features illustrating the different distributions of WDS and NDS. (Color figure online)

voice activity detection is not conducted before computing the frame-wise F0 values. Therefore, the resulting curves should be regarded as representing a noisy distribution of F0 values. It may be observed that the F_0 values for WDS tend to frequent at the comparatively lower end of the spectrum than the normal speech (see Fig. 1(a)). The peaks in the histogram of driving speech (green curve) is slightly shifted towards lower pitch in comparison to others class (blue curve). This pattern is consistently observed across all the F_0 values. The deviation observed here may not be stark because of the limited size of dataset. Nevertheless, the slight difference observed provides evidence for the hypothesis that WDS deviates from normal speech. It may be the case that the drivers exclude excitement in their voice to compensate for the cognitive overload during driving, leading to a slightly reduced pitch than normal.

The local tempo of speech signals used in this work has been estimated by computing Cyclic Tempograms [9]. The method computes local auto-correlations of the onset strength envelope. A measure to represent the tempo for each consecutive short-term window is proposed as a ratio of the mean (μ) and standard deviation (σ) of its autocorrelation function. The histograms of local tempo values for WDS and normal speech are illustrated in Fig. 1(b). It may be observed that the driver's speech tends to display a comparatively higher tempo than normal speech.

The spectral bandwidth and spectral roll-off point for the driver's speech and normal speech are illustrated in Fig. 1(c) and Fig. 1(d). The distribution of spectral bandwidth and roll-off point for the driver's speech tend to be lower than normal speech. These observations indicate that the spectral components of the driver's speech tend to be concentrated at the lower end of the spectrum compared to normal speech. Thus, it may be assumed that cognitive overload during driving makes the speaker lower his/her pitch (see Fig. 1(a)) and the corresponding harmonics as an involuntary reaction to diverted attention.

The characteristic differences between the driver's speech and normal speech may be utilized to distinguish them. The next section elaborates on the various approaches employed in this study for performing the classification.

4   Driving Speech Detection

This section describes the approaches explored in this initial study of distinguishing WDS from normal speech. As discussed in Sect. 3, various signal characteristics of WDS are observed to be distinct from that of normal speech. The perceptual discrimination of the two speaking states may be comparatively easier for humans. However, constructing systems for efficient automatic classification of these two speaking states might not be as straightforward. This study explores and utilizes four feature extraction strategies commonly employed in audio classification tasks in the literature. Additionally, three types of classifiers are utilized for the task at hand. The details regarding the features and classifiers used in this research are elaborated in the following subsections.

4.1   Features Sets

This work explores four standard feature sets to detect WDS. The audio signals are sampled at 16000 Hz. A short-term processing window size of 25 ms with a shift of 10 ms is chosen. The features are computed at a segment level. Various segment sizes are considered to find the optimal duration. The different features used in this work are described below.

Mel Frequency Cepstral Coefficients (MFCC). It is one of the most popular spectral features employed in different audio classification tasks, like impulse acoustic event detection [25], sentiment analysis from speech [18], voice assistant systems [1], and others. Yin et al. [27] have also employed MFCCs for detecting cognitive load from speech. MFCCs represent the vocal tract characteristics of the speaker. Since the speech signal produced while driving is expected to differ from normal speech, MFCC features (F_M) may help discriminate the speaking states.

OpenSMILE Functionals Features. The OpenSMILE toolkit [7] is a popular open-source library to extract common speech features. The toolkit can extract features at the short-term window level (low-level descriptors) or segment level (functionals). The toolkit has been previously used in multiple audio processing tasks, like emotion recognition [6], fake speech detection [12], detecting paralinguistic cues in speech [3], and others. This work explores the openSMILE functionals feature set (F_O) in discriminating WDS from normal speech.

Table 1. Classifier hyper-parameter tuning.

Classifier	Parameter	Range
DNN	Num layers	$[1, 2, 3, 4]$
	Num nodes	$[2^5, 2^6, 2^7, 2^8]$
SVM	Cost	$[2^{-4}, 2^{-3}, 2^{-2}, 2^{-1}, 2^0, 2^1, 2^2, 2^3, 2^4]$
	Gamma	$[2^{-4}, 2^{-3}, 2^{-2}, 2^{-1}, 2^0, 2^1, 2^2, 2^3, 2^4]$
RF	Num Trees	$[10, 20, 30, 40, 50, 60, 70, 80, 90]$
	Max Depth	$[1, 2, 3, 4, 5]$

X-Vectors Embeddings. X-Vectors were introduced by Snyder et al. [24] to provide state-of-the-art performance in text-independent speaker recognition/verification tasks. X-Vectors are deep embeddings extracted from a special type of neural network called Time-Delay Neural Networks (TDNN). X-Vectors are shown to capture speaker characteristics very well. Additionally, these features were shown to represent spoken content and channel-related information [21]. Various other audio processing tasks were also attempted using X-Vectors, like emotion recognition [19], detecting Parkinson's disease from speech [17], and others. Since X-Vectors are shown to capture speaker and channel information well, it is explored in this work (F_X) to detect WDS.

Wav2vec 2.0 Embeddings. Recently, Baevski et al. [4] published their wav2vec 2.0 model designed to learn robust representations in a self-supervised manner for better speech transcription. Subsequently, the wav2vec 2.0 model was successfully employed in emotion recognition [20], language identification [8], pronunciation assessment [13], and others. Considering the success of this model in various speech processing tasks, embeddings obtained from the original pre-trained wav2vec 2.0 model (F_{W2V}) were also explored as a feature for classifying WDS from normal speech.

4.2 Classification Setup

This work is modeled as a binary classification task to distinguish between WDS and normal speech. Three standard classifiers have been employed to perform the classification, viz. Random Forests (RF), Support Vector Machines (SVM), and Deep Neural Networks (DNN). The classifiers have some hyperparameters that must be tuned to obtain optimal performance. Table 1 lists the hyperparameters for each tuned classifier, along with the range of values tested. For the DNN classifier, the number of hidden layers and the number of hidden nodes were tuned. For the SVM classifier, the Cost and Gamma parameters were optimized. Finally, for the RF classifier, the best number of trees and their maximum depths were searched. The parameter tuning was performed on a validation set extracted from the training data. The test set was kept untouched at this stage. The

Table 2. Performance of classifying driving speech and normal speech. F_{All} indicates the combination of the different feature sets. The best performance is highlighted as **bold**, while the second best is highlighted with an <u>underline</u>.

Classifier	Feature	Metric	500 ms	1 s	3 s	5 s	10 s
DNN	F_M	Accuracy	41.76	44.95	37.82	37.59	50.77
		F1-score	40.51	44.71	37.74	37.43	47.92
	F_O	Accuracy	52.03	43.30	32.80	41.07	55.45
		F1-score	44.44	43.02	31.99	38.85	51.36
	F_X	Accuracy	43.45	56.59	58.24	60.13	45.52
		F1-score	38.61	53.58	53.81	55.74	39.58
	F_{W2V}	Accuracy	46.73	50.54	67.20	37.76	35.03
		F1-score	45.57	46.16	53.72	37.76	34.96
	F_{All}	Accuracy	62.39	42.33	52.14	42.16	59.90
		F1-score	57.82	41.16	50.47	42.04	55.90
SVM	F_M	Accuracy	74.53	74.39	73.36	74.44	73.19
		F1-score	66.98	66.94	65.17	66.22	63.62
	F_O	Accuracy	73.50	76.55	77.18	76.95	78.49
		F1-score	62.09	64.69	64.60	65.60	61.22
	F_X	Accuracy	74.10	74.04	74.04	74.04	74.04
		F1-score	43.52	42.54	42.54	42.54	42.54
	F_{W2V}	Accuracy	66.91	67.20	69.31	70.51	71.36
		F1-score	53.40	54.50	57.26	58.60	59.20
	F_{All}	Accuracy	74.10	74.04	74.04	74.04	74.04
		F1-score	42.56	42.54	42.54	42.54	42.54
RF	F_M	Accuracy	74.94	74.84	72.85	70.62	66.40
		F1-score	58.77	61.18	60.39	59.72	53.32
	F_O	Accuracy	<u>78.01</u>	**80.09**	**80.43**	**79.12**	**79.01**
		F1-score	**71.10**	**74.96**	**75.94**	**75.10**	**75.72**
	F_X	Accuracy	73.93	73.76	<u>80.15</u>	<u>77.47</u>	<u>78.15</u>
		F1-score	47.35	54.12	<u>72.54</u>	70.54	73.63
	F_{W2V}	Accuracy	74.10	73.99	73.93	74.22	75.07
		F1-score	42.56	42.52	43.55	43.24	49.46
	F_{All}	Accuracy	**78.68**	<u>78.78</u>	76.38	76.78	77.35
		F1-score	<u>69.10</u>	<u>72.47</u>	71.00	<u>71.82</u>	<u>74.21</u>

classification results on the unseen test set, as reported in Table 2, are obtained using the optimized classifier parameters. The classification results are discussed in the next subsection.

4.3 Performance Analysis

The classification results presented in Table 2 are computed for the unseen test set. In addition to the individual feature sets (see Subsect. 4.1), the study also reports results for an early-fusion combination of all feature sets. The performance metrics used for evaluation are accuracy and F1-score. It is important to note that the contributed dataset has a notable imbalance between the two categories. Consequently, using accuracy alone may not accurately reflect the true performance. Instead, F1-score is employed, as it takes into account the imbalance in the data by considering the harmonic mean of precision and recall values.

Few observations may be derived from the results presented in Table 2. First, the combination of the openSMILE feature set and the RF classifier emerges as the most effective in classifying WDS from normal speech. Second, the RF classifier outperforms the DNN and SVM classifiers. This could be attributed to the DNN classifier being hindered by insufficient data for training the model. Third, X-Vectors exhibit the second-best performance after the openSMILE features, suggesting that speech features and speaker representations play a crucial role in detecting WDS. Fourth, while there is no prominent trend in the performance with increasing segment sizes, most improved performances are achieved with 1s and 3s segments.

The above analysis of the driver's speech detection performance indicates that the current proposal has some significant shortcomings that must be addressed. First, the data collected is insufficient to train decent classifier models, and therefore, the dataset should be expanded in future research. Second, better performance may be obtained with the X-Vectors and wav2vec 2.0 features if the pre-trained models for extracting the embeddings are fine-tuned on the WDS dataset. Nevertheless, the present work provides some insights into the challenges of detecting a driver's speech. Additionally, the contributed dataset might spark interest within the research community and encourage innovative approaches to address this problem.

5   Conclusions

This work represents an initial attempt to detect While-Driving Speech (WDS) in real driving scenarios. Additionally, the research contributes a corpus containing speech data recorded during natural driving situations. A comparative analysis is conducted between WDS and regular speech using various features, including F_0, the ratio of mean and standard deviation of autocorrelation of onset strength envelope, spectral bandwidth, and spectral roll-off. Slight differences in the distribution of these features are observed for both speech classes.

Furthermore, WDS and normal speech are classified using different sets of features, including MFCC, openSMILE feature set, X-vectors, and Wav2vec 2.0 embeddings, with three classifiers. The combination of the openSMILE feature set and the Random Forest classifier yields the best performance. In the future, the dataset contributed in this work will be expanded with additional manually labeled videos, enhancing its utility for further research and development.

References

1. Ahmed, S.F., Jaffari, R., Jawaid, M., Ahmed, S.S., Talpur, S.: An MFCC-based secure framework for voice assistant systems. In: International Conference on Cyber Warfare and Security (ICCWS), pp. 57–61 (2022). https://doi.org/10.1109/ICCWS56285.2022.9998446
2. Angkititrakul, P., Petracca, M., Sathyanarayana, A., Hansen, J.H.: UTDrive: driver behavior and speech interactive systems for in-vehicle environments. In: 2007 IEEE Intelligent Vehicles Symposium, pp. 566–569 (2007)
3. Ashok, A., Pawlak, J., Paplu, S., Zafar, Z., Berns, K.: Paralinguistic cues in speech to adapt robot behavior in human-robot interaction. In: 9th IEEE RAS/EMBS International Conference for Biomedical Robotics and Biomechatronics (BioRob), pp. 1–6 (2022)
4. Baevski, A., Zhou, Y., Mohamed, A., Auli, M.: wav2vec 2.0: a framework for self-supervised learning of speech representations. Adv. Neural Inf. Process. Syst. **33**, 12449–12460 (2020)
5. Bořil, H., Sadjadi, S.O., Kleinschmidt, T., Hansen, J.H.L.: Analysis and detection of cognitive load and frustration in drivers' speech. In: Interspeech, pp. 502–505 (2010)
6. Devi, C.A., Renuka, D.K.: Multimodal emotion recognition framework using a decision-level fusion and feature-level fusion approach. IETE J. Res. 1–12 (2023)
7. Eyben, F., Wöllmer, M., Schuller, B.: Opensmile: the munich versatile and fast open-source audio feature extractor. In: ACM International Conference on Multimedia, pp. 1459–1462 (2010)
8. Fan, Z., Li, M., Zhou, S., Xu, B.: Exploring wav2vec 2.0 on speaker verification and language identification. arXiv preprint arXiv:2012.06185 (2020)
9. Grosche, P., Müller, M., Kurth, F.: Cyclic tempogram-a mid-level tempo representation for music signals. In: IEEE International Conference on Acoustics, Speech and Signal Process (ICASSP), pp. 5522–5525. IEEE (2010)
10. Hansen, J.H., Busso, C., Zheng, Y., Sathyanarayana, A.: Driver modeling for detection and assessment of driver distraction: examples from the UTDrive test bed. IEEE Signal Process. Maga. **34**(4), 130–142 (2017)
11. Kristjansson, T., Deligne, S., Olsen, P.: Voicing features for robust speech detection. In: Interspeech, pp. 369–372 (2005)
12. Kumar, D., Patil, P.K.V., Agarwal, A., Prasanna, S.R.M.: Fake speech detection using OpenSMILE features. In: Prasanna, S.R.M., Karpov, A., Samudravijaya, K., Agrawal, S.S. (eds.) SPECOM 2022. LNCS, vol. 13721, pp. 404–415. Springer, Cham (2022). https://doi.org/10.1007/978-3-031-20980-2_35
13. Lin, B., Wang, L.: Exploiting information from native data for non-native automatic pronunciation assessment. In: IEEE Spoken Language Technology Workshop (SLT), pp. 708–714 (2023)

14. Liu, S., et al.: The empathetic car: exploring emotion inference via driver behaviour and traffic context. In: Proceedings of the ACM on Interactive, Mobile, Wearable and Ubiquitous Technologies, vol. 5, no. 3, pp. 1–34 (2021)
15. Martelaro, N., Teevan, J., Iqbal, S.T.: An exploration of speech-based productivity support in the car. In: CHI Conference on Human Factors in Computing Systems, CHI 2019, pp. 1–12. Association for Computing Machinery, New York (2019)
16. Moreno, A., et al.: SPEECHDAT-CAR: a large speech database for automotive environments. In: 2nd International Conference on Language Resources and Evaluation (LREC), pp. 1–6 (2000)
17. Moro-Velazquez, L., Villalba, J., Dehak, N.: Using X-vectors to automatically detect Parkinson's disease from speech. In: IEEE International Conference on Acoustics, Speech and Signal Processing (ICASSP), pp. 1155–1159 (2020)
18. Murugaiyan, S., Uyyala, S.R.: Aspect-based sentiment analysis of customer speech data using deep convolutional neural network and BiLSTM. Cogn. Comput. 1–18 (2023)
19. Pappagari, R., Wang, T., Villalba, J., Chen, N., Dehak, N.: X-vectors meet emotions: a study on dependencies between emotion and speaker recognition. In: IEEE International Conference on Acoustics, Speech and Signal Processing (ICASSP), pp. 7169–7173 (2020)
20. Pepino, L., Riera, P., Ferrer, L.: Emotion recognition from speech using wav2vec 2.0 embeddings. In: Interspeech, pp. 3400–3404 (2021)
21. Raj, D., Snyder, D., Povey, D., Khudanpur, S.: Probing the information encoded in X-vectors. In: IEEE Automatic Speech Recognition and Understanding Workshop (ASRU), pp. 726–733 (2019)
22. Sathyanarayana, A., Sadjadi, S.O., Hansen, J.H.L.: Leveraging speech-active regions towards active safety in vehicles. In: IEEE International Conference on Emerging Signal Processing Applications, pp. 48–51 (2012)
23. Shokouhi, N., Sathyanarayana, A., Sadjadi, S.O., Hansen, J.H.: Overlapped-speech detection with applications to driver assessment for in-vehicle active safety systems. In: IEEE International Conference on Acoustics, Speech and Signal Processing (ICASSP), pp. 2834–2838 (2013)
24. Snyder, D., Garcia-Romero, D., Sell, G., Povey, D., Khudanpur, S.: X-Vectors: robust DNN embeddings for speaker recognition. In: IEEE International Conference on Acoustics, Speech and Signal Processing (ICASSP), pp. 5329–5333 (2018)
25. Svatos, J., Holub, J.: Impulse acoustic event detection, classification, and localization system. IEEE Trans. Instrument. Meas. 72, 1–15 (2023). https://doi.org/10.1109/TIM.2023.3252631
26. Wood, C., Torkkola, K., Kundalkar, S.: Using driver's speech to detect cognitive workload. In: SPECOM, pp. 215–222 (2004)
27. Yin, B., Ruiz, N., Chen, F., Khawaja, M.A.: Automatic cognitive load detection from speech features. In: 19th Australasian Conference on Computer-Human Interaction: Entertaining User Interfaces, OZCHI 2007, pp. 249–255. Association for Computing Machinery, New York (2007)

Regularization Based Incremental Learning in TCNN for Robust Speech Enhancement Targeting Effective Human Machine Interaction

Kamini Sabu[1]([✉]), Mukesh Sharma[1], Nitya Tiwari[2], and M. Shaik[1]

[1] Samsung R & D Institute Bangalore, Bangalore, India
{kamini.sabu,s.chandrakan,m.shaik}@samsung.com
[2] Indian Institute of Technology Bhubaneswar, Bhubaneswar, India
nityatiwari@iitbbs.ac.in

Abstract. In general, the performance of deep learning based speech enhancement degrades in presence of unseen noisy environments for any signal-to-noise ratio (SNR) conditions. Although model adaptation techniques may help in improving the performance, they lead to catastrophic forgetting of the previously learned knowledge. Under such conditions, incremental learning or life-long learning has been reported to help in gradually learning the new tasks while maintaining the existing inferred knowledge. In this work, we propose a regularization-based incremental learning strategy for adapting temporal convolutional neural network (TCNN) based speech enhancement novel framework named as RIL-TCN. We investigate the effect of incorporating various weight regularization strategies such as curvature and path regularization on time-domain Scale-Invariant SNR (SI-SNR) loss function associated with TCNN based enhancement framework. We evaluate and compare the performance of our proposed model with the state-of-the-art frequency domain incremental learning model using objective measures such as SI-SNR and PESQ (Perceptual Evaluation of Speech Quality). We show that our proposed approach outperforms on unseen noises from standard CHiME-3 corpus compared to competitive TCNN baseline.

Keywords: Speech Enhancement · Incremental Learning · Life-Long Learning · Adaptation · TCN

1 Introduction

With the advent of various speech applications such as voice assistants, conversational dialogue systems, smart appliances, automotives, etc., the accurate human speech recognition has become more and more important irrespective of background noise conditions [8,19,24]. The multimedia applications further require that the voice/audio fed to human ears should be without any traces of perceptible noise [38]. With the smart appliances being accessible anytime anywhere and entertainment modes being handy on smartphones, there is pressing need to recognize long distance commands or to suppress background noise during video conference in crowded places [38]. The background audio noise has become inevitable and an increasingly challenging problem. Speech enhancement by suppression of background noise plays an important role in improving human speech perception [20, 38] and automatic speech recognition [24] across noisy environments. Several signal processing based noise suppression algorithms [5, 6, 31] have been proposed earlier. These generally involve estimation of noise statistics from the noisy speech signal and using it for estimating a gain function to obtain enhanced speech signal. Performance of these algorithms is dependent on the noise estimation. An under-estimation of noise results in residual noise whereas over-estimation causes speech distortions. An estimation of noise statistics is generally based on certain assumptions made for clean speech and noisy speech distributions. Therefore, the signal processing based speech enhancement methods perform poorly when these assumptions are not valid.

More recently, supervised deep learning based speech enhancement techniques that use parallel noisy and clean speech data for enhancement have been proposed [21, 29, 30]. These speech enhancement techniques learn speech and noise characteristics from the training data without making any assumptions about speech and noise distributions. They generally carry out enhancement using a forward transformation to the time-frequency (T-F) representation, mask estimation, and obtaining an enhanced T-F representation to resynthesize the time domain output using inverse transformation. These methods use ideal binary mask (IBM) or ideal ratio mask (IRM) or fast fourier transform (FFT) mask as training targets [34]. However, these techniques enhance only the spectral magnitude while retaining the noisy phase. This may lead to perceptual roughness in the processed output due to disassociation of the enhanced magnitude and noisy phase [11, 25]. The accurate phase information also helps with improved speech recognition accuracy leading to efficient human-machine interaction. For a combined magnitude and phase enhancement, time domain speech enhancement from raw waveform using deep neural networks with encoder-decoder based architecture have been proposed in [7, 12, 14]. A temporal convolutional network (TCN) was used between encoder and decoder to obtain enhanced representation in [27]. TCNN using 2-D convolutional encoder-decoder layers with skip connections and TCN to directly obtain the enhanced representation was reported in [28]. Inspired from [27] and [28], a multilayer encoder-decoder based architecture with a TCN-based gain function estimator for speech enhancement has been proposed in [16].

Although, deep learning based speech enhancement techniques perform well when the characteristics of noise in the test data is similar to that used in training, the performance degrades in presence of unseen noisy environments [32, 37]. Direct fine-tuning of a pre-trained model for adaptation to new noises and to improve the performance in a target domain has been proposed in [3, 35]. However, direct adaptation to a new environment generally leads to "catastrophic forgetting" of the previously learned environments. Incremental learning or life-long learning aims at gradually learning the new tasks while maintaining the existing knowledge [4,9]. A regularization-based incremental learning strategy for adapting speech enhancement model has been proposed in [18] to improve the performance for new noise environments while maintaining the performance on previously learned noise types. Curvature-based regularization [15] and path optimization augmenting approach [36] were used for obtaining the regularization terms. The technique involved use of time-frequency (T-F) representation and regularization of frequency domain signal-to-distortion ratio loss function. However, the effect of these regularization strategies has not been studied for time-domain speech enhancement models and loss functions.

Following sections present the speech enhancement framework, regularization based incremental learning strategy, evaluation and comparison with state-of-the-art techniques, and conclusions.

2   Proposed Speech Enhancement Framework

Figure 1 shows the proposed architecture that uses multilayer encoder-decoder and TCN for speech enhancement. Multilayer encoder and decoder helps learn long-range dependencies, while TCN separator obtains the enhanced speech mask. The mask multiplied with noisy encoded representation results in enhanced encoded representation, which is finally transformed by the decoder to an enhanced time-domain output. The encoder-decoder layers use 1-D convolutional operations. Earlier investigations using objective measures and t-SNE (t-distributed stochastic neighbor embedding) analysis in [16] showed that a two-layer encoder-decoder architecture results in a noise-independent representation appropriate for speech enhancement. Thus, we use two-layer encoder-decoder architecture.

We divide the noisy input into overlapping frames with M samples and a shift of S samples. The first encoder layer applies a linear transformation and transforms input frame with M samples to a representation with N samples. The second layer applies a non-linear transformation using N kernels of size 3 and parametric rectified linear unit (PReLU) as the activation function. For mask estimation, we use TCN separator consisting of stacks of eight convolutional blocks with dilation factors of 1, 2, 4, ..., and 128. Three such stacks are concatenated to capture long-range dependencies without a significant increase in model size. The encoded noisy input multiplied with mask estimated using TCN is given as input to the decoder. The decoder consists of the same number of non-linear convolutional layers as used in the encoder and a final linear transformation layer that converts N-sample representation to M-sample time-domain output. The enhanced output is resynthesized using overlap-add procedure.

3   Regularization Strategy for Incremental Learning

Weight regularization strategy involves using a special regularization term, generally added to the loss function, with an objective to mitigate the catastrophic

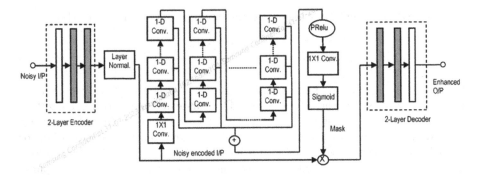

Fig. 1. Time-domain enhancement model with 2-layer encoder-decoder and TCN for mask estimation (adapted from [16]).

forgetting. It involves constraining the update of weight parameters that contribute more for the previous task so that the model can retain some of the previous knowledge while acquiring new knowledge. We use regularization term obtained as the weighted average of curvature-based regularization [15] and path optimization augmenting approach [36] as described in [18].

In the curvature based regularization strategy, the loss function is formulated as:

$$L^t(\theta) = L_{new}(\theta) + \lambda \Sigma_i F_{\theta_i} (\theta_i^t - \theta_i^{t-1})^2 \tag{1}$$

where L^t is the total loss for t^{th} task, L_{new} is the loss in the new environment, θ_i^t and θ_i^{t-1} are the ith parameters in the current and the previous environments, λ is a hyperparameter, and F_{θ_i} is the diagonal element of the Hessian matrix of the previous loss L_{old} for old parameters θ^{t-1}.

While curvature based regularization strategy captures local curvature information around θ^*, path optimization-based approach uses the information over the optimization path on the loss surface. For a task t, the path optimization augmenting approach involves use of importance scores in the regularization term. The importance score is given as:

$$S_{\theta_i}^t = \Sigma_{t' < t} \frac{\Delta L_i t'}{\Delta \theta_i^{t'2} + \epsilon} \tag{2}$$

where t' are the tasks previous to task t, $\theta_i^{t'}$ is the ith parameter of the model trained on t', $\Delta \theta_i^{t'} = \theta_i^{t'} - \theta_i^{t'-1}$, $\Delta L_i t'$ is the derivative of loss $L^{t'}$ with respect to i^{th} parameter $\theta_i^{t'}$, and ϵ is a positive valued hyperparameter. A weighted average of curvature and path regularization terms is used to obtain the average loss.

$$\bar{L\theta}_i^t = L^t(\theta) + \frac{\lambda}{2}(F_{\theta_i}^t + S_{\theta_i}^t)(\theta_i^t - \theta_i^{t-1})^2 \tag{3}$$

The speech enhancement model based on TCN uses scale-invariant signal-to-noise ratio (SI-SNR) as objective function for training with Adam [13] optimizer.

The SI-SNR loss function for the proposed speech enhancement model is calculated as:

$$SI - SNR = 10log_{10}\frac{||(<s', s>s)/||s||^2||^2}{||s' - s||^2} \tag{4}$$

where s' is the estimated enhanced speech signal, s is the target clean speech signal, $<s, s> = ||s||^2$ is the signal power. The curvature and path regularization strategies have been explored earlier in the context of speech enhancement [18] for a frequency domain loss function. Here, we carry out the investigation for time-domain SI-SNR loss, as it would indicate the effect of weight regularization on a speech enhancement model aiming at combined magnitude and phase enhancement.

4   Experiments

The experiments for speech enhancement were carried out using a pre-train dataset (D0) and four adaptation datasets (D1, D2, D3, D4). The corresponding pre-trained model and regularized models are M0 and (M1, M2, M3, M4). Both datasets used clean speech from "train-clean-360" subset of publicly available Librispeech [26] dataset. The noisy mixtures in the pre-train dataset were generated using babble, cafeteria, pedestrian, and street noises from CHiME-3 [2] dataset at 0, 5, and 10 dB SNRs. To evaluate the speech enhancement models in presence of unseen noisy environments, the noisy mixtures in the adaptation datasets were created at 0, 5, and 10 dB SNRs using four noises from Demand dataset [33]: office noise for D1, living room noise for D2, kitchen noise for D3, and washing noise for D4. The pre-train dataset consisted of 544, 68, and 68 h of train, validation, and test data, respectively. Each adaptation dataset was much smaller and consisted of 17, 5, and 5 h of train, validation, and test data, respectively.

Earlier investigations on class incremental learning have showed a significant effect of class ordering on the performance [22]. Metrics such as class confusion matrix have been used earlier to order the classes for class incremental learning tasks. In the current investigation, there are no new classes to add to the output. Instead, we propose to use Jensen-Shannon divergence [23] between the distribution of clean data and the distributions of the noisy adaptation data for deciding the order of adaptation. Jensen-Shannon divergence is a symmetric measure based on Kullback-Leibler divergence and it measures similarity between two probability distributions. The scores for office, living room, kitchen, and washing noise were 6.0×10^{-2}, 4.9×10^{-2}, 5.3×10^{-2}, and 6.8×10^{-2}, respectively. As a lower Jensen-Shannon divergence score indicates higher similarity between distributions, the order of adaptation data was chosen as D2, D3, D1, and D4. Therefore, the models M2, M3, M1, and M4 represent the M0 model adapted on {D2}, {D2, D3}, {D2, D3, D1}, and {D2, D3, D1, D4} respectively. The objective scores for models adapted using Jensen-Shannon divergence metrics were in general better than those obtained from random ordering.

The proposed speech enhancement framework used causal convolutions. The network parameters were chosen as L = 16, S = 8, and N = 128. For training, the learning rate was initially set as 10^{-3} and was halved every 3 epochs for no change in validation SI-SNR. For pre-trained model, the training was carried out till the validation SI-SNR reached 13 dB, or for 200 epochs, whichever was achieved earlier. The training was carried out for 30 epochs for regularized models. The LSTM-based speech enhancement using regularization based incremental learning (SERIL) [18] was used as baseline. The parameters and the training epochs were chosen according to [17]. Directly fine-tuned version of TCN based architecture [16] was used as the baseline, to evaluate the performance in terms of catastrophic forgetting effect. The performance evaluation was carried out using objective measure of speech quality PESQ [1] and scale-invariant source-to-noise ratio for enhanced outputs.

5 Results

Initial evaluation was carried out using SI-SNR measure. To analyze the effect of regularization based incremental learning on TCN based time-domain speech enhancement framework (RIL-TCN). Table 1 shows average SI-SNR scores for five models (M0, M1, M2, M3, M4) and for four adaptation datasets (D1, D2, D3, D4). It can be seen from the table that the scores for all the adapted models are higher than M0. Further, model Mi gives the highest SI-SNR scores (given in bold) for the datasets Di i.e. the last dataset used for adaptation of ith model. M4 model adapted using all four adaptation datasets results in higher overall SI-SNR scores considering all datasets.

Table 1. SI-SNR scores averaged over 0, 5, 10 dB SNR for five RIL-TCN models (M0, M1, M2, M3, M4) and for four adaptation datasets (D1, D2, D3, D4)

	D1	D2	D3	D4
M0	7.68	6.72	8.78	7.50
M1	**14.60**	9.78	10.95	10.47
M2	8.30	**12.94**	7.87	10.66
M3	13.64	7.23	**12.87**	10.07
M4	12.05	11.82	11.19	**14.00**

The TCN-based architecture uses the time-domain SI-SNR as loss function whereas the baseline SERIL uses frequency-domain signal-to-distortion ratio as the loss function. PESQ was used as objective measure for comparing their performance. Table 2 shows the average PESQ scores five models (M0, M1, M2, M3, M4) and for four adaptation datasets (D1, D2, D3, D4) calculated for proposed RIL-TCN architecture and SERIL baseline architecture. Considering all models

Table 2. PESQ scores averaged over 0, 5, 10 dB SNR for five models (M0, M1, M2, M3, M4) and four adaptation datasets (D1, D2, D3, D4) calculated for proposed TCN-based architecture (RIL-TCN) and SERIL baseline architecture.

	RIL-TCN (Proposed)				SERIL [18]			
	D1	D2	D3	D4	D1	D2	D3	D4
M0	3.63	**3.71**	2.99	3.30	3.21	3.29	2.68	2.87
M1	**3.67**	3.55	2.59	3.36	3.45	3.55	2.71	2.99
M2	3.66	3.59	2.56	3.27	3.30	3.50	2.57	2.91
M3	3.54	3.68	**3.05**	3.41	3.49	3.57	2.98	3.12
M4	3.57	3.44	2.66	**3.53**	3.49	3.63	2.82	3.27

Table 3. PESQ and SI-SNR scores averaged over 0, 5, 10 dB SNR for RIL-TCN pre-trained model M0, model M4, and directly fine-tuned model (FT) on dataset D0.

Metrics	RIL-TCN (Proposed)			SERIL [18]		
	M0	M4	FT	M0	M4	FT
PESQ	2.67	2.14	1.90	2.56	2.29	2.10
SI-SNR	12.25	8.57	6.60	12.53	10.43	6.71

and adaptation noise datasets, RIL-TCN architecture has higher PESQ scores than SERIL baseline.

The PESQ and SI-SNR scores were obtained for pre-train test dataset D0 using pre-trained model M0 and the model M4, for evaluating the performance of RIL-TCN in terms of catastrophic forgetting effect. The scores were also obtained using directly fine-tuned model (FT). The average PESQ and SI-SNR scores are given in Table 3. The scores for M4 are lower than M0 but higher than FT, indicating that incremental learning using weight regularization results in optimal model weight adjustment to minimize the forgetting effect as compared to direct fine-tuning. The scores for SERIL are also shown in Table 3. It was observed that scores for SERIL model obtained using pre-train test dataset D0 are in general higher than RIL-TCN. This indicates that the frequency-domain speech enhancement framework results in higher improvement for noises from CHiME-3 dataset used for creating D0. However, the time-domain enhancement framework is suitable for the noises from Demand dataset. Thus, there is a need for investigating a speech enhancement framework that combines time and frequency domain losses for improving performance in presence of different noisy environments. Architectures like TFCN (Temporal-Frequential Convolutional Network) could also be tried [10].

6   Conclusions

We proposed a regularization based incremental learning strategy for adapting time-domain TCN based speech enhancement model. It aims to improve the performance for new noise environments while maintaining the performance on previously trained noises. The TCN model gives around 13% better PESQ scores compared to the architecture used in SERIL. The RIL strategy tends to improve the performance for both SERIL and RIL-TCN. The SI-SNR scores for model M4 tuned on more diverse data are higher than the model FT tuned only on the same domain data by 2–3 dB. This indicates the benefit of RIL strategy not only in the diminished forgetting effect, but also in the more well-regularized training avoiding the over-fitting. To the best of our knowledge, this work is the first attempt to perform regularization based incremental learning using TCNN framework for robust speech enhancement. Thus, future work involves investigation using combined time and frequency domain losses for improving performance in presence of different noise environments.

References

1. Perceptual evaluation of speech quality (pesq): An objective method for end-to-end speech quality assessment of narrow-band telephone networks and speech codecs, rec. itu-t p. 86 (2001)
2. Barker, J., Marxer, R., Vincent, E., Watanabe, S.: The third 'chime' speech separation and recognition challenge: dataset, task and baselines. In: 2015 IEEE Workshop on Automatic Speech Recognition and Understanding (ASRU), pp. 504–511 (2015). https://doi.org/10.1109/ASRU.2015.7404837
3. Biswas, R., Nathwani, K., Abrol, V.: Transfer learning for speech intelligibility improvement in noisy environments. In: Proceedings of the Interspeech 2021, pp. 176–180 (2021). https://doi.org/10.21437/Interspeech.2021-150
4. Choy, M.C., Srinivasan, D., Cheu, R.L.: Neural networks for continuous online learning and control. IEEE Trans. Neural Networks 17(6), 1511–1531 (2006). https://doi.org/10.1109/TNN.2006.881710
5. Cohen, I.: Noise spectrum estimation in adverse environments: improved minima controlled recursive averaging. IEEE Trans. Speech Audio Process. 11(5), 466–475 (2003). https://doi.org/10.1109/TSA.2003.811544
6. Ephraim, Y., Malah, D.: Speech enhancement using a minimum-mean square error short-time spectral amplitude estimator. IEEE Trans. Acoust. Speech Signal Process. 32(6), 1109–1121 (1984). https://doi.org/10.1109/TASSP.1984.1164453
7. Fu, S.W., Tsao, Y., Lu, X., Kawai, H.: Raw waveform-based speech enhancement by fully convolutional networks. In: 2017 Asia-Pacific Signal and Information Processing Association Annual Summit and Conference (APSIPA ASC), pp. 006–012 (2017). https://doi.org/10.1109/APSIPA.2017.8281993
8. Gnanamanickam, J., Natarajan, Y., Sri Preethaa, K.R.: A hybrid speech enhancement algorithm for voice assistance application. Sensors (Basel) 21(21), 7025 (2021). https://doi.org/10.3390/s21217025

9. Goodfellow, I.J., Mirza, M., Da, X., Courville, A.C., Bengio, Y.: An empirical investigation of catastrophic forgeting in gradient-based neural networks. In: Bengio, Y., LeCun, Y. (eds.) 2nd International Conference on Learning Representations, ICLR 2014, Banff, AB, Canada, April 14–16, 2014, Conference Track Proceedings (2014). https://arxiv.org/abs/1312.6211

10. Jia, X., Li, D.: TFCN: temporal-frequential convolutional network for single-channel speech enhancement. arXiv (2022)

11. Kim, D., Han, H., Shin, H.K., Chung, S.W., Kang, H.G.: Phase continuity: Learning derivatives of phase spectrum for speech enhancement. In: ICASSP 2022–2022 IEEE International Conference on Acoustics, Speech and Signal Processing (ICASSP), pp. 6942–6946 (2022). https://doi.org/10.1109/ICASSP43922.2022.9746087

12. Kim, J.H., Yoo, J., Chun, S., Kim, A., Ha, J.W.: Multi-domain processing via hybrid denoising networks for speech enhancement. arXiv (2018)

13. Kingma, D.P., Ba, J.: Adam: a method for stochastic optimization. In: 3rd International Conference on Learning Representations, ICLR 2015, San Diego, CA, USA, May 7–9, 2015, Conference Track Proceedings (2015)., https://arxiv.org/abs/1412.6980

14. Kinoshita, K., Ochiai, T., Delcroix, M., Nakatani, T.: Improving noise robust automatic speech recognition with single-channel time-domain enhancement network. In: ICASSP 2020–2020 IEEE International Conference on Acoustics, Speech and Signal Processing (ICASSP), pp. 7009–7013 (2020). https://doi.org/10.1109/ICASSP40776.2020.9053266

15. Kirkpatrick, J., et al.: Overcoming catastrophic forgetting in neural networks. Proc. Natl. Acad. Sci. 114(13), 3521–3526 (2017). https://doi.org/10.1073/pnas.1611835114

16. Kishore, V., Tiwari, N., Paramasivam, P.: improved speech enhancement using TCN with multiple encoder-decoder layers. In: Proceedings of the Interspeech, 2020, pp. 4531–4535 (2020). https://doi.org/10.21437/Interspeech.2020-3122

17. Lee, C.C.: Seril (2020). https://github.com/ChangLee0903/SERIL

18. Lee, C.C., Lin, Y.C., Lin, H.T., Wang, H.M., Tsao, Y.: SERIL: noise adaptive speech enhancement using regularization-based incremental learning. In: Proceedings of the Interspeech 2020, pp. 2432–2436 (2020). https://doi.org/10.21437/Interspeech.2020-2213

19. Lei, P., Chen, M., Wang, J.: Speech enhancement for in-vehicle voice control systems using wavelet analysis and blind source separation. IET Intel. Transport Syst. 13(4), 693–702 (2019)

20. Li, Y., Chen, F., Sun, Z., Ji, J., Jia, W., Wang, Z.: A smart binaural hearing aid architecture leveraging a smartphone app with deep-learning speech enhancement. IEEE Access 8, 56798–56810 (2020). https://doi.org/10.1109/ACCESS.2020.2982212

21. Lu, X., Tsao, Y., Matsuda, S., Hori, C.: Speech enhancement based on deep denoising autoencoder. In: Proceedings of the Interspeech 2013, pp. 436–440 (2013). https://doi.org/10.21437/Interspeech.2013-130

22. Masana, M., Twardowski, B., van de Weijer, J.: On class orderings for incremental learning (2020)

23. Menéndez, M., Pardo, J., Pardo, L., Pardo, M.: The Jensen-Shannon divergence. J. Franklin Inst. 334(2), 307–318 (1997). https://doi.org/10.1016/S0016-0032(96)00063-4

24. Nair, G.G., Kumar, C.S.: Speech enhancement system for automatic speech recognition in automotive environment. In: 2021 12th International Conference on Computing Communication and Networking Technologies (ICCCNT), pp. 01–07 (2021). https://doi.org/10.1109/ICCCNT51525.2021.9579986
25. Paliwal, K., Wójcicki, K., Shannon, B.: The importance of phase in speech enhancement. Speech Commun. **53**(4), 465–494 (2011). https://doi.org/10.1016/j.specom.2010.12.003
26. Panayotov, V., Chen, G., Povey, D., Khudanpur, S.: Librispeech: an ASR corpus based on public domain audio books. In: 2015 IEEE International Conference on Acoustics, Speech and Signal Processing (ICASSP), pp. 5206–5210 (2015). https://doi.org/10.1109/ICASSP.2015.7178964
27. Pandey, A., Wang, D.: A new framework for supervised speech enhancement in the time domain. In: Proceedings of the Interspeech 2018, pp. 1136–1140 (2018). https://doi.org/10.21437/Interspeech.2018-1223
28. Pandey, A., Wang, D.: TCNN: temporal convolutional neural network for real-time speech enhancement in the time domain. In: ICASSP 2019–2019 IEEE International Conference on Acoustics, Speech and Signal Processing (ICASSP), pp. 6875–6879 (2019). https://doi.org/10.1109/ICASSP.2019.8683634
29. Park, S.R., Lee, J.W.: A fully convolutional neural network for speech enhancement. In: Proceedings of the Interspeech 2017, pp. 1993–1997 (2017). https://doi.org/10.21437/Interspeech.2017-1465
30. Qian, K., Zhang, Y., Chang, S., Yang, X., Florêncio, D., Hasegawa-Johnson, M.: Speech enhancement using Bayesian Wavenet. In: Proceedings of the Interspeech 2017, pp. 2013–2017 (2017). https://doi.org/10.21437/Interspeech.2017-1672
31. Rangachari, S., Loizou, P.C.: A noise-estimation algorithm for highly non-stationary environments. Speech Commun. **48**(2), 220–231 (2006). https://doi.org/10.1016/j.specom.2005.08.005
32. Sivaraman, A., Kim, M.: Efficient personalized speech enhancement through self-supervised learning. IEEE J. Sel. Topics Sig. Process. **16**(6), 1342–1356 (2022). https://doi.org/10.1109/JSTSP.2022.3181782
33. Thiemann, J., Ito, N., Vincent, E.: The diverse environments multi-channel acoustic noise database (DEMAND): a database of multichannel environmental noise recordings. In: Proceedings of Meetings on Acoustics, vol. 19, no. 1, p. 035081 (2013). https://doi.org/10.1121/1.4799597
34. Wang, Y., Narayanan, A., Wang, D.: On training targets for supervised speech separation. IEEE/ACM Trans. Audio Speech Lang. Process. **22**(12), 1849–1858 (2014). https://doi.org/10.1109/TASLP.2014.2352935
35. Yosinski, J., Clune, J., Bengio, Y., Lipson, H.: How transferable are features in deep neural networks? In: Proceedings of the 27th International Conference on Neural Information Processing Systems - Volume 2. p. 3320–3328 (2014)
36. Zenke, F., Poole, B., Ganguli, S.: Continual learning through synaptic intelligence. In: Proceedings of the 34th International Conference on Machine Learning, pp. 3987–3995 (2017)
37. Zezario, R.E., Fuh, C.S., Wang, H.M., Tsao, Y.: Speech enhancement with zero-shot model selection. In: 2021 29th European Signal Processing Conference (EUSIPCO), pp. 491–495 (2021). https://doi.org/10.23919/EUSIPCO54536.2021.9616163
38. Zhang, G., Yu, L., Wang, C., Wei, J.: Multi-scale temporal frequency convolutional network with axial attention for speech enhancement. In: ICASSP 2022–2022 IEEE International Conference on Acoustics, Speech and Signal Processing (ICASSP), pp. 9122–9126 (2022). https://doi.org/10.1109/ICASSP43922.2022.9746610

Candidate Speech Extraction from Multi-speaker Single-Channel Audio Interviews

Meghna Pandharipande$^{(\boxtimes)}$ and Sunil Kumar Kopparapu⬤

TCS Research, Tata Consultancy Services Limited, Mumbai, India
{meghna.pandharipande,sunilkumar.kopparapu}@tcs.com
http://www.tcs.com

Abstract. Video interviews are increasingly common, initially due to travel restrictions during the pandemic and now extended for economic reasons. However, in many developing nations, limited bandwidth makes video interviews impractical, leading to a preference for telephonic interviews. These interviews are often recorded for audit and analysis purposes. A candidate's performance in an interview depends not only on their knowledge but also on how they respond to the interviewer. Both the content of their responses and their communication skills influence the overall selection process. For any downstream interview analysis or automation, a reliable method is needed to identify speech segments spoken by the candidate in a multi-speaker, single channel interview conversation. In this paper, we propose a pipeline to accurately identify candidate speech segments. This pre-processing step is crucial for analyzing various aspects of a candidate's interview performance, such as answer analysis, confidence level, and emotional expression.

Keywords: Speaker diarization · Binary classifier · Candidates speech · Late fusion

1 Introduction

Candidate interviewing is a vital stage in any enterprise recruitment process. If done effectively, this process enables the employer to determine, with confidence, if an applicant's skills, experience and personality meet the job's requirement. Online video based job interviewing is not new, many enterprises adopt this mode especially when they do not want to fly-in candidates who live in far geographies. However, due to pandemic and unprecedented challenge in conducting face to face interviews, focus has been to shift to online interviews [11]. Commercial platforms that allow conducting virtual interviews have the facility to record the interview sessions as well. Most enterprises record interviews for different purposes like (a) internal audit, (b) to identify any deficiencies in their hiring process, (c) as a proof, especially when there is a contest from candidate that has not been selected [13], etc. The recorded online interviews [19] are multi-speaker, single channel audio data [4].

© The Author(s), under exclusive license to Springer Nature Switzerland AG 2023
A. Karpov et al. (Eds.): SPECOM 2023, LNAI 14338, pp. 210–221, 2023.
https://doi.org/10.1007/978-3-031-48309-7_18

Evaluating the performance of a candidate after an interview can offer added value and insights [20]. Any analysis, manual or automated, concerning the candidate, requires extracting the speech utterances corresponding to the candidate from a single channel multi speaker audio recording. The process of identifying *who spoke when*, also called Speaker diarization (SD), is critical in several downstream speech applications dealing with multi-speaker speech like online interviews, team meeting, news broadcasts, voice based contact center conversations, etc. [8]. Speaker diarization task is especially challenging when the audio stream contains an unknown amount of speech from an unknown number of speakers [1] because the process of SD involves partitioning an audio stream into homogeneous segments according to the speaker's identity [12]. Conventional SD systems use two stages speaker segmentation: aiming at finding (a) speaker change points in a multi-speaker audio stream, and (b) grouping together speech segments which identify individual speakers across the conversation, called speaker clustering. Conventional SD systems rely on differences in how people sound acoustically to distinguish the speakers in the conversations.

A range of downstream analysis, in an audio interview setting, become possible by extracting audio responses uttered by the candidate. For example, speech segments associated with the candidate can be analyzed from the answer evaluation [6] perspective to assess subject knowledge; assess behaviour and soft-skills of the candidate [18] by analyzing para-linguistic parameters to determine emotion, confidence etc. Irrespective of the downstream task, in the context of interview recordings, identifying accurately, all the speech segments spoken by the candidate in a single channel, multi-speaker audio recording is very crucial. In this paper, we propose a system to extract candidate spoken speech segments from and an interview recording. The proposed system uses (a) a standard SD system and (b) a custom built trained neural network model to classify an audio segment as a question or an answer. The final extraction of candidate spoken speech is based on fusing the decision from these two individual systems. We demonstrate improved performance on real interview audio data using the proposed approach. The rest of the paper is organized as follows, in Sect. 2 we formulate the problem, describing the complete system in Sect. 3. We have explained the complete experimental setup in Sect. 4 followed by experimental results and discussion. We conclude in Sect. 5.

2   Problem Formulation

Let $a(t), 0 \leq t \leq T$, be an interview recording of length T between n interviewers and a candidate such that $a(t)$ has speech spoken by $(n+1)$ speakers, in a single audio channel. The task at hand is to identify all the speech segments spoken by the candidate. Typically, this objective is achieved by a SD system which identifies, say a set of N segments, $\mathcal{A} = \{a_i(t)\}_{i=1}^{N}$ based on speaker change detection and then each segment, $a_i(t)$ is labeled as one of the $(n+1)$ speakers. The set of audio segments, $\mathcal{A}_c \subset \mathcal{A}$, labeled as the candidate speaker by the SD system become the audio segments spoken by the candidate. The task at hand is to reliably identify all $a_i(t) \in \mathcal{A}_c$. The set of audio segments, $\mathcal{A}_c$, can help in downstream applications, for example to assess the performance of the candidate in an interview. Note that $\mathcal{A}_c \subset \mathcal{A}$ and contains all the audio segments spoken by the candidate *only*.

Generally a pre-trained SD model can be used for speaker diarization [9,10,17] to identify the set of speech segments $\mathcal{A}_c$ spoken by the candidate. One of the drawbacks of a SD system is that there is no inherent capability to *identify* which of the $(n+1)$ speaker label corresponds to the candidate speaker. Aside of this, our analysis on in-house interview recordings showed them to be erroneous on two counts, namely, (a) speech segments actually spoken by the candidate were missed and marked as being spoken by one of the interviewer or (b) the speech segments spoken by one of the interviewers were assigned to the candidate. This observation together with the fact that most often the candidate responds (answers, A) to the queries (questions, Q) by the interviewers motivates our approach towards building a robust mechanism to identify candidate speech. We hypothesize that if we are able to determine if the speech segment is a "question" or an "answer" we could effectively use it to better identify audio segments spoken by the candidate. This is the main contribution of this paper.

We build a binary class audio classifier, called QA classifier, trained to classify a given utterance, into either a Q or an A. We propose the use of late fusion to combine the output of a pre-trained SD and the trained QA classifier to achieve better extraction of candidate speech in the interview conversation. We describe this in more detail in the next section.

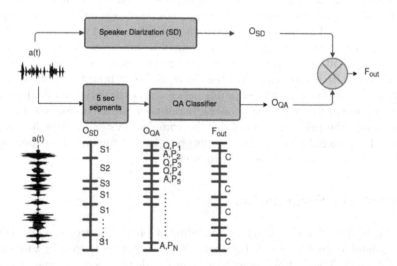

Fig. 1. Proposed approach to identifying candidate spoken speech, schematic.

3   Candidate Speech Identification

The audio conversation $a(t)$ is directly passed through the SD system and in parallel, $a(t)$ is divided into 5 s non-overlapping segments and is passed through the trained QA classifier (see Fig. 1), the output of these two individual blocks is fused to identify the speech segments spoken by the candidate in audio conversation. Note that while the SD block takes the entire audio conversation $a(t)$ as input and outputs unequal length speech segments with speaker label (O_{SD}); the QA system takes a fixed length (5 s) utterances and labels them as Q or A along with a confidence score, namely, ($O_{\mathrm{QA}}, p_{\mathrm{QA}}$). The outputs O_{SD} and O_{QA}, as seen in Fig. 1, are fused to get the desired output, namely, speech segments spoken by the candidate. We use the pre-trained Kaldi based SD [10] implementation[1] and we trained a QA classifier ourselves.

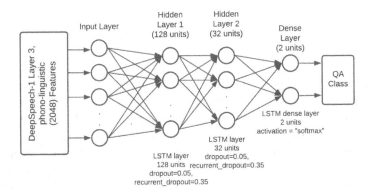

Fig. 2. QA classifier architecture is composed of two LSTM layers and a dense layer.

We now describe the training of the QA classifier. We use an end-to-end fully connected deep LSTM network [21] for classifying a given audio utterance as a Q or an A. Specifically, QA classifier is composed of two LSTM layers and a dense layer to consolidate output as shown in Fig. 2. We use Adam optimizer with categorical-crossentropy loss function to back propagate the error and modify the weights of the network. The learning rate is fixed at 0.001.

We use embeddings derived from Mozilla's **DeepSpeech** [14] as input speech features to the QA classifier. Note that **DeepSpeech** is an end-to-end pre-trained deep network model that converts speech into alphabets based on the Connectionist Temporal Classification (CTC) loss function. The 6 layer deep model is pre-trained on 1000 h of speech from the LibriSpeech corpus [16]. All the 6 layers, except the 4th, have feedforward dense units; the 4th layer itself has recurrent units as seen in Fig. 3.

---

[1] We do not describe this in this paper.

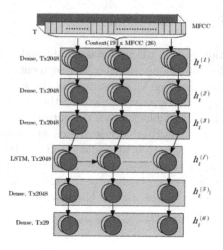

Fig. 3. DeepSpeech Architecture [14].

A speech utterance $x(t)$ is segmented into K frames, as is common in speech processing, namely, $x^\tau(t)$ $\forall \tau \in [0, K-1]$. Each frame $x^\tau(t)$ is of duration 25 min s and is represented by 26 Mel Frequency Cepstral Coefficients (MFCCs), namely, $\vec{f}_\tau$. Subsequently the complete speech utterance $x(t)$ can be represented as a sequence namely, $\{\vec{f}_\tau\}_{\tau=0}^{K-1}$. The input to the DeepSpeech is $\{\vec{f}_{\tau-9} \cdots \vec{f}_{\tau+9}\}$, namely, 9 preceding and 9 succeeding frames. The output of the DeepSpeech model is a probability distribution over an alphabet set $\mathcal{E}$ of a particular language. In case of English language, $\mathcal{E} = (a, b, \cdots, z, \diamond, \square, \prime)$ and $|\mathcal{E}| = 29$. Note that there are three additional outputs, namely, $\diamond$, $\square$, and $\prime$ corresponding to *unknown*, *space* and an *apostrophe* respectively in $\mathcal{E}$ in addition to the 26 known English letters. The output at each frame, τ is

$$c_\tau^* = \max_{\forall k \in \mathcal{E}} P\left((c_\tau = k) \mid \left\{\vec{f}_{\tau-9}, \cdots, \vec{f}_\tau, \cdots, \vec{f}_{\tau+9}\right\}\right) \tag{1}$$

where $c_\tau^* \in \mathcal{E}$.

We hypothesize that for any given utterance, the embeddings from the initial layers of DeepSpeech mostly capture the *acoustic content* of the utterance while the embeddings from layers close to the output are expected to capture properties related to the *linguistic content* of the utterance. We further hypothesize that embeddings from an intermediate layer of DeepSpeech is most suitable for QA classification because these embeddings contain both acoustic cues (*assertiveness, emphasis, stress* which are predominantly observed in questions utterances) as well as linguistic cues (words like *What, How, Why, When, Where, Which* again observed in question utterances). Our hypothesis is substantiated by our initial study on spoken language understanding [2,3] where we showed that the embeddings from the 3rd layer of DeepSpeech capture both the acoustic and the linguistic cues optimally. In all our experiment, in this paper, we use the output embeddings from the 3rd layer as input features of size 2048, to incorporate the deep encoded phono-linguistic features, for the QA classification task. Subsequently the input to the QA classifier is a vector of length 2048 extracted from 5 s audio segments as seen in Fig. 2.

4   Experimental Setup and Results

We use the MIT job interview (MIT-JI) dataset [15] to train a QA classifier. The entire MIT-JI dataset has 138 audio-video recordings, totaling 10.5 h from 69 internship-seeking undergraduates[2]. The MIT-JI consist of two session per candidate. Further a single recording session consists of several question and answer interactions between the interviewer and the candidate.

Keras [5] was used to train the QA classifier shown in Fig. 2. The MIT-JI audio data is split in 80 : 20 ratio for training and testing. Further each utterance (labelled as Q or A) is segmented into non-overlapping segments of 5 s duration and a 2048 length vector (embedding) extracted from DeepSpeech 3rd layer (Fig. 3). The performance of the trained QA classifier on MIT-JI (test set not part of the training set) ranged between 82% and 88% across 5 fold cross validation. We chose the trained model that gave the best performance (88%) as the QA classifier in all our experiments.

Table 1. TCS-TI interview data details. Duration and number of interviewers. Total number of speakers including the candidate is $m + 1$.

Interviews	Duration (mm:ss)	m $(S_1, \cdots, S_m)$
TCS-TI#1	30:01	2
TCS-TI#1	27:05	3
TCS-TI#3	18:07	2
TCS-TI#4	21:16	3
TCS-TI#5	26:08	3
TCS-TI#6	14:44	2
TCS-TI#7	32:08	2
TCS-TI#8	34:52	3
TCS-TI#9	12:17	1
TCS-TI#10	28:01	3
TCS-TI#11	12:50	1
TCS-TI#12	32:72	3

For identifying the candidate spoken segments from interview conversation, we considered 12 real audio technical interviews (TCS-TI; Table 1) between the

---

[2] We used only the audio recordings for training the QA classifier.

candidate and the interviewers ranging between 1 and 3 for our experimental analysis. The duration of the technical interviews ranged between 12 and 35 minutes. The interview conversation was recorded on Microsoft Teams platform (MP4) and the audio stream (WAV, mono, 16 bit, 16 kHz) was extracted using sox[3] utility. All the 12 audio files in TCS-TI dataset were manually segmented to extract the candidate speech and the interviewer speech. Note that TCS-TI data was not part of the train data used to build the QA classifier.

Each of these 12 interview audio files is then passed through the SD module to obtain an output of *unequal* duration segments, denoted by the start time (t_i^{sd}) of the segment, the duration (d_i) of the segment, and a corresponding speaker label L_i^{sd}, namely, $(t_1^{sd}, d_1, L_1^{sd}), (t_2^{sd}, d_2, L_2^{sd}), \cdots, (t_n^{sd}, d_n, L_n^{sd})$. Typically SD needs to be initialized with number of speakers, say, m. This implies $L_i^{sd} \in \{S_1, S_2, \cdots, S_m\}$. The same audio file, which is part of the TCS-TI dataset, is split into non-overlapping segments of 5 s duration (say K segments) and passed through the QA classifier (see Note 1). The output of the QA classifier is a label $L_j^{qa} \in \{Q, A\}$ for $j = 1, 2, \cdots, K$ with a probability score, p_j namely, $(t_1^{qa}, D, L_1^{qa}, p_1), (t_2^{qa}, D, L_2^{qa}, p_2), \cdots, (t_K^{qa}, D, L_K^{qa}, p_K)$ where $t_{i+1}^{qa} = t_i^{qa} + D$ and $D = 5$ s.

Note 1. *Note that the QA classifier has been trained on MIT-JI dataset which is different and non-overlapping with the TCS-TI dataset.*

Note 2. *We used non-overlapping segments of 5 s in this set of experiments because we observed that most candidates seems to speak in longish utterances during formal interviews.*

Algorithm 1. Fusing the output of SD and QA classifier.

1: Given: Output of SD; $(t_i^{sd}, d_i, L_i^{sd})\}_{i=1}^n$
        ▷ n audio segments; $L_i^{sd} \in \{S_1, S_2, \cdots, S_m\}$; m is # of interviewers
2: Given: Output of QA classifier; $\{(t_j^{qa}, D, L_j^{qa}, p_j)\}_{j=1}^K$
        ▷ K audio segments; $L_j^{qa} \in \{Q, A\}$ and $\{p_j\}_{j=1}^K > 0.5$; $D = 5$ s
3:
4: **for** $k \leftarrow 2$ to $(n-1)$ **do**   ▷ Adjust the SD outputs
5:    $t_k'^{sd} = \text{SPEAKERCHANGE}(t_k^{sd}, 3D)$
6: **end for**
7:
8: **for** $k \leftarrow 1$ to $(n-1)$ **do**   ▷ Identify speaker change in SD
9:    Find $\{t^{qa}\} \in [t_k'^{sd}, t_{k+1}'^{sd}]$
10:    $\{L^{qa}\} \leftarrow \{t^{qa}\}$ ▷ L^{qa} corresponding to t^{qa}
11:    $L'^{qa} = \text{MEDIANFILTER}(\{L^{qa}\}, 2)$
12:    $\{t^{qa}\} \leftarrow \{L'^{qa}\}$
13: **end for**   ▷ All t^{qa} with $(L'^{qa} = A)$ is candidate speech

---

[3] https://sox.sourceforge.net/.

The outputs of the SD block, $\{(t_i^{sd}, d_i, L_i^{sd})\}_{i=1}^n$, and the QA classifier block, $\{(t_j^{qa}, D, L_j^{qa}, p_j)\}_{j=1}^K$, are then fused as described in Algorithm 1 to make a decision. The fusing mechanism does two things, namely, (a) refines the speaker change boundaries output by SD (Line 4 to 6, Algorithm 1) followed by (b) median filtering using a kernel of size 5 ($= 2l + 1$) on the labels (Q, A) within the refined speaker change regions (Line 8 to 13, Algorithm 1) so that the labels are smooth.

We now describe the fusion decision in detail (see Algorithm 1 and 2). For every output t^{sd} of the SD we collect all the QA segments which are within 15 s ($3D$; Line 5, Algorithm 1) to the left (denoted by "$-$") and 15 s to the right (denoted by "$+$", Algorithm 2). If the QA segments to the left and the QA segments to the right show different labels (see Line 12, Algorithm 2) then we retain the original output of SD (Line 13, Algorithm 2) else (when the left QA segment and the right QA segment have the same label) we try to find t'^{sd} recursively. Note that at the end of this process the number of SD segments do not change (Line: 5, Algorithm 1).

Note 3. *Note that the function* SPEAKERCHANGE *(Line 1 to 17, Algorithm 2) calls the function* ADJUST *(Line 26 to 31, Algorithm 2) which in turn calls the function* SPEAKERCHANGE.

Table 2. Experimental results based on individual interview Conversations.

TCS-TI Dataset	Ground Truth Seg (Cand, Inter)	SD Seg (Cand, Inter)	SD Acc (%)	SD+ QAAcc (%)	Cand Speech Acc (%)	
					SD	SD+ QA
TCS-TI#1	145 (97, 48)	99 (74,25)	64.19	77.70 (↑ 13.51)	76.29	82.47 (↑ 6.19)
TCS-TI#2	163 (103, 60)	98 (71,27)	56.97	70.71 (↑ 13.75)	68.93	74.76 (↑ 5.83)
TCS-TI#3	106 (73, 34)	74 (56, 18)	65.36	76.18 (↑ 10.83)	77.78	84.72 (↑ 6.94)
TCS-TI#4	96 (65, 31)	57 (44, 13)	54.81	66.72 (↑ 11.91)	67.69	75.38 (↑ 7.69)
TCS-TI#5	102 (77, 25)	61 (53, 8)	50.42	64.31 (↑ 13.90)	68.83	76.62 (↑ 7.79)
TCS-TI#6	83 (53, 30)	49 (37, 12)	54.91	69.40 (↑ 14.50)	69.81	75.47 (↑ 5.66)
TCS-TI#7	148 (102, 46)	102 (76, 26)	65.52	78.24 (↑ 12.72)	74.51	80.39 (↑ 5.88)
TCS-TI#8	152 (111, 41)	97 (81, 16)	56.00	66.02 (↑ 10.02)	72.97	78.38 (↑ 5.41)
TCS-TI#9	76 (52, 24)	45 (35, 10)	54.49	66.67 (↑ 12.18)	67.31	75.00 (↑ 7.69)
TCS-TI#10	117 (82, 35)	76 (62, 14)	57.80	71.46 (↑ 13.66	75.61	82.93 (↑ 7.32)
TCS-TI#11	97 (68, 29)	68 (53, 15)	64.83	77.38 (↑ 12.55)	77.94	82.35 (↑ 4.41)
TCS-TI#12	137 (101, 36)	92 (79, 13)	57.16	73.53 (↑ 16.36)	78.22	83.17 (↑ 4.95)
Overall Performance			59.00	72.12 (↑ **13.13**)	73.35	79.55 (↑ **6.20**)

Algorithm 2. Supporting functions to Algorithm 1

1: **function** SPEAKERCHANGE(t_k^{sd}, d)
2:     Find $\{t^{qa-}\} \in [t_k^{sd} - d, t_k^{sd}]$
3:     **for** $t_j^{qa} \in \{t^{qa-}\}$ **do**
4:         $pQ^- = pQ^- + \text{STRENGTH}(L_j^{qa}, p_j, Q); pA^- = pA^- + \text{STRENGTH}(L_j^{qa}, p_j, A)$
5:     **end for**
6:
7:     Find $\{t^{qa+}\} \in [t_k^{sd}, t_k^{sd} + d]$
8:     **for** $t_j^{qa} \in \{t^{qa+}\}$ **do**
9:         $pQ^+ = pQ^+ + \text{STRENGTH}(L_j^{qa}, p_j, Q); pA^+ = pQ^+ + \text{STRENGTH}(L_j^{qa}, p_j, A)$
10:     **end for**
11:
12:     **if** $((pQ^- > pA^-)\&(pA^+ > pQ^+)|(pQ^- < pA^-)\&(pA^+ < pQ^+))$ **then**
13:         $t_k'^{sd} = t_k^{sd}$
14:     **else**
15:         $t_k'^{sd} = \text{ADJUST}(t_k^{sd}, 3D)$
16:     **end if**
        return $(t_k'^{sd})$
17: **end function**
18:
19: **function** STRENGTH(L^{qa}, p, X)
20:     $pX = 0$
21:     **if** $(L^{qa} == X)$ **then**
22:         $pX = p$
23:     **end if**
        return pX
24: **end function**
25:
26: **function** ADJUST(t_k^{sd},d)
27:     Find $\{t^{qa*}\} \in [t_k^{sd} - d, t_k^{sd} + d]$
28:     **for** $t_j^{qa} \in \{t^{qa*}\}$ **do**
29:         $t' = \text{SPEAKERCHANGE}(t_j^{qa}, d)$
30:     **end for**
        return t'
31: **end function**
32:
33: **function** MEDIANFILTER($\{L^{qa}\}, l$)
34:     $C = |L^{qa}|; L'^{qa} = L^{qa}$ ▷ C is size of $\{L^{qa}\}$
35:     **for** $i \leftarrow (l+1)$ to $(C - (l+1))$ **do**
        $L_i' = \text{majority}(L_{i-l}^{qa} : L_{i+l}^{qa})$ ▷ Example QQAQA is replaced by QQQQA
36:     **end for**
37:     **for** $i \leftarrow (l+1)$ to $(C - (l+1))$ **do**
38:         $L_i'^{qa} = L_i'$
39:     **end for**
        return L'^{qa}
40: **end function**

The smoothing (Line 8 to 13, Algorithm 1) happens on the QA segment labels which appear in between two adjacent SD time stamps, namely, $[t_k^{\prime sd}, t_{k+1}^{\prime sd}]$. We collect the QA label sequence $\{L^{qa}\}$ and do a 3×1 median filtering on the labels (Line 35 to 36, Algorithm 2). These labels $L_i^{\prime qa}$ are the final labels of the interview recording and all t^{qa} with the label, $L^{\prime qa} ==$ A, correspond to the candidate speech.

The performance on 12 interview recordings from the TCS-TI dataset is shown in Table 2. The first column shows the ground truth. For example TCS-TI#1 has a total of 145 segments of which 97 segments correspond to candidate speech and 48 segments correspond to the interviewer speech. As can be seen for TCS-TI#1 the SD module produced only 99 segments (of the possible 145 segments) resulting in a performance of 64.19%. When 5 s audio segments of TCS-TI#1 are passed through the QA classifier a total of 109 segments[4] were labeled as either Q or A. The decision level combining of SD and QA classifier output, as described in Algorithm 1 results in an overall performance of 77.70%, an absolute improvement of 13.51%. As can be seen in Table 2 the use of QA classifier labels helps in better identification of speech spoken by candidate and the interviewer; there is an overall absolute improvement of 13.13% on the entire TCS-TI database.

As mentioned earlier, our interest is in the candidate segments which enables downstream candidate performance analysis. Again taking TCS-TI#1 as an example, the proposed method is able to identify 80 of the 97 candidate spoken segments correctly leading to a performance of 82.47%; in comparison using SD, only 74 of the 97 candidate spoken segments are identified correctly, suggesting that the proposed use of QA classifier helps in identifying candidate spoken speech. We can observe that there is an absolute performance improvement in recognizing candidate speech by 6.2% (see Table 2). We observed that the candidate segments which were not identified correctly were mostly the "start" and "end" segments of the answers being spoken by the candidate. The overall performance of the system on 12 interview recordings showed an ability to identify the candidates speech segments from an interview conversation with an accuracy of 79.55%.

5   Conclusion

The ability to identify the speech segments in an audio interview conversation corresponding to a candidate is crucial for downstream candidate performance analysis. We showed that, typical speaker diarization systems do not work very well on real audio conversations. In this paper, motivated by the observation that a candidate majorly responds to questions posed by an interviewer, we propose to use a QA classifier trained on publicly available dataset. The input to the QA classifier were embeddings from the 3rd layer of `DeepSpeech` pretrained model which captures both the acoustic and linguistic features in an utterance. The overall system, to identify candidate speech segments, involved

---

[4] If two adjacent 5 s segments get the same label we count the two segments as one.

fusing the output from both SD and 2-layer-deep LSTM QA classifier. The overall system shows an absolute performance improvement of 13.13% in identifying both candidate and interviewer speech segments and an absolute improvement of 6.20% in identifying speech segments spoken by the candidate. We plan to use this segmented candidate speech for downstream processing in an in-house interview bot system which is being built to provide assistance to interviewers [7]. For example, we can uses the candidate speech segments to automatically grade the response of the candidate among other things.

References

1. Anguera, X., Bozonnet, S., Evans, N., Fredouille, C., Friedland, G., Vinyals, O.: Speaker diarization: a review of recent research. IEEE Trans. Audio Speech Lang. Process. **20**(2), 356–370 (2012)
2. Bhosale, S., Chakraborty, R., Kopparapu, S.K.: Deep encoded linguistic and acoustic cues for attention based end to end speech emotion recognition. In: 2020 IEEE International Conference on Acoustics, Speech and Signal Processing (ICASSP), pp. 7189–7193. IEEE (2020)
3. Bhosale, S., Sheikh, I., Dumpala, S.H., Kopparapu, S.K.: End-to-end spoken language understanding: bootstrapping in low resource scenarios. In: Proceedings of the Interspeech 2019, pp. 1188–1192 (2019)
4. Chandratre, S., Soman, A.: Preparing for the interviewing process during coronavirus disease-19 pandemic: Virtual interviewing experiences of applicants and interviewers, a systematic review. PLoS ONE **15**(12), e0243415 (2020)
5. Chollet, F., et al.: Keras (2015). https://github.com/fchollet/keras
6. Das, B., Majumder, M., Phadikar, S., Sekh, A.A.: Automatic question generation and answer assessment: a survey. Res. Pract. Technol. Enhanc. Learn. **16**(1), 5 (2021). https://doi.org/10.1186/s41039-021-00151-1
7. Dasgupta, A., et al.: Method and system for providing assistance to interviewers. https://patents.google.com/patent/US20230109692A1/ (US20230109692A1 filed April 2023)
8. El-Khoury, E., Senac, C., Pinquier, J.: Improved speaker diarization system for meetings. In: 2009 IEEE International Conference on Acoustics, Speech and Signal Processing, pp. 4097–4100. IEEE (2009)
9. Huggingface: speaker-diarization.   https://huggingface.co/pyannote/speaker-diarization (pyannote/speaker-diarization@2022072, 2022)
10. Jamiroquai88: Speaker diarization using kaldi. https://github.com/Jamiroquai88/VBDiarization
11. Jones, R.E., Abdelfattah, K.R.: Virtual interviews in the era of covid-19: a primer for applicants. J. Surg. Educ. **77**(4), 733–734 (2020)
12. Joshi, A., Kumar, M., Das, P.K.: Speaker diarization: a review. In: 2016 International Conference on Signal Processing and Communication (ICSC), pp. 191–196. IEEE (2016)
13. Langer, M., König, C.J., Hemsing, V.: Is anybody listening? the impact of automatically evaluated job interviews on impression management and applicant reactions. J. Manag. Psychol. **35**, 271–284 (2020)
14. Mozilla: Deepspeech (2019). https://github.com/mozilla/DeepSpeech/releases

15. Naim, I., Tanveer, M.I., Gildea, D., Hoque, M.E.: Automated analysis and prediction of job interview performance. IEEE Trans. Affect. Comput. $9(2)$, 191–204 (2018)
16. Panayotov, V., Chen, G., Povey, D., Khudanpur, S.: Librispeech: an ASR corpus based on public domain audio books. In: 2015 IEEE international conference on acoustics, speech and signal processing (ICASSP), pp. 5206–5210. IEEE (2015)
17. Park, T.J., Koluguri, N.R., Balam, J., Ginsburg, B.: Multi-scale speaker diarization with dynamic scale weighting (2023). https://docs.nvidia.com/deeplearning/nemo/user-guide/docs/en/stable/asr/speaker_diarization/models.html
18. Rasipuram, S., Jayagopi, D.B.: Automatic multimodal assessment of soft skills in social interactions: a review. Multimedia Tools Appl. $79(19\text{--}20)$, 13037–13060 (2020)
19. Salmons, J.: Online Interviews in Real Time. Sage, Thousand Oaks (2009)
20. Volle, L.M.: Analyzing oral skills in voice e-mail and online interviews. Lang. Learn. Technol. $9(3)$, 146–163 (2005)
21. Zhu, W., et al.: Co-occurrence feature learning for skeleton based action recognition using regularized deep LSTM networks. In: Proceedings of the AAAI Conference on Artificial Intelligence, vol. 30 (2016)

Post-processing of Translated Speech by Pole Modification and Residual Enhancement to Improve Perceptual Quality

Lalaram Arya[✉] and S. R. Mahadeva Prasanna

Indian Institute of Technology Dharwad, Dharwad 580011, India
{202021004,prasanna}@iitdh.ac.in

Abstract. The perceptual quality of translated speech depends on the quantity of speech data used for training. The translation speech quality is poor when the system is trained with less data. The quality improves by gradually adding more speech data for training. This work demonstrates the significance of post-processing of translated speech by signal processing for improving perceptual quality. Initially, the target speech original residual is used to replace the translated speech residual. It is then replaced using the weighted residual obtained by speech enhancement. The pole modification of translated speech is also done. Finally, both weighted residual and pole modifications are combined. All the experiments show improvement in perceptual quality.

Keywords: Speech-to-speech translation (S2ST) · Weighted LP residual · Speech enhancement · Pole modification

1 Introduction

Speech-to-speech translation involves the translation of speech from one language to speech in another language [1]. Conventionally, it can be done using the cascaded system where three modules, namely, Automatic speech recognition (ASR), Machine translation (MT), and Text to speech (TTS), are cascaded to generate the translated speech of target language [7,9]. The issue with this approach is since modules depend on one other output, the error propagates from one module to another [14,16]. To avoid this issue, researchers have devised an end-to-end system approach that can generate direct target speech from the source speech [6]. Direct speech-to-speech translation (DS2ST) allows the source language speech to be directly translated into the target language speech. This problem is approached in two ways. Firstly, by making use of the mapping function that exists between the source and target languages [4]. Secondly, by taking advantage of the mapping function between the discrete representations of the source and target language speech [5]. Because, DS2ST requires fewer decoding steps than cascaded systems, it has lower error propagation between modules,

© The Author(s), under exclusive license to Springer Nature Switzerland AG 2023
A. Karpov et al. (Eds.): SPECOM 2023, LNAI 14338, pp. 222–232, 2023.
https://doi.org/10.1007/978-3-031-48309-7_19

lower computational cost, and lower inference latency. Furthermore, DS2ST is an excellent method for assisting translation in spoken languages that do not have written transcripts [15]. The DS2ST is difficult because it requires direct mapping of lexicon information from the source language to lexical information of the target language, as in MT. Also, it has to capture the vocal tract, excitation source, and long-term information from both languages, as in ASR and TTS [11].

In DS2ST, the translation quality suffers as the translated speech is generated using the direct mapping of source and target language speech [2]. Due to limited speech data, direct mapping may not be able to capture all the nuances. Figure 1 (a) to (c) shows the waveforms of the 25 ms window speech signal, where for (a) original recorded speech, (b) translated utterance from DS2ST system trained with 500 utterances, and (c) waveform of the translated utterance from DS2ST system trained with 5000 utterances. Figure 1 (d) to (f) depicts the extracted Linear Prediction (LP) spectrum of the 25 ms window speech signal, where for (d) original target speech, (e) translated speech using 500 utterances, and (f) translated speech using 5000 utterances. Figure 1 (g) to (i) plots the LP residual of the 25 ms window speech signal where (g) for the original target speech, (h) for the translated speech using 500 utterances, and (i) for the translated speech using 5000 utterances.

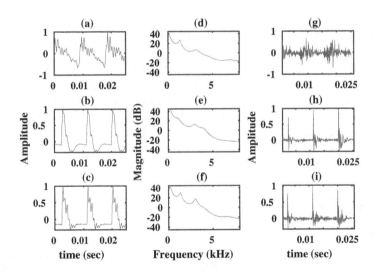

Fig. 1. Comparison in 25 ms window speech signal, LP spectrum and LP residual of target speech, translated utterance by DS2ST system trained on 500 and 5000 utterances

Figure 1 shows that when the DS2ST system is trained with less data (500 utterances), the vocal tract and the residual information are not properly mapped. When we increase the data (5000 utterances), the mapping of the vocal tract and the residual information gets improved. Instead of training with more speech data, can we try to achieve the same by post-processing of translated speech using suitable speech signal processing methods? For instance, SincNet uses an array of parameterized sinc functions to help the network find the essential features as a pre-processing in the deep learning tasks [13]. Motivated by this, similar to the SincNet pre-processing, the post-processing of the translated speech may help to improve the relatively poor LP spectrum and the LP residual (Fig. 1 (e) and (h)) of the translated speech from the DS2ST system trained on less data [10]. This work demonstrates the significance of post-processing in the DS2ST system to improve the quality of translated speech. To achieve that, four experiments are carried out. Firstly, the target speech original residual replaces the translated speech residual. We hypothesize that improved residual may have effect on perceptual quality. However, we always do not get access to the target speech. In the second experiment, hence it is replaced using the weighted residual obtained by speech enhancement (SE). The pole modification of translated speech is performed next to improve LP spectrum nature. In the last experiment, both weighted residual and pole modification are combined to further improve perceptual quality.

The rest of the paper is organized as follows: In Sect. 2, Bi-LSTM based DS2ST system is explained. In Sect. 3, different SE approaches are discussed. Section 4 discusses the experimental setup and evaluation. Finally, in Sect. 5, the paper is concluded.

2   Direct Speech-to-Speech Translation

DS2ST is a process for translating speech in one language to speech in another without the use of text. The overall schema of the DS2ST system is depicted in Fig. 2. Firstly, three features are extracted from the given speech data: Mel-frequency cepstral coefficients (MFCC), F_0, and aperiodic components. The Bi-LSTM network layers are used to transform MFCC (excluding energy features).

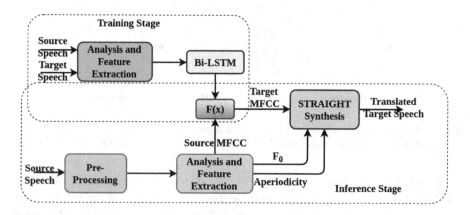

Fig. 2. Overall DS2ST framework

Because F_0 and aperiodic components lack linguistic information, we can use them directly with transformed MFCC to synthesize the target speech. The system processes the entire utterance in order to preserve the wide range of context in both forward and backward directions of the Bi-LSTM.

2.1 Training Stage

Sequence and context are essential factors in language translation. Hence back-propagation through time (BPTT) is suitable for the task [18]. During the training phase, we recorded parallel utterances in a lab environment. The source and target utterances are aligned using DTW and then padded before being fed to the Bi-LSTM during training. The Bi-LSTM learns the mapping between source and target MFCCs. The same can be used for deriving target MFCCs for the given source MFCCs during inference.

2.2 Inference Stage

The whole utterance of the source language is provided to the translation system during the inference stage. The necessary speech parameters (F_0, MFCC, and aperiodicity) are obtained from the source utterance. The MFCCs are processed through the framework shown in Fig. 2. The Bi-LSTM provides target MFCCs. The target language speech is then synthesized using the STRAIGHT vocoder with the aid of modified MFCCs, F_0, and aperiodic components.

3 Speech Enhancement

This section discusses different SE techniques to improve the perceptual quality of the translated speech generated from the DS2ST system trained on less data. SE involves enhancing the vocal tract information and excitation source information. The enhancement of vocal tract information can be achieved by modifying the spectral peaks corresponding to the formants. The same can be achieved by pole modification. The excitation source information can be enhanced by processing the LP residual. This can be achieved by deriving suitable weight functions that can enhance the regions around the glottal closure instants. The weight functions can be both fine and gross weight functions. The use of gross weight function is mostly, in case of degraded speech with external noise. In the present case of translated speech, only fine weight function may suffice. This work, therefore, uses pole modification and weighted residual generation using fine weight function as signal post-processing steps for improving perceptual quality.

3.1 Pole Modification

The LP spectrum's envelope can be used as a representation of the vocal tract structure. The LP spectrum represents the resonant frequencies (formants) and

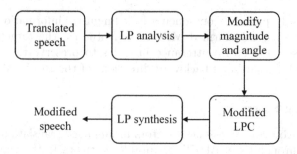

Fig. 3. Procedure for pole modification

their bandwidths in the input speech signal. The Bi-LSTM learns the mapping between source and target speech LP spectra. Good learning leads to proper reconstruction of target LP spectrum. The same involves proper reconstruction of peaks and their bandwidths around the target speech formants. From the point of view of signal processing, the angle and location of the poles in the z-plane are related to the vocal tract resonances and their bandwidths. Moving the pole positions in the z-plane makes it possible to change the formant frequencies of the system transfer function [12]. The magnitude and angle of the poles are varied using certain factors in accordance with the necessary alteration in formant frequencies. The essential steps for pole modification are shown in Fig. 3. The linear prediction coefficients (LPCs) are recomputed using the new poles. These LPCs can be used for synthesis of target speech. Due to pole modification, the formants are expected to become prominent and hence, may result in enhanced speech.

3.2 Residual Enhancement by Weighting

The vocal tract system can be represented as a time-varying all-pole filter in linear prediction (LP) analysis. If a speech signal is depicted by $s(n)$, then the estimated sample at an instant n is determined by

$$\hat{s}(n) = -\sum_{k=1}^{p} a_k s(n-k) \tag{1}$$

where a_k is the set of LP coefficients. The residual error is determined by the following relationship

$$l(n) = s(n) - \hat{s}(n) \tag{2}$$

If glottal closure instants (GCIs) are treated as a shifted train of impulses, the fine weight function $wf(n)$ is drawn by

$$w_f(n) = \left(\sum_{k=1}^{N_k} \delta(n - i_k) \right) * h_w(n) \tag{3}$$

where, N_k is the total number of GCIs found, and i_k is the estimated location of a GCI [8]. The minimum value, $w_f(n)$ is set to a T threshold [3]. The weight function, $w_f(n)$ is multiplied by the residual signal, $l(n)$ to produce the weighted LP residual signal (WLPR), $r_w(n)$, from which the temporally enhanced speech signal, $s_t(n)$ can be generated.

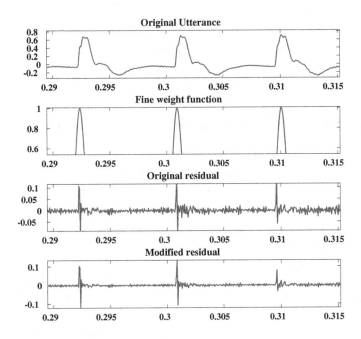

Fig. 4. Residual enhancement of translated speech by weighting

This is shown in Fig. 4, where the first subplot shows the recorded speech signal, second, the fine weight function $w_f(n)$, third, the LP residual signal derived from the speech signal, and the last, the modified LP residual signal, $r_w(n)$.

3.3   LP Residual Replacement

The residual of translated utterances can be replaced with the residual of the target utterance to enhance the perceptual quality of the translated utterances containing corresponding target utterances. As shown in Fig. 5, LP analysis has been performed to derive the LP coefficients and LP residual for both the translated and target utterances. In the first case, the modified translated speech is synthesized with the help of the translated utterance's LP coefficients and the target utterance's LP residual. In the second case, the target utterance is weighted using the fine weight function derived by LP analysis. The weighted residual is then used for synthesizing target speech.

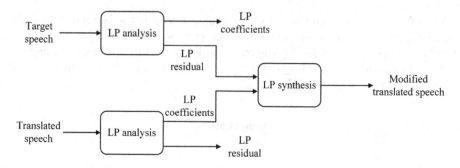

Fig. 5. Modification of translated speech by changing residual

4   Experimental Setup, Results and Discussion

Firstly we have described the dataset considered for the experimental evaluations in this section. A brief description of the DS2ST system setup used for the evaluation follows next. The experimental findings used to validate the efficacy of the proposed strategy are then described.

4.1   Dataset Description

We recorded the data internally for this study in a lab setting. For the DS2ST work, we have recorded parallel data in Hindi and English from a single speaker, where we have considered Hindi as the target language and English as the source language. We have collected 7.76 h of data in total, with 7,000 utterances in each language. All of the 7000 utterances have the same linguistic content. 500 is used for the inference out of the 7000. Out of remaining data, 10% utterances are used for development and the rest are for training. The recorded utterances were sampled at 16 kHz with a mono channel.

4.2   Experimental Setup

This experiment uses the parallel DS2ST data set discussed in the Sect. 4.1. Before being fed into the network, the data is first cleaned using an endpoint detection algorithm that takes out the non-speech elements at the beginning and the end of the utterance. The mapping function is then estimated by aligning the source and target utterances with dynamic time warping (DTW) and padding them with zero. To extract MFCC, the voice signal is windowed by 20 ms and given a 5 ms frame shift. A 25-dimensional mfcc feature was fed into the Bi-LSTM network.

In this study, a four-layer Bi-LSTM network has been used to set up the DS2ST system. The Bi-LSTM network consists of a total $[25, 256, 256, 256, 256, 25]$ units. The Bi-LSTM network can gather speech context in forward and backward directions since each hidden layer comprises forward and backward LSTM layers. Before feeding the data for training, training data is modified to have zero mean and unit variance for each dimension. With a learning rate of $1.0 * 10^{-5}$ and momentum of 0.9, BPTT has been employed. The Bi-LSTM model was trained using CUDA-capable deep learning tools [17]. The model needs to be trained for about 12 h. The 10th order LP analysis has been done using the Matlab tool for the pole modification and the weighted LP residual in post-procession.

4.3   Performance Evaluation and Discussion

The bilingual assessment understudy (BLUE) score is typically used as an objective metric to evaluate the translation quality of the S2ST system [4,5]. The experiments used the data discussed in Sect. 4.1, where a single speaker repeated the same message every time. Thus, mean cepstral distortion (MCD), which measures translation quality has been used to evaluate the enhanced performance in this work.

Objective Evaluation. Figure 6, (a) to (g) shows the waveforms of the 25 ms speech signal, where for (a) original target speech, (b) translated speech generated by the DS2ST system trained with 500 utterances, (c) translated speech generated by the DS2ST system trained with 5000 utterances, (d) enhanced translated speech by residual replacement, (e) enhanced translated speech by pole modification, (f) enhanced translated speech by weighted residual, (g) enhanced translated speech by both pole modification and weighed residual. Similarly, (h) to (n) represents the corresponding LP spectrum and (o) to (u) shows the LP residual of the same 25 ms speech signal.

Initially, the residual of translated speech generated from the DS2ST system trained with less data (0.27 h) is replaced with the residual of target speech as shown in Fig. 5. It can be seen from Fig. 6 (d), (k), and (r) that after replacing the LP residual of translated speech, the waveform, peaks of the LP spectrum and the LP residual are improved. The peaks of the LP spectrum are now more prominent compared to (i) and are closer to (j), similarly, the LP residual is also improved. The perceptual quality of the translated speech is observed to be enhanced, which can be verified from Table 1. The MCD score of enhanced translated speech by LP residual replacement is less than the original translated speech.

Next, the pole modification of the translated speech is done with a factor, α of 0.9. Comparing Fig. 6 (e), (l) and (s) with (b), (i) and (p), it can be seen that the pole modification also contributes to enhancing the translated speech. Analyzing plot (l), it can be observed that the LP spectrum peaks are prominent, which means it contains enhanced vocal tract information than in plots (i). The improvement also can be verified by the reduction in the MCD score from Table 1. The MCD score is less for the translated speech by pole modification compared to the translated speech by the DS2ST system trained with 500 utterances. Compared to the residual replacement technique, pole modification is lagging in performance slightly. Still, the benefit is that it can enhance the perceptual quality of translated speech even when the target speech is not available.

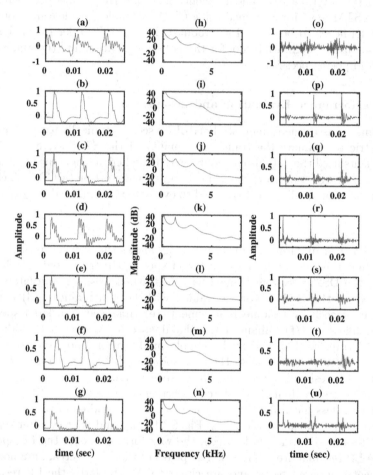

Fig. 6. Comparison in the waveform, LP spectrum, LP residual of original, translated and enhanced translated speech using different enhancement techniques

In the third case, the weighted residual enhancement is performed. Comparing Fig. 6 (f), (m), and (t) with (b), (i) and (p), we can see an improvement in the perpetual quality of the translated speech. The LP residual in (t) is improved than the (p) and also, the LP spectrum in (m) is slightly improved than (i). The improvement in MCD value can verify the same from Table 1. Compared to the residual replacement technique, the weighted residual enhancement is slightly lagging in performance. Still, the benefit is that it can enhance the perceptual quality of translated speech even when target speech is not available.

Last, the pole modification followed by the weighted residual is done where the benefits of both techniques have been taken. Pole modification improves the

Table 1. Improvement in MCD for DS2ST by applying different enhancement techniques

SE Techniques	Training utterances	MCD
No	500	7.181
No	5000	6.261
Residual replacement	500	6.461
Pole modification	500	6.682
Weighted residual	500	6.619
Pole + weighted residual	500	6.592

vocal tract information and the weighted residual improves the LP residual of the translated speech. Figure 6 (g), (n), and (u) shows the improvement in LP spectrum peaks and the LP residual information compared to (b), (i), and (p). The Table 1 also reflects the same that the MCD score is less for the enhanced translated speech than the translated speech from the DS2ST system trained on less data.

5 Conclusion and Future Work

In this paper, a method to enhance the perceptual quality of translated speech by the DS2ST system trained with less data is proposed. Initially, the translated speech is enhanced by changing the LP residual of the translated with the LP residual of the original target speech. Secondly, the pole modification is done and in the third weighted residual enhancement is done. Lastly, both weighted residual and pole modification are combined to enhance the translated speech. It is found that all four techniques perform well and improve the translation perceptual quality. Out of all the LP residual replacement provides the best performance by improvement in MCD by 6.461. On the other hand, other techniques can enhance the perceptual quality of translated speech even when target speech is not available. The improvement by combination is still not significant and needs further exploration. In the future, we will focus on improving naturalness and speaker-specific information in the DS2ST system trained on spontaneous and real-time speech.

Acknowledgment. We would like to thank the "AnantGanak" high-performance computation (HPC) facility at IIT Dharwad for enabling us to conduct our experiments.

References

1. Arora, K., Arora, S., Roy, M.: Speech to speech translation: a communication boon. CSI Trans. ICT **1**, 207–213 (2013)
2. Arya, L., Agarwal, A., Mishra, J., Mahadeva Prasanna, S.R.: Analysis of layer-wise training in direct speech to speech translation using BI-LSTM. In: 2022 25th Conference of the Oriental COCOSDA International Committee for the Co-ordination and Standardisation of Speech Databases and Assessment Techniques (O-COCOSDA), pp. 1–6 (2022)
3. Deepak, K.T., Prasanna, S.R.M.: Foreground speech segmentation and enhancement using glottal closure instants and MEL cepstral coefficients. IEEE/ACM Trans. Audio Speech Lang. Process. **24**(7), 1205–1219 (2016)
4. Jia, Y., et al.: Direct speech-to-speech translation with a sequence-to-sequence model. In: INTERSPEECH, pp. 1123–1127 (2019)
5. Lee, A., et al.: Direct speech-to-speech translation with discrete units. In: Association for Computational Linguistics, pp. 3327–3339 (2022)
6. Liu, Y., et al.: End-to-end speech translation with knowledge distillation. In: INTERSPEECH, pp. 1128–1132 (2019)
7. Morimoto, T., et al.: ATR's speech translation system: ASURA. In: Proceedings of the 3rd European Conference on Speech Communication and Technology (Eurospeech 1993), pp. 1291–1294 (1993)
8. Murty, K.S.R., Yegnanarayana, B.: Epoch extraction from speech signals. IEEE Trans. Audio Speech Lang. Process. **16**(8), 1602–1613 (2008)
9. Nakamura, S., et al.: The ATR multilingual speech-to-speech translation system. IEEE Trans. Audio Speech Lang. Process. **14**(2), 365–376 (2006)
10. Nomo Sudro, P., Prasanna, S.: Enhancement of cleft palate speech using temporal and spectral processing. Speech Commun. **123**, 70–82 (2020)
11. Rabiner, L.R., Schafer, R.W., et al.: Introduction to digital speech processing. Found. Trends® Signal Process. **1**(1–2), 1–194 (2007)
12. Rao, K.S., Yegnanarayana, B.: Voice conversion by prosody and vocal tract modification. In: 9th International Conference on Information Technology (ICIT 2006), pp. 111–116 (2006)
13. Saritha, B., Shome, N., Laskar, R.H., Choudhury, M.: Enhancement in speaker recognition using sincnet through optimal window and frame shift. In: 2022 2nd International Conference on Intelligent Technologies (CONIT), pp. 1–6 (2022)
14. Seligman, M., Waibel, A., Joscelyne, A.: Taus speech-to-speech translation technology report. De Rijp: TAUS BV, pp. 1–58 (2017)
15. Tjandra, A., Sakti, S., Nakamura, S.: Speech-to-speech translation between untranscribed unknown languages. In: Automatic Speech Recognition and Understanding Workshop (ASRU), pp. 593–600 (2019)
16. Wahlster, W.: Verbmobil: Foundations of Speech-to-Speech Translation. Springer, Heidelberg (2013). https://doi.org/10.1007/978-3-662-04230-4
17. Weninger, F.: Introducing CURRENNT: the Munich open-source CUDA recurrent neural network toolkit. J. Mach. Learn. Res. **16**(17), 547–551 (2015)
18. Werbos, P.: Backpropagation through time: what it does and how to do it. Proc. IEEE **78**(10), 1550–1560 (1990)

Region Normalized Capsule Network Based Generative Adversarial Network for Non-parallel Voice Conversion

Md. Tousin Akhter[1], Padmanabha Banerjee[2], Sandipan Dhar[1(✉)],
Subhayu Ghosh[1], and Nanda Dulal Jana[1(✉)]

[1] Department of Computer Science and Engineering,
National Institute of Technology Durgapur, Durgapur, West Bengal, India
{sd.19cs1101,sg.22cs1101}@phd.nitdgp.ac.in, nandadulal@cse.nitdgp.ac.in
[2] Department of Electronics and Communication Engineering, Jalpaiguri
Government Engineering College, Jalpaiguri, West Bengal, India

Abstract. Voice conversion (VC) involves altering the vocal characteristics of a source speaker to resemble those of a target speaker while maintaining the same linguistic content. Recently, researchers have turned to deep generative models, particularly generative adversarial network (GAN) models, for VC studies due to their superior performance compared to statistical models. However, there is a noticeable disparity in naturalness between real speech samples and those generated by state-of-the-art (SOTA) VC models. This study introduces an enhanced GAN model for non-parallel VC, which employs mel-spectrograms as the speech feature. The enhanced GAN model incorporates a region normalization technique in the generator and a discriminator based on capsule networks (Caps-Net), to improve the quality of the generated speech samples. The proposed model is evaluated using the VCC 2018 and CMU Arctic datasets. The experimental outcomes demonstrate that the region normalization technique-based Caps-Net GAN (RNCapsGAN-VC) model outperforms the SOTA MaskCycleGAN-VC model in terms of both objective and subjective evaluations considering less training time.

Keywords: Generative adversarial network (GAN) · Voice conversion (VC) · Region normalization technique · Capsule network based discriminator

1 Introduction

Voice conversion (VC) [20, 26] is a speech synthesis process that converts the vocal texture of a source speaker to a target speaker without altering the linguistic content of the source speaker's speech. It has a wide variety of applications in various domains, such as the entertainment industry, military applications, and healthcare technology, to name a few [4].

© The Author(s), under exclusive license to Springer Nature Switzerland AG 2023
A. Karpov et al. (Eds.): SPECOM 2023, LNAI 14338, pp. 233–244, 2023.
https://doi.org/10.1007/978-3-031-48309-7_20

VC processes can be mainly divided into two categories based on the content of the speech corpus, i.e., parallel VC and non-parallel VC [4]. On the other hand, based on the type of mapping from the source-to-target domain, it is divided into two additional categories: one-to-one and many-to-many VC. In the early stage of the developments of VC, statistical models such as gaussian mixture models (GMMs) [22,27], phonetic posteriorgram (PPG) based models [21] etc. [1,3], were widely used. Eventually, in the recent era of artificial intelligence (AI), the deep learning (DL) models appeared as a better alternative over the conventional models [11].

Among the DL models, generative adversarial networks (GANs) [6] have been widely used for the VC task due to their capability of performing efficient style transfer from source to target domain. Based on the preceding works of GAN-based VC [20], it is observed that the successive models of CycleGAN-VC [9,11] have the potential ability to perform the VC task. Although, most of these models rely on multiple speech features for the VC process [2,24]. This limits the ability of the VC models to capture the fine time-frequency relationship of the speech data. In this context, MaskCycleGAN-VC [10] showed notable performance improvement by considering mel-spectrogram as the only input feature. Although, there is still a significant difference between the generated speech samples of existing VC models and the real speech samples, in terms of speaker similarity and speech quality. To generate more natural-sounding speech, we put forth an improved GAN model with region normalization technique in the generator and a capsule network based discriminator, referred as RNCapsGAN-VC model in this work.

In our proposed RNCapsGAN-VC model we incorporates the region normalization technique in the intermediate stage of the generator network to address the covariate shift [25] problem. Covariate shift refers to a notable alteration in the distribution of neural network model layers caused by changes in network parameters during training. Previous works on GAN-based VC [9–11] primarily utilized the instance normalization technique, but research suggests that region normalization provides better results in image style transfer tasks [25]. Additionally, we integrated a Caps-Net based discriminator into our enhanced GAN model. Caps-Net offers equivariance properties that overcome the translation invariance problem of convolutional neural networks (CNNs), making the discriminator more effective in classifying real and generated mel-spectrograms based on formant patterns [7]. Our implementation of Caps-Net utilizes a self-attention mechanism based routing algorithm to improve the feature representation [17]. We evaluated the performance of our proposed RNCapsGAN-VC model on the VCC 2018 [16] and CMU Arctic datasets [14], using objective evaluation metric (i.e. mel cepstral distortion (MCD) [5]), and subjective evaluation metric (i.e. mean opinion score (MOS) [20]), to assess the quality and vocal texture similarity of the generated speech samples as compared to the original speech samples. We have also provided the mel-spectrograms generated by RNCapsGAN-VC and MaskCycleGAN-VC for visual comparison. Apart from that we have conducted an ablation study to evaluate the impact of region normalization technique and Caps-Net discriminator in the overall performance of the proposed model. Based on both objective and subjective evaluation metrics, our proposed RNCapsGAN-VC model outperformed the state-of-the-art (SOTA) MaskCycleGAN-VC model. It is also observed that our proposed model obtained significant result as compared to SOTA VC model in less training iteration, which indicates the effectiveness of the model for non-parallel VC.

2   Proposed Model

We present a comprehensive explanation of the framework of the proposed RNCapsGAN-VC model, accompanied by a detailed description of the loss functions. In Fig. 1, we denote $x \in X$ as the mel-spectrogram of the source speaker, and m as the mask, where $x, m \in \mathbb{R}^{c \times h \times w}$ (where c, h, w are channel, height and width respectively). The mask m is used to obtain the masked mel-spectrogram x', where the black region in Fig. 1 corresponds to the masked region, and rest of the region represents the unmasked region. The masked mel-spectrogram x' of the source speaker is obtained by element-wise multiplication between x and m (i.e. $x' = x \odot m$) [10]. Similarly, the masked mel-spectrogram of the target

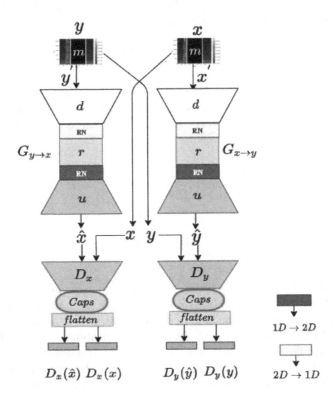

Fig. 1. The complete framework of the proposed RNCapsGAN-VC model.

speaker y' is obtained by element-wise multiplication between y and m (i.e. $y' = y \odot m$).

As illustrated in Fig. 1, the generator $G_{X \rightarrow Y}$ maps x' from the source domain X to the target domain Y and generates the synthesized mel-spectrogram $\hat{y}$. Similarly, the generator $G_{Y \rightarrow X}$ maps y' from the source domain Y to the target domain X and generates $\hat{x}$. Both $G_{X \rightarrow Y}$ and $G_{Y \rightarrow X}$ are generators based on region normalization techniques. Additionally, the discriminators D_X and D_Y of RNCapsGAN-VC are Caps-Net discriminators to estimate the similarity between the given original mel-spectrogram and the synthesized mel-spectrogram.

2.1 Region Normalized Technique-Based Generator

The architectural framework of the RNCapsGAN-VC generators consists of a combination of downsample block $d(.)$, residual summation block $r(.)$ and upsample block $u(.)$. Additionally, a 2-dimensional convolution to 1-dimensional convolution, i.e. $2D \rightarrow 1D$ CNN $(d_{2 \rightarrow 1}(.))$ is used between the downsample and residual blocks, and an 1-dimensional convolution to 2-dimensional convolution, i.e. $1D \rightarrow 2D$ CNN $(u_{1 \rightarrow 2}(.))$ block is used in the intermediate stage between the residual and upsample blocks. The region normalization technique is incorporated in both $d_{2 \rightarrow 1}(.)$ and $u_{1 \rightarrow 2}(.)$ block. The overall architectural framework of the RNCapsGAN-VC generator $G(.)$ is depicted in Eq. (1),

$$G(.) \rightarrow u(u_{1 \rightarrow 2}(r(d_{2 \rightarrow 1}(d(.))))). \tag{1}$$

The components of $G(.)$ consist of basic operations, including the convolution operation $(Conv(.))$, instance normalization $(IN(.))$, region normalization $(RN(.))$ [25], gated linear unit $(GLU(.))$, and pixel shuffler $(PS(.))$. Thus, the components of $G(.)$ can be represented as follows:

$$d(.) \rightarrow GLU(IN(Conv2D(.))), \tag{2}$$

$$d_{2 \rightarrow 1}(.) \rightarrow RN(Conv1D(.)), \tag{3}$$

$$u_{1 \rightarrow 2}(.) \rightarrow RN(Conv1D(.)), \tag{4}$$

$$r^i \rightarrow r^{i-1} \oplus IN(Conv1D(GLU(IN(Conv1D(r^{i-1}))))), \tag{5}$$

$$u(.) \rightarrow GLU(IN(PS(Conv2D(.)))). \tag{6}$$

In Eq. (3) and Eq. (4), the region normalization technique is employed in both $d_{2 \rightarrow 1}(.)$ and $u_{1 \rightarrow 2}(.)$. Equation (5) demonstrates the fundamental structure of the ith residual summation block (wherein this study, six such blocks are utilized). In Eq. (5), the operator $\oplus$ denotes the concatenation operation.

In the region normalization technique (RN(.)), batch normalization is applied separately to the masked and unmasked regions of the input matrix $x', y' \in \mathbb{R}^{n \times c \times h \times w}$, where n represents the batch size. In this study, n is set to 1. Each channel c of the input matrix is associated with a corresponding mask m (i.e., $x'_{n,c}, y'_{n,c} \in \mathbb{R}^{h \times w}$), and these matrices are divided into k regions. In this work, k

is considered as 2, representing the unmasked and masked regions. Subsequently, $x'_{n,c}$ is computed as follows,

$$x'_{n,c} = R^1_{n,c} \cup R^2_{n,c} \cup \dots \cup R^k_{n,c}. \tag{7}$$

Here, $R^k_{n,c}$ is the kth region of the input mel-spectrogram. In a similar manner $y_{n,c}$ is also computed. Thereafter, region normalization technique is applied in each of the k regions based on the following computation,

$$\hat{R}^k_{n,c} = \frac{1}{\sigma^k_{n,c}}(R^k_{n,c} - \mu^k_{n,c}). \tag{8}$$

The mean (denoted as $\mu^k_{n,c}$) and standard deviation (denoted as $\sigma^k_{n,c}$) are computed to perform region normalization on each of the k regions, as described in [25]. The region-wise normalization mechanism of RN(.) [25] addresses the covariate shift problem that occurs during the mapping of input features from the source to the target domain. The primary goal of incorporating the region normalization technique in the proposed RNCapsGAN-VC model is to achieve better quality natural-sounding speech, by obtaining the formant structure of the mel-spectrogram in an efficient manner.

2.2 Caps-Net Discriminator

Caps-Net is an improvised CNN [19] model composed of convolutional layer, primary capsule layer and secondary capsule layer. The convolution layer obtain high level feature from the input data in terms of feature vectors. The feature vectors are passed through a depth-wise separable convolution layer to obtain the final feature representation by reducing the training parameters. This feature representation is reshaped to obtain the primary capsules which retains the feature information. The primary capsules utilise squashing algorithm [18] as an activation function to determine the information of orientational and relative spatial relationship among the existing features in terms of probability. The weighted sum of all the prediction vectors (i.e. the feature vectors in terms of probability) are then routed using dynamic routing algorithm [18] and passed to the secondary capsule layer. In this work, self attention [23] mechanism based routing algorithm [18] is incorporated to enhance the overall effectiveness of the model by selectively focusing on important elements of the primary capsule layer, while reducing the computational time. In Fig. 2, the schematic overview of the self attention mechanism based efficient Caps-Net discriminator is shown. The Caps-Net discriminator D_X and D_Y can be written as follows,

$$D_X(.) \rightarrow CapsNet(.), \tag{9}$$

$$D_Y(.) \rightarrow CapsNet(.). \tag{10}$$

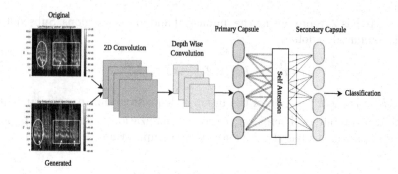

Fig. 2. Schematic overview of the self attention mechanism based efficient Caps-Net discriminator.

where, the outputs of D_X and D_Y are the last layer flatten vector (1 dimensional latent representation of features) obtained from the secondary capsule layer output of the respective discriminators. The discriminator incorporated in the RNCapsGAN-VC model works as a critic that measures the similarity between real and generated speech feature.

2.3 Loss Functions

Generator Loss. The generator $G_{X \to Y}$ and $G_{Y \to X}$ learns the target distribution Y and X by minimizing the generator least squares loss $\mathcal{L}_{gen}^{X \to Y}$ and $\mathcal{L}_{gen}^{X \to Y}$ as shown in Eq. (11) and Eq. (12),

$$\mathcal{L}_{gen}^{X \to Y} = \frac{1}{2}\mathbb{E}_{x \sim P_x}(D_Y(G_{X \to Y}(x) - 1))^2, \tag{11}$$

$$\mathcal{L}_{gen}^{Y \to X} = \frac{1}{2}\mathbb{E}_{y \sim P_y}(D_X(G_{Y \to X}(y) - 1))^2. \tag{12}$$

Here, $\mathcal{L}_{gen}^{X \to Y}$ and $\mathcal{L}_{gen}^{Y \to X}$ indicates generator loss functions following the syntax $\mathcal{L}_{gen}^{s \to t}$, such that $s \in$ source domain and $t \in$ target domain.

Cycle-Consistency Loss. The cycle-consistency loss preserves the contextual information by minimizing the L_1 loss between the original input x and its cycled from $G_{Y \to X}(G_{X \to Y}(x))$, and similarly for y and $\mathcal{L}_{cyc}^{Y \to X \to Y}$. The loss function can be stated as below,

$$\mathcal{L}_{cyc}^{X \to Y \to X} = \mathbb{E}_{x \sim P_x}||G_{Y \to X}(G_{X \to Y}(x)) - x||_1, \tag{13}$$

$$\mathcal{L}_{cyc}^{Y \to X \to Y} = \mathbb{E}_{y \sim P_y}||G_{X \to Y}(G_{Y \to X}(y)) - y||_1. \tag{14}$$

Here, $\mathcal{L}_{gen}^{X \to Y \to X}$ and $\mathcal{L}_{gen}^{Y \to X \to Y}$ indicates cycle-consistency loss functions in terms of the generators following the syntax $\mathcal{L}_{gen}^{s \to z \to t}$, such that $s \in$ source domain, $z \in$ intermediate target domain and $t \in$ final target domain.

Identity Loss. Apart from the cycle-consistency loss for better generator training, identity loss is also used to minimize the loss of information while intra-domain mapping. The mathematical formulation of the identity loss $\mathcal{L}_{id}^{X \to Y}$ and $\mathcal{L}_{id}^{Y \to X}$ are shown in Eq. (15) and Eq. (16) respectively.

$$\mathcal{L}_{id}^{X \to Y} = \mathbb{E}_{y \sim P_y} \|G_{X \to Y}(y) - y\|_1, \tag{15}$$

$$\mathcal{L}_{id}^{Y \to X} = \mathbb{E}_{x \sim P_x} \|G_{Y \to X}(x) - x\|_1. \tag{16}$$

Discriminator Loss. The last layer flattened vector obtained using D_X and D_Y corresponding to real and synthesized speech features are compared inorder to compute the discriminator loss $\mathcal{L}_{disc}^{Caps_X}$ and $\mathcal{L}_{disc}^{Caps_Y}$ using L_2 loss function [8]. The discriminator loss measures the similarity between the latent representations of the real and the synthesized mel-spectrogram, as shown in Eq. (17) and Eq. (18),

$$\mathcal{L}_{disc}^{Caps_X} = (D_X(x) - D_X(\hat{x}))^2, \tag{17}$$

$$\mathcal{L}_{disc}^{Caps_Y} = (D_Y(y) - D_Y(\hat{y}))^2. \tag{18}$$

3 Experimental Design

3.1 Dataset Description

The models under consideration were trained and tested using the VCC 2018 [16] and CMU Arctic [14] speech datasets, for both inter and intra-gender voice conversion. In the VCC 2018 dataset, the considered speakers were VCC2-TM1/-SM3/-TF1/-SF3. In the CMU Arctic dataset, the considered speakers were cmu-us-bld-Arctic/-rms-Arctic/-clb-Arctic/-slt-Arctic. In both the VCC-2018 and CMU Arctic datasets, a total of 81 speech samples were used for training, and 35 speech samples were used for evaluation. In this work, the CMU Arctic dataset is also considered in non-parallel setting [13] as that of VCC 2018.

3.2 Training Details

For training the RNCapsGAN-VC model, Adam optimizer [12] is used with learning rate 1×10^{-4}. The RNCapsGAN-VC model is trained for 5×10^2 epochs (i.e. 40.5k iterations) considering VCC 2018 dataset and CMU Arctic dataset. The mini-batch size is considered as 1. In this work, pretrained MelGAN vocoder [15] is used for mel-spectrogram to audible speech synthesis. The size of the mel-spectrograms considered here is $2 \times 80 \times 64$. In MaskCycleGAN-VC [10], the model is trained for 6.172×10^3 epochs (i.e. 500k iterations) considering VCC-2018 dataset. Whereas, considering CMU-Arctic dataset MaskCycleGAN-VC model is trained for 1×10^3 epochs (i.e. 80k iterations) in the same machine configuration as the RNCapsGAN-VC model is executed.

3.3 Experimental Setup

The proposed RNCapsGAN-VC model is executed on a Dell Precision 7820 workstation running Ubuntu 18.04 64 bit Operating System. The workstation is equipped with an Intel Xeon Gold 5215 2.5 GHz processor, 96 GB RAM, and an Nvidia 16 GB Quadro RTX5000 graphics card. All experiments for this project are conducted using Python 3.6.9, with Pytorch 1.1.2 and Numpy 1.19.5 libraries. The audible speech samples are preprocessed using Librosa 0.9.1.

4 Results and Discussion

4.1 Objective Evaluation

The average MCD values of the proposed RNCapsGAN-VC and MaskCycle GAN-VC model-generated speech samples are provided in Table 1. The samples are generated using both the VCC 2018 and CMU Arctic datasets[1]. Lower values of the objective evaluation metrics indicate higher speaker similarity. In Table 1, it can be observed that the MCD values of RNCapsGAN-VC are lower than those of MaskCycleGAN-VC for both intra-gender (M-M, F-F) and inter-gender (M-F, F-M) voice conversion (VC). However, it is also noticeable that for CMU-Arctic dataset MaskCycleGAN-VC obtained lower MCD score (i.e. 7.12) than RNCapsGAN-VC (i.e. 7.23) for male to male (M-M) VC condition.

Table 1. MCD values for VCC 2018 and CMU-Arctic dataset.

Dataset	Models	M-M	F-F	M-F	F-M
MCD					
VCC 2018	**RNCapsGAN-VC**	**7.26**	**6.63**	**6.65**	**6.68**
	MaskCycleGAN-VC	7.45	6.85	6.76	7.84
CMU-Arctic	**RNCapsGAN-VC**	7.23	**7.68**	**8.00**	**7.98**
	MaskCycleGAN-VC	**7.12**	7.81	8.20	8.07

In this work, an ablation study is conducted to evaluate the performance of the proposed RNCapsGAN-VC model for each contribution. Table 2 presents the results, where RNCapsGAN-VC(1) refers to the RNCapsGAN-VC model without capsule network discriminator (replaced by patchGAN discriminator of MaskCycleGAN-VC), and RNCapsGAN-VC(2) represents the RNCapsGAN-VC without region normalization technique based generator (replaced by instance normalization technique based generator of MaskCycleGAN-VC). The ablation study is conducted using the VCC 2018 dataset considering 500 epochs.

---

[1] The generated speech samples and code implementation can be found at https://github.com/BlueBlaze6335/RNCapsGAN-VC.

Table 2 demonstrates that the MCD values of RNCapsGAN-VC(2) are consistently lower than those of RNCapsGAN-VC(1). This suggests the effectiveness of the capsule network discriminator in the RNCapsGAN-VC model. However, it is noteworthy that the inclusion of the region normalized generator, along with the capsule network discriminator in the RNCapsGAN-VC model, yields significant improvements in terms of speaker similarity, as observed in Table 2.

Table 2. MCD values for ablation study.

Models	M-M	F-F	M-F	F-M
MCD				
RNCapsGAN-VC	**7.26**	**6.63**	**6.65**	**6.68**
RNCapsGAN-VC(1)	7.56	6.72	6.75	7.09
RNCapsGAN-VC(2)	7.46	6.64	6.70	6.98

For a visual comparison between MaskCycleGAN-VC and RNCapsGAN-VC generated speech samples, the mel-spectrograms of source, target, MaskCycleGAN-VC and RNCapsGAN-VC for both intra-gender and inter-gender VC are provided in Fig. 3. In Fig. 3, it is well observed that the amplitude (loudness) and frequency (pitch) components of the RNCapsGAN-VC generated mel-spectrogram is highly similar to the corresponding target mel-spectrogram of each VC type. Moreover, the generated samples of RNCapsGAN-VC model successfully retained the formant patterns of the source mel-spectrogram without any distortion, which implies the effectiveness of the proposed model for the non-parallel VC task. Though, it is also noticeable that the mel-spectrograms of MaskCycleGAN-VC obtained significant similarity as that of the RNCapsGAN-VC, but the training epochs required in MaskCycleGAN-VC is approximately twelve times more than the proposed RNCapsGAN-VC model. This indicates the superiority of our proposed model in terms of robustness and adaptability.

4.2 Subjective Evaluation

Subjective evaluations were conducted to measure the naturalness of the generated speech samples using the Mean Opinion Score (MOS) [20] metric. The MOS values were obtained by considering a total of 15 volunteers. In the MOS test, each volunteer was provided with their original speech samples, as well as speech samples generated by RNCapsGAN-VC and MaskCycleGAN-VC. The MOS values, along with their corresponding 95% confidence intervals, are presented in Table 3 for both the VCC 2018 and CMU-Arctic datasets. Higher MOS values indicate high speaker similarity and naturalness from human hearing perspective. The MOS values presented in Table 3 indicate that the speech samples generated by RNCapsGAN-VC have higher scores compared to those generated by MaskCycleGAN-VC. This suggests that the proposed RNCapsGAN-VC model outperforms MaskCycleGAN-VC in terms of subjective evaluation, demonstrating its superiority in generating speech samples with better perceived naturalness.

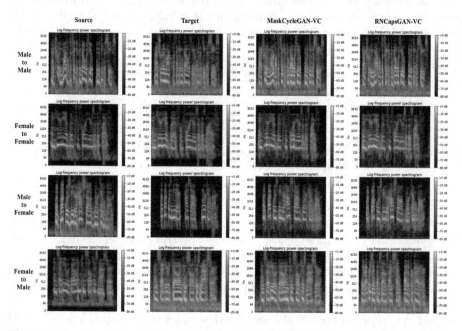

Fig. 3. Mel-spectrograms of source, target, MaskCycleGAN-VC and RNCapsGAN-VC generated speech sample for intra-gender and inter-gender VC.

Table 3. MOS for naturalness with 95% confidence intervals.

Dataset	Models	M-M	F-F	M-F	F-M
VCC 2018	**RNCapsGAN-VC**	**3.5 ± 0.19**	**3.9 ± 0.23**	**3.3 ± 0.35**	**3.1 ± 0.47**
	MaskCycleGAN-VC	3.1 ± 0.32	2.9 ± 0.42	2.6 ± 0.23	2.9 ± 0.24
CMU-Arctic	**RNCapsGAN-VC**	**3.4 ± 0.42**	**3.6 ± 0.20**	**3.2 ± 0.15**	**3.6 ± 0.13**
	MaskCycleGAN-VC	2.9 ± 0.15	3.1 ± 0.41	3 ± 0.04	3 ± 0.05

5   Conclusion

This work introduces a novel GAN model, the RNCapsGAN-VC, specifically designed for mel-spectrogram based voice conversion (VC). The RNCapsGAN-VC model consists of a region-normalized generator and a Caps-Net discriminator. The utilization of a region-normalized generator and a Caps-Net discriminator aims to enhance the generation of mel-spectrograms by capturing the target distribution more effectively than the state-of-the-art MaskCycleGAN-VC model. The proposed model is evaluated on the VCC 2018 and CMU Arctic speech datasets, employing both objective and subjective evaluation measures. The results of these evaluations consistently demonstrate the superiority of the RNCapsGAN-VC model. Furthermore, it can also be concluded from the experimental results that the proposed model showed better performance in less training epochs than the considered SOTA VC model. This indicates the high robustness and adaptability of the proposed model for the non-parallel VC task. Moving forward, there are opportunities to further enhance the performance of GAN-based VC models, particularly in the context of inter-gender voice conversion. Additionally, the potential of the RNCapsGAN-VC model in speech enhancement for the generated speech samples could be explored in future investigations.

References

1. Abe, M., Nakamura, S., Shikano, K., Kuwabara, H.: Voice conversion through vector quantization. In: International Conference on Acoustics, Speech, and Signal Processing, ICASSP 1988, vol. 1, pp. 655–658 (1988). https://doi.org/10.1109/ICASSP.1988.196671
2. Chen, Y.N., Liu, L.J., Hu, Y.J., Jiang, Y., Ling, Z.H.: Improving recognition-synthesis based any-to-one voice conversion with cyclic training. In: ICASSP 2022, pp. 7007–7011 (2022). https://doi.org/10.1109/ICASSP43922.2022.9747140
3. Coto-Jiménez, M., Goddard-Close, J., Martínez-Licona, F.M.: Quality assessment of HMM-based speech synthesis using acoustical vowel analysis. In: Ronzhin, A., Potapova, R., Delic, V. (eds.) SPECOM 2014. LNCS (LNAI), vol. 8773, pp. 368–375. Springer, Cham (2014). https://doi.org/10.1007/978-3-319-11581-8_46
4. Dhar, S., Jana, N.D., Das, S.: An adaptive learning based generative adversarial network for one-to-one voice conversion. IEEE Trans. Artif. Intell. 4, 92–106 (2022). https://doi.org/10.1109/TAI.2022.3149858
5. Du, H., Tian, X., Xie, L., Li, H.: Optimizing voice conversion network with cycle consistency loss of speaker identity. In: 2021 IEEE SLT, pp. 507–513 (2021). https://doi.org/10.1109/SLT48900.2021.9383567
6. Goodfellow, I., et al.: Generative adversarial nets. In: Advances in NIPS, vol. 27. Curran Associates, Inc. (2014)
7. Jaiswal, A., AbdAlmageed, W., Wu, Y., Natarajan, P.: CapsuleGAN: generative adversarial capsule network. In: Leal-Taixé, L., Roth, S. (eds.) ECCV 2018. LNCS, vol. 11131, pp. 526–535. Springer, Cham (2019). https://doi.org/10.1007/978-3-030-11015-4_38
8. Jolicoeur-Martineau, A.: The relativistic discriminator: a key element missing from standard GAN. arXiv arXiv:1807.00734 (2019)
9. Kaneko, T., Kameoka, H., Tanaka, K., Hojo, N.: CycleGAN-VC2: improved cycleGAN-based non-parallel voice conversion. In: ICASSP, vol. 2019, pp. 6820–6824 (2019)
10. Kaneko, T., Kameoka, H., Tanaka, K., Hojo, N.: MaskCycleGAN-VC: learning non-parallel voice conversion with filling in frames. In: ICASSP, pp. 5919–5923 (2021)

11. Kaneko, T., Kameoka, H.: CycleGAN-VC: non-parallel voice conversion using cycle-consistent adversarial networks. In: 2018, 26th EUSIPCO, pp. 2100–2104 (2018). https://doi.org/10.23919/EUSIPCO.2018.8553236

12. Kingma, D.P., Ba, J.: Adam: a method for stochastic optimization. arXiv preprint arXiv:1412.6980 (2014)

13. Kishida, T., Nakashika, T.: Non-parallel voice conversion based on free-energy minimization of speaker-conditional restricted Boltzmann machine. In: 2022 Asia-Pacific Signal and Information Processing Association Annual Summit and Conference (APSIPA ASC), pp. 251–255 (2022). https://doi.org/10.23919/APSIPAASC55919.2022.9980151

14. Kominek, J., Black, A.W.: The CMU arctic speech databases. In: SSW (2004)

15. Kumar, K., et al.: MelGAN: generative adversarial networks for conditional waveform synthesis. In: NeurIPS (2019)

16. Lorenzo-Trueba, J., et al.: The voice conversion challenge 2018: promoting development of parallel and nonparallel methods. In: Odyssey (2018)

17. Mazzia, V., Salvetti, F., Chiaberge, M.: Efficient-CapsNet: capsule network with self-attention routing. Sci. Rep. **11**(1), 14634 (2021)

18. Mazzia, V., Salvetti, F., Chiaberge, M.: Efficient-CapsNet: capsule network with self-attention routing. CoRR abs/2101.12491 (2021). https://arxiv.org/abs/2101.12491

19. Sabour, S., Frosst, N., Hinton, G.E.: Dynamic routing between capsules. arXiv arXiv:1710.09829 (2017)

20. Sisman, B., Yamagishi, J., King, S., Li, H.: An overview of voice conversion and its challenges: from statistical modeling to deep learning. IEEE/ACM Trans. Audio Speech Lang. Process. **29**, 132–157 (2021)

21. Sun, L., Li, K., Wang, H., Kang, S., Meng, H.M.: Phonetic posteriorgrams for many-to-one voice conversion without parallel data training. In: 2016 IEEE International Conference on Multimedia and Expo (ICME), pp. 1–6 (2016)

22. Uchida, H., Saito, D., Minematsu, N., Hirose, K.: Statistical acoustic-to-articulatory mapping unified with speaker normalization based on voice conversion. In: Proceedings of the INTERSPEECH 2015, pp. 588–592 (2015). https://doi.org/10.21437/Interspeech.2015-209

23. Vaswani, A., et al.: Attention is all you need. In: NIPS (2017)

24. Wu, J., Polyak, A., Taigman, Y., Fong, J., Agrawal, P., He, Q.: Multilingual text-to-speech training using cross language voice conversion and self-supervised learning of speech representations. In: ICASSP 2022, pp. 8017–8021 (2022). https://doi.org/10.1109/ICASSP43922.2022.9746282

25. Yu, T., et al.: Region normalization for image inpainting. In: AAAI (2020)

26. Yun, Y.-S., Jung, J., Eun, S.: Voice conversion between synthesized bilingual voices using line spectral frequencies. In: Ronzhin, A., Potapova, R., Fakotakis, N. (eds.) SPECOM 2015. LNCS (LNAI), vol. 9319, pp. 463–471. Springer, Cham (2015). https://doi.org/10.1007/978-3-319-23132-7_57

27. Zahariev, V., Azarov, E., Petrovsky, A.: Voice conversion for TTS systems with tuning on the target speaker based on GMM. In: Karpov, A., Potapova, R., Mporas, I. (eds.) SPECOM 2017. LNCS (LNAI), vol. 10458, pp. 788–798. Springer, Cham (2017). https://doi.org/10.1007/978-3-319-66429-3_79

Speech Enhancement Using LinkNet Architecture

Anuj Patel[2(✉)], G. Satya Prasad[1], Sabyasachi Chandra[1], Puja Bharati[1], and Shyamal Kumar Das Mandal[1]

[1] Indian Institute of Technology, Kharagpur, India
gsatyaprasad@kgpian.iitkgp.ac.in
[2] Pandit Deendayal Energy University, Gandhinagar, India
anujtpatel2004@gmail.com

Abstract. Speech enhancement techniques play a vital role in enhancing the clarity and overall quality of audio signals, addressing issues like background noise, reverberation, and channel impairments that often degrade speech intelligibility. Neural network models, including DNNs, CNNs, RNNs, and VAEs, have demonstrated their effectiveness in improving speech quality by decoding noisy speech inputs, capturing intricate patterns, and extracting relevant information. Evaluation metrics like PESQ and STOI are commonly employed to assess the performance of speech enhancement algorithms. STOI measures the understandability of enhanced speech using short-time spectral information, while PESQ evaluates the subjective quality of enhanced speech compared to the original clean speech. Moreover, recent advancements in speech enhancement research have shown that employing LinkNet, a specific neural network architecture, can significantly surpass the efficiency of other models. LinkNet has demonstrated superior performance in enhancing speech signals by effectively mitigating noise, reducing artifacts, and enhancing the overall intelligibility of the output. Its architecture incorporates innovative techniques that facilitate the extraction of meaningful features from noisy speech inputs, leading to remarkable results in terms of speech quality improvement. By leveraging LinkNet, researchers and practitioners can further advance the field of speech enhancement and achieve outstanding outcomes in terms of audio clarity and intelligibility.

Keywords: Speech enhancement · Deep learning · Convolutional neural networks · Auto encoder · UNET · LinkNet-speech

1 Introduction

Speech enhancement techniques have undergone extensive research and development to enhance speech quality in the presence of diverse noise sources. Traditional approaches, including spectral subtraction [1], Wiener filtering [8], statistical model-based methods [5], and subspace algorithms [3,6], have been

A. Karpov et al. (Eds.): SPECOM 2023, LNAI 14338, pp. 245–257, 2023.
https://doi.org/10.1007/978-3-031-48309-7_21

widely employed to mitigate the deleterious effects of noise and improve speech intelligibility and quality. However, recent advancements in deep learning have introduced novel avenues for speech enhancement, particularly by leveraging the spectrogram representation of audio signals as training data.

Deep learning techniques, such as Convolutional Neural Networks (CNN), have demonstrated remarkable capabilities in capturing local dependencies in the spectral domain. By training CNN on large datasets consisting of spectrograms, these models can effectively learn speech enhancement filters that adaptively attenuate noise components [15]. Moreover, Recurrent Neural Networks (RNN) and Long Short-Term Memory (LSTM) networks have demonstrated their efficacy in capturing temporal dependencies in sequential data. When applied to speech enhancement tasks, RNNs and LSTMs can exploit the sequential nature of spectrograms to enhance speech quality further [13].

Auto-encoder architectures have also emerged as a prominent approach in speech enhancement. These architectures are trained to reconstruct clean speech from noisy input spectrograms, leveraging the denoising capabilities of deep neural networks. By learning to represent and reconstruct the underlying clean speech, auto-encoders effectively suppress noise and improve speech intelligibility [9].

The primary advantage of these deep learning methods is their capability to acquire intricate mappings between noisy and clean speech signals. By operating directly on the spectrogram representation of audio, these models can capture intricate patterns and dependencies that exist within the data. This enables these methods to effectively differentiate between speech and noise elements, resulting in improved speech signal quality and enhanced perceptual intelligibility. As a result, these advanced techniques have the potential to revolutionize speech communication by enabling clearer and more intelligible speech in various noisy environments.

Furthermore, this paper proposes a novel architecture known as LinkNet, which has demonstrated superior performance in terms of PESQ (Perceptual Evaluation of Speech Quality) metrics and the enhancement of speech quality. The LinkNet architecture represents an exciting advancement in the field of speech enhancement, offering promising prospects for real-world applications where speech quality is of paramount importance.

2 Speech Enhancement

In real-life settings, speech signals frequently experience the presence of noise, encompassing both stationary and non-stationary components. The connection between the clean speech signal $s(t)$, convolutional noise $h(t)$, additive noise $n(t)$, and the resultant noisy speech signal $y(t)$ can be expressed as [18]:

$$y(t) = s(t) * h(t) + n(t) \tag{1}$$

To tackle this problem, various speech enhancement techniques have been developed. These methods strive to enhance the quality and comprehensibility of speech signals by utilizing signal processing approaches. One frequently employed tool is the Short-Time Fourier Transform (STFT), which examines the speech signal in both the time and frequency domains. The STFT equation can be expressed as:

$$X(k, l) = \sum_{n=0}^{N-1} x(n)w(n - l)e^{-j2\pi kn/N} \tag{2}$$

In the given equation, $X(k, l)$ denotes the STFT coefficient at frequency bin k and time frame l. Here, $x(n)$ represents the input speech signal, $w(n - l)$ denotes the window function centered at frame l, N is the window length, and j stands for the imaginary unit [11].

Analyzing the magnitude of STFT coefficients allows for the creation of a spectrogram, which visually displays the energy distribution of the speech signal across different frequencies and time intervals. The spectrogram provides insights into the spectral properties of the speech signal, including the presence of noise elements and their changes over time.

Speech enhancement techniques frequently rely on the spectrogram to identify and reduce noise components while preserving crucial speech details. Methods such as spectral subtraction and Wiener filtering operate within the spectrogram domain, with the objective of estimating the clean speech signal based on the noisy spectrogram.

In general, speech enhancement techniques make use of signal processing tools like the STFT and leverage the spectrogram to enhance the quality and comprehensibility of speech signals by mitigating the impact of noise. These methods play a vital role in enhancing speech communication in diverse real-world situations.

3   Deep Learning Approaches

The objective of speech enhancement is to enhance the clarity and comprehensibility of speech signals that are affected by background noise or other forms of distortions. Deep learning models can be trained to denoise such speech signals by learning the underlying patterns and dependencies between the noisy input x and the desired denoised output y.

To train the model, a dataset consisting of pairs of noisy speech samples and their corresponding clean or denoised versions is required. The mel spectrogram is a commonly used representation of audio signals, obtained by applying a Fourier transform to short segments of the signal and then taking the logarithm of the resulting mel-frequency spectrogram. This representation captures the spectral content of the audio over time. The deep learning architecture is constructed to estimate the denoised speech y using predictions derived from the noisy speech x. Throughout the training process, the model's parameters, which encompass weights and biases, are adjusted to minimize the disparity between the predicted values and the desired targets.

The Mean Squared Error (MSE) is a commonly used loss function in various machine learning and deep learning applications, especially in regression tasks.

It measures the average squared difference between the predicted values and the target values. MSE is a popular choice because it heavily penalizes larger errors due to the squaring operation, which can make it sensitive to outliers.

$$MSE = \frac{1}{n} \sum_{i=1}^{n} (y_i - \hat{y}_i)^2 \tag{3}$$

where: - n is the total samples in the dataset. - y_i represents the target (denoised) value for the i-th sample. - $\hat{y}_i$ represents the predicted value for the i-th sample. By minimizing the Mean Absolute Error during training, the model learns to approximate the denoised speech accurately and improves its performance in reducing noise and enhancing the quality of the input speech signals. There are many deep learning architectures for Speech Enhancement using mel spectrogram as follows:

3.1   Encoder Decoder Architecture - 2DCNN

The encoder-decoder architecture introduced in [17] for speech enhancement tasks is built upon a convolutional neural network (CNN) and has demonstrated encouraging outcomes. The architecture comprises two key elements: the encoder and the decoder.

The encoder component comprises multiple layers, including convolutional layers, batch normalization [7], max-pooling, and ReLU activation [10]. These layers collaborate to extract and encode the pertinent features from the input spectrogram. The convolutional layers apply filters to capture local patterns in the spectrogram, while the batch normalization normalizes the activations to improve training stability. By employing max-pooling layers, the spatial dimensions of the feature maps are reduced, resulting in efficient feature compression. The utilization of the ReLU activation function introduces non-linearity, thereby improving the model's ability to capture intricate relationships within the data.

On the other hand, the decoder component is responsible for reconstructing the enhanced spectrogram. It consists of convolutional layers, batch normalization, and up-sampling layers. The convolutional layers decode the compressed features and restore spatial information. The batch normalization helps in maintaining the stability of the model during training. The up-sampling layers increase the spatial dimensions of the feature maps, facilitating the reconstruction process.

In this specific application, the last softmax layer typically found in classification tasks has been replaced with a convolutional layer [12]. This modification aims to better suit the reconstruction process required in speech enhancement tasks. The utilization of this encoder-decoder architecture allows for effective feature compression and reconstruction, leading to improved outcomes in comparison to traditional speech enhancement methods.

3.2   Autoencoder with Skip Connections

The autoencoder based on a CNN with skip connections consists of an encoder for feature extraction, utilizing 3×3 convolutional layers and down-sampling through convolution with a stride of 2. The decoder employs deconvolution for reconstruction, allowing learnable upsampling. Shortcut connections ensure pixel-wise correspondence by adding feature maps with their corresponding deconvolutional layers as shown in Fig. 1. The network investigates supervised pre-training's influence and focuses on reconstruction performance, rather than complex architectures, to enhance image restoration tasks.

The encoding process can be represented as:

$$\hat{Z} = \text{Encoder}(X) = \text{Conv\_3x3}(\text{Conv\_3x3}(\dots(\text{Conv\_3x3}(X)))) \qquad (4)$$

where X represents the input image and Z denotes the encoded features. The decoding process can be represented as:

$$\hat{X} = \text{Decoder}(Z) = \text{Deconv\_3x3}(\text{Deconv\_3x3}(\dots(\text{Deconv\_3x3}(Z)))) \qquad (5)$$

where $\hat{X}$ represents the reconstructed output image.

To ensure pixel-wise correspondence and enable information flow between the encoder and decoder, skip connections are implemented. The presence of skip connections enables the incorporation of feature maps from the encoder to their respective deconvolutional layers in the decoder.

$$\hat{X} = \text{Decoder}(Z) + \text{Encoder}(X) \qquad (6)$$

Overall, this approach utilizes a simple architecture with skip connections to enhance image restoration tasks, focusing on the reconstruction performance while investigating the impact of supervised pre-training [4].

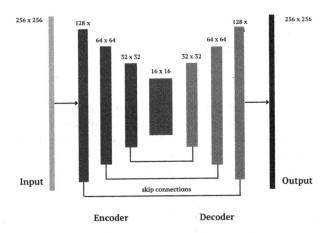

Fig. 1. Diagram of Encoder-Decoder architecture with skip connections based on CNN [4].

3.3   UNet

The U-Net architecture is widely employed in speech enhancement applications to enhance the quality and comprehensibility of speech signals. It is composed of a contracting path and an expansive path.

In the contracting path, there are consecutive 3×3 convolutions, ReLU activation, and 2×2 max pooling operations to achieve downsampling. This path is responsible for extracting relevant features from the input noisy speech signals. The number of feature channels doubles at each downsampling step, allowing for an increased representation capacity.

The expansive path of the architecture involves upsampling, using a 2×2 convolution to decrease the number of feature channels, combining with the corresponding cropped feature map from the contracting path, and applying further convolutions with ReLU activation. This path aims to restore the spatial information and enhance the quality of the denoised speech. By concatenating the feature maps from the contracting path, the network can effectively utilize both local and global information for denoising. The additional convolutions refine the feature maps and further enhance the denoised speech representation.

In the last layer of the network, a 1×1 convolution is utilized to transform the feature vectors into the intended denoised speech output.

As shown in Fig. 2, the U-Net for speech enhancement typically consists of 23 convolutional layers. It combines convolutional and pooling operations to capture hierarchical features and spatial information effectively. Shortcut connections are incorporated to preserve detailed information during the encoding and decoding processes.

The input tile size should be chosen appropriately to ensure consistent tiling of the output denoised speech signals. This allows for seamless processing of the input speech signals and consistent enhancement results [14].

4   Experimental Setup

4.1   Data Preprossessing

The dataset used in this experiment was obtained from the DataShare Platform of the University of Edinburgh. The average size of audio clips were around 3 s in which the noise was added manually to generate the dataset for speech research domain. It consists of audio files containing both cleaned speech and noisy speech recordings. To preprocess the data for speech enhancement, several steps were taken. Firstly, the audio files were loaded and subjected to the Short-Time Fourier Transform (STFT), which generated spectrograms representing the frequency content over time. The STFT is a commonly used technique for analyzing the frequency content of audio signals. Next, a logarithmic operation was applied to convert the spectrograms into log-mel spectrograms, which are expressed in decibels (dB).

Since the duration of the audio clips varied, it was important to ensure a consistent input shape for the model. To achieve this, extra padding was added

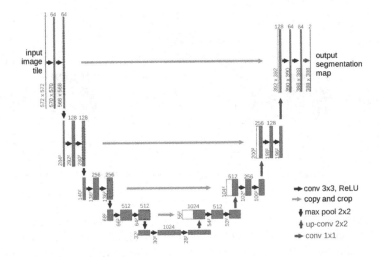

Fig. 2. Diagram of UNET architecture [14].

to each spectrogram. This padding ensured that all spectrograms had the same dimensions, which is necessary for the model's input requirements. Additionally, for computational efficiency, all padded spectrograms were resized to a standardized dimension of 256×256. This resizing step allowed the model to effectively handle spectrograms of varying lengths while reducing computational cost and reduce memory storage for training data. Like unequal size of spectograms is not the good idea with which we should work.

Furthermore, the preprocessed data was split into 660 training and 164 testing audio files. The model acquired the ability to reduce noise and enhance the quality of the provided speech signals through its training process. Flow of model training can be visualized from Fig. 3.

In the given diagram or pipeline, the model undergoes training using the preprocessed data. Once the audio is inputted into the model or speech enhancer, the inverse Short-Time Fourier Transform (STFT) operation needs to be performed to reconstruct the clean waveform of the audio. This reconstruction process results in enhanced speech quality and improved intelligibility. Overall, the data preprocessing steps and the training process play a crucial role in achieving effective speech enhancement outcomes.

4.2 Network Architecture

LinkNet-Speech is a specialized architecture that focuses on enhancing speech by regenerating high-quality spectrograms from audio data. The model utilizes convolution and full-convolution operations for processing spectrograms, employing strided convolutions for downsampling and upsampling techniques to restore the original resolution. The model's capacity to grasp intricate patterns and improve the input's denoising is boosted by the incorporation of BatchNormalization and

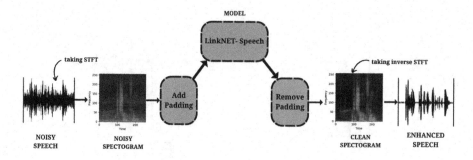

Fig. 3. Flowchart of LinkNet-Speech Training.

ReLU non-linearity following every convolutional layer. The structure comprises an encoder on the left and a decoder on the right. The encoder commences with an initial block, which carries out a 7×7 convolution with a stride of 2, along with spatial max-pooling utilizing a 3×3 kernel and a stride of 2. Residual blocks, referred to as encoder-block(i), are utilized within the encoder to capture and retain important features from the spectrogram. The decoder employs similar blocks to reconstruct the spectrogram with improved clarity. LinkNet-Speech adopts a ResNet18 encoder, known for its lighter weight compared to other architectures, yet it outperforms larger architectures in terms of speech enhancement for spectrogram regeneration. An innovative aspect of LinkNet-Speech is the establishment of connections between the encoder and its corresponding decoder, allowing the model to recover lost spatial information during downsampling and leverage it during upsampling, resulting in improved spectrogram regeneration. The use of full-convolution in the decoder enhances the upsampling process, enabling the model to reconstruct the spectrogram with finer details and improved accuracy. This approach significantly improves the efficiency of the network, making speech enhancement feasible for audio spectrograms [2]. Proposed model architecture diagram is provided in Fig. 4.

By utilizing the proposed approach of training the model within the LinkNet-Speech architecture, wherein the training dataset comprises clean audio spectrograms as the ground truth and noise audio spectrograms as the input images, it is possible to achieve the reported outcomes as discussed in the Results section. This training methodology involves supplying the model with an extensive collection of paired data, encompassing clean audio spectrograms and their corresponding noisy counterparts. Throughout the training process, the LinkNet-Speech model is able to acquire a deep understanding of the intricate relationship between the denoised and noisy speech spectrograms. Leveraging the inherent capabilities of the architecture, the model effectively learns to generate outputs that closely align with the desired clean audio spectrograms when provided with the corresponding noisy input spectrograms.

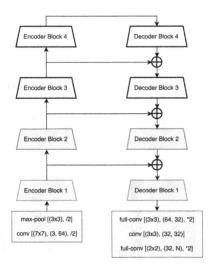

Fig. 4. LinkNet-Speech architecture [2].

5   Results

To evaluate the fidelity of the improved speech, we employed objective metrics that meticulously quantified diverse facets of the generated output. The proposed model was trained on the Kaggle platform, specifically on a GPU P100. The training dataset consisted of 80%(1200 audio files) of the original data, while the remaining 20% (240 audio file) was used for testing. One of the objective measures employed is PESQ (Perceptual Evaluation of Speech Quality). The range of PESQ scores varies from −0.5 to 4.5, where higher values indicate enhanced quality [16]. Table 1 presents the results and comparision between other architectures at constant epochs = 50, providing a comparative reference by including scores obtained directly from the noisy signals and signals filtered using other methods.

Table 1 and Fig. 5(*left*) provides a comparison of different models based on their performance metrics, including loss (MAE), STOI (Short-Time Objective Intelligibility) score, and time per epoch. Among the models evaluated, the proposed LinkNet-Speech model demonstrates superior performance. Graph of training losses of 4 architectures has been shown in Fig. 6. It achieves the lowest loss of 0.7124, outperforming the Autoencoder (CNN), Autoencoder with Skip connection (CNN), and UNet models. Moreover, LinkNet-Speech achieves the highest STOI score of 96.5419% and PESQ of 3.6403 indicating its ability to effectively enhance speech intelligibility. Remarkably, the model achieves this impressive performance while maintaining the same time per epoch as the Autoencoder (CNN) model. These findings highlight the potential of the LinkNet-Speech model as an effective approach for speech-related tasks, offering improved accuracy and intelligibility without sacrificing computational efficiency. Spectogram Outputs of cleaned *vs* noisy audio inputs is compared in Fig. 7.

Table 1. Model Performance Comparison.

Model	Loss (MAE)	STOI (%)	time/epoch (sec)
Autoencoder (CNN)	1.2020	60.4018	3
Autoencoder with Skip Conn. (CNN)	0.8450	89.2511	5
UNet	0.7159	90.0897	4
LinkNet-Speech (Proposed)	**0.7124**	**96.5419**	**3**

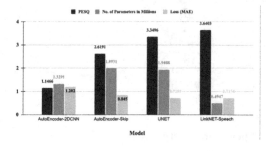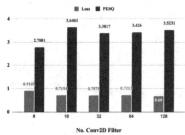

Fig. 5. (*left*): Comparision of Model vs Loss(MAE), PESQ, No. of Parameters(in millions). (*right*): No. of Conv2D Filters vs Loss(MAE), PESQ.

Table 2 and Fig. 5(*right*) showcases the relationship between the number of convolutional filters in a model and its performance metrics. As the number of filters increases, there is a notable improvement in both the loss and STOI (Short-Time Objective Intelligibility) metrics. The decrease in loss indicates that a higher number of filters allows the model to better minimize the discrepancy between predicted and target outputs.

Similarly, the increasing STOI percentage suggests that the additional filters enhance the model's ability to capture finer acoustic details, leading to improved intelligibility in the output signals. However, it's important to note that the increase in filter count also results in more parameters, making the model more computationally demanding and potentially requiring more resources for training and inference. The result achieved with 16 convolutional filters stands out as

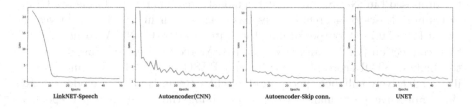

Fig. 6. Training Loss of different architecture.

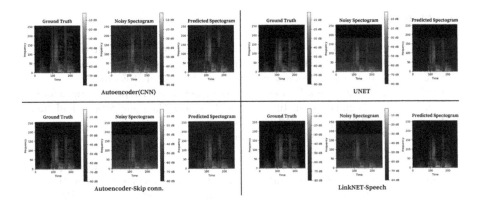

Fig. 7. Output Comparison of different architecture.

Table 2. Variation of No. of Conv.Filters.

No. of Conv.Filters	Loss	STOI (%)	Parameters (mill.)
8	0.9101	87.3745	0.1246
16	0.7154	96.5419	0.4947
32	0.7071	92.6047	1.9709
64	0.7213	97.2291	7.8679
128	0.6800	96.7056	31.4400

highly convincing. With a loss of 0.7154, a PESQ score of 3.6403, and an STOI of 96.5419%, the model demonstrates impressive performance.

6   Conclusion

In summary, this research paper aimed to compare the performance of various architectures, including Autoencoder (CNN), Autoencoder with skip connections, UNet, and LinkNet-Speech, in the task of denoising speech audio. The evaluation and analysis revealed that LinkNet-Speech consistently outperformed the other architectures in terms of generating higher quality clean speech from noisy input. This superiority can be attributed to LinkNet-Speech's unique architectural design, which enables it to effectively capture relevant spectral and temporal features, resulting in enhanced speech restoration. The findings of this study suggest that LinkNet-Speech holds great potential as a powerful architecture for speech enhancement tasks. However, further research is needed to investigate its performance in different noise scenarios, assess its generalization capabilities, and validate its effectiveness on larger and more diverse datasets. Overall, this research demonstrates that LinkNet-Speech offers significant advancements in generating improved clean speech from noisy audio compared to existing architectures, providing a promising direction for future speech enhancement techniques.

References

1. Berouti, M., Schwartz, R., Makhoul, J.: Enhancement of speech corrupted by acoustic noise. In: ICASSP 1979. In: IEEE International Conference on Acoustics, Speech, and Signal Processing, vol. 4, pp. 208–211. IEEE (1979)
2. Chaurasia, A., Culurciello, E.: Linknet: Exploiting encoder representations for efficient semantic segmentation. In: 2017 IEEE Visual Communications and Image Processing (VCIP), pp. 1–4. IEEE (2017)
3. Dendrinos, M., Bakamidis, S., Carayannis, G.: Speech enhancement from noise: a regenerative approach. Speech Commun. **10**(1), 45–57 (1991)
4. Dong, L.F., Gan, Y.Z., Mao, X.L., Yang, Y.B., Shen, C.: Learning deep representations using convolutional auto-encoders with symmetric skip connections. In: 2018 IEEE International Conference on Acoustics, Speech and Signal Processing (ICASSP), pp. 3006–3010. IEEE (2018)
5. Ephraim, Y.: Statistical-model-based speech enhancement systems. Proc. IEEE **80**(10), 1526–1555 (1992)
6. Ephraim, Y., Van Trees, H.L.: A signal subspace approach for speech enhancement. IEEE Trans. Speech Audio Process. **3**(4), 251–266 (1995)
7. Ioffe, S., Szegedy, C.: Batch normalization: accelerating deep network training by reducing internal covariate shift. In: International Conference on Machine Learning, pp. 448–456. PMLR (2015)
8. Lim, J., Oppenheim, A.: All-pole modeling of degraded speech. IEEE Trans. Acoust. Speech Signal Process. **26**(3), 197–210 (1978)
9. Lu, X., Tsao, Y., Matsuda, S., Hori, C.: Speech enhancement based on deep denoising autoencoder. In: Interspeech, vol. 2013, pp. 436–440 (2013)
10. Nair, V., Hinton, G.E.: Rectified linear units improve restricted Boltzmann machines. In: Proceedings of the 27th International Conference on Machine Learning (ICML-2010), pp. 807–814 (2010)
11. Nawab, S., Quatieri, T., Lim, J.: Signal reconstruction from short-time Fourier transform magnitude. IEEE Trans. Acoust. Speech Signal Process. **31**(4), 986–998 (1983)
12. Park, S.R., Lee, J.: A fully convolutional neural network for speech enhancement. arXiv preprint arXiv:1609.07132 (2016)
13. Parveen, S., Green, P.: Speech enhancement with missing data techniques using recurrent neural networks. In: 2004 IEEE International Conference on Acoustics, Speech, and Signal Processing. vol. 1, pp. 1–733. IEEE (2004)
14. Ronneberger, O., Fischer, P., Brox, T.: U-net: convolutional networks for biomedical image segmentation. In: Navab, N., Hornegger, J., Wells, W.M., Frangi, A.F. (eds.) MICCAI 2015. LNCS, vol. 9351, pp. 234–241. Springer, Cham (2015). https://doi.org/10.1007/978-3-319-24574-4_28
15. Tamura, S., Waibel, A.: Noise reduction using connectionist models. In: ICASSP-1988, International Conference on Acoustics, Speech, and Signal Processing, pp. 553–556. IEEE (1988)
16. Union, I.: Wideband extension to recommendation p. 862 for the assessment of wideband telephone networks and speech codecs. International Telecommunication Union, Recommendation P. 862 (2007)

17. Vincent, P., Larochelle, H., Lajoie, I., Bengio, Y., Manzagol, P.A., Bottou, L.: Stacked denoising autoencoders: learning useful representations in a deep network with a local denoising criterion. J. Mach. Learn. Res. **11**(12), 1–38 (2010)
18. Yuliani, A.R., Amri, M.F., Suryawati, E., Ramdan, A., Pardede, H.F.: Speech enhancement using deep learning methods: a review. Jurnal Elektronika dan Telekomunikasi **21**(1), 19–26 (2021)

ATT:Adversarial Trained Transformer for Speech Enhancement

Aniket Aitawade[✉] ⓘ, Puja Bharati ⓘ, Sabyasachi Chandra ⓘ,
G. Satya Prasad , Debolina Pramanik ⓘ, Parth Sanjay Khadse ⓘ,
and Shyamal Kumar Das Mandal ⓘ

Speech Processing Lab, Indian Institute of Technology Kharagpur, Kharagpur, India
{aniketaitawade,gsatyaprasad,debolina96,parthkhadse}@kgpian.iitkgp.ac.in,
{pujabharati,sabyasachichandra}@iitkgp.ac.in, sdasmandal@cet.iitkgp.ac.in

Abstract. Speech enhancement is crucial in various applications where background noise or interference affects the quality of speech signals. Traditional signal processing techniques have limitations in handling complex and non-stationary noise sources, leading to sub-optimal performance in real-world scenarios. In recent years, research has been increasing on machine learning and deep learning-based algorithms for speech enhancement. This paper presents a novel method called Adversarial Trained Transformer (ATT) for speech enhancement. The generator component of ATT is based on a transformer architecture, which utilizes multi-head attention and LSTM-embedder layers to capture temporal dependencies and local structure in the speech signals. The discriminator component, on the other hand, employs convolutional layers for binary classification. The effectiveness of the ATT method is demonstrated through experiments conducted on the VoiceBank+DEMAND dataset. The outcomes reveal noteworthy enhancements in different speech quality metrics in comparison to other baseline methods. Furthermore, the ATT model achieves superior performance while utilizing a comparatively smaller number of parameters when compared to alternative models. The generator of ATT model has 6.57 million parameters while the generator of SEGAN has 74.13 million parameters. The results show that the suggested ATT architecture has a lot of promise for improving speech quality, and it presents a viable strategy that combines the benefits of transformer-based models with adversarial training.

Keywords: Adversarial trained transformer · Generative adversarial etwork · Speech enhancement · Transformer

1 Introduction

Speech enhancement plays a pivotal role in numerous applications, including telecommunication systems, voice assistants, hearing aids, and communication

A. Karpov et al. (Eds.): SPECOM 2023, LNAI 14338, pp. 258–270, 2023.
https://doi.org/10.1007/978-3-031-48309-7_22

channels impaired by background noise or interference. Traditional signal processing techniques have achieved considerable success but often struggle to handle complex and non-stationary noise sources, leading to sub-optimal performance in real-world scenarios [3]. Hence in recent years, more research is going on in machine learning, deep learning-based algorithms for speech enhancement.

Traditional algorithms like spectral subtraction and wiener filter give good performance for stationary noises and they require less computing power hence still they are useful in speech enhancement of portable devices [3,16,17]. But these traditional algorithms fail when given non-stationary noises or noises with low Signal to Noise ratio.

Then comes the deep learning era where deep learning models were performing better than these traditional algorithms and hence major research is going on in deep learning-based algorithms.

Artificial Neural Networks or Deep Neural Networks are used for speech enhancement but later it was observed that these models are not giving desired results because they can't analyze temporal features [15]. Hence some researchers used Convolutional Neural Networks for speech enhancement as convolutional models can very well learn spatial dependencies [5]. Then convolutional models got developed and used as an encoder-decoder structure [6,13]. Some researchers brilliantly used FFT loss while training time domain autoencoder networks [4].

Later on, it was observed that 1D convolution only extracts information from the current frame. But each frame is dependent on its neighbor frames hence there was a need to use frame dependencies. So researchers have taken 2D spectrogram as input and used 2D convolution [10]. While some researchers have used RNN, LSTM for extracting frame dependencies [11].

RNN, LSTM work sequentially hence they are getting replaced by a transformer that learns sequence dependencies and also does parallel operations and hence efficient use of GPU is possible. Various researchers have proposed different transformer architectures for speech enhancement. Mainly they have used frequency spectrum rather than time domain signal for enhancement [18].

At the same time convolutional architecture was also evolving and the Generative Adversarial Network (GAN) has gained recognition as a promising deep learning architecture in the domain of speech enhancement. Until GAN we were using a general loss function that calculates L1 or L2 norm between desired and produced outputs. But due to GAN, we got a completely new loss function. SEGAN was one of the first models which uses GAN for speech enhancement applications that completely work in the time domain [7]. Since then many GAN-based methods have been proposed, and many of these methods have assumed that the phase spectrum doesn't play a much important role in the perseverance of speech in the human auditory system. Hence they only modified the magnitude spectrum of the noisy signal and used the noisy phase spectrum to reconstruct the enhanced signal.

In this paper, we have proposed a novel method that takes advantage of both GAN and transformer. In short, we are training transformer-based architecture with adversarial learning and we observed that it produces far better results than when only trained by L2 norm loss function.

The contributions of this paper are as follows:

- We introduce the Adversarial Trained Transformer (ATT) method for speech enhancement, combining the advantages of transformer-based models and adversarial training.
- We conduct experiments on the VoiceBank+DEMAND dataset and demonstrate the effectiveness of the proposed ATT method in improving speech quality metrics.
- We show that the ATT model achieves superior performance while having a relatively lower number of parameters compared to other baseline models, making it more efficient and practical for real-world applications.

The remainder of this paper is organized as follows: Sect. 2 provides an overview of the Adversarial Trained Transformer (ATT) architecture, including the generator and discriminator components. Section 3 describes the experimental setup, including the dataset and implementation details. Section 4 presents the experimental results and performance evaluation. Finally, Sect. 5 concludes the paper and discusses future directions.

2   Adversarial Trained Transformer

2.1   Overall Network Overview

The overall network architecture of ATT is shown in Figs. 1 and 2 Network consists of two main models generator and a discriminator. While training we will be using both models but for testing, we will be using a generator only.

We have designed a generator of LSTM-embedder, MultiHeadAttention, and linear layer which is similar to the encoder of transformer architecture [14]. The generator takes input in shape as $F \times N$ where F is nothing but the number of input frames while N is the dimension of the input vector. The generator will produce an output of the same shape.

We have designed the discriminator in such a way that it will take input in pairs so that we can add the effect of a noisy audio sample in the discriminator. This input pair should consist of one noisy sample along with either a clean or enhanced sample. But output labels for the discriminator change as per the input pair. If we give input as a noisy and clean spectrum then the output label should be "REAL" while if we provide input as a noisy and enhanced spectrum then the label should be "FAKE". As we can see discriminator is nothing but a binary classifier.

A generator uses adversarial training to learn how to do the mapping. As a result, Generator tries to trick Discriminator by modifying its parameters such that Discriminator accepts Generator's output as legitimate. As the Discriminator improves at recognising realistic properties in its input during backpropagation, the Generator modifies its settings to get closer to the real data manifold

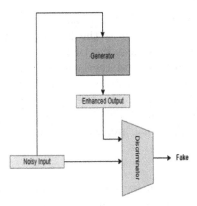

Fig. 1. Discriminator detects input pair as FAKE.

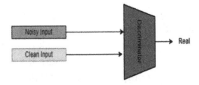

Fig. 2. Discriminator detects input pair as REAL.

defined by the training data. Generator and Discriminator play a minimax game as part of this adversarial learning process. Cross entropy loss will be our initial instinct when selecting the loss function for the discriminator, but prior research has shown that it suffers from vanishing gradients because of the sigmoid in cross-entropy loss, as a result, we will be using the least square loss function described in the Eqs. 1 and 2 as studies have shown that it performs better for speech enhancement applications.

$$\min_{D} V_{ATT}(D) = \mathbf{E}_{x_{noise},x_{clean}}[(D(x_{noise},x_{clean}) - 1)^2]$$
$$+ \mathbf{E}_{x_{noise}}[(D(x_{noise},G(x_{noise})))^2] \tag{1}$$

$$\min_{G} V_{ATT}(G) = \mathbf{E}_{x_{noise}}[(D(x_{noise},G(x_{noise})) - 1)^2] \tag{2}$$

In preliminary studies, we found that it was helpful to reduce the distance between the output of the generator and the clean signal by adding a secondary component to the generator's loss. We used the L1 norm to calculate this distance because it has been shown to be successful in the field of image processing [2,8] and also in speech enhancement [7]. By doing this, we allow the adversarial component to add more precise and accurate results. The new hyperparameter λ controls the size of the L1 norm. As a result, the generator loss that we select as the one in Eq. 2 becomes:

$$\min_{G} V_{ATT}(G) = \mathbf{E}_{x_{noise}}[(D(x_{noise},G(x_{noise})) - 1)^2] + \lambda\|G(x_{noise}) - x_{clean}\|_1 \tag{3}$$

This loss function mentioned in Eq. 3 has two terms. The first term is the adversarial loss, which is the same as the loss function that we used in the previous section. The second term is the L1 loss, which measures the distance between the generator's output and the clean signal. The hyperparameter λ controls the weight of the L1 loss. In this experiment value of λ is set to 100.

We found that adding the L1 loss to the generator's loss function improved the performance of the generator. This is because the L1 loss encourages the generator to produce outputs that are closer to the clean signal.

2.2 Generator

The magnitude spectra of the noisy speech input is a sequence of frames which is represented as $[x_1, x_2, ...x_t, ...x_T]$, where each x_t is the magnitude spectrum of the noisy speech at a particular frame t. The total number of frames in the speech segment is denoted by the letter T.

We use a linear transformation with softmax to transform the input into N-dimensional vectors, just like other sequence models. The architecture of the ATT generator shown in Fig. 3 is made up of a stack of identical layers. Framing, LSTM-embedder, multi-head attention, and linear layer are the four elements that make up each layer. These components are applied in order, with a residual and layernorm layer following each component.

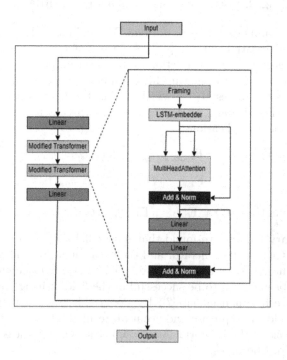

Fig. 3. Generator of ATT model.

Framing and LSTM-Embedder. Speech already has a strong local structure, thus modeling this localization attribute in speech enhancement systems is both desired and necessary to increase speech enhancement performance. To do this, we shall discuss LSTM-embedder in this part [18].

We are taking an N-dimensional input vector as a feature for each time frame but we want to fine-tune the feature by using LSTM-embedder. LSTM-embedder will take input as M number of N-dimensional vector as input and will give output as a single N-dimensional vector. We are using this LSTM-embedder so that we can again extract some local temporal information before giving it to our main transformer model.

We will pad the N-dimensional vector of zeros before the first frame and then We will do framing of input which is of shape $(F + M - 1) \times N$ with a window of M and overlap of 1 which produce output as $F \times M \times N$. We can consider this framing as a part of data preprocessing. The output we got from framing will be given to LSTM-embedder.

We are using LSTM-embedder as a position embedding algorithm, it adeptly captures the sequential information within each window in a comprehensive manner. Moreover, the sliding operation seamlessly incorporates global sequential information.

In our work, we use an LSTM-embedder to process short sequences of data within fixed-size local windows. This is because long-term dependencies are not necessary for these short sequences. The computation for processing these short sequences is independent, which makes parallelization straightforward and greatly reduces computational complexity.

Multihead Attention. The multi-head attention (MHA) mechanism has the ability to capture long-term dependencies because it allows each position to attend to all preceding positions [14]. This means that the representation of each position is influenced by the representations of all other positions, even those that are far apart in the sequence. This allows the MHA mechanism to capture long-range dependencies, which is important for our speech enhancement tasks.

The MHA mechanism, shown in Fig. 4, allows for direct connections between all positional pairs. In particular, each position in the MHA mechanism attends to preceding positions, acquiring a collection of attention scores that enhance its representation. When provided with the current representations $k_1, k_2, ..., k_N$ the updated representation l_t can be computed as follows:

$$l_t = MHA(k_1, k_2, ..., k_t) = concatenation(head_1(k_t), ..., head_i(k_t))W^o \quad (4)$$

In the provided equation, MHA denotes the multi-head attention function, Concatenation represents the concatenation of outputs from multiple attention heads ($head_1, ..., head_i$), and W^o is a weight matrix. This computation allows the model to effectively capture and integrate long-term dependencies across

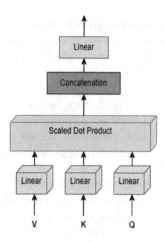

Fig. 4. Multi Head Attention.

positions in the sequence, thereby enhancing the representation of each position by incorporating information from other positions.

Within the MHA, the notation $head_i(h_t)$ represents the output of the ith attention head, while W^o corresponds to a linear projection. The attention function employed is the scaled dot product, as illustrated in Fig. 4. To be more specific, the computation of $head_i(h_t)$ involves calculating a weighted sum of all value vectors. These weights are determined by applying the attention function to each pair of $< query, key >$ elements:

$$\{\alpha_1, ..., \alpha_n\} = softmax(\frac{< q, k_1 >}{\sqrt{d_k}}..., \frac{< q, k_n >}{\sqrt{d_k}})$$

$$head_i(h_t) = \sum_{j=1}^{n} \alpha_j v_j \tag{5}$$

In Eq. 5, dimension of k_i is d_k and MHA mechanism uses three types of vectors: key, query, and value vectors denoted as k_i, q and v_i respectively, and calculated by Eq. 6

$$q, k_i, v_i = W^q h_t, W^k h_i, W^v h_i \tag{6}$$

where $W^q \in R^{d_N \times d_k}$, $W^k \in R^{d_N \times d_k}$ and $W^v \in R^{d_N \times d_k}$ are projection matrices.

In this study, we use 4 parallel attention heads (h = 4). This means that the MHA mechanism projects the input vectors into 4 separate query, key, and value spaces. The dimensions of the key, query, and value spaces are all set to 128 i.e. d_k=128.

It is important to note that each attention head has its own distinct set of projection matrices. This means that each attention head is able to learn different aspects of the input vectors.

Linear Layer. Like a conventional transformer, we have used two linear layers each containing N number of neurons with ReLU activation.

2.3 Discriminator

The discriminator network shown in Fig. 5 is composed of a series of one-dimensional strided convolutional layers. The number of filters for each layer increases as the network progresses so that the depth of the network increases as the width decreases. This allows the discriminator to learn increasingly complex features from the input data. It consists of 4 convolutional layers with filters 16,32,64 and 128 respectively with kernel size 31 and stride 2 followed by batch normalisation and LeakyRelU with alpha value 0.3. Then flatten layer is used followed by a linear layer with 100 neurons. The final layer of the discriminator is a classification neuron with a sigmoid activation function. The sigmoid activation function allows the discriminator to output a probability between 0 and 1, which represents the likelihood that the input data is real or fake.

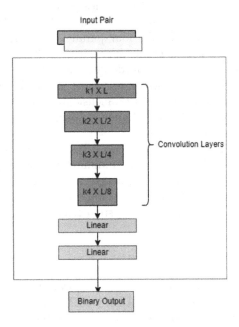

Fig. 5. Discriminator of ATT model.

3   Experimental Setup

3.1   Data Set

To ensure that our results are comparable to other studies, we used the Voice-Bank+DEMAND dataset, which is a commonly used dataset for speech research.

This dataset contains the speech recordings of 30 speakers, with 28 speakers used for training and 2 speakers used for testing. For training, there are 11,572 pairs of clean and noisy speech samples, and for testing, there are 824 clean and noisy speech pairs. To generate the noisy speech, clean speech is mixed with noise from the DEMAND dataset. The training set included 40 noise conditions, while the test set consisted of 20 noise conditions which are completely different from the training set.

3.2   ATT Setup

In this study, the sampling rate for all speech sounds was set at 16 kHz. Each individual time frame had a duration of 32 ms, which was equivalent to using a 512-point Short-Time Fourier Transform (STFT) with a spectral dimension of 257. There was a 50% overlap between consecutive time frames. The training speech samples all have a duration of two seconds. If a speech segment lasts longer than two seconds, it will be cut into slices of two seconds each. The last slice will be padded with zeros to 2 s if it is less than that amount.

The proposed ATT's generator is made up of two modified transformers, each of which has two linear layers, four paralleled attention layers, and one layer each of framing and LSTM-embedder with M=3 and N=512. Since both the input and the output are magnitude spectra, they both have 257 dimensions. Before the modified transformer, a layer of linear processing is stacked to transform the speech spectrum into 512-dimensional feature vectors. SEGAN [7] and SETransformer [18] are used as standard speech enhancement systems for comparison.

During the training phase, the Adversarial Trained Transformer(ATT) model underwent 100 epochs of training. The minimum batch size used was 32, and the learning rates for both the generator and discriminator were set to 0.0002. RMSProp was used as the optimizer. The model was trained on the system with NVIDIA RTX A5000 GPU and 32 GB system RAM.

4   Experimental Results

The proposed ATT speech enhancement algorithm was compared to other speech enhancement methods using the VoiceBank+DEMAND dataset. The results in Table 2 show that the proposed ATT algorithm achieved significantly better results than other methods in terms of PESQ [9], STOI [12] and CBAK [1].

As shown in Table 1, the ATT generator has 6.57 million parameters, which is much lower than the SEGAN generator, which has 74.13 million parameters. The SEtransformer has the same 6.57 million parameters as the generator of the proposed ATT model, but because we are using adversarial training to train it, ATT is producing superior results.

To illustrate the enhancing effect of the proposed ATT algorithm, a speech sample that is severely muddled by noise from the test set was used. Two

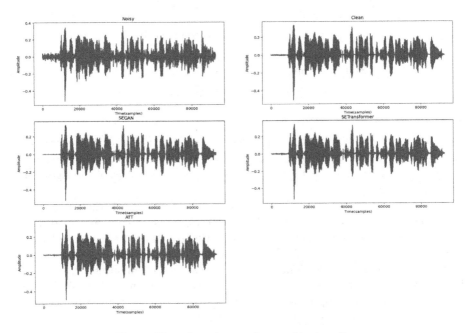

Fig. 6. Time domain waveforms of test audio.

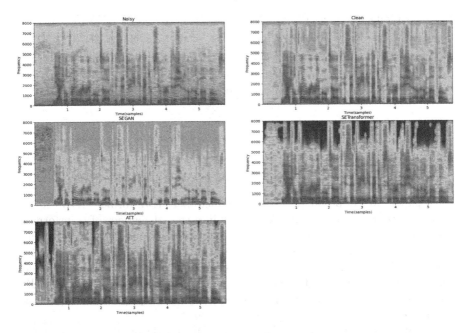

Fig. 7. Spectrograms of test audio.

Table 1. Number of learning parameters of models.

Model	Parameters(Million)
SEGAN Generator	74.13
SETransformer	6.57
ATT Generator(Proposed)	**6.57**

methods (SEGAN, SETransformer) from the comparison algorithm were chosen to compare the impact on the spectrogram and time-domain waveform of the enhanced voice in order to more clearly illustrate the effect of the algorithm suggested in this paper.

Figures 6 and 7 shows ATT-enhanced speech samples with their respective time-domain waveforms along with their spectrograms, in comparison to noisy speech, SEGAN-enhanced speech, SETransformer-enhanced speech, and clean speech. We can observe that ATT-enhanced speech can effectively reduce interference noise in the speech signal and can be close to clean speech in both the frequency domain and time domain. Also, we can make an additional observation that SEGAN is suppressing the unvoiced part of speech by considering it as noise, in this view also ATT performs better.

Table 2. Experimental results on the VoiceBank+DEMAND dataset.

Model	PESQ	CSIG	STOI	CBAK	SSNR	COVL
Noisy	1.96	3.33	0.92	2.44	1.68	2.62
SEGAN	2.16	**3.54**	0.93	3.00	**8.47**	**2.84**
SETransformer	2.45	1.01	0.93	2.99	8.18	1.26
ATT(Proposed)	**2.55**	2.22	**0.93**	**3.14**	8.26	2.35

5   Conclusion

In this paper, we proposed the Adversarial Trained Transformer (ATT) architecture for speech enhancement. ATT combines the advantages of transformer-based models and adversarial training to achieve superior performance in enhancing speech signals. The generator component of ATT utilizes a modified transformer architecture, incorporating multi-head attention and LSTM-embedder layers to capture global and local dependencies in the speech signals. The discriminator component, employing convolutional layers, plays a crucial role in guiding the generator through adversarial learning.

Experimental results on the VoiceBank+DEMAND dataset demonstrated the effectiveness of the proposed ATT method, showing significant improvements in various speech quality metrics. As we can observe in Table 2 proposed ATT model has the highest PESQ score and CBAK score which are 2.55 and 3.14 respectively which is a major improvement compared to other baseline models. The ATT model achieved superior performance with relatively fewer parameters, making it more efficient and practical for real-world applications.

The findings of this study highlight the potential of the proposed ATT architecture for speech enhancement. Future research can focus on further improvements to the ATT model, such as incorporating additional techniques or exploring different architectures to enhance its performance.

References

1. Hu, Y., Loizou, P.C.: Evaluation of objective quality measures for speech enhancement. IEEE Trans. Audio Speech Lang. Process. **16**(1), 229–238 (2007)
2. Isola, P., Zhu, J.Y., Zhou, T., Efros, A.A.: Image-to-image translation with conditional adversarial networks. In: Proceedings of the IEEE Conference on Computer Vision and Pattern Recognition, pp. 1125–1134 (2017)
3. Loizou, P.C.: Speech Enhancement: Theory And Practice. CRC Press, Boca Raton (2013)
4. Pandey, A., Wang, D.: A new framework for CNN-based speech enhancement in the time domain. IEEE/ACM Trans. Audio, Speech Lang. Process. **27**(7), 1179–1188 (2019)
5. Pandey, A., Wang, D.: TCNN: temporal convolutional neural network for real-time speech enhancement in the time domain. In: ICASSP 2019–2019 IEEE International Conference on Acoustics, Speech and Signal Processing (ICASSP), pp. 6875–6879. IEEE (2019)
6. Park, S.R., Lee, J.: A fully convolutional neural network for speech enhancement. arXiv preprint arXiv:1609.07132 (2016)
7. Pascual, S., Bonafonte, A., Serra, J.: SEGAN: speech enhancement generative adversarial network. arXiv preprint arXiv:1703.09452 (2017)
8. Pathak, D., Krahenbuhl, P., Donahue, J., Darrell, T., Efros, A.A.: Context encoders: feature learning by inpainting. In: Proceedings of the IEEE Conference on Computer Vision and Pattern Recognition, pp. 2536–2544 (2016)
9. Rec, I.: P. 862.2: Wideband extension to recommendation p. 862 for the assessment of wideband telephone networks and speech codecs. International Telecommunication Union, CH-Geneva (2005)
10. Shahriyar, S.A., Akhand, M.A.H., Siddique, N., Shimamura, T.: Speech enhancement using convolutional denoising autoencoder. In: 2019 International Conference on Electrical, Computer and Communication Engineering (ECCE), pp. 1–5 (2019). https://doi.org/10.1109/ECACE.2019.8679106
11. Sun, L., Du, J., Dai, L.R., Lee, C.H.: Multiple-target deep learning for LSTM-RNN based speech enhancement. In: 2017 Hands-free Speech Communications and Microphone Arrays (HSCMA), pp. 136–140. IEEE (2017)
12. Taal, C.H., Hendriks, R.C., Heusdens, R., Jensen, J.: An algorithm for intelligibility prediction of time-frequency weighted noisy speech. IEEE Trans. Audio Speech Lang. Process. **19**(7), 2125–2136 (2011)
13. Tawara, N., Kobayashi, T., Ogawa, T.: Multi-channel speech enhancement using time-domain convolutional denoising autoencoder. In: INTERSPEECH, pp. 86–90 (2019)

14. Vaswani, A., et al.: Attention is all you need. In: Advances in Neural Information Processing Systems, vol. 30 (2017)
15. Xu, Y., Du, J., Huang, Z., Dai, L.R., Lee, C.H.: Multi-objective learning and mask-based post-processing for deep neural network based speech enhancement. arXiv preprint arXiv:1703.07172 (2017)
16. Yang, L.P., Fu, Q.J.: Spectral subtraction-based speech enhancement for cochlear implant patients in background noise. J. Acoust. Soc. Am. **117**(3), 1001–1004 (2005)
17. Yu, D., Deng, L., Droppo, J., Wu, J., Gong, Y., Acero, A.: A minimum-mean-square-error noise reduction algorithm on Mel-frequency cepstra for robust speech recognition. In: 2008 IEEE International Conference on Acoustics, Speech and Signal Processing, pp. 4041–4044. IEEE (2008)
18. Yu, W., Zhou, J., Wang, H., Tao, L.: Setransformer: speech enhancement transformer. Cogn. Comput. **14**, 1–7 (2022). https://doi.org/10.1007/s12559-020-09817-2

Human Identification by Dynamics of Changes in Brain Frequencies Using Artificial Neural Networks

Daniyar Wolf(ORCID), Yaroslav Turovsky(ORCID), Roman Meshcheryakov(ORCID),
and Anastasia Iskhakova(✉) (ORCID)

V. A. Trapeznikov Institute of Control Sciences of Russian Academy of Sciences, Moscow,
Russia
runsolar@mail.ru, shumskaya.ao@gmail.com

Abstract. The article considers the problem of improving the methods of human identification using biometric features, in particular, the signals of an electroencephalogram. The authors present the results of scientific research into human identification by dynamics of frequency changes of the brain using the known architecture of artificial neural networks: AlexNet and Mobile Net 2. The basic hypothesis is formulated that the waves registered by sensors from head leads are unique for each person. The authors describe the preparation of experimental data on the basis of electroencephalogram signals received as a result of experiments on the formation of steady-state visual evoked potentials in a group of people with the subsequent creation of an applied database. The achievability of the set task was based on assessments of the relevance and representativeness of the obtained data. Frequency-time characteristics were taken as training datasets. Using deep machine learning technology, two classification models are obtained that allow identifying the identity of a person with a probability of 70%. The evaluation of the adequacy of the obtained classification models is carried out with PCA and t-SNE algorithms; the efficiency of their work is evaluated. The results of deep machine learning and machine classification tasks were confirmed by assessments of the adequacy of the obtained models. As a result, the authors confirm the main hypothesis.

Keywords: Electroencephalogram · Human-Machine Interaction ·
Brain-Computer Interface · Biometric Personal Characteristic · Identification ·
Automation of Identification Processes · Machine Learning · Processing of
Bioelectric Signals · Data Analysis

1 Introduction

The identification of a person by their biometric data has long been a topic of research, but its relevance has not diminished. The development of technologies and tools for reading and processing data makes it possible to explore new biometric parameters which may be more reliable in terms of user spoofing and intruder actions. On the other hand, the application of identification tools extends far beyond the familiar security systems of a decade ago. Today, human biometric recognition technologies are actively implemented and continue to be reinforced in smart city systems, crime prevention, criminal detection, medical manipulation, multifactor systems for providing access to restricted data and premises, and so on. All of this makes possible the idea of a new level of development of identification technologies, the need to develop directions related to new biometric parameters, and increase the level of their detection efficiency.

From the information security point of view, the creation of new identification methods will allow improving identification procedures in the system; and also in case of the application of new, more exact (individually non-repeatable) features, increase the accuracy of the authentication procedure. It should be also noted that the use of new biometric features, in particular bioelectrical signals, should take into account the peculiarities of their reading, the preparation of this process, and be applied to the appropriate tasks.

In this paper, we consider the problem of studying the possibility of human identification by the signals of the electroencephalogram, that is, the presence in the electroencephalogram (EEG) signals of individual identification characteristics that can distinguish and uniquely identify the person.

2   Bioelectric Signals in Process Automation Tasks

Developments and research that allow humans to interact directly with technology, excluding any physiological activity, are becoming increasingly widespread and relevant. Such developments are related to advances in data processing, and hence to a deeper exploration of complex-structured data, including EEG. The reading and analysis of bioelectrical signals is a rapidly developing field in science and technology. It finds its application in the diagnostics of various diseases, in improving the quality of life of people with disabilities, and in the sport of great achievements. This area is closely related to human health, so two aspects are extremely important: the safety of the person at the time of reading their bioelectrical signals and the accuracy of the data transfer. The difficulty of recording bioelectric signals consists in the fact that such signals are weak, at the same time there is a significant level of interference – noises inside the human body, and artifacts – noises from the measuring instruments, the frequency range of which interferes with the reading of bioelectric signals, sometimes overlapping them.

The relevance of developments in the field of systems through which it is possible to establish a brain-computer interface (BCI) is confirmed by the fact that at the moment there are already a number of studies devoted to this topic. In 2017 Elon Musk in his speech said: "Humans must merge with machines, or become irrelevant in the AI age". The point of this statement makes precise practical sense. Computers can exchange data at the speed of a trillion bits per second. At the same time, humans are limited in the speed of exchange, given the necessary actions to transmit it. The basic mode of human communication is a system composed of nerve and muscle tissues, and the signals of typing into a computer using the fingers of the hand through the keyboard are transmitted within 10 bits per second.

The examples of the latest developments show the progressive application of bioelectric signals to solving numerous practical and scientific problems of our time.

In 2020, researchers at Pusan National University in South Korea developed an original brain-machine interface technology. The researchers proposed a simplified synchronized hybrid system for multiple command control with electroencephalograph signals in the motor cortex. The proposed system can issue 38 control commands, which only require the user to focus on the stimulus and blink their eyes [1].

In 2022, during the presentation of the N1 neurochip, Elon Musk's company, Neuralink, demonstrated the ability of "telepathic typing" of a text. In the presentation, a monkey typed a text on a computer using the power of its mind. The device converted neural impulses into data, which was interpreted by the computer using an artificial neural network [2].

In the same year, 2022, the company Synchron (a competitor to Neuralink) received permission for human experiments and conducted research with four people in Australia, implanting their device into a patient from the United States. In contrast to the technology offered by Neuralink, Synhcron technology is characterized by a lower degree of invasiveness – a thin sensor is inserted into a cerebral vessel via an artery in the patient's neck, and there is no need to penetrate the cranium [3].

In 2023, Elon Musk's company received approval from the U.S. Food and Drug Administration for the first clinical human trial of an invasive neuro-interface to establish a high-speed connection between the human brain and computer hardware.

Another study was conducted by researchers at the National Tsing Hua University in Taiwan. In their research, the researchers emphasized the importance of BCI for people with motor neuron disease (MND) who are unable to move on their own. The article mainly proposed a brain-computer interface (BCI) based on wireless electroencephalography and a drive circuit for direct current motors to control electric wheelchairs via a Bluetooth interface for paralyzed patients [4].

S. Rihana, P. Damien, and T. Moujaess aimed to detect eye blink signals from EEG signals in their work. The researchers collected data, described the methods used for preprocessing EEG signals, and classified eye blink signals using a probabilistic neural network as a binary classifier. Their ultimate goal was to apply the obtained database in neurorehabilitation applications for patients with motor impairments [5].

Thus, it is evident that research aimed at developing brain-computer interface technology will allow people with various disorders, such as those recovering from stroke or suffering from amyotrophic lateral sclerosis and unable to speak, to treat conditions such as Parkinson's disease, dementia, etc.

However, the aforementioned studies do not address the topic of human identification based on brain wave patterns. It is one thing to control devices - effectors, computers, etc., but it would also be beneficial for a system to be able to identify the owner of a neurointerface based on the dynamics of brain activity.

Thus, this scientific study attempts to verify the hypothesis that the waves detected by sensors on the scalp are unique to each individual. If this is indeed the case, clusters should be obtained that could be used to determine decision boundaries.

Hypothesis formulation. Presumably, during successive cycles of the formation of steady-state visually evoked potential (SSVEP), the brain produces waves unique to each individual, consisting in changes in the frequency-time characteristics of the registered signal, which differ from the frequency of photo-stimulation.

3 Collection and Preparation of Experimental Data

Electroencephalograms with steady-state visually evoked potentials (SSVEPs) were taken as the data for the study. They are signals that the brain generates in response to visual stimulation. When the retina is excited by flashes of frequency ranging from 3.5 to 75 Hz, the brain generates electrical activity with the flash frequency [6–10].

This potential has found wide application in the tasks of development and further modification of neuro-interfaces as one of the well-detectable phenomena of brain activity. At the same time, as statistical material on the performance of this type of NCI-IBC is accumulated, it becomes obvious that the stability of this interface can vary quite widely even for the same user. From this, one can assume that the available electroencephalograms with the SSVEP may contain information related to a specific person. Thus, the main goal is to isolate such unique features from the basic signals from the EEG. SSVEPs, in the authors' opinion, have obvious practical application in non-traditional control systems. The visual keyboard is an example: the operator looks at visual stimuli and depending on where he looked the command for control is selected. In comparison to auditory evoked potentials, it can be stated that there is as yet no tool for unambiguous sound selection by humans.

A group of 30 subjects of both sexes aged between 17 and 23 years (12 females and 18 males) with no neurological or psychiatric pathologies was formed for the study. Before the experiment, the participants did not take any psychotropic drugs and had normal or corrected-to-normal vision.

The electroencephalogram data were registered with a Neuron-Spectr-4VP device (Neurosoft LLC, Russia) [11, 12]. Electroencephalogram data were recorded on leads $O1$, $O2$, Oz, $P3$, $P4$, and Pz with a sampling frequency of 5000 Hz, with the cutoff filter on and high- and low-frequency filters off. It is the leads $O1$, $O2$ from the occipital part of the head that are responsible for the evoked potentials, so they were used as identification leads. Photostimulation was performed at frequencies 1, 8, and 14 Hz. The duration of each SSVEP session was 15 s. The total number of spectrograms that were studied in training was 5580 samples. 80% of this number was used for model training and 20% was used as a test sample.

To eliminate "parasitic" frequencies, all signals were pre-processed with a 6th order Butterworth bandpass filter (order) with 2 Hz (lowcut) to 35 Hz (highcut) bandwidth. Further, all signals were grouped by photostimulation frequencies (1, 8, and 14 Hz), by groups of leads "$O1$", "$O2$", "Oz", "$P3$", "$P4$", and "Pz" for each subject. The subjects were also assigned an ordinal number from 1 to 30. Given the sampling rate, three data matrices were obtained after grouping:

$N = 30 \times M = 75000 \times V = 6$ elements, where:
N is the ordinal number of the subject;
M is the number of samples in the signal (number of measurements per time);
V is the number of signals in the group for each subject (also, let this value denote a set consisting of {"$O1$", "$O2$", "Oz", "$P3$", "$P4$", "Pz"}).

As an example of the resulting data structure, Fig. 1 shows two groups with EEG-SSVEP data for the two frequencies: 8 and 14 Hz.

It is evident from the obtained data structures that there are sufficiently large sets of M for set V. To reduce the dimensionality of V, we carried out resampling of each signal in the groups to $M = 25000$, with the unchanged data structure.

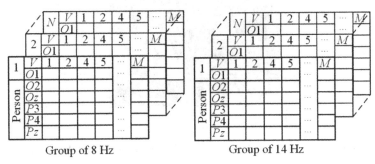

Group of 8 Hz   Group of 14 Hz

Fig. 1. Structure of the EEG input data with SSVEP for each subject in the 8 and 14 Hz frequency groups. Same for the 1 Hz group.

Note that after applying the filter, there are no data with photostimulation at 1 Hz. Such data is considered to be a group of signals without photostimulation.

Next, from the obtained data groups, it was necessary to extract sufficiently representative and separable features for subsequent deep machine learning and classification. The dynamics of frequency changes on a time scale was chosen as the features for training and classification, for this purpose the short-time Fourier transform was applied. As a result, the sets of spectrograms were obtained for each set V, for each subject. Each spectrogram was divided into 32×32 fragments with an overlap window of 25%. Moreover, this allowed us to carry out augmentation of the available experimental data.

Each feature M was divided into parts of 1260 samples into steps of 625 samples (data augmentation). In total, for each lead, we received 1140 samples for the subsequent deep machine learning of the neural network.

Figure 2 shows the EEGs with the SSVEP in the frequency-time sweep for the $O2$ zone. Thus, we obtained training sets in the form of personal "frequency maps" with signals for each subject [13, 14].

4   Results of Deep Machine Learning and Machine Classification

Two well-known neural network architectures, AlexNet and MobileNet 2, were chosen for deep machine learning. It is logical to assume that if the existing well-known neural network architectures can handle this task, there is little point in considering derivative or own implementations.

In the deep machine learning experiment, the configurations of the selected neural networks did not differ from their classical variants. AlexNet neural network implementation was done according to research paper [15], and MobileNet 2 architecture according to research paper [16]. Note that the choice of these neural networks was not random. Both network models operate on the principle of convolutional neural networks (CNN), which have proven their effectiveness in image recognition tasks.

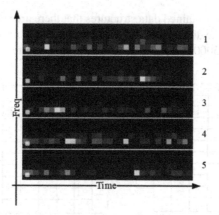

Fig. 2. A set of trained EEG spectrograms for deep machine learning.

The key idea of CNN is the local connectivity and distribution of weights of neurons that are combined into layers. Each neuron in a layer receives input from the set of neurons located in the previous layer. The activations computed by each nucleus are collected into matrices, which are called feature maps and represent the actual outputs of the convolutional layers. The last layer of CNN is the output layer of the actual prediction network; it consists of fully connected neurons so that each of them takes all outputs of the previous layers as input.

The basic idea of machine classification was that a frequency-time spectrum is fed to the input of the neural network as features. Then, the pre-trained neural network evaluated which of the EEG signal belonged to which subjects.

It took about 300 epochs to train the AlexNet network, and about 600 epochs for MobileNet 2 (Fig. 3).

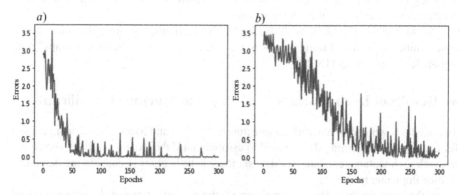

Fig. 3. Machine learning error curves for the SNS models: a) AlexNet; b) and MobileNet.

From the obtained curves of machine learning errors, it can be said that AlexNet learns better and faster, but this does not affect the final result of the machine classification inference of the obtained models.

The machine classification results are shown in the Table 1.

Table 1. Estimation of the machine classification.

Neural Network	1 Hz stimulation		8 Hz stimulation		14 Hz stimulation	
	Test data	Train data	Test data	Train data	Test data	Train data
AlexNet	73.47	99.55	65.94	99.33	72.49	99.82
MobileNet 2	72.40	98.39	68.72	98.40	71.32	97.51

The machine classification results shown in the Table 1 indicate that the selected neural networks show almost the same accuracy in recognizing a person by their EEG. The probability of human identification is almost 70%. Obviously, this value can be improved by the additional configuration of neural network architectures with the addition of different mathematical blocks. The authors did not set themselves the task of obtaining 100% accuracy in human identification, as the sufficient condition was to evaluate the separability of EEG data by subjects and the ability of typical algorithms of neural networks to distinguish people by this data [17]. We can also conclude from the obtained estimations that the SSVEP does not affect the results of the classification estimations. This is proved by the experiment with 1 Hz stimulation from the table. Generalization in a group machine learning model on a set of test data and predicting categorical labels

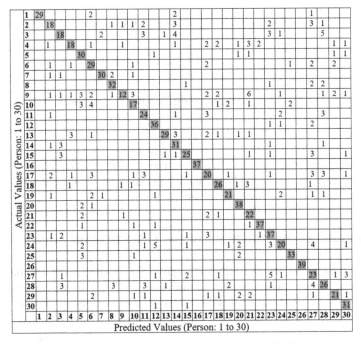

Fig. 4. Confusion matrix for the pre-trained AlexNet.

for each input data instance for 30 subjects show a fairly good prediction score: in the range of 70%.

The validity of the resulting classification models can be assessed by the Confusion matrices shown in Fig. 4 and 5.

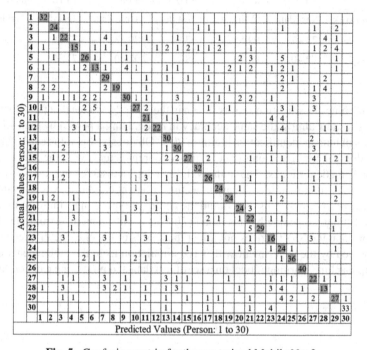

Fig. 5. Confusion matrix for the pre-trained Mobile Net 2.

The matrices (in Fig. 4 and 5) contain the number of true positives, true negatives, false positives and false negatives, for the AlexNet and Mobile Net 2 models on the test data. The presented confusion matrices indicate a different level of classification of individuals - in the range from 12 to 38. The reason for such a scatter of values is that classification is performed by two different neural network models.

Thus, we have obtained two classification models for human identification based on the dynamics of brainwave frequency changes.

5 Evaluation of the Adequacy of the Classification Models

We were mostly interested in another key question, which was the adequacy of the obtained classification models based on the applied CNN. Are the resulting models really that good at identifying a person based on impulses emitted by the brain? In formal words, what is the representativeness of the obtained experimental data used in the task of machine learning, and how adequate are the obtained classification models on their basis in general.

To answer this question, we performed a dual visual evaluation of the representativeness of the experimental data using the principal component analysis (PCA) and the t-SNE algorithm.

The classical approach to principal component extraction boils down to a few simple steps:

Step 1. Standardize the d-dimensional data set.

Step 2. Build the covariance matrix.

Step 3. Decompose the covariance matrix into its eigenvectors and eigenvalues (eigenvalue; characteristic numbers).

Step 4. Sort eigenvalues in descending order to rank the corresponding eigenvectors.

Step 5. Select k eigenvectors that correspond to the k largest eigenvalues, where k is the dimensions of the new feature subspace.

Step 6. Build a projection matrix W of the "top" k eigenvectors.

Step 7. Transform the d-dimensional input dataset X using the projection matrix W, to obtain a new k-dimensional feature subspace.

However, in our case, we already had two trained classification models, which have the operator properties of projecting data from one space into another (projectors). In turn, the obtained EEG spectrograms (experimental data) were taken as multidimensional random variables (all training features were taken as sets of random vectors), where the position of the center is also the mathematical expectation of its projections on the axis of principal components. Applying the PCA algorithm using two obtained classification models (at the deep machine learning stage for AlexNet and Mobile Net 2), we obtained an orthogonal linear transformation which allowed us to map the data from the original multidimensional feature space into a new two-dimensional space, which further allowed us to visualize them and draw some conclusions (Fig. 6).

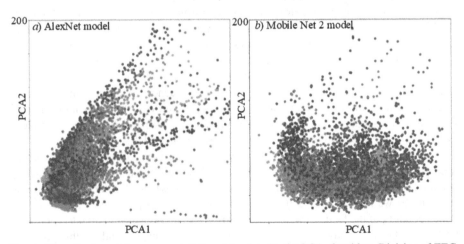

Fig. 6. Visualization of the representativity of the data by the PCA algorithm. Division of EEG data into two-dimensional PCA space: a) for AlexNet model; b) for Mobile Net 2 model.

In Fig. 6, we can observe the distribution of the features in the form of color groups. The feature groups are nested inside each other and layered in the two-dimensional space. In the context of dimensionality reduction, the selection of features can be understood as an approach to data compression in order to preserve most of the meaningful information. The resulting graphs can be interpreted as projections onto new directions of maximum variance (new subspaces).

Unfortunately, cluster separability is not evident in the PCA graphs. One may note that PCA directions are extremely sensitive to data scaling, so an additional evaluation was carried out using the t-SNE algorithm.

The t-SNE algorithm refers to multiple feature learning methods and was published in 2008 by Lawrence van der Maaten and Jeffrey Hinton [18]. The classical SNE was proposed by G.E. Hinton and S.T. Roweis in 2002 [19]. The application of the t-SNE algorithm allowed us to nonlinearly decrease the data dimensionality to 2 and to carry out revisualization.

As in the case of PCA, there was already an initial data set (including classification models) described by multidimensional random vectors with a space dimension substantially greater than 3. It was necessary to obtain new variables existing in two- or three-dimensional space, which would preserve the structure and regularities in the original data as much as possible. SNE begins by converting the multidimensional Euclidean distance between points into conditional probabilities that reflect the similarity of the points.

In Fig. 7 we can observe good spatial separability of the EEG data in the form of clear, distinct clusters. However, some clusters appear to be quite distant from their main groups. Such results may indicate a distinctive feature of EEG signals taken from different leads of the head of the same subject.

In rare cases, the clusters in Fig. 7 have an oblong shape. The reason is that the t-SNE algorithm tends to expand the denser areas of the data.

Let us remind you that we used the frequency-time spectrum as a feature for deep machine learning. No additional specific operations were performed to further extract the features from the available spectrograms. Of course, it was possible to reduce the dimensionality of the features by the above-considered algorithms and perform deep machine learning based on them, but we evaluated the ability of neural networks to perform the task of human identification based on the frequency-time spectrum in general. I.e., downscaling of informative features was carried out only for evaluation of relevance and representativeness of the available data for their separability, with subsequent evaluation of the adequacy of the obtained classification models.

The main goal of this work was to show the possibility of classifying individuals using known convolutional neural network architectures based on data from evoked potentials. These convolutional neural networks were chosen not by chance, as the training features were ordinary spectrograms, and no additional procedures to reduce the dimensionality of the features were performed. It was also considered that the representation of only truth matrices would be insufficient in this paper. And for this purpose, non-linear dimensionality reduction techniques were applied in order to visualize the available multidimensional dataset.

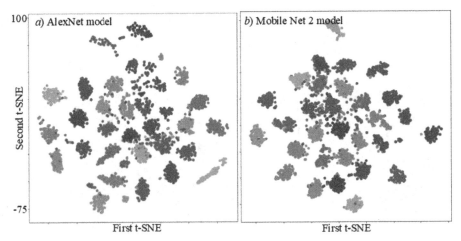

Fig. 7. Visualization of the representativeness of the data by the t-SNE algorithm. Divi-sion of EEG data in a two-dimensional t-SNE space: a) for the AlexNet model; b) for the Mobile Net 2 model. We can consider each cluster to be the brain activity of a single individual.

First, the PCA algorithm was applied, and the distribution of feature clusters PCA 1 – PCA 2 for AlexNet and Mobile Net 2 showed different localization of features for the same informant (Fig. 6). This is due to the fact that the applied PCA design algorithm uses two different trained neural network models mentioned above. That is, the informant is the same, but two different trained neural network models were fed to the input of the PCA algorithm. It can be considered that the visual representation is a slice-projection on one of the planes of the multidimensional space (by principal components).

The same is true for Fig. 7, but the t-SNE algorithm shows a clearer localization of trait clusters. This indicates the obvious representativeness of the experimental data (in contrast to PCA), and therefore explains that individuals can be separated from each other using artificial neural networks.

Thus, the presented results of the machine classification in Sect. 3 are confirmed by the conducted additional estimations of the chosen PCA and t-SNE algorithms, which indicate a visually distinctive non-linear separability of the available initial features, which in turn allows us to confirm the adequacy of the obtained classification models within 70%.

If we represent the obtained data in a single three-dimensional space, we can obtain a geometric structure similar to the model of the expanding universe [20]. It can be assumed that in its general population people's thoughts are scattered similarly to how galaxies and their clusters are scattered in the universe. Of course, 30 subjects are only a small sample of the general population of all people, but this comparison takes place within the law of large numbers. It is likely that people's thoughts, similarly to galaxies, occupy certain places in space and time (Fig. 8).

Based on the results of this study, we can conclude that the dynamics of changes in brain frequencies in each person has its own unique character, by which these persons can be identified.

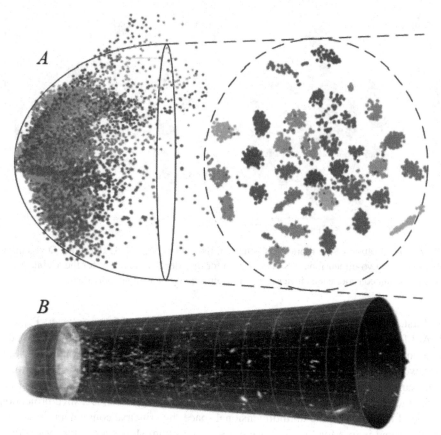

Fig. 8. Visualization and comparative analogy of two models: A) the data model under study; B) the model of the expanding universe [20].

6   Conclusion

Statistical information was collected to confirm the main hypothesis. Obtaining statistical data was achieved by creating technical conditions and organizational arrangements for a scientific experiment with a group of 30 subjects of both sexes. The experiment was provided with specialized medical measuring equipment of high-resolution electroencephalograph type.

Achievability of the set task and 70% achievement of the expected results were based on the estimates of relevance and representativeness of the received data. The frequency-time response was taken as a training dataset. The results of deep machine learning and machine classification tasks were confirmed by estimates of the adequacy of the models obtained.

The scientific results highlighted in the article are of practical interest and can be used in the development of new types of human biometric identification.

Acknowledgements. The study was financially supported by the Russian Science Foundation under scientific project No. 23–19-00664.

References

1. Yang, D., Nguyen, T.H., Chung, W.Y.: A bipolar-channel hybrid brain-computer interface system for home automation control utilizing steady-state visually evoked potential and eye-blink signals. Sensors (Basel) **20**(19), 5474 (2020). https://doi.org/10.3390/s20195474. PMID: 32987871; PMCID: PMC7582823
2. Suthar, A.: Neuralink technology: the future of neural engineering. J. Biomedical Sciences **10**(S6), 003 (2021)
3. Synchron Announces First Human U.S. Brain-Computer Interface Implant. https://www.bus inesswire.com/news/home/20220719005248/en/Synchron-Announces-First-Human-U.S.-Brain-Computer-Interface-Implant. Accessed 25 June 2023
4. Lin, J.-S., Yang, W.-C.: Wireless brain-computer interface for electric wheelchairs with EEG and eye-blinking signals. Int J Innov Comput Inf Control **8**, 6011–6024 (2012)
5. Rihana, S., Damien, P., Moujaess, T.: EEG-eye blink detection system for brain computer interface. In: Pons, J., Torricelli, D., Pajaro, M. (eds) Converging Clinical and Engineering Research on Neurorehabilitation. Biosystems & Biorobotics, vol 1. Springer, Berlin, Heidelberg (2013). https://doi.org/10.1007/978-3-642-34546-3_98
6. Tao, T., Yi, X., Xiaorong, G., Shangkai, G.: Chirp-modulated visual evoked potential as a generalization of steady state visual evoked potential. J. Neural Eng. **9**(1), 016008 (2011). https://doi.org/10.1088/1741-2560/9/1/016008
7. Kwak, N.-S., Müller, K.-R., Lee, S.-W.: Toward exoskeleton control based on steady state visual evoked potentials. 2014 International Winter Workshop on Brain-Computer Interface, BCI 2014, 1–2, Gangwon, Korea (2014). https://doi.org/10.1109/iww-BCI.2014.6782571
8. Balnytė, R., Uloziene, I., Rastenytė, D., Vaitkus, A., Malcienė, L., Laučkaitė, K.: Diagnostic value of conventional visual evoked potentials applied to patients with multiple sclerosis. Medicina **47**(5), 263–269 (2011)
9. Markand, O.: Visual Evoked Potentials, Springer Cham (2020)
10. Chaudhary, U., Birbaumer, N., Curado, M.R.: Brain-machine interface (BMI) in paralysis. Ann. Phys. Rehabil. Med. **58**(1), 9–13 (2015). https://doi.org/10.1016/j.rehab.2014.11.002
11. NEURON-SPECTRUM-4/EPM 21-channel Upgradeable EEG System with EP Capabilities. https://neurosoft.com/en/catalog/eeg/neuron-spectrum-4epm
12. do Espírito-Santo, R.B., Dias, G.C.B., Bortoloti, R., Huziwara, E.M.: Effect of the number of training trials on the event-related potential correlates of equivalence relations. Learning & Behavior **48**, 221–233 (2020)
13. Wolf, D.A., Turovsky, Y.A., Meshcheryakov, R.V., Iskhakov, A.Y., Iskhakova, A.O.: EEG signal Auto Encoder, computer software. https://www1.fips.ru/iiss/document.xhtml?faces-redirect=true&id=d4eb144baee4f995556af206cde9da36. Accessed 31 May 2023. (In Russ.)
14. Meshcheryakov, R.V., Wolf, D.A., Turovsky, Y.A.: An autocoder of the electrical activity of the human brain. Bulletin of the South Ural State University, Series "Mathematics. Me-chanics. Physics" **15**(1), 34–42 (2023). https://doi.org/10.14529/mmph230104. (In Russ.)
15. PyTorch Implemention of MobileNet V2. https://github.com/d-li14/mobilenetv2.pytorch. Accessed 25 June 2023
16. Torchvision. https://github.com/pytorch/vision/blob/main/torchvision/models/alexnet.py. Accessed 25 June 2023

17. Turovsky, Y., Wolf, D., Meshcheryakov, R., Iskhakova, A.: Dynamics of frequency characteristics of visually evoked potentials of electroencephalography during the work with brain-computer interfaces. In: Prasanna, S.R.M., Karpov, A., Samudravijaya, K., Agrawal, S.S. (eds) Speech and Computer. SPECOM 2022. Lecture Notes in Computer Science, vol 13721. Springer, Cham (2022). https://doi.org/10.1007/978-3-031-20980-2_57
18. Maaten, L.v.d., Hinton, G.: Visualizing data using t-SNE. J. Machine Learning Research 9, 2579–2605 (2008)
19. Hinton, G., Roweis, S.: Stochastic neighbor embedding. Adv. Neural. Inf. Process. Syst. 15, 833–840 (2002)
20. Helge, K., Lemaitre, G. In: Gillispie, Charles, Dictionary of Scientific Biography. Scribner & American Council of Learned Societies, New York, pp. 542–543 (1970)

Speech Prosody

Analysis of Formant Trajectories of a Speech Signal for the Purpose of Forensic Identification of a Foreign Speaker

Rodmonga Potapova[1,3,4,4]($\boxtimes$) (iD), Vsevolod Potapov[2,4] (iD), and Irina Kuryanova[3,4] (iD)

[1] Institute of Applied and Mathematical Linguistics, Moscow State Linguistic University, 38 Ostozhenka Street, Moscow 119034, Russia
rkpotapova@yandex.ru
[2] Centre of New Technologies for Humanities, Lomonosov Moscow State University, Leninskije Gory 1, 119991 Moscow, Russia
[3] Experimental Phonetic Laboratory of Criminalistics for Speech Translation, Institute of Applied and Mathematical Linguistics, Moscow State Linguistic University, 38 Ostozhenka Street, Moscow 119034, Russia
[4] Department of Forensic Linguistics, Moscow Research Center, 5 Nizhnyaya Syromyatnicheskaya Street, Moscow 105120, Russia

Abstract. The solution of the fundamental tasks of modern forensics (identification and verification of a person by voice and speech, as well as profiling of a person by voice) is based on a comprehensive study of phonograms during phonoscopic examination. Currently, the scope of forensic phonetics and speech acoustics is increasingly in demand, while there is still a range of problems that require additional in-depth research from specialists. For a long time, the problem of studying foreign speech in a language unfamiliar to an expert has been relevant and extremely difficult for modern forensics. This task is especially complicated in the study of languages that have been little studied, taking into account the linguistic specifics of the analyzed languages, in particular, Romani. In this regard, one of the most promising is the language-independent automated method of formant analysis proposed in this paper, which makes it possible to study the segment parameters of a speech signal by an expert who does not speak the language spoken by a suspect.

Keywords: Phonoscopic Examination · Romani · Identification · Verification · Profiling · Formant Alignment

1 Introduction

The widespread use of various technical means of communication has led to an increase in the mobility and latency (stealthy) of the process of transmitting speech information. The growing interest in voice biometric technologies is caused by such practical tasks of modern forensics as confirmation (verification) of a certain personality, identification of a speaker and speech portrait of an individual (profiling the individual personality characteristics of a person by voice). Identification is the recognition of a speaker according

© The Author(s), under exclusive license to Springer Nature Switzerland AG 2023
A. Karpov et al. (Eds.): SPECOM 2023, LNAI 14338, pp. 287–300, 2023.
https://doi.org/10.1007/978-3-031-48309-7_24

to the principle "one out of many" (on a closed set of "samples"); verification is confirmation that the voice sample belongs to a specific speaker according to the principle "he/she – not he/she" (object recognition is built from two alternatives: "own" ↔ "alien") [1, 2]. Of particular difficulty is the solution of these tasks in relation to foreign language speech [3]. Numerous experiments on the speaker recognition strategy, the choice of a system of parameters that allow analyzing the speech signal based on acoustic parameters and auditory perception, decision-making methodologies and much more are discussed in detail in the works by Rodmonga K. Potapova (for example, [4–9]).

Identification of the most complete set of identifying features of a speaker, differentiation of group and individual features, taking into account sociolinguistic parameters, assessment of the stability of features and the degree of their manifestation requires the use of various methods for studying voice and speech (for example, [10–14]). However, the matrix of speech acoustic features traditionally used in Russia for identifying Russian speakers is too limited for conducting identification studies involving foreign speech. The need for an expert, who is not a native speaker of the language under study, to establish the key characteristics of foreign language speech in order to identify a speaker, necessitated new fundamental methodological developments.

2 Solution of the Task of Identification in Relation to the Romani Language

Since the beginning of the 21st century, works on the study of identification-significant characteristics based on the material of the Romani language have become of particular relevance to expert research on the identification of persons speaking a foreign language. The Romani language, due to the forced migration of the Gypsies from their original places of residence (India), does not have a clearly defined distribution area and a single standardized norm today. Having retained typological closeness to the Middle Indian and Modern Indian languages, the ethnic groups of the Gypsies speak various dialects, which are more or less influenced by the languages used in their residence areas. Due to its heterogeneity, the Romani language can be classified as a multi-dialect system, which is influenced by language contacts with native speakers of the dominant language in a certain territory [15, 16].

An analysis of available sources showed that there were no speech databases in the Romani language, especially those suitable for developing systems for identifying speakers, to date. Due to the lack of any information about the distribution of speech phenomena in the Romani language, as well as the inability of involving a professional linguist (a native speaker of the Romani language), in expert research, the most promising direction was the search for new complex language-independent automatic and automated methods that allow studying segmental and suprasegmental parameters of the speech signal by an expert who does not speak the language spoken by a suspect.

In order to develop algorithms for identifying speakers of the Romani language, the research team of the Speech Technology Center (St. Petersburg) collected a speech database in the Romani language. The fundamental requirements for the speech database in the Romani language for the subsequent development of computer methods for the segmental analysis of spoken language were the phonetic representativeness of the material, which refers to the presence of all phonemes of the Romani language in their main realization variants (positional and contextual), as well as the presence of contexts, contributing to the manifestation of the well-known regional and individual variability of Gypsy speech.

The speakers had to be Gypsies who speak the Romani language as their native and primary language. To ensure representativeness of various realizations of the Romani language, it is necessary that speakers represented the main dialects most common among Gypsies, as well as various gender, age and educational social groups. The speakers pronounced both prepared reference speech material (a set of phonetically and melodically representative phrases) and spontaneous speech: a monologue (a story about events, about self, a description of an object) and dialogues with various communicative objectives (a conversation on an arbitrary or given topic, including general and specific questions, echo questions, responses, exclamations, requests, incentives). The speakers' speech was recorded in several sessions; the total duration of speech in the Romani language of each speaker is about 10–15 min. For each speaker, a standard questionnaire was filled-in: gender, age, education, place of birth, place of attendance of elementary school, type of dialect (according to the proposed classification), knowledge of the Russian language, knowledge of other languages. All speakers were recorded under the same acoustic and communication conditions. The speakers' membership in groups of one or another dialect type was verified by professional linguists: specialists in the Romani language and its dialects.

The text material in the Romani language prepared to collect the speech database meets the above requirements. It ensures a representation of the full range of phonemes of the Romani language; occurrence of phonemes in contexts of greatest differentiation of their realization options; a complete representation of the main communicative types of utterances; the presence of contexts that contribute to the manifestation of regional and/or individual phonetic variability.

The developed linguistic maps containing isoglosses of the main phonetic features of the Romani language dialects confirm that it is not the characteristics of the Romani dialects themselves that determine pronunciation differences between representatives of various Romani groups, but rather the phonetic features of the linguistic environment. Thus, modern differences between the Romani dialect groups are mainly caused by the typological and genetic features of the foreign language environment, where a certain Romani group lives, as well as differences in the degree and nature of the assimilation of foreign language interference features of a particular Romani group. The processes of phonetic modification, which resulted in modern inter-dialect differences in phonetic systems and in the pronunciation of some common Gypsy words, are closely related to the history of Gypsy migration, their movement across Europe and splitting into smaller groups.

The collected speech database made it possible to establish which features should be identified and used in the analysis of phonograms of a speech signal in order to maximize the reliability of identifying a Romani speaker. At the initial stages of the study [5, 16], the method of structural-melodic analysis of a speech signal at the suprasegmental level of spoken speech was described in detail. This study is focused on the consideration of an automated method for identifying Romani speakers at the segment level based on a universal acoustic-linguistic platform for the study of voice and speech for forensic purposes developed by SIS II (Speech Technology Center, St. Petersburg).

2.1 Method

The speaker identification method based on the ratios of formant frequencies on the reference fragments of the speech signal (the "formant alignment" method) is based on the study of identical instantaneous articulations (vocal tract configurations) in an arbitrary phonetic context. In contrast to the well-known methods of phonetic-spectral analysis [17–19] or microanalysis traditionally used in Russia in the analysis of the speech of Russian speakers, this approach involves identification and numerical comparison of special fragments within the studied speech material: not spectrograms of the same phonemes in the same context, but spectrograms of sounds corresponding to phonetically identical articulations, which, in turn, meets the task of identifying a speaker speaking a language unfamiliar to the expert. The study of speech signals includes numerical comparison of the positions of at least the first three formants F1 – F3 of sounds corresponding to phonetically identical articulations, which are determined based on the analysis of formant trajectories constructed automatically.

The speaker identification algorithm based on formant alignment of reference fragments consists of the following main steps:

1. Identification of formant trajectories of the phonograms being compared using a specially developed automatic formant extractor, which is part of the hardware-software complex. Formant trajectories for speech signals are selected automatically using an algorithm implemented based on the calculation of the LPC (linear prediction coefficient) filter. The LPC filter is a spectral model of the voice path. The maximum amplitude-frequency response (AFR) characteristics of this filter correspond in position and width to the formant frequencies of the vocal path. Linear prediction coefficients are calculated on each frame of the speech signal. Next, an LPC filter is built, its AFR characteristics are calculated and the values of the formant maxima are obtained. A special algorithm for tracing these formant maxima makes it possible to construct formant trajectories. Recommended parameter values are set by default. The algorithm for constructing formant trajectories includes the following steps: mapping a sequence of data vectors (frames) into a sequence of maxima of the spectrum of the linear prediction filter and mapping a sequence of vectors of maxima in a trajectory.

2. Automatic search in the sample phonogram (for which the identity of the speaker has been established) for reference fragments (RFs) corresponding to the representative values of the first two semantically distinctive formant frequencies of the most contrasting types of Gypsy speech phonemes /a/, /o/, /e/, /ı/. Traditionally, these are F_1 and F_2 and their localization on the formant frequency scale. Examples of search results for representative formant vectors in a sample phonogram and extracted reference fragments are shown in Figs. 1–2.

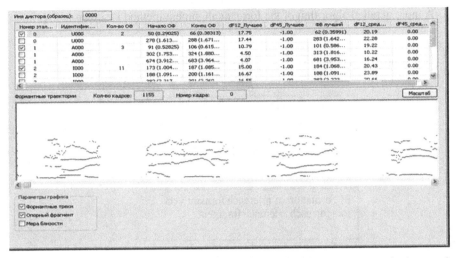

Fig.1. Window with the results of searching for representative formant vectors in the sample phonogram.

Данные		Идентификатор	F1, Гц	dF1, %	F2, Гц	dF2, %	F3, Гц	dF3, %
Идент.	U000	U000	480.00	1.88	1002.00	3.39	2125.00	0.38
		A000	772.00	2.98	1640.00	3.11	2786.00	2.15
F1, Гц	480.00	A001	619.00	1.62	1340.00	1.12	2456.00	1.38
dF1	1.88	A002	792.00	3.91	1434.00	4.95	2843.00	1.86
F2, Гц	1002.00	A003	747.00	4.28	1336.00	1.65	2739.00	4.64
dF2	3.39	I000	245.00	4.08	1960.00	3.01	2610.00	3.79
F3, Гц	2125.00	I001	250.00	1.20	2142.00	1.35	2546.00	1.02
dF3	0.38	I002	297.00	4.71	1792.00	1.12	2304.00	0.87
		I003	259.00	3.86	2220.00	3.78	2910.00	1.72
F4, Гц	3457.00	I004	251.00	1.59	2183.00	0.60	2768.00	2.31
dF4	3.70	I005	271.00	1.48	2145.00	3.50	2557.00	2.46
		I006	276.00	2.17	2019.00	4.06	2601.00	3.34
F5, Гц	5124.00	I007	268.00	2.24	1821.00	0.49	2644.00	0.34
dF5	0.02	I008	294.00	4.42	1795.00	1.62	2575.00	1.28
		I009	225.00	4.89	1734.00	3.00	2394.00	1.17
F6, Гц	0.00	I010	274.00	1.09	1965.00	2.04	2711.00	3.02
		I011	262.00	3.05	1918.00	3.81	2679.00	3.17
dF6	0.00	I012	263.00	1.14	1863.00	2.09	2493.00	2.57
		I013	262.00	1.53	1849.00	1.41	2336.00	1.46
		I014	224.00	4.02	1871.00	2.62	2730.00	2.45

Fig.2. Window with a list of reference fragments characteristic of the sample phonogram.

3. Construction of personal samples of Gypsy vowels in the speaker's speech according to the reference fragments found in the sample phonogram based on representative values of formant frequencies.

4. Automatic search in the disputed phonogram (for which the identity of the speaker has not been established) for reference fragments corresponding to the constructed samples of the speaker's voice (personal samples) according to the values of formant frequencies.

5. Comparison and verification of the match (by a given threshold) of characteristic reference fragments in the sample and disputed phonograms and making an identification decision.

A more detailed algorithm of the formant alignment method is shown in Fig. 3.

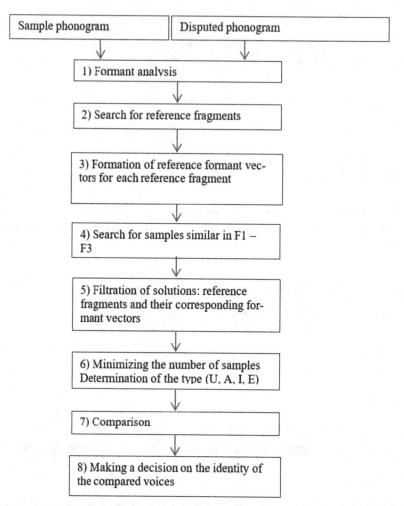

Fig. 3. Algorithm of the formant alignment method.

Formant tracks of the two phonograms being compared are analyzed in the same way. The identification decision for a pair of compared phonograms is made on the basis of calculating the percentage of reference fragments of the disputed phonogram that matched the voice samples from the total number of identified reference fragments. This percentage determines the "distance" between the phonograms under study. The decision-making mechanism uses automatically calculated values for false rejection (FR) of the speaker and false acceptance (FA) of the speaker, where FR is a measure of matching features, and FA is a measure of mismatched features [5, 16]. When FR > FA, the identification result is positive, and it is concluded that "The same speaker is recorded on the phonograms." When FR < FA, the result is negative, and it is concluded that "Different speakers are recorded on the phonograms."

The effectiveness of the speaker identification method based on the ratios of formant frequencies in the reference fragments of the speech signal is largely based on how successfully the formant trajectories are obtained. The correctness of the algorithm can be confirmed by the comparability of its results with the results obtained by other (alternative) methods, as well as by the repeatability (stability) of its results. To check the correctness of the algorithm for constructing formant trajectories, two types of experiments were performed: (a) comparison of formant trajectories and spectrograms for the same phonograms; (b) comparison of trajectories obtained for identical phonograms (for one speech signal and different distortions).

2.2 Comparison of Formant Trajectories and Spectrograms of Identical Speech Signals

The spectrograms of speech signals were obtained using the SIS II identification module "LPC frequency response" implemented in a specialized audio editor. In a number of cases, for the same signal, differences were observed between the pattern of spectrogram maxima and formant trajectories. These differences are due to the difference in the parameters of the algorithms (the number of LPCs), the difference in the methods for estimating the LPCs and the trajectory tracing algorithm. Thus, the LPC frequency responses (in spectrograms) calculated with different values of the algorithm parameters can differ significantly in the number and position of the maxima (such parameters, for example, are the frame size, frequency resolution, type of weighting window, etc.). Thus, it makes sense to compare formant trajectories only with a spectrogram constructed using the same algorithm parameters. In addition, part of the information that is present on the spectrogram is not displayed in formant trajectories (the set of points of the trajectories is poorer compared to the set of maxima of the LPC frequency response). This is due to the fact that the algorithm for constructing trajectories imposes restrictions on the set of events (combinations of spectrum maxima). Some events (for example, the splitting of the spectrum maximum) are simplified by the tracing algorithm.

Thus, the study of the algorithm correctness showed that even for identical signals, objectively determined differences in spectrograms and trajectories are possible. Such differences are related to the properties of statistical estimates and are not a manifestation of the incorrect operation of the algorithm itself. In general, a comparison of formant trajectories and spectrograms of identical speech signals showed that formant trajectories demonstrate good agreement with the spectrogram maxima. However, there may be differences between the formant trajectories and the maxima of the spectrograms, due to the difference in the models used for the assessment. In this regard, formant trajectories obtained for different audio recordings should be compared using the same models (algorithm parameters).

2.3   Comparison of Formant Trajectories for Speech Signals Recorded Under Different Conditions

From the comparison made for the similarity of the spectrograms of the speech signal and formant trajectories, it follows that the formant trajectories constructed for audio recordings of the same speaker are comparable only with the same values of the algorithm parameters. However, in real conditions there are additional factors that affect the accuracy (and comparability) of formant trajectories, for example, the recording channel (microphone, telephone, room reverberation time), additive noise of the channel, audio signal sampling frequency. The effects of these factors were tested using model experiments. The effect of the frequency response of the recording channel (filter with a bandwidth of 300 – 3600 Hz) is shown in Fig. 4.

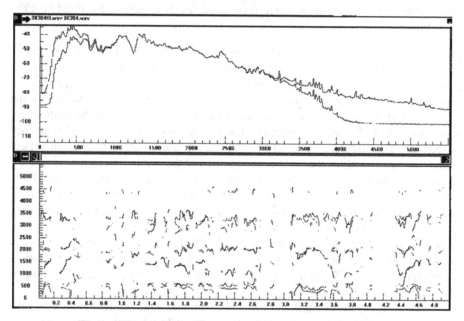

Fig. 4. Effect of the frequency response of the recording channel.

The upper graph shows the spectra of the original and filtered signal; the lower graph shows trajectories for the formants of the original signal and the signal passed through a filter with a bandwidth of 300 – 3600 Hz. From the plot of formant trajectories, it follows that the frequency response of the channel affects the position and number of formants. After the signal passed through the channel, the fifth formant disappeared, and the rest formants were displaced.

The effect of additive noise on the extraction of formant trajectories is shown in Fig. 5. The upper graph shows the spectra of the original and noisy signal; the lower graph shows trajectories for the formants of the original and noisy signal. It follows from the graph of formant trajectories that additive noise affects the position of the formants (in a monochrome figure, the displacement is expressed as a neighborhood of two similar trajectories).

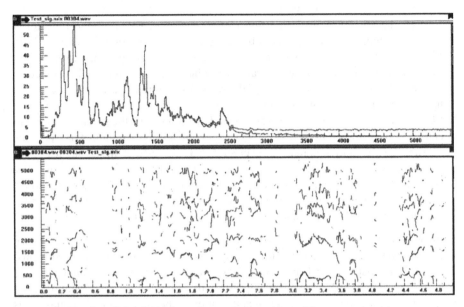

Fig. 5. Effect of additive noise on the extraction of formant trajectories.

The effect of the signal sampling frequency was also studied experimentally. It was established that formant trajectories constructed for the same signal digitized with different sampling frequencies are incompatible. This is due to two factors. First, within the additional frequency range (a signal with a higher sampling frequency), there are signal and noise components that affect the model and spectrum of the signal. Secondly, even in the absence of such an additional signal component in the high-frequency region, the spectral model tends to approximate the spectrum over the entire frequency range, which leads to its change over the entire frequency range (redistribution of degrees of freedom).

Thus, the linear prediction model turned out to be a formant estimation tool that is sensitive to the effect of channel characteristics and sampling frequency. The obvious solution to this problem is to bring all records to a common (standard) sampling frequency. To use the method as a working tool of an automated system, it is necessary to ensure the immunity of the method to distorting factors, as well as to take into account possible discrepancies in the algorithm for searching for similar (close) formant trajectories.

3   Results of the Investigation

To obtain reliable results, the following factors must be considered:

1. Effect of the amplitude-frequency response characteristic (AFC) of the phonogram recording channel. Strong roll-offs of the channel AFC lead to displacements in the spectral maxima, which in turn lead to an error in determining the frequency value of the corresponding formant.
2. Effect of the signal-to-noise ratio value. Correct determination of formant trajectories for vowel sounds in a signal is possible if the signal-to-noise ratio is at least 12 dB. With the deterioration of this parameter, the relatively weak spectral maxima of the third and fourth formants are not always determined correctly; as a result, the method based on the statistical processing of the relations of formant trajectories does not have reliable material to work with.
3. Reverberation effect. The studies carried out have shown that the spectral distortions caused by the reverberation effects displace the formants in the region of the spectrum maxima. In the time domain, the reverberation echo destroys the dynamics of the formants, causing the effect of "pulling" the formant trajectory. In the case of a significant difference in the values of the reverberation echo parameters in the sample and disputed phonograms, the reliability of the statistical analysis of the reference fragments obtained on such material is significantly reduced.

In order to check the correctness of the automatic extraction of formant trajectories, it is recommended to construct dynamic spectrograms of the phonograms being compared using the FFT (Fast Fourier Transform) method, regardless of which method was used to extract them, with the subsequent imposition of formant trajectories automatically extracted by the system. To ensure the manifestation of the high-frequency components of the spectrum, signal normalization is used. To normalize the signal, it is necessary to define the frequency to be boosted and the boost level. To set these parameters correctly, it is necessary to analyze the middle spectrum of the signal. Figure 6 shows an example of analyzing the middle spectrum of the speech signal power to determine the normalization parameters.

Fig. 6. Example of determining the parameters of speech signal normalization.

When analyzing a dynamic LPC spectrogram, in some cases, non-tonal segments of the signal can be reflected on it as tonal ones (i.e., as segments that have a formant structure). To analyze the correctness of constructing formant tracks, the expert needs to listen to a speech fragment, analyze the location of the formants on the dynamic spectrogram, and then check their compliance with the formant trajectories automatically extracted on the fragment under study. Figure 7 shows errors in the automatic extraction of formant trajectories.

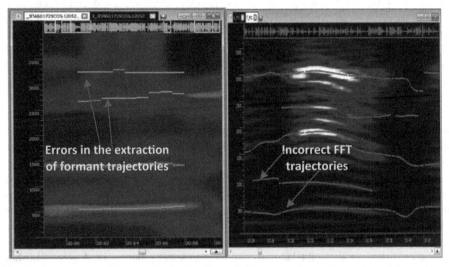

Fig. 7. Spectrogram of the speech signal with overlaid formant images in the LPC (left) and FFT (right) modes.

By virtue of the fact that the generalized samples include non-contrasting types of phonemes and also taking into account that the boundaries of the automatic search for reference fragments are quite wide, the number of reference fragments corresponding to one type of phonemes may include fragments corresponding to another type of phonemes (for example, the number of A-type reference fragments can include O-type fragments, etc.). Errors in automatic formant extraction are eliminated using the editing mode; this process involves correction of the formant trajectory in accordance with the dynamic spectrogram.

In addition, to work with this method, it is necessary to comply with the speech signal suitability criteria, which include the duration of the speech signal (more than 180 s for the sample phonogram, more than 40 s for the disputed phonogram), the signal-to-noise ratio of more than 10 dB, the reverberation time of less than 600 ms. To identify persons speaking a language unfamiliar to the expert, the phonogram must ensure the representativeness of the selected reference fragments, and the completeness and accuracy of the identified and analyzed identification characteristics are directly dependent on the expert's experience and competency.

4 Conclusion

The deliverables of the study of the Romani language showed that, subject to the requirements for the suitability of phonograms, the result of identification studies by the method of formant comparison of the reference fragments of the speech signal (formant alignment method) makes it possible to identify stable identification features associated with the spectral characteristics of an individual's speech. The results of the experiments indicate the universality and fundamental possibility of using the voice and speech analysis method proposed in this work to make a reasonable identification decision regarding foreign speakers by an expert who does not speak the language being studied. Thus, the study of the interdependence between the qualifications of auditors and the completeness and accuracy of identifying informative features of unprepared foreign language speech made it possible to establish a direct relationship between the experience and training of an expert in the field of forensic identification by voice and speech and the completeness and accuracy of the analysis of spoken language. The completeness and accuracy of identifying segmental characteristics of foreign language speech, in turn, has a significant impact on the correctness and reliability of the identification decision about the similarity or dissimilarity of the voice and speech of the persons participating in the conversation. In addition, it has been experimentally established that knowledge of the perceived language certainly simplifies the process of perception, primary recognition and identification analysis of the speech characteristics of the speaker's voice, but does not preclude a correct assessment of the voice characteristics at the segment level by an experienced expert who does not speak the language perceived during the phonoscopic examination. Thus, the reliability of the identification decision depends not so much on the expert's proficiency in the language the speaker speaks, but on the degree of his/her training and experience in the field of forensic identification of speakers by voice and speech. Thus, processing of foreign language (Gypsy) spontaneous speech using this method indicates the relative language independence of the method in relation to the Romani language.

However, it should be noted that it is necessary to use a set of identification methods (both automated and automatic, available to the expert) when making a generalized decision about the similarity or difference between voice and speech on the phonograms being compared [20]. Separately recorded values calculated on reference fragments may be the same for various speakers. The features identified by an expert in relation to foreign language speech acquire identification significance only in combination with each other, in terms of their frequency and repeatability.

Thus, the use of automatic identification methods (especially when the object of study is a language unfamiliar to the expert and little studied from a linguistic point of view) seems to be the most relevant. The identification of foreign speakers using the SIS II acoustic-linguistic platform, in addition to the described formant alignment method, involves the use of an automatic method for constructing a mathematical model of the speaker's voice based on normal mixture distributions (GMM, Gaussian mixture models), a method based on spectral-formant representations, as well as an automatic method based on pitch statistics. Approbation and validation of these automatic methods in relation to various rare languages are a promising prospective for further research of this kind.

References

1. Potapova, R.K., Mikhailov, V.G.: Fundamentals of Speech Acoustics. Moscow State Linguistic University "Rema", Moscow (2012) (in Russian)
2. Potapova, R.K., Potapov, V.V.: Language, Speech, Personality. Languages of Slavic culture, Moscow (2006). (in Russian)
3. Potapova, R., Potapov, V., Kuryanova, I.: Acoustic correlates of the native language speaker identity. Vestnik Moskovskogo Universiteta. Seriya 9. Philology **4**, 39–49 (2022)
4. Potapova, R.K.: Speech: Communication, Information, Cybernetics. Radio and Communication, Moscow (1997). (in Russian)
5. Potapova, R., Potapov, V., Kuryanova, I.: Forensic identification of foreign-language speakers by the method of structural-melodic analysis of phonograms. In: Prasanna, S.R.M., Karpov, A., Samudravijaya, K., Agrawal, S.S. (eds) Speech and Computer. SPECOM 2022. Lecture Notes in Computer Science, LNAI 13721, Springer, Cham, pp. 567–578 (2022). https://doi.org/10.1007/978-3-031-20980-2_48
6. Potapova, R.K., Potapov, V.V.: Auditory Perception of Speech by Non-Native Speakers. The Phonetician. CL–78, pp. 6–12 (1998)
7. Potapova, R.K.: Subject-oriented perception of foreign-language speech. Voprosy Jazykoznanija **2**, 46–65 (2005). (in Russian)
8. Potapova, R.K.: Acoustic-linguistic decoding of a speech signal as a basic component of phonoscopic analysis in forensic science. In: Kirin V.I. (ed.) Proceedings of the international conference "Informatization and information security of law enforcement agencies". Moscow, Administration Academy of the Ministry of Internal Affairs of Russia, pp. 34–335 (1994) (in Russian)
9. Potapova, R.K., Potapov, V.V.: Perceptual-auditory features of the identification of a foreign-language speaker. Vestnik of Moscow State Linguistic University. Humanities, **3**(771), 80–92 (2017) (in Russian)
10. Künzel, H.J.: Sprechererkennung: Grundzüge forensischer Sprachverarbeitung. Kriminalistik Verlag, Heidelberg (1987)
11. Hollien, H.: The Acoustics of Crime: The New Science of Forensic Phonetics. Plenum Press, New York; London (1990)
12. Hollien, H.: Forensic: Voice Identification. Academic Press, London; San Diego (2002)
13. Gibbons, J.: Forensic Linguistics: An Introduction to Language in the New Justice System. Carlton, Blackwell Publ, Malden; Oxford (2003)
14. Hudson, T., McDougall, K., Hughes, V.: Forensic phonetics. In: Setter, J., Knight, R.-A. (eds.) Cambridge Handbook of Phonetics, pp. 631–656. CUP, Cambridge (2021)
15. Potapov, V.V.: A short linguistic reference-book: Languages and Writing. Moscow, the Foundation "Development of fundamental linguistic studies" (2014) (in Russian)
16. Kuryanova, I.V.: Identification features of foreign-language speakers (forensic aspect): PhD thesis. Moscow, Moscow State Linguistic University (2020) (in Russian)
17. Koenig, B.E.: Spectrographic voice identification: a forensic survey. J. Acoust. Soc. Am. **79**(6), 2088–2090 (1986)
18. Künzel, H.J.: Current approaches to forensic speaker recognition. In: Proc. ESCA Workshop on automatic speaker recognition identification, Martigny, Switzerland, April 5–7, pp. 135–141 (1994)

19. McDermott, M.C., Owen, T., McDermott, F.M.: Voice identification: The Aural/Spectrographic Method. Electronic resource: http://www.forensictapeexpert.com/published/voiceidaural.htm
20. Goloschapova, T.I.: Advanced directions of forensic research of sound recordings in ethnic languages. In: Kirin. V.I. (ed.) Proceedings of the International Conference "Informatization and Information Security of Law Enforcement Agencies". Moscow, Administration Academy of the Ministry of Internal Affairs of Russia, pp. 337–341 (2009) (in Russian)

Gestures vs. Prosodic Structure in Laboratory Ironic Speech

Polina Vasileva⬧, Uliana Kochetkova(✉)⬧, and Pavel Skrelin⬧

Saint Petersburg University, Saint Petersburg 199034, Russia
st076593@student.spbu.ru, {u.kochetkova,p.skrelin}@spbu.ru

Abstract. The current paper deals with paralinguistic means of irony expression in Russian laboratory speech and their synchronization with different parts of prosodic structure of the utterance. The role that gestures and prosodic characteristics of laboratory speech play in irony perception is also studied. The research is based on the part of the multimodal ironic speech corpus built at the Department of Phonetics of Saint Petersburg State University. The total of 744 audio-visual stimuli were analysed using Praat, Wave Assistant and ELAN software and then corrected manually. The material includes pairs of homonymous ironic and non-ironic target utterances that allowed making a consistent comparison. The results of the acoustic and paralinguistic analyses showed that gestures are synchronized with the nucleus in most of ironic and non-ironic utterances, the head movements prevail in both speech types, the repetitive head movements are more frequent in ironic speech. As opposed to the actors' speech in films and series, there is no significant correspondence between pitch movement and gesture direction. Series of perceptual experiments, in which single- and multichannel signals were suggested, confirms the hypothesis about prevalence of the visual channel.

Keywords: Irony · Gestures · Prosodic Structure · F0 Direction · Acoustic Analysis · Perceptual Experiments

1 Introduction

The interaction of various channels of information transmission in communication becomes an increasingly popular area of research in modern linguistics, psychology and cognitive science [11, 13, 17, 18, 21]. It becomes obvious that studying exclusively the language channel of information is unproductive, since communication is multimodal, that is, several modes are used for its functioning and perception. It is noted that paralinguistic cues play a greater role in recognition than prosodic and semantic ones [1]. Research on the multimodality of oral speech has practical significance: as part of the creation of ECA (embedded computational agents), visual assistants, interfaces, robots, developers are faced with the question of recreating the paralinguistic behaviour of a person accompanying speech activity to express various emotions and give naturalness, friendliness, improving communication between a computer agent and a user. In addition, information about the visual cues of a person's emotional and physical state is necessary for correct speech recognition and the formation of a suitable response by the agent.

A. Karpov et al. (Eds.): SPECOM 2023, LNAI 14338, pp. 301–313, 2023.
https://doi.org/10.1007/978-3-031-48309-7_25

From this point of view, emotional evaluative statements are of particular interest, notably the ironic statements, in which the speaker means something opposite to what he says. The correct interpretation of such statements with irony-negation is highly important in human-machine communication. Irony-negation is a complex phenomenon and is expressed at different levels: lexical, grammatical, stylistic, phonetic and paralinguistic [6, 10, 12, 27–29]. In a situation where relying on context or lexical markers is impossible, acoustic cues and paralinguistic means (gestures and facial expressions) play an important role in recognizing irony.

The relevance of the current study lies in the fact that at the moment the paralinguistic cues of irony-negation and their synchronization with the prosodic structure of the utterance have not been studied on the material of the Russian language.

1.1 Gestures Description

There are two main functions of gesticulation – communicative and speech-assisted. The opinions of researchers on which of them is paramount vary. The communicative function is that gestures are carried out primarily for the listener: they help to fully understand the speaker and convey additional information that is not verbally voiced (that is, they are in the nature of compensation). Proponents of this idea (D. McNeill, A. Kendon, C. Nobe) believe that gestures and speech are formed in consciousness simultaneously and are divided into different channels of information transmission later [14–16, 22, 24, 25]. By the speech-aid function, researchers mean the use of gestures by the speaker for their own convenience (for example, in a situation of remembering low-frequency vocabulary). As proof, the researchers cite the argument that gesticulation is used even in situations where the listener does not see the gesture (for example, during a telephone conversation) or in monologue statements.

Adam Kendon in the work "Gesture: Visible Action as Utterance" [16] proposed to distinguish gestures by the following parameters: the obligation of accompanying speech, the presence or absence of systematic language features in gestures, regularity or spontaneity of the gesture. David McNeill created a generally accepted classification of gestures based on these parameters – the "Kendon continuum" [22]. He arranged various types of gestures along a certain axis: Gestures – Emblems – Pantomime – Sign Languages, in which he considered as gestures (gesticulation) only gestures accompanying speech (co-speech gestures).

Each gesture consists of a set of features that define its character. These signs include gesticulating organ, direction of movement, multiplicity (repetitiveness), trajectory, configuration of the gesticulating organ (palm) [4, 23]. In our study we analyse three parameters: the gesticulation organ, direction, and multiplicity.

1.2 Synchronization with Prosodic Structure

In spontaneous speech, a gesture is not always synchronized with the linguistic phenomenon [8, 13] to which it relates; it may anticipate or delay relative to the semantic component that caused it, especially in unprepared speech [25, 26]. It is noted that temporal coordination between gestures and prosody is stronger than between gestures and speech in general [30]. Studies on the material of different languages have shown that there is a correlation between gestures and changes in the frequency response and the amplitude of the speech signal [3, 9]. Many studies have confirmed that in most cases the stressed part of gestures coincides with stressed syllables and the intonation centre (the nucleus) of the utterance [30]. The coincidence of the direction of movement of the F0 with the direction of the gesture is noted [5]. Nobe made the observation that the stroke, which is the main part of the gesture, precedes or coincides with the acoustic peak of the utterance (the peak of F0 or intensity) [25].

One of the objectives of the study is to determine the presence or absence of synchronization of facial expressions and gestures with the intonation centre (the nucleus) of an ironic utterance, as well as comparison with the synchronization of facial expressions and gestures with the intonation centre (the nucleus) of neutral homonymous utterances.

1.3 Paralinguistic Characteristics of Ironic Speech

A characteristic element of paralinguistics in ironic statements is laughter. Listeners can also use laughter in response to signal that they have recognized the irony in the speaker's utterance [2]. Research by R. Kreutz and J. Kochi, devoted to the comparison of facial expressions in ironic and neutral statements based on the material of the English language, showed that the main difference is that speakers smile more in an ironic situation [7, 20]. However, S. Attardo's research conducted on the material of American comedies [1] has the opposite results: speakers most often use an emotionless face (blank face) in ironic situations. Another paralinguistic cue of irony is the reduction of eye contact with the interlocutor in comparison with non-ironic situations [31], as well as the "rolling" of the eyes, squinting, winking, wide-open eyes [1]. It is noted that speakers use eyebrows (raised or "frown") as a gesticulator to convey ironic meaning [31].

Various head movements (nods, tilts, circular movements) are also used by speakers in addition to ironic statements [1]. The multiplicity of these movements is highlighted in comparison with the gestures accompanying neutral statements. In the study of ironic actor's speech, conducted on the material of the Russian language, the presence of hyperarticulation and the labialization of the non-labial vowels in ironic utterances is noted. Similar phenomena were not found in neutral statements [19]. The work of S. Gonzalez-Fuente, V. Escandell-Vidal and Pilar Prieto "Gestural codas pave the way to the understanding of verbal irony" [8] is devoted to the influence of gestures reproduced after an ironic utterance. The study revealed that such gestures play a significant role for the recognition of irony in the absence of contextual markers of the modality of utterance. The results of previous studies on gestures accompanying ironic speech were also confirmed, namely that emotionlessness is one of the key markers of irony.

2 Material and Method

Homonymous target fragments of ironic and non-ironic utterances from the corpus of laboratory ironic speech developed at the Department of Phonetics of St. Petersburg State University served as the material for the study. A part of the corpus consists of sets of short texts. Mini-texts include ironic or non-ironic utterances representing various sentence types with homonymous target fragments. One mini-text consists of 1–3 sentences providing sufficient context for an ironic or a non-ironic target fragment, a target fragment includes 1–5 words. For example, there are two mini-texts with the same target fragment – *"pozhaleyut"* (*'they will feel sorry'*): an ironic text *"Pozhaleyut! Kak zhe! Zhdi ot nih!"* (*They will feel sorry < for me >, yeah, well, expect from them'*) and a non-ironic one *"On ochen' lyubil naveshchat' roditelej – vsegda prigreyut, nakormyat, pozhaleyut..."* (*'he loved to visit his parents very much – they had always warmed him, fed him, felt sorry for him'*).

Audio and video recordings were conducted simultaneously. The video was recorded at a frame rate of 100 frames per second. The speakers were recorded in close-up (that is, the speaker's head, neck, and shoulders are visible on the recording), which influenced the use of gestures.

In the current study, an analysis of one of the sets of 60 mini-texts was carried out. Audio and video recordings of 12 speakers (7 men and 5 women) were selected. There was a slight gender imbalance in speakers, as there was no intention to compare male and female ironic speech in this study. A total of 744 stimuli were analyzed. The acoustic and paralinguistic analysis of the material was carried out.

The target fragments of ironic and neutral statements of each of the speakers were cut out in the Movavi Video Editor 23 program. Frame-by-frame video viewing mode was used for segmentation accuracy. The audio recordings were segmented and annotated using the Wave Assistant and Praat software, then corrected manually. At different levels in the TextGrid file, the boundaries of words, the vowel in the intonation centre of the utterance and the syllable in which it is located were annotated; also, at a separate level, the mini-text, of which this target fragment was extracted, was indicated. Next, video files and textgrid files containing an annotation were combined in the ELAN program (Fig. 1). A new annotation level was created – the "par" level, where gestures and facial expressions were marked up. The following designations were used: he (head), eb (eyebrows), e (eyes), sh (shoulders), ha (arm), lh (laughter). If different gestures were played at the same time, the "par 1" and, in some cases, "par 2" and "par 3" levels were created.

Gestures were described by the following parameters:

- the organ of gesticulation (head, eyebrows, eyes, lips, shoulders, hands);
- the direction of movement of the gesture (vertically (up/down) and horizontally);
- the multiplicity of the gesture (single /multiple, multiple gestures were considered to consist of several movements of the gesticulator relative to one axis (horizontal or vertical));
- the part of the target fragment with which the gesture was synchronized: the first syllable/the first stressed syllable (if the target fragment consisted of two or more words)/the intonation centre of the utterance/ the post-centre of the utterance/ throughout the entire fragment; the nature of the movement (for the eyes): squinted, wide open.
- Laughter was singled out separately as a paralinguistic component. Individual phases of the gesture were not highlighted in the frame of the current study.

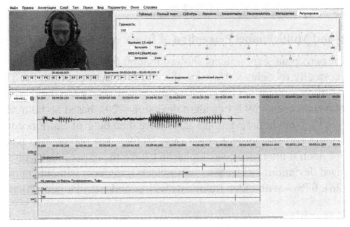

Fig. 1. Example of annotation using ELAN software.

2.1 Perceptual Experiments

In order to determine what role the visual cues of irony-negation play in recognizing the ironic meaning of an utterance, a series of perceptual experiments was conducted, including three different experiments. In the first experiment, the participants were asked to determine the character of the utterance (ironic or non-ironic) by listening to an audio recording of the target fragment. In the second experiment, the auditors had to determine the character of the utterance by watching video clips without sound, relying only on paralinguistic cues. In the third experiment, participants determined the character of the utterance after watching a video clip with sound, relying on both acoustic and visual cues.

6 phrases were selected for each of the speakers: 3 with ironic and 3 with non-ironic meaning. The material for the experiment was processed manually, as follows:

1) The target fragments of statements were segmented and sliced in the Movavi Video Editor 23 program. Each target fragment was saved in two versions: with sound and without sound.
2) Audio recordings corresponding to them were selected from the body of ironic speech for the cut target fragments.

Questionnaires for surveys were created in the SoSci Survey web application. Three questionnaires were compiled: to determine the modality of the target fragments based on audio recordings, video recordings without sound, video recordings with sound. On the first page of each of the questionnaires, the participants were offered instructions and an example of irony-negation for the correct passage of the survey.

A survey on the recognition of acoustic cues of irony-negation was accomplished by 46 participants. 32 participants took part in a survey on the recognition of the visual cues of irony-negation. 33 participants participated in a survey on the recognition of acoustic cues, the same number of participants was in the last experiment on visual cues of irony-negation.

3   Results

3.1   Single- and Multichannel Perception of Ironic and Non-ironic Utterances

The results of perceptual experiments showed that 60.6% of fragments of ironic utterances were correctly recognized by more than 60% of auditors (Fig. 2). The average percentage of irony recognition based on acoustic cues was 56% (standard deviation – 26), based on visual cues – 59% (standard deviation – 29), based on both acoustic and visual cues – 65% (standard deviation – 23). More than 60% of auditors correctly recognized the same percentage neutral phrases (60.6%), but the average percentage of recognition of neutral utterances was higher: 62% for the experiment with audio fragments (standard deviation – 21), 68% – with video fragments without sound (standard deviation – 28), 67% – with video fragments with sound (standard deviation – 24).

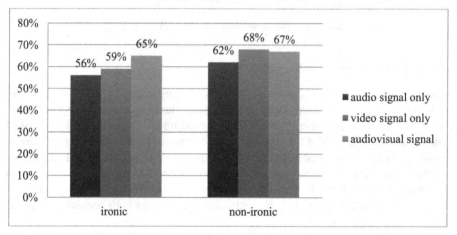

Fig. 2. Perception of ironic and non-ironic utterances due to the single- or multichannel perception.

The results of the perceptual experiments were subjected to statistical analysis. The difference in the recognition of ironic and non-ironic statements was statistically significant ($p < 0.05$). The interaction of audio cues and visual cues of utterances was verified using r-Pearson correlation analysis. It was found that for neutral statements, the relationship between the results of experiments with audio fragments and video fragments with sound is strong on the Cheddock scale (Pearson coefficient = 0.8); the relationship between the results of experiments with video fragments without sound and video fragments with sound is also strong (Pearson coefficient = 0.7). For ironic statements, the relationship between the results of the experiment with audio fragments and video fragments with sound is strong on the Cheddock scale (Pearson coefficient = 0.7), but for experiments with video fragments without sound and with sound, the Pearson correlation coefficient is -0.06.

The speaker's facial expressions and gestures improved the recognition of irony; however, it is worth noting that all ironic statements were correctly recognized in each of the 3 experiments by more than 60% of the auditors.

3.2 Gestures

The analysis of the paralinguistic means showed that in the majority of both ironic (87%) and non-ironic (86%) statements, speakers use head movements. Single head movements prevail (excursion - single percussive movement-recursion (it is also possible that there is no excursion and/or recursion)), however, in ironic statements, multiple head movements are more common – in 15% of statements than in non-ironic – in 7% of statements.

In ironic statements, the movement of the head was carried out vertically in 54% of cases (92% of them - downward movement), horizontally – in 46% of cases. The upward movements of the head are characteristic for the design of non-ironic inter-rogative utterances, while the gesture is synchronized with the intonation centre of the utterance.

In 20% of ironic and 12% of neutral statements, the speakers used facial move-ments with their eyebrows (raised/furrowed eyebrows; movement with one eyebrow), an example is given in Fig. 3.

Fig. 3. An example of facial movement with eyebrows (furrowed eyebrows) in the ironic statement "Professional".

Eyes were used as a gesticulator by only one speaker out of 12 (speaker F006) in 15% of ironic utterances and 20% of non-ironic utterances (Fig. 4).

Fig. 4. An example of facial movement with eyebrows (raised eyebrows) and eyes in a neutral statement "Professional!"

Due to the special properties of the laboratory video recording of reading, the hands practically did not get into the frame, so the use of this gesticulator was noted in speech of two speakers. One female speaker used her hand in 5% of ironic utterances and in 10% of non-ironic utterances and one male speaker used his hand only in one statement – non-ironic. A characteristic paralinguistic component in ironic utterances is laughter. Laughter (as well as a smile) was used by most speakers to convey an ironic meaning.

3.3 Synchronization

Synchronization with the Nucleus. During the analysis of the material, it was found out that the percentage of synchronization of facial expressions and gestures with the intonation centre of the utterance is 70% for ironic target fragments and 72% for neutral target fragments (Fig. 5).

Fig. 5. An example of synchronization with the intonation centre in the statement "Baggage!"

Synchronization with the First Syllable. It was noted that the gestures accompanying both ironic and non-ironic speech are also synchronized with the first syllable of the utterance: the gesture was synchronized with the first syllable of the utterance in 40% of ironic utterances and 32% of non-ironic utterances. In statements consisting of 2 or more words, the gesture coincided with the first stressed syllable of the statement (45% of ironic statements of 2 or more words and 72% of non-ironic statements of 2 or more words). The illustration is given bellow (Fig. 6).

Synchronization with Post Nuclear Part. It was noted that gestures can synchronize with the post-centre of the utterance (18% of ironic utterances and 9% of non-ironic utterances).

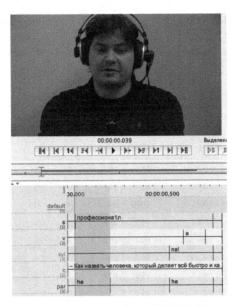

Fig. 6. Example of synchronization with the first syllable in the statement "Professional".

The information about co-speech gestures and their synchronisation with the into-nation centre (nucleus) in ironic and non-ironic utterances is given below in Tables 1 and 2.

Table 1. Co-speech gestures in ironic utterances.

Speaker	Synchronization with the nucleus (% of utterances)	Repetitiveness	Head	Eyebrows	Lips	Shoulders	Hands	Eyes	Laughter
1 (M)	75%	31%	80%	25%	10%	0%	0%	0%	10%
2 (F)	80%	50%	95%	0%	0%	10%	0%	0%	0%
3 (F)	80%	10%	75%	10%	20%	5%	5%	15%	5%
4 (F)	80%	10%	85%	20%	10%	0%	0%	0%	0%
5 (M)	55%	0%	45%	30%	5%	0%	0%	0%	0%
6 (M)	80%	0%	90%	15%	0%	5%	0%	0%	0%
7 (F)	75%	15%	95%	10%	15%	0%	0%	0%	5%
8 (M)	70%	5%	95%	20%	0%	0%	0%	0%	0%
9 (M)	85%	15%	100%	10%	0%	0%	0%	0%	5%
10(M)	60%	10%	100%	45%	0%	0%	0%	0%	0%
11 (F)	50%	20%	100%	0%	15%	0%	0%	0%	5%
12(M)	50%	10%	85%	0%	5%	0%	0%	0%	0%

Table 2. Co-speech gestures in non-ironic utterances.

Speaker	Synchronization with the nucleus (% of utterances)	Repetitiveness	Head	Eyebrows	Lips	Shoulders	Hands	Eyes	Laughter
1 (M)	65%	20%	80%	20%	0%	0%	0%	0%	0%
2 (F)	90%	10%	95%	0%	0%	0%	0%	0%	0%
3 (F)	85%	100%	90%	20%	10%	0%	10%	20%	5%
4 (F)	85%	5%	90%	0%	5%	0%	0%	0%	0%
5 (M)	45%	10%	55%	15%	5%	0%	0%	0%	0%
6 (M)	75%	100%	85%	5%	0%	5%	0%	0%	0%
7 (F)	60%	100%	100%	0%	5%	0%	0%	0%	0%
8 (M)	75%	10%	95%	25%	0%	0%	0%	0%	0%
9 (M)	75%	10%	80%	15%	10%	0%	0%	0%	0%
10(M)	70%	5%	80%	25%	0%	0%	0%	0%	10%
11 (F)	85%	5%	95%	10%	15%	0%	0%	0%	0%
12(M)	50%	5%	85%	0%	0%	0%	0%	0%	0%

Direction of movement of the gesticulator and the F0 direction in the intonation centre of the utterance. According to the results of a comparative analysis, it was found out that the movement of F0 and gestures in the intonation centre of the utterance coincide in 25% of cases for ironic utterances and in 67% of cases for non-ironic utterances. The results obtained do not coincide with the results of the study of the interaction of

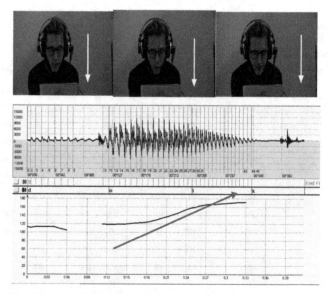

Fig. 7. Example of discrepancy between the F0 movement direction and head gesture direction.

acoustic and visual cues in ironic actor's speech [Kochetkova et al. 2022]. It is assumed that the results could be affected by the absence of interlocutors when recording speech in the laboratory. In addition, irony is a complex phenomenon for both perception and reproduction, especially when reading, and not in conditions of spontaneous speech (Fig. 7).

4 Conclusion

In the course of this study, it was revealed that the paralinguistic cues of irony-negation are synchronized with the intonation centre (nucleus) of the utterance in 70% of cases. It was noted that other parts of the utterance (the first syllable or the first stressed syllable) are also distinguished by paralinguistic elements. As a result of perceptual experiments, it was found that gestures accompanying ironic speech can have the character of both parallelism and compensation, which depends on the individual strategy of the speaker, but in general, the video sequence improves the recognition of irony, which indicates the importance of visual cues of modality.

Neutral utterances have a greater percentage of synchronization with the intonation centre of the utterance than ironic ones. In both ironic and neutral utterances, there is a tendency to highlight the first syllable or first stressed syllable using gestures. Gesticulation in ironic utterances is characterized by a greater complexity of movements; speakers use more gesticulators to express ironic meaning. Laughter and smile were observed as markers of irony. Multiple movements are more common when making ironic statements than non-ironic ones.

The results obtained in the current study will be verified at the next step of the analysis on the whole Multimodal corpus of Russian ironic speech. We should note that the material included only the monologues, so one can suppose that the absence of the interlocuter could slightly affect the performance of irony. But, if we would enlarge the corpus embedding spontaneous dialogues, it would make impossible the comparison of the homonymous target fragments, which allowed us to make a paired statistical analysis.

The perspective of the study is the analysis of the ratio of segmental (acoustic and /or articulatory) characteristics and facial gestures (the presence of labialization, hyperarticulation, etc.), as well as the analysis of acoustic and paralinguistic cues of irony in various languages, as the linguistic and cultural variety can affect the way irony is present in speech, gestures and facial expressions.

References

1. Attardo, S., Eisterhold, J., Hay, J., Poggi, I.: Multimodal markers of irony and sarcasm. Humor Int. J. Humor Res. **16**(2), 243–260 (2003)
2. Attardo, S., Pickering, L., Baker, A.A.: Prosodic and multimodal markers of humor in conversation. Pragmatics Cogn. **19**(2), 224–247 (2011)
3. Badin, P., Bailly, G., Revéret, L., Baciu, M., Segebarth, C., Savariaux, C.: Three-dimensional articulatory modeling of tongue, lips and face, based on MRI and video images. J. Phonetics **30**(3), 533–553 (2002)
4. Birdwhistell, R.L.: Kinesics and context: essays on body motion. Communication University of Pennsylvania Press, Philadelphia, PA (1970)

5. Bolinger, D.: Intonation and gesture. Am. Speech **58**, 156–174 (1983)
6. Braun, A., Schmiedel, A.: The phonetics of ambiguity: a study on verbal irony. Cultures and Traditions of Wordplay and Wordplay Research, De Gruyter, Berlin, pp. 111–136 (2018)
7. Caucci, G.M., Kreuz, R.J.: Social and paralinguistic cues to sarcasm. Humor: Int. J. Humor Res. **25**(1), 1–22 (2012)
8. Gonsalez-Fuente, S., Escandell-Vidal, V., Prieto, P.: Gestural codas pave the way to the understanfing of verbal irony. J. Pragmatics **90**, 26–47 (2015)
9. Graf, H.P., Cosatto, E., Strom, V., Huang, F.J.: Visual prosody: facial movements accompanying speech. In: Proceedings of AFGR, pp. 96–102 (2002)
10. Grice, H.P.: Logic and Conversation. Speech Acts [Syntax and Semantics 3]. eds. Peter Cole and Jerry Morgan, Academic Press, New York, pp. 41–58 (1975)
11. Grishina, E.A.: Russian gesticulation from a linguistic point of view (corpus studies) [Russkaya zhestikulyaciya s lingvisticheskoj tochki zreniya (korpusnye issledovaniya)] - M.: YASK: Yazyki slavyanskoj kul'tury (2017)
12. Haiman, J.: Talk Is Cheap: Sarcasm, Alienation, and the Evolution of Language. Oxford University Press (1998)
13. Karpin´ski, M., Jarmołowicz-Nowikow, E., Malisz, Z.: Aspects of gestural and prosodic structure of multimodal utterances in Polish task-oriented dialogues. In: Speech and Language Technology, vol. 11, pp. 113–122 (2009)
14. Kendon, A.: Some relationships between body motion and speech. In: Seigman, A., Pope, B. (eds.) Studies in Dyadic Communication, pp. 177–216. Pergamon Press, Elmsford (1972)
15. Kendon, A.: Gesticulation and speech: two aspects of the process of utterance. In: Key, M.R. (ed.) The Relationship of Verbal and Nonverbal Communication, pp. 207–227. Mouton and Co., The Hague (1980)
16. Kendon, A.: Gesture: Visible Action as Utterance. Cambridge University Press (2004)
17. Kibrik, A.A.: Multimodal linguistics. A. A. Kibrik // Cognitive research: collection of scientific papers [Mul'timodal'naya lingvistika / A. A. Kibrik // Kognitivnye issledovaniya : sbornik nauchnyh trudov]. vol. 4. – Moscow : "Institut psihologii RAN", pp. 135–152 (2010)
18. Kita, S.: The temporal relationship between gesture and speech: A study of Japanese-English bilinguals. Chicago, IL: Department of Psychology, University of Chicago. – 1990 (1990)
19. Kochetkova, U.E., Evdokimova, V.V., Skrelin, P.A., German, R.D., Novoselova, D.D.: Interplay of visual and acoustic cues of irony perception: a case study of actor's speech. Artificial Intelligence and Natural Language, V. 1731, Springer Nature, Cham, pp. 82—94 (2022)
20. Kreuz, R.J., Roberts, R.M.: Two cues for verbal irony: hyperbole and the ironic tone of voice. Metaphor Symbol. Activity **10**(1), 21–31 (1995)
21. Lapaire, J.-R.: Grammar, gesture and cognition: insights from multimodal utterances and applications for gesture analysis. Visnyk of Lviv University. Philology Series **52**, 88–103 (2011)
22. McNeill, D.: Hand and mind: What gestures reveal about thought. University of Chicago Press (1992)
23. Morris, T., Elshehry, O.: Real-Time Fingertip Detection for Hand Gesture Recognition. Advanced Concepts for Intelligent Vision Systems (2002)
24. Munhall, K.G., Jones. J.A., Callan, D.E., Kuratate, T., Vatikiotis-Bateson, E.: Visual prosody and speech intelligibility. Psychol. Sci. **15**(2), 133–137 (2004)
25. Nobe, S.: Representational gestures, cognitive rhythms, and acoustic aspects of speech: a network/threshold model of gesture production. Unpublished dissertation, University of Chicago (1996)
26. Nobe, S.: Where to most spontaneous representational gestures actually occur with respect to speech? In: McNeill, D. (ed.) Language and Gesture Cambridge University Press, pp. 186–198 (2000)

27. Searle, R.J.: Expression and Meaning: Studies in the Theory of Speech Acts. Cambridge University Press, Cambridge (1979)
28. Simpson, P.: That's not Ironic, that's just Stupid!: towards an eclectic account of the discourse of irony. In: Dynel, M. (eds.) The Pragmatics of Humour across Discourse Domains, John Benjamins, pp. 33–50 (2011)
29. Sperber, D., Wilson, D.: Relevance: Communication and Cognition. Oxford: Blackwell (1986/1995)
30. Wagner, P., Malisz, Z., Kopp, S.: Gesture and speech in interaction: an overview. Speech Commun. **57**, 209–232 (2014)
31. Williams, J.A., Burns, E.L., Harmon, E.A.: Insincere utterances and gaze: Eye contact during sarcastic statements. Perceptual and Motor Skills **108**, 565–572 (2009)

Sounds of <sil>ence: Acoustics of Inhalation in Read Speech

Priyankoo Sarmah[(⊠)] [ID], Wendy Lalhminghlui[ID], and Neeraj Kumar Sharma[ID]

Indian Institute of Technology Guwahati, Guwahati 781039, India
{priyankoo,wendy,neerajs}@iitg.ac.in

Abstract. In spoken conversations, inhalations are associated with the initiation of speech. In multiparty conversations, inhalations are crucial as they signal turn-taking. However, in read speech, inhalations are not considered as holding any crucial information and hence are often omitted from the analysis, marked with a <sil> annotation. In this work, we demonstrate that the acoustics of inhalations may not be completely 'silent' and contain useful cues correlated with the contiguous linguistic sounds. Using a read speech database of Mizo, we show that the acoustics of inhalations show prominent anticipatory effects and are often correlated with the formants of the following vowel sounds.

Keywords: Acoustics of inhalation · Formants · Speech initiation

1 Introduction

How speakers begin to speak has been of interest to speech scientists in recent years as it provides insights into the cognitive aspects of speech planning and also helps in the development of better automatic speech recognition (ASR) systems. In continuous speech, be it spontaneous or read, speakers have to inhale in order to sustain speaking. While such inhalations are considered 'pre-speech' elements with discourse functions, such as turn-taking and preparing the listener to start hearing speech, they are believed to be devoid of any linguistic-phonetic content [12,13]. In the present paper, it is argued that acoustic characteristics of inhalation in speech are strongly correlated with the acoustic characteristics of contextual phonemes.

Previous studies have shown a strong positive correlation between the length of inhalation and the duration of the following breath group. It is also argued that inhalation duration also differed according to the syntactic boundaries [11,17]. In the case of German spontaneous speech, it has been shown that increased syntactic complexity and possibly, the cognitive load associated with the spoken tasks, may result in longer inhalations in the 'pre-speech' phase. While not much interest is observed in acoustically analyzing the inhalation breaths, they are, nevertheless, considered relevant for modeling more natural-sounding synthesized speech [3]. In the case of ASRs, it has been shown that accuracy could be improved by explicitly modeling the breath sounds in continuous speech [4].

© The Author(s), under exclusive license to Springer Nature Switzerland AG 2023
A. Karpov et al. (Eds.): SPECOM 2023, LNAI 14338, pp. 314–321, 2023.
https://doi.org/10.1007/978-3-031-48309-7_26

As mentioned earlier, attempts at investigating the acoustic properties of inhalations are rare. Recently, it has been shown that speech preparation consists of mouth opening for inhalation, and hence, it is possible that such opening may correlate with the articulatory gestures required for the following speech sound production [10]. In characterizing inhalation noises, it has also been noticed that inhalations are accompanied by silence on both sides [16]. While it has been postulated to be associated with changing motor gestures, part of such silences may also be associated with the adjustment of articulatory gestures. Previous studies have also shown that inhalation noises are characterized by lower intensity (compared to other speech sounds) and highly variable duration [14]. Another study that examined the acoustic properties of breath sounds concluded that intensity, the center of gravity (COG), and the first formant (F1) are positively correlated to the speed of inhalation [15]. While these few studies have investigated the acoustic properties of inhalation in speech to a certain extent, the correlation with the contextual segments is yet to be investigated.

Furthering the understanding of the effect of contextual segments on the acoustics of inhalations in speech, in the current study, we attempt to see how acoustic characteristics of the preceding and following vowels in a spoken utterance affect the acoustics of the inhalation. Most of the inhalation noises recorded in our lab showed evidence of formants in them. The existence of formants is confirmed by previous studies that report that inhalation while producing speech, involves mouth opening [10]. However, it has also been reported that such formants produced in inhalation are typically stable. In the current study, we report a strong correlation between the formant values associated with inhalation and the following vowels.

2   Methodology

This section provides an overview of the methodology adopted in this study. In the subsection immediately following this, we provide a detailed description of the speech database used in this study. This will be followed by a description of the acoustic and statistical methods used.

2.1   Speech Database and Annotation

The material used for the speech recording consists of 2 Mizo passages which are Mizo folktales recorded by 12 Mizo native speakers (10 female, 2 male). The speakers were 20 to 25 years old at the time of recording the speech data. The speech recordings took place in a quiet room in Shillong and Aizawl using a TASCAM DR 100 MK II audio recorder connected to a Shure SM 10 unidirectional head-mounted close-talk microphone. The participants were provided printed material on a paper sheet and requested to read as naturally as possible.

The recorded speech was transferred to a PC for further analysis. Since the inhalation occurs in the area of silence between the closure of the preceding speech and the onset of the following speech, this silence part is segmented and annotated as the inhalation area by using Praat [2]. The second author confirmed by listening that the <sil> marked intervals were actually inhalation noises and involved the opening of the mouth. After all the inhalation noises were marked, in total 1408 inhalation noises were extracted for analyses from the speech data.

2.2 Acoustic and Statistical Analyses

In order to analyze the acoustic and temporal characteristics of the inhalations, we used a Praat script to extract the duration of each sentence and the inhalations. We also extracted the number of inhalations in each sentence in order to ascertain the average number of inhalations per second. Apart from the temporal characteristics, we also extracted the formant frequencies, namely the first formant (F1) and the second formant (F2) from each of the inhalation noises and from the vowels preceding and following the inhalations. In order to analyze the extracted raw data, we used descriptive statistics and some simple statistical measures, such as Pearson correlation coefficient to ascertain the relationship between inhalation duration and sentence duration and between F1 and F2 of the inhalation noise and those of the contextual vowels. The statistical analyses were conducted using R [9]. Some exploratory statistics were conducted with the *lme4* package on R and the post-hoc analyses conducted using the *car* and *emmeans* packages [1,6,7].

3   Results

3.1   Amount of Inhalation in Speech

The Mizo data we used for analysis, consisted of individual sound files that consisted of one written sentence, that were usually spoken with several inhalations. Hence, we calculated the number of inhalations per second which yielded an average of 0.36 inhalations per second with a standard deviation of 0.09. Figure 1 shows the average per second inhalations in speech for each speaker in the speech database used in this work. As seen from the figure, except for speaker F39, all other speakers had a very similar number of inhalation instants in speech. A linear mixed effects model with speaker as a fixed effect and sentences as random effects showed a significant effect of the speaker on average inhalation per second. A posthoc analysis of the model showed that only speaker F39 was significantly different from all the other speakers. Hence, the results of this speaker may be considered outliers in our analysis.

We also plotted the duration of the written sentences in speech along with the total duration of inhalation that occurred in speaking each sentence. The average ratio of inhalation and spoken sentence duration was about 13%. The duration of inhalation seemed to be positively correlated with the total duration of the sentences they were produced in. This correlation is shown in Fig. 2. As seen in the figure, the correlation is positive with an R of 0.73 with significant p values. Hence, as reported in previous works, we show that there is a strong correlation between the duration of inhalation and the duration of sentences produced following inhalation. This supports the claim that inhalations play an important role in speech planning.

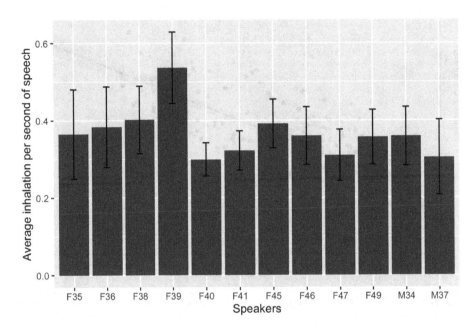

Fig. 1. Average inhalation per second for all speakers with standard deviations as error bars.

3.2 Correlation Between Formants in Inhalation and Contextual Vowels

It has been shown in the previous literature that inhalations during speech may involve the gesture of an open mouth. Hence, we assume that the articulatory gestures during inhalations may be influenced by the preceding or the following phonetic segments. Hence, in the current work, from the speech database, we extracted the inhalations that are either preceded by or followed by vowel sounds. This resulted in all five vowels in Mizo, namely, /a, i, u, e and o/, occurring in the pre-inhalation context. However, in the post-inhalation context, only three vowels, namely, /a, i, u/ occurred in the database. In total, for the pre-inhalation context, there were 884 tokens whereas 440 tokens could be considered for the post-inhalation context.

Average formant values extracted from the inhalation noises and following and preceding vowels are plotted in Fig. 3. In the case of the preceding vowels, Fig. 3a shows a significant correlation in terms of the F1 values with an R score of 0.17 while in terms of $F2$ values, the R score is of 0.27 as seen in Fig. 3b. The

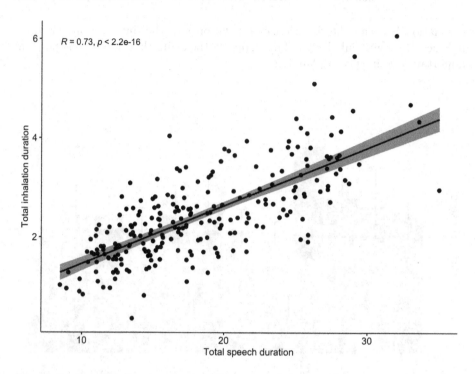

Fig. 2. Scatter plot showing the correlation between inhalation duration and speech duration in each sentence.

formant values of the following vowels also show a significant correlation with the formant values of the inhalation noises. As seen in Fig. 3c, the correlation in terms of the F1 values is 0.12. The F2 values of the following vowels show a stronger correlation with an R score of 0.34.

As the following F2 of vowels showed the strongest correlation with the F2 values extracted from the preceding inhalation noise, in Fig. 4, we present a scatterplot showing the correlation between the two, separated by vowel types. As expected, the F2 values of the following three vowels are distinct in the scatterplot. However, it is also noteworthy that the F2 values of the corresponding preceding inhalations are also clustered separately according to the vowels. We consider this as a piece of strong evidence showing how the inhalation preceding vowels are colored by the acoustic properties of the following vowels.

4 Discussion and Conclusion

In the recent works on the acoustic analysis of inhalations in speech, it has been shown that the inhalations provide discoursal cues in conversations that signal turn-taking and initiation of speech [5]. While the role of breath sounds has been acknowledged to be important in modeling synthetic speech [8], not much

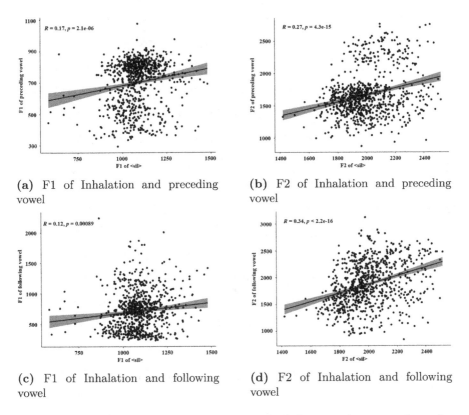

(a) F1 of Inhalation and preceding vowel

(b) F2 of Inhalation and preceding vowel

(c) F1 of Inhalation and following vowel

(d) F2 of Inhalation and following vowel

Fig. 3. Scatter plots showing formants values of inhalation and contextual vowels

effort has gone into in-depth acoustic analysis of inhalations. It has also been shown that explicit modeling of such sounds aids ASR systems by reducing the possibility of confusing breathing sounds as phonemic units in speech. Nevertheless, these inhalation sounds are often considered part of noise modeling and are not believed to contain any linguistic information. As a result of this, the inhalation sounds are often reduced to a <sil> annotation in conventional speech data curation. However, considering the efforts that go into speech planning, it seems unlikely that humans will not utilize the so-called pre-speech periods in preparing themselves for forthcoming articulations. As shown in this study, the duration of inhalations before reading a sentence aloud is about 13% of the total duration of the following breath group. Also, it is remarkable that on average every 3 s of speech is preceded by an inhalation.

As these inhalations are performed with the mouth open, there is a fair chance that the speakers also configure their vocal tract for the production of the impending linguistic-phonetic units. In this study, we have shown that such a mouth opening during the inhalation phase results in formant generation, and the quality of these formants are strongly correlated with the following vowels than the preceding ones. In the current study, we have shown that specifically

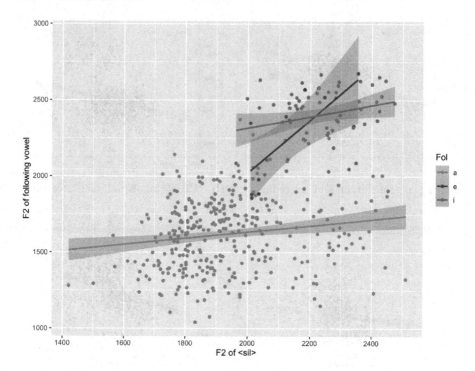

Fig. 4. Scatter plot of F2 in inhalation separated by following vowels

the F2 of the following vowel is strongly correlated with the F2 produced while inhaling with the mouth open. This can be considered a coarticulatory effect of the following vowel on breathing. While it has been claimed that nasal inhalation may also be performed while speaking, in our data of read speech, almost all inhalations are oral.

In this study, we limited our investigation only to the oral vowels. However, we have noticed that preceding nasal consonants, the inhalations also become quite nasal. Hence, in future, we intend to look into the effect of various consonantal sounds on inhalation noises while reading written texts. Apart from that we also intend to look into the speech databases of various languages and investigate if the patterns we observed in the current study are language-specific or language-independent.

References

1. Bates, D., Mächler, M., Bolker, B., Walker, S.: Fitting linear mixed-effects models using lme4. J. Stat. Softw. **67**(1), 1–48 (2015). https://doi.org/10.18637/jss.v067.i01
2. Boersma, P., Weenink, D.: Praat: doing phonetics by computer [computer program]. Version 6, 1 (November 2020). http://www.praat.org/

3. Braunschweiler, N., Chen, L.: Automatic detection of inhalation breath pauses for improved pause modelling in HMM-TTS. In: ISCA Speech Synthesis Workshop, pp. 1–6 (2013)

4. Butzberger, J., Murveit, H., Shriberg, E., Price, P.: Spontaneous speech effects in large vocabulary speech recognition applications. In: Speech and Natural Language: Proceedings of a Workshop Held at Harriman, New York, February 23–26, 1992 (1992)

5. Ćwiek, A., Włodarczak, M., Heldner, M., Wagner, P.: Acoustics and discourse function of two types of breathing signals. In: Nordic Prosody, Trondheim, Norway, 10–12 August, 2016, pp. 83–91. Peter Lang Publishing Group (2017)

6. Fox, J., Weisberg, S.: An R Companion to Applied Regression. Sage, Thousand Oaks CA, third edn. (2019). https://socialsciences.mcmaster.ca/jfox/Books/Companion/

7. Lenth, R.V.: emmeans: Estimated Marginal Means, aka Least-Squares Means (2022). https://CRAN.R-project.org/package=emmeans, r package version 1.8.1-1

8. Prakash, J.J., Murthy, H.A.: Analysis of inter-pausal units in indian languages and its application to text-to-speech synthesis. IEEE/ACM Trans. Audio, Speech, Lang. Process. **27**(10), 1616–1628 (2019)

9. R Core Team: R: A Language and Environment for Statistical Computing. R Foundation for Statistical Computing, Vienna, Austria (2022). https://www.R-project.org/

10. Rasskazova, O., Mooshammer, C., Fuchs, S.: Temporal coordination of articulatory and respiratory events prior to speech initiation. In: Interspeech, pp. 884–888 (2019). https://doi.org/10.21437/Interspeech. 2019–2876

11. Rochet-Capellan, A., Fuchs, S.: The interplay of linguistic structure and breathing in German spontaneous speech. In: Interspeech, pp. 2014–2018 (2013). https://doi.org/10.21437/Interspeech. 2013–478

12. Scobbie, J.M., Schaeffler, S., Mennen, I.: Audible aspects of speech preparation. In: International Congress of Phonetic Sciences (ICPhS), pp. 1782–1785 (2011)

13. Trouvain, J., Möbius, B., Werner, R.: On acoustic features of inhalation noises in read and spontaneous speech. In: 1st International Seminar on the Foundations of Speech: Breathing, Pausing, and Voice (2019)

14. Trouvain, J., Werner, R., Möbius, B.: An acoustic analysis of inbreath noises in read and spontaneous speech. In: International Conference Speech Prosody, Tokyo. pp. 789–793 (2020)

15. Werner, R., Fuchs, S., Trouvain, J., Möbius, B.: Inhalations in speech: acoustic and physiological characteristics. In: Interspeech, pp. 3186–3190 (2021). https://doi.org/10.21437/Interspeech. 2021–1262

16. Werner, R., Trouvain, J., Fuchs, S., Möbius, B.: Exploring the presence and absence of inhalation noises when speaking and when listening. Int. Semin. Speech Prod, ISSP (2020)

17. Winkworth, A.L., Davis, P.J., Ellis, E., Adams, R.D.: Variability and consistency in speech breathing during reading: Lung volumes, speech intensity, and linguistic factors. J. Speech Lang. Hear. Res. **37**(3), 535–556 (1994)

Prolongations as Hesitation Phenomena in Spoken Speech in First and Second Language

Natalia Bogdanova-Beglarian[1] ⬡, Kristina Zaides[1,2](✉) ⬡, Daria Stoika[1,3] ⬡, and Xiaoli Sun[4] ⬡

[1] Saint Petersburg State University, St. Petersburg, Russia
n.bogdanova@spbu.ru, zaides.kristina@gmail.com
[2] Tel Aviv University, Tel Aviv, Israel
[3] Main Administration of the Internal Affairs Ministry of the City of St. Petersburg and the Leningrad Oblast, St. Petersburg, Russia
[4] Southeast University, Nanjing, China

Abstract. The article considers sound prolongations as one of the most typical hesitation phenomena of spontaneous spoken speech in any language. The material for the analysis was 40 monologues-descriptions, partly taken from the corpus of Russian monologue speech "Balanced Annotated Text Library", and partly recorded specifically for this study. The monologues were recorded from 4 groups of speakers: 10 Russians and 30 Chinese, of whom 10 described the comic strip in Russian and Chinese, and another 10 only in Chinese. The analysis showed that the appearance of prolongations correlates with the language factor: bilinguals use them more often than monolinguals. More prolongations were found in full-fledged words (not pragmatic markers), but most of them are function words and pronouns. In Russian speech, the percentage of prolongations is also high in pragmatic markers, especially in the word *vot*, which appears in spoken discourse most often as a hesitative boundary marker. Thus, it turned out that even language proficiency does not make the Russian colloquial speech of the Chinese as natural as one of the native speakers. Prolongations predominate in vowels and sonorants; they are frequent at the end of a word and in single-letter words. Often prolongations become a component of an extended hesitation chain that includes other hesitative units (physical hesitation pauses, breaks, repetitions, vocalizations, etc.). The data obtained can be useful in all aspects of applied linguistics: from linguodidactics and linguistic expertise to automatic speech processing systems and the creation of artificial intelligence.

Keywords: Spontaneous Monologue · Monologue-Description · Hesitation Phenomenon · Prolongation · Monolingual · Bilingual · Hesitation Chain

1 Introduction

Spontaneous speech generation, which accompanies all our everyday spoken communication, inevitably forces speakers to act in conditions of time deficit, when they have to think and speak at the same time, cf.: "in real communication conditions, during natural spontaneous dialogue [the same applies, presumably, to a spontaneous monologue

A. Karpov et al. (Eds.): SPECOM 2023, LNAI 14338, pp. 322–338, 2023.
https://doi.org/10.1007/978-3-031-48309-7_27

as well.—Authors] the production of a text (utterance) essentially occurs in 'extreme conditions'—with a lack of time and the absence of the opportunity to carefully plan the strategy" [13: 162]. Such "extreme conditions" pose many problems for the speaker related to the formulation of a thought, the selection of words that would best express this thought, and the correction of inevitable inaccuracies, stipulations, and even mistakes. This complex speech and thought activity often leads to a "gap between thoughts and language", which is expressed "in speech hesitations, false starts, and reformulations that abound in everyday speech" [5: 64].

Hesitation phenomena, or *signs of spontaneity*, that accompany speech production are characteristic of spontaneous speech in any language, and the speech of any speakers, regardless of their social and/or psychological characteristics. One of these hesitation phenomena are *prolongations of sounds* [1, 9, 18], both vowels (*vo-o-ot, nu-u-u ('well')*) and consonants (*s-skazal ('said'), khodim-m-m ('we walk')*). Such prolongations on monosyllabic (and one-phonemic) words (*a-a ('but'), i-i ('and'), v-v ('in')*) should be distinguished from insertions of non-speech sounds (*vocalizations*). The criterion for their differentiation can be the presence or absence of grammatical meaning of these units within the text.

This kind of material is of interest in various aspects. In this paper, it is considered from the point of view of general linguistics (speech in the native and non-native language, the speech of monolinguals or bilinguals, as well as the characteristics of prolongations), but it can also be considered in terms of sociolinguistics (men and women speech, the influence of the level of Chinese proficiency in Russian on their speech, including the appearance of prolongations as a hesitating phenomenon) and psycholinguistics (texts produced by speakers with different psychological characteristics). This approach allows applying the study results in linguodidactics, for the creation of speech portraits of both individual speakers and various social groups. The results can be useful for linguistic expertise and linguocriminalistics, as well as for automatic natural language processing systems and the creation of artificial intelligence.

2 Material and Methodology

To obtain the material, 4 groups of texts were recorded from:

1) Russian monolinguals speaking Russian as their native language (R)—10 texts;
2) Chinese monolinguals who speak Chinese as their native language and do not know Russian (Ch-Ch)—10 texts;
3) bilingual Chinese speaking Chinese as their native language and know Russian (Ch-Ch1)—10 texts;
4) the same bilingual Chinese speaking Russian as their second language (Ch-R)—10 texts.

Calling speakers *monolinguals* or *bilinguals*, we take into account only their attitudes towards Russian and Chinese. Moreover, in this paper, we use the term 'bilingual' in its wider meaning to describe a person who can speak two languages or frequently uses them both in a relevant language environment while studying one of them, e.g., Chinese and Russian. Thus, Russian monolinguals speak Russian as their native language and do not know Chinese; Chinese monolinguals speak Chinese as their native language and do not know Russian. Accordingly, Chinese bilinguals, in addition to their native Chinese, also speak Russian (they study it). At the same time, both Russians and Chinese may be proficient in some other foreign languages (third, fourth, etc.), which in this case is not taken into account in any way.

All speakers are from the same age group: they are students and graduate students 20–29 years old. The groups of speakers are balanced by gender (5 men and 5 women in each group); the group of Russian monolinguals is balanced in terms of psychotype (5 extroverts and 5 introverts); for the group of Chinese, it was not possible to achieve such a balance. For the Chinese speaking Russian, the level of Russian as a foreign language proficiency (TORFL) is also taken into account (5 speakers with B2 level and 5 with C1 level). To define the psychotype, the speakers were psychologically tested (test by H. Eysenck, which all speakers passed in their native language). The level of TORFL for the Chinese was determined at the place of their study: a lower level B2 (TORFL-2) or higher C1 (TORFL-3), according to the Russian State Testing System for Foreign Citizens. Some of the texts were borrowed from the corpus of monologues "Balanced Annotated Text Library" [2], other texts, primarily in Chinese, were recorded specifically for this study.

The initial stimulus for the production of the monologue in all cases was the image with the plot— H. Bidstrup's comic strip "Hair loss treatment". The speakers were asked to describe this comic while looking at it, i.e., to compose a story based on the picture. All speakers are familiar with this genre of spoken monologue: for native speakers, this was an exercise for speech development in elementary school; the Chinese often performed such exercises during Russian language lessons at the university.

2.1 Prolongations of Vowels and Consonants in Russian

When determining the duration of a hesitation prolongation of a particular sound, the following factors were taken into account:

- change (difference) in the amplitude of the oscillation of the vocal folds, with fixation of the appearance of two-peak vowels (oscillographic analysis);
- change in sound quality; for example, when a vowel is represented by a non-basic or reduced allophone, the main allophone may become clearer ('ne' [n'ee]) during lengthening, and at the absolute end of the word the vowel may turn into a reduced one ('na' [naъ]) (spectral analysis);
- the average duration of sound in speech.

The average duration of vowels and consonants in Russian speech was determined based on the experimental data from some of the main phonetic studies [4, 7, 8, 11, 17, 19, 24], as well as on the extended expert experience of the authors in the analysis of spontaneous speech. Table 1 shows the values of the average duration for those Russian sounds, the hesitation lengthening of which was found in the material.

The duration of sounds in speech is very variable and depends on many factors: the type of a sound (for example, occlusive consonants are shorter than fricative ones; closed vowels are shorter than mid and open vowels), the position of sound in the word and the place of stress, the number of sounds in a word, the type of a syllable (closed or open), the quality of an adjacent consonant, the position of a phonetic word in a phrase, the length of a phrase itself and the communicative type of a phrase [21: 184], the speech rate. In [7], for speech synthesis, the following average values of the duration of sounds are indicated: for vowels—180 ms, for consonants—95 ms; the range of vowel duration is 30–300 ms [7: 216]. In other papers, the range of vowel duration is 60–200 ms [4, 19, 24].

Table 1. The average duration of Russian sounds with prolongation in the study material.

Type of sound	Sound	Average duration, ms
Vowels	/i ы u e o a/	130
Occlusive plosive sonorants	/m n n'/	100
Obstruent fricative consonants	/s s' z f/	100
Obstruent occlusive plosive consonants	/k t t'/	80

Considering the above experimental data, to describe Russian hesitation prolongations, in this paper it was decided to analyze only those sounds whose duration exceeds 180–200 ms (for vowels) and 95–100 ms (for consonants).

2.2 Prolongations of Vowels and Consonants in Chinese

Standard Chinese (Mandarin) phonology is based on the Beijing dialect. A Mandarin syllable consists of three components: an initial (consonant), a final (vowel), and a tone [10]. There are 22 initials in Chinese and three types of final sounds: simple finals, compound finals, and nasal finals. The 6 simple finals *a, o, e, i, u, ü* are the most fundamental elements of Chinese vowels. There are 13 compound finals and 14 nasal finals in Chinese. In addition, two semi-vowels *y* and *w* can be distinguished in Chinese. The tone is the pitch contour of the syllable. Mandarin has four contour tones and a neutral tone used on weak syllables. All syllables in Chinese must have a final, but many syllables exist with no initial, for example, 爱 *ai* and 五 *wu*.

Each Chinese character is spoken as one syllable. Chinese words are made up of one, two, or more characters (syllables). In Chinese, there are whole syllables that are not divided into an initial consonant sound and a final. There are 16 in total.

The prolongation is presented in Chinese native speech in both content words and function words, but "due to the particularity of Chinese syllables (most Chinese syllables are open syllables and closed syllables ending in nasal consonants), only word-ending vowels and nasal consonants appear prolongation" [22: 119]. There are both single vowels and compound vowels in the vowels where prolonged sounds occur. Nasal consonants that tend to be elongated are *n* and *ng* [id.], and the results of this study also confirm this.

The data obtained in this study shows that the prolongations in Chinese may be related to the tone. The soft tone is the easiest to prolong, followed by the first and fourth tones, and the least elongated sounds are the second and third tones. In addition to being influenced by the phonemic rules, the frequency of prolongations is also influenced by personal characteristics, such as expressiveness and psychological factors.

Prolongation in Chinese is the duration of a sound that usually exceeds the average duration of the same sound. The average duration of Chinese vowels is presented in Table 2.

Table 2. The average duration of Chinese vowels.

Vowel	Average duration, ms
Simple final	104–118 ms
Compound final	154–158 ms
Nasal final	160 ms

Feng Long's research data on the sound duration of Beijing dialect shows that the average duration of the simple final in the front syllable is 104 ms, and the average duration of the simple final in the following syllable is 118 ms, and the simple final in the back syllable is 14 ms longer than the simple final in the front syllable [6]. This study did not directly count the average duration of compound finals, but we can infer that the average duration of compound finals is about 40 ms longer than that of simple finals by comparing the average duration of syllables with simple finals and syllables with compound finals. Furthermore, it can be inferred that the average duration of the compound finals in the front syllable is about 154 ms, and the average duration of the compound finals in the back syllable is 158 ms. Because the prolongation in this study only occurs in the following syllables, here we only need to consider the average duration of the finals in the back syllables. Since no literature was found about the average duration of nasal finals, we measured and calculated the average duration of nasal finals in the material. The results show that the average length of Chinese nasal finals is 160 ms.

Qi Shiqian and Zhang Jialu analyzed 7 male and 6 female speech excerpts, and obtained the average length of the 22 initials in Mandarin [16], as shown in Table 3.

Table 3. The average duration of Chinese initials.

Consonant	Aver. Dur. (ms)	Consonant	Aver. Dur. (ms)	Consonant	Aver. Dur. (ms)
b	14.2	g	23.2	sh	138.6
p	98.2	k	94.4	r	56.3
m	71.3	h	106.6	z	53.9
f	106.6	j	55	c	126.9
d	9.6	q	143.7	s	140.3
t	106.3	x	129.1	ng	134.2
l	63.9	zh	21.1		
n	61.5	ch	108.9		

The pronunciation of the whole syllable will remain the same as the consonant even after adding a vowel behind the consonant (*zhi, chi, shi, ri, zi, ci, si*) or as the vowel even after adding a semi-vowel *y* behind the vowel (*ye, yi, yin, ying, wu, yu, yue, yun, yuan*). Therefore, the overall sound length of the whole syllables can refer to the average length of the actual pronunciation of initials or finals.

2.3 Problems of Analysis and Decisions Made

In the process of analyzing sound prolongations by instrumental methods (oscillographic and spectral analysis), some disagreements arose with the results of the initial auditory analysis carried out by the transcribers: some of the Ps identified by ear were not confirmed instrumentally. Thus, the following inconsistencies were identified.

1. When a vowel appeared at the junction with another vowel, auditory analysis determined the sound prolongation due to the merging of neighboring vowels, although instrumental analysis showed that there was no prolongation in these cases, the duration of the vowels falls within the average sound range.
2. In two cases, a vowel prolongation was noted after long fortis fricative [s], [s']: *volosy:* (*'hair'*), *eliksi:r* (*'treatment'*). The duration of the fricatives in these words was 334 and 216 ms, respectively, while the duration of the vowels following them fell into the average values.
3. Quite often, in the course of auditory analysis, a prolongation was noted in the words *vot* and *nu* (*'well'*), which, as a rule, appear in speech not as particles, but as pragmatic markers of one or another functional type [3], which could affect the subjective perception of duration, not supported by instrumental analysis.
4. In several cases, the speaker's hesitation was mistaken for the sound prolongation in the course of auditory analysis.

In all these cases, the data obtained after the instrumental analysis and correction were used for further investigation.

In the monologue of the speaker 8Ch-R, prolongations of vowels were annotated, which were not hesitative, but emphatic. This kind of elongation of a sound was also not considered hesitation prolongation.

2.4 Phonetic Properties of Prolongations

Before proceeding to the description of the results obtained during the study, it is interesting to note several phonetic features of prolongations in the Russian speech of Russian and Chinese speakers.

Thus, Russians often have prolongations with a change in sound quality, the transition of a vowel into vocalizations *m-m, e-e: dlya:* + *m-m* [dl'a ⊆:m:] (*'for m-m'*), *no:* + *m-m* [nó:m:] (*'but m-m'*), *on:* + *e-e* [ón:ɛ:] (*'he e-e'*), *i:* + *e-e* [i ❹:ɛ:] (*'and e-e'*), *no:* + *e-e* [nó:ɛ:] (*'but e-e'*). In prolongations produced by the Chinese speakers, the retention of the sound quality or its transition to a reduced one is more often observed.

Let us illustrate such an elongation using the example of the two longest prolongations: in Russian speech, it is the prolongation in the conjunction *i* (*'and'*) with the duration of 1104 ms (see Fig. 1), in Chinese speech, it is the prolongation of the final vowel [a] in the word *zavtra* (*'tomorrow'*) with a duration of 1314 ms (see Fig. 2).

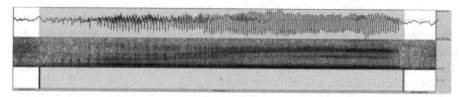

Fig. 1. Oscillogram and spectrogram of the conjunction 'i' ('and') from the speech of a Russian monolingual.

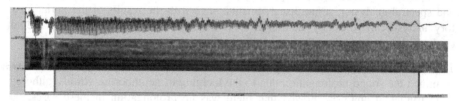

Fig. 2. Oscillogram and spectrogram of the final vowel [a] in the word 'zavtra' ('tomorrow') from the Russian speech of a bilingual Chinese.

The spectrogram of the vowel [i] shows a change in its quality—the frequencies F1 and F2 change: F1 rises from 222 Hz to 510 Hz, and F2 drops from 2123 Hz to 1614 Hz. Thus, [i] becomes more open and moved back, i.e., approaching the sound [e]. The spectrum of the vowel [a] is more stable: being at the absolute end of the word, the vowel becomes reduced (there is a slight decrease in F2).

Another feature noted in the Russian speech of bilingual Chinese is the hesitative lengthening of final plosives:

- *otrezat':* (*'to cut off'*): [t'] 351 ms—strengthening of the affrication of the soft [t'] with the transition to the affricate [ts'];
- *tak:* (*'so'*): [k] 428 ms—h-sounded fricatization [k];
- *budet:* (*'will be'*): [t] 183 ms—long-term plosive and enhanced explosion phase;
- *raschosyvat'* (*'to comb'*): [t'] 611 ms—strengthening of the affrication of the soft [t'] with the transition to the affricate [ts'] with a vowel overtone after the consonant.

All these features are taken into account in the further analysis of prolongations.

3   Results

3.1   Quantitative Overview

The monologues-descriptions that have become the object of analysis differ primarily in their volume in words/tokens: the longest monologues were in Russian, both for Russian monolinguals (2216 tokens) and for bilingual Chinese (1984 tokens); significantly (2–3 times) shorter are monologues in Chinese: 974 in the Ch-Ch1 group (bilingual Chinese) and 694 in the Ch-Ch group (monolingual Chinese). In other words, in their native language, within the same type of text, speakers of different languages produced monologues of fundamentally different volumes: Russian monolinguals produced very large monologues, and monolingual Chinese—more than 3 times shorter. The reason for such a significant difference should be determined, apparently, by the structural features of the languages used, since the bilingual Chinese also produced larger texts in Russian than Chinese. However, the monologue length can be also influenced by various factors, such as the speaker's gender, age, speech rate, etc., which are not considered in this study.

Table 4 shows the general quantitative data on prolongations in the monologues of all groups of speakers.

Table 4. General quantitative data on prolongations in monologues of all speakers.

Group	R	Ch-R	Ch-Ch1	Ch-Ch
Total	69	171	49	7
% of all prolongations	23.3	57.8	16.6	2.4
Proportion of words (per 100 words)	3.1	8.6	5.0	1.0
Proportion of duration (per 100 s)	6.9	9.7	4.5	1.2
Mean (per text)	6.9	17.1	4.8	0.8
Median (per text)	7.0	16.0	3.5	1.0
Standard deviation	4.5	9.4	3.0	0.9

Table 4 shows that bilingual Chinese (Ch-R) use Ps as a hesitation phenomenon most often: their monologues-descriptions in non-native Russian contain more than half (57.8%) of all identified P, the maximum is reached also in all other respects: 8,6 prolongations per 100 words, average 17.1 (±9.4) and median 16.0 per one monologue.

Chinese monolinguals (Ch-Ch), who speak their native language, use the least number of prolongations. Interestingly, Russian monolinguals use almost a quarter (23.3%) of all identified prolongations. It can be assumed, therefore, that the factor of spontaneity "outweighs" the factor of the native or non-native language of speech production since the native speakers of two languages use different number of prolongations in their spontaneous monologues.

The Kruskal–Wallis test [12] was used to compare medians, which showed that all median values differ significantly: statistic = 25.554183644461276; pvalue = 1.18234602351863e-05.

3.2 Frequency List of Words with Prolongations in Russian and Chinese

Tables 5 and 6 show the lists of the most frequently elongated words from the analyzed monologues for both languages.

It can be seen that in the Russian material (see Table 5) the maximum of prolongations (which mark, as it was said, speech disfluencies) can be found in the conjunction i ('and') (the absolute maximum: more than a third of all prolongations in both cases, i.e., in a speech in a native and a non-native language), as well as in forms of the personal pronoun on/nego ('he/his'), replacing the name of the main character of the comic strip in monologues-descriptions. The appearance in this top of the only content (not a pronoun) word volosy ('hair') is explained by the topic of the comic and, consequently, the main topic of all monologues-descriptions.

Table 5. TOP-5 elongated words in Russian speech.

#	Word	Total	Number R	% of all R	Number Ch-R	% of all Ch-R
1	i ('and')	91	24	34.8	67	39.2
2	on/nego ('he/his')	22	5	7.2	17	9.9
3	volosy ('hair')	9	2	2.9	7	4.1
4	na ('on')	8	2	2.9	6	3.5
5	vot ('well')	8	8	11.6	0	0

Also noteworthy is a high percentage of prolongations in the word *vot* (*'well'*) in the speech of Russian monolinguals—11.6%, which exceeds the percentage in *on/nego* (*'he/his'*) (7.2%). This can be easily explained by the fact that *vot* is high-frequent in Russian speech in the role of primarily a pragmatic marker, including the boundary-hesitative [15: 91–109], which is within the list of hesitation phenomena. Interestingly, in the Russian speech of Chinese bilinguals, there are no prolongations in this word, i.e., the Chinese, even those who speak Russian well, do not fully master the arsenal of hesitation phenomena that native speakers have. It can be assumed that the ability to use such "signs of colloquialism" can serve as one of the criteria for good (natural) colloquial Russian speech for foreigners.

Table 6. TOP-5 and TOP-2 elongated words in Chinese speech (*These words are untranslatable particles).

Ch-Ch1				Ch-Ch			
#	Word	Number Ch-Ch1	% of all Ch-Ch1	#	Word	Number Ch-Ch	% of all Ch-Ch
1	yi ge ('one')	9	18.4	1	de*	3	42.8
2	de*	7	14.3	2	you yu ('because')	1	14.3
3	zhe ge ('this')	5	10.2				
4	ne*	4	8.3	2	qu ('go')	1	14.3
5	dan shi ('but')	3	6.2	2	le*	1	14.3
5	ran hou ('and then')	3	6.2	2	dao ('arrive')	1	14.3
5	ta ('he')	3	6.2				

Table 6 shows that in Chinese speech, too, most of the hesitation prolongations (i.e., the speaker's disfluencies) are not in content words, but in auxiliary particles, discourse or pragmatic markers. Thus, the auxiliary particle *de* (的/得/地) can be used after definition and indicate a qualitative, possessive attribute (*tu tou de: nan zi*); is used as a suffix for a state verb (*gao xing de: mo shang qu*); is used as a suffix of a verb that accompanies an adverbial mode of action (*zhang de: yue lai yue kuai*). *Yi ge* (*'one'*) is a counter word, after which a noun is usually searched, and *zhe ge* (*'this'*) is a demonstrative pronoun or a hesitation marker, an analog of the Russian markers *eto* and *eto samoye* [15: 432–458] (about the method of searching for analogs of Russian verbal hesitative markers using parallel text analysis, see [20]).

3.3 Position of Prolongation

Table 7 shows data on the prolongation position within a word.

Table 7. Number of prolongations in different positions in a word (abs./relat. (%)).

Position in word	R	Ch-R	Ch-Ch1	Ch-Ch	Total
Single-letter words	25/36.2	73/42.7	0/0	0/0	98/33.1
Word beginning	4/5.8	6/3.5	0/0	0/0	10/3.4
Within a word	13/18.8	19/11.1	0/0	0/0	32/10.8
Word end	27/39.1	73/42.7	49/100.0	7/100.0	156/52.7

Table 7 suggests that a higher number of prolongations as hesitation phenomena occurs at the end of a word (52.7%)—in the speech of all groups of speakers. At the same time, in the Chinese speech of all Chinese speakers (Ch-Ch1 and Ch-Ch), prolongations appear only in this position.

The second most common type is the prolongations of single-letter words (33.1%), and in the Russian speech of bilingual Chinese (Ch-R), their number coincides with such in the position at the end of the word (42.7% each).

Prolongations occur least often at the beginning of a word (3.4%). Apparently, the process of hesitation begins towards the end of the pronounced word, when the speaker begins to think about the next word or portion of the text.

Let us further consider the results of quantitative and qualitative analysis of particular sounds prolongations in Russian and Chinese spontaneous speech.

3.4 Prolongations of Vowels and Consonants

In general, the number of vowel Ps in a speech in both languages predominates consonant Ps: 198 (83%) vs. 42 (17%) in Russian and 48 (86%) vs. 8 (14%) in Chinese.

Data on prolongations of particular sounds are presented in Tables 8, 9, 10 and 11.

Table 8. Number of vowel prolongations in Russian speech of Russians and Chinese.

#	Vowel	% of all R	Vowel	% of all Ch-R
1	i	45.6	i	42.1
2	o	19.3	a	15.8
3	a	8.8	o	11.6
4	ы	5.3	u	4.3
5	e	3.5	ы	3.6
6	u	1.7	e	3.1

Most often in Russian speech, speakers of both groups (R and Ch-R) elongate the sound [i], the range of the prolongation duration of this vowel for Russian monolinguals is 205–1104 ms, for bilingual Chinese—212–919 ms. The sound [o] (208–625 ms) is the second most frequent sound with prolongations among Russian speakers, and the sound [a] (218–1314 ms)—among the Chinese. The Chinese speech is characterized by prolongations of the final [a] in content words (*produvtsa:* (*'seller'*), *segodnya:* (*'today'*), *rasteniya:* (*'plants'*)), while Russians elongate [a] more often in functional words (*na:* (*'on'*), *dlya:* (*'for'*), *ta:k* (*'thus'*)). As noted above, in the speech of bilingual Chinese, the sound [a] in the word *zavtra* (*'tomorrow'*) is the most often elongated (see Fig. 2).

Table 9. Number of consonant prolongations in Russian speech of Russians and Chinese.

#	Consonant	% of all R	% of all Ch-R
1	n	10.5	7.9
2	n'	3.5	0.6
3	z	1.7	0
4	s	0	4.9
5	s'	0	1.2
6	m	0	1.8
7	t	0	0.6
8	t'	0	1.2
9	k	0	0.6
10	f	0	0.6

Of the consonants in Russian speech, speakers of both groups most often elongate [n], the range of the duration of this prolongation for Russian monolinguals is 180–412 ms, for bilingual Chinese—211–619 ms. Frequently, such a prolongation is placed in the pronoun *on:* (*'he'*). The remaining consonants are elongated mainly in the Russian speech of the Chinese and mainly in content words (*volos:y* (*'hair'*), *s:mog* (*'could'*), *s:nom* (*'by dream'*), *vecherom:* (*'in the evening'*), *budet:* (*'will'*), etc.), which is not typical for Russian speech.

Table 10. Number of vowel prolongations in Chinese speech of Chinese monolinguals and bilinguals.

#	Vowel	% of all Ch-Ch1	#	Vowel	% of all Ch-Ch
1	e	63.4	1	e	57.1
2	a	10.0	2	u	28.6
2	i	10.0	3	ao	14.3
2	ou	10.0			
3	iu	1.2			
3	u	1.2			
3	ü	1.2			

Most often, in Chinese speech, speakers from both groups (Ch-Ch and Ch-Ch1) elongate the vowel [e], the range of the duration of this prolongation is 263–586 ms for Chinese monolinguals, and 169–789 ms for Chinese bilinguals. For Chinese monolinguals, the prolongation is most often found at the end of the auxiliary particle *de* (3 out of 7 cases; 42.9%). Chinese bilinguals' speech also is characterized by prolongations at the end of the auxiliary particle *de* (12 out of 41 cases; 29.2%), the counter word *yi ge* (*'one'*) (7 uses; 17.1%), the pragmatic marker or demonstrative pronoun *zhe ge* (*'this'*) (5; 12.2%). In second place by frequency among Chinese bilinguals, there are three elongated vowels [a], [i], [ou], and their prolongation duration range is 257–445 ms, 433–655 ms, and 188–385 ms, respectively. Other vowels are rarely elongated.

Table 11. Number of consonant prolongations in Chinese speech of Chinese monolinguals and bilinguals.

#	Consonant	% of all Ch-Ch1
1	sh	62.5
2	z	12.5
2	ng	12.5
2	n	12.5

It should be noted that in the Chinese speech of Chinese monolinguals there are no consonant prolongations. Of the consonants in the Chinese speech of bilingual Chinese, *shi* is most often elongated in conjunctions *dan shi* (*'but'*) and *ke shi* (*'however'*), which is an inseparable syllable in Chinese and is pronounced the same as the consonant sound [sh]. The range of duration of this prolongation in Chinese bilinguals' speech is

345–869 ms. In contrast to the result of the study by Teng Hai and Li Yifang [22], the prolongations of the nasal consonants [ng] and [n] in the present study are unique cases and take second place, behind the consonant [sh].

Table 12 summarizes the data by sound types.

Table 12. Number of consonant prolongations of different types of sounds.

Sound types	R	Ch-R	Ch-Ch1	Ch-Ch	Total
Fricative obstruent consonants	1/1.4	15/8.8	6/12.2	0/0	22/7.4
Sonorant	10/14.5	16/9.4	2/4.1	0/0	28/9.5
Vowels	58/84.1	140/81.9	41/83.7	7/100.0	246/83.1

Table 12 confirms the data presented at the beginning of this section that most prolongations were found in vowels (83.1%), the difference between consonants of different types is insignificant.

3.5 Isolated Prolongations and Prolongations in Hesitation Chain

The standalone prolongations are two times rarer (30%) than the prolongations within a hesitation chain (70%). It can be explained by the fact that the single prolongation does not usually provide enough time for word search and speech planning. However, the length of a hesitation chain produced by the speakers can be influenced by their language knowledge: the second language speakers use longer hesitation chains than the first language speakers. A hesitation chain can consist of different items: hesitation pauses (filled and silent), word repetitions, word breaks, sighs, and other types of verbalized speech disfluencies. The average length of the chain among the first language speakers is two items, while the average length of the chain among the second language speakers is four items, and the difference is statistically significant, according to the Mann–Whitney U test (statistic = 3966.0, pvalue = 5.01748542859133e-05) [14].

The most common sequence in a hesitation chain that includes Ps is the prolongation and one or two hesitation pauses (36%). Among them, the sequences with a short unfilled hesitation pause are taken the first place (22%). The 'prolongation + long unfilled hesitation pause' is the second most common type (9%). At last, the 'prolongation + filled hesitation pause' are 3%. 2% of cases are the 'prolongation + filled hesitation pause + short unfilled hesitation pause'. Other types of hesitation chains form 64%.

Within the language groups, the ratio remains relatively similar.

Note that almost all cases with the prolongation and short hesitation pause are such that the pause follows the P. Thus, the prolongation signals that there is a disfluency that is happening now, and a pause is needed to find a way to resolve this disfluency.

The length of a hesitation chain lies in the range 2–13 units. Figure 3 shows the number of hesitation chains with prolongations among all the speakers.

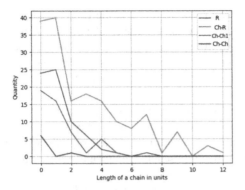

Fig. 3. Number of hesitation chains with prolongations in Russian and Chinese speech.

The trend in usages of hesitation chains with prolongations is that the longer the chain is, the rarer it appears in spoken speech. 39% of all hesitation chains with prolongations are sequences of two elements.

The longest hesitation chain in the material consists of 13 elements, including filled and unfilled long and short hesitation pauses, a break, and a repetition, as well as there are three cases of a 12-elements chain (for the signs of the orthographic representation of corpus materials, see: [23]):

(1) *ran'she o... () odin muzhchina / e-y () u nego () u nego net () volos:y u... volosOv // n-n (...) e-y eto: (...) ochen' (...) y-yn (...) g... e-y e-y (...) yemu ochen' grustno* (1Ch-R, w., 23)
before o... one man / e-y () he () he doesn't have () hair h... hair // n-n (...) e-y this (...) very (...) y-yn (...) s... e-y e-y (...) he is very sad.

However, all such cases with the longest hesitation chains belong to the speaker 1Ch-R, which has II level of Russian as a foreign language. So, the length of the chain can be potentially affected by the level of Russian as a foreign language knowledge in this way that the speakers with lower Russian level use longer hesitation chains. We tested this hypothesis, and it was confirmed: the average length of the chain among the II-level speakers was 4.6 units, the average length of the chain among the III-level speakers was 3.2. The difference between the means was statistically significant, according to the Mann–Whitney U test (statistic = 4507.0, pvalue = 0.006).

4 Conclusion

The study allowed to draw several preliminary conclusions on prolongations based on the analysis of the material.

The monologue-description has various signs of spontaneity, among which a significant place in speech of all groups of speakers is taken by prolongations of sounds, both vowels and consonants.

Most of the prolongations were found in the Russian speech of bilingual Chinese (Ch-R)—more than half of the total number of prolongations. The least number of prolongations was found in the monologues of monolingual Chinese (Ch-Ch). Quite many prolongations were also observed in Russian speech—almost a quarter of the total. Apparently, the factor of spontaneity of speech in this respect is much stronger than the factor of the native language.

In the Russian speech of both Russians and Chinese, the maximum prolongations in the material fall on the conjunction *i* (*'and'*) and forms of the pronoun *on/nego* (*'he/his'*); in Chinese speech—on the structural particle *de* (*'of'*), the counter word *yi ge* (*'one'*) and the demonstrative pronoun/discourse-pragmatic marker *zhe ge* (*'this'*) (analogs of the Russian PM *eto* and *eto samoye*).

Of the content parts of speech, only the word *volosy* (*'hair'*) is in the TOP-5 most frequent Russian words with prolongations, which is easily explained by the topic of the comic strip being described.

In general, in both languages, there were more prolongations in full-fledged words than in markers, although in the Russian speech of Russians, the percentage is also high for PM, especially in the word *vot* (*'well'*).

Prolongations at the end of a word and in single-letter words clearly predominate.

There are much more prolongations of vowels than of consonants, and of the latter—of sonorants. In the Russian speech of Russians, vowel extensions [i] and [o] predominate, in the Russian speech of the Chinese—[i] and [a]. Of the Russian consonants, this type of hesitation most often occurs in the sound [n] in the speech of Russians and the sounds [n] and [s] in the speech of the Chinese. In the Chinese speech of Chinese bilinguals and monolinguals, the prolongation of the vowel [e] predominates. In the Chinese speech of Chinese monolinguals, there is no prolongation of consonants. Of the consonants in the Chinese speech of Chinese bilinguals, [sh] is most often elongated.

Prolongations can more often be found within the hesitation chain, and the second language speakers (Chinese speakers who know Russian), especially those with a lower level of language proficiency, use longer hesitation chains than the first language speakers. 39% of all hesitation chains with prolongations are sequences of two elements, one of them, in addition to the prolongation, tends to be an unfilled hesitation pause.

The study allowed us to obtain a lot of specific data on prolongations as a type of hesitation phenomena that is characteristic of the speech of any speaker and in any language. This is a universal phonetic and discourse feature of spoken speech, which must be taken into account in all applied aspects of linguistics: from linguodidactics and linguistic expertise to automatic speech processing systems and the creation of AI.

Acknowledgements. The research was conducted was partially supported by St. Petersburg State University, project #94033528 "Modeling of Russian Megalopolis Citizens' Communicative Behavior in Social, Speech and Pragmatic Aspects Using Artificial Intelligence Methods".

References

1. Betz, S., Eklund, R., Wagner, P.: Prolongation in German. In: Eklund, R. (ed.) Proceedings of DiSS 2017, Royal Institute of Technology, Stockholm, Sweden, 5–8 (2017)

2. Bogdanova-Beglarian, N.V., Blinova, O.V., Zaides, K.D., Sherstinova, T.Yu.: Korpus «Sbalan-sirovannaya annotirovannaya tekstoteka» (SAT): izucheniye spetsifiki russkoy monologich-eskoy rechi [Corpus "Balanced Annotated Text Library" (SAT): studying the specificity of Russian monological speech]. In: Proceeding of the V.V. Vinogradov Institute of the Russian language RAS. Iss. 21. Natsional'nyy korpus russkogo yazyka: issledovaniya i razrabotki [Russian National Corpus: research and development]. Moscow, 111–126 (2019)
3. Bogdanova-Beglarian, N.V.: Predisloviye redaktora [Editor's preface]. In: Pragmaticheskiye markery russkoy povsednevnoy rechi: slovar'-monografiya [Pragmatic markers of Russian everyday speech: dictionary-monograph]. St. Petersburg, pp. 5–52 (2021)
4. Bondarko, L.V.: Zvukovoy stroy sovremennogo russkogo yazyka [Sound system of the modern Russian language]. Moscow, 175 p. (1977)
5. Cheyf, U.: Na puti k lingvistike, osnovannoy na myshlenii [Toward a thought-based inguis-tics]. In: Yazyk i mysl': sovremennaya kognitivnaya lingvistika [Language and Thought: Modern Cognitive Linguistics]. Moscow, pp. 60–88 (2015)
6. Feng, L.: The duration of rhyme and tone in Beijing discourse flow. In: Lin Tao, Wang Lijia, etc. Beijing phonetic experiment record. Peking University Press, pp. 131–159 (1985). 冯隆. 北京话语流中声韵调的时长. 选自林焘、王理嘉等著. 北京语音试验录. 北京大学出版社
7. Fonetika spontannoy rechi [Phonetics of spontaneous speech]. Leningrad, 243 p. (1988)
8. Geyl'man, N.I. Foneticheskiye kharakteristiki spontannoy rechi (eksperimental'no-foneti-cheskoye issledovaniye na materiale soglasnykh) [Phonetic characteristics of spontaneous speech (experimental phonetic consonant research)] Ph.D. thesis abstract, Leningrad, 16 p. (1983)
9. Gósy, M., Eklund, R.: Segment prolongation in Hungarian. In: Proceedings of DiSS 2017, Royal Institute of Technology, Stockholm, Sweden, 29–32 (2017)
10. Huang, B., Liao, X.: Modern Chinese. Beijing Higher Education Press, 643 p. (2002). 黄伯荣, 廖序东. 现代汉语(增订三版). 北京高等教育出版社
11. Krivnova, O.F.: Dlitel'nost' kak sredstvo realizatsii slovesnogo udareniya v tekste (sopostavi-tel'nyy analiz raznykh sposobov otsenki vyrazhennosti udareniya v slove) [Duration as a means of realizing verbal stress in a text (comparative analysis of different methods for assessing the severity of a word stress)]. In: Yazyk i rech': problemy i resheniya: Sb. trudov k yubileyu L.V. Zlatoustovoy [Language and speech: problems and solutions: Coll. of scientific papers for the anniversary of L.V. Zlatoustova]. Moscow, pp. 77–99 (2004)
12. Kruskal, W.H., Wallis, W.A.: Use of ranks in one-criterion variance analysis. J. Am. Stat. Assoc. **47**, 260, 583–621 (1952)
13. Levitskiy, Yu.A.: K voprosu o vtoroy kommunikatsii [To the question of the second commu-nication]. In: Problemy sotsio- i psikholingvistiki [Problems of socio- and psycholinguistics]. Iss. 15. Perm socio-psycholinguistic school: ideas of three generations, to the 70th anniversary of Alla Solomonovna Stern, Coll. articles, Perm, pp. 159–167 (2011)
14. Mann, H.B., Whitney, D.R.: On a test of whether one of two random variables is stochastically larger than the other. In: Annals of Mathematical Statistics, 18, 50–60 (1947)
15. Pragmaticheskiye markery russkoy povsednevnoy rechi: slovar'-monografiya [Pragmatic markers of Russian everyday speech: dictionary-monograph]. St. Petersburg, 520 p. (2021)
16. Qi, S., Zhang, J.: Analysis of consonant length in Mandarin Chinese. J. Acoustics **7**(1), 8–13 (1982). 齐士钤, 张家騄. 汉语普通话辅音音长分析. 声学学报
17. Russkaya fonetika v razvitii: foneticheskiye «Ottsy» i «Deti» nachala XXI v. [Russian phonet-ics in development: phonetic "Fathers" and "Children" of the beginning of the XXI century]. V.V. Vinogradov Institute of the Russian language RAS, Moscow, 464 p. (2013)
18. Seifart, F., et al.: The extent and degree of utterance-final word lengthening in spontaneous speech from 10 languages. Linguistics Vanguard, 7 (2021)

19. Shcherba, L.V.: Russkiye glasnyye v kachestvennom i kolichestvennom otnoshenii [Russian vowels in qualitative and quantitative respects]. Leningrad, 155 p. (1983)
20. Sun, X.: The ways of translating pragmatic marker ETO SAMOE (based on the material of parallel Russian and Chinese literary texts). Commun. Stud. **8**(2), 323–332 (2021)
21. Svetozarova, N.D.: Prosodicheskaya organizatsiya vyskazyvaniya i intonatsionnaya sistema yazyka [Utterance prosodic organization and language intonation system] Doctoral dissertation. Leningrad, 514 p. (1983)
22. Teng, H., Li, Y.: The commonality and characteristics of the hesitant dragging phenomenon in natural spoken Russian and Chinese. In: Journal of Shanxi Datong University (Social Science Edition) **3**, 116–120 (2022). 滕海, 李毅芳. 俄语和汉语自然口语犹豫型拖音现象的共性及特性. 山西大同大学学报(社会科学版)
23. Zaides, K.D.: Ob unifikatsii razmetki korpusa "Sbalansirovannaya annotirovannaya tekstoteka" [On the standardization of the corpus "Balanced Annotated Text Library"]. In: Trudy mezhdunarodnoy konferentsii «Korpusnaya lingvistika-2019» [Proceedings of the international conference "Corpus linguistics-2019"]. St. Petersburg, pp. 332–339 (2019)
24. Zlatoustova, L.V.: Foneticheskiye yedinitsy russkoy rechi [Phonetic Russian speech units] Moscow, 105 p. (1981)

Study of Indian English Pronunciation Variabilities Relative to Received Pronunciation

Priyanshi Pal[1(✉)], Shelly Jain[2], Chiranjeevi Yarra[2], Prasanta Kumar Ghosh[1], and Anil Kumar Vupalla[2]

[1] Electrical Department, Indian Institute of Science, Bengaluru 560012, India
priyanshipal53@gmail.com, prasantg@iisc.ac.in
[2] Language Technologies Research Center, IIIT Hyderabad, Hyderabad 500032, India
{chiranjeevi.yarra,anil.vuppala}@iiit.ac.in

Abstract. Analysis of Indian English (IE) pronunciation variabilities is useful in ASR and TTS modelling for the Indian context. Prior works characterised IE variabilities by reporting qualitative phonetic rules relative to Received Pronunciation (RP). However, such characterisations lack quantitative descriptors and data-driven analysis of diverse IE pronunciations, which could be due to the scarcity of phonetically labelled data. Furthermore, the versatility of IE stems from the influence of a large diversity of the speakers' mother tongues and demographic region differences. To address these issues, we consider the corpus Indic TIMIT and manually obtain $13,632$ phonetic transcriptions in addition to those parts of the corpus. By performing a data-driven analysis on $15,974$ phonetic transcriptions of 80 speakers from diverse regions of India, we present a new set of phonetic rules and validate them against the existing phonetic rules to identify their relevance. Finally, we test the efficacy of Grapheme-to-Phoneme (G2P) conversion developed based on the obtained rules considering Phoneme Error Rate (PER) as the metric for performance.

Keywords: Indian English · Pronunciation analysis · Received pronunciation · Phonetic rules · Phonetic rule validation

1 Introduction

India is a linguistically diverse country having more than $1,369$ mother tongues [5]. The various languages spoken in India use a vast number of vowels and consonants [12]. Indian English (IE) pronunciation is affected by the varying influence of Indian native languages, which use many of these vowels and consonants. These variations pose a challenge in automatic speech recognition (ASR) and text-to-speech (TTS) synthesis systems in the Indian context. Consequently, these systems are rendered ineffective or yield performance degradation, which could be due to the inadequacy of labelled pronunciation data, which is lacking for Indian English speech [22].

[24] concluded that for better pronunciation modelling of a language that is non-native to the speaker, the characteristics of the speaker's native language must be considered in the modelling. Additionally, the differences in the phonemic inventory of various native Indian languages and English play a crucial role in a non-native Indian speaker's pronunciation of English phonemes. Typically, a non-native English speaker is inclined to map English phonemes to the closest phoneme in their native language [19]. As suggested in [13], a phoneme set developed to incorporate distinct characteristics of IE phonology can facilitate better pronunciation models for non-native speech. Approaches such as appropriate selection and optimisation of the phoneme set considered can increase the effectiveness of speech systems for non-native speech. [23] reported that speech recognition was more effective with phoneme set selection techniques for phoneme and word level speech recognition.

Considering these factors, there is a need to study IE pronunciations at the phonetic level to improve the speech systems for Indian speakers. Prior studies in the Indian context done to facilitate the adaptability of speech systems for non-native Indian speech are as follows. [1] reported phoneme selection rules for better naturalness and intelligibility in TTS for Marathi. [22] showed that certain IE accents are more recognisable than others, suggesting their suitability as canonical IE accents. [8] developed a linguistically-guided IE pronunciation dictionary for ASR by modifying the North American English (NAE) pronunciations in CMU (Carnegie Mellon University) Dictionary (often referred as CMU-dict) [25] to IE using observed IE phonological features. For the few phonemes listed for comparison between NAE and IE pronunciations in IPA, the methodology to obtain phonological features of IE is unclear since ARPAbet is used in CMUdict. Hence, the peculiarities of IE obtained by comparing the canonical NAE pronunciations seem unsuitable. Other works in the Indian context have also studied phonetics and its influences, especially for particular Indian native languages. For instance, [16] examined Telugu speakers' L2 English phonetics.

Prior works lack approaches that focus on analysing sizeable datasets which are diverse in IE pronunciation variabilities using data-driven means. Typically, this results in capturing very few pronunciation variabilities in IE. Qualitative observations about various IE phonetic features can be informative; however, additional quantitative metrics can reveal the prevalence and significance of those observations. Furthermore, the data-driven rules are inherently dependent on the properties of the data used. In order to study the characteristics of IE using phonetic transcriptions, it must be ensured that the latter is reliable, consistent and representative of IE. This paper addresses these gaps by performing a data-driven analysis of phonetic transcriptions obtained by considering speech recordings in a linguistically diverse, Indic TIMIT corpus [27]. We gather existing qualitative phonetic rules relative to Received Pronunciation (RP) and report quantitative metrics to represent the prevalence of the phonetic features in IE and their probability of being representative of IE. We also present new rules found through our data analysis, which have not been discussed in the existing literature. Finally, we demonstrate the benefits of the obtained rules in building a Grapheme-to-Phoneme (G2P) conversion system for the automatic generation of IE pronunciations.

2   Data Annotation and Pre-processing

2.1   Indic TIMIT Corpus

We consider the speech data from Indic TIMIT [27] corpus for our work. In the corpus, 80 Indian English L2 speakers were considered from 6 regions of India, namely – North-East, East, North, Central, West, and South. From all these regions, speakers were recorded while speaking TIMIT stimuli [28], where each speaker was recorded for $2,342$ stimuli. The age of subjects ranged from 18-60 years. Cumulatively from all 80 speakers, a total of 240 h of speech data was obtained. From the considered 6 regions, a total of 5 groups were formed based on regions of the speakers' native language. The number of subjects in each group is 16 and they were gender balanced. The details of the groups are as described below:

> *Group 1 (North East and East Regions)*: Maithili, Nepali, Oriya, Bengali, Assamese, Dimasa, Mog, and Manipuri.
> *Group 2 (North and Central Regions)*: Malwi, Marwari, Punjabi and Hindi.
> *Group 3 (West Region)*: Gujarati, Konkani, and Marathi.
> *Group 4 (Upper South Region)*: Kannada and Telugu
> *Group 5 (Lower South Region)*: Malayalam and Tamil.

The languages in these groups were identified based on their originating language families and also by considering how they are influenced by other language families. The languages in Groups 1, 2, and 3 originate from the Indo-Aryan language family, except for Dimasa, Mog and Manipuri, which are Tibeto-Burman languages. Assamese and Nepali are influenced by the Tibeto-Burman language family. Assamese and Bengali are also influenced by Austro-Asiatic language family. The languages in Groups 4 and 5 originate from Dravidian language family, wherein languages in the former group are also influenced by Indo-Aryan language family. The considered languages in these groups are spoken in proximate regions. Using information from these groups, further annotation is done. Since a large majority of the Indian population speak the languages considered in the corpus, subjects from these native languages were considered sufficient to cover the accent variabilities in IE.

2.2   Data Preparation

In Indic TIMIT, two linguists had transcribed a subset of the recordings of speakers that have native languages from all the 5 groups, totalling $2,342$. Apart from the pre-existing subset in the Indic TIMIT corpus, we collected annotations for $13,632$ recordings, totalling $15,974$ phonetic transcriptions for the analysis. They were phonetically transcribed sequentially into a total of 5 groups such that each group covered languages from all 5 region-based groups. This was done by considering one of the linguists who annotated a subset of transcriptions for Indic TIMIT Corpus. The linguist is affiliated with Spire Lab at the Electrical Engineering Department, Indian Institute of Science. We believe that the collected phonetic transcriptions could include the phonetic variations resulting from different native languages of the Indian population. A total of 108 IPA symbols were used for transcribing. The consistency of transcriptions was accessed by calculating Intra-Rater Agreement using Cohen's Kappa Score [6] for each group separately by repeating a sub-set of 200 files. The mean Cohen's Kappa Score was 0.827 across all groups, which indicates strong agreement. To perform an analysis of IE pronunciation, a pronunciation lexicon (containing words and respective phonetic pronunciations) was created considering the 15,974 transcriptions from all 5 groups. The lexicon contains 16,664 entries, each containing words and their corresponding pronunciation using IPA notation. Considering the existing literature in which IE pronunciation variations were described relative to RP, we also considered the RP canonical transcriptions obtained using BEEP pronunciation lexicon [17] to compare with IE for the analysis. The phone set of the BEEP lexicon is an extension of ARPAbet [18]. It was converted into IPA for comparison with phone-level IPA transcriptions of our speech data. The words (in the created lexicon from phonetic transcriptions) which contained "-" (ex: audio-visual) and were absent in the BEEP lexicon were added by considering the pronunciations of individual words already available in the lexicon. The phonetic transcriptions in our lexicon were mapped to that of the RP for the words common between our created and BEEP lexicons.

3   Indian English in Linguistic Literature

The influence of Indian native languages on the L2 English of Indian speakers attributes to the characteristic features of Indian English. Few linguistic works discussed these characteristics of IE relative to RP in the past, as mentioned in Table 1 and within this section. Considering these, we have assimilated the phonetic rules mentioned in the works. The phonetic rules based on English pronunciation, spoken by the Indian population regardless of their native language, are considered as *General IE Phonetic Rules* in Table 1. These features have been collectively described in the literature as characteristic identifiers of IE. The table also includes the phonetic rules which are specific to the native language of a speaker.

3.1   Context Dependent Phonetic Rules

Certain phonetic rules are based on the context, such as the position of vowels and consonants in a word. Found from literature, these are categorised into context dependent phonetic rules.

1. **Insertion or Omission of Phoneme:** In regions like Uttar Pradesh and Bihar, a short vowel /ɪ/ is prefixed at word-initial positions, as the following:

Table 1. Phonetic Rules mentioned in Literature.

General IE Phonetic Rules				Native Language Specific Phonetic Rules				
No.	RP	IE		No.	RP	IE	Native Language	References
1	/ɛ/	/e/ or /eː/	[3]	1	/ʃ/	/s/	Hindi, Telugu, Bengali, Bihari	[15,21]
2	/ʌ/	/ə/	[3]	2	/z/	/s/	Hindi, Telugu, Bengali, Bihari	[15]
3	/d/, /t/	/ɖ/, /ʈ/	[2,14,20,26]	3	/ɪ/	/i/	Assamese, Bengali, Bihari Hindi, Oriya	[3]
4	/θ/	/t̪ʰ/, /t̪/	[7,15]	4	/v/	/bh/	Bengali, Oriya, Assamese	[15]
5	/ð/	/ɖ/	[7,15]	5	/ʒ/	/dʒ/	Kashmiri	[15]
6	/n/, /l/	/ə n/, /ə l/	[2]	6	/f/	/ph/	Gujarati, Marathi	[15]

"speech" becomes [ɪspiːtʃ] and "school" becomes [iskuːl] [11,14]. Few speakers add a semivowel before an initial vowel. Some examples would be, "every" ([jevri]), "about" ([jebaut]), and "old" ([woːld]) [26]. Conversely, according to [14], sometimes people also tend to omit the semivowels /j/ and /w/. "Yet" is realized as [ɛt], "won't" as [oːnt].

2. **Rhoticity:** In words ending with the letter 'r', rhoticity is found in the IE pronunciation [26]. For example, as "letter" ends with /r/, it is realised as [ər]. However, whether IE is rhotic or non-rhotic is not unanimously concluded in the literature. [20] mentioned that although non-rhoticity is not governed by region, it is prevalent across regions.

3. **Monophthongisation of Diphthongs:** A majority of the Indian population uses monophthongs in their English, whereas diphthongs are used in RP [10]. For the diphthongs /eɪ/ and /aʊ/, the corresponding monophthongs /eː/ and /oː/ are used [2]. In certain contexts, such as word-final positions, these long vowels can be reduced to short vowels. For instance, in words like "today", these vowels are reduced to /e/ and /o/ [15]. In words similar to "near" and "square" where the vowel is succeeded by /r/ (i.e. /rV/), such as "period" and "area", IE generally uses /i/ and /e/ instead of /ɪə/ and /eə/ respectively [26].

4. **Word-specific Contexts:** 1) In the "-ed" inflexions which follow voiceless consonants, IE shows a greater use of /d/ over /t/. Some examples include words like "traced" as [treːsd] (IE) instead of [treːst] (RP), and "packed" as [pækd] (IE) in place of [pækt] (RP) [14].
2) Double consonants in written English are often geminated. Few examples are: "matter" [mættər], "innate" [ɪnneːt], and "illegal" [ɪlliːgəl] [10].

4 Data Analysis

4.1 Procedure

In our data analysis, we aim to observe the variabilities of phonemes used in IE to those in RP. For this, we employ the many-to-many (m2m) aligner [9], which performs alignment followed by classification. Firstly, the phonemes in RP and IE pronunciation are aligned such that one or many phonemes of RP have the corresponding aligned IE phoneme(s) and vice versa. In addition to these alignments, we also obtain a confidence score from the m2m aligner indicating the likelihood between each set of aligned phonemes. We consider this confidence value (C.V.) for our analysis. Typically, m2m aligner is used for the prediction of phonemes, given graphemes. Therefore, the source is graphemes and the target is phonemes. In our analysis, we consider the source as RP phonemes and the target as IE phonemes for various words in the lexicon. We chose the maximum length specification in m2m aligner as 2 for obtaining alignments. The classification method provides C.V. for each aligned set of phonemes. Since C.V. indicates the likelihood of the IE phoneme(s) for a corresponding RP phoneme(s), we consider these values to validate the rules (phoneme mappings between IE and RP) obtained from the analysis based on aligned set of phonemes with the existing rules reported in the literature. We also consider the normalised frequency (N.F.) of occurrence corresponding to that rule, to indicate how recurrently it is observed. The frequency of occurrence of a rule is normalised by the total number of occurrences of RP phonemes of that rule.

The C.V. and N.F. both range from 0 to 1. The rules with C.V. of 0.10 and above are considered in this analysis. Furthermore, a minimum frequency of occurrence of 150 is also ensured for each rule to avoid C.V. and N.F. values derived from the low frequency of occurrence of the rule in the data. We grouped the phonetic rules into three categories in Table 2 based on their occurrence in literature, dataset, and as found using data-driven method:

- **Category 1** - *Phonetic rules mentioned in literature and observed in the dataset:* This contains IE phonetic rules, which were validated on the corpus by using data-driven methods.
- **Category 2** - *Phonetic rules observed in the dataset, but not discussed in literature:* This consists of phonetic rules which were observed with high C.V. and N.F.. However, discussion regarding them was not found in the linguistic works we studied.
- **Category 3** - *Phonetic rules mentioned in the literature but not observed in dataset:* The phonetic rules listed in this category have been discussed in the literature; however, they were either not present in our dataset or were not prominent enough to cross our thresholds for C.V. and frequency of occurrence. We also report the phoneme observed (Obs. IE) in our data in place of the expected phoneme (Exp. IE), which is mentioned in the literature and the C.V. and N.F. corresponding to Obs. IE.

4.2   Discussion

Category 1. The rules in rows 1–8 correspond to general IE features mentioned in the literature, were prominent in our dataset, indicated by high C.V. and N.F. values. For the rule in row 8, although for the phoneme /l/ in R.P, the most commonly observed corresponding phoneme in IE is /l/ in our data, there is a significant presence of usage of /ə l/ as well. Therefore, this phoneme

Table 2. IE Phonetic Rules relative to RP for all three categories. '*' Indicates Native language specific IE rules.

Category 1					Category 2					Category 3				
No.	RP	IE	C.V.	N.F.	No.	RP	IE	C.V.	N. F.	No.	RP	Exp. IE	Obs. IE	C.V.	N.F.
1	/ɛ/	/e/	0.917	0.912	1	/ʊ/	/u/	0.980	0.747	1	/n/	/ə n/	/n/	0.873	0.902
2	/ʌ/	/ə/	0.94	0.932	2	/aʊ/	/au/	0.576	0.569	2(t)	*/ʃ/	/s/	/ʃ/	0.402	0.375
3	/d/	/ɖ/	0.964	0.820	3	/j ʊ/	/u/	0.765	0.835	2(h)	*/ʃ/	/s/	/ʃ/	0.336	0.334
4	/t/	/ʈ/	0.964	0.851	4	/ɝ/	/ə r/	0.866	0.525	2(b)	*/ʃ/	/s/	/ʃ/	0.47	0.420
5	/θ/	/t̪ʰ/	0.502	0.453	5	/ɑ/	/a r/	0.624	0.237	3(t)	*/ʃ/	/s/	/ʃ ə/	0.508	0.416
6	/θ/	/t̪/	0.45	0.381	6	/ɪ d/	/e ɖ/	0.912	0.373	3(h)	*/ʃ/	/s/	/ʃ ə/	0.481	0.399
7	/ð/	/ɖ/	0.737	0.669	7	/ʃ n/	/ə n/	0.843	0.893	3(b)	*/ʃ/	/s/	/ʃ ə/	0.461	0.389
8	/l/	/ə l/	0.159	0.183	8	/ə n/	/e n/	0.729	0.451	4	*/v/	/b h/	/v/	0.964	0.942
9(t)	*/z/	/s/	0.607	0.584						5	*/f/	/p h/	/f/	0.984	0.984
9(h)	*/z/	/s/	0.557	0.552						6	/oʊ/	/oː/	/o/	0.925	0.731
9(b)	*/z/	/s/	0.537	0.592						7	/eɪ/	/eː/	/e/	0.953	0.727
10	*/ɪ/	/i/	0.837	0.818						8	/ɒ/	/ɔː/	/ɔ/	0.871	0.654

insertion happens sometimes, as mentioned in Table 1 under 3.1. For rules in row numbered 9, the native languages are Hindi and Bihari (h), Telugu (t) and Bengali (b). Row 10 is applicable for Hindi, Bengali, Assamese, and Oriya native languages are applicable. For these native language specific rules, only the transcriptions obtained from the native speakers of those languages are considered.

Category 2. The phonetic rule in row 1 has not been discussed in literature where comparisons between the RP /ʊ/ and IE /u/ have been made.

Consequently, it is possible that as a result of the phonetic rule in row 1, the rule in row 2 can be observed wherein, for the diphthong /aʊ/, /au/ is observed instead. There might also have been diphthongs where this replacement could be seen; however, such phonetic rules would not have met either the C.V. or minimum frequency of occurrence criteria in our dataset. Its influence can also be seen in the rule of row 3. However, the rule in row 3 also suggests the deletion of a phoneme. For example, as mentioned in Sect. 3 that in certain contexts, the semivowels /j/ and /w/ are omitted. Therefore, further investigations regarding the context of usage could be helpful in understanding the presence of this rule. The rules in rows 4 and 5 could suggest mild rhoticity in the speakers' accents, as mentioned in point 4 of Sect. 3. In the rule corresponding to row 6, the usage of retroflex /ɖ/ is clear from the validation of the rule in Category 1, row 3. However, there is little information regarding the presence of /e/ in /e ɖ/ or /ɪ/ in /ɪ d/.

Syllabification of /n/ and /l/ as /ə n/ and /ə l/ is discussed in [2]. The presence of rule in row 7 could indicate phoneme insertion, particularly in words ending with "-tion". For example, in the word "absorption", the RP pronunciation can be [əbsɔpʃn], whereas [əbsɔpʃən] can be the IE alternative. This may also be associated with the discussion in [15], where the insertion of /ə/ in a word-final cluster like "lm" in words such as "film" i.e./fɪləm/ is mentioned. In

346 P. Pal et al.

order to conclusively understand these phonetic rules, analysis of contexts along with native language is needed for the rules in rows 6, 7 and 8.

Category 3. Row 1 follows the description of syllabification [2]. However, unlike the schwa insertion in /ə l/ for /l/, presence of /ə n/ wasn't observed for /n/. Instead, the prevalent usage was closer to RP phoneme /n/. The rules in rows numbered 2 and 3 share the same native languages as row numbered 9 in Category 1. Row 4 applies to Bengali, Oriya and Assamese speakers and row 5 for Gujarati or Marathi speakers. These are mentioned in rows 1, 4 and 6 in Table 1 under native language specific rules, as found in the literature. Following the rules in rows numbered 2,4 and 5, we observed the phonemes in IE (Obs. IE) of the corresponding native languages to be the same as RP. In row 2, apart from the occurrences where the IE phoneme /ʃ/ is the same as RP, we also observed /ʃ ə/ in IE, which is listed in row number 3. This could indicate the presence of /ə/ phoneme insertion.

In row 4, the prominent usage of the phoneme /v/ instead of /b h/ indicates a possibly vanishing /v/-/b h/ substitution. Similarly, row 5 indicates that /f/ was retained in its original form.

The rules in rows 6, 7 and 8 correspond to the diphthongs in RP, often substituted as monophthongs in IE. Contrary to the phonemes being substituted by a long vowel, we observed a wide usage of short vowels with high prominence. However, in certain contexts such as the ones which are mentioned in Sect. 3.1, IE often has short vowels substituting diphthongs.

Apart from the phonetic rules discussed above, the rules for the following phonemes /əʊ/, /ɛə/, /ɪe/ , /ɑː/, /ɔː/ couldn't be analysed as they are absent in the considered RP canonical transcriptions. Description for some of the rules related to them are as follows. In [3], the rule consists of RP phoneme /ɑː/ and its corresponding IE phoneme /aː/. Additionally, IE /ɒː/ is mentioned for RP /ɔː/ in another rule.

Finally, in addition to the rules mentioned in this category, with reference to point 5 under native-specific language features in Table 1, the phonetic rule specified for the Kashmiri native language is not analysed due to its absence in the languages considered in Indic TIMIT corpus.

Context Dependent Phonetic Rules. For the words ending with "-ed", the usage of IE /d/ instead of RP /t/ was barely observable. In our RP pronunciations for "-ed" ending words, instead of /t/, we observed /d/. This is contradictory to the description in 4. (Word-specific Contexts) under Sect. 3.1. Furthermore, the IE phoneme /ḍ/ for those words was observed in place of RP phoneme /d/, which is expected.

Many Indian languages have gemination in their verbal and orthographic forms, which explains the expectation for a native Indian language speaker to influence their L2 English similarly. However, a possible explanation for the absence of this behaviour in our data could be that speakers pronounced the correct phonetic sequence in the limited words where the context was applicable.

For gemination, we considered words with consonants such as "ll", "nn" and "tt". Very few instances of gemination by Indian speakers were observed. Lastly, we consider the insertion rule corresponding to /ɪ/ insertion as mentioned in point 1, particularly for words starting with "s". We consider Hindi speakers to validate /ɪ/ insertion. There were very rare instances where this was observed to happen. Apart from this, when word-initial positions were considered for semi-vowel insertion, the occurrences were very few.

4.3   Efficacy of G2P System Based on Phonetic Rules

We consider the Sequitur G2P conversion system [4] to show the effectiveness of the phonetic rules obtained from the proposed analysis. For the experimentation, we consider three pronunciation lexicons.

Table 3. Phoneme Error Rate (PER) for the lexicons.

Lexicon	IE	RP	IE_PRAG
PER	7%	47%	25%

The first one is referred to as IE lexicon, which is described in Sect. 2.2. It is constructed using unique pairs of words in the stimuli and their respective annotated phonetic transcriptions. Since the IE lexicon is obtained from phonetically annotated transcriptions for each word, the maximum performance can be achieved. Thus, IE lexicon can be considered as oracle lexicon. The second lexicon is referred to as RP lexicon, which is the BEEP pronunciation lexicon. Finally, the third one is referred to as IE_PRAG (**P**honetic **R**ule based **A**utomatically **G**enerated) lexicon, constructed from rules in Table 2 by substituting the phonemes of RP column in all the pronunciation sequences in the RP lexicon with the phonemes of IE column. Each substitution rule is applied to the fraction (equal to the N.F. in the table) of all possible candidates in the RP lexicon for the rule, chosen randomly. It is observed that the unique words vary in IE_PRAG, RP and IE lexicon. Thus, a similar approach mentioned in Sect. 2.2 is used to consider unique words common across all three. These are found to be a total of 6,720 out of which the pronunciation entries correspond to 5,376 (randomly chosen) words from all three lexicons for training the G2P system and the entries of the remaining words for testing. We consider Phoneme Error Rate (PER) as the metric for the evaluation on the test set. From the PER reported in Table 3 with all three lexicons, it is observed that the PER with IE_PRAG lexicon is lesser than that of the RP lexicon. This shows the benefit of the phonetic rules obtained from the proposed analysis for building a lexicon for IE automatically with G2P. Hence, IE_PRAG lexicon could be helpful in building better ASR and TTS in the Indian context.

5   Conclusion

Addressing the need to study and analyse IE pronunciation, we used a data-driven approach to explore the pronunciation variabilities of IE relative to RP.

For this, we phonetically transcribed 13, 632 utterances taken from the Indic TIMIT speech corpus. Considering a total of 15, 974 phonetic transcriptions, we presented a methodology to extract phonetic rules and validate them for their relevance and significance in the Indian context. We believed that the indicative rules helped determine relevant IE phonetic tendencies with higher confidence. Furthermore, we compared the performance of G2P conversion using lexicons constructed with and without the phonetic rules obtained in the proposed analysis. Further investigation is needed to analyse the quality of the new set of rules based on the influences from the native language-specific patterns. Additionally, inclusion of more annotators for phonetic transcriptions and their inter-annotator agreement can be presented with more data availability. Future directions include identifying the reasons for the absent rules reported in the analysis as well as further investigating the performance changes in ASR or TTS systems using the reported rules , along with incorporating other automatic G2P systems. Lastly, the examination of various phonetic combinations within speech signals remains a potential avenue for exploration.

References

1. Anil, M.C., Shirbahadurkar, S.D.: Phoneme selection rules for Marathi text to speech synthesis with Anuswar places. In: Thampi, S.M., Bandyopadhyay, S., Krishnan, S., Li, K.-C., Mosin, S., Ma, M. (eds.) Advances in Signal Processing and Intelligent Recognition Systems, pp. 501–509. Springer, Cham (2016). https:// doi.org/10.1007/978-3-319-28658-7_42
2. Bansal, R.K.: The pronunciation of English in India. Studies in the pronunciation of English: a commemorative volume in honour of AC Gimson, pp. 219–230 (1990)
3. Bansal, R.K., Harrison, J.B.: Spoken English: A Manual of Speech and Phonetics. Sangam (1994)
4. Bisani, M., Ney, H.: Joint-sequence models for grapheme-to-phoneme conversion. Speech Commun. **50**(5), 434–451 (2008)
5. Chandramouli, C., General, R.: Census of India 2011. Provisional Population Totals. New Delhi: Government of India, pp. 409–413 (2011)
6. Cohen, J.: A coefficient of agreement for nominal scales. Educ. Psychol. Measur. **20**(1), 37–46 (1960)
7. Gargesh, R.: Indian English: Phonology. In: A handbook of varieties of English, pp. 992–1002. De Gruyter Mouton (2008)
8. Huang, X., Jin, X., Li, Q., Zhang, K.: On construction of the ASR-oriented Indian English pronunciation dictionary. In: Proceedings of the 12th Language Resources and Evaluation Conference, pp. 6593–6598 (2020)
9. Jiampojamarn, S., Kondrak, G., Sherif, T.: Applying many-to-many alignments and hidden markov models to letter-to-phoneme conversion. In: Human Language Technologies 2007: The Conference of the North American Chapter of the Association for Computational Linguistics; Proceedings of the Main Conference, pp. 372–379. Association for Computational Linguistics, Rochester, New York (2007). https://www.aclweb.org/anthology/N/N07/N07-1047
10. Kachru, B.B.: English in South Asia, The Cambridge History of the English Language, vol. 5, pp. 497–553. Cambridge University Press (1994). https://doi.org/10. 1017/CHOL9780521264785.011

11. Kachru, B.B.: Asian Englishes: beyond the canon, vol. 1. Hong Kong University Press (2005)
12. Kishore, S., Kumar, R., Sangal, R.: A data driven synthesis approach for Indian languages using syllable as basic unit. In: Proceedings of International Conference on NLP (ICON), pp. 311–316 (2002)
13. Kumar, R., Gangadharaiah, R., Rao, S., Prahallad, K., Rosé, C.P., Black, A.W.: Building a better indian english voice using" more data". In: SSW, pp. 90–94. Citeseer (2007)
14. Mesthrie, R.: Introduction: varieties of English in Africa and south and southeast Asia. In: 4 Africa, South and Southeast Asia, pp. 23–34. De Gruyter Mouton (2008)
15. Pingali, S.: Indian English. Edinburgh University Press (2009)
16. Pisegna, K., Volenec, V.: Phonology and phonetics of 12 Telugu English. Studies in Linguistics and Literature 5, 46–69 (02 2021). https://doi.org/10.22158/sll.v5n1p46
17. Robinson, T.: Beep dictionary. BEEP dictionary (1996)
18. Robinson, T., Fransen, J., Pye, D., Foote, J., Renals, S.: Wsjcamo: a British English speech corpus for large vocabulary continuous speech recognition. In: 1995 International Conference on Acoustics, Speech, and Signal Processing. vol. 1, pp. 81–84. IEEE (1995)
19. Saikia, R., Singh, S.R.: Generating Manipuri English pronunciation dictionary using sequence labelling problem. In: 2016 International Conference on Asian Language Processing (IALP), pp. 67–70 (2016). https://doi.org/10.1109/IALP.2016.7875936
20. Sailaja, P.: Indian English: features and sociolinguistic aspects. Lang. Linguist. Compass 6(6), 359–370 (2012)
21. Sirsa, H., Redford, M.A.: The effects of native language on Indian English sounds and timing patterns. J. Phon. 41(6), 393–406 (2013)
22. Sitaram, S., Manjunatha, V., Bharadwaj, V., Choudhury, M., Bali, K., Tjalve, M.: Discovering canonical Indian English accents: a crowdsourcing-based approach. In: Proceedings of the Eleventh International Conference on Language Resources and Evaluation (LREC 2018) (2018)
23. Vazhenina, D., Markov, K.: Phoneme set selection for Russian speech recognition. In: 2011 7th International Conference on Natural Language Processing and Knowledge Engineering, pp. 475–478. IEEE (2011)
24. Vignesh, S.R., Shanmugam, S.A., Murthy, H.A.: Significance of pseudo-syllables in building better acoustic models for Indian English TTS. In: 2016 IEEE International Conference on Acoustics, Speech and Signal Processing (ICASSP), pp. 5620–5624 (2016). https://doi.org/10.1109/ICASSP.2016.7472753
25. Weide, R.: The carnegie mellon pronouncing dictionary [cmudict. 0.6]. Version 0.6. Available at [www. speech. cs. cmu. edu/cgi-bin/cmudict] (2005)
26. Wells, J.C.: Accents of English: Volume 3: Beyond the British Isles, vol. 3. Cambridge University Press (1982)
27. Yarra, C., Aggarwal, R., Rajpal, A., Ghosh, P.K.: Indic timit and indic English lexicon: A speech database of Indian speakers using timit stimuli and a lexicon from their mispronunciations. In: 2019 22nd Conference of the Oriental COCOSDA International Committee for the Co-ordination and Standardisation of Speech Databases and Assessment Techniques (O-COCOSDA), pp. 1–6. IEEE (2019)
28. Zue, V., Seneff, S., Glass, J.: Speech database development at MIT: Timit and beyond. Speech Commun. 9(4), 351–356 (1990)

Multimodal Collaboration in Expository Discourse: Verbal and Nonverbal Moves Alignment

Olga Iriskhanova[ID], Maria Kiose[✉][ID], Anna Leonteva[ID], Olga Agafonova[ID], and Andrey Petrov[ID]

Institute of Linguistics of Russian Academy of Sciences, Moscow State Linguistic University, Ostozhenka 38, 19013 Moscow, Russia
maria_kiose@mail.ru

Abstract. The paper explores multimodal collaboration in expository discourse considering verbal and nonverbal moves used by the participants in turn-taking. It reports the results of an experiment which tested speech, gesture and gaze alignment as affected by intentional and spontaneous communication. The results based on the 46-min long pilot subcorpus (out of 640-min long collected database) reveal that collaborative expository discourse is vastly multimodal where nonverbal moves in contact-establishing gesture and face-oriented gaze modulate each type of verbal move. Despite the fact that verbal moves do not manifest specific alignment with nonverbal moves, there are several tendencies in their distribution, for instance, verbal request move and elaboration moves are more frequently accompanied by nonverbal moves than other verbal moves. The study also shows that verbal and nonverbal moves alignment is not modulated by either intentional or spontaneous collaboration since there are no distinctions observed in the nonverbal move use with either common or new topic elaboration move, which proves that more intricate patterns of moves are exploited to provide intentionality and spontaneity in expository discourse.

Keywords: Multimodal behavior · Expository discourse · Collaboration · Speech · Gaze · Gesture

1 Introduction

In the study, we address the problem of multimodal collaboration modulated by a problem-solving task. Whereas there is extensive research on communicative moves of collaborative discourse ([1–3], among the many) as well as on the discursive markers which shape them in communicative modalities, speech ([4–6], among the many), gaze [7, 8] and gesture [9, 10], little is still known on how these moves are accomplished multimodally to achieve a specific discourse task, single and common for all the participants (cf. [11]). Additionally, recent studies develop the view that speech and multimodal alignment of speech, gaze and gesture in collaboration are dependent on the distribution of communicative moves (intentional and/or spontaneous) [12–14]; however, this view has not been statistically attested.

A. Karpov et al. (Eds.): SPECOM 2023, LNAI 14338, pp. 350–363, 2023.
https://doi.org/10.1007/978-3-031-48309-7_29

To explore the alignment of speech, gaze and gesture during a problem-solving collaborative task, we conduct a pilot experiment where the participants have to identify the differences between the pairs of synonyms and adopt a common decision. To obtain multimodal data, we record the participants' speech, gesture (using motion capture equipment), and gaze (using head-mounted eye trackers) for each pair of participants. In the study we develop three hypotheses. Hypothesis 1: following [12], collaborative expository discourse manifests multimodal patterns with gesture and gaze nonverbal moves accompanying different types of verbal moves. Hypothesis 2: different verbal moves (in **request, response** and **topic elaboration**) manifest specific alignment with nonverbal moves, i.e., in gesture (in **contact-establishing gestures**) and in gaze (in **face-oriented gaze**). This hypothesis is rooted in speech, gaze and gesture alignment studies which claim that multimodal behavior is highly dependent on the communicative role of the discourse participants [3, 8]. Hypothesis 3: this alignment is modulated by either intentional or spontaneous collaboration. With intentional collaboration being more oriented towards participants' involvement into discourse [12], we expect that speech, gaze and gesture will adopt a more interlocutor-oriented stance.

Overall, the study reveals i) the distribution of verbal and nonverbal communicative moves in this discourse type, ii) the distinctions between verbal and nonverbal moves, iii) the differences between intentional and spontaneous collaboration appearing in verbal and nonverbal moves.

The paper is structured as follows. In Sect. 2 we present the theoretical framework on Speech, gaze and gesture alignment in problem-oriented discourse task. In Sect. 3 we describe the methods and experiment design. Section 4 displays the results and their discussion. In Sect. 5 major conclusions and final remarks are presented.

2   Theoretical Framework

2.1   Verbal and Nonverbal Communicative Moves in Collaborative Communication

Turn-taking is a crucial aspect of collaborative communication, as it helps speakers maintain a fluid conversation by using both verbal moves such as requests, responses, topic elaboration moves and nonverbal moves such as gestures and gaze. To explore the verbal moves, the studies most commonly consider the discourse markers, for instance fillers, adjacency pairs, and backchanneling which help speakers organize the conversation by weaving turns and ideas together [15, 16], as well as lexical, grammatical and phonetic cues appearing within the verbal moves or at turn boundaries [17, 18]. Both discourse markers and cues allow the speaker to shape a verbal move as a discourse component and consequently allow the researcher to identify the move type and its boundaries.

The studies of collaborative discourse distinguish three types of verbal moves as collaborative discourse components, which are verbal request, verbal response, and topic elaboration [4, 13]. In [12] it was shown that in narrative discourse 1) these moves can be modulated by nonverbal moves, for instance, gesture and gaze, and 2) these moves can shape collaborative communication as intentional, spontaneous and unrealized; however, the author does not provide any data which might prove the specificity of their multimodal distribution. For this reason, we will consider two types of topic elaboration move, common and new topic elaboration, with the first being a component of intentional collaboration, and the second – a component of spontaneous collaboration. Additionally, while multimodal behavior in collaboration is thoroughly explored in multiple studies [19–21] the distinction between intentional and spontaneous collaboration in verbal turn-taking is commonly described via the use of discourse markers like hesitation marks, repetitions, etc. [14], which can serve as indirect verbal moves; however, their alignment with gesture and gaze is mostly neglected.

It is noteworthy that the distribution of multimodal communicative moves may be discourse dependent [1, 5, 6, 12]. In this study, we address the expository discourse [15] in which collaboration was stimulated by a problem-solving task, single and common for all the discourse participants or interlocutors. In expository discourse, the object of reference is construed as having fuzzy boundaries; therefore, identifying these boundaries while contrasting different object of reference can serve as a common task or problem which the interlocutors can solve.

Overall, following [4, 12, 13], we distinguish several verbal moves, which are 1) verbal request, 2) verbal response, and topic elaboration of two types, 3) common topic elaboration move and 4) new topic elaboration move, and also 5) indirect verbal move.

2.2   Verbal and Nonverbal Alignment in Collaborative Communication

The collaborative nature of discourse shapes both verbal and nonverbal moves of inter-locutors. Importantly, gestures in dialogues have been regarded as discourse markers [22] which together with prosody and syntax help to define the basic units of communication [23]. These gestures are used to engage the listener and might entail social affordances as these gestures are thought to invoke behavioral response, facilitate sensorimotor patterns of brain activations that determine specific behavioral responses, thus evoking social interactions [24]. They are regarded as a direct reference to the interlocutor due to their form and direction: finger(s) and/or palm(s) are oriented towards the interlocutor [25]. The importance of such gestures has been highlighted in the results of different studies. Holler in her study (2010) discusses the role of gestures used in communicating the shared information. The results indicate that if the participants shared some common ground, they used more interactive gestures [25]. In the current paper gestures with similar functions and used for similar purposes are termed contact-establishing gestures, as we regard them as a communicative nonverbal move used to address the interlocutor, maintain their attention, appeal to their position in the discussion, ask for the opinion or agreement or to even appease the interlocutor, i.e., they are used in collaborative communication and can be regarded as one of its markers.

Nonverbal properties of the dialogical communication are not limited solely to the body movements. Eye gaze is also regarded as an important part of the dialogue as it helps in establishing contact and adds to turn taking. Scholars established various findings in terms of possible gaze patterns during conversation, especially while turn taking and turn yielding [26]. Kendon (1967) conducted pioneering research [27] where he concluded that eye gaze regulates and monitors turn taking. i.e., in order to concentrate and plan their utterance speakers avert their gaze [28, 29], whereas at the end of the turn they shift their gaze towards the interlocutor to indicate the end of their turn or to verify the availability of the other party to speak next, thus offering the floor to speak next [30–32]. Argyle and Cook (1976) found that 60% of the conversation involves gaze and 30% involves the eye contact (when interlocutors look at each other) [33]. For these reasons, in this paper, we mostly focus on face-oriented gaze as manifesting the discourse function of contact retaining. The face orientation of the gaze is determined by the location of the eye-tracker red focal point indicating the pupil's activity on the face of the interlocutor.

Overall, we consider contact-establishing gestures and face-oriented gaze as two types of nonverbal moves which can modulate the verbal moves. Additionally, the alignment of gesture and gaze in modulating these moves may play a part; for this reason, we attest this alignment type separately.

3   Data and Methods

3.1   Experiment Design and Data

To collect the data, we conducted an experimental study, where participants were asked to find one main trait that differs one synonym from the other in given pairs. In total they were provided with the pairs of synonyms in the Russian language, which were "fire – flame", "deadman – corpse", "battle – fight", "nonsense – rubbish", "punishment – penalty", "ideal – perfection", "lie – falsehood", "fear – apprehension", "burden – load", "effort – diligence", "duty – obligation", "line – lineament", "roar – howl", "obscurity – darkness". All the participants were male and female students aged 18–21 from linguistic and non-linguistic faculties, previously acquainted. Before the experiment the participants signed the agreement and were first outfitted with motion capture system (Perception Neuron Motion Capture), which included a hand band, gloves and upper body straps; and eye-tracker (Tobii Pro Glasses 2, 1920 × 1080, 25 FPS). The setting of the experiment consisted of a plastic table, as motion capture system is very sensitive to any magnetic impulse, and white screen for better gesture recognition as all motion capture system is black (see Fig. 1).

Fig. 1. Experiment setting.

The recording of the experiment was performed with three cameras. The first camera (Sony HXR-NX30P, 1920x1080 FHD, 25 FPS with the ECM-XM1 mounted shotgun microphone) was filming both participants from aside; two other cameras were built in the eye-tracking glasses, which allowed to obtain a frontal view of each participant. After the calibration of the eye-tracker and the motion capture was fulfilled, the participants started the communication; the limit of time was set on 30 min for a pair of participants.

The tools used for analyzing the material were: annotating software ELAN (Max Planck Institute for Psycholinguistics) (see Fig. 2), motion capture software Axis Neuron, eye tracking software Tobii Pro Glasses Controller. In the experiment we compiled a 640-min long corpus. For this pilot study, we used a 46-min long multimodal corpus which consisted of 28 collaboration (joint action) units or problem-solving tasks of the same type in expository discourse.

3.2   Methods

To proceed, we used multimodal analysis annotating communicative moves of two types, verbal and nonverbal. As described above (see Sects. 2.1 and 2.2) we annotated five types of verbal moves: direct – verbal request, verbal response, common topic elaboration move, new topic elaboration move, and indirect verbal move. To identify these, we relied on the discursive markers as well as on the language cues [3, 6, 12]. We also annotated three types of nonverbal moves: contact-establishing gesture, face-oriented gaze, and combinations of contact-establishing gesture and face-oriented gaze separately.

The coded annotation procedure was performed in ELAN. As seen in Fig. 2, in ELAN we created several tiers manifesting direct verbal moves for left and right interlocutor (the interlocutors located to the left and to the right) separately, indirect verbal moves for left and right interlocutor separately, gesture moves for left and right interlocutor separately, gaze moves for left and right interlocutor separately.

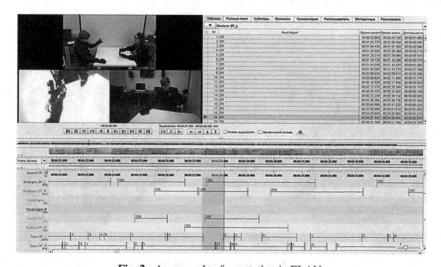

Fig. 2.   An example of annotation in ELAN.

While determining the frequency of the moves within the corpus we identified the cases of synchronized use of each verbal move type and each nonverbal move type, not the cases of their single uses. In this study, we did not consider the cases of nonverbal move use which were not accompanied by verbal moves.

Since the pilot annotated corpus is not large, we mostly used descriptive statistics to explore verbal and nonverbal communication moves; however, to test Hypotheses 2 and 3 we applied a series of contingency tests to determine the distinctions in nonverbal moves modulating different types of verbal moves. Still, further annotations of the compiled database will allow to identify significant differences in the moves and also to disclose the individual preferences in multimodal collaborative behavior.

4 Results and Discussion

4.1 Communicative Moves Within a Collaborative Act

First, two poles of collaborative communication were identified, the pole of intentional collaboration with common topic elaboration move as its nucleus, and spontaneous collaboration with new topic elaboration move as its nucleus. Preliminary data analysis showed that a collaborative act did not necessarily contain all types of verbal moves, for instance verbal request was not present in all acts and not all acts were finalized with a verbal response. Their distribution was not dependent on whether the act was intentional or spontaneous – both topic elaboration moves could precede, be accompanied or be followed by these move types. Therefore, we considered common and new topic elaboration moves as a nuclear and obligatory component of a collaborative act, and verbal request, verbal response and indirect verbal moves as its optional or non-nuclear components.

Second, we identified the basic discourse functions of verbal and nonverbal moves[1]. The verbal request to perform a joint action can be used to attract attention e.g., *послушай меня* (listen to me); *ну пожалуйста* (but please), to state the conditions for the communication in *у нас есть еще три минуты* (we have three more minutes), request for repetition in *прости, что?* (sorry, what?) and request for clarification in *почему а если это вообще не человек?* (why and if it's not a person at all?). The response serves to express consent in *да я тоже с тобой согласна* (yes, I also agree with you), discord in *ну нет это уже такая…* (but no, this is a…), hesitation in *нууу это когда* (wellll it's when), assessment in *здесь нет разницы* (there's no difference) or in *очень странно* (very weird) or emotion in *я с ума сойду* (I'll go crazy). The topic elaboration move includes giving additional information or details on the topic, information sequencing in *если все допустим объяло пламя все сгорело в пламени* (if everything is enflamed and has burnt down), restating in *ну пара человек ну в смысле ПВП какое-то* (well a couple of people it's like sort of PVP) and also summarizing of what has been said in *короче огонь более нейтральное* (so the fire is more neutral).

Contact-establishing gestures are used to address the interlocutors, maintain their attention, appeal to them, ask for the opinion, etc. In the example below (Fig. 3) we can

---

[1] Below, we present the examples of their use omitting the punctuation marks in verbal moves, leaving them only when they are necessary to understand the contents of the moves.

see that both speakers use similar gestures to address each other during the discussion. The speaker on the right uses this gesture while restating but the use of the gesture adds the addressing to the interlocutor asking for the confirmation of the statement. The speaker on the left disagrees and highlights the disagreement by using a similar gesture to address the other speaker and to strengthen her point.

Fig. 3. An example of contact-establishing gestures. Speaker Right: По сути это как вектор (so it's sort of a vector). Speaker Left: Нет. Вектор имеет направленность. Линия это просто такая фигня которая проходит через две точки (No. A vector has a direction. A line is such a trifle that passes through two points).

The eye gaze was annotated according to two major areas of interest (AOI): face of the interlocutor and somewhere else (see Fig. 4 and Fig. 5).

Fig. 4. Face-oriented gaze.

Overall, we found that maintaining gaze on the listener is performed in order to indicate the importance of what is being said or to check the reaction (understanding, agreement or disagreement, attention, availability) of the listener.

Fig. 5. Face-averted gaze.

4.2 Communicative Moves Distribution in Collaborative Expository Discourse

To test hypothesis 1 claiming that collaborative expository discourse is vastly multimodal with gesture and gaze non-verbal moves accompanying different types of verbal moves, we identified 1) the number of verbal moves and nonverbal moves accompanying the verbal moves which shape collaborative expository discourse and 2) the distribution of single verbal moves as accompanied by nonverbal moves. With the total number of moves equal to 2458, we observe the following distribution of moves (see Fig. 6).

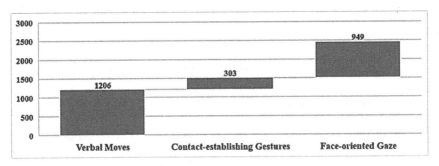

Fig. 6. Communicative moves distribution (in fractions and in absolute values).

Figure 6 shows that 25 per cent of verbal moves are accompanied with contact-establishing gestures and almost 79% of verbal moves proceeded with face-oriented gaze, which manifests the general alignment pattern of verbal and nonverbal moves in collaborative expository discourse and specifies the results found in [29, 32]. Additionally, we found that both contact-establishing gestures and face-oriented gaze appeared in 305 cases which means that both nonverbal modalities shaped 25.3% of all the verbal moves in the discourse, which elaborates on the data received in [7, 8, 12].

Since the verbal moves involve verbal request, verbal response, common topic elaboration, new topic elaboration, and indirect verbal move, we identified the distribution of nonverbal moves, contact-establishing gestures (CE Gesture), face-oriented gaze (FO Gaze) and both contact-establishing gestures and face-oriented gaze (CE Gesture and FO Gaze) accompanying each of these moves (see Table 1).

Table 1. Verbal and nonverbal moves distribution.

Types of verbal moves	Total	With CE Gesture	With FO Gaze	With both CE Gesture and FO Gaze
Verbal Request	156	55	130	51
Verbal Response	237	39	175	38
Common Topic Elaboration	353	106	312	111
New Topic Elaboration	209	64	179	59
Indirect Verbal Move	251	39	153	46

Table 1 shows that all types of verbal moves are frequently accompanied with contact-establishing gesture and face-oriented gaze. To test Hypothesis 2 claiming that different verbal moves (in request, response and topic elaboration) in collaborative expository discourse manifest specific alignment with nonverbal moves, we considered the distribution of their relative values in discourse. Relative values distribution (see Fig. 7) allows to determine the prevalence of either verbal or nonverbal moves as modulated by the move type.

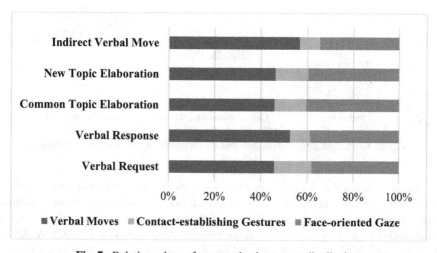

Fig. 7. Relative values of communicative moves distribution.

As seen from Fig. 7, verbal request move and elaboration moves are more frequently accompanied by nonverbal moves; still, the distribution of contact-establishing gestures is higher with verbal requests, which is a multimodal evidence of the higher necessity to establish the contact at this verbal move rather than to retain it. At the response move, the role of contact-establishing gesture is lower; however, the frequent use of face-oriented gaze proves that retaining contact is important. Indirect verbal moves are less frequently accompanied by nonverbal moves. Since the use of indirect verbal moves evidences in favor of a speaker's need to form an opinion of a discourse event [14] and a consequent lower involvement into cooperation, this may serve as a possible explanation to the decrease in the nonverbal manifestation of these moves. Further studies of the distribution of verbal and nonverbal moves in collaborative expository discourse can help identify the distinctions which might evolve.

4.3 Multimodal Intentional and Spontaneous Collaboration

Since our third hypothesis claimed that verbal and nonverbal alignment was modulated by either intentional or spontaneous collaboration displayed primarily in the use of common or new topic elaboration, we explored the differences in the distribution of contact-establishing gestures, face-oriented gaze and both contact-establishing gestures and face-oriented gaze accompanying each of these moves. Contingency tests determined that no distinctions in multimodal behavior are observed between common topic elaboration and new topic elaboration moves with $\chi2 = 0.012$ at $p = 0.914$ for verbal moves and CE Gesture, $\chi2 = 0.06$ at $p = 0.806$ for verbal moves and FO Gaze, and $\chi2 = 0.347$ at $p = 0.557$ for verbal moves and CE Gesture with FO Gaze. The results suggest that while these verbal moves display the nuclei of joint action acts, they do not manifest multimodal specificity which conforms to the results obtained in [12]. Presumably, the differences between intentional or spontaneous collaboration do not lie in its multimodal character, but in the presence of the non-nuclear components of joint action acts as well as in the presence of the clusters of elaboration moves.

The results manifest that only 27.8% of topic elaboration moves (common and new topic elaboration) are stimulated by a direct verbal request, which means that to initiate an elaboration move, the expository discourse participants are guided by either nonverbal moves or indirect verbal moves of the interlocutor. Additionally, the prevailing number of responses over requests suggests that the participants do not perform responses only to express consent, hesitation, assessment or emotion in relation to the question posed in the request, but they frequently assess the joint action itself. For instance, in ‖ Participant 1: *пламя любви* (the flame of love)/Participant 2: *смех* (laughter)/*ну да* (well yes)/*и все допустим объяло пламя все сгорело в пламени* (and everything well was in flame everything was burning in flame)/Participant 2: *ну да* (well yes) ‖ there appear two direct responses (well yes) which are not initiated by any direct request of the interlocutor, but express agreement with the joint action. Therefore, responses in expository discourse commonly appear not only after direct requests but following topic elaboration moves.

The results also show that common topic elaboration prevails over new topic elaboration moves. New topic elaboration moves help initiate each joint action unit like in ‖ Participant 2: *ну мне кажется схватка это когда такое типа два ну типа да человек на человека ну у них схватка* (well it seems to me that a battle is when well two well person onto a person well they have a battle)/Participant 2: *ага* (yes)/Participant 1: *когда вдвоем* (when there are two of them /Participant 2: *А битва это когда глобально много народа* (and the battle is when there is globally a lot of people)/Participant 1 (simultaneously): *Битва это когда не знаю ну короче район на район просто* (A battle is when I don't know well in short the region onto region simply)‖. Still, with 28 probes of collaborative expository discourse (joint action units), we observe that new topic elaboration moves do not only initiate the joint action but help develop it in case no agreement is presently achieved. In ‖ Participant 1: *ну допустим мы придем к соглашению что мертвец лучше чем труп* (well, presumably we will come to an agreement that a corpse is better than a dead man) / Participant 2: *да они вообще разные* (but they are completely different)/Participant 1: *им вообще пофигу* (they don't care)/Participant 2: *ну да* (well, yes)/Participant 1: *ну мертвец это более низкочастотное слово* (a corpse has lower frequency)‖ we find that while not being satisfied with attesting the fact that *мертвец* and *труп* do display specificity with *мертвец* being "better" than *труп*, Participant 1 starts elaborating a new topic focusing on the corpus frequency contrasts of two words. The second observed use of new topic elaboration moves within the joint action unit is found when the participants do not directly contrast the notions but corroborate the uniqueness or specificity of either of them, like in ‖ Participant 2: *схватка еще может быть родовая* (fight may be when a person is born)[2] ‖, in which the participant suggests an earlier unnoticed meaning of a word *схватка* to provoke further specification of two synonyms.

We also observe that indirect verbal moves frequently appear to express response (most commonly, with sound combinations manifesting indirect consent or discord, but also emotion and hesitation); still, we presume that in major cases they provoke further topic elaboration acting as both indirect response (to what has been said before) and indirect request (to proceed with topic elaboration). The data show that prolonged pauses, hesitation sounds, laughter, repetitions can stimulate the interlocutor to contribute a new elaboration move. For instance, in ‖ Participant 2: *ты идеал* (you are an ideal)/Participant 1: *смех* (laughter)/Participant 2: *смех* (laughter)/Participant 2: *совершенство* (perfection) ‖ where Participant 2 contributes a new elaboration move following his prior one interposed with an indirect verbal move (emotion) expressed by both participants. Similar situation is frequently observed with direct verbal responses which can also evoke further topic elaboration and often do not even interrupt the speech flow of the participant. In ‖ Participant 2: *сказать то что ты говоришь это ложь* (to say what you say is a lie)‖ Participant 1: *ага* (yes) ‖ *а вранье это когда например про тебя кто-то плохо сказал что-то* (and falsehood is when for example about you someone said something bad)‖ Participant 1: *да здесь нет разницы* (well, there is no difference)‖ *нелицеприятно о тебе высказался* (said something displeasing about you)‖ there are two interposing moves of participant 1 which do not break the speech flow of participant 2 but possibly stimulate his more persistent topic elaboration. However, further contingency tests to determine whether indirect responses multimodally resemble either a request or a response, revealed that indirect verbal moves display similar distribution of nonverbal moves with response and distinctions with request with $\chi 2 = 12.758$ at $p < 0.001$ for verbal moves and CE Gesture, $\chi 2 = 3.98$ at $p = 0.047$ for verbal moves and FO Gaze, and $\chi 2 = 5.335$ at $p = 0.021$ for verbal moves and CE Gesture with FO Gaze.

---

[2] In this meaning the word *fight* is not used in the English language.

Overall, the results show that the distribution of direct and indirect verbal moves as well as the distribution of nonverbal moves do not display a straightforward dependency on the collaboration type, intentional or spontaneous, but reveal several distinctive tendencies. However, we expect to reveal more precise distinctions within a larger corpus.

5 Final Remarks

In the study, we tested three hypotheses: the first, claiming that collaborative expository discourse is vastly multimodal with verbal moves frequently accompanied by gaze and gesture nonverbal moves, the second, that different verbal moves manifest specific alignment with nonverbal moves, and the third, claiming that verbal and nonverbal moves alignment is modulated by either intentional or spontaneous collaboration manifested via common and new topic elaboration.

The results support the first hypothesis. We found that 25 per cent of verbal moves were accompanied with contact-establishing gestures and almost 79% of verbal moves proceeded with face-oriented gaze, which manifest the general alignment pattern of verbal and nonverbal moves in collaborative expository discourse. Still, a collaborative act did not necessarily contain all types of verbal moves, for instance verbal request was not present in all acts and not all acts were finalized with a verbal response.

The second hypothesis was verified. The results showed that verbal request move and elaboration moves were more frequently accompanied by nonverbal moves. Additionally, indirect verbal moves were less frequently accompanied by nonverbal moves.

The third hypothesis was not verified. The distribution of direct and indirect verbal moves as well as the distribution of nonverbal moves in the pilot corpus did not display a straightforward dependency on the collaboration type, intentional or spontaneous; therefore, a larger corpus might suffice to specify this distribution.

Overall, the study has shown that while collaboration in a problem-solving discourse task is highly multimodal, the alignment of verbal and nonverbal moves as well as the distribution of intentional or spontaneous collaboration moves is modulated by various factors besides the move type.

Acknowledgements. The research presented in Sections 1 and 2 is part of the project "Multimodal research of the speaker's communicative behavior in different discourse types" (075–03-2020–013) carried out at Moscow State Linguistic University. The research presented in Sections 3, 4, and 5 is part of the project "Kinesic and vocal aspects of communication: parameters of variance" (FMNE-2022–0015) carried out at the Institute of Linguistics RAS.

References

1. Ono, T., Thompson, S.A.: Interaction and syntax in the structure of conversational discourse: collaboration, overlap, and syntactic dissociation. In: Hovy, E.H., Scott, D.R. (eds.) Computational and Conversational Discourse, pp. 67–96. Springer Berlin Heidelberg, Berlin, Heidelberg (1996). https://doi.org/10.1007/978-3-662-03293-0_3

2. Clancy, B., McCarthy, M.: Co-constructed turn-taking. In: Aijmer, K., Rühlemann, C. (eds.) Corpus pragmatics: A handbook, pp. 430–453 (2014)
3. Kibrik, A.A., Korotaev, N.A., Podlesskaya, V.I.: Chapter 1. Russian spoken discourse: Local structure and prosody. In: Izre'el, S., Mello, H., Panunzi, A., Raso, T. (eds.) In Search of Basic Units of Spoken Language: A Corpus-Driven Approach, pp. 35–76. John Benjamins Publishing Company, Amsterdam (2020). https://doi.org/10.1075/scl.94.01kib
4. Lerner, G.H.: Collaborative turn sequences. In: Lerner, G.H. (ed.) Conversation analysis: Studies from the first generation, pp. 225–256. John Benjamins, Philadelphia (2004)
5. Sacks, H.: Lectures on Conversation. Basil Blackwell, Oxford (1992)
6. Grenoble, L.: Syntax and co-constructed turns in Russian dialogue. Issues Linguist. 1, 25–36 (2008). (in Russian)
7. Richardson, D., Dale, R., Tomlinson, J.: Conversation, gaze coordination, and beliefs about visual context. Cogn. Sci. 33, 1468–1482 (2009)
8. Brône, G., Feyaerts, K. & Oben, B.: Multimodal turn-taking in dialogue: on the interplay of eye gaze, speech and gesture. Proceedings of AFLiCo5: Empirical approaches to multi-modality and to language variation, 21–22 (2013)
9. Bangerter, A.: Using pointing and describing to achieve joint focus of attention in dialogue. Psychol. Sci. 15, 415–419 (2004)
10. Mol, L., Krahmer, E., Maes, A., Swerts, M.: Adaptation in gesture: converging hands or converging minds? J. Mem. Lang. 66, 249–264 (2012)
11. Maman, L., et al.: GAME-ON: a multimodal dataset for cohesion and group analysis. IEEE Access, 8, 124185–124203 (2020)
12. Korotaev, N.A. Collaborative constructions in Russian conversations: a multichannel perspective. Computational Linguistics and Intellectual Technologies. Papers from the Annual International Conference "Dialogue" (2023) 22, 250–258 (2023)
13. Mondada, L.: L'organisation séquentielle des ressources linguistiques dans l'élaboration collective des descriptions. Langage et Société 89(1), 9–36 (1999)
14. Bogdanova-Beglarian, N., Blinova, O., Sherstinova, T., Gorbunova, D., Zaides, K., Popova, T.: Pragmatic Markers in Dialogue and Monologue: Difficulties of Identification and Typical Formation Models. In: Karpov, A., Potapova, R. (eds.) SPECOM 2020. LNCS (LNAI), vol. 12335, pp. 68–78. Springer, Cham (2020). https://doi.org/10.1007/978-3-030-60276-5_7
15. Longacre, R.: The grammar of discourse. Plenum, New York (1983)
16. Hughes, R.: Teaching and Researching: Speaking, 2nd edn. Routledge, London (2010)
17. Thornbury, S., Slade, D.: Conversation: From Description to Pedagogy. Cambridge University Press, Cambridge (2006)
18. Levinson, S.C.: Turn-taking in human communication – origins and implications for language processing. Trends Cogn. Sci. 20(1), 6–14 (2016)
19. Bohus, D., Horvitz, E.: Facilitating multiparty dialog with gaze, gesture, and speech. In: Proceedings of the International Conference on Multimodal Interfaces and the Workshop on Machine Learning for Multimodal Interaction (ICMI-MLMI), Beijing, China, 8–12 November 2010, 1–8. New York, NY: ACM (2010)
20. Hessels, R.S., Benjamins, J.S., van Doorn, A.J., Koenderink, J.J., Hooge, I.T.C.: Perception of the potential for interaction in social scenes. i-Perception 12(5), 204166952110402 (2021). https://doi.org/10.1177/20416695211040237
21. Goodwin, C.: Action and embodiment within situated human interaction. J. Pragmat. 32(10), 1489–1522 (2000)
22. Kendon, A.: Gestures as illocutionary and discourse structure markers in Southern Italian conversation. J. Pragmat. 23(3), 247–279 (1995)
23. Ford, C., Fox, B.A., Thompson, S.A.: Practices in the construction of turns: The 'TCU' revisited. Pragmatics 6(3), 427–454 (1996)

24. Curioni, A, Knoblich, G.K., Sebanz, N., Sacheli, L.M. The engaging nature of interactive gestures. PLoS ONE **15**(4), e0232128 (2020)
25. Holler, J.: Speakers' use of interactive gestures as markers of common ground. In: S. Kopp and I. Wachsmuth (eds.) GW 2009, Lecture Notes in Computer Science 5934, pp. 11–22. (2010)
26. Degutyte, Z., Astell, A.: The role of eye gaze in regulating turn taking in conversations: a systematized review of methods and findings. Front. Psychol. **12**, 616471 (2021)
27. Kendon, A.: Some functions of gaze-direction in social interaction. Acta Physiol (Oxf.) **26**, 22–63 (1967)
28. Cummins, F.: Gaze and blinking in dyadic conversation: a study in coordinated behaviour among individuals. Lang. Cogn. Process. **27**, 1525–1549 (2012)
29. Ho, S., Foulsham, T., Kingstone, A.: Speaking and listening with the eyes: gaze signaling during dyadic interactions. PLoS ONE **10**, e0136905 (2015)
30. Rutter, D.R., Stephenson, G.M., Ayling, K., White, P.A.: The timing of looks in dyadic conversation. British J. Social Clin. Psychol. **17**, 17–21 (1978)
31. Brône, G., Oben, B., Jehoul, A., Vranjes, J., Feyaerts, K.: Eye gaze and viewpoint in multimodal interaction management. Cogn. Linguist. **28**(3), 449–483 (2017)
32. Kendrick, K.H., Holler, J.: Gaze direction signals response preference in conversation. Res. Lang. Soc. Interact. **50**, 12–32 (2017)
33. Argyle, M., Cook, M.: Gaze and Mutual Gaze. Cambridge University Press, London (1976)

Association of Time Domain Features with Oral Cavity Configuration During Vowel Production and Its Application in Vowel Recognition

Arup Saha[1]([⊠]) [ID], Tulika Basu[1] [ID], and Bhaskar Gupta[2]

[1] CDAC-Kolkata, Kolkata, India
{arup.saha,tulika.basu}@cdac.in
[2] Jadavpur University, Kolkata, India

Abstract. In speech processing, the vowels play an important role in identifying the intended meaningful unit required for specific speech-based applications. To facilitate the quick extraction of the parameter for further processing, the time domain feature of the acoustic signal proves to be quite useful. To prove the usefulness of time domain parameters in speech processing, current study aims at mapping of the time domain parameters viz. Extrema rate, zero-crossing rate, perturbation area, and peak to peak distance with the physiological process involved in the vowel production and finally followed by their application in vowel recognition. To achieve the first objective, k-means clustering algorithm has been used on each of the parameters. The second objective is being achieved through the classification of the vowels using the random forest algorithm. To conduct the experiment, seven oral Bangla vowels from LDC-IL database for the Indic language has been used. Around 750 steady parts of the abovementioned vowels have been manually extracted for the study. It has been observed that the time domain parameters correlate well with the oral cavity configuration during vowel production. Moreover, recognition rate of Bangla vowels comes out to be 93% which seems very encouraging.

Keywords: Vowel · Bengali · Bangla · Time Domain Parameter

1 Introduction

The technological advancement in the development of the human-computer interface has gained a significant place in the current decade. This is mainly attributed to the increased demands of using the digital platform for accessing knowledge and applying it for the betterment of life. Moreover, immense enhancement in computation power, digital connectivity and efficient algorithms for computation using AI have added an extra mileage towards its need for the development of an efficient system.

The success of the development of an efficient human-computer interface requires the information-rich correct input to the system. The perfect candidate for such input is speech [1] as it is one of the important communication vehicles for expressing thoughts and emotions. The building of the adequately efficient speech recognition system will

A. Karpov et al. (Eds.): SPECOM 2023, LNAI 14338, pp. 364–379, 2023.
https://doi.org/10.1007/978-3-031-48309-7_30

serve as an initial step to achieve the above purpose [2]. The last few decades have witnessed the development of various time domain, frequency domain, and hybrid algorithms for speech recognition.

It has been observed that the efficiency of the speech recognition system is highly enhanced by using the bottom-up approach of recognition, where the text is identified from the speech signal through a sequence of combination and refinement of knowledge base with speech parameters at various stages of processing [3]. The aforesaid approach is very much similar to the process by which human beings decode the speech from the spoken signal [4]. It is worth mentioning here that as the recognition of the consonant is not up to the expectation [5], so to identify the spoken word correctly from the utterance, one has to heavily rely on the correct recognition of the vowels [6]. Apart from speech recognition, the vowel classification system is also used in the speaker identification and verification system [7], language recognition system [8] and emotion recognition from speech [9].

In classifying vowels, so far, several frequency-domain parameters viz. MFCC, LPC, formants etc. have been used [10]. MFCC in Neural Network with Parametric Bias is used in vowel recognition system [11]. Few other time-domain parameters like zero-crossing rate, shimmer, jitter, etc. have been used for vowel recognition purposes [12, 28]. Recently wavelet parameters, which are considered to be time-domain parameters, have been used for the classification of vowels in a noisy environment [13]. One of the main advantages of using the time domain parameters is its simplicity of being extracted from the signal itself in comparison to the frequency-domain parameter where the process of extraction is very complex. To overcome this problem, the researchers started looking into time-frequency domain parameters i.e. parameters related to both time and frequency domain [14–17]. In this approach, the researchers are using time-frequency domain parameters in the neural networks to achieve the desired result [18]. To mention, one such combination is phase and magnitude of spectra in the frequency domain and temporal information of the wave file in the time domain [19].

In this present work an attempt has been made to correlate four-time domain parameters viz., peak-to-peak distance, extrema rate, zero-crossing rate and perturbation area with the qualitative aspects of vowel that has been reflected in tongue height and position of vowels. Finally, to test the effectiveness of those four time domain parameters in classifying vowels, four classifier of different genre namely Naïve Bayes (NB), Multi-Layer Perceptron (MLP), Random Forest (RF) and Support Vector Machine(SVM) have been employed. The work is unique in a way that no such time domain parameter correlates well with oral cavity configuration i.e. the qualitative aspects of vowels. The usefulness of the TDP may be attributed towards its simple extraction mechanism; which can be used for the development of low memory-based devices.

Moreover, all the data has been manually selected after careful listening and segmented and finally no work with time domain parameter has been done in Bangla which is a low resource language.

Rest of the paper is organized as follows. Section 2 contains introduction to Bangla Language followed by a vowel production mechanism. This section also contains the definition of the proposed time-domain parameters and their correlation with oral cavity configuration during vowel production. Section 3 deals with the experimental details of the work to meet the above said objectives. The results of the experiment have been enumerated in Sect. 4. The discussion of results has also been written in this section. Section 5 contains conclusion and finally followed by references.

2 Methodology

A brief discussion about the Bangla language and the vowel production mechanism along with the mapping with tongue height and position have been presented in Sect. 2.1 and Sect. 2.2 respectively. Section 2.3 provides a detailed methodology for the extraction of the proposed TDP. The algorithm used for the classification of the vowel using the proposed TDP is given in Sect. 2.4.

2.1 Brief Description of Bangla Language

The current literature survey indicates that the Bangla language ranked fifth as the most spoken native language of the world [20] with approximately 265 million people [21]. It is not only one of the 22 scheduled languages of India and official language of the states of West Bengal and Tripura but also the national language of Bangladesh. The Bangla language belongs to the Indo-Aryan group of languages [22]. The present study is based on the Standard Colloquial Bangla (SCB) [23]. The Bangla Language consists of 47 phonemes out of which 33 are consonants and the rest are vowels (both oral and nasal). In this study we have included only oral vowels (excluding diphthongs and nasal vowels).

2.2 Vowel Production Mechanism and Mapping to Tongue Height and Position

The physiological process involved in the production of the speech as well as vowels is as follows. During the time of articulation, the lungs get compressed to exhale the air forcefully to pass through the glottis which is the narrow opening in the vocal folds located at the larynx. Then the air passes through three main cavities of the vocal tract viz., the pharyngeal, oral, and nasal cavity; and finally exited through the mouth and nose. One of the main functions of the glottis is to modulate the airflow that passes through it. This is done by varying the frequency of opening and closing of the flaps in the glottis. The mechanism of opening and closing the glottis go through the following process. At first, the glottis opens due to the high pressure of air built inside the lungs. As the air rapidly moves through the glottis, the pressure around the glottis decreases following Bernoulli's principle. Hence the glottis once again collapses back to its original position. This causes a buzzing sound from which the voiced sounds are generated. During the vowel production, the air puff so formed is passed through the constriction, formed between palate and the hump of the tongue in the oral cavity. The constriction at the oral cavity divides it into two resonating cavities viz., front and back cavity. The length of these resonating cavities gets changed at the position where the constriction is formed.

Depending on the position of the constriction and the height of the tongue hump, the quality (different resonating frequencies) of the vowel is added. The height and place of the constriction of the tongue hump as depicted in the IPA chart is given in Fig. 1

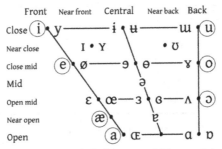

Fig. 1. Bangla vowel in IPA chart.

[24]. It has been worth mentioning here that Peterson and Barney have shown that first formant frequency (F1) roughly represents the tongue height whereas the second formant frequency (F2) approximately represents the tongue position [25].

The encircled vowels in Fig. 1 represent the Bangla vowel in the IPA chart [26]. On careful observation of Fig. 1, one can conclude that /i/ and /u/, /o/ and /e/ and finally /ɔ/, /a/ and /æ/ can form separate groups based on the height of the tongue hump. On the other hand, /u/, /o/, / ɔ / and /a/, /ɔ/, /e/, /i/ can form two distinctive groups on the basis of the tongue hump position during the articulation of the vowel.

2.3 Time Domain Parameters (TDP)

In the time domain representation, the shape of the waveform for each of the vowels shows some distinctive characteristics like high frequency, peak to peak distance, zero-crossing, randomness etc. The description of each of the TDP is given below:

Extrema Rate (ER). It is defined as the total number of peaks and valleys of the signal. For the given window in one second. This is likely to be influenced by the frequency of the higher resonant bands. It is defined in Eq. 1.

$$E = (V + P)/N \tag{1}$$

where V is the cardinality of the set of valleys $\{\xi_V\}$ and P is the cardinality of the set of peaks $\{\zeta_P\}$. N is the window length for which the data is being extracted. Each of the elements of the above-said valley series $\{\xi_V\}$ should satisfy the following condition $x[n+1] \geq x[n] \leq x[n-1]$ except the condition $x[n+1] = x[n] = x[n-1]$. Similarly, the elements of the peak series should satisfy the following condition $x[n+1] \leq x[n] \geq x[n-1]$ except for the condition $x[n+1] = x[n] = x[n-1]$. Here $x[n]$ represent the elements of the signal. Figure 2. Gives the extrema points of the signal and is indicated by the circle.

Peak-to-Peak Distance (PPD). It is defined as the distance between the largest maxima and smallest minima for a given window. This is likely to capture the location of the frequency of the lowest frequency band which is defined in equation in 2.

$$PPD = |Dist(Max(\{\zeta_P\})) - Dist(Min(\{\xi_V\}))| \tag{2}$$

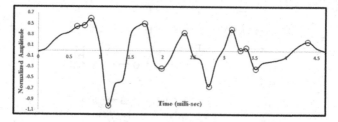

Fig. 2. Extrema points.

where Dist is the distance function used for calculating the distance of the position of the maximum amplitude peak and minimum amplitude valley from the start of the analysis frame. Max and Min represent the maximum and minimum function respectively for finding the maximum amplitude of the peak in the series $\{\zeta_P\}$ and minimum amplitude of the valley in the series $\{\xi_V\}$. The PPD is given in Fig. 3.

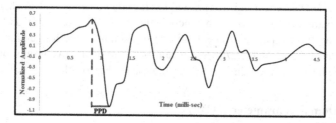

Fig. 3. Peak-to-peak distance.

Perturbation Area (PA). It is defined as the area enclosed between the curves joining positive and negative peak. It is used to capture the intensity of high resonating band. The PA is shown in Fig. 4.

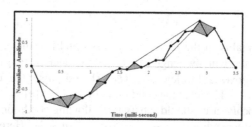

Fig. 4. PA as indicated by the grey color area.

Zero-Crossing Rate (ZCR). It is defined as the number of times the signal has crossed the zero-line or its amplitude changes from negative to positive and vice-versa for a given window in one second. It is a measure of dominant frequency in signal [3].

Figure 5 gives the zero crossings of the signal and is indicated by the circle.

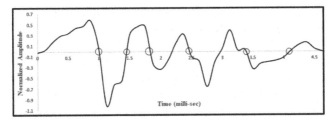

Fig. 5. Zero crossing of the signal.

2.4 Algorithms

In this study, k-means algorithm with the weighted Euclidean distance function has been used mainly for clustering of the Bangla vowels. On the other hand NB, MLP, RF, and SVM algorithm are used for classification of the vowels.

3 Experimental Details

The detailed experimental technique has been enumerated in this section through three sub-sections. Section 3.1 contains the details about the conversational speech database together with the number of sound segments taken for training and testing purposes. A detailed experimental process for the extraction of the TDP and the mapping of the proposed TDP with a speech production system has been explained in Sect. 3.2. Section 3.3 gives an inside view of training and testing of the vowel recognition system using the proposed TDP.

3.1 Data Gathering and Preparation

In this work LDC-IL conversational speech database (8 kHz, 8 bit) for the Indic language is used for training and testing of the vowels. Around 750 Bangla vowel segments (comprising all the vowels are carefully segmented manually by the native linguists and stored for the experiment. In the first experiment all the vowel segments have been used whereas in the second experiment, among 750 segments, around 66% are used for training and around 34% have been taken for testing purpose.

3.2 Experimental Procedure

Based on the objective of the study, the experiment is broken into two parts viz. Mapping of the TDP with height and position of the tongue and secondly developing the vowel recognition system with the proposed TDP. The details of the experiments have been discussed in the following sub-sections.

Mapping of the Proposed TDP with Speech Production System
The process of mapping of the proposed time domain parameter starts with the extraction of the parameter from the raw speech signal. After that, process of mapping the parameter

with tongue height and tongue position of vowels is done through a clustering algorithm which has been enumerated in subsequent sections.

Extraction of Parameter

The process of extraction of the TDP involves in the careful selection of the steady-state [26] of the vowel segment from the CVC syllable which is indicated in the Fig. 6. This is done to avoid the unsteady parameter values in the transition region. In Fig. 6 "T" represents the transition state and "S" represents the steady state of the vowel.

After that, the vowel segment undergo the process of amplitude normalization for further processing. The equation for amplitude normalization is given in Eq. 3.

$$x[i] = x[i] / (Max(x[0, ..., n-1]) - Min(x[0, ..., n-1])) \qquad (3)$$

where Max () and Min () are functions used for finding the maximum and minimum values respectively of the amplitude in the given series and i refers to the sample number.

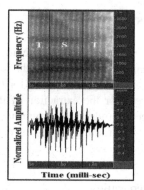

Fig. 6. Time-frequency domain representation of vowel /a/.

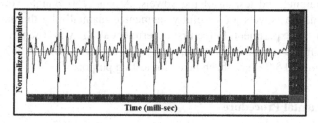

Fig. 7. Pitch marked boundary signal of vowel /a/.

The pitch period of the resultant processed segment is extracted by using the Phase Space Algorithm [27]. The pitch boundary marked signal is given in Fig. 7. The pitch boundary marker obtained in the above step has been corrected through the epoch detection algorithm [27]. The corrected pitch boundary marked by the vertical lines is given in Fig. 8.

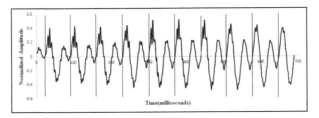

Fig. 8. Corrected pitch boundary.

Mapping of Parameter

Once the value of the proposed parameter set is obtained, the frequency distribution of the parameter set is plotted. The frequency distribution plot not only gives an initial idea of the number of clusters in the dataset but also provides preliminary values of the mean and standard deviation value to the clustering algorithm. Here we have considered the initial standard deviation value to be $\pm$ 40% of the mode value of the cluster as we have considered the distribution of the data in the cluster to be normal. In this experiment, we have used the k-means clustering algorithm using the Euclidean distance metric to determine the final mean and standard deviation of the cluster. The clustering algorithm continues to run over n number of epochs until the difference between values of the previous and current mean of the cluster is not less than constant ϖ;. Here we have considered ϖ; to be 0.05. On obtaining the final mean and standard deviation of the clusters for a particular TDP, the membership of individual vowel samples to the clusters is being determined. This is done by comparing the distance (i.e. weighted Euclidean distance) of the individual sample of vowels with the c number of clusters in that data distribution. The sample which is closer to the cluster (i.e. having minimum distance) is assigned to it.

3.3 Recognition System

Another objective of the current study is to develop the vowel recognition system using the proposed four TDP. Like any other recognition system, our system is also consisted of training and testing modules. The input to both the training and testing module comes from the feature extraction module, which directly converts the raw vowels speech segment into a TDP set. In the training module, the mean and standard deviation of each of the TDP for every vowel is calculated and stored. Once the model parameters are estimated from the training module with 10-fold cross-validation, testing has been done using the model parameters. The obtained results are discussed in Sect. 4.

4 Result and Discussion

One of the main objectives of this paper is to establish the relationship of the proposed TDP with the height and position of the tongue during articulation which has been discussed in following sub-sections.

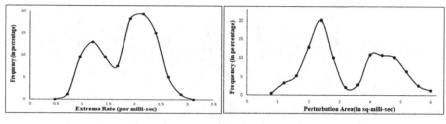

Fig. 9. Frequency distribution of PA and ER across Bangla vowels.

4.1 ER and PA

The frequency distribution of ER and PA across Bangla vowels are given in Fig. 9. It is evident from Fig. 9 that there are two distinct clusters for both the parameter value. Using the procedure as explained in 3.2 the final value of the cluster points are obtained. Table1 and Table 2 give the percentage of distribution of ER and PA respectively for Bangla vowels in each of the clusters along with the total cluster content. It is interesting to note from Table 1 that all the instances (100%) of /u/, /o/ and /ɔ/ go to Cluster 1 whereas the majority of the instances (81.55%) of /a/, /æ/, /e/, and /i/ go to Cluster-2.

Table 1. Distribution of vowels in clusters (in %) using ER.

Vowels	/u/	/o/	/ɔ/	/a/	/æ/	/e/	/i/
Cluster-1	100	100	100	19.92	6.53	21.53	19.85
Cluster-2	0	0	0	80.07	93.46	78.46	80.14

Table 2. Distribution of vowels in clusters (in %) for PA.

Vowels	/u/	/o/	/ɔ/	/a/	/æ/	/e/	/i/
Cluster-1	100	100	100	10.71	0	0	0
Cluster-2	0	0	0	89.29	100	100	100

Similarly, it can be observed from Table 2 that Cluster-1 contains /u/, /o/ and /ɔ/ whereas Cluster-2 contains /a/, /æ/, /e/, and /i/. Moreover, the presence of each of the vowel in their respective cluster is quite remarkable as indicated by the high classification percentage. The total recognition of Cluster-1 and Cluster-2 comes out to be 96.55% and 100% respectively. Besides 10.71% false inclusion of /a/ in Cluster-1, no such false inclusion is seen. Applying the analogy of the vowel groups as stated in Sect. 2.2, it can be stated that Cluster-1 represents back vowels while Cluster-2 represents front vowels. Hence we can conclude that ER denotes the position of the tongue hump i.e. back and front position of the tongue during articulation.

The average value of the ER of the Bangla vowels is given in Fig. 10. It is interesting to observe from Fig. 10. That the values of ER of the Bangla vowels gradually increase from /u/ to /i/. The decreasing value of ER towards back-to-front vowels corresponds well with the second formant frequency (F2) of the vowels [26].

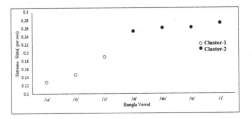

Fig. 10. Average value of ER for Bangla vowels.

Similarly Fig. 11 represents the plot of the average value of the PA which indicates that /u/, /o/ and /ɔ/ form one cluster and /a/, /æ/, /e/, and /i/ form another. Like ER, the values of the PA also gradually increase from /u/ to /i/ confirming its correspondence with the second formant frequency (F2). It is interesting to observe that Cluster-1(back vowels) shows a better accuracy rate than Cluster-2 (front vowels) for both ER and PA.

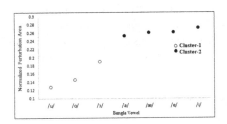

Fig. 11. Mean value of PA for Bangla vowels.

4.2 PPD and ZCR

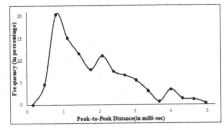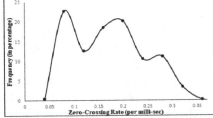

Fig. 12. Frequency distribution of PPD and ZCR across Bangla vowels.

Figure 12 gives the distribution of the PPD and ZCR of Bangla vowels. It is evident from the below figure that the given data have three clusters as indicated by the mode.

The same process of clustering and weighted Euclidean distance function have been applied on the PPD and ZCR values to get final mean and standard deviation of clusters.

Table 3 presents the percentage of distribution of Bangla vowels in each cluster. It is evident from Table 3 that Cluster-1 contains /u/ and /i/, Cluster-2 contains /o/, /e/ and part of /i/ and finally Cluster-3 contains /ɔ/, /a/ and /æ/. It has been observed that quite a percentage of vowel /i/ has been falsely included in Cluster-2. Similarly, apart from Cluster-2, vowel /o/ has been distributed into Cluster-1 and Cluster-3 also.

Table 3. Distribution of vowels in clusters (in %) using PPD.

Vowels	/u/	/o/	/ɔ/	/a/	/æ/	/e/	/i/
Cluster-1	92.59	27.54	0	0	0	9.62	60
Cluster-2	7.41	57.97	2	0	0	78.08	40
Cluster-3	0	14.49	98	100	100	12.30	0

Just like Table 3, Table 4 contains the content of each clusters using the same procedure described above. It is evident from Table 4 that Cluster-1 contains /u/ and /i/, Cluster-2 contains /o/ and /e/ and finally Cluster-3 contains /ɔ/, /a/ and /æ/. Moreover, intended vowel content in each of the clusters is more than 80%. The recognition rate of the intended vowel classes into their cluster is more than 93%. So, it can be assumed that based on the classification of the cluster, the grouping of the vowels is done correctly.

Table 4. Distribution of vowels in clusters based on percentage of ZCR.

Vowels	/u/	/o/	/ɔ/	/a/	/æ/	/e/	/i/
Cluster-1	92.54	1.41	1.37	0	0	8.97	81.48
Cluster-2	7.46	98.59	0	0	0	89.74	5.56
Cluster-3	0	0	98.63	100	100	1.28	12.96

The average value of PPD for each of vowels is given in Fig. 13. Figure 13 reflects the fact that the PPD values form three clusters just like position of Bangla vowels in the IPA chart which shows three divisions based on the tongue height i.e. close, close-mid and open. One can say that the position of Bangla vowel /ɔ/ as shown in the IPA chart indicates its position as open-mid but it has been found by plotting formant frequency in [26] the position of /ɔ/ is open and more closer to vowel /ɒ/ of the IPA chart. Apart from this it has also been observed from Fig. 13 that /a/ has the lowest PPD value whereas /u/ has the highest value which is quite opposite to the values of first formant frequency [F1] as shown in [25].

Figure 14 represents the average value of the ZCR across Bangla vowels. It is observed from the figure that ZCR clusters the vowels into three groups just like PPD. But here we can observe different scenario from Fig. 13. Here the values of /u/ and /i/

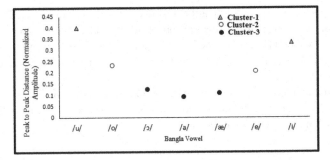

Fig. 13. Plot of average PPD of Bangla vowels.

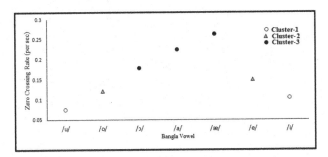

Fig. 14. Mean value of ZCR across Bangla vowels.

have lowest ZCR whereas vowel /æ/ has the largest one confirming its correspondence with first formant frequency [F1]. Using the same equivalence process as stated in the previous section we can conclude that both PPD and ZCR represent tongue height i.e. close, close-mid, and open.

4.3   Classification of Vowel

In the second part of the experiment we have conducted vowel recognition using TDP. The result has been enumerated below as confusion matrix.

Table 5. Confusion matrix of Bangla vowel using RF classifier.

	u	o	ɔ	a	æ	e	i
u	**100**	0	0	0	0	0	0
o	1.41	**95.77**	1.41	0	0	1.41	0
ɔ	0	1.18	**92.94**	4.71	0	1.18	0
a	0	0	5.95	**94.05**	0	0	0
æ	0	0	0	4	**94.67**	1.33	0
e	0	0	0.93	0	1.85	**92.59**	4.63
i	0	0	0	0	0	11.11	**88.89**

Table 5 represents the classification result of Bangla vowels using RF classifier. It is interesting to note that the recognition of all the individual vowels is more than 90% except /i/ which is 88.89%. The main reason for the low recognition rate of /i/ in comparison to others is due to the false classification of /i/ as /e/. The overall recognition rate is 93.93%.

The confusion matrix for recognition of Bangla vowel using MLP Classifier is given in Table 6. The overall recognition rate is 90%. The recognition rate is low due to misclassification of /u/ as /o/ and /e/ as /i/.

Table 6. Confusion matrix of Bangla vowel using MLP classifier.

	u	o	ɔ	a	æ	e	i
u	**88.46**	11.54	0	0	0	0	0
o	11.29	**87.1**	1.61	0	0	0	0
ɔ	0	5.56	**90.28**	4.17	0	0	0
a	0	0	3.57	**92.86**	3.57	0	0
æ	0	0	0	3.51	**92.98**	3.51	0
e	0	0	0	0	5.32	**82.98**	11.7
i	0	0	0	0	0	4.76	**95.24**

Table 7 represents the recognition of the vowels using NB classifier. The overall recognition rate is 82%. The main reason of the low accuracy of NB Classifier is that /o/ misclassified as /u/, /ɔ/ as /o/ or /a/ and /æ/ as /e/. But it is interesting to observe that the misclassified vowels get confused with its neighboring vowel only.

Table 7. Confusion matrix of Bangla vowel using NB classifier.

	u	o	ɔ	a	æ	e	i
u	**93.59**	6.41	0	0	0	0	0
o	17.74	**70.97**	11.29	0	0	0	0
ɔ	0	13.89	**75**	11.11	0	0	0
a	0	0	5.36	**83.93**	10.71	0	0
æ	0	0	0	3.51	**77.19**	19.3	0
e	0	0	0	0	1.06	**82.98**	15.96
i	0	0	0	0	0	14.29	**85.71**

Table 8 represents the recognition of the vowels using SVM classifier. The overall recognition rate is 82%. SVM classifier shows almost similar trend as NB classifier except the percentage of classification rate in each class. Here also /u/ is misclassified as /o/, /o/ is misclassified as /u/ and /ɔ/, /a/ has been mostly misclassified as /æ/, /æ/ has been mainly misclassified as /e/, /e/ is mostly misclassified as /i/ and similarly /i/ with /e/. Only incase of vowel /ɔ/ the two classifiers depicts slightly different picture when in

NB classifier /ɔ/ is misclassified as /o/ and /a/, SVM classifier misclassifies /ɔ /as /o/, /a/ and /u/ respectively.

Table 8. Confusion matrix of Bangla vowel using SVM classifier.

	u	o	ɔ	a	æ	e	i
u	**92.31**	7.69	0	0	0	0	0
o	14.52	**72.58**	11.29	0	0	1.61	0
ɔ	4.17	9.72	**73.61**	12.5	0	0	0
a	0	0	1.79	**87.5**	10.71	0	0
æ	0	0	0	5.26	**64.91**	29.82	0
e	0	0	0	0	3.19	**87.23**	9.57
i	0	0	0	0	0	11.9	**88.1**

5 Conclusion

Experimental findings show that four TDP play an important role in discriminating vowels of Bangla. Further we have been able to map those parameters with the oral cavity configuration during vowel production also. PA and ER map to the tongue position whereas PPD and ZCR map to the height of the tongue. The above-said mapping has been done by using the k-means clustering algorithm with the weighted Euclidean distance classifier. The RF, MLP, Bayes and SVM classification algorithm have been used for the training and classification of the recognition model. It has been seen that RF algorithm outperforms other classification algorithm using the TDP having recognition rate of 93.93%. In the future scope we will include cross lingual comparative study on vowel recognition using both time and frequency domain parameters.

References

1. Yu, Y.: Research on speech recognition technology and its application. In: International Conference on Computer Science and Electronics Engineering, 2012, pp. 306–309 (2012)
2. Tadeusiewicz, R.: Speech in human system interaction. In: 3rd International Conference on Human System Interaction, Rzeszow, 2010, pp. 2–13, https://doi.org/10.1109/HSI.2010.551 4597
3. Siniscalchi, S.M., Svendsen, T., Lee, C.: A bottom-up modular search approach to large vocabulary continuous speech recognition. IEEE Trans. Audio, Speech, Lang. Process. 21(4), pp. 786–797
4. Allen, J.B.: How do humans process and recognize speech? IEEE Trans. Speech Audio Process. 2(4), 567–577 (1994)
5. Cole, R.A., Yan, Y., Mak, B., Fanty, M., Bailey, T.: The contribution of consonants versus vowels to word recognition in fluent speech. In: IEEE Conference on Acoustics, Speech, and Signal Processing Conference Proceedings, pp. 853–856 vol. 2 (1996)

6. Mathad, V.C., Liss, J.M., Chapman, K., Scherer, N., Berisha, V.: Consonant-vowel transition models based on deep learning for objective evaluation of articulation. In: ACM Trans. Audio, Speech, Lang. Process. **31**, pp. 86–95, 202

7. Daqrouq, K., Tutunji, T.A.: Speaker identification using vowels features through a combined method of formants, wavelets, and neural network classifiers. Appl. Soft Comput. **27**, 231–239 (2015)

8. Panchanan, S., Saha, A., Kr. Datta, A.: Automatic spoken language identification for indian languages using relative abundance model (Ram). In: FRSM, 2017 pp. 271–276, Rourkela, India (2017)

9. Vlasenko, B., Prylipko, D., Philippou-H€ubner, D., Wendemuth, A.: Vowels formants analysis allows straightforward detection of high arousal acted and spontaneous emotions. In: Proceedings 12th Annual Conference International Speech Communication Association, 2011, pp. 1577– 1580 (2011)

10. Paulraj, M.P., Yaacob, S.B., Nazri, A., Kumar, S.: Classification of vowel sounds using MFCC and feed forward Neural Network. In: 5th International Colloquium on Signal Processing & Its Applications, 2009, pp. 59–62 (2009)

11. Kanda, H., Ogata, T., Takahashi, T., Komatani, K., Okuno, H.G.: Phoneme acquisition model based on vowel imitation using recurrent neural network. In: Proceedings of RSJ International Conference on Intelligent Robots and Systems, Kyoto, 2009, pp. 5388–5393 (2009)

12. Koolagudi, S., Shivakranthi, B., Rao, K.S., Ramteke, P.B.: Contribution of telugu vowels in identifying emotions. In: Proceedings International Conference Advances Pattern Recognition, pp. 1–6 (2015)

13. Nagy, Z., Vrba, K.: Noise-resistant feature extraction using 2D techniques. In: Proceedings Asia-Pacific Conference on Circuits and Systems, Singapore, pp. 397–400 (2002)

14. Aissa-El-Bey, A., Linh-Trung, N., Abed-Meraim, K., Belouchrani, A., Grenier, Y.: Underdetermined blind separation of nondisjoint sources in the time-frequency domain. IEEE Trans. Signal Process. **55**(3), 897–907 (2007)

15. Linh-Trung, N., Belouchrani, A., Abed-Meraim, K., Boashash, B.: Separating more sources than sensors using time-frequency distributions. EURASIP J. Appl. Signal Process. **17**, 2828–2847 (2005)

16. Yilmaz, O., Rickard, S.: Blind separation of speech mixtures via time-frequency masking. IEEE Trans. Signal Process. **52**(7), 1830–1847 (2004)

17. Barkat, B., Abed-Meraim, K.: Algorithms for blind components separation and extraction from the time-frequency distribution of their mixture. EURASIP J. Appl. Signal Process. **13**, 2025–2033 (2004)

18. Lim, T.Y., Yeh, R.A., Xu, Y., Do, M.N., Hasegawa-Johnson, M.: Time-frequency networks for audio super-resolution. In: 2018 IEEE International Conference on Acoustics, Speech and Signal Processing (ICASSP), Calgary, AB, 2018, pp. 646–650 (2018)

19. Jiaxing, Y., Kobayashi, T., Higuchi, T.: Vowel Recognition Based on FLAC Acoustic Features and Subspace Classifier. In: Proceedings of on Signal Processing, Beijing, 2010, pp. 530–533

20. "The World Factbook". www.cia.gov. Central Intelligence Agency

21. Gary, J., Rubino, C.: Facts about the world's languages: An encyclopedia of the world's major languages, past and present, pp.65–71. New York

22. Hammarström, H.: Linguistic diversity and language evolution. J. Lang. Evol. **1**(1), 19–29 (2016)

23. Bhattacharya, K.: Bengali Phonetic Reader, Central Institute of Indian Languages, (1999)

24. The International Phonetic Association, "Handbook of the International Phonetic Association", Cambridge University Press

25. Peterson, G.E., Barney, H.L.: Control Methods used in Study of Vowels. J. Acoust. Soc. Am. **24**(2), 175–184 (1952)

26. Basu, T., Saha, A.: Qualitative and quantitative classification of bangla vowel, year of pub. In: Proceedings of Oriental COCOSDA-2011, Taiwan, pp. 54–59 (2011)
27. Chowdhury, S., Datta, A.K., Chaudhuri, B.B.: Pitch detection algorithm using state phase analysis. J. Acous. Soc. Ind **28**(1–4), 247–250 (2020)
28. Eyben, F., et al.: The Geneva minimalistic acoustic parameter set (gemaps) for voice research and affective computing. IEEE Trans. Affect. Comput. **7**(2), 190–202 (2016). https://doi.org/ 10.1109/TAFFC.2015.2457417

Prosodic Interaction Models in a Conversation

Anastasia Gorbyleva[(✉)]

Diplomatic Academy of the Ministry of Foreign Affairs of the Russian Federation, 53/2, Build. 1 Ostozhenka St., Moscow 119992, Russian Federation
a.gorbyleva@dipacademy.ru

Abstract. Spoken dialogue systems are increasingly being developed to process the linguistic aspect of communication, yet they meet difficulties to capture the complex dynamics of social interaction. In particular, prosodic accommodation of conversational partners governed by the need for social approval has proved to enhance effectiveness of conversation. Providing automatic systems with the capacity to exhibit accommodation could improve their efficiency and make machines more likable and user-friendly. This article investigates the occurrence of mutual adaptation in human-human interaction, presenting the results on the dynamics of prosodic convergence and divergence in naturally occurring spoken dialogues by means of pitch and pitch range. The converging points are recurring lexemes – keywords produced by both speakers – showing evidence for thematic and prosodic unity of accommodation. Three prosodic interaction models are observed: convergence – divergence; convergence – intensified convergence; divergence – convergence. The three models of interaction show structural variance, convergence being their common feature. The results of the Mann-Whitney test show evidence that in the middle of a dyad the distinction in pitch between interlocutors is significantly less than at the end.

Keywords: Prosodic Accommodation · Interactional Linguistics · Convergence · Dialogue

1 Introduction

In human-human conversation, dialogue participants often adapt their manner of speaking to that of the other participants. This phenomenon manifests itself in different ways at the lexical, syntactic and phonetic levels. The result of the accommodation process is convergence, which manifests itself in the repetition of syntactic structures, lexical units and phonetic characteristics of the speech of two interlocutors in the process of dialogue. In its early days, Communication Accommodation Theory explained convergence in terms of the need for approval and likability and divergence in terms of strive for distinctiveness [14]. Later, cognitive function was introduced stating that speaker A converges to speaker B to facilitate comprehension and enforce effectiveness of communication [15].

In human-computer interaction, e.g. with spoken dialogue systems, people are also observed to adapt their manner of speaking in similar ways. However, this behavior is not always suitable for interaction with machines. Typically, users of dialogue systems,

A. Karpov et al. (Eds.): SPECOM 2023, LNAI 14338, pp. 380–388, 2023.
https://doi.org/10.1007/978-3-031-48309-7_31

when misunderstood, hyperarticulate, lower the speech rate, increase the loudness, insert pauses between the words, i.e. employ the strategy to increase intelligibility with other humans [11]. Unfortunately, this strategy doesn't work for a spoken dialogue system and in fact has the opposite effect elevating failures in human-machine communication.

Conversation is a two-party process, and as people adapt their speaking manner, the same adaptability skills would be expected from the spoken dialogue systems. However, at present, no dialogue system is available to process the complex dynamics of social interaction and, in particular, interpersonal prosodic accommodation, nor do any clear measures exist that quantify its dynamics [4]. Providing automatic systems with the capacity to exhibit accommodation could improve their efficiency. By converging speech manner to that of a human, a spoken dialogue system would become more similar to its interlocutor and thus would appear more likable.

However, natural conversation analysis yet needs to be improved, before introducing accommodation to automatic speech processing. Numerous studies have documented the phenomenon of phonetic convergence: the process by which speakers alter their speaking manner on some phonetic level mimicking that of their interlocutor. It has been observed at many levels including pause and utterance duration [7], vocal intensity [10], and vowel quality [2, 8]. Previous research on prosodic adaptation has seen laboratory experiments using the shadowing method [1, 6], repetitions while performing tasks according to the road map [12] and negotiations between two participants in computer games working from different computers [9]. However, the study of unprepared speech is a new and more difficult task of identifying the convergence of participants in a naturally occurring conversation without a preliminary structured discourse program.

The goal of this study is to find relevant signs of convergence of prosodic parameters based on thematic unity in a friendly conversation. We will focus on global (throughout the whole dialogue) prosodic features determined by the speakers' interaction. In the current study we will measure pitch and pitch range parameters correlated with three stages of conversation (beginning, middle, end).

2   Methodology

2.1   Data

The material under analysis is based on the dialogues of the Santa Barbara Corpus of Spoken American English [5]. The Corpus presents a large body of recorded conversations of naturally occurring spoken interaction from all over the United States and as a whole consists of 60 recordings approximately 20 min each. The majority of the recordings are a personal, face-to-face conversation between two or more people. The corpus is annotated according to the social factors of the interlocutors, such as gender, age, state of origin, educational level, occupation, and ethnicity (white, black, Chicano, Crow Indian, Hispanic). In order to preserve the anonymity of the interlocutors, personal names and any other information that could potentially lead to identification of an individual have been changed.

For this study 12 dialogues (24 speakers) were selected taking into account the balanced gender distribution in pairs: male - male, female - female, male - female. The duration of each dialogue is on average 20 min, which in total rounds to 240 min of recorded speech (four hours). Speakers represent different regions of the United States, overwhelmingly West Coast (California - 11 speakers), Northeast (Montana - 2 speakers), Northwest (Wisconsin - 4 speakers, Idaho - 3 speakers), South (Louisiana - 2 speakers) and East Coast (Massachusetts - 2 speakers). The speakers are predominantly white, although one African American, three Native Americans, and two Hispanics are also represented.

2.2 Procedure

The experimental research comprises three steps:

1 compiling a corpus of recurring lexemes;
2 electronic-acoustic measurements;
3 statistical processing.

For the preliminary research (step 1), it was necessary to perform a verbal analysis of transcriptions of dialogues compiled by the authors of the corpus. This stage consisted in the search for recurring keywords - lexemes present in the output of the first interlocutor (A) repeated in the response turns of the second interlocutor (B). The method of verbal text analysis was applied to the selected corpus (12 dialogues, 24 speakers) with a total duration of four hours. Within each dialogue, at the beginning, middle and end of the dialogue, we identified recurring lexemes associated with the topic of the conversation. The choice of these lexical units is justified by the fact that both interlocutors produce them at short intervals during the dialogue. In each dialogue, from 8 to 11 recurring words were identified, with a total of 107 lexemes.

2.3 Measurements

In step 2 we intend to find evidence of mutual adaptation, determine the degree of convergence, as well as to identify and classify the models of interaction in the dialogue. The following prosodic characteristics of lexemes were determined and measured by means of Praat [3]:

- mean pitch (Herz, Hz);
- minimum pitch (Hz);
- maximum pitch (Hz);
- pitch range (semitone, st). The pitch range shows the ratio between the maximum and minimum pitch within each word. It was calculated using the following equation:

$$n = 12\log_2\left(\frac{f_n}{f_0}\right) \tag{1}$$

Here, f_n is the maximum pitch (F0 $_{max}$); f_0 is the minimum pitch (F0 $_{min}$); n is the pitch range value.

In overall, the narrow corpus consists of 642 scores of pitch (Hz) and 214 scores of pitch range (st), in total, the narrow corpus amounts to 856 numerical values.

For statistical processing (step 3) the Mann-Whitney test was run, in order to identify statistically significant differences between the three groups (beginning, middle and end of the dialogue). Statistical procedures were performed in JAMOVI program [16].

3   Results

In this section we will look at the data to identify the interaction models in the conversation. To find evidence of convergence, we measured the delta, i.e. the distance, between interlocutors in terms of pitch and pitch range within every recurring lexeme. By comparing the deltas in the dyads under analysis we can observe three interaction models:

1. Model 1: convergence – divergence. Prosodic features of two interlocutors converge towards the middle of conversation, then they diverge towards the end.
2. Model 2: convergence – intensified convergence. Prosodic features of two interlocutors converge towards the middle of conversation and go on converging towards the end.
3. Model 3: divergence – convergence. Prosodic features of two interlocutors diverge towards the middle of conversation, then converge towards the end.

3.1   Model 1: Convergence – Divergence

The analysis of the delta in pitch and pitch range reveals that in four out of 12 analyzed dyads the pitch dynamics of the two interlocutors go towards each other, their pitch parameters converge towards the middle of the dialogue, then by the end of the dialogue the values diverge, going back to interlocutors' individual characteristics.

For instance, in dialogue 7 the mean value of the delta between the interlocutors demonstrates that from the beginning to the middle of the conversation, the interlocutors' parameters get closer, the difference between them decreases (from 2.8 st to 1.9 st), which is a manifestation of convergence. By the end of the conversation, the speakers of dialogue 7 show signs of divergence, the difference between them increases to 6.2 st. The dynamics is repeated at the pitch level (see Fig. 1).

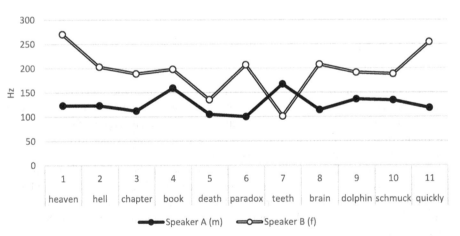

Fig. 1. Model 1: dynamics of pitch (Hz) variability in dialogue 7 (male – female).

3.2   Model 2: Convergence – Intensified Convergence

In four out of 12 dyads we can observe model 2 when the interlocutors' parameters approach in the middle of the dialogue, and this process intensifies towards the end of the conversation. In this case average delta indicators are lower than the initial ones, and the final indicators are even lower than the middle ones.

For example, our findings show that in dialogue 6 the delta between the interlocutors in terms of pitch range changes according to the development of the conversation: there is a significant convergence from the beginning to the middle of the conversation (from 12.9 st to 4.9 st) and an even greater convergence from the middle to the end of the conversation (from 4.9 st to 1.8 st). The average pitch level of recurring lexemes also shows a high degree of convergence; we can see that the speakers step by step repeat the pitch level of their interlocutor (see Fig. 2).

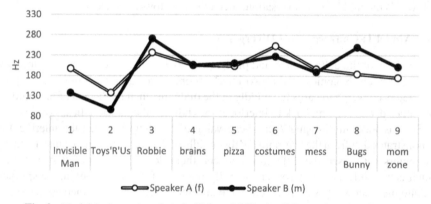

Fig. 2.   Model 2: dynamics of pitch (Hz) variability in dialogue 6 (male – female).

3.3   Model 3: Divergence – Convergence

For four out of 12 analyzed dialogues, the third model of interaction is observed, in which the interlocutors' parameters diverge in the middle of the dialogue, and converge again towards the end. For example, when analyzing dialogue 12, the mean values of the delta of pitch range allow us to conclude that there is an insignificant degree of divergence in the middle of the conversation (from 2.3 st to 2.9 st) and convergence towards the end of the conversation (from 2.9 st to 1.6 st).

The dynamics of interaction between interlocutors on the level of pitch confirms the conclusions based on the pitch range parameter. The divergence in the middle of the conversation is observable over the values for the word *cars*, by the end of the conversation there is a gradual convergence of values for the words *firestone, Samurai, insurance* (see Fig. 3).

One particularly important factor is that in half of the dialogues there is synchrony, or step-by-step accordance. The trajectory of the pitch movement of one partner fluctuates,

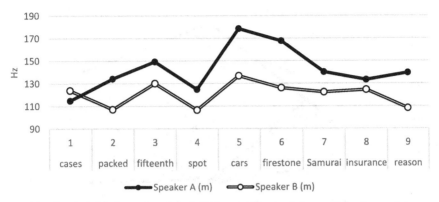

Fig. 3. Model 3: dynamics of pitch (Hz) variability in dialogue 12 (male – male).

rising and falling, and the trajectory of the second partner simultaneously repeats these dynamics, which is indicative of a parallel development of the conversation.

To examine the degree of convergence, we calculated the delta between the mean pitch values of Speaker A and Speaker B for each recurring lexeme. The delta of the mean pitch values at the beginning of the conversation ranges from 0 to 7 semitones, with mean delta being 3 st. In the middle of a conversation, on average, the delta is smaller, declining to 2 st. At the end of the conversation, the delta between the two interlocutors increases significantly and amounts to 5 st (see Table 1). This indicates that, on average, the tendency towards the pitch convergence within keywords in the middle of a conversation is dominant.

Table 1. Delta of the pitch (mean) between two interlocutors for 12 dialogues (st).

Dialogue №	Beginning	Middle	End
1	2	0	8
2	1	1	9
3	4	1	2
4	4	1	2
5	6	4	9
6	2	0	2
7	7	3	9
8	0	2	6
9	2	6	3
10	1	1	0
11	6	6	6
12	2	4	3
Mean	**3**	**2**	**5**

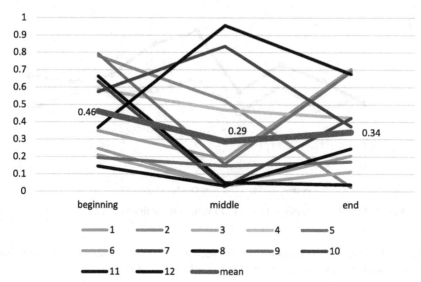

Fig. 4. Dynamics of pitch distance between interlocutors for random fragments in 12 conversations.

The results of the Mann-Whitney test support our conclusions. The test was run with the variable "delta of the mean pitch values between interlocutors" and the factor "phase of the dialogue" (categories – beginning, middle, end). The results revealed a significant difference ($p = .027$) in the pitch delta between interlocutors in the middle and the end of the dialogues, proving that in the middle of a dyad the distinction in pitch between interlocutors is significantly less than at the end.

In order to verify the obtained conclusions about the dynamics of convergence / divergence between the two interlocutors, we extracted random fragments up to 10 s from the beginning, the middle and the end of 12 dialogues. For every fragment mean pitch was measured and again the delta between speakers' values was calculated. As seen in Fig. 4, the dynamics for random speech fragments replicates the dynamics for keywords: on average, the difference between speakers' pitch levels decreases towards the middle of dialogues (convergence) and increases towards the end (divergence).

4   Conclusions and Discussion

Interactive technologies have been developed with the assumption that the user and the computer take turns in a question-answer based interaction which fails to capture the complex dynamics involved in social interactions that require a set of not only linguistic, but also cognitive and social skills. In particular, it has long been observed that such phenomena as prosodic accommodation, turn-takings and overlaps require coordination and adaptation on the part of conversational partners [13].

In this study, we find evidence that prosodic convergence is correlated with thematic unity of conversation. We established three interaction models (convergence – divergence; convergence – intensified convergence; divergence – convergence). Despite the structural variance of models, convergence is a common feature for each of them. The most characteristic dynamics of bilateral verbal interaction is that speakers converge, reducing the interval of pitch distances. Finally, our data shows tendency toward prosodic convergence in the middle and divergence at the end of a conversation.

One possible explanation for this is that all participants in the dialogue express their mutual desire for agreement and understanding (through convergence). At the same time, they strive to emphasize distinctiveness and reinforce one's positive sense of identity (through divergence). Both strategies appear in all the 12 analyzed conversations at different stages of conversation. This corresponds to the spontaneous essence of naturally occurring speech, in contrast to controlled experiments, for example, the coordination of players in computer games, aimed at performing one pragmatic task and limited by the conditions of the experiment.

Thus, we assume that lack of convergence on the part of the automatic systems in the human-computer interaction hinders the perception of such communication as natural. In order to facilitate man-machine communication, spoken dialogue systems have to reckon with dynamicity of human interaction, including prosodic convergence governed by the need for social approval. The findings of the present research, including prosodic interaction models, might contribute to this purpose.

References

1. Babel, M.: Evidence for phonetic and social selectivity in spontaneous phonetic imitation. J. Phon. **40**, 177–189 (2012)
2. Babel, M.: Phonetic and Social Selectivity in Speech Accommodation: Doctoral dissertation. University of California, Berkeley (2009)
3. Boersma, P., Weenink, D.: Praat: doing phonetics by computer (Version 6.0.14). http://www.praat.org/. Accessed 14 Feb 2022
4. De Looze, C., Scherer, S., Vaughan, B., Campbell, N.: Investigating automatic measurements of prosodic accommodation and its dynamics in social interaction. Speech Commun. **58**, 11–34 (2014)
5. Du Bois, J.W., et al.: Santa Barbara Corpus of Spoken American English, Parts 1–4. Linguistic Data Consortium, Philadelphia (2005)
6. Goldinger, S.: Echoes of echoes? An episodic theory of lexical access. Psychol. Rev. **105**, 251–279 (1998)
7. Jaffe, J., Feldstein, S.: Rhythms of Dialogue. Academic Press, New York (1970)
8. Kholiavin, P., Menshikova, A., Kachkovskaia, T., Kocharov, D.: Estimating social distance between interlocutors with MFCC-based acoustic models for vowels. In: Ekštein, K., Pártl, F., Konopík, M. (eds) Text, Speech, and Dialogue. TSD 2021. Lecture Notes in Computer Science, vol. 12848. Springer, Cham (2021). https://doi.org/10.1007/978-3-030-83527-9_47
9. Levitan, R., Hirschberg, J.: Measuring acoustic-prosodic entrainment with respect to multiple levels and dimensions. In: Interspeech, pp. 3081–3084 (2011)
10. Natale, M.: Convergence of mean vocal intensity in dyadic communication as a function of social desirability. J. Pers. Soc. Psychol. **32**(5), 790–804 (1975)
11. Oviatt, S., Bernard, J., Levow, G.-A.: Linguistic adaptations during spoken and multimodal error resolution. Lang. Speech **41**(3–4), 419–442 (1998)
12. Pardo, J.S.: On phonetic convergence during conversational interaction. J. Acoust. Soc. Am. **119**(4), 2382–2393 (2006)

A. Gorbyleva

13. Shevchenko, T., Gorbyleva, A.: Temporal concord in speech interaction: overlaps and interruptions in spoken American English. In: Karpov, A., Potapova, R. (eds) Speech and Computer. SPECOM 2020. Lecture Notes in Computer Science, vol. 12335. Springer, Cham (2020). https://doi.org/10.1007/978-3-030-60276-5_47
14. Street, R. Jr., Giles, H.: Speech accommodation theory: a social cognitive approach to language and speech behavior. In: Social Cognition and Communication, pp. 193–226. Sage Publications, Beverly Hills (1982)
15. Thakerar, J.N., Giles, H., Cheshire, J.: Psychological and linguistic parameters of speech accommodation theory. Adv. Soc. Psychol. Lang. **205**, 205–255 (1982)
16. The jamovi project. jamovi (Version 1.2) (2020). https://www.jamovi.org. Accessed 20 Apr 2022

Natural Language Processing

Development and Research of Dialogue Agents with Long-Term Memory and Web Search

Kirill Apanasovich⬤, Olesia Makhnytkina^(✉)⬤, and Yuri Matveev⬤

ITMO University, Saint Petersburg 197101, Russian Federation
{apan.kirill,yunmatveev,makhnytkina}@itmo.ru

Abstract. This paper describes the training process of neural network that can extract additional knowledge from the Internet and long-term memory with the goal to improve the quality of generated dialogue responses. Modern language models, due to their large size and high-quality data, can generate meaningful texts, including dialogues with other speakers. Meanwhile, their knowledge is frozen in time by the data they were trained on. Without re-training, such models are not able to acquire new relevant knowledge. We propose one of the possible solutions to this problem, in which the neural network model will be able to use the knowledge received from the Internet and long-term memory to generate dialogue responses. Using these methods we improved BLEU-1 metric by 43% and BLEU-2 metric by 45% on Toloka Persona Chat Rus dataset.

Keywords: Internet search · Long-term memory · Knowledge extraction · Dialogue agent

1 Introduction

In the last few years, significant progress has been made in the field of dialogue agents using modern neural network models [18] and having many learning parameters, which in some cases reaches 175 billion parameters [16]. Such models are trained on large amounts of data that makes them able to generate meaningful texts. However, the knowledge of such models is frozen in time, as without further training they will not be able to obtain new relevant information.

To solve this problem, the neural network model can be trained to use information from the Internet. One such solution is the SeeKeR [15]. This model is based on a modular architecture, in which several tasks are executed sequentially by the same model, and the output after one task is used in the input on the next. The SeeKeR model solves the generating a search query, extracting useful knowledge from texts obtained from the Internet and generating a reply tasks.

Using this approach, the models outperform previous solutions in terms of using relevant and reliable information in their responses. On the other hand, the model was trained to conduct dialogue only in English and it is not able to use the long-term memory module. For this reason, we developed a model with a similar architecture but trained to generate dialogue responses using both the knowledge from the web search and long-term memory. In addition, we investigated the Fusion-in-Decoder mechanism (FiD) [5] in the problems of extracting relevant knowledge and generating responses, while in the original model it was used only for knowledge extraction.

With these methods, we implemented a model that can generate dialogue responses in Russian and can get relevant information from different sources. Our best model with 737 million trainable parameters shows improvement in BLEU-1 metric by 43% and BLEU-2 metric by 45% on Toloka Persona Chat Rus dataset. It also shows that using Fusion-in-Decoder method in dialogue response generation step provides a small improvement in BLEU-1 metric by 6% and BLEU-2 metric by 3% compared to the same model without it.

2   Related Work

Open-Domain Dialogue Models. This paper is based on the task of dialogue modelling. There are many different models for it that were created earlier. According to the method of creating a dialogue response, models can be either retrieval or generative. Based on the input context, retrieval models determine the best answer from the candidates available in their database [12,13]. Generative models sequentially generate token by token, with each new generated token added to the end of the input context [12]. Alternatively, a hybrid approach can be used that uses both ranking and generative models [10].

Among generative models, there may be models with a relatively small number of parameters such as DialoGPT [24] with 762 million parameters or TransferTransfo [19] with 124 million parameters. To achieve better results, larger models can be used, for example, Meena [1] with 2.6 billion parameters or BlenderBot [14] with 9.1 billion parameters. There are also models that were made according to a multi-module architecture. In the P^2 model [9], the Receiver module works with the personas of the speakers, and the transmitter module is responsible for generating responses. Another example is the Adapter-bot model [8], where the generated response depends on the dialogue context and the meta-knowledge added to it. To do this, using the dialogue manager, an adapter layer is defined that generates a response. In the meantime, it has been shown that large pre-trained [22] models in zero-shot mode can generate dialogue responses with similar results to smaller models, that were fine-tuned for this task.

Models Using Knowledge from the Internet. In the task of using additional knowledge from the Internet, based on the SeeKeR model, a large model BlenderBot 3 [16] with 175 billion parameters was developed. This model has a module which decides whether to use web search or not. In addition, knowledge from the Internet can receive Sparrow model [4], that was trained to use web search with the help of human judgements. Lamda model [17] in order to get additional knowledge was trained to call an external information retrieval system that returns snippets of content from the Internet. All these models have been trained to communicate with the user. Another example is the WebGPT [11], but it is used for the Question-Answering task.

Models Using Knowledge from Long-Term Memory. In addition to the Internet, the source of knowledge can be its own long-term memory. For the first time this mechanism was used in the BlenderBot 2 model [20]. Its necessity was justified by the fact that the dialogue models showed good results on short dialogues but were unable to memorize long dialogues. In the already mentioned BlenderBot 3, this mechanism is implemented in such a way that during the dialogue the model can remember new facts about its speaker and to remember facts about itself. Just like with web search, the BlenderBot 3 model has a module that decides whether long-term memory should be accessed or not. A similar to BlenderBot 2 memory mechanism was implemented in the PLATO-LTM [21].

3   Methods

3.1   Overview of Datasets

There are 4 datasets that were used during fine-tuning in this paper.

Toloka Persona Chat Rus[1]. Dataset of 10013 dialogues in Russian. It contains profiles describing a speaker's persona and dialogues between them. In each dialogue, each speaker is assigned his persona in the form of 5 short sentences, for example, "I draw", "I live abroad" or "I have a snake". In total, 1505 different personas are represented in this dataset.

Dataset collection took place in 2 stages. On the first stage with the help of crowdworkers, personas were collected containing information about a speaker, his hobbies, profession, family, and life events. Of these, those that are best suited for dialogue were selected. At the second stage, the participants were asked to play the role of a person described by one of these profiles and communicate with each other. The purpose of each dialogue was to learn more about each other and talk about yourself. The received dialogues were checked by other performers.

Wizard of Internet [7]. A dataset of 9633 dialogues that was collected to teach neural network models to use Internet search. To do this, the speakers were paired to conduct a dialogue with each other. The former can use the Internet search, while the latter does not, but he has an assigned persona that describes his interests. The purpose of the dialogue is to discuss these assigned interests. This approach is explained by the fact that, according to the authors' assumptions, the dialogue between a human and a neural network will take place in a similar form: the conversation will be focused on the interests of a human, and the bot will use a search engine to find out details about them.

---

[1] https://toloka.ai/datasets.

The dialogue can be started by either of the two interlocutors. If the first one starts it, then he is recommended to start with an introduction that meets the interests of the second. For example, if he knows that the second interlocutor is interested in tennis, then he can take the latest news about tennis and start with an interesting point found among these news. If the dialogue is started by a person with a person, then his goal is to communicate more based on their interests, for example, in this case they could communicate on the topic of tennis. The structure of the dataset includes: dialogues, search queries and lists of sentences received from the Internet for these queries. This dataset is presented in English. For further training of the model, all his remarks were translated into Russian. For this, a model-translator Opus-mt[2] was used.

Sberquad [3]. Dataset of sets of questions and answers. In addition to them, there is a context in the form of several sentences, such that inside one of them is presented the answer to the question. The context was collected from Wikipedia pages, and questions and answers were formed manually in such a way that the answer to the question must be contained in the context. In total, the dataset contains 73,000 questions.

Miracl [23]. Dataset with questions and answers to them. Each question is accompanied by a set of documents, some of which are marked as those where there is a correct answer, and one where there is no answer to the question. In total, the dataset contains 5935 questions and 47021 documents in Russian.

3.2   Model Architecture

The model operation process is shown in the Fig. 1. In this process were used a generative language model which is based on Encoder-Decoder transformer architecture. All tasks are performed sequentially by one model:

Search Query Generation. At this stage the dialogue history and persona if it exists are fed to the model. Model has to generate a search query. With this query will be received a text from the Internet in the future. On the other hand, there is a chance that the model will decide that the search is not needed. In this case, a special token will be generated that indicates that the search is not needed, and therefore the next two steps are skipped. The Wizard of Internet dataset was used to train the model on this task. Since this dataset was translated into Russian automatically, it is used only in this task.

Long-Term Memory and Candidates Ranking. With the help of web search, obtaining highly specialized knowledge can be difficult. Also, this knowledge may be inaccurate. In this regard, long-term memory was used. In further experiments, knowledge related to speech technologies was collected in it. The

---

[2] https://huggingface.co/Helsinki-NLP/opus-mt-tc-big-en-zle.

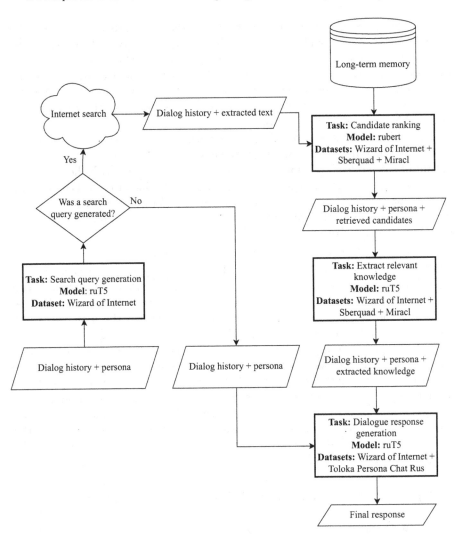

Fig. 1. The process of generating a response to a model that uses the Internet as a source of new knowledge.

data inside the memory can be extended, but during the dialogue it remains static.

A large amount of text can be received from the Internet and with addition of long-term memory knowledge, there may not be enough computing resources to use the model after training. Therefore, for the pre-selection of relevant knowledge, a retrieval model based on the ruBERT-base[3] model was trained. This retrieval model replicates the Dense Passage Retrieval [6]. The whole text are

---

[3] https://huggingface.co/sberbank-ai/ruBert-base.

splitted into a list of candidates, where the candidate in this case can be either a single sentence or a paragraph. Next, the dialogue history and each candidate are fed to the model separately. Received from the model embeddings are used then to calculate a dot product between the dialogue history embeddings and the candidate embeddings, which presents the similarity score of the dialogue history and each candidate. Thus, the N candidates that have the greatest score are used later in the dialogue model.

Since the candidates are processed separately from the context, the candidates' embeddings from long-term memory will always be the same at the output of the model. Therefore, in long-term memory, along with the initial text of candidates, they are assigned their embeddings obtained from this model. The datasets were used to train the retrieval model are Wizard of Internet, Sberquad and Miracl. All of them are containing questions, answers, and the candidates where answers are presented.

Extracting Relevant Knowledge. Here the dialogue history, persona if it exists and a set of retrieved candidates obtained earlier are fed into the model as inputs. For Encoder-Decoder models, the Fusion-in-Decoder method can be used. With this method each candidate are concatenated with the dialogue history and persona and processed inside the Encoder block independently from other candidates. The Decoder block works with the concatenation of all outputs from the Encoder. This method is particularly effective when the size of candidates is too large to submit them all together to the model. In this task Sberquad, Miracl and Wizard of Internet datasets were used for learning. In addition to it, the dataset of dialogues in Russian language Toloka Persona Chat Rus was used. Following this [2] solution, the entities are retrieved from the replies, that are used as knowledge. The target knowledge here are those entities, that are presented both in the dialogue history and the target response.

Dialogue Response Generation. In the final task the dialogue history, persona and knowledge gained on the previous step are used as the input of the model. In this step Wizard of Internet and Toloka Persona Chat Rus datasets were used. This problem can be solved by the usual method, feeding the combination of dialogue history, persona and knowledge to the model. Another way would be to use the Fusion-in-Decoder method like in the extracting relevant knowledge task. Given the specificity of this method, only the most recent response from the dialogue history will be used as context, and all previous replies will be used as candidates.

4   Experiments

Two pretrained models were used for the experiments: ruT5-base[4] and ruT5-large[5]. It is an Encoder-Decoder model with the same architecture but different

---

[4] https://huggingface.co/sberbank-ai/ruT5-base.
[5] https://huggingface.co/sberbank-ai/ruT5-large.

Table 1. Description of the special tokens.

Token name	Description
user1 persona	Token is listed before the first speaker's persona
user2 persona	Token is listed before the second speaker's persona
user1 reply	Token is specified before the reply of the first speaker
user2 reply	Token is specified before the reply of the second speaker
knowledge info	Token specified before the extracted knowledge
no knowledge	Token is specified when the model has not found a relevant knowledge
no search query	Token is specified when the model has decided not to use web-search
do search	Token is specified in the input where the model has to generate a search query
do knowledge	Token is specified in the input where the model has to extract a relevant knowledge
do response	Token is specified in the input where the model has to generate a reply
search result	When a model generates a search query, the token must be first in the answer
knowledge result	When a model extracts relevant knowledge, the token must be first in the answer
response result	When a model generates a reply, the token must be first in the answer

configuration of some hyperparameters. In particular, ruT5-base model has 12 layers of Encoder and Decoder blocks, with 222 million learning parameters. In ruT5-large model, the Encoder and Decoder blocks consist of 24 layers, and the number of parameters reaches 737 million. Both models have 32,101 tokens.

Special tokens have been added to separate the tasks from each other and individual context elements, the purpose of which is specified in the Table 1. The last three special tokens were used due to the fact that in experiments conducted without them, both models often confused the tasks with each other and in the end the results were significantly worse.

The comparison also involved models who were trained to generate a response by their input dialogue history and persona. In fact, these models perform only the last task described earlier and without the use of additional knowledge. Such models have been trained based on ruT5-large and rugpt3-large-based-on-gpt2[6], which is a Decoder-model with 760 million parameters.

All models were fine-tuned on 1 RTX 3090ti GPU. For ruT5-large model were used the gradient accumulation technique with 64 accumulation steps. Here were

---

[6] https://huggingface.co/sberbank-ai/rugpt3large_based_on_gpt2.

used the AdamW optimizer with the linear warmup of 100 steps and a maximum learning rate of 1e–5. The whole training process on 2 epochs took about 36 h.

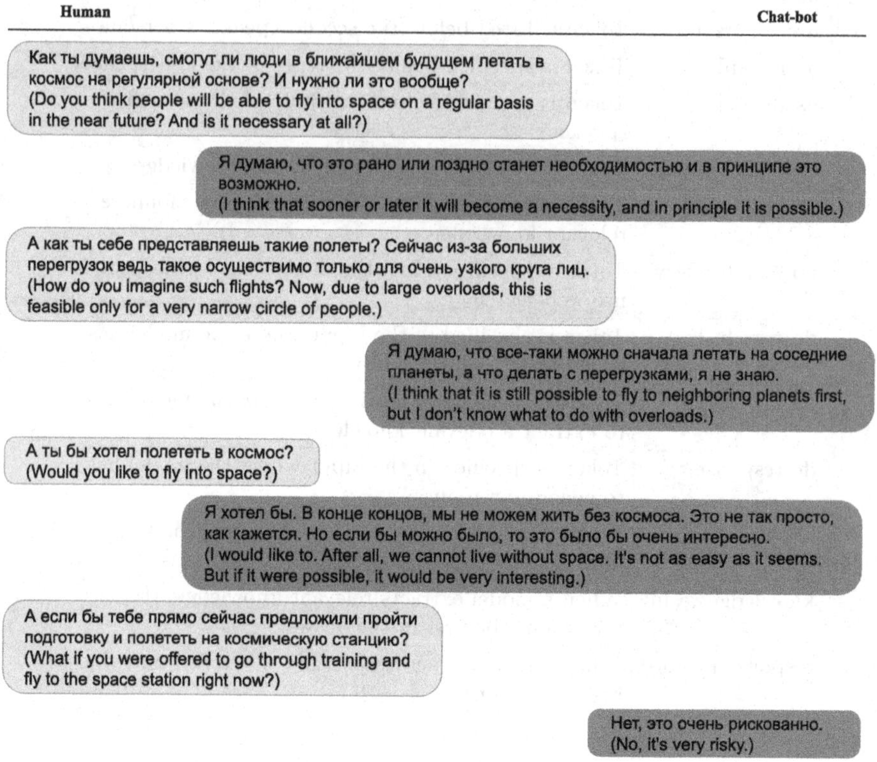

Human		Chat-bot

Как ты думаешь, смогут ли люди в ближайшем будущем летать в космос на регулярной основе? И нужно ли это вообще?
(Do you think people will be able to fly into space on a regular basis in the near future? And is it necessary at all?)

Я думаю, что это рано или поздно станет необходимостью и в принципе это возможно.
(I think that sooner or later it will become a necessity, and in principle it is possible.)

А как ты себе представляешь такие полеты? Сейчас из-за больших перегрузок ведь такое осуществимо только для очень узкого круга лиц.
(How do you imagine such flights? Now, due to large overloads, this is feasible only for a very narrow circle of people.)

Я думаю, что все-таки можно сначала летать на соседние планеты, а что делать с перегрузками, я не знаю.
(I think that it is still possible to fly to neighboring planets first, but I don't know what to do with overloads.)

А ты бы хотел полететь в космос?
(Would you like to fly into space?)

Я хотел бы. В конце концов, мы не можем жить без космоса. Это не так просто, как кажется. Но если бы можно было, то это было бы очень интересно.
(I would like to. After all, we cannot live without space. It's not as easy as it seems. But if it were possible, it would be very interesting.)

А если бы тебе прямо сейчас предложили пройти подготовку и полететь на космическую станцию?
(What if you were offered to go through training and fly to the space station right now?)

Нет, это очень рискованно.
(No, it's very risky.)

Fig. 2. Example of model chatting with a human. Green boxes of the left are the human's replies and blue boxes are model's replies. (Color figure online)

To compare models, perplexity, BLEU-1, BLEU-2 and F1 metrics are used. For F1 metric in the context of dialogue, precision is the fraction of words in the predicted response that are contained in the gold response, and recall is the fraction of words in the gold response that were in the predicted response. The Table 2 shows the comparison of models with each other. The results for each model were gotten using Toloka Persona Chat Rus dataset. For models that use Internet search and long-term memory, separate results are calculated using the FiD method when generating replica and without it. In addition, the results of the original SeeKeR model have been added to the table. But the results cannot be fully compared as this model works only on English, while others work on Russian.

The Table 3 shows the model results for each task. They show that the task of learning is the simplest for the model. This is explained by the fact that this

Table 2. Comparison of models without obtaining additional knowledge and with obtaining through an Internet search and a long-term memory. In cases when the FiD method was used while generating the reply, metrics were provided separately for each model that uses Internet search.

Model name	ppl ↓	F1 ↑	BLEU-1 ↑	BLEU-2 ↑
rugpt3-large-based-on-gpt2	9,48	–	0,22	0,20
ruT5-large	13,64	–	0,23	0,11
ruT5-base with external knowledge	10,33	24,8	0,31	0,28
+ *FiD in response*	10,34	23,8	0,31	0,27
ruT5-large with external knowledge	10,33	26,3	0,31	0,28
+ *FiD in response*	**8,86**	**27,1**	**0,33**	**0,29**
SeeKeR [15]	8,60	24,5	–	–

Table 3. Model results for different tasks.

Model name	Search task		Knowledge task		Response task	
	BLEU-1/2	ppl	BLEU-1/2	ppl	BLEU-1/2	ppl
t5-base with internet	0,35/0,20	9,88	0,72/0,66	1,48	0,31/0,28	10,33
+ *FiD in response*	0,35/0,20	11,25	0,68/0,60	1,53	0,31/0,27	10,34
t5-large with internet	**0,35/0,19**	**9,79**	0,72/0,66	1,47	0,31/0,28	10,33
+ *FiD in response*	0,34/0,17	9,78	**0,75/0,69**	**1,48**	**0,33/0,29**	**8,864**

task was meant as a task of copying - from the set of candidates it was necessary only to copy the necessary information. There is no need to generate new text.

The Fig. 2 shows a fragment of a dialogue with one of the resulting models based on the ruT5-large model.

5 Conclusion

In this work, we presented a model that can use the search on the Internet and a data stored in a long-term memory in order to obtain relevant knowledge from them and use it when generating a dialogue response. The results show that such a solution is superior to conversational language models, which generate a reply only depending on the existing dialogue history and the speakers' personas, if they are given.

Dividing the whole process into subtasks also allows us to add new modules or remove unnecessary ones. For example, there is a possibility to remove a long-term memory module if there is no need to receive and store highly specialized knowledge.

Acknowledgment. The research was financially supported by the Russian Science Foundations (project 22-11-00128).

References

1. Adiwardana, D., et al.: Towards a human-like open-domain chatbot. arXiv preprint arXiv:2001.09977 (2020)
2. Adolphs, L., Shuster, K., Urbanek, J., Szlam, A., Weston, J.: Reason first, then respond: modular generation for knowledge-infused dialogue. arXiv preprint arXiv:2111.05204 (2021)
3. Efimov, P., Chertok, A., Boytsov, L., Braslavski, P.: SberQuAD – Russian reading comprehension dataset: description and analysis. In: Arampatzis, A., et al. (eds.) CLEF 2020. LNCS, vol. 12260, pp. 3–15. Springer, Cham (2020). https://doi.org/10.1007/978-3-030-58219-7_1
4. Glaese, A., et al.: Improving alignment of dialogue agents via targeted human judgements. arXiv preprint arXiv:2209.14375 (2022)
5. Izacard, G., Grave, E.: Leveraging passage retrieval with generative models for open domain question answering. arXiv preprint arXiv:2007.01282 (2020)
6. Karpukhin, V., et al.: Dense passage retrieval for open-domain question answering. arXiv preprint arXiv:2004.04906 (2020)
7. Komeili, M., Shuster, K., Weston, J.: Internet-augmented dialogue generation. arXiv preprint arXiv:2107.07566 (2021)
8. Lin, Z., Madotto, A., Bang, Y., Fung, P.: The adapter-bot: all-in-one controllable conversational model. In: Proceedings of the AAAI Conference on Artificial Intelligence, vol. 35, pp. 16081–16083 (2021)
9. Liu, Q., et al.: You impress me: dialogue generation via mutual persona perception. arXiv preprint arXiv:2004.05388 (2020)
10. Matveev, Y., Makhnytkina, O., Posokhov, P., Matveev, A., Skrylnikov, S.: Personalizing hybrid-based dialogue agents. Mathematics 10(24), 4657 (2022)
11. Nakano, R., et al.: WebGPT: browser-assisted question-answering with human feedback. arXiv preprint arXiv:2112.09332 (2021)
12. Posokhov, P., Apanasovich, K., Matveeva, A., Makhnytkina, O., Matveev, A.: Personalizing dialogue agents for Russian: retrieve and refine. In: 2022 31st Conference of Open Innovations Association (FRUCT), pp. 245–252. IEEE (2022)
13. Posokhov, P., Matveeva, A., Makhnytkina, O., Matveev, A., Matveev, Y.: Personalizing retrieval-based dialogue agents. In: Prasanna, S.R.M., Karpov, A., Samudravijaya, K., Agrawal, S.S. (eds.) International Conference on Speech and Computer, pp. 554–566. Springer, Heidelberg (2022). https://doi.org/10.1007/978-3-031-20980-2_47
14. Roller, S., et al.: Recipes for building an open-domain chatbot. arXiv preprint arXiv:2004.13637 (2020)
15. Shuster, K., Komeili, M., Adolphs, L., Roller, S., Szlam, A., Weston, J.: Language models that seek for knowledge: modular search & generation for dialogue and prompt completion. arXiv preprint arXiv:2203.13224 (2022)
16. Shuster, K., et al.: Blenderbot 3: a deployed conversational agent that continually learns to responsibly engage. arXiv preprint arXiv:2208.03188 (2022)
17. Thoppilan, R., et al.: Lamda: language models for dialog applications. arXiv preprint arXiv:2201.08239 (2022)
18. Vaswani, A., et al.: Attention is all you need. Adv. Neural Inf. Process. Syst. 30, 1–11 (2017)
19. Wolf, T., Sanh, V., Chaumond, J., Delangue, C.: TransferTransfo: a transfer learning approach for neural network based conversational agents. arXiv preprint arXiv:1901.08149 (2019)

20. Xu, J., Szlam, A., Weston, J.: Beyond goldfish memory: long-term open-domain conversation. arXiv preprint arXiv:2107.07567 (2021)
21. Xu, X., et al.: Long time no see! open-domain conversation with long-term persona memory. arXiv preprint arXiv:2203.05797 (2022)
22. Zhang, S., et al.: Opt: open pre-trained transformer language models. arXiv preprint arXiv:2205.01068 (2022)
23. Zhang, X., et al.: Making a MIRACL: multilingual information retrieval across a continuum of languages. arXiv preprint arXiv:2210.09984 (2022)
24. Zhang, Y., et al.: DialoGPT: large-scale generative pre-training for conversational response generation. arXiv preprint arXiv:1911.00536 (2019)

Pre- and Post-Textual Contexts in Assessment of a Message as Offensive or Defensive Aggression Verbalization

Liliya Komalova(⊠)

Institute of Scientific Information for Social Sciences of the Russian Academy of Sciences,
Nakhimovsky Prospect, Moscow 51/21 117418, Russia
komalova@inion.ru

Abstract. Contrary to the public stereotype that aggression is evil, scientific paradigm attributes aggression the fundamental importance for humans as biological and social beings. Despite the fact that most definitions of the aggression concept are based on the desire of an individual to harm another person, many aggressive actions do not have the goal of causing harm and damage. Aggression can serve the purpose of increasing self-esteem, self-affirmation, social and psychological adaptation, self-preservation. It is conditionally possible to distinguish offensive, defensive and instrumental types of aggression that are detected by people in verbal communication. Defensive type of aggression is aimed at maintaining an optimally stable psychological state of the individual under negative influence from the outside world. The paper describes an experiment on classification of written communication assessed as aggression verbalization. We explore messages in Russian language extracted out of the VKontakte social network site in interpretations given by a group of Russian natives. We confirm the assumption that the presence of pre- and post- textual contexts changes the result of classification of a written message: the message that previously (without any contexts) was assessed as offensive aggression verbalization, within textual contexts (messages provoking aggressive verbal reaction in response) is being assessed as defensive aggression verbalization.

Keywords: Pragmatic Linguistics · Verbalized aggression · Written communication · Social network site · Defensive aggression

1 Introduction

Different linguists classify speech behavior as cooperative, centered or conflictive. Researchers take into account the specifics of interaction and relationship with a partner in communicative activity and the possibilities to cooperate [9, 11, 21, 22, 25]. These classifications assign to the conflictive (confrontational) type of speech behavior the intention to cause harm, without considering it as a possible productive form of defense or an instrument required by the communicative situation (see [13, 15]).

1.1 Types of Aggression

The study of the issue of defensive aggression verbalization in Internet-mediated communication must begin with the definition of the aggression concept itself. D. Myers defines aggression as physical or verbal behavior aimed at causing damage / causing harm. At the same time, in the broad sense of the word, aggression is understood as the intentional actions of two or more persons, one of which is the aggressor (who attacks), the other is the victim (the one who is physically or verbally attacked) [18]. According to many researchers [2–6, 16, 17, 19, 26, 27], aggression reflects the hostility, negative attitude of a person, and aggressiveness (predisposition to an attacking type of behavior). Aggression can be aimed both at causing real physical harm or material damage, and at causing psycho-emotional harm to a person [10].

Despite the fact that most definitions of the aggression concept are based on the desire of an individual to harm another person, "many aggressive actions do not have the goal of causing harm and damage. Aggression can serve the purpose of increasing self-esteem, self-affirmation, social and psychological adaptation, self-preservation" [1]. At the same time aggression can be realized as an instrument, when an individual chooses an aggressive form of influence to achieve a goal different than causing harm. It should be noted that the main motivation for such actions is the desire to achieve subjectively significant benefits, ignoring the attitude of others to these actions, therefore this behavior is motivated, as a rule, by a socially disapproved or relatively approved desire [1].

It is conditionally possible to distinguish offensive, defensive and instrumental types of aggression. The latter "acts as a means of achieving the goals and motives of non-aggressive content (for example, education through punishment, a shot at a bandit who has taken a hostage, etc.). Thus, causing damage is instrumental in nature, being a condition for achieving other goals, and not an end in itself" [1, 7].

E. Fromm considers defensive aggression as a factor in the biological adaptation of a living creature, arguing that the defensive aggression of an animal is more pronounced than in humans. Defensive aggression does not tend to destroy simply for the sake of destroying. At its core, defensive aggression is a natural response to an emerging threat [8]. However, there is a significant difference between human being and animal. In people, defensive aggression can occur not only in case of a real threat to life [24], but also in response to a threat to other people, their status, image, property, as well as in response to potential threats and things that threaten individual's or other people's mental health.

In addition, defensive aggression can be considered as a way of psychological defense, as an unconscious process aimed at minimizing negative experiences [20] in order to create conditions that maximize the adaptability and balance of the psyche. At the same time, defensive aggression is always a response to an attack from outside [22]. In general, the functions of defensive aggression can be represented as follows:

– own protection, i.e. protecting yourself and your interests;
– protection of other individuals and their interests;
– removal of psycho-emotional stress in a situation of pressure from the outside;
– desire to protect yourself from outside interference, i.e. the desire to oppose oneself to imposed ideas;

– removal of the feeling of one's own guilt for any misconduct (in case of unreasonable aggression on the part of another individual).

Thus, defensive aggression is aimed at maintaining an optimally stable psychological state of the individual under negative influence from the outside.

2 Experimental Research on Defensive Aggression Verbalization

2.1 Research Material

To run an experiment we extracted and analyzed a set of written messages on VKontakte social network site given by real people in real communication in Russian language. The choice of topics for the analyzed messages was determined by the socially significant nature of the discussion (mandatory vaccination, prohibition of abortions). Those topics were of interest because when discussing them, the communicants formulated clear positions, speaking "for" and "against" a certain thesis.

For the experiment, we took ten communicative situations out of real messaging continuum, which were built according to the following scheme:

1 an initial real message is a verbal provocation from the so called aggressor (Communicant-1);
2 verbalization of a defensive verbal response from the so called victim (Communicant-2);
3 a new verbal provocation or verbalization of a defensive response from the so called aggressor (Communicant-1).

Each threesome consisted of messages previously classified as aggression verbalization, based on the criteria for human subjects and manual annotation described in [12, 13] and presented at SPECOM 2013–2018. For the experimental design it was important that previous and subsequent messages were classified as verbalized aggression.

Out of the total number of situations, in five cases (five threesomes) a female communicant acted as the so called victim (Communicant-2), in the remaining five cases, a male acted as the so called victim.

The hypothesis of the experiment was the assumption that the result of the assessment of a stimulus message representing aggression verbalization will change in favor of evaluating the message as a defensive type of aggression, provided that the nearest textual context contains verbal provocation in the form of verbalized offensive aggression.

2.2 Research Procedure

A group of recipients were asked to assess each communicative situation and go through the protocol of observation.

The experiment was conducted in four sessions. In the first session, it was proposed to analyze the sample (message of the so called victim "Communicant-2") without any textual contexts (Table 1). In the second session, a sample was analyzed with a previous ("left") context (a message that provoked defensive aggression verbalization and was placed before the message of the so called victim) (Table 2). In the third session, the sample was analyzed with the subsequent ("right") context (the message that followed after the implementation of defensive aggression verbalization and was located after the message of the so called victim) (Table 3). In the fourth session, the sample was analyzed in two contexts (the message of the so called victim, preceded by the message of the provocateur and closed by the verbalized response of the provocateur) (Table 4).

Table 1. An example of the analyzed message without any textual contexts.

Russian transliteration	Translation into English
Communicant-2:	Communicant-2:
…, da my uzhe ponyali, chto Vy posledstvie intsesta. Nam Vas zhal. No vy ne rasstraivaites, vse u vas budet khorosho	…, we already understood that you are the result of incest. We feel sorry for you. But don't worry, everything will be fine

Table 2. An example of the analyzed message with textual pre-context.

Russian transliteration	Translation into English
Communicant-1:	Communicant-1:
Estestvenno,oni tam do sikh por s baranami chshpokhayutsya, kakie im tekhnologii 😔	Naturally, they are still chshpokhayutsya with sheep there, what technologies do they need 😔
Communicant-2:	Communicant-2:
… Pod barany ty vidimo podrazumevaesh sebya i takikh kak ty !!	By sheep you apparently mean yourself and people like you !!

Table 3. An example of the analyzed message with textual post-context.

Russian transliteration	Translation into English
Communicant-2:	Communicant-2:
…, ogo otkuda togda geneticheskie zabolevaniya peredayushchiesya po materinskoy linii? I gde takaya alternativnaya biologiya? Na md sajtakh? Ochen pokhozhe po urovnyu intellekta	…, wow, where do genetic diseases transmitted through the maternal line come from then? And where is this alternative biology? On md web-sites? Very similar in terms of intelligence
Communicatnt-1:	Communicatnt-1:
Chitaj glazami, a ne drugimi organami. "Nositel informatsii"	Read with your eyes, not with other organs. "Information carrier"

2.3 Tasks for the Recipients

The recipients in the process of analyzing the stimulus material performed the following tasks. It was necessary to:

Table 4. An example of the analyzed message with both pre- and post-textual contexts.

Russian transliteration	Translation into English
Communicatnt-1: … u zaabortnykh zombulyak voobshche logika poroj sryvaetsya. Eto ikh istinnoe amplua. "prervi beremennost, a to u tebya poly eshcho ne pomyty". Ikh vyskazyvaniya – eto sam po sebe silnejshij demotivator Communicant-2: …, dura nabitaya, bolshinstvo storonnits abortov imeyut detej i znayut o tom, chto takoe otvetstvennost. Eto tolko takie nishchenki, kak ty i tebe podobnye, starayutsya lyudej v svoe boloto zatashchit i glumitsya Communicatnt-1: … Ooospodi 👎😩😔💀 … Eta imbetsilka dazhe ne mozhet na golovy natyanut, o chem ya. S kem my tut dialog vedem?… Sborishche odnokletochnykh. I eto nanyali, chtoby dvigat oborty v strane? Big farma! Ne nanumaj po objyavleniyam!	Communicatnt-1: … in general, the logic of for-abortion zombulyaks sometimes breaks down. This is their true role. "abort the pregnancy, otherwise your floors have not been washed yet." Their statements are the strongest demotivator in themselves Communicant-2: … Fool stuffed, most abortion supporters have children and know what responsibility is. It's only beggars like you and people like you who try to drag people into their swamp and mock Communicatnt-1: … Lllord 👎😩😔💀 … This imbecile can't even put it on her head, what am I talking about. Who are we talking to here?… A bunch of unicellular. And it was hired to promote abortion in the country? Big pharma! Do not hire from ads!

1. determine whether verbalized aggression is present in the test sample (only in the first session);
2. determine the type of aggression (offensive or defensive);
3. indicate on the basis of what linguistic means the respondents concluded that the analyzed message is verbalized aggression (only in the first session).

2.4 Respondents' Demographic Data

Participants were asked to answer a series of questions regarding their demographic data (biological sex, age, type of professional activity, city of birth and residence, level of education, diploma specialty).

The survey was created and conducted using the Google Forms platform. A total number of 20 respondents took part in the survey (Table 5). The experiment involved adult subjects who speak Russian language. All of them were Internet users, in particular, VKontakte social network site's users. Mostly students were involved in the experiments.

All the respondents were informed about the condition of their participation in the experiment and signed an informed consent.

3   Results

3.1   Out-Of-Context Message Assessment

Before entering the experimental procedure, the respondents got acquainted with the memo, which revealed the content of aggression and the difference between offensive and defensive types of aggression.

Table 5. Respondents' demographic characteristics (in absolute measures).

Respondents' age	Respondents' sex	
	males	females
18–24 years olds	8	12
Level of education	males	females
master's degree	2	0
bachelor degree	4	8
vocational technical school	0	2
secondary education (11 grades)	2	2
Type of professional activity	males	females
I'm only working	0	1
I'm studying and working	5	5
I'm only studying	3	5
I'm not studying nor working	0	1

During the first experimental session the respondents assessed whether the stimuli messages verbalized aggression. The results of this session are presented in Table 6.

The respondents' agreement was 94%. Among the grounds for agreeing to the presence of verbalized aggression in these samples, the respondents indicated:

- indignant tone and categoricalness while expressing one's own opinion;
- repeated use of questions, which is a common means of expressing irritation in the course of communication;
- use of lexemes with a negative connotation related to the semantic field "aggression" (see [12, p. 94–116]) with the meaning of destructive actions;
- presence of lexemes containing a marked prefix with an estimated value;
- use of sarcasm, expressed through vocabulary with positive connotations, which contrasts with negatively colored vocabulary.

Sample No. 3 caused the most doubts when assessing it for the presence of verbalized aggression. Doubts can be explained by:

- neutral tone of reasoning;
- absence of lexemes containing only negative characteristics for the nomination, the contextual use of which can be regarded as aggressive or offensive;
- absence of lexemes in figurative meanings with a contemptuous, derogatory, abusive coloring.

Table 6 also shows the results of respondents' assessment of verbalized aggression types (offensive / defensive). In the majority of the analyzed messages without (out of) context, the respondents assessed messages as a verbalization of an offensive type of aggression.

Further, when analyzing each sample, the respondents could identify several categories of language means that, in their opinion, indicate verbalized aggression (see more about markers [12, p. 61–68]). The results of respondents' assessment of the stimulus

Table 6. How respondents assessed the analyzed messages without any textual contexts (in %).

Number of the assessed sample (message of the so called victim – Communicant-2)	Message verbalizes aggression		Type of verbalized aggression	
	yes	no	offensive	defensive
(7) Z...i sranye klavishnye geroi, kotorye tolko tut mogut strochit pro drugie narody a v litso skazat ochko szhimaetsya / Z...i fucking keyboard heroes who only here can scribble about other nations and say something in the face the arsehole shrinks	100	0	90	10
(8) V Rossiyu prishla tretiya volna. Ne zametili? U NEvaktsinirovannykh stalo eshcho bolshe shansov pouchastvovat v estestvennom otbore. Uspekhov. / The third wave has come to Russia. Did not notice? The NOT-vaccinated became even more likely to participate in natural selection. Good luck	85	15	90	10
(5) Dura nabitaya, bolshinstvo storonnits abortov imeyut detej i znayut o tom, chto takoe otvetstvennost. Eto tolko takie nishchenki, kak ty i tebe podobnye, starayutsya lyudej v svoe boloto zatashchit i glumitsya. / Fool stuffed, most abortion supporters have children and know what responsibility is. It's only beggars like you and people like you who try to drag people into their swamp and mock	95	5	75	25
(2) Da my uzhe ponyali, chto Vy posledstvie intsesta. Nam Vas zhal. No vy ne rasstraivaites, vse u vas budet khorosho. / We already understood that you are the result of incest. We feel sorry for you. But don't worry, everything will be fine	95	5	70	30
(1) Ogo otkuda togda geneticheskie zabolevaniya peredayushchiesya po materinskoy linii? I gde takaya alternativnaya biologiya? Na md sajtakh? Ochen pokhozhe po urovnyu intellekta / Wow, where do genetic diseases transmitted through the maternal line come from then? And where is this alternative biology? On md web-sites? Very similar in terms of intelligence	95	5	65	35

(continued)

Table 6. (*continued*)

Number of the assessed sample (message of the so called victim – Communicant-2)	Message verbalizes aggression		Type of verbalized aggression	
	yes	no	offensive	defensive
(6) A Vy ne plodites? Sami ponyali, chto napisaly? Ok, esli agressivnykh sobak mozhno otstrelivat, to mozhno tak zhe postupat s agressivnymi lyudmi?) vozmozhno s Vami, sudya po stilyu myshleniya?)K slovy, v protsesse prodolzheniya roda uchastvyet ne 1 subjekt) Tak chto kogda ploditsya nachnete Vy, ne zabudte utopit detej v vedre ili vybrosit v pakete na musorku, kak kotyat i shchenkov, raz vy schitaete razumnym provodit takuyu analogiyu / And you, don't you breed? Did you understand what you wrote? Ok, if you can shoot aggressive dogs, then you can do the same with aggressive people?) It is possible with you, judging by the style of thinking?) By the way, more than 1 subject is involved in the process of procreation) So when you start to breed, do not forget to drown children in a bucket or thrown in a bag in the trash, like kittens and puppies, since you think it is reasonable to draw such an analogy)	100	0	60	40
(9) a zarazhayutsya, boleyut, gibnut lyudi bez 'b...go tsirka", tak? yazyk prikusi! / and people get infected, get sick, die without a "fucking circus", right? bite your tongue!	95	5	50	50
(3) Pro muzha tut voobshche rechi net. Nais sposob govorit pro nego, chtoby obestsenit zaslugi etoj mamy: a ot nee nichego drugogo i ne ozhidalos, muzh-to rabotaet! A mb ona vdova. A mb u nee ne muzh, a zhena (privet, eko). Da i kak-to vy sebya pereotsenivaete. Chel, esli ty v lyuboj novosti vidish zdorovogo bogatogo papika, otrefleksiruj eto, my ne osudim. / There is no mention of a husband at all. Nice way to talk about him in order to devalue the merits of this mother: and nothing else was expected from her, her husband is at work! And maybe she is a widow. And maybe she has not a husband, but a wife (hello, eco). And yes, you overestimate yourself. Man, if you see a healthy rich daddy behind any news, reflect on it, we will not condemn	80	20	50	50

(*continued*)

Table 6. (*continued*)

Number of the assessed sample (message of the so called victim – Communicant-2)	Message verbalizes aggression		Type of verbalized aggression	
	yes	no	offensive	defensive
(10) Nu mozhno skazat, chto d…ka tut tolko ty. My ne znaem, cherez chto on proshel. / Well, we can say that only you are moron here. We don't know what he went through	100	0	40	60
(4) Pod barany ty vidimo podrazumevaesh sebya i takikh kak ty !! / By sheep you apparently mean yourself and people like you !!	95	5	40	60

material (Table 7) indicate that the most frequent marker of aggression verbalization are lexical means (43.09%), followed by syntactic-stylistic means (30,35%), grammatical means (14,36%) and punctuation means (12,2%).

Table 7. How respondents evaluate language means marking verbalized aggression in the analyzed messages (in %).

Number of the assessed sample	Language means marking aggression verbalization			
	lexical	grammatical	syntactic-stylistic	punctuation
1	35,48	6,45	58,06	0
2	39,39	12,12	45,45	3,03
3	31,82	18,18	29,55	20,45
4	39,02	9,76	9,76	41,46
5	50	16,67	27,78	5,56
6	35,29	23,53	31,37	9,8
7	80	8	12	0
8	34,29	11,43	48,57	5,71
9	37,5	14,58	29,17	18,75
10	76	16	8	0
Total	43,09	14,36	30,35	12,2

3.2 In-Context Message Assessment

During the second, third and fourth sessions, the respondents were asked to determine the type of verbalized aggression (offensive or defensive) in messages within pre- and post- textual contexts. The results obtained are presented in Tables 8, 9, 10.

Table 8. Comparing respondents' evaluations towards the analyzed messages without any textual context and messages with pre- textual context (in %).

Number of the assessed sample (message of the so called victim – Communicant-2)	Type of verbalized aggression			
	offensive		defensive	
	without any context	with pre-textual context	without any context	with pre-textual context
(7)	90	30,4	10	69,6
(8)	90	45	10	55
(5)	75	50	25	50
(2)	70	52,4	30	47,6
(1)	65	85	35	15
(6)	60	40	40	60
(9)	50	47,6	50	52,4
(3)	50	56,5	50	43,8
(10)	40	45	60	55
(4)	40	61,9	60	38,1

In the presence of the previous (pre- textual) context, there is a sharp (45–59,6%) decrease in the share of assessments "offensive aggression" in relation to messages No. 7 and 8, which, out of context, the respondents assessed as offensive aggression with the highest level of consistency. For samples No. 5, 2, 1, 6, and 9, which are less unambiguous in the respondents' assessments, there is a tendency to evaluate messages as verbalizations of defensive aggression. Along with this, when assessing samples No. 3, 10, 4 with the previous (pre- textual) context, the respondents tend to believe that they represent a verbalization of offensive aggression. In general, it can be said that the presence of the previous (pre- textual) context in the communicative situation of defensive aggression verbalization by the so called victim (Communicant-2) helps to recognize the defensive nature of responsive aggression.

The tendency to recognize the defensive type of responsive aggression is also characteristic of messages with a subsequent (post- textual) context.

When assessing the messages in contexts on both sides (pre- and post- textual contexts), the respondents are even more inclined to characterize these messages as defensive form of aggression verbalization.

The objectiveness of received results were verified with chi-square test: for offensive aggression verbalization shifts from non-context to within contexts are statistically significant at $\chi^2 = 13,6$ and ρ-value $< 0,001$; for defensive aggression verbalization at $\chi^2 = 15,514$ and ρ-value $< 0,001$.

Table 9. Comparing respondents' evaluations towards the analyzed messages without any textual context and messages with post- textual context (in %).

Number of the assessed sample (message of the so called victim – Communicant-2)	Type of verbalized aggression			
	offensive		defensive	
	without any context	with post-textual context	without any context	with post-textual context
(7)	90	63,6	10	36,4
(8)	90	40,9	10	59,1
(5)	75	42,8	25	57,2
(2)	70	45,4	30	54,6
(1)	65	52,8	35	47,2
(6)	60	52,8	40	47,2
(9)	50	20	50	80
(3)	50	61,9	50	38,1
(10)	40	40	60	60
(4)	40	63,6	60	36,4

Table 10. Comparing respondents' evaluations towards the analyzed messages without any textual context and messages with both pre- and post- textual contexts (in %).

Number of the assessed sample (message of the so called victim – Communicant-2)	Type of verbalized aggression			
	offensive		defensive	
	without any context	with pre- and post- textual context	without any context	with pre- and post- textual context
(7)	90	20	10	80
(8)	90	38,8	10	61,2
(5)	75	38	25	62
(2)	70	45,4	30	54,6
(1)	65	52,8	35	47,2
(6)	60	14,2	40	85,8
(9)	50	45,4	50	54,6
(3)	50	50	50	50
(10)	40	52,8	60	47,2
(4)	40	57,1	60	42,9

4 Conclusion

Contrary to the public stereotype that aggression is evil, scientific paradigm attributes aggression the fundamental importance for humans as biological and social beings.

Aggression can be considered both as a way of attack and as a way of defense. In the second case, aggression is manifested in response to situations that pose danger and threat to the individual.

In practice, in speech communication, it is difficult to determine the type of aggression, since both offensive and defensive types of aggression are implemented using similar language means.

In the course of the experimental research described in this paper, an attempt was made to identify the degree of influence of pre- and post- textual contexts on the classifying of defensive form of aggression verbalization. The working hypothesis was confirmed based on the analysis of respondents' assessments of messages without context and in different textual contexts. The results obtained allow us to conclude that the presence of both previous (pre- textual) and subsequent (post- textual) contexts equally affects the classification of the type of aggression verbalized in written communication on social network site VKontakte in Russian language (based on the experimental data).

We believe that there are lot of speech features that help automatic systems detect verbal, prosodic and non-verbal signals and signs of aggression as a complex emotional state and behavior. We also believe that results of our research contribute to the understanding of the type of verbalized aggression in written speech on social network site VKontakte. Especially in case of detecting the real aggressor based on his / her speech behavior. For example in legal framework expertise covers a controversial message. Our approach recommends also expertise pre- and post- messages on verbalized aggression to decide whether the controversial message verbalizing defensive or offensive type of aggression. In this regard, in written speech communication, when determining the pragmatic orientation of verbalized aggression to attack or to defend, the textual context should be taken into account as one of the mandatory parameters for assessing the speech behavior of a person.

Small sample size of the analyzed messages as well as analyzing respondents may reduce the generalizing ability of the research results. But we suppose that "small data approach[1]" can be implemented in repeated experiments with similar design that increases validity of the results. For example, similar results were obtained in research applied to explore assessment of verbalized aggression type on Twitter messages [14].

Acknowledgements. The research is carried out within the framework of the state assignment to Institute of Scientific Information for Social Sciences of the Russian Academy of Sciences, project "Linguacultural aspects of civilizational contradictions".

References

1. Banshikova, T.N.: Aggression as a conceptual concept. Concept **8**, 71–75 (2013). (in Russian)

---

[1] See, for example: https://www.bbvaopenmind.com/en/technology/digital-world/small-data-vs-big-data-back-to-the-basics/

2. Baron, R., Richardson, D.: Aggression. Saint-Petersburg, Piter (2014) (in Russian)
3. Bass, A.H.: Instrumentality of aggression, feedback, and frustration as determinants of physical aggression. J. Pers. Soc. Psychol. **3**(2), 153–162 (1966)
4. Bass, A.H.: Physical aggression in relation to different frustrations. J. Abnorm. Soc. Psychol. **67**, 1–7 (1963)
5. Berkowitz, L.: Aggression: its causes, consequences, and control. Saint-Petersburg, Praim-Evroznak (2007)
6. Dollard, J., Doob, L.W., Miller, N.E., Mowrer, H.O., Sears, R.R.: Frustration and Aggression. Yale University Press, New Heaven (1939)
7. Feshbach, S.: The function of aggression and the regulation of aggressive drive. Psychol. Rev. **71**, 257–272 (1964)
8. Fromm, E.: The Anatomy of Human Destructiveness. AST, Moscow (2020). (in Russian)
9. Gerasimova, A.V., Sorokina, J.A.: The role of lexical means in the disclosure of the linguistic personality dynamics. Moscow, Moscow Region State University (2020) (in Russian)
10. Iljasov, F.N.: Political marketing. Art and Science to Win the Elections. IMA-press, Moscow (2000) (in Russian)
11. Issers, O.S.: Communicative Strategies and Tactics in Russian Speech. Lki, Moscow (2008). (in Russian)
12. Komalova, L.R.: Aggressogen Discourse: the Multilingual Aggression Verbalization Typology. Sputnik, Moscow (2020). (in Russian)
13. Komalova, L.R.: Interpersonal communication: from conflict to consensus. INION RAN, Moscow (2016). http://inion.ru/site/assets/files/2556/2016_mon_mezhlichnostnaia_komm unikatciia-1.pdf (in Russian)
14. Komalova, L., Kulagina, D.: Perceiving speech aggression with and without textual context on Twitter social network site. In: Karpov, A., Potapova, R. (eds.) SPECOM 2021. LNCS (LNAI), vol. 12997, pp. 348–359. Springer, Cham (2021). https://doi.org/10.1007/978-3-030-87802-3_32
15. Komalova, L.R., Sadova, E.R.: Pragmatic vector of verbalized aggression within internet mediated communication: textual context dimension. Sci. J. Volgograd State Univ. Linguist. **3**, 77–89 (2022). https://doi.org/10.15688/jvolsu2.2022.3.7 (in Russian)
16. Kornadt, H.J.: Aggressionsmotiv und Aggressionhemmung. Band 1, 2. Bern, Huber (1982)
17. Matsumoto, D.: Psychology and Culture. Praim-Evroznak, Moscow (2006). (in Russian)
18. Mayers, D.: Social Psychology. Saint-Petersburg, Piter (2019) (in Russian)
19. Nalchadzhjan, A.A.: Human Aggressiveness. Saint-Peresburg, Piter (2007) (in Russian)
20. Nikolskaya, I.M., Granovskaja, R.M.: Psycological Protection in Children. Rech, Moscow (2006). (in Russian)
21. Panchenko, N.N.: Communicative Linguistics. Linguistic Russia: Volgograd scientific fields and schools (pp. 262–283). Volgograd, Volgogradskoe nauchnoe izdatelstvo (2012) (in Russian)
22. Petrova, N.E., Raciburskaja, L.V.: Language of Modern Media: Means of Speech Aggression. Flinta, Nauka, Moscow (2017). (in Russian)
23. Sedov, K.F.: Types of linguistic personality based on the ability to cooperate in speech behavior. Issues of speech communication (pp. 6–12). Saratov, Saratov State University (2000) (in Russian)
24. Tarasenko, A.V.: Aggression and ways to prevent from it. Young Scientist **12**, 196–199 (2017). (in Russian)
25. Tretyakova, V.S.: Speech conflictology: problems, tasks, perspectives. Bulletin of Chelyabinsk State University **1**(292), 279–282 (2013) (in Russian)
26. Trifonov, E.V.: Psychophysiology of professional activity. Saint-Petersburg (1996) (in Russian)
27. Zillmann, D.: Hostility and aggression. New York, Hillsdale, L. Erlbaum Associates (1979)

Boosting Rule-Based Grapheme-to-Phoneme Conversion with Morphological Segmentation and Syllabification in Bengali

Krishnendu Ghosh[1]([✉])([iD]), Sandipan Mandal[2], and Nilay Roy[3]

[1] Techno International New Town, Kolkata, India
krishnendu.ghosh@tint.edu.in
[2] Theta One Software, Kolkata, India
[3] Indian Institute of Technology Kharagpur, Kharagpur, India

Abstract. This paper presents a novel approach to enhance rule-based Bengali grapheme-to-phoneme (G2P) conversion by leveraging morphological segmentation and syllabification techniques. In this approach, input words are first morphologically segmented into valid morphological chunks, each having a different stem and semantic. Applying the G2P rules on each of these chunks, their pronunciations are generated. An intermediate pronunciation for the whole input word is attained by merging these pronunciations. Using syllabification, this intermediate pronunciation is further divided into valid syllabic sequences that offer accurate morphological boundaries. Finally, the final pronunciation is achieved using syllable-specific orthographic rules on these syllabic sequences. The performance of the proposed G2P approach is assessed using measures representing (i) direct accuracy and (ii) enhancements in different speech-related applications. According to the performances noted for the direct accuracy-based measures, the proposed approach predicted the appropriate pronunciations for about 90% cases, especially for compound and inflected words. This performance is around 22% and 10% better than the performance of a rule-based system and a previous state-of-the-art system, respectively. On the other hand, application-based measures guarantee that the generated phone sequences (i) sound natural and (ii) improve the quality of speech synthesis and recognition systems. These quantitative and qualitative assessment plans answered research questions pertinent to speech and linguistics.

Keywords: Grapheme-to-phoneme conversion · Morphology · Syllable · Text-to-speech synthesis · Speech recognition

1 Introduction

Grapheme-to-phoneme conversion is a crucial step in natural language processing tasks [18]. Grapheme is the smallest unit in scripts, and the phoneme is the basic

A. Karpov et al. (Eds.): SPECOM 2023, LNAI 14338, pp. 415–429, 2023.
https://doi.org/10.1007/978-3-031-48309-7_34

speech unit. Consequently, G2P conversion involves transforming the written representation of a word (graphs) into corresponding pronunciation (phonemes). G2P conversion is one of the key modules for generating natural and intelligible speech by text-to-speech synthesis (TTS) systems [17,19], as its accuracy or phonetic smoothness affects the quality of an automatic speech recognition (ASR) system [18]. The complexity of G2P conversion is compounded by various challenges, including the inherent complexity and irregularities of the concerned languages, inconsistencies in orthographic systems, and many-to-many grapheme-to-phoneme mappings [9]. In the context of the Bengali language, the challenges can be itemized as follows.

- **Complex Orthographic System:** Bengali scripts consist of characters formed with vowels and consonants, representing syllables rather than individual phonemes. So, it is challenging to establish a one-to-one correspondence between graphs and phonemes.
- **Ambiguity and Irregularities:** Approaches pertaining to Bengali language suffers due to multiple and many-to-many grapheme-to-phoneme mappings, irregular spellings, and phonetic variations [10].
- **Morphological Complexity:** Bengali has a rich morphology with various prefixes, suffixes, and word formation. Without knowledge of the morphological structure of words, one cannot develop an accurate G2P conversion module [5].
- **Limited Linguistic Resources:** Unlike English or Mandarin, Bengali lacks the necessary resources (like pronunciation dictionaries, lexicons, and annotated datasets). Consequently, it poses challenges in developing data-driven and rule-based G2P approaches in Bengali [1,10].
- **Dialectal Variations:** Bengali exhibits regional dialectal variations in terms of pronunciation and vocabulary [1]. However, the present study considers the colloquial Bengali pronunciations used in Kolkata as standard.

The present study addresses these challenges by proposing an approach to enhance the performance of a rule-based G2P conversion module using two linguistic techniques: morphological segmentation and syllabification. The study aims to capture linguistic and phonological patterns by breaking down Bengali words into morphemes and syllables. Morphological segmentation addresses the intricacies associated with morphology, while syllabification contributes to an accurate representation of the syllabic structure [15]. These techniques are integrated into the existing rule-based framework to enhance phoneme predictions and complement the existing conversion rules.

This paper is structured as follows. Section 1 provides an overview of grapheme-to-phoneme (G2P) conversion approaches, particularly in Bengali. Section 2 examines the current state-of-the-art G2P systems, highlighting their limitations and setting the context for further research. Section 3 describes the proposed G2P approach integrating morphological segmentation and syllabification into a rule-based framework. Section 4 provides an overview of the database used and the subjects participating in the assessment tasks. Section 5 sets up the experiments, presents the results, and analyzes the findings. Finally, the paper concludes in Sect. 6, summarizes the contributions of this paper and outlines plans and potential avenues for further research.

2 Literature Survey

Previous research on G2P Conversion has employed various techniques, broadly categorized into rule-based methods, instance-based learning methods, memory-based learning methods, statistical methods, and machine learning-based approaches. Each of these categories is elaborated further.

- **Rule-based Methods:** Rule-based methods rely on predefined conversion rules mapping graphemes to phonemes based on linguistic knowledge and resources. Linguists and experts typically handcraft these rules. Rule-based approaches are primarily used in Bengali G2P conversion incorporating linguistic patterns, orthographic rules, and phonological information specific to Bengali [1,8,9]. However, it is challenging to develop a minimal rule set [20,23]. Moreover, constructing a rule yields a set of exceptions.
- **Instance-based Learning Methods:** The instance-based learning tool constructs a classification tree based on data categorized by specific features. The process begins with an empty tree, and the original dataset is partitioned into subsets using the most predictive feature. This iterative process continues on each subset until the leaves of the classification tree can accurately classify any object into the required class or until no more attributes are available [6,14].
- **Memory-based Learning Methods:** This approach initiates by creating a memory base. Subsequently, it searches within the memory base to identify the most similar record with the highest frequency, which yields the class for the given data. The method relies on language-specific patterns but may be time-consuming [13,22].
- **Machine Learning based methods:** Machine learning techniques, such as Artificial Neural Networks (ANNs) and Deep Learning models, have been applied for Bengali G2P Conversion. These models get trained on large datasets and learn to generate pronunciations. Recurrent Neural Networks (RNNs) and Long Short-Term Memory (LSTM) networks are commonly used for sequence-to-sequence mapping in G2P conversion tasks. Machine learning-based approaches have shown promising results in capturing complex patterns and improving the accuracy of Bengali G2P Conversion.
- **Statistical Methods:** Statistical models use large annotated datasets to understand the statistical patterns and grapheme-to-phoneme mappings associated with the concerned language. These models utilize techniques like Hidden Markov Models (HMMs), Maximum Entropy (MaxEnt) models, or Conditional Random Fields (CRFs) [2,3,11]. Nevertheless, it is important to note that these statistical models demand a substantial volume of labeled data to effectively capture the statistical regularities and patterns involved in Bengali grapheme-to-phoneme (G2P) conversion.

2.1 Limitations

Although the approaches mentioned earlier have contributed towards achieving quality G2P conversion methods, they also have some limitations. Manual methods for generating pronunciation dictionaries are next to impossible, given that the language is dynamic and alive, like Bengali. Rule-based methods rely on expert knowledge and must address several issues related to phonetic, contextual, and morphological factors [8]. Nonetheless, their performance is limited due to a lack of accurate morphological analyzers. Statistical models and machine learning-based approaches require substantial amounts of accurately annotated data, which is rare for low-resource languages like Bengali. Due to their phonetic nature, rule-based methods are preferred for Bengali G2P conversion. Recent research combines different approaches and leverages additional linguistic techniques to improve basic Bengali G2P conversion methods. Consequently, the present work combines two linguistic techniques: morphological segmentation and syllabification, to boost the performance of rule-based G2P conversion.

2.2 Objective

The present work integrates morphological segmentation and syllabification to boost performances of the rule-based G2P approach in Bengali. In light of this objective, we also investigate how the proposed G2P approach (i) performs for different types of words (simple, compound, or inflected) and (ii) affects the performance of end-to-end speech systems like TTS and ASR. Considering these objectives, the present work outlines the research questions mentioned below.

- **RQ1:** Does the proposed approach improve the performance of rule-based G2P conversion module?
- **RQ2:** For which types of words does the proposed approach improve the performance of the rule-based G2P conversion module the most?
- **RQ3:** With the proposed approach, are there significant improvements in the performance of a text-to-speech synthesis (TTS) system?
- **RQ4:** With the proposed approach, are there significant improvements in the performance of an automatic speech recognition (ASR) system?

3 Proposed G2P Conversion Approach

This section elaborates on the working details of the proposed G2P approach for integrating morphological segmentation and syllabification into a rule-based G2P conversion framework. This proposed approach is realized over four modules: (1) Morphological Segmentation, (2) Rule-based G2P Conversion, (3) Syllabification, and (4) Pronunciation Refining, as illustrated in Fig. 1.

'Morphological Segmentation' module divides input words into valid morphological chunks, each having a different stem and semantic. Applying the G2P rules on each chunk, their pronunciations are generated in the 'Rule-based G2P Conversion' module. An intermediate pronunciation for the whole input

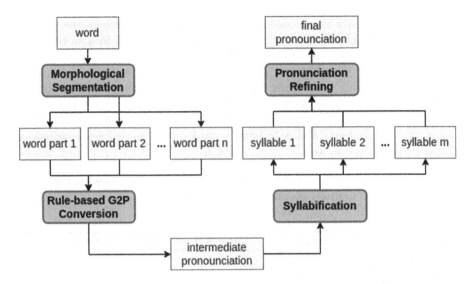

Fig. 1. Block diagram of the proposed G2P conversion approach.

word is attained by merging these pronunciations. The 'Syllabification' module once again divides this intermediate pronunciation into valid syllabic sequences which present accurate morphological boundaries. Finally, the final pronunciation is achieved by applying syllable-specific rules and clubbing pronunciations for the syllabic sequences in the 'Pronunciation Refining' module.

3.1 Morphological Segmentation

Morphological segmentation is a linguistic technique that involves breaking down words into their constituent morphemes, the smallest meaningful units of a word [15]. For example, morphological segmentation of the compound word "শ্রীরামকৃষ্ণ" /shriiraamakrishna/[/ʃrirəmkriʃno/] presents three morphemes "শ্রী" /shrii/[/ʃri/], "রাম" /raam/[/rəm/] and "কৃষ্ণ" /krishna/[/kriʃno/] . In the context of G2P conversion, morphological segmentation is crucial in capturing the morphological structure and variations in the target language for the following reasons.

- **Improved Accuracy:** G2P conversion systems can capture the underlying morphological structure by breaking words into constituent morphemes, allowing for more accurate phoneme predictions.
- **Enhanced Contextual Appropriateness:** Morphological segmentation helps G2P conversion systems consider the context and meaning of words. Different morphemes may have distinct phonetic properties or influence the pronunciation of neighbouring morphemes. This segmentation module enables the conversion system to generate contextually appropriate pronunciations.

This is particularly important in languages like Bengali, where the pronunciation of a grapheme can vary based on its position within a word or the presence of neighbouring morphemes.

- **Robustness to Word Variations:** Morphological segmentation aids in handling variations in word forms due to inflectional or derivational processes. By identifying the morphemes within a word, the G2P conversion system can generalize the pronunciation patterns across different word forms. This improves the system's ability to handle word variations and generate consistent phoneme predictions.

This morphological segmentation module proposes the following algorithm to determine valid morphemes out of input words.

Algorithm 1. Determining valid morphemes present in an input word

---

Algorithm(w) $\rightarrow M(w)$
Input: A word w, a list of valid words VW
Output: A set of valid morphemes $M(w)$
Step 1: Initialize input and output.
Step 2: if: $w \in VL$, then append w in $M(w)$ and return $M(w)$.
Step 3: else: get the largest possible string $p1$ from the left part of w such that $p1 \in VL$, append $p1$ in $M(w)$, and return $Algorithm(p2)$ considering that w is formed by concatenating $p1$ and $p2$.

3.2   Rule-Based G2P Conversion

Rule-based G2P conversion is the module where orthographic rules are applied on each valid morpheme or word-chunks to generate their pronunciations. The current study realizes this module in two steps: Grapheme-to-phoneme Mapping and Pronunciation Generation following [9].

Grapheme-to-Phoneme Mapping. Grapheme-to-phoneme mapping is a one-to-one mapping of each grapheme present in the word with the corresponding phoneme. For this, the longest possible sequence of characters, a valid graph, is considered.

Pronunciation Generation. After the grapheme-to-phoneme mapping, the phone sequences are modified using three types of grapheme-to-phoneme conversion rules: (1) basic orthographic rules, (2) special rules and (3) schwa deletion rules.

1. Basic orthographic rules:
   Based on phonetics, if a specific series of phones always or in some special conditions generates a particular phoneme sequence as its pronunciation, then it is an orthographic rule. The general format is ABC $\rightarrow$ ADC. To illustrate,

if, in a word, a consonant is repeated, i.e., there is the same consonant in consecutive positions and is followed by "অ", then that "অ" is transformed into "ও".

Example: "দত্ত" /datta/ [dɔtto].

2. Special orthographic rules:

Special orthographic rules have a limited and narrower scope, built for the exceptions and the words which require special attention. For instance, if there is "ক্ষ" in the starting position of a word, then it is transformed into "খ". Again, in other than starting position, if in a word there is "ক্ষ", it is transformed into "কখ".

Example:

"ক্ষমতা" /kshhamataa/ [kʰ motɐ], "সক্ষমতা" /sakshhamataa/ [sɔkkʰ motɐ]

3. Schwa deletion rules:

Dependent vowel "অ" or schwa, which may occur anywhere in a word, is sometimes uttered and sometimes not. For example, if the schwa is the last letter of the word and it is preceded by "হ", then the schwa is retained and pronounced as "ও".

Example: "দুরূহ" /duruha/ [duruho], "দুরূহ" /ratna/ [rɔtno]

In this rule-based approach, a sequence of rules is employed, and the test word undergoes a step-by-step application of these rules. As each rule modifies the word in the sequence, the resulting graph sequence ultimately produces the final pronunciation of the word.

3.3 Syllabification

Syllabification is a language-dependent procedure where syllables structure varies with language. The syllable structure in Bengali is shown in Table 1, where C and V represent consonants and vowels, respectively.

Table 1. Valid syllable structure in Bengali.

Syllable Structure	Example	Syllable Structure	Example
V	অ	VC	ইম
CV	রা	CVC	রাম
CVCC	রামস*	CCV	শ্রা
CCVC	শ্রম	CCVCC	স্পার্ট*
CCCV	জ্ঞা	CCCVC	চ্ছাস
CCCVCC	রাম*		

In this step, pronunciation generated by the orthographic rules for other than compound words in the previous step is syllabified. The syllabification is performed according to Algorithm 2:

Algorithm 2. Determining syllable boundaries for an input word

---

Input: Syllable sequence ss

Output: A set of syllable boundary $SB(ss)$

Step 1: For word-medial intervocalic CC sequences, a syllable boundary is introduced between the two Cs except in cases where /r/ or /l/ is the second member.

Step 2: In word-medial CC sequences with /r/ or /l/ as the second member, the first member of the sequence is geminated, forming a CCC sequence (i.e., CCr/l). A syllable boundary is then inserted between the first and second members of the CCC sequence. The first C becomes the coda of the syllable to the left, while the second and third Cs form the onset cluster of the following syllable.

Step 3: In word-medial CCC sequences, the third member is always /r/. In this case, the syllable boundary is located immediately after the first member. The first C becomes the coda of the preceding syllable, while the second and third Cs form the onset cluster of the following syllable.

Step 4: The word-medial CCCC sequence contains only one instance, namely /kr/. The syllable boundary is positioned between the 2nd and 3rd members.

3.4   Pronunciation Refining

After syllabifying the pronunciation, the phone sequences are merged and compared to ensure that the resultant pronunciation is formed using valid syllable constructs only. Accordingly, syllable-specific grapheme-to-phoneme rules are applied to the input graph sequences to make pronunciation more accurate and valid.

4   Corpus and Participants

In this section, we provide an overview of the dataset employed in our study and introduce the subjects who took part in the annotation task aimed at evaluating the proposed system.

4.1   Corpus

The present study collected a text corpus from different domains like politics, entertainment, sports, stories and textbooks on history, geography, science and literature. A total of 200,078 unique words was collected from this text corpus. The details of the corpus collected are shown in Table 2.

Table 2. Database Statistics: Distribution of the words.

Number of words	Number of Bengali words	Number of Foreign words
200,078	152,147	47,931

152,147 Bengali words were manually checked to obtain: simple words, compound words with two chunks, and compound words with more than two chunks, respectively represented as WP1, WP2, and WP3+, in Table 3.

Table 3. Database Statistics: Distribution of the Bengali words.

WP1	WP2	WP3+
28,832	95,231	28,084

4.2 Participants

Pronunciations predicted by the proposed G2P approach can be assessed by comparing them with gold standards in pronunciation dictionaries. However, linguists or experts should be assigned to check the pronunciation of an unseen word. Similarly, participants were required for subjective or qualitative analysis of TTS systems. The present study assigns linguists to ask 20 native Bengali speakers to test TTS systems. 20 Bengali native speakers (14 male and 6 female) are our university students aged 18–24.

5 Experiments, Results, and Findings

This section devises experiments for answering the research questions mentioned in Sect. 1. The results and findings of these experiments are also highlighted.

5.1 Answering RQ1: Evaluating Proposed G2P Approach

Research question RQ1 is answered by comparing the performances of the proposed G2P approach against three baselines: a rule-based G2P approach from [9], a subword-based G2P approach from [8], and a memory-driven G2P approach from [7]. The rule-based approach used phonetic features to generate sets of orthographic, schwa deletion, and special rules. Subword-based approach boosted the rule-based approach using a segmentation method similar to the current morphological segmentation. However, it considers only a few common suffixes to address the inflected words, unlike the current work that (i) considers all possible morphemes and (ii) addresses inflected and compound words. Performances of G2P approaches are analyzed using four standard measures: word-level accuracy (WLA), phone-level accuracy (GLA), mean normalized Levenshtein distance (MNLD) for classification accuracy, and conditional relative entropy (CRE) for validation of phonetic smoothness. WLA is a simple word-by-word comparison between the exact and predicted pronunciation. GLA measures the percentage of the graphs for which phones are correctly predicted. MNLD for two strings is defined as the minimum number of edit operations (Levenshtein distance) to convert one string into the other divided by the length of the reference string [21] while LD is determined using the Wagner-Fisher algorithm [24]. The CRE measure determines the phonetic smoothness of the predicted pronunciation [21]. This measure is crucial in incorporating the G2P approach in TTS or ASR systems. Pronunciations predicted by four baselines and the current proposed G2P approaches are compared against the gold standards using four measures, with higher values being better for WLA and GLA and lower values being better for MNLD and CRE. Accordingly, these two categories of measures are denoted with ↑ and ↓, respectively, in Table 4.

Table 4. Performance of the baseline and proposed G2P approaches.

Method	WLA ↑	GLA ↑	MNLD ↓	CRE ↓
Rule-based G2P approach	67.47 %	75.78 %	0.13	2.19
Rule-based + subword-based approach	72.21 %	78.49 %	0.08	1.77
Rule-based + memory-driven approach	79.18 %	**82.66 %**	**0.04**	1.34
Rule-based + proposed G2P approach	**89.36 %**	80.64 %	**0.04**	**1.06**

Table 4 shows that the proposed method outperforms all baseline approaches across various metrics, except for GLA. This performance is attributed towards the effectiveness of morphological segmentation and syllabification modules.

5.2   Answering RQ2: Evaluating Proposed G2P Approach

The proposed G2P approach is expected to handle compound, inflected words using morphological segmentation and syllabification. Accordingly, we analyzed the performances of the proposed approach on three datasets: one having simple words, second one having compound and inflected words, and the third having foreign words. Performances are analyzed using the same four measures: word-level accuracy (WLA), phone-level accuracy (GLA), mean normalized Levenshtein distance (MNLD), and conditional relative entropy (CRE). The result has been discussed in Table 5.

Table 5. Performance of proposed G2P models for different test-set.

Datasets	WLA ↑	GLA ↑	MNLD ↓	CRE ↓
Bengali words	88.19 %	**96.47 %**	0.04	1.23
Compound and Inflected words	**88.47 %**	83.35 %	**0.03**	**0.98**
Foreign words	80.11 %	77.23 %	1.02	2.94
Total words	89.36 %	80.64 %	0.04	1.06

According to Table 5, the proposed approach performed as expected: better for the compound and inflected words than simple words. Foreign words are not addressed by the rules or the proposed modules of segmentation or syllabification. Accordingly, the proposed approach's performance for foreign words is not at par.

5.3   Answering RQ3: Evaluating TTS System

With the proposed G2P approach, the change in the performance of a TTS system is analyzed in this section. The basic TTS system is an unrestricted unit-selection based system that considers syllables as basic units and is developed using the Festival framework [4]. We developed different TTS systems without any G2P approach, with all three baselines and our proposed G2P approach. 20 sentences and a paragraph synthesized by these TTS systems were subjectively tested for naturalness and intelligibility. Listening tests were conducted using 20 native Bengali participants to judge the quality of synthesized speech on a 5-point Likert scale (1 representing very bad and 5 representing very good) for each sentence. The subjects submitted their opinion scores for each sentence as instructed in Table 6.

Table 6. Instruction for evaluating the quality of synthesized speech.

Point	Quality of sentence
1	Poor speech with distortion and low intelligibility
2	Poor speech with distortion but intelligible
3	Good speech with less distortion and intelligible
4	Excellent speech quality with less naturalness
5	As good as natural speech

Averaging the opinion scores obtained from all the participants over all the sentences, a mean opinion score (MOS) is achieved. Whether the proposed G2P approach positively affected the performance of the TTS system where it was integrated is determined by considering changes in this MOS value. The mean opinion scores (MOS) provided by all evaluators for each sentence were compared before and after employing these approaches, as mentioned in Table 7. The results in terms of MOS for all sentences demonstrated improvement after incorporating the proposed G2P approach.

Table 7. MOS comparison of TTS systems with the different G2P approaches.

TTS Systems	MOS
TTS system without any G2P approach	3.7
TTS system with rule-based G2P approach	4.0
TTS system with rule-based and subword-based G2P approach	4.1
TTS system with rule-based and memory-driven G2P approach	4.1
TTS system with rule-based and proposed G2P approach	**4.2**

According to Table 7, integrating the proposed approach with TTS systems achieved better MOS than others, as expected and statistically significant as we tested using paired t-test.

5.4 Answering RQ4: Evaluating ASR System

This section analyzes the performances of ASR systems when integrated with the proposed G2P approach. The present study developed two different ASR systems: (i) the first one with a rule-based G2P approach and (ii) another with the proposed G2P approach on three different speech data: (i) isolated speech, (ii) continuous speech, and (iii) spontaneous speech. The ASR systems were developed using CMU Sphinx Recognizer [12]. Isolated speech was collected as the speakers had been asked to read 20 sentences from independent and different domains, continuous speech was collected by reading 20 paragraphs with 15–20 sentences, and spontaneous speech was collected as the speakers had not been prompted with a specific topic or discourses. Performances of these ASR systems were assessed using four standard metrics: Word Error Rate (WER), Word Match Rate (WMR), Mean Normalized Levenshtein Distance (MNLD), and word information lost (WIL) [16], as presented in Table 8.

Table 8. Accuracy of proposed G2P models for ASR systems.

Types of G2P approaches and speech	WER ↓	WMR ↓	MNLD ↓	WIL ↓
Rule-based System on Isolated speech	10.35 %	17.28 %	0.15	1.03
Rule-based System on Continuous speech	12.62 %	18.86 %	0.17	1.21
Rule-based System on Spontaneous speech	14.93 %	19.64 %	0.18	1.29
Proposed System on Isolated speech	**7.18 %**	**8.9 %**	**0.1**	**0.93**
Proposed System on Continuous speech	9.62 %	10.85 %	0.13	1.11
Proposed System on Spontaneous speech	10.39 %	11.03 %	0.14	1.27

According to Table 8, the ASR system with the proposed G2P approach performs better for isolated speech than all other speech types and statistically significant as we tested using paired t-test. This performance can be attributed to the current system's capacity to generate phonetically smooth speech. Incorporating contextual complexities in continuous data and unseen data in spontaneous data, performances were meagerly hampered.

6 Conclusion

The method proposed in this study holds significant importance for both text synthesis and speech recognition, particularly for Indian languages. The key characteristics of the method are as follows:

1. With this method, using a manual dictionary without compromising word coverage is no longer required. Accordingly, developing a faster speech system like TTS or ASR systems is possible.
2. Although not an out-of-the-box approach for converting graphs into phones, the proposed approach provides a novel technique to address the problem.
3. The segmentation process aims to extract the necessary morphological information for resolving ambiguity in predicting word pronunciation rather than precisely segmenting words into valid morphemes.
4. Accuracy of the proposed approach relies heavily on the list of valid words. Approximately 4% of errors occurred due to compound or inflected words out of the total 10.64%. If all valid words were present in the list, errors due to inflection could be significantly reduced.

Following future research directions, the proposed paper's approach can be extended, refined, and applied to various real-world scenarios, ultimately enhancing the performance of rule-based grapheme-to-phoneme conversion for Bengali and other languages.

1. Handling Out-of-Vocabulary (OOV) Words: This is important as real-world text often contains new or rare words not covered by the existing rules.
2. Data Augmentation: This can help improve the generalization of the model and its ability to handle various linguistic variations in Bengali.
3. Leveraging Neural Networks: Neural networks may capture more complex patterns and dependencies in the grapheme-to-phoneme mapping, improving performance.
4. Error Analysis and Refinement: Based on the analysis, refine the rules and linguistic techniques to address specific weaknesses in the current approach.
5. Multilingual Approaches: Explore the possibility of developing multilingual or cross-lingual G2P models that can handle grapheme-to-phoneme conversion for multiple languages, leveraging shared linguistic properties.

Acknowledgement. We would like to express our sincere gratitude to Mr Prabhat Mukherjee for his contribution in collecting data and generating the pronunciation dictionary and Mr Nilay Roy for his guidance as a linguist. We also acknowledge the collaborative spirit of the students of KIIT University in the evaluation tasks.

References

1. Basu, J., Basu, T., Mitra, M., Mandal, S.K.D.: Grapheme to phoneme (g2p) conversion for bangla. In: 2009 Oriental COCOSDA International Conference on Speech Database and Assessments, pp. 66–71. IEEE (2009)
2. Bellegarda, J.R.: Unsupervised, language-independent grapheme-to-phoneme conversion by latent analogy. Speech Commun. **46**(2), 140–152 (2005)
3. Bisani, M., Ney, H.: Joint-sequence models for grapheme-to-phoneme conversion. Speech Commun. **50**(5), 434–451 (2008)
4. Black, A.W., Lenzo, K.A.: Building synthetic voices. Lang. Technol. Ins. Carnegie Mellon Univ. Cepstral LLC **4**(2), 62 (2003)

5. Choudhury, M.: Rule-based grapheme to phoneme mapping for Hindi speech synthesis. In: 90th Indian Science Congress of the International Speech Communication Association (ISCA), Bangalore, India. Citeseer (2003)
6. Dietterich, T.G., Hild, H., Bakiri, G.: A comparative study of id3 and backpropagation for English text-to-speech mapping. In: Machine Learning Proceedings 1990, pp. 24–31. Elsevier (1990)
7. Ghosh, K., Rao, K.S.: Memory-based data-driven approach for grapheme-to-phoneme conversion in Bengali text-to-speech synthesis system. In: 2011 Annual IEEE India Conference, pp. 1–4. IEEE (2011)
8. Ghosh, K., Rao, K.S.: Subword based approach for grapheme-to-phoneme conversion in Bengali text-to-speech synthesis system. In: 2012 National Conference on Communications (NCC), pp. 1–5. IEEE (2012)
9. Ghosh, K., Reddy, R.V., Narendra, N., Maity, S., Koolagudi, S., Rao, K.: Grapheme to phoneme conversion in Bengali for festival based TTS framework. In: 8th International Conference on Natural Language Processing (ICON). Macmillan Publishers (2010)
10. Ghosh, K., Sreenivasa Rao, K.: Data-driven phrase break prediction for Bengali text-to-speech system. In: Parashar, M., Kaushik, D., Rana, O.F., Samtaney, R., Yang, Y., Zomaya, A. (eds.) IC3 2012. CCIS, vol. 306, pp. 118–129. Springer, Heidelberg (2012). https://doi.org/10.1007/978-3-642-32129-0_17
11. Jiampojamarn, S., Kondrak, G., Sherif, T.: Applying many-to-many alignments and hidden markov models to letter-to-phoneme conversion. In: Human Language Technologies 2007: The Conference of the North American Chapter of the Association for Computational Linguistics; Proceedings of the Main Conference, pp. 372–379 (2007)
12. Lee, K.F., Hon, H.W., Reddy, R.: An overview of the sphinx speech recognition system. IEEE Trans. Acoust. Speech Signal Process. **38**(1), 35–45 (1990)
13. Lehnert, W.G.: Case-based problem solving with a large knowledge base of learned cases. In: Proceedings of the Sixth National Conference on Artificial Intelligence, vol. 1, pp. 301–306 (1987)
14. Lucassen, J., Mercer, R.: An information theoretic approach to the automatic determination of phonemic baseforms. In: ICASSP 1984. IEEE International Conference on Acoustics, Speech, and Signal Processing, vol. 9, pp. 304–307. IEEE (1984)
15. Macherey, K., Dai, A.M., Talbot, D., Popat, A.C., Och, F.: Language-independent compound splitting with morphological operations. In: Proceedings of the 49th Annual Meeting of the Association for Computational Linguistics: Human Language Technologies, HLT 2011, vol. 1, pp. 1395–1404. Association for Computational Linguistics (2011)
16. Morris, A.C., Maier, V., Green, P.: From WER and RIL to MER and WIL: improved evaluation measures for connected speech recognition. In: Eighth International Conference on Spoken Language Processing, pp. 2765–2768 (2004)
17. Murthy, H.A., Bellur, A., Viswanath, V., Narayanan, B., Susan, A., Kasthuri, G.: Building unit selection speech synthesis in Indian languages: an initiative by an Indian consortium. In: Proceedings of COCOSDA (2010)
18. Narendra, N., Rao, K.S., Ghosh, K., Reddy, V.R., Maity, S.: Development of bengali screen reader using festival speech synthesizer. In: 2011 Annual IEEE India Conference, pp. 1–4. IEEE (2011)
19. Narendra, N., Rao, K.S., Ghosh, K., Vempada, R.R., Maity, S.: Development of syllable-based text to speech synthesis system in Bengali. Int. J. Speech Technol. **14**, 167–181 (2011)

20. Oakey, S., Cawthorn, R.: Inductive learning of pronunciation rules by hypothesis testing and correction. In: IJCAI, pp. 109–114. Citeseer (1981)
21. Reichel, U.D., Schiel, F.: Using morphology and phoneme history to improve grapheme-to-phoneme conversion. In: Proceedings of the Eurospeech, pp. 1937–1940 (2005)
22. Stanfill, C.: Memory-Based Reasoning Applied to English Pronunciation. Thinking Machines Corporation, Cambridge (1987)
23. Van Coile, B.: Inductive learning of pronunciation rules with the depes system. In: IEEE International Conference on Acoustics, Speech, and Signal Processing, pp. 745–748. IEEE Computer Society (1991)
24. Wagner, R.A., Fischer, M.J.: The string-to-string correction problem. J. ACM (JACM) **21**(1), 168–173 (1974)

Revisiting Assessment of Text Complexity: Lexical and Syntactic Parameters Fluctuations

Alexandra Vahrusheva[1] ⓘ, Valery Solovyev[1(✉)] ⓘ, Marina Solnyshkina[1] ⓘ,
Elzara Gafiaytova[1] ⓘ, and Svetlana Akhtyamova[2] ⓘ

[1] Kazan Federal University, 420008 Kazan, Russia
Maki.solovyev@mail.ru
[2] Kazan National Research Technological University, Kazan, Russia

Abstract. In this article we share findings on linguistic complexity fluctuations of Russian middle school textbooks. The study partially confirmed the null hypothesis that textbook syntactic complexity grows universally over the course of a single school year. The Research Corpus was compiled of 104 textbooks used in 12 subject domains in Russian middle schools. In accordance with school semesters (Fall-Spring), we divided each textbook into two parts and examined 208 texts for 47 quantitative parameters measured with RuLingva (rulingva.kpfu.ru). After considering dynamics of the values of each parameter for Fall and Spring semesters, we narrowed the parameters list down to syntactic (average word length, average sentence length, Flesch-Kincaid grade level) and lexical (lexical diversity and frequency) clusters. We identified and scrutinized three types of text complexity fluctuations: simultaneous increase of both clusters of parameters, opposite dynamics and independent fluctuations. The majority of textbooks demonstrate lexical and syntactic clusters' "trade-off"" when the lexical complexity increase triggers the syntactic complexity decrease thus balancing the joint complexity. We also discuss the assumptions that underline the concept of complexity fluctuations and algorithms of its measurements in an effort to put the issue on the agenda of researchers and education authorities. Our findings can be useful for scholars, academicians and education policy makers at the national and regional levels.

Keywords: Text Complexity · Textbook · Readability · Syntactic Complexity · Lexical Complexity · Fluctuations

1 Introduction

Research on linguistic complexity of instructional (academic) texts have thus far mainly been focused on separate factors or clusters of parameters such as morphological, lexical, syntactic, and discourse a sum of which define as total or joint text complexity [8]. The starting assumption employed as a working hypothesis in numerous studies and ubiquitously acknowledged is that complexity as a quantifiable measure can be estimated based on values (indices) of complexity predictors. The list of these predictors may include, but not limited to, morphemes of a certain type (e.g. genitive case in Russian), long or

© The Author(s), under exclusive license to Springer Nature Switzerland AG 2023
A. Karpov et al. (Eds.): SPECOM 2023, LNAI 14338, pp. 430–441, 2023.
https://doi.org/10.1007/978-3-031-48309-7_35

rare words, distance to the main verb in a sentence, etc. [11]. Another most significant implication of text complexity theory includes insights into complexity continuity, i.e. gradual cognitive and linguistic complexity growth across grades from elementary to high school [12].

Text complexity as one of the most important cognitive characteristics of a text largely predetermines readers' success in comprehension and reduces the risk of demotivation against reading. Accurate assessment of text complexity allows to identify priority target audience. The latter has numerous implications for computational linguistics including the task of automatic identification of complexity of texts of different types. The intensive studies on complexity of educational [23], legal [3], medical [15] and texts of other discourse types proved their value in numerous fields where verbal communication is vitally important. The current status of theoretical research in this area is provided in [5].

High school textbooks used throughout a school year present a specific genre and as they are quite extensive in length, assessment of their complexity implies additional difficulties. Textbook content complexity is expected to grow throughout a school year so that educational material changes from simpler to more complex. Content complication causes numerous questions on the nature of material presentation and its complexity characteristics. Until now, most of the research on complexity, beginning with the classic Flesch-Kincaid Grade Level formula [9], has dealt with the formal characteristics of texts, such as sentence and word length. It is logical to raise the question: Should syntactic complexity of texts also increase along with the lexical complexity, or should textbooks authors save students of cognitive overload and reduce syntactic complexity while lexical complexity grows (mostly due to the terminology density)?

The present contribution is a part of a larger project exploring text complexity predictors with the focus on how separate syntactic and lexical text complexity predictors fluctuate on one complexity level, i.e. within texts of a certain grade and a subject domain. The null hypothesis of this study is that academic texts of a predefined grade level complexity (i.e., text books for 7th graders) and a subject domain (i.e., Mathematics, IT, and Natural Science) exhibit quantitative differences in lexical and syntactic metrics at the beginning and end of a school year thus realizing complexity growth continuity from grade to grade.

Our main research objective is to observe and describe trajectories of lexical and syntactic parameters dynamics across 2–11 grades in Russian academic texts of 12 domains, i.e. Art, Biology, Science, Geography, History, IT, Mathematics, Technology, Music, Physics, Ecology, and Social studies for school. We also aim at providing researchers with a practical and reproducible route to developing new language resources for Russian as a low-resource language.

2   Literature Review

The contemporary paradigm regards 'grade level complexity' as a quantifiable phenomenon matching texts of certain linguistic parameters and students of a certain grade able to independently read and comprehend texts [6]. Although all researchers take for granted that 'grade level complexity' grows from year to year and children are expected to read increasingly complex texts each school year, the ideas on specifics of how linguistic parameters in different languages fluctuate from the start to the end of a school year are few if any [7].

Complexity theory suggests that text complexity is a phenomenon of manifold interactions among constitutive elements, a function of numerous factors which may develop multidirectional dynamics or operate in opposing directions [21]. Text complexity varies across the academic discourse as a result of text parameters change: text factors may compound or mitigate each other. Attempts to isolate the influence of a particular factor in explaining text complexity change is not only impossible, but also wrongheaded. Automatic text complexity assessment algorithms realized in Coh-Metrix (tool.cohmetrix.com), TextInspector (textinspector.com), Tekstomer (textometr.ru) and RuLingva (rulingva.kpfu.ru) are in fact similar and present metrics of numerous text parameters which are not assigned to grade levels. The only exceptions are two: (1) readability indices measured with Flesch-Kincaid grade level (further FKGL) or lexical complexity estimated with vocabulary lists (A1–C2, CEFR) in TextInspector and Tekstomer.

As for readability indices they are sufficiently well characterized in [20, 22], so here we dare to offer readers only information on the Russian readability formula, FKGL (SIS), which was designed in 2018 by a group of Russian scholars on Corpus of Russian academic texts and validated in numerous studies in Russia and abroad [19]. The formula employs two metrics, i.e. average word and sentence length: FKGL $(SIS)^1 = -11.97 + 0.36 \times ASL + 5.76 \times ASL$, where ASL is average sentence length, AWL – average word length [19]. Lexical complexity in texts for native readers unlike in texts for non-native speakers is traditionally measured based on the age of acquisition [4], lexical diversity and vocabulary frequency [8]. The use of vocabulary lists corresponding a range of language proficiency levels is ubiquitously practiced to select foreign language teaching materials, although similar practice is still very rare when educational materials are selected for native speakers. The reason for the latter is typically explained by impossibility to compile corresponding vocabulary lists [14].

The index of lexical diversity indicates how wide the range of the text author's vocabulary is. The idea behind the parameter is the following: the more various vocabulary is used in the text, the more challenging is the text for comprehension.

Modern discourse complexology developed numerous techniques and algorithms to measure lexical diversity, although Type Token ratio is still the most validated and acknowledged. In contemporary studies the classical TTR formula [13] is normalization to 1000 tokens: TTR (per 1000 tokens) = Types/Tokens.

As for word frequency profiles, they are determined based on frequency lists compiled based on the data of national corpora. Researchers of the Russian language by default use Frequency dictionary [16] to determine the frequency level of each word in a text under study.

As for text complexity models based on a combination of syntactic and lexical features, which researchers define as rather helpful [17], little has been done in the area [1] and their compatibility for the Russian language is still being a research niche.

---

1 SIS in FKFL(SIS) stands for the initials of the formula developers, i.e. Solovyev, Ivanov, Solnyshkina [19].

3 Methods and Data

Our study was carried out in three stages described below:

(1) Dataset: preparation, 'cleaning', and pre-processing.

The corpus for this study was compiled of 104 textbooks on 12 subjects (Art, Biology, Science, Geography, History, IT, Mathematics, Technology, Music, Physics, Ecology, and Social studies) from the Federal list of textbooks of the Russian Federation [10], with the total size of the corpus amounting to 2,589,521 tokens (see Table 1). Russian Academic Corpus (further RAC), originally compiled by researchers of Lab "Text Analytics" at Kazan Federal University in 2018, has since been updated and by now its size has reached over 10 mln. Tokens [24]. In 2018, RAC comprised texts included into the Federal List of Textbooks recommended for use in schools of General Education of the Russian Federation of that period (inlnk.ru/ZZyK5e) and has been updated and improved since then by including there books of the later versions of the Federal Lists (surl.li/lktpb, fpu.edu.ru/). The general law "On the Standard Period for Using Textbooks" says that "Educational organizations have the right, for a period of five years, to use textbooks purchased before the relevant order of the Ministry of Education and Science came into force, although they are excluded from the federal list of textbooks" (https://inlnk.ru/PmklL5). It was later specified in Order of the Ministry of Education dated September 21, 2022 №. 858 permitting schools to use textbooks from the previous list until September 25, 2025 (surl.li/lktow).

We also divided texts of each textbook into two parts – Fall and Spring semesters respectively thus preparing them for contrasting metrics of each semester. In total we received 208 texts of 104 textbooks which is viewed as a representative sample of 941 books in the Federal list of textbooks thus ensuring validity of the research results [2].

(2) On Stage II of the research we processed each text with the help of the automatic analyzer of Russian texts RuLingva (rulingva.kpfu.ru) and measured metrics of 47 linguistic features in each of them. The profiler is in the public domain of Kazan Federal University enabling users to upload large texts (up to 50000 tokens), estimate metrics of numerous parameters and download metrics in spreadsheets.

(3) Based on immediate observation of the 47 complexity metrics dynamics through the school year, from Fall to Spring semester, we narrowed the list to five metrics estimating syntactic and lexical complexity. We employed a discriminant analysis to identify text features as measures contributing to text complexity prediction [see 25, 26]. The list of the selected statistically significant syntactic parameters includes Flesch-Kincaid Grade Level index (FKGL(SIS)), Average Sentence Length and Average Word Length, while lexical complexity manifests itself in Vocabulary Frequency, and lexical diversity, measured as Type Token Ratio.

Statistical processing of the obtained data was carried out using StatSoft Statistica program which we also used to visualize interim and final results of the research (see Figs. 1, 2, 3, and 4).

Table 1. Corpus size.

Discourse domain	Number of textbooks	Grades
Art	5	2–4
Biology	12	5–7
Science	9	2–4
Geography	8	5–8, 10–11
History	11	5–7, 10–11
IT	12	2–4, 7
Mathematics	8	2–3
Music	4	2–4
Physics	6	7–9
Ecology	3	2–3, 8
Social studies	14	5–11
Technology	12	2–4
Total: 2,589,521 tokens	104	2–11

4   Analysis

The analysis revealed two patterns of FKGL (SIS) dynamics, i.e. increasing and decreasing: in 56 of 104 textbooks reviewed, the arithmetic mean of FKGL (SIS) in Spring Semester appears to be lower than in Fall Semester. E.g. 7.57 against 7.54 in Bio_6_Si (Table 2 below). However, the difference is typically very small and does not exceed one grade level (for the full dataset see Fig. 1 below and Dataset FPU at https://clck.ru/U7sCt).

No uniform trend in the dynamics of the Flash-Kincaid index for all textbooks is observed: FKGL (SIS) grows in Art, Mathematics, Social Studies and Science textbooks, which indicates their gradually increasing complexity, while Ecology, IT and Biology textbooks demonstrate the opposite.

Similar estimates on all the selected parameters presented in Figs. 5, 6, 7, and 8 (see at Laboratory website https://clck.ru/U7sCt) indicate manifold dynamics of parameters. E.g., frequency index decreases in all Ecology, partly in Music, Art, Technology, Physics, IT and Social Studies textbooks. The reverse trend can be traced in Mathematics textbooks.

As for syntactic and lexical complexities we identified four patterns.

In 43 textbooks we observe increase of only lexical, but not syntactic complexity. In 32 textbooks we registered concurrent growth of both lexical and syntactic complexity have increased, while in 23 textbooks only syntactic, but not lexical complexity arises. In 6 textbooks texts became simpler syntactically and lexically by the end of the school year. Thus, in 66 textbooks out of 104 (almost two-thirds of the dataset), we observe a trade-off when while metrics of one of the clusters of parameters grow, metrics of another drop. And lexical complexity, as expected, increases in the majority of textbooks – 75, while syntactic demonstrates growth in 55 textbooks.

Below we consider two interesting cases in more detail.

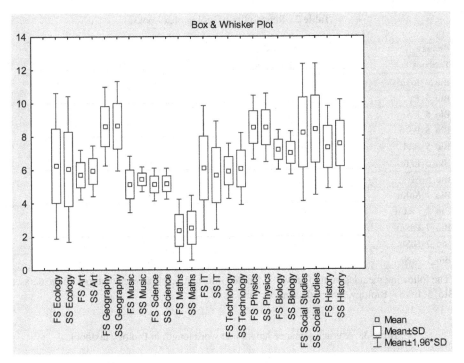

Fig. 1. Range of FKGL (SIS) metrics in fall (FS) and spring semesters (SS).

The readability of Spring semester in 11 biology textbooks out of 12 is lower than in Fall semester.

Considering that FKGL (SIS) is a function of average word and sentence length, we focus on the fluctuations of these metrics first.

The data in Table 3 indicate obvious wobbling of the sentences length metrics and its fluctuations in opposite directions, while the average word length has a much better visible co-dependence with FKGL (SIS): it is less in Spring semester in those 11 textbooks which reveal a lower FKGL (SIS) (cf. Table 2 and Table 3). We apply the statistical criterion – T-test to determine the level of statistical significance of this pattern. To justify the possibility of its application, we first check the normality of the distribution of values (Fig. 2, Fig. 3).

The data obtained (K-S $p > .20$; Lilliefors $p > .20$; Shapiro-Wilk $p = .69$) allow us to conclude that the distribution of both features is normal, which, in turn, allows us to use parametric methods for data processing. The parameters under consideration (Fall and Spring Semesters) demonstrate a strong statistically significant correlation – 0.92 (Fig. 4).

In Spring Semester, the average value of the parameter decreases from 2.64 to 2.61. The application of the criterion for dependent variables T-test for Dependent Samples results in $p = 0.011$ (Table 4), which means the significance of the change in the mean values of the two samples.

Table 2. Readability of biology textbooks.

Biology	FKGL (SIS)	
Textbook	Fall Semester	Spring Semester
Bio_5_IoVa[a]	7.03	6.49
Bio_5_Pa	8.03	7.58
Bio_5_PiSo	6.49	6.44
Bio_5_PoNi	7.34	6.99
Bio_5_SiPl	6.14	6.05
Bio_5_PrTu	6.63	6.56
Bio_6_Si	7.57	7.54
Bio_7_SuKu	7.58	7.53
Bio_7_MaCh	6.65	6.18
Bio_7_PaSu	7.94	8.08
Bio_7_NiSh	7.27	7.04
Bio_7_ViNi	7.65	7.61

[a]The following metadescription provides detailed information about each textbook in the dataset: Bio_5_IoVa – Biology, 5th grade, authors' initials.

Table 3. Average sentence length and word length in Biology textbook.

Textbook	Average sentence length		Average word length	
	Fall Semester	Spring Semester	Fall Semester	Spring Semester
Bio_5_IoVa	10.1	9.93	2.67	2.58
Bio_5_Pa	11.91	11.43	2.73	2.68
Bio_5_PiSo	10.24	10.66	2.56	2.53
Bio_5_PoNi	11.01	11.7	2.66	2.56
Bio_5_SiPl	9.75	10.3	2.54	2.49
Bio_5_PrTu	10.92	10.71	2.55	2.55
Bio_6_Si	10.97	11.09	2.71	2.69
Bio_7_SuKu	9.6	9.72	2.79	2.78
Bio_7_MaCh	12.03	11.03	2.48	2.46
Bio_7_PaSu	12	12.16	2.71	2.72
Bio_7_NiSh	11.27	11.53	2.64	2.58
Bio_7_ViNi	11.59	11.21	2.68	2.7

The decrease in syntactic complexity in Spring semester, according to our assumptions, should be accompanied by an increase in complexity in some other aspect. Table 5 below shows the values of the TTR parameter, which reflects texts lexical diversity. The higher the TTR value, the greater the lexical complexity of the text, the more difficult the textbook to understand.

Table 5 illustrates another pattern of complexity predictors behavior: TTR as a lexical complexity indicator in Spring Semester in 9 out of 12 textbooks is higher than in Fall

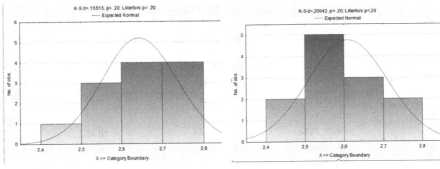

Fig. 2. Distribution of values of average word length of words in Biology textbooks in Fall Semester.

Fig. 3. Distribution of values of average word length of words in Biology textbooks in Spring Semester.

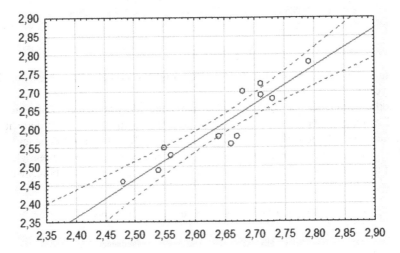

Fig. 4. Correlation of average word length in Biology textbooks of Fall and Spring semesters. The X-axis shows the values for Fall Semester.

Table 4. T-test for dependent samples.

Variables	Mean	Std.Dv	N	Diff	Std.Dv	t	df	p*	Confidence	Confidence
Fall Semester	2.64	0.092	12							
Sping Semester	2.61	0.100	12	0.03	0.03	3.059	11	0.011	0.009	0.057

*Marked differences are significant at $p < 0.05$

Semester. Thus, for Biology domain, lexical complexity increase is compensated with a

Table 5. TTR lexical diversity metric in biology textbooks.

#	Textbook	TTR	
		Fall Semester	Spring Semester
1.	Bio_5_IoVa	0.44	0.42
2.	Bio_5_Pa	0.44	0.48
3.	Bio_5_PiSo	0.46	0.47
4.	Bio_5_PoNi	0.44	0.46
5.	Bio_5_SiPl	0.46	0.49
6.	Bio_5_PrTu	0.42	0.41
7.	Bio_6_Si	0.44	0.47
8.	Bio_7_SuKu	0.47	0.5
9.	Bio_7_MaCh	0.47	0.45
10.	Bio_7_PaSu	0.46	0.47
11.	Bio_7_NiSh	0.44	0.46
12.	Bio_7_ViNi	0.41	0.46

decrease in syntactic complexity, thus keeping joint text complexity stable through the school year.

Another parameter that characterizes lexical complexity is frequency of words. The general assumption here is as follows: the rarer the word, the more difficult it is to understand [18]. Table 6 shows metrics of FKGL (SIS) and words frequency of (the number of occurrences per million tokens) in IT textbooks. We also highlighted the cases of metrics increase through a school. As we can see, for all 12 textbooks with only

Table 6. FKGL (SIS) and frequency in IT textbooks.

IT Textbook	FKGL (SIS)		Frequency	
	Fall Semester	Spring Semester	Fall Semester	Spring Semester
Inf_2_BePa_1	4.82	4.36	244.26	182.52
Inf_2_MaCh_1	6.42	6.52	298.02	254.52
Inf_2_RuSe_1	4.53	4.67	239.28	264.64
Inf_3_BePa_1	4.21	3.36	178.96	155.5
Inf_3_MaCh_1	7.77	7.12	291.36	252.44
Inf_3_MoMo_1	6.27	5.73	224.51	183.35
Inf_4_BePa_1	5.27	5.37	159.73	188.37
Inf_4_GoGo_2	2.79	2.96	192.18	237.7
Inf_4_MaCh_2	6.11	6.37	268.13	275.79
Inf_4_MoMo_2	6.93	6.44	218.55	201.12
Inf_7_BoBo_2	9.36	8.9	205.56	169.16
Inf_7_GeYu_1	8.69	6.19	213.49	203.24

any exception, one of the two parameters contributing to joint complexity increases, while the other decreases. Probability of random coincidence is $p < 0.005$. Thus, here we observe, in its purest form, an example of a balance of joint complexity.

5 Conclusion

The present study focuses on linguistic complexity fluctuations of Russian school textbooks. We scrutinized the dynamics of three syntactic and two lexical text parameters, comparing their values in texts studied in Fall and Spring Semesters of the academic year. We used the dataset of 104 textbooks of 12 domains, i.e. Art, Biology, Science, Geography, History, IT, Maths, Technology, Music, Physics, Ecology, and Social studies.

In this study we asked two simple research questions:

Does readability, as a central contributor to text syntactic complexity, increase through a school year?

Do lexical and syntactic clusters of parameters manifest the same or similar propensity to form a higher joint text complexity by the end of a school year?

The answer to both proved to be a resounding 'negative'.

We revealed readability increase in the textbooks on Art, Mathematics, Social Studies and Science textbooks, while FLGL in Ecology, IT and Biology textbooks decreases by the end of the school year. Lexical complexity increased in 75 textbooks while syntactic complexity grew only in 55 books.

The majority of textbooks (66 of 104) reveal the so-called trade-off of syntactic and lexical parameters, i.e. concurrent growth of the one cluster and fall of the other. As human capacity for attention is limited, textbook writers, seeking for readers' attention, tend to trade-off syntactic with lexical complexity thus balancing increase of the one with decrease of the other.

Based on the research findings we offer a valid algorithm of measurement and monitoring classroom books complexity which may considerably contribute to progress in the country's educational policy. The research findings may also have implications for curriculum replanning.

Acknowledgements. This research was supported by the Kazan Federal University Strategic Academic Leadership (Priority 2030).

References

1. Balakrishna, S.V.: Analyzing Text Complexity and Text Simplification: Connecting Linguistics, Processing and Educational Applications. Ph.D. thesis (2015)
2. Biber, D.: Representativeness in corpus design. Liter. Linguist. Comput. **8**(4), 243–257 (1993)
3. Blinova, O., Tarasov, N.: Complexity metrics of Russian legal texts: selection, use, initial efficiency evaluation. In: Papers from the Annual International Conference "Dialogue" (2022), pp. 1017–1028. https://doi.org/10.28995/2075-7182-2022-21-1017-1028
4. Botarleanu, R.-M., Dascalu, M., Watanabe, M., Crossley, S.A.: Age of exposure 2.0: estimating word complexity using iterative models of word embeddings. Behav. Res. Methods **54**(1), 3015–3042 (2022). https://doi.org/10.3758/s13428-022-01797-5

5. Churunina, A.A., Solnyshkina, M.I., Yarmakeev, I.E.: Lexical diversity as a predictor of complexity in textbooks on the Russian language. Russ. Lang. Stud. **21**(2), 212–227 (2023)
6. Crossley, S.A., Skalicky, S.: Examining lexical development in second language learners: an approximate replication of Salsbury, Crossley & McNamara (2011). Lang. Teach. **52**(3), 1–21 (2017)
7. Elmore, J., Hiebert, E.H.: Text complexity and the early grades: the fuss and how recent research can help. Phi Delta Kappan **97**(8), 60–65 (2015)
8. DuBay, W.H. The principles of readability. Impact Information: Costa Mesa, CA. (2004)
9. Flesch, R.: A new readability yardstick. J. Appl. Psychol. **32**, 221–233 (1948)
10. Fpu.edu.ru. Order of the Ministry of Education of Russia No. 254. (2020)
11. Gatiyatullina, G., Solnyshkina, M., Solovyev, V., Danilov, A., Martynova, E., Yarmakeev, I.: Computing Russian morphological distribution patterns using RusAC online server. In: Proceedings - International Conference on Developments in eSystems Engineering, DeSE, art. no. 9450753, pp. 393–398 (2020)
12. Goldman, S.R., Lee, C.D.: Text complexity. Element. School J. **115**, 290–300 (2014)
13. Guiraud, P.: Problèmes et méthodes de la statistique linguistique. Dordrecht: Reidel, D. Harley, B., & King, M. L. Verb lexis in the written compositions of young L2 learners. Stud. Second Lang. Acquisit. **11**, 415–440 (1989)
14. Laposhina, A.N., Lebedeva, M.Yu.: Textometr: an online tool for automated complexity level assessment of texts for Russian language learners. Russ. Lang. Stud. **19**(3), 331–345 (2021)
15. Lina Sulieman, L., Robinson, J.R., Jackson, G.P.: Automating the classification of complexity of medical decision-making in patient-provider messaging in a patient portal. J. Surg. Res. **255**, 224–232 (2020)
16. Lyashevskay, O.N., Sharoff, S.A.: New Russian frequency dictionary (2009). http://dict.rus lang.ru/freq.php. Accessed 28 Dec 2021
17. Santini, M., Jönsson, A.: Pinning down text complexity - an exploratory study on the registers of the Stockholm-Umeå corpus (SUC). Regist. Stud. **2**(2), 306–349 (2020)
18. Solovyev, V., Andreeva, M., Solnyshkina, M., Zamaletdinov, R., Danilov, A., Gaynutdinova, D.: Computing concreteness ratings of Russian and English most frequent words: contrastive approach. In: Proceedings - International Conference on Developments in eSystems Engineering, DeSE, art. no. 9073272, pp. 403–408 (2019)
19. Solnyshkina, M., Ivanov, V., Solovyev, V.: Readability formula for Russian texts: a modified version. In: Batyrshin, I., Martínez-Villaseñor, M.L., Ponce Espinosa, H.E. (eds.) MICAI 2018. LNCS (LNAI), vol. 11289, pp. 132–145. Springer, Cham (2018). https://doi.org/10.1007/978-3-030-04497-8_11
20. Solnyshkina, M.I., Harkova, E.V., Kazachkova, M.B.: The structure of cross-linguistic differences: meaning and context of 'readability' and its Russian equivalent 'chitabelnost.' J. Lang. Educ. **6**(1), 103–119 (2020)
21. Solnyshkina, S.I., Kiselnikov, A.S.: Complexity of the text: stages of study in Russian applied linguistics. Quest. Cognit. Linguist. **1**, 18–40 (2022)
22. Solnyshkina, M.I., Solovyev, V.D., Gafiatova, E.V., Martynova, E.V.: Text complexity as an interdisciplinary problem. Quest. Cognit. Linguist. **1**, 18–40 (2022)
23. Solovyev, V., Solnyshkina, M., Ivanov, V., Batyrshin, I.: Prediction of reading difficulty in Russian academic texts. J. Intell. Fuzzy Syst. **36**(5), 4553–4563 (2019)
24. Solnyshkina, M., Solovyev, V., Ivanov, V., Danilov, A.: Studying text complexity in Russian Academic Corpus with multi-level annotation. CEUR Worksh. Proc. **2303**, 1–11 (2018)

25. Kupriyanov, R.V., Solnyshkina, M.I., Dascalu, M., Soldatkina, T.A.: Lexical and syntactic features of academic Russian texts: a discriminant analysis research result. Theor. Appl. Linguist. **8**(4), 105–122 (2022)
26. Churunina, A.A., Solnyshkina, M.I., Yarmakeev, I.E.: Lexical diversity as a predictor of the complexity of textbooks on the Russian language. Rusistika. Russ. Stud. **21**(2), 212–227 (2023)

Analysis of Natural Language Understanding Systems with L2 Learner Specific Synthetic Grammatical Errors Based on Parts-of-Speech

Snehal Ranjan[1]([✉]), Sai Kalyan Nanduri[1], Prakul Virdi[2],
and Chiranjeevi Yarra[1]

[1] International Institute of Information Technology Hyderabad, Hyderabad, India
snehal.ranjan@research.iiit.ac.in, chiranjeevi.yarra@iiit.ac.in
[2] Indian Institute of Technology Delhi, Delhi, India

Abstract. Second language learners often make grammatical mistakes, which can impact the performance of Spoken Language Understanding (SLU) systems. SLU systems consist of two key components: Automatic Speech Recognition (ASR) and Natural Language Understanding (NLU). This work focuses on the effects of grammatical errors which were synthetically generated by manipulating Parts of Speech (POS) tokens on the NLU module. Our analysis comprises three main aspects. Firstly, we assess the impact of grammatical errors on the overall performance of NLU systems, specifically in the domains of Intent Detection and Slot Filling. Secondly, we investigate NLU performance concerning POS tags. Lastly, we utilize an Attention-based NLU model to evaluate the significance of different POS. This study evaluates NLU models on ATIS and SNIPS datasets for Intent Detection and Slot Filling tasks with introduced grammatical errors, leading to a significant performance drop as large as 4.7% for Intent Detection and 5.1% for Slot Filling. However, training on datasets with synthetic errors helps mitigate this drop, and the models are shown to be sensitive to increasing levels of corrupted tokens. Additionally, attention analysis reveals Proper Nouns' higher weights in determining intent, while specific POS corruption, particularly Auxiliary Verbs and Nouns, is more likely to cause intent misclassification.

Keywords: Speech recognition · Human-computer interaction · Spoken language understanding · Language learning

1 Introduction

Spoken Language Understanding (SLU) have gained significant popularity in recent years, as it provides a way for humans to interact with machines in a natural mode of communication. SLU systems are crucial as they are responsible for accurately interpreting and processing language.

SLU (Spoken Language Understanding) systems play a pivotal role in various tools, such as digital assistants, and are extensively utilized by individuals not only in their native languages but also in non-native languages [11]. Consequently, these SLU systems must be capable of effectively process and comprehend non-native characteristics of speech.

However, SLU systems have a limitation in working with speech that contains non-native grammatical errors [21]. This research paper aims to investigate the effectiveness of SLU systems in processing speech that contains non-native grammatical errors and highlight the reasons why SLU systems fail in such cases.

SLU systems are primarily designed to recognize and interpret native speech, which is produced by individuals who are native speakers of a particular language. The effectiveness of SLU systems in recognizing native speech can be attributed to the large datasets used to train them [19], or the constituent modules like [2] which contain ample examples of native speech. Consequently, the statistical models used by these systems are better suited to the patterns and structures of native speech.

Non-native speakers of a language often make errors, which can include pronunciation, grammar, or syntax errors. These errors are often caused by the influence of the speaker's native language, which can have different patterns and structures [10]. Non-native grammatical errors pose a significant challenge for SLU systems because the statistical models used by these systems are not equipped to handle the varied patterns and structures of non-native speech.

When non-native grammatical errors are introduced into speech, the effectiveness of SLU systems is significantly reduced. The errors can lead to incorrect interpretations of the spoken language, resulting in inaccurate transcriptions or misinterpretations of the speaker's intent. Additionally, non-native errors can cause ASR systems to misinterpret common words, resulting in a failure to recognize the intended meaning of an utterance [18].

SLU systems, which are the core component of interfaces like Dialog Systems, have a limitation in processing non-native speech. The challenges posed by non-native grammatical errors can lead to incorrect interpretations, resulting in inaccurate transcriptions and by extension misinterpretations of the speaker's intent. The investigation of the effectiveness of SLU systems in processing speech that contains non-native grammatical errors is crucial to improving speech technology's accuracy.

Previous research efforts in the domain have primarily concentrated on enhancing model performance by proposing novel architectures or addressing specific issues related to individual modules like noisy environments [1] or large scale NLU. Many studies have focused on developing new models or refining existing ones to improve overall accuracy and robustness.

In [14], the researchers propose an end-to-end SLU pipeline. This pipeline is designed to specifically target and mitigate errors stemming from the ASR component. The authors of [15] introduce an augmentation strategy for training SLU models. This strategy involves simulating errors during the training process to enhance the model's robustness against variations and imperfections commonly encountered in real-world scenarios. By exposing the model to synthetic errors, the authors aim to create a more resilient system that can effectively handle diverse speech patterns, accent variations, and other sources of noise commonly encountered in spoken language. In [16], integration of a word confusion network is proposed into the SLU framework. This integration allows for effective error mitigation by incorporating information about potential word confusions and their likelihoods. The focus of these works lies predominantly on refining architectures, proposing novel training strategies, or incorporating error mitigation techniques, rather than delving into the intricacies and unique challenges posed by non-native language inputs.

This work aims to explore the effect of non-native speech on SLU systems. We evaluate the performance of NLU models on input with grammatical errors, to explore the degradation of performance of State of the Art models on the tasks of Intent Detection and Slot Filling on the Airline Travel Information Systems (ATIS) and SNIPS Natural Language Understanding benchmark datasets. We also conduct an analysis of the errors made by SLU systems when presented with grammatically erroneous input. Specifically, we examine the error rates with respect to the different Parts of Speech (POS) for the task of Intent Detection. We found that the performance of State of the Art NLU models drop considerably when presented with inputs that had L2 learner inspired grammatical errors. We also found certain POS to be more important, corruption of which had a higher chance of resulting in an error.

2 Background

One of the most common ways of building a SLU system is connecting an Automatic Speech Recognition (ASR) and a Natural Language Understanding (NLU) system in a cascaded fashion [9,12]. The ASR module transcribes spoken language into text, which is then used by the NLU module to extract semantic information.

To perform Intent Detection, which is the process of identifying the underlying purpose or goal expressed in a user's input text or speech, one of the common approaches involves the use of Long Short-Term Memory (LSTM) [7] models. LSTM models are recurrent neural networks that are capable of sequentially processing the input sequence and capturing long-term dependencies.

Slot Filling, another NLU task, which involves extracting specific pieces of information (slots) from a user's input that correspond to essential entities or parameters necessary to fulfill the user's intent is also very well suited for models built using LSTM. In this approach, the input sequence is fed into the LSTM model, and the final hidden state or output is used for intent classification while the intermediate representations are used for Slot Filling. However, a drawback of this approach is that the intent model may assign higher importance to tokens observed in the later parts of the sequence, potentially overlooking important information from the earlier parts.

On the other hand, an Attention Module [17] provides equal access to all tokens in the input sequence, regardless of their position. This module allows the model to dynamically assign weights to each token based on its relevance to the task at hand. The attention mechanism calculates these weights by considering the interaction between each token and the context vector, which summarizes the information learned from the entire input sequence. By using the attention weights as a proxy for the importance of certain tokens, the model can make more informed intent classification decisions.

A model with attention mechanism will have a more comprehensive understanding of the entire input sequence. For example, for a user input, "Find me a Chinese restaurant nearby that serves vegetarian dishes", a usual NLU models that is based on sequential processing like LSTM is likely to put higher weight on latter tokens "vegetarian dishes", but the attention model would prioritize tokens for intent classification based on their importance. This would mean that the tokens "Chinese restaurant" would also get high importance.

This attention based approach enables the model to capture both local and global dependencies and make more accurate intent predictions. Attention-based NLU models have shown promising results in various natural language understanding tasks, providing a more robust and interpretable approach for intent detection and classification.

One of the advantages of incorporating an attention layer into the NLU model for intent classification is the increased interpretability it offers. The attention layer assigns weights to each token in the input sequence, indicating their relative importance in making the intent classification decision. These attention weights provide valuable insights into which tokens the model focuses on and considers most relevant for determining the intent. By examining the attention weights, one can gain a better understanding of the model's decision-making process and identify the tokens that contribute significantly to the intent classification.

3 Methods

Table 1. Dataset Statistics.

Dataset	Train Size	Test Size	# Intent Classes	# Slot Classes	Mean # Tokens per Utterance
ATIS	4478	893	21	120	12.28
SNIPS	13084	700	7	72	10.0

To assess the impact of grammatical errors on the performance of Natural Language Understanding (NLU) models, we conducted experiments using three models, proposed in [13,20] and [4]. These models were chosen based on their State of the Art performance on the ATIS and SNIPS benchmarks. These are referred to as SF-ID-Network-For-NLU (SF-ID), Bi-Model-Intent-And-Slot (Bi-Model) and StackPropagation-SLU (Stack) respectively. By evaluating these models in the presence of grammatical errors, we aimed to understand how robust they are in handling linguistic variations and to gauge their overall performance in real-world scenarios.

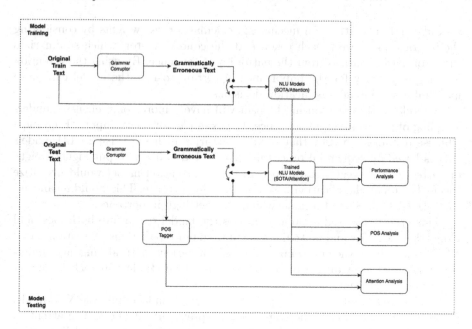

Fig. 1. Workflow for the conducted analysis.

The ATIS [6] and SNIPS [3] benchmarks provide standardized datasets that are widely used for evaluating the performance of NLU models. These datasets include utterances that cover various intents and are representative of the tasks performed in the respective domains. Statistics for the datasets can be found in Table 1.

Figure 1 presents a comprehensive overview of the analysis workflow, which was undertaken to evaluate the impact of grammatical errors on the performance of the models. The initial step of this study involved training two distinct versions of each model, with one version trained on the original, error-free text from the dataset(s) and the other on the grammatically erroneous version of the same text.

Following the model training, the test set was utilized to assess the performance of each model variant. To gain further insights into the impact of errors on the model's performance, an additional analysis was conducted by passing the data through a Part of Speech (POS) tagger in the spaCy toolkit [8]. This POS information allowed us to categorize the errors based on their corresponding parts of speech, such as nouns, verbs, adjectives, and so forth. Evaluating the model's performance along different POS provided valuable information about which linguistic elements were more susceptible to errors and which parts of speech might have a greater influence on the overall performance of the models.

3.1 Synthesizing Grammatical Errors

We utilized the tool introduced in [5] to synthesize grammatically erroneous sentences by introducing grammatical errors. The tool offered four operations: insert, delete, substitute, and move, enabling us to create random syntactic noise and change word forms. We also removed quotes from the corpus to generate additional variations.

For a given input sentence, the tool applies the above stated operations and introduces noise. By utilizing POS information, the tool has the capability to replace words with incongruent versions. This means that words can be replaced with others that might not belong to the same POS category, allowing us to study the impact of a wide variety of grammatical errors on the performance of NLU tasks. This is particularly crucial as real-world non-native language usage often involves instances where words may be used in unconventional ways.

3.2 Intent Detection and Slot Filling Performance

In our experiments, we trained the three models using the regular train splits available in the dataset. The models were trained to learn the relationships between input utterances and their corresponding intents and slots based on this clean and error-free training data.

To evaluate the impact of grammatical errors on the performance of the models, we conducted testing on two versions of the test splits. The first version is the original test split, which contains naturally occurring utterances without any introduced errors. This allows us to assess the models' performance under normal conditions and compare it to their performance on the clean training data.

The second version of the test split was included modifications for synthetic grammatical errors. These errors were introduced by corrupting specific parts-of-speech (POS) in the utterances, simulating common grammatical mistakes that users might make in real-world interactions. By testing the models on this modified split, we aimed to evaluate their ability to handle and understand utterances with grammatical errors, which are more representative of the variability and challenges encountered in real-world language understanding scenarios.

By comparing the models' performance on the original test split versus the modified split with introduced grammatical errors, we can gain insights into their robustness and adaptability to linguistic variations.

To explore strategies for mitigating the impact of grammatical errors on NLU model performance, we trained the models on a modified version of the training data. By introducing synthetic grammatical errors into the original training data, we aimed to expose the models to linguistic variations and errors commonly found in real-world user inputs. This training approach sought to enhance the models' ability to handle and adapt to grammatical errors.

3.3 POS Analysis

To gain a deeper understanding of the effects of specific kinds of grammatical errors on the performance of the NLU models, we categorized the utterances based on the type of part-of-speech (POS) that was intentionally corrupted to introduce the error. This categorization allowed us to examine the impact of different types of grammatical errors on the models' performance.

By grouping the utterances based on the POS that was modified, we were able to analyze how each specific type of error affected the models' ability to understand and classify the intent correctly.

By comparing the performance of the models on the original, error-free versions of the utterances to their performance on the modified versions with introduced errors within each group of POS, we could identify patterns and trends. This analysis enabled us to assess which specific types of grammatical errors had the most significant impact on the models' accuracy and whether certain POS categories were more challenging for the models to handle.

3.4 Attention Analysis

As an alternative approach to analyzing the importance of specific parts-of-speech (POS) for intent classification, we trained an attention-based NLU model on the task of intent classification. This model incorporated an attention mechanism, which allowed us to explore the relative importance of different POS for each intent class.

By analyzing the attention weights assigned by the model, we could determine which POS received higher weights, indicating their significance in determining the intent class.

4 Results

Table 2. NLU model performance on ATIS and SNIPS with and without grammatical errors.

			ATIS			SNIPS		
			SF-ID	Bi-Model	Stack	SF-ID	Bi-Model	Stack
Intent Accuracy	O-Train	O-Test	95.63	95.18	96.19	97.00	97.42	97.71
		E-Test	95.18	94.40	93.50	95.85	92.71	96.14
	E-Train	O-Test	96.19	95.40	93.72	97.00	96.28	96.85
		E-Test	96.19	95.63	94.28	97.14	96.14	97.42
Slot F1 Score	O-Train	O-Test	97.94	97.81	97.45	94.00	95.32	95.40
		E-Test	97.15	97.09	96.66	90.87	90.21	92.24
	E-Train	O-Test	97.82	97.73	97.40	92.46	93.18	93.79
		E-Test	97.90	97.70	97.50	93.53	94.28	95.08

Table 3. Cumulative Intent Accuracy and Slot F1-Score with Increased Errors on ATIS and SNIPS.

	ATIS						SNIPS					
	SF-ID		Bi-Model		Stack		SF-ID		Bi-Model		Stack	
# Corrupted	Intent	Slot	Intent	Slot	Intent	Slot	Intent	Slot	Intent	Slot	Intent	Slot
0	95.28	98.47	94.88	98.05	94.86	97.41	97.64	96.10	94.44	95.75	96.32	94.58
1	96.11	97.83	95.26	97.57	94.53	96.85	96.26	93.68	93.42	93.81	96.25	93.93
2	95.60	97.47	94.95	97.29	94.13	96.92	96.15	92.25	93.63	91.70	96.44	92.80
3	95.44	97.42	94.74	97.29	93.72	96.77	96.06	91.14	92.57	90.73	96.08	92.32
4	95.35	97.26	94.66	97.19	93.47	96.73	96.02	90.89	92.76	90.39	96.13	92.28
5	95.17	97.18	94.38	97.12	93.49	96.70	95.82	90.92	92.64	90.22	96.14	92.24
6	95.17	97.17	94.39	97.10	93.50	96.66	95.85	90.91	92.70	90.25	96.14	92.24
7	95.17	97.17	94.39	97.10	93.50	96.66	95.85	90.91	92.70	90.25	96.14	92.24
8	95.17	97.17	94.39	97.10	93.50	96.66	95.86	90.87	92.71	90.21	96.14	92.24
9	95.18	97.15	94.40	97.09	93.50	96.66	95.86	90.87	92.71	90.21	96.14	92.24

4.1 Intent Detection and Slot Filling

Table 2 provide insights about the performance of the NLU models on the ATIS and SNIPS datasets for the tasks of Intent Detection and Slot Filling. The table demonstrate the performance of the models across different variations of the train and test splits. Notably, there is a clear drop in performance for the models trained on the original train split (O_train) when transitioning from testing on the original test split (O_test) to the test split with introduced grammatical errors (E_test). This drop indicates the challenges posed by grammatical errors in real-world language understanding scenarios.

The results obtained from training the models on a modified version of the train split (E_train) indicate a potential mitigation strategy for addressing the drop in model performance caused by grammatical errors. By training the models on a train split that includes synthetic grammatical errors, we observe a recovery of a significant portion of the performance loss when tested on the modified test split with introduced errors. For example, the Stack model lost 2.69% Intent Accuracy on ATIS when tested on grammatically erroneous version but training on synthetic dataset allowed us to recover 0.78%.

Table 3 provides a quantitative understanding of how the models' performance deteriorates as the number of corrupted tokens (# Corrupted) increases. This tells us that most models become progressively worse as the tokens are replaced and information available is diminished which makes the task more challenging. This information helps us gauge the sensitivity of the models to different levels of grammatical errors and provides insights into their robustness and generalization capabilities.

4.2 POS Analysis

Table 4 presents the results of POS analysis experiments. It shows the drop in performance with respect to POS that were corrupted in the input sentence. A larger value indicates a larger effect. This provides us with valuable insights

Table 4. Increase in Error Rates per POS when tested on Grammatically Erroneous data for ATIS and SNIPS.

POS	ATIS			SNIPS		
	SF-ID	Bi-Model	Stack	SF-ID	Bi-Model	Stack
ADJ	0.00	0.00	0.00	0.02	0.06	0.00
AUX	0.02	0.04	0.04	0.01	0.04	0.04
DET	0.01	0.00	0.02	0.00	0.07	0.02
NOUN	0.03	0.11	0.03	0.03	0.05	0.03
NUM	−0.01	0.00	0.00	0.02	0.03	0.00
PRON	0.00	0.00	0.00	0.00	0.00	0.2
PROPN	0.01	−0.01	0.01	−0.01	0.05	0.00
VERB	0.00	0.00	0.00	0.03	0.09	0.04

into the impact of specific POS on the performance of the model for the task of Intent Detection.

We can see that certain POS like Auxiliary Verbs and Noun had a consistently large effect across the three models and both of the datasets.

4.3   Attention Analysis

Table 5. Mean Attention Weights per POS on ATIS and SNIPS.

POS	ATIS	SNIPS
ADJ	0.06	0.06
ADP	0.12	0.04
ADV	0.04	0.10
AUX	0.05	0.05
CONJ	0.00	0.00
CCONJ	0.01	0.04
DET	0.04	0.04
INTJ	0.01	0.07
NOUN	0.04	0.09
NUM	0.05	0.05
PART	0.19	0.04
PRON	0.10	0.05
PROPN	0.10	0.19
PUNCT	0.00	0.04
SCONJ	0.07	0.09
SYM	0.00	0.00
VERB	0.05	0.13
X	0.33	0.33
SPACE	0.13	0.00

The results presented in Table 5 provide insights into the attention analysis conducted in our study. It demonstrates the average attention weights assigned to different parts of speech (POS) during the intent classification task. A higher value represents indicates that more attention was paid to that particular POS which indicates that it played an important role in the classification decision of the model. We can observe that certain POS like Proper Noun and Adposition (Prepositions + Postpositions) receive higher attention weights, for both datasets, indicating their perceived importance in determining the intent of a given utterance. Please Note that X refers to 'other' which are tokens that couldn't be tagged into any of the presented POS.

5 Discussion

The findings from our study offer valuable insights into the impact of grammatical errors on the performance of Natural Language Understanding (NLU) models, specifically in the context of Intent Detection. Understanding and mitigating the effects of grammatical errors is crucial for developing robust and accurate NLU systems that can effectively handle real-world language variations. Our research highlights several key findings that can be useful for further advancements in this field.

Firstly, our experiments demonstrate a clear drop in performance when NLU models are tested on utterances with introduced grammatical errors compared to the original, error-free test data. This emphasizes the challenges posed by grammatical errors and highlights the need for addressing this issue to improve the overall performance and usability of NLU systems.

Secondly, by training the models on a modified version of the train split that includes synthetic grammatical errors, we observe a significant mitigation of the performance drop. This suggests that training models on data that resemble real-world language variations can enhance their robustness and adaptability, enabling them to handle grammatical errors more effectively during inference.

Furthermore, our analysis at the POS level provides valuable insights into the importance of specific parts-of-speech (POS) for intent classification. Certain POS, when corrupted, were found to have a greater impact on intent misclassification. This understanding enables us to focus on improving the models' handling of these specific POS categories and develop targeted strategies for addressing their challenges.

Overall, our findings contribute to the progress of NLU research by highlighting the significance of addressing grammatical errors, providing mitigation strategies, and emphasizing the importance of certain POS in intent classification. These insights can guide the development of more robust and accurate NLU systems, enhancing their performance in real-world scenarios where users may express their intents with grammatical variations. By improving the models' ability to handle grammatical errors, we can ensure more reliable and effective communication between users and NLU systems, thereby advancing the field of natural language understanding.

6   Conclusions

In this work, we presented an analysis of the performance of state-of-the-art Natural Language Understanding (NLU) models when exposed to grammatically erroneous input and the impact of such input on the overall model performance. We conducted a comprehensive analysis to understand how these models handle errors introduced in the input data and to identify any potential limitations or challenges they may face in processing non-standard or non-native language.

Our analysis also explored possible mitigation strategies to recover some of the performance loss. We observed that training the models on modified versions of the training data with grammatical errors could partially mitigate the drop in performance. This finding suggests that exposing the models to diverse and error-prone data during training can enhance their robustness and ability to handle grammatical errors in real-world scenarios.

Overall, our study sheds light on the performance of state-of-the-art NLU models when dealing with grammatically erroneous input. Understanding these limitations is crucial for improving the reliability and effectiveness of NLU systems, especially in situations where non-standard or non-native language is encountered. The insights gained from this analysis can inform the development of enhanced NLU models and strategies to handle grammatical errors more effectively in various applications, such as voice assistants, chatbots, and natural language processing systems.

7   Future Work

Future work can focus on the exploration of diverse error synthesis methods, rooted in linguistic insights, to generate errors that closely mimic the linguistic challenges posed by non-native speakers.

References

1. Ali, M.N., Schmalz, V.J., Brutti, A., Falavigna, D.: A speech enhancement front-end for intent classification in noisy environments. In: 2021 29th European Signal Processing Conference (EUSIPCO), pp. 471–475 (2021). https://doi.org/10.23919/EUSIPCO54536.2021.9616322
2. Amodei, D., et al.: Deep speech 2: end-to-end speech recognition in English and Mandarin. In: Proceedings of Machine Learning Research, vol. 48, pp. 173–182. PMLR, New York (2016). https://proceedings.mlr.press/v48/amodei16.html
3. Coucke, A., et al.: Snips voice platform: an embedded spoken language understanding system for private-by-design voice interfaces. ArXiv arxiv:1805.10190 (2018)
4. E, H., Niu, P., Chen, Z., Song, M.: A novel bi-directional interrelated model for joint intent detection and slot filling. In: Proceedings of the 57th Annual Meeting of the Association for Computational Linguistics, pp. 5467–5471. Association for Computational Linguistics, Florence (2019). https://doi.org/10.18653/v1/P19-1544. https://aclanthology.org/P19-1544

5. Foster, J., Andersen, O.: GenERRate: generating errors for use in grammatical error detection. In: Proceedings of the Fourth Workshop on Innovative Use of NLP for Building Educational Applications, pp. 82–90. Association for Computational Linguistics, Boulder (2009). https://aclanthology.org/W09-2112
6. Hemphill, C.T., Godfrey, J.J., Doddington, G.R.: The ATIS spoken language systems pilot corpus. In: Speech and Natural Language: Proceedings of a Workshop Held at Hidden Valley, Pennsylvania, 24–27 June 1990 (1990). https://aclanthology.org/H90-1021
7. Hochreiter, S., Schmidhuber, J.: Long short-term memory. Neural Comput. 9(8), 1735–1780 (1997). https://doi.org/10.1162/neco.1997.9.8.1735
8. Honnibal, M., Montani, I.: spaCy 2: natural language understanding with Bloom embeddings, convolutional neural networks and incremental parsing (2017). https://spacy.io/usage/linguistic-features
9. Horlock, J., King, S.: Discriminative methods for improving named entity extraction on speech data. In: Proceedings 8th European Conference on Speech Communication and Technology (Eurospeech 2003), pp. 2765–2768 (2003). https://doi.org/10.21437/Eurospeech.2003-737
10. Lee, J., Seneff, S.: An analysis of grammatical errors in non-native speech in English. In: 2008 IEEE Spoken Language Technology Workshop, pp. 89–92 (2008). https://doi.org/10.1109/SLT.2008.4777847
11. Pal, D., Arpnikanondt, C., Funilkul, S., Varadarajan, V.: User experience with smart voice assistants: the accent perspective. In: 2019 10th International Conference on Computing, Communication and Networking Technologies (ICCCNT), pp. 1–6 (2019). https://doi.org/10.1109/ICCCNT45670.2019.8944754
12. Palmer, D.D., Ostendorf, M.: Improving information extraction by modeling errors in speech recognizer output. In: Proceedings of the First International Conference on Human Language Technology Research, pp. 1–5 (2001). https://aclanthology.org/H01-1034
13. Qin, L., Che, W., Li, Y., Wen, H., Liu, T.: A stack-propagation framework with token-level intent detection for spoken language understanding. In: Proceedings of the 2019 Conference on Empirical Methods in Natural Language Processing and the 9th International Joint Conference on Natural Language Processing (EMNLP-IJCNLP), pp. 2078–2087. Association for Computational Linguistics, Hong Kong (2019). https://doi.org/10.18653/v1/D19-1214. https://aclanthology.org/D19-1214
14. Rao, M., Raju, A., Dheram, P., Bui, B., Rastrow, A.: Speech to semantics: improve ASR and NLU jointly via all-neural interfaces. ArXiv arxiv:2008.06173 (2020)
15. Simonnet, E., Ghannay, S., Camelin, N., Estève, Y.: Simulating ASR errors for training SLU systems. In: Proceedings of the Eleventh International Conference on Language Resources and Evaluation (LREC 2018). European Language Resources Association (ELRA), Miyazaki (2018). https://aclanthology.org/L18-1499
16. Simonnet, E., Ghannay, S., Camelin, N., Estève, Y., de Mori, R.: ASR error management for improving spoken language understanding. In: Interspeech 2017, Stockholm, Sweden (2017). https://hal.science/hal-01526298
17. Vaswani, A., et al.: Attention is all you need. In: Guyon, I., et al. (eds.) Advances in Neural Information Processing Systems, vol. 30, pp. 1–11. Curran Associates, Inc. (2017)
18. Vu, N.T., Wang, Y., Klose, M., Mihaylova, Z., Schultz, T.: Improving ASR performance on non-native speech using multilingual and crosslingual information. In: Annual Conference of the International Speech Communication Association, pp. 11–15 (2014)

19. Wang, P., Wei, L., Cao, Y., Xie, J., Nie, Z.: Large-scale unsupervised pre-training for end-to-end spoken language understanding. In: ICASSP 2020–2020 IEEE International Conference on Acoustics, Speech and Signal Processing (ICASSP), pp. 7999–8003 (2020). https://doi.org/10.1109/ICASSP40776.2020.9053163
20. Wang, Y., Shen, Y., Jin, H.: A bi-model based RNN semantic frame parsing model for intent detection and slot filling. In: Proceedings of the 2018 Conference of the North American Chapter of the Association for Computational Linguistics: Human Language Technologies, vol. 2 (Short Papers), pp. 309–314. Association for Computational Linguistics, New Orleans (2018). https://doi.org/10.18653/v1/N18-2050, https://aclanthology.org/N18-2050
21. Yin, F., Long, Q., Meng, T., Chang, K.W.: On the robustness of language encoders against grammatical errors. In: Proceedings of the 58th Annual Meeting of the Association for Computational Linguistics, pp. 3386–3403. Association for Computational Linguistics (2020). https://doi.org/10.18653/v1/2020.acl-main.310. https://aclanthology.org/2020.acl-main.310

On the Most Frequent Sequences of Words in Russian Spoken Everyday Language (Bigrams and Trigrams): An Experience of Classification

Maria V. Khokhlova[1]([⊠]) [iD], Olga V. Blinova[1,2] [iD], Natalia Bogdanova-Beglarian[1] [iD], and Tatiana Sherstinova[1,2] [iD]

[1] Saint Petersburg State University, St. Petersburg, Russia
{m.khokhlova,o.blinova,n.bogdanova,t.sherstinova}@spbu.ru
[2] HSE University, St. Petersburg, Russia

Abstract. The article provides a description of the most frequent bigrams and trigrams obtained using the n-gram analysis technique on a representative sample of Russian spoken language. N-gram analysis allows identifying frequent lists of sequences consisting of n graphical words, which is important for describing corpus material in various theoretical and applied aspects. The source data for applying this technique was a sample of 388 episodes of everyday speech communication from the ORD corpus (about 110 hours of audio). The results of the n-gram analysis in the form of frequency lists of word sequences allow constructing a typology of the most common bigrams and trigrams in Russian oral communication and lead the study equally to the levels of grammar, pragmatics, lexicon, and phraseology. The list of the most frequent bigrams and trigrams contains grammatical structures (U TEBYA, YA NE PONIMAYU, MNE KAZHETSYA), idioms (in a broad sense of the term) (VSYO RAVNO, TO ZHE SAMOE), introductory units (TAK SKAZAT', S DRUGOY STORONY), as well as a number of sequences typical only for oral speech, such as one-word pragmatic markers (NU VOT, KAK BY, NU V OBSHCEM), amplifications (DA-DA, TAK-TAK-TAK), and hesitations-vocalizations (E-E, M-M-M). The obtained frequency lists can be useful for solving many modern applied natural language processing tasks.

Keywords: Everyday Russian · Spoken Speech · N-gram · N-gram-Analysis · Grammatical Structure · Construction · Pragmatic Marker · Vocalization · Amplification · Everyday Communication

1 Introduction

According to dictionary definitions, a 'structure' refers to the 'arrangement and relationship between constituent parts of something, or the device and organization' [1]. When applied to language, especially oral speech, the term 'construction' is more commonly used than 'structures.' This term pertains to 'combinations of words viewed from their grammatical relations' [2]. Simplistically, a construction is always more than one word, and these words must be interconnected in a specific manner, making them describable from an 'arrangement and relation' perspective within a certain structure. Words are predominantly grammatically linked, although exceptions exist, as will be illustrated in this article.

The interest in constructions has given rise to many distinctive research directions within linguistics, most notably Construction Grammar (CxG) [3], which is closely connected to phraseology. This indicates that the boundary between grammar and lexis is often blurred, diffuse, and permeable. It is not surprising that the range of units typically described in terms of constructions, collocations, colligations, collocations or collostructions (the latter a term still unsettled in its Russian spelling; from 'collocation + construction'), phrasemes and semi-phrasemes, phrase schemas, idioms, form-idioms, speech or discursive formulas, etc., is so vast and varied. This is evident in the extensive literature on these topics, which includes the works of various linguists such as L.S. Beylinson, E.G. Borisova, P.A. Bychkova, D.O. Dobrovolsky, S.Yu. Zhukova, V.P. Zakharov, L.L. Iomdin, M.V. Kopotev, T.A. Maisak, T.Yu. Paveleva, E.V. Rakhilina, T.I. Steksova, M.V. Khokhlova, A.O. Chernousova, E.V. Yagunova, M. Benson, Ö. Dahl, Ch.J. Fillmore, A.E. Goldberg, R. Jackendoff, P. Kay, A. Makkai, M.C. O'Connor, P. Pecina, J. Sinclair, among others.

Within certain interpretations of Construction Grammar, both 'regular constructions' (or 'constructs') and 'irregular constructions' - those that are semantically non-compositional and/or syntactically opaque - are identified. For more on this, see, for example, [4, 5]. According to this approach, knowledge of a language can be encapsulated through the knowledge of its constructions (or more precisely, a network of constructions, often referred to as a 'construction'). In this context, the phenomena of interest to a linguist studying constructions may include structures whose meaning can be fully derived from the values of their constituents, structures whose formation can be explained based on existing syntactic rules, structures whose meaning cannot be predicted from the combination of the meanings of their constituents, and structures whose form cannot be (or cannot completely be) predicted based on grammatical rules. What binds this diverse series together is primarily the feature of being multi-worded, and secondly, stability, defined here as the relatively high frequency of co-occurrence of the structural elements, a concept which can be referred to as 'construction in a broad sense'.

The method of n-gram analysis is traditionally employed when identifying multi-word units and dividing them into classes based on various criteria, such as their compositional or idiomatic nature.

More specifically, the search for such units across various corpora depends on the particular interests of the researchers. They first must select a method for the search itself, followed by a method for description. In this work, we utilise the method of extracting n-grams from a corpus of data and we discuss the results of its application in the extraction and classification of bigrams and trigrams.

2 Materials and Methodology of N-gram Analysis

N-grams represent sequences of textual graphic units on the same level, typically letters or words, with their frequency lists traditionally utilized in contemporary applications of natural language processing. The variable 'N' can represent any positive integer, signifying the number of units considered within a sequence. Frequently, small values of N, from 1 to 5, are employed. In this study, n-grams are utilized to count sequences of graphic words based on transcriptions from spontaneous oral speech recordings. Here, a graphic word is defined as any sequence of letters separated by a space or a non-letter character, such as a hyphen.

A large number of Russian words can be categorized as 1-grams (unigrams), examples being TAK, VOT, DOM, SOLNCE, and GULYAT', among others. Certain words fall into the 2-grams (bigrams) category, including compound conjunctions like TAK KAK, POTOMU CHTO, KAK BUDTO, and all hyphenated words such as PREMYER-MINISTR, GENERAL-LEYTENANT, KRESLO-KROVAT', KAKOY-NIBUD', KAKOY-TO, and KRASNO-KIRPICHNY. Specific compound phrases qualify as 3-grams (trigrams), such as VSLEDSTVIE TOGO CHTO, V PROSHLOM GODU, and NI O CHEM.

N-gram analysis enables not only the identification of compound words but also the recognition of concepts and names composed of several graphic words, for example, KRASNAYA PLOSHCHAD', ZIMNYAYA KANAVKA, BOL'SHOY DRAMATICH-ESKIY TEATR, and KURSY POVYSHENIYA KVALIFIKATSII. The automatic identification of such words and stable combinations surpasses the capabilities of a standard frequency lexeme (unigram) dictionary, hence the prevalent use of n-grams. Additionally, n-gram analysis serves as a convenient instrument for identifying not just compound words and names, but also frequent and stable phrases, collocations, and constructions, among others (see above) [6].

In the current study, n-gram analysis is utilized as a supplementary tool for generating all potential sequences of graphic words, using a representative sample of transcribed oral speech as source material. This process was based on a dataset comprised of 388 instances of everyday speech communication, taken from the "One Speech Day" (OSD) corpus [7] (for more details, refer to [8]). The recordings in question were made in 2007 and between 2014-2016, yielding approximately 110 hours of spoken content, devoid of extended pauses.

The chosen instances encapsulate a wide range of daily verbal communication in Russian: informal household chats, professional dialogues at work, casual conversations with colleagues, as well as interactions with friends, acquaintances, relatives, and diverse customer-service related communication scenarios, such as those occurring in shops, medical centers, customer service departments, etc. The recordings were collected from informants spanning various social and professional groups (refer to [9] for further details).

Transcriptions from the OSD corpus were carried out within the ELAN multimedia annotation environment [10], and stored in its supported format (*.eaf). For the purpose of automatically calculating n-grams from transcriptions, the "Phrases" tier was extracted [11]; it should be noted that information concerning the speakers and the specific circumstances of communication was not considered at this stage of the research. The transcription texts underwent preprocessing to preserve the phrase and response boundaries, as well as speaker changes within speech-overlapping fragments. The n-gram count was facilitated by the AntConc tool [12], generating frequency lists of all bigrams and trigrams. The study delves into an in-depth examination of the 200 most frequent sequences within each of these categories of units.

The traditional expectations a linguist might hold when using the n-gram analysis methodology can be readily conceptualized: among bigrams, for instance, one might anticipate prepositional-case word forms like U REKI, DLYA MENYA, or other syntactically cohesive forms such as NE KHOCU, TRI CHASA, MNOGO LET, SAMYJ UMNYJ, CHASHCHE VSEGO, KHOCU SPAT', BYL BOLEN. These can be effortlessly associated with particular structures, as well as single-word lemmas featuring hyphenated spellings like KTO-TO, KOGDA-NIBUD', VO-VTORYKH. When examining trigrams, one could expect roughly similar units, but possibly complicated by particles or other means, like NE PRISHEL ZHE, RESHIL STAT' VRACHEM, NI PRI CHEM, as well as combinations incorporating lexically integral units with hyphenated spellings (e.g., CHTO-TO TAM, V OBSCHEM-TO, etc.). In essence, one would anticipate the n-gram analysis to yield primarily grammatical structures or a variety of constructions, which would subsequently be convenient to describe from various perspectives.

However, the top-200 samples obtained for bigrams and trigrams yielded slightly different outcomes. A pilot analysis of the first 20 units from the 2- and 3-gram frequency lists revealed the genuine set of most frequent sequences of this kind in Russian speech, and whether all of them can be classified as 'structures' in the conventional sense of the term. We will examine both lists in further detail below.

3   Analysis of Bigrams in Contemporary Russian Oral Discourse: Frequency Characteristics and Typology of Units Obtained with Quantitative Data

A method for manual annotation (determining their linguistic status) was developed for the first 20 units from the bigram list (see Table 1).

These initial 20 units from the bigram frequency list have unveiled virtually their entire linguistic diversity present in the corpus material:

- Vocalizations (VOK) (EH EH, M M, A A) - these are a type of hesitation phenomena, one of the non-verbal methods used to fill pauses during hesitation. Vocalizations refer to "speech-like" sounds, or sounds of a "non-phonemic character". Such elements are often considered a form of speech disruption, where the smooth flow of speech is interrupted. They are akin to a "pause that the speaker utilizes to prepare the next portion and/or (when combined with correction) - to deliberate on the potential method of correcting the preceding portion" of the text [13].
- Amplifications (AMPL) (DA DA) - these are specific repetitive units, often created by repeating syllables such as OP-OP-OP, TO-TO-TO, TA-TA-TA, TAK-TAK-TAK, and so on. In everyday speech, they frequently function as pragmatic markers (PM). (For further details about the class of amplified units, refer to [14, 15: 462–465].
- Compound conjunctions (CONC) (TO EST', POTOMU CHTO).
- Pragmatic markers (PM) - these include basic multi-word units, their structural variants, or chains (NE ZNAYU, NU VOT, KAK BY). (For more details on PMs, refer to a specialized dictionary of such units: [15]).

Table 1. Most frequent bigrams of everyday Russian speech (top-20).

Rank	Type	Freq	NormFreq = ipm	Status
1	e-e	3746	4217	VOK
2	u menya	2157	2428	PPF
3	to yest'	1926	2168	CONC
4	u nas	1635	1840	PPF
5	ya ne	1572	1769	BIGRAM
6	potomu chto	1551	1746	CONC
7	da-da	1525	1717	AMPL
8	ne znayu	1512	1702	PM
9	nu vot	1338	1506	PM
10	m-m	1312	1477	VOK
11	kak by	1252	1409	PM
12	chto-to	1166	1312	LEMMA
13	u tebya	878	988	PPF
14	nu da	866	975	2 PART
15	vot eto	856	964	2 FREQUENT/fragment PM
16	a-a	834	939	VOK
17	kak-to	779	877	LEMMA
18	nu ya	775	872	BIGRAM
19	vot tak	761	857	2 FR/PM
20	ya govoryu	737	830	PREDIC

In the analysis of spoken language, ambiguous decisions or the polyfunctionality of linguistic units led to a total exceeding 100%, which is considered quite normal. Choices were often made in favor of pragmatic markers (PMs), as opposed to grammatical units or forms. This was based on contextual analysis within large speech corpora.

For instance, NE ZNAYU in the frequency list is more likely a pragmatic marker (possibly indicating hesitation, metacommunication, or approximation) rather than a verb with negation. Such a marker is frequently used in speech and ranks 16th in a list of 60 PMs, with an incidence per million (IPM) of 237 for 300.000 word usages.

Furthermore, an examination of the most frequent bigrams from the list revealed interesting grammatical insights. The most frequent combinations from the Prepositional-Case Forms (PPF) class were three pronoun forms in the genitive case: U MENYA, U NAS, U TEBYA. The elevated frequency of these forms is supported by data from the spoken subcorpus of the National Corpus of the Russian Language. For example, U MENYA has 23.5 thousand entries, significantly more than DLYA MENYA with 2.5 thousand entries, and OT MENYA with 860 entries. A similar pattern is observed with U NAS and U TEBYA.

In terms of frequency of occurrence in the ORD (Oral Russian Discourse) dataset, vocalizations form the following chain: EH-EH (rank 1), MM-MM (rank 10), AH-AH (rank 16). These "priorities" of Russian oral communication can be considered nationally conditioned. For example, it is known that in the spoken Russian of Chinese speakers, vocalizations of the "i-" or "n-" types dominate.

The only predicative structure in the top-20 list is YA GOVORYU (I speak), which is likely not a complete verb but a pragmatic marker indicating foreignness. This marker's frequency is quite high, with the base form "GOVORIT" (says) ranking 6th and having an IPM of 767 per 300.000 word usages in the annotated ORD subcorpus. The form "GRYU/GORYU" (I say/speak) is only less frequent than the form "GRIT" (says) and its many pronunciation variants.

The statistics of the types of bigrams in the corpus material of the present study for the 200 most frequent sequences are presented in Table 2.

The analysis of the 200 most frequent units obtained through n-gram analysis revealed several additional types that were not encountered in the first 20 units:

- Idioms (IDIOMA) - both actual idioms (VSE RAVNO, CHTO TAKOE) and potential idioms that allow for alternative interpretations (NU CHTO, I CHTO, KAK ETO). Idioms are understood broadly as speech expressions that are used as a whole, cannot be further decomposed, and their meaning cannot be derived from the meanings of their constituent words (see, for example: [16, 17].
- Negations (OTRIC) (NE KHOCU, NE OCHEN', NE BYLO).
- Introductory units (VVODN) (MNE KAZHETSYA, TAK SKAZAT').
- Discourse words (DISC) (POTOM) (for more information on discourse words in the Russian language, see: [18]).

Once again, the list includes ambiguous units: 2 CHAST/PM (VOT TAK, NU ETO, TAK VOT), 2 CHAST/PM fragment (VOT ETO), BIGRAMMA/IDIOMA (NU CHTO, I CHTO), PM/IDIOMA/BIGRAMMA (KAK ETO), PPΦ/PM (V ETOM), and others. There are also combinations of units indicated with a plus sign (+) in the table: CHAST + PM (A TAM), VOK + CHAST (E NU), CHAST + VOK (VOT E), KONK + DISC (A POTOM). One usage remained only hypothetical: CHTO TAM (PM?).

The final quantitative data for the bigrams are as follows (units with double interpretation were counted twice):

- 40.8% of the identified bigrams do not have any specific status - neither grammatical nor pragmatic. They are merely frequent combinations of frequently occurring graphic words, such as YA PROSTO (I simply), A V (and in), A ON (but he), CHTO ONA (what she), and so on. Transitioning directly from these units to the description of grammar can be challenging. However, in the context of contextual and discourse analysis, this data can prove to be valuable.
- 14.7% of the bigrams turned out to be pragmatic markers or fragments of pragmatic markers, such as NU VOT (well, here), TY ZNAYESH' (you know), DUMAYU CHTO (I think that), VOT ETO (here it is), which confirms the observation of their increased frequency in oral discourse (see, for example, corresponding data in: [19]).
- Another 10.6% of the bigrams are combinations of two particles, such as TAK A (so but), NE NU (not well), DA NET (yes no), DA NU (yes well), which further confirms the overall higher occurrence of particles in oral speech compared to written speech (see corresponding data in: [20: 299]). This indicates that n-gram analysis can be

Table 2. Statistics of bigram types in the corpus material.

Status	Absolute Count	Relative Count (%)
2 PART	15	7.6
2 FR/PM	7	3.5
2 FREQUENT/fragment PM	1	0.5
AMPL	6	3.0
BIGRAM	80	40.4
BIGRAM/IDIOMA	4	2.0
BIGRAM/PM	1	0.5
BIGRAM/PM fragment	2	1.0
BIGRAM/FREQUENT + PM	1	0.5
INTRODUCTION	2	1.0
INTRODUCTION/PM	1	0.5
WOK	4	2.0
WOK + CHAT	1	0.5
IDIOM	4	2.0
CONC	6	3.0
KONK + DISC	1	0.5
LEMMA	11	5.6
PM	11	5.6
PM/BIGRAM	1	0.5
PM/IDIOMA/BIGRAM	1	0.5
PM?	2	1.0
PREDIC	5	2.5
PF	10	5.1
PF/PM	1	0.5
NEGATIVE	7	3.5
PM fragment	5	2.5
FREQUENT	7	3.5
PART + WOK	1	0.5
TOTAL	198	

utilized for describing particles, although manual analysis of the context can introduce significant corrections to the obtained data.

Thus, even at the stage of processing bigrams, the methodology used in this study can provide insights across all linguistic levels, although it requires some manual adjustment of the results.

4 Analysis of Trigrams in Contemporary Russian Oral Discourse: Frequency Characteristics and Typology of the Obtained Units with Quantitative Data

The analysis of trigrams in contemporary Russian oral discourse reveals intriguing findings. The top-20 positions of the corresponding frequency list are presented in Table 3.

Exactly half of the trigrams in this list represent more or less explicit pragmatic markers (with the same caveat about the usage statistics of such forms in the corpus material as a whole: it is precisely on the basis of these data that decisions were made about the status of this or that unit in the current work), 25% of trigrams somehow include vocalizations, there are combinations of particles with conjunctions (NU TO EST') or prepositional phrases (A U MENYA) and for the first time in the upper frequency vocabulary zone (that is, among the most frequent) appeared what can be attributed to idioms, i.e., to stable and reproducible units (NU I CHTO).

Table 3. Most frequently occurring trigrams in everyday Russian speech (top-20).

Rank	Type	Freq	NormFreq = ipm	Status
1	da-da-da	688	774	AMPL
2	ya ne znayu	557	627	PM
3	na samom dele	286	322	PM
4	vot tak vot	264	297	PM
5	nu v obshchem	210	236	PM
6	vot e-e	190	214	PM + VOK
7	ya dumayu chto	170	191	PM
8	vot eto vot	167	188	PM
9	potomu chto ya	144	162	TRIGRAM
10	nu kak by	139	156	PM
11	e-e nu	138	155	VOK + CHAT
12	e-e-e	138	155	VOK
13	i daleye	135	152	PM
14	nu ne znayu	126	142	PM
15	e-e v	124	140	VOK + PROPOSITION
16	nu to yest'	123	138	TRIGRAM
17	a u menya	114	128	TRIGRAM
18	nu i chto	113	127	IDIOM
19	chto u nas	112	126	TRIGRAM
20	m-m-m	105	118	VOK

Expanding the material to 200 units changes little in the pilot quantitative data, but against the backdrop of bigrams, trigrams as sequences of graphic words have become more "recognizable": among them are many clear pragmatic markers (YA NE ZNAYU, NU V OBSCHEM, YA DUMAYU CHTO, VOT ETO VOT), more or less explicit idioms (in the same broad understanding discussed above) (CHTO ETO TAKOE, NU I CHTO, TO ZHE SAMOE, NU CHTO TY), and other trigrams, not claiming the status of grammatical structures or stable constructions, yet represent quite frequent sequences, from which, like from bricks, Russian oral discourse is formed: NU TO EST', TO EST' YA, U MENYA EST', TAM CHTO-TO, A U NAS, MNE KAZHETSYA CHTO and so on.

The last group includes predicative structures: YA NE MOGU, YA NE PONY-MAYU, YA NE HOCU. It is curious that all of them are built "in a negative key": apparently, a person is significantly more likely to deny his actions or states than to affirm them. The structures YA MOGU, YA HOCU, YA PONYMAYU among the 200 most frequent bigrams in the annotated OR corpus did not occur. Let's note once again that the construction YA NE ZNAYU, externally similar to the ones under consideration, is not attributed to predicative structures, but to pragmatic markers, for which there is an explanation. Based on observations of corpus material, about half (48.7%) of all uses of this construction act in oral discourse as PM-hesitatives, cf.:

- *v obshchem Kirill% / ya ne znayu / eto prosto / *P pritcha vo yazytsekh // ya / voobshche ne znayu kak s nim obshchat'sya uzhe* [7]

    *in general, Kirill% / I don't know / this is just / *P a parable in tongues // I / generally don't know how to communicate with him anymore* [7]

    (note the presence of a full-fledged predicative unit "I generally don't know" next to the PM; the difference between them is visible to the naked eye);

- *okazyvaetsya / tam vot s eh... s etogo vhoda / *V tam u nih vot k... / vsyakie konferents-zaly / i tam ustraivayut / *P vsyakogo roda (eh...eh) vot takie (eh...eh) kak eto skazat' / (...) *V nu vot (eh...eh) vsyakogo roda tam ya ne znayu / vystupleniya / *V (eh...eh) obrazovatel'nye takie / nu she... shou(?) *N* [7].

    *it turns out / there with eh... from this entrance / *V there they have... / various conference halls / and there they organize / *P all sorts of (eh...eh) these (eh...eh) how to say / (...) *V well (eh...eh) all sorts of there I don't know / performances / *V (eh...eh) educational ones / well she... show(?) *N* [7].

The hesitational nature of the unit under consideration is often emphasized with additional hesitational markers, such as eh...eh, how to say, well, there, etc., which are especially numerous in the second of the given examples (for more details on this PM, see: [15: 259–263]). New units that have not been mentioned before among trigrams appeared as adverbial expressions: V ETOM GODU (this year), V PROSHLOM GODU (last year), DO SIX POR (still). As before, the list of the most frequent units includes vocalizations (M-M-M, E-E-E), amplifications (DA-DA-DA, NET-NET-NET, TAK-TAK-TAK) and introductory units (PO KRAYNEY MERE, NA SAMOM DELE).

Overall, the material of trigrams revealed much more "recognizable" (and, accordingly, useful in various applied aspects of speech processing, up to the creation of artificial intelligence systems) than the material of bigrams. The application of the n-gram analysis method in this case also takes corpus research not only into grammar, but also into pragmatics, lexis, and idiomatics to an equal extent.

Let's compare the obtained data with the results of using another technique for annotating corpus material for our purposes, namely - the keyness metric, which allows to assess the significance of a word or phrase in the focus corpus (ORD) relative to a larger volume corpus (reference corpus, in this case for Russian language it is the Internet-corpus ruTenTen) [21]:

$$keyness = \frac{f\,(focus) + 1}{f\,(reference) + 1}$$

This metric allows identifying not so much frequent words or phrases that are characteristic of the language as a whole, but those of them that occur in a specific corpus, while their frequency indicators in general for other texts are not so high. According to the keyness measure, the following are among the most frequently encountered trigrams in the corpus: YA NE ZNAYU (I don't know), NU V OBSCHEM (Well, in general), VOT TAK VOT (So it is), VOT ETO VOT (This is it), NU TO EST (Well, that is), NU KAK BY (Well, as if), TO EST VOT (That is), TO EST TAM (That is there), NU NE ZNAYU (Well, I don't know), TO EST YA (That's me), POTOMU CHTO YA (Because I), TO EST ETO (That's it), YA DUMAYU CHTO (I think that), V OBSCHEM-TO (In general), A CHTO TY (And what about you). Obviously, how close this list is to those units that were obtained using n-gram analysis. In this case, the results confirm that the frequency of these units in the ORD corpus exceeds the indicators that can be observed in a large neutral corpus, - therefore, they are indeed characteristic of spoken language and are its markers.

5   Conclusion

Wrapping up our discussion, we note that the n-gram analysis method we utilized in this research proved to be quite effective for developing a classification of bigrams and trigrams. This technique provides insight into grammatical structures, established constructions in spoken discourse (both actual and potential), pragmatic markers, while also unveiling numerous other pathways for analyzing corpus data. Importively, this method accurately illustrates the proportion of lexicogrammatical and pragmatic units in our speech and the balance between 'significant' and 'insignificant' entities (from a traditional lexicogrammatical perspective), which is both crucial and intriguing for a multifaceted examination of oral communication.

Indeed, the implementation of this methodology allowed us to observe oral discourse, particularly its grammar, from a somewhat new perspective. It is clear that not only significant grammatical structures or overtly stable units deserve highlighting and linguistic description for various purposes, but also common sequences of words. The gap between 'significant' and 'insignificant' components, though pragmatically or functionally critical in our spoken language, is so large that neglecting this 'insignificant' aspect would be entirely unreasonable. Both automatic speech recognition systems and speakers of other languages engaging in Russian-language communication primarily perceive the entire stream of speech - the full 'sound mass' of this communication - and not just its meaningful elements. The perception of this 'sound mass' always precedes comprehension, and understanding is aided not only by the ability to sift the 'wheat from the chaff' (which is technically difficult to formalize, hence foreigners often take years to learn Russian and still consistently fall short of perfect proficiency, especially on a perceptual level), but also through the simple recognition of frequent sound sequences - the foundational 'bricks' of discourse. This recognition can aid in successfully navigating this 'sound mass' within the perceived speech flow.

Therefore, both the methodology described and the data obtained about the most common bi- and trigrams can prove to be very useful. From a theoretical standpoint, these can be used in developing a theory of conversational speech, usage-based linguistics (as suggested by [22]), or when outlining the grammar of speech. They can also be employed for various practical applications related to natural language processing and modeling, including the development of artificial intelligence.

Acknowledgements. The presented research was supported by the Russian Science Foundation, project No. 22-18-00189 "Structure and functionality of stable multiword units in Russian everyday speech".

References

1. MAS. In: Evgenieva, A.P. (ed.) Dictionary of the Russian Language in Four Volumes, vol. IV. S – Ya, 790p. Russian Language, Moscow (1988)
2. MAS. In: Evgenieva, A.P. (ed.) Dictionary of the Russian Language in Four Volumes, vol. II. K – O, 736p. Russian Language, Moscow (1986)
3. Fillmore, Ch.J., Kay, P., O'Connor, M.C.: Regularity and idiomaticity in grammatical constructions: the case of let alone. Language **64**(3), 501–538 (1988)
4. Hilpert, M.: Construction Grammar and its Application to English, p. 220. Edinburgh University Press, Edinburgh (2014)
5. Dobrovolsky, D.O.: Grammar of constructions and phraseology. Quest. Linguist. **3**, 7–21 (2016)
6. Sherstinova, T.: The syntax of everyday russian speech through the prism of N-gram analysis. In: Glazunova, O.I., Rogova, K.A. (eds.) Russian Grammar: Structural Organization of Language and Processes of Language Functioning, pp. 454–466. LENAND, Moscow (2019)
7. ORD Corpus of Russian Everyday Speech. https://ord.spbu.ru/. Accessed 01 Apr 2023
8. Bogdanova-Beglarian, N.V., Blinova, O.V., Martynenko, G.Ya., Sherstinova, T.Yu.: Corpus of the Russian language of everyday communication "one speech day": current state and prospects. In: Moldovan, A.M. (ed.) Proceedings of the V.V. Vinogradov Institute of the Russian Language, National Corpus of the Russian Language: Research and Development, Rep. ed. Issue of V.A. Plungyan, no. 21, pp. 101–110. IRYA RAN, Moscow (2019)
9. Russian Language of Everyday Communication: Features of Functioning in Different Social Groups. In: Bogdanova-Beglarlan, N.V. (ed.) Collective Monograph, 244p. LAIKA, St. Petersburg (2016)
10. Wittenburg, P., Brugman, H., Russel, A., Klassmann, A., Sloetjes, H.: ELAN: A Professional Framework for Multimodality Research. In: Proceedings of LREC 2006 Fifth International Conference on Language Resources and Evaluation, Genoa, pp. 1556–1559 (2006)
11. Sherstinova, T.: The structure of the ORD speech corpus of Russian everyday communication. In: Matoušek, V., Mautner, P. (eds.) TSD 2009. LNAI, vol. 5729, pp. 258–265. Springer, Heidelberg (2009)
12. Anthony, L.: *AntConc* (Version 4.2.0) [Computer Software]. Waseda University, Tokyo (2023). http://www.laurenceanthony.net/software.

13. Podlesskaya, V.I., Kibrik, A.A.: Correction of failures in oral spontaneous speech: the experience of corpus research. In: Kobozeva, I.M., Narinyani, A.S., Selegey, V.P. (eds.) Computational Linguistics and Intellectual Technologies: Proceedings of the International Conference "Dialogue 2005". RGGU, Moscow (2005). http://www.dialog-21.ru/media/2416/podlesskaya-kibrik.pdf.

14. Sherstinova, T.Yu.: On repetitions of discursive words in everyday speech communication (based on the Russian language). In: Monakhov, S., Vasilyeva, I., Khokhlova, M. (eds.) Proceedings of the 45th International Philological Conference (IPC-2016). Advances in Social Science, Education and Humanities Research (ASSEHR), vol. 122, pp. 480–483. Atlantis Press (2016)

15. PM. In: Bogdanova-Beglarian, N.V. (ed.) Pragmatic Markers of Russian Everyday Speech: Dictionary-Monograph, 520p. Nestor-History, St. Petersburg (2021)

16. Akhmanova, O.S.: Dictionary of Linguistic Terms, p. 607. Soviet Encyclopedia, Moscow (1966)

17. Liu, D.: Phraseological Units in the Russian Everyday Speech: Typology and Functioning, 389p. Ph.D. Thesis, St. Petersburg (typescript) (2019)

18. Baranov, A.N., Plungyan, V.A., Rakhilina, E.V.: Guide to the Discursive Words of the Russian Language, p. 208. Pomovsky and Partners, Moscow (1993)

19. Sherstinova, T.Yu.: The most common words of everyday Russian speech (in terms of gender and depending on the conditions of communication. In: Selegey, V.P. (ed.) Computational Linguistics and Intelligent Technologies. Based on the Materials of the Annual International Conference "Dialogue", vol. 15, no. 22, pp. 616–631. RGGU, Moscow (2016)

20. Sound Corpus as a Material for the Analysis of Russian Speech. In: Bogdanova-Beglarian, N.V. (ed.) Collective Monograph. Part 2. Theoretical and Practical Aspects of the Analysis. Volume 1. On Some Features of Oral Spontaneous Speech of Various Types. Sound Corpus as a Material for Teaching the Russian Language to Foreign Audiences, 396p. Faculty of Philology of St. Petersburg State University, St. Petersburg (2014)

21. Kilgarriff, A.: Simple maths for keywords. In: Proceedings of Corpus Linguistics Conference CL 2009. University of Liverpool, UK (2009). https://ucrel.lancs.ac.uk/publications/cl2009/.

22. Tomasello, M.: Constructing a Language: A Usage-Based Theory of Language Acquisition, p. 388. Harvard University Press, Harvard (2003)

Child Speech Processing

Recognition of the Emotional State of Children by Video and Audio Modalities by Indian and Russian Experts

Elena Lyakso[1]([✉]) [iD], Olga Frolova[1] [iD], Aleksandr Nikolaev[1] [iD], Egor Kleshnev[1] [iD], Platon Grave[1] [iD], Abylay Ilyas[1] [iD], Olesia Makhnytkina[2] [iD], Ruban Nersisson[3] [iD], A. Mary Mekala[4] [iD], and M. Varalakshmi[4] [iD]

[1] The Child Speech Research Group, St. Petersburg State University, St. Petersburg, Russia
lyakso@gmail.com
[2] ITMO University, St. Petersburg, Russia
[3] School of Electrical Engineering, Vellore Institute of Technology, Vellore, India
[4] School of Computer Science and Engineering, Vellore Institute of Technology, Vellore, India

Abstract. The paper presents the results of perceptual experiment by Indian and Russian experts for recognition of the emotional states of Russian children by video and audio modalities. The participants of the study were 64 Russian children (32 – boys & 32 – girls) aged 5–16 years and 26 adults. Video and audio recordings of child's emotion expression were made in the laboratory condition in a testing of the Child Emotional Development Method (CEDM), in tasks to depict "joy – neutral (calm state) – sadness – anger" in facial expressions and in voice, pronouncing words and phrases that reflect different emotional states. The design of the dataset is presented, the research procedure is described, video and audio fragments correctly recognized by Russian and Indian experts are analyzed. It was shown that Indian and Russian experts are able to recognize the basic emotions "joy – sadness – anger" and neutral state by facial expression, voice, and speech of Russian children. Experts better recognize joy and sadness from video, anger and sadness from audio. Both Indian & Russian experts recognize emotional states of girls by video and audio better vs. emotional states of boys. Universal and specific feature of both the cultures for recognizing the children's emotions are revealed. The paper described limitation and depicted the future research.

Keywords: Emotional State · Perceptual Experiment · Children · Video and Audio Modalities · Russian experts · Indian experts

1 Introduction

The problem of cross-cultural recognition of emotions by audio and video modalities is widely studied on the basis of different cultures [1–3]. The recognition of adults' emotions – in simulated situations using face images [4, 5], voice & speech [3, 6] and multimodal [7] are most studied. It is noted that when recognizing emotions, the age [8] and gender [9] of the person who is demonstrating and recognizing emotions

[10] are significant. The natural, spontaneous manifestation of emotions is difficult to analyze due to the impossibility of recreating situations of natural manifestation of emotions on a valid sample of informants. Creating datasets for cross-cultural emotion recognition is an independent task, as it requires careful selection of material [11]. A more difficult task is to recognize the emotional states of children. The manifestation of emotional states in facial expressions, voice, speech, behavior depends on the children's age, their upbringing and education. The wild manifestation of emotions at an early age of children is replaced by a restrained one, which is due to the requirements of society and culture [12–14]. Therefore, one of the promising areas of research is the cross-cultural recognition of children's emotions.

The goal of the study was to reveal the specificity of recognition of the emotional state of children by their facial expressions and speech by experts from two different cultures – Indian and Russian.

2 Methods

2.1 Participants of the Study

The participants of the study were 64 Russian children (32 – boys & 32 – girls) aged 5–16 years. By age and gender, the distribution of children was as follows: 5–7 y – 7 boys, 10 girls; 8–11y – 13 boys, 8 girls; 12–14 years – 6 boys, 5 girls; 15–16 years – 6 boys, 9 girls. 1 expert cut fragments (see 2.3); 5 adults, the research team of the Child Speech Research Group of St. Petersburg University (5 experts-1, age – 35.8 ± 18.0 years – mean ± standard deviation) selected fragments of audio and video recordings for tests; 10 Russian experts (age – 44.7 ± 10.2 years) and 10 Indian experts (age – 35.9 ± 6.0, specialties in the field of speech and information technology) viewed the video tests and listened to the audio tests.

2.2 Data Collection

Video and audio recordings of emotion expression were made in the laboratory condition in a testing of the Child Emotional Development Method (CEDM) [15].

CEDM is designed to assess the emotional development of children by determining the ability to express their own emotions, the adequacy of emotions, recognizing the emotional states of others. The approach is based on adapted methods and scales, assessment criteria and methodological approaches tested in a number of studies, depending on the age of the children, their developmental characteristics, language and culture of the country of residence of the child [16–19]. The approach includes two blocks – information about the development of the child obtained from parents; methods for children testing, including interview methods, psychological tests, play situations. For assessment scores on the 4-point Likert scale were used [20].

The procedure for testing the children was recorded on a video camera and tape recorder. For video recording of facial expression of children, a SONY HDR-CX560 video camera (maximum resolution 1920 × 1080 at 50 frames per second) was used, which was located at a distance of 1 m from the child's face. To record children's speech,

Marantz PMD660 tape recorder with a SENNHEIZER e835S external microphone was used. The microphone was set at a distance of 30–50 cm from the child's face. Audio files were saved in.wav format, 48000 Hz, 16 bits. The total recording time for each child was 1–1.5 h.

Non-parametric criteria – Spearmen correlation (p < 0.05), Mann-Whitney test, regression analysis, multiple regression analysis were used.

The parents of the children participating in the study signed an informed consent approved by the Ethics Committee of St. Petersburg State University. Permission to use video and audio recordings for research was obtained from parents.

2.3 Dataset

For this study, we selected emotion audio & video data from the recording files of the child testing procedure using CEDM, in tasks to depict emotional states "joy – neutral (calm state) – sadness – anger" in facial expressions and in voice, pronouncing words and phrases that reflect different emotional states. This task was designed to show how children could demonstrate different states in vocal and facial expressions. Example words for emotions: /Sadness: sadness, longing, hard, sad, crying; Joy: joy, beautiful, cool, super/. Examples of phrases for emotions: /Neutral: I'm fine. Sadness: I'm sad, sad time. Anger: I like to hit and break everything. Crush and bite when everyone got me. Joy: I like when everything is beautiful!/. Simulated acting emotions are used to produce emotional video [21]. The design of the experiment (Fig. 1):

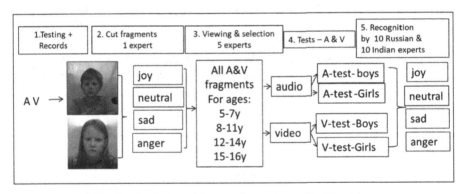

Fig. 1. The design of the experiment. A – audio, V – video.

1. Child testing and audio and video recording.
2. Cut fragments: from long files (recording of the all testing), experts (one expert for each child age: 5–7 years old; 8–11 years old; 12–14 years old; 16–16 years old) cut out fragments corresponding to the task:

    Video: To depict in facial expression joy, a neutral (calm) state, state of sadness, anger – for 4 fragments per child (one fragment corresponds one emotion according to the task given to the children);

Audio: 8 fragments for each child – 4 fragments contain words and 4 fragments contain phrases reflecting 4 emotional states (Table 1).

To cut video fragments, the program "Pinnacle Studio 1.0.0.155" was used; to cut audio fragments "Cool Edit Pro" sound editor was used. Thus, segmentation was carried out so that each audio and video fragment corresponded to the task performed by the child.

3. Viewing and selecting: 5 experts-1 listened to and reviewed all segments. If all experts agreed to attribute the fragment to a certain emotion (kappa Cohen's coefficient – 1.0), then this fragment was selected.
4. From all the fragments selected by 5 experts-1, the same number of fragments for each emotion were taken for audio and video tests. 2 audio tests were created (containing audio fragments of boys – test A1 and girls – test A2) and 2 video tests (containing videos of boys – test V1 and girls – test V2) (Table 2).
5. Recognition of the emotional state of children by video and audio modalities by 10 Indian and 10 Russian experts.

A similar approach to the selection of emotional video fragments was used by other researchers: initial selection, then two other researchers performed an emotion recognition task by watching videos without sound to make sure that emotions could be evoked without understanding the language; final selection [11].

Table 1. Dataset: selection of audio and video fragments.

Information about children				Total number of A & V fragments		The number of selected of A & V fragments by 5 experts-1	
Child age, y	Child, n	Boys	Girls	Video fragments	Audio fragments	Video fragments	Audio fragments
5–7	17	7	10	68	136	40	57
8–11	21	13	8	84	168	24	56
12–14	11	6	5	44	88	15	13
15–16	15	6	9	60	120	29	48
Total	64	32	32	256	512	118	174

To justify the involvement in the study of 10 experts (Russian and Indian), we conducted a special perceptual experiment. We created the audio test that included meaningless speech material from Russian and Indian Tamil-speaking children, which Russian and Indian Tamil-speaking experts unequivocally attributed to the corresponding emotion "joy – neutral – sadness – anger" [14]. The use of meaningless speech material does not allow listeners to rely on linguistic information, and when recognizing emotions to take into account only the prosodic features of speech [14]. The test was taken for listening by 100 people – 60 native Russian speakers (age: 35.5 ± 15 y), 40 foreigners (age: 20.5 ± 3.1 y; language – Arabic, Farsi, lack of knowledge of Russian; also

Russian listeners did not speak Tamil). Analysis of the results of the perceptual experiment showed that listeners give the correct answers when recognizing emotions from children's speech (Table 2), but with different probabilities compared to recognition by experts from previous study. Correct recognition with an increase in the number of listeners, but the number of correct answers is somewhat less can be explained by the individual characteristics of people and the specifics of perception as a cognitive process [22].

Table 2. Confusion matrix for recognition by Russian and foreign listeners of the emotional states of children (Indian & Russian) by audio test (% of answers).

	joy		neutral		sadness		anger	
	R	F	R	F	R	F	R	F
joy	**73**	**53**	23	34	3	3	1	10
neutral	15	29	**78**	**66**	5	5	2	0
sadness	0	7	9	16	**91**	**77**	0	0
anger	15	31	15	12	6	**6**	**64**	**51**

2.4 Data Analysis

The study includes perceptual study, spectrographic analysis of speech, automatic analysis of facial expression in FaceReader program.

Perceptual Study: Video and audio tests were created for the perceptual experiment. The video tests for boys (n = 27) and for girls (n = 27) included for 45 fragments, mixed in a random order (Table 3). Before each video fragment, the number was inserted. The duration of the fragments was from 3 to 4 s, the pause between the fragments was 5 s. Each of the video fragments was included in the test once. The video test was presented without sound from a monitor of a personal computer. Before the experiment, in the questionnaire, the experts indicated their gender and age. Watching the tests, experts noted the emotional state of the children, choosing one of the four proposed categories: joy, neutral, sadness, anger.

The audio tests for boys (n = 26 boys) and for girls (n = 27 girls) included for 48 fragments, mixed in a random order. Each speech signal was repeated once in the test, the pause between speech signals was 5 s. The audio test was presented to experts in an open field.

Instructions for Russian and Indian experts differed. Since the speech data of Russian children linguistically reflected emotion, the instruction for Russian experts was as follows: When listening to audio tests please ignore the linguistic context, be guided by the voice features, since the real emotional state of the child may not correspond to the given one. Indian experts could only focus on the voice features. Listening to the tests, experts noted the emotional state of the children, choosing one of the four proposed categories: joy, neutral, sadness, anger.

Table 3. Tests information.

Tests		joy	neutral	sadness	anger	Total
Video	test V1-b	15	15	5	10	45
	test V2-g	15	19	6	5	45
Audio	test A1-b	12	12	12	12	48
	test A2-g	12	12	12	12	48

Watching video tests and listening to audio tests were individual. There was no preliminary training of experts.

Confusion matrixes for perceptual experiments were prepared. We counted recall, precision, F-1 score for each emotion, Unweighted Average Recall (UAR) – for all emotions [23]. Agreement between experts and listeners is assessed using the Cohen's kappa statistic (k) [24, 25]. Relative strength of agreement was associated with kappa statistics: slight (0.00–0.20), fair (0.21–0.40), moderate (0.41–0.60), substantial (0.61–0.80), and almost perfect (0.81–1.00) [26].

Spectrographic Analysis of the speech material was carried out in the Cool Edit Pro sound editor. The spectral characteristics of speech were automatically calculated, based on the algorithms implemented in the Cool Edit Pro sound editor. We analyzed the acoustic features of speech correctly classified by both Indian and Russian experts. The duration (ms) of fragments, words, stressed vowels and stationary vowel section was calculated. Pitch values (F0, Hz) – average, F0 max, F0 min, and intensity values (E, dB) were determined. The range of F0 was calculated by subtracting the minimum F0 from the maximum F0 values: F0 range = F0max – F0min; the ratio of intensities corresponding to F0max – E0max and F0min – E0min normalized with respect to E0 – E0max/E0, E0min/E0, the ratio E0max/E0min were calculated. Acoustic features are chosen as the most significant in the analysis of emotional speech [8, 27].

Automatic Analysis of facial expression in FaceReader program: Analysis of facial expression was performed in the FaceReader v.8.0 program (Noldus Information Technology, Netherlands) [28]). Based on the algorithms embedded in the program, the following parameters are determined: the time during which the child demonstrates a certain emotional state in facial expression (as a percentage of the time of the video fragment), arousal, and the valence of the emotions. The data obtained from the automatic analysis of children's facial expression were compared with the results of a perceptual experiment.

3   Results

3.1   Perceptual Experiment

Recognition of the Emotional State of Children by Facial Expression. An analysis of the perceptual experiment showed that by video fragments of boys Russian experts better recognize joy (89% correct answers) and neutral state (77%); for girls – joy state

(94%) with a high recognition of anger, sadness and a neutral state. Indian experts better recognized by boy's facial expressions the joy state (94%) and sadness state (86%) vs. anger and neutral state; by girl's facial expressions – joy state (98%), anger (94%) and sadness state (93%). The Unweighted Average Recall (UAR) was – 0.745 (for boys), 0.832 (for girls) – for Russian experts; 0.75 (for boys), 0.87 (for girls) – for Indian experts (Table 4). Indian and Russian experts demonstrated moderate agreement in recognizing all emotional states by video for boys (Cohen's kappa coefficient = 0.522), substantial agreement – for girls (0.634). Maximum agreements between exerts was revealed for recognition of joy state: for boys – substantial (0.735), for girls – perfect (0.883) (see Table 6).

Table 4. Confusion matrix for recognition by Indian and Russian experts of the emotional states of Russian boys and girls by facial expressions by video fragments (% of answers).

Boys video fragments (test V1-b)

	joy		neutral		sadness		anger	
	I	R	I	R	I	R	I	R
joy	**94**	**89**	6	8	0	3	0	0
neutral	3	5	**61**	77	30	17	6	1
sadness	2	0	4	28	**86**	**70**	8	2
anger	19	11	17	13	5	14	**59**	**62**
Recall	0.94	0.89	0.61	0.77	0.86	0.7	0.59	0.62
Precision	0.80	0.85	0.69	0.61	0.71	0.67	0.81	0.95
F1-score	0.86	0.86	0.65	0.68	0.78	0.68	0.68	0.75
UAR	I = **0.750**; R = **0.745**							

Girls video fragments (test V2-g)

	joy		neutral		sadness		anger	
	I	R	I	R	I	R	I	R
joy	**98**	**94**	2	1	0	5	0	0
neutral	3	**2**	**63**	**81**	25	14	9	3
sadness	0	5	3.5	13	**93**	**80**	3.5	2
anger	0	0	2	8	4	14	**94**	**78**
Recall	0.98	0.94	0.63	0.81	0.93	0.80	0.94	0.78
Precision	0.97	0.93	0.89	0.79	0.76	0.71	0.88	0.94
F1-score	0.98	0.94	0.74	0.80	0.84	0.75	0.91	0.85
UAR	I = **0.870**; R = **0.832**							

Note: I-Indian experts; R-Russian experts; UAR- Unweighted Average Recall

Indian and Russian experts better recognize all emotional states by video test of girls than by video test of boys.

Recognition of the Emotional State of Children by the Speech. The Indian and Russian experts recognize the anger state (72.5% & 82.5% – corresponding for Indian and Russian experts) and sadness (63% & 87.5%) – namely emotions with negative valence better than joy and neutral state by speech of boys. For girl's speech, Indian experts recognize all the states with better recognition the anger (70%) and sadness state (68%). Russian experts worse recognized the joy state (71%) vs. sadness (91.5%), anger (82%) and neutral (80%) states. Russian experts better recognized all emotions by boys and girls speech vs. Indian experts. The UAR was 0.616 (for boys) and 0.674 (for girls) – for Indian experts; 0.785 (for boys) and 0.811 (for girls) – for Russian experts (Table 5). Indian and Russian experts demonstrated moderate agreement in recognizing all emotional states by speech of boys (0.431) and girls (0.496). Maximum agreements between experts was revealed for recognition of anger state – substantial agreement (0.569 – for boys & 0.565 – for girls) (see Table 6).

Table 5. Confusion matrix for recognition by Indian and Russian experts of emotional states by speech of boys and girls (% of answers).

Boys audio fragments (test A1-b)								
	joy		neutral		sadness		anger	
	I	R	I	R	I	R	I	R
joy	**53**	**68**	16	26	3	5	28	1
neutral	13	4	**58**	**76**	21	19	8	1
sadness	2	0	30	12.5	**63**	**87.5**	5	0
anger	12.5	1	11	14	4	2.5	**72.5**	**82.5**
Recall		0.68	0.58	0.76	0.63	0.88	0.73	0.83
Precision		0.93	0.50	0.59	0.69	0.77	0.64	0.98
F1-score		0.79	0.54	0.67	0.66	0.82	0.68	0.89
UAR	I = **0.616**; R = **0.785**							
Girls audio fragments (test A2-g)								
	joy		neutral		sadness		anger	
	I	R	I	R	I	R	I	R
joy	**62**	**71**	12	19	3	2.5	23	7.5
neutral	4	4	**69**	**80**	21	15	6	1
sadness	2.5	0	19	7.5	**68.5**	**91.5**	10	1
anger	8	1	21	15	1	2	**70**	**82**
Recall	0.62	0.71	0.69	0.80	0.69	0.92	0.7	0.82
Precision	0.81	0.93	0.57	0.66	0.73	0.82	0.64	0.90
F1-score	0.70	0.81	0.62	0.72	0.71	0.87	0.67	0.86
UAR	I = **0.674**; R = **0.811**							

Table 6 presented data about agreement in recognizing the emotional states of children via facial expressions by video and speech by audio fragments by Indian and Russian experts.

3.2 Characteristics of Video and Audio Fragments Correctly Recognized by Indian and Russian Experts (Probability 0.75–1.0)

Characteristics of Facial Expressions by Video Fragments: Automatic analysis of boy's and girl's facial expressions in the FaceReader 8.0 program showed that children's facial expressions correspond mainly to a neutral state and joy state (Table 7).

The facial expression of children in a state of joy is characterized by positive valence (0.451 – for boys, 0.438 – for girls); state of sadness (−0.097/−0.248 – for boys/girls), anger (−0.297/−0.177) and neutral state (−0.199/−0.014) – by negative valence. The highest arousal was revealed for the joy state (0.514/0.47 – for boys & girls); the least arousal – for neutral state for boy's and girl's (0.21/0.262) facial expressions.

Table 6. Expert's agreement in recognizing the emotional states of children via video and audio fragments (Cohen's kappa coefficient).

Modality		Emotions	Indian experts	Russian experts	Indian & Russian
Video	Boys	Joy	0.769	0.730	0.735
		Neutral	0.424	0.528	0.420
		sadness	0.515	0.388	0.383
		anger	0.470	0.598	0.458
		all	0.564	0.579	0.522
	Girls	joy	0.934	0.852	0.883
		neutral	0.523	0.601	0.520
		sadness	0.591	0.411	0.453
		anger	0.669	0.675	0.650
		all	0.685	0.646	0.634
Audio	Boys	joy	0.295	0.684	0.397
		neutral	0.293	0.446	0.286
		sadness	0.355	0.606	0.470
		anger	0.535	0.808	0.569
		all	0.337	0.618	0.431
	Girls	joy	0.509	0.697	0.551
		neutral	0.374	0.463	0.338
		sadness	0.502	0.683	0.549
		anger	0.491	0.756	0.565
		all	0.458	0.635	0.496

Table 7. Facial expression of boys and girls, % of the time (FaceReader 8.0).

Boys video fragments

Emotional state	joy	neutral	sadness	anger	fear	surprise	disgust
joy	**0.542**	0.299	0.013	0.061	0.029	0.019	0.001
neutral	0.006	**0.802**	0.158	0.145	0.013	0.02	0.002
sadness	0.012	0.802	**0.106**	0.026	0.004	0.022	0.12
anger	0.064	0.389	0.02	**0.353**	0.022	0.004	0.147

Girls video fragments

joy	**0.486**	0.355	0.018	0.022	0.008	0.016	0.01
neutral	0.064	**0.816**	0.058	0.032	0.007	0.025	0.019
sadness	0.061	0.535	**0.307**	0.016	0.004	0.01	0.003
anger	0.056	0.678	0.023	**0.23**	0.009	0.009	0.007

Note: Rows correspond to real emotional states; columns correspond to emotional states highlighted by the FaceReader 8.0 program

Acoustic Features of Speech: The correlation was revealed between emotional state of children and: child gender – $F(1,156) = 11.066$ p < 0.001 ($R^2 = 0.066$ β $= -0.25$) – in the recognized fragments in the speech, emotions are reflected better in the boys speech vs. girls speech (Regression analysis); speech fragments duration – $F(1,34) = 4.513$ p < 0.04 ($R^2 = 0.117$ β $= 0.342$); intensity E0max/E0min – F $(2,33) = 3.095$ p < 0.01 ($R^2 = 0.158$ β $= 0.442$); words duration – $F(1,156) = 4.261$ p < 0.04 ($R^2 = 0.027$ β $= -0.163$). According to Multiple Regression analysis, the correlation was revealed between emotional state of children and children age and acoustic features of speech (Table 8).

It is shown that: the state of joy is characterized by maximum average pitch values of words vs. sadness and neutral states (p < 0.001 – Mann Whitney U test), maximum values F0 max for words and vowels vs. sadness, neutral state (p < 0.001), and anger state (p < 0.05). Joy is characterized by the maximum pitch range [max–min] for words and vowels (p < 0.05) vs. sadness and neutral, and for speech fragments (p < 0.05) vs. sadness state only.

The anger state is characterized by short words duration compared to the corresponding data for sadness (p < 0.00001), joy (p < 0.0001), neutral state (p < 0.001), maximum intensity E0max/E0min of stress vowels (p < 0.05) and high values of pitch (there is no significant difference for the joy state).

The sadness state is characterized by the significantly longer words and stress vowels duration vs. neutral, joy and anger states.

Differences in the acoustic features between boys and girls were revealed in the pitch range for joy state (p < 0.05 – for girls is higher than for boys) and for neutral state (p < 0.05 – for boys it is higher than for girls); intensity E0max/E0min values for sadness state (p < 0.05 – higher in words and vowels in boys speech); the duration of words in sadness state is higher in girls vs. boys speech (p < 0.05).

Table 8. The correlation between acoustic features of speech and types of emotions & children age (Multiple Regression analysis data).

R^2	F	Independent variable	β	SE β	B	SE B	t	p
Dependent variable: Emotions 0.232	F(10,130) 3.92						141	
		D-v	−.195	.089	−.002	.001	−2.172	.03
		F0 av-v	−.636	.289	−.010	.004	−2.020	.02
		F0max-v	−.623	.310	−.009	.004	−2.005	0.04
		F0st-v	1.00	.335	.0159	0.005	3.00	.003
0.063	F(2,141) 4.71	F0-v (max-min)	−.178	.085	−.006	.003	−2.093	.003
		E0max/E0min	.235	.085	.049	.017	2.756	.006
age 0.395	F(2,154) 50.473						154	
		F0 av-words	−.643	.064	−.043	.004	−9.930	.0001
0.448	F(10,129) 10.486						129	
		F0 max-v	−.623	.264	−.038	.016	−2.360	.01

R^2—correlation coefficient (R) squared; SE—standard error; β—standardized, B—unstandardized regression coefficients; p—a number describing how likely it is that data would have occurred under the null hypothesis of statistical test. D-v—vowel duration, v-vowels, av-average, st-stationary part

4 Discussion and Future Work

The results of the study showed the ability of people belonging to different linguistic groups and cultures (India and Russia) to recognize the emotions of Russian children by their facial expressions and speech, with better emotions recognition by facial expressions than by voice. These data confirm the classical studies of P. Ekman [1] on the universality of the basic emotions "joy – sadness – anger", determined by facial expression. 10 Indian and 10 Russian experts took part in our study, which is primarily due to the ethical aspects, which allow working with video recordings only by the scientific team of the project. An ethical framework must be observed when using any data obtained from research participants, as noted in other studies [29, 30]. We justified the participation of a small number of experts in the perceptual experiment by conducting an additional auditory experiment. The results showed that the number of listeners did not significantly affect the result, and that non-linguistic listeners were able to correctly recognize children's emotions from their speech.

Indian and Russian experts better recognized child's emotions by video vs. speech; joy and sadness by facial expression; anger and sadness – by speech.

When creating the dataset, we used Child Emotional Development Method (CEDM) [15], in tasks to depict emotional states "joy – neutral (calm state) – sadness – anger" in facial expressions and in voice, pronouncing words and phrases that reflect different emotional states. Children were not taught to depict emotions, their manifestations were almost spontaneous.

Predominant number of works are devoted to the study of the reflection of emotions in the facial expression of adults [31–34]. In the evolution the visual sensory system has become the leading one in humans. Vision plays a prominent role in the overall functioning of the brain, providing the lion's share of information about the outside world [35]. In a behavioral and neurophysiological study, the authors [10] compared the simultaneous responses in recognizing emotions (anger, fear, joy and neutral) from the faces of adults and children. It was observed that participants made fewer errors when matching adult faces compared to children's face. The same brain regions were involved in processing adult and child faces, activation of the face processing neural network was higher for adults than for children. Negative and neutral facial stimuli produced the greatest effects for adults, for children – happy face stimuli [10]. Earlier in our work, it was shown that adults recognized from photographs of children aged 4–7 years, joy and sadness state better than fear and anger [36]. These data and the data of the present study obtained for children in a wide age range using video are consistent.

It was expected that Russian experts recognize emotions from the speech of Russian children better than Indian ones. They had linguistic cues despite being given instruction. It is important that the data of the perceptual experiment and the acoustic analysis of speech confirmed the previously obtained data for 8–12 years old children [14, 27].

Despite the novelty of the obtained results, the work has limitations.

Limitation: Current study includes audio and video data from Russian children only. Comparative cross-cultural study of Russian and Indian children will be the next step of our research. There is lack of native speakers with or without everyday experience of interacting with children for perceptual experiment.

Future: Cross-cultural and cross-linguistic recognition of emotional states "joy – neutral (calm) – sadness – anger" by humans and automatically using mono (A, V) and multimodal (A + V). Obtaining data on Indian children's reflection of emotional state in facial expressions and voice features.

5 Conclusion

It was shown that Indian and Russian experts are able to recognize the basic emotions "joy – sadness – anger" and neutral state by facial expression, voice and speech of Russian children. Experts better recognize joy and sadness from video, anger and sadness from audio. Both Indian & Russian experts recognize emotional states of girls by video and audio fragments better vs. boys. Cultural peculiarities are associated with better recognition by Russian experts a neutral state by facial expressions of children, by Indian experts – sadness state by the facial expressions of boys, sadness and anger state – by girls.

The data of automatic analysis of video in the FaceReader program correspond to the results of the perceptual experiment. FaceReader detects joy and neutral states more accurately than the other emotions. When recognizing the emotions of children in their speech, Indian and Russian experts rely on the pitch values, pitch range, pitch intensity and duration of stressed vowels in words.

The novelty of the work lies in the identified possibility of cross-cultural (India-Russia, Tamil – St. Petersburg) recognition of emotions by the facial expressions of children; confirmation of the classical works of basic emotions on the material of facial expressions of children. Revealing acoustic features of emotional speech correctly classified by experts into "joy – neutral – sadness – anger" states complement the previously obtained data.

Acknowledgements. This study is financially supported by the Russian Science Foundation (project 22-45-02007) – for Russian researches; DST/INT/RUS/RSF/P-57/2021 – for Indian researches.

References

1. Ekman, P.: Basic emotions. In: Dalgleish, T., Power M.J. (eds.) Handbook of Cognition and Emotion, pp. 45–60. John Wiley & Sons, Ltd, Hoboken (1999)
2. Sauter, D.A., Eisner, F., Ekman, P., Scott, S.K.: Cross-cultural recognition of basic emotions through nonverbal emotional vocalizations. Proc. Natl. Acad. Sci. U.S.A. **107**(6), 2408–2412 (2010)
3. Jiang, X., Paulmann, S., Robin, J., Pell, M.D.: More than accuracy: nonverbal dialects modulate the time course of vocal emotion recognition across cultures. J. Exp. Psychol. Hum. Percept. Perform. **41**, 597–612 (2015)
4. Zhang, L., et al.: ARFace: attention-aware and regularization for face recognition with reinforcement learning. IEEE Trans. Biomet. Behav. Ident. Sci. **4**(1), 30–42 (2022)
5. Barrett, L.F., Adolphs, R., Marsella, S., Martinez, A.M., Pollak, S.D.: Emotional expressions reconsidered: challenges to inferring emotion from human facial movements. Psychol. Sci. Publ. Interest **20**(1), 1–68 (2019). https://doi.org/10.1177/1529100619832930
6. Laukka, P., Elfenbein, H.A.: Cross-cultural emotion recognition and in-group advantage in vocal expression: a meta-analysis. Emot. Rev. **13**(1), 3–11 (2021)
7. Proverbio, A.M., Camporeale, E., Brusa, A.: Multimodal recognition of emotions in music and facial expressions. Front. Hum. Neurosci. **11** (2020)
8. Goy, H., Pichora-Fuller, M.K., van Lieshout, P.: Effects of age on speech and voice quality ratings. J. Acoust. Soc. Am. **139**(4), 1648–1659 (2016)
9. Lausen, A., Schacht, A.: Gender differences in the recognition of vocal emotions. Front. Psychol. **9** (2018)
10. Marusak, H.A., Carré, J.M., Thomason, M.E.: The stimuli drive the response: an fMRI study of youth processing adult or child emotional face stimuli. Neuroimaging **83**, 679–689 (2013)
11. Chen, H., Chin, K.L., Tan, C.B.Y.: Selection and validation of emotional videos: dataset of professional and amateur videos that elicit basic emotions. Data Brief **34**, 106662 (2020)
12. Kaya, H., Salah, A.A., Karpov, A., Frolova, O., Grigorev, A., Lyakso, E.: Emotion, age, and gender classification in children's speech by humans and machines. Comput. Speech Lang. **46**, 268–283 (2017)
13. Amorim, M., Anikin, A., Mendes, A.J., Lima, C.F., Kotz, S.A., Pinheiro, A.P.: Changes in vocal emotion recognition across the life span. Emotion **21**(2), 315–325 (2021)
14. Lyakso, E., Ruban, N., Frolova, O., Mekala, M.A.: The children's emotional speech recognition by adults: cross-cultural study on Russian and Tamil language. PLoS ONE **18**(2), e0272837 (2023)

15. Lyakso, E., Frolova, O., Kleshnev, E., Ruban, N., Mekala, M., Arulalan, K.V.: Approbation of the Child's Emotional Development Method (CEDM). In: Companion Publication of the 2022 International Conference on Multimodal Interaction (ICMI 2022 Companion), New York, pp. 201–210 (2022)
16. Hart, S., Jacobsen, S.L.: Zones of proximal emotional development – psychotherapy within a neuroaffective perspective. J. Infant Child Adolesc. Psychother. 17(1), 28–42 (2018)
17. Hart, S., Jacobsen, S.L.: The emotional development scale: assessing the emotional capacity of 4–12 year olds. J. Infant Child Adolesc. Psychother. 18(2), 185–195 (2019)
18. Sappok, T., Budczies, J., Dziobek, I., Bölte, S., Dosen, A., Diefenbacher, A.: The missing link: delayed emotional development predicts challenging behavior in adults with intellectual disability. J. Autism Dev. Disord. 44(4), 786–800 (2014)
19. Sappok, T., et al.: Scale of emotional development—short. Res. Dev. Disabil. 59, 166–175 (2016)
20. Likert, R.: A technique for the measurement of attitudes. Archiv. Psychol. 22, 5–55 (1932)
21. Profyt, L., Whissell, C.: Children's understanding of facial expression of emotion: I. Voluntary creation of emotion-faces. Percept. Motor Skill. 73(1), 199–202 (1991)
22. Heald, S.L., Nusbaum, H.C.: Speech perception as an active cognitive process. Front. Syst. Neurosci. 8 (2014)
23. Dalianis, H.: Evaluation metrics and evaluation. In: Clinical Text Mining, pp. 45–53. Springer, Cham (2018). https://doi.org/10.1007/978-3-319-78503-5_6
24. Md Juremi, N.R., Zulkifley, M.A., Hussain, A., Zaki W.M.D.: Inter-rater reliability of actual tagged emotion categories validation using Cohen's Kappa coefficient. J. Theor. Appl. Inf. Technol. 95, 259–264 (2017)
25. Bobicev, V., Sokolova, M.: Inter-annotator agreement in sentiment analysis: machine learning perspective. In: Recent Advances in Natural Language Processing Meet Deep Learning, Varna, pp. 97–102 (2017)
26. Landis, J.R., Koch, G.G.: The measurement of observer agreement for categorical data. Biometrics 33(1), 159–174 (1977)
27. Lyakso, E., Frolova, O., Ruban, N., Mekala, A.M.: The child's emotional speech classification by human across two languages: Russian & Tamil. LNAI 12997, 384–396 (2021)
28. FaceReader v.8.0 Program. https://www.noldus.com/facereader
29. Takasaki, K., Stransky, D.A., Miller, G.: Psychogenic nonepileptic seizures: diagnosis, management, and bioethics. Pediatr. Neurol. 62, 3–8 (2016)
30. O'Sullivan, S., et al.: Legal, regulatory, and ethical frameworks for development of standards in artificial intelligence (AI) and autonomous robotic surgery. Int. J. Med. Robot. Comput. Assist. Surg. 15(1), e1968 (2019)
31. Song, Z.: Facial expression emotion recognition model integrating philosophy and machine learning theory. Front. Psychol. 12 (2021)
32. Kumar, M., et al.: Transfer learning based convolution neural net for authentication and classification of emotions from natural and stimulated speech signals. J. Intell. Fuzzy Syst. 41(1), 213–224 (2021)
33. Agarwal, A., Susan, S.: Emotion recognition from masked faces using inception-v3. In: Proceedings of 5th International Conference on Recent Advances in Information Technology (RAIT), Dhanbad (2023)
34. Dores, A.R., Barbosa, F., Queirós, C., Carvalho, I.P., Griffiths, M.D.: Recognizing emotions through facial expressions: a largescale experimental study. Int. J. Environ. Res. Public Health 17(20), 7420 (2020)
35. Hegdé, J.: Neural mechanisms of high-level vision. Compr. Physiol. 8(3), 903–953 (2018)
36. Lyakso, E.E., Frolova, O.V., Grigorev, A.S., Sokolova, V.D., Yarotskaya, K.A.: Recognition by adults of emotional state in typically developing children and children with autism spectrum disorders. Neurosci. Behav. Physiol. 47(9), 1051–1059 (2017)

Effect of Linear Prediction Order to Modify Formant Locations for Children Speech Recognition

Udara Laxman Kumar[1]([✉]), Mikko Kurimo[2], and Hemant Kumar Kathania[1]

[1] Department of Electronics and Communication Engineering,
National Institute of Technology Sikkim, Ravangla, India
{phec220031,hemant.ece}@nitsikkim.ac.in
[2] Department of Information and Communication Engineering, Aalto University,
Espoo, Finland
mikko.kurimo@aalto.fi

Abstract. Children's speech recognition shows poor performance as compared to adult speech. Large amount of data is required for the neural network models to achieve good performance. A very limited amount of children's speech data is publicly available. A baseline system was developed using adult speech for training and children's speech for testing. This kind of system suffers from mismatches between training and testing speech data. To overcome one of the mismatches, which is formant frequency locations between adults and children, in this paper we have explored the effect of linear prediction order to modify the formant frequency locations. The explored method studies for narrowband and wideband speech and found that they gave reductions in word error rate (WER) for GMM-HMM, DNN-HMM, and TDNN acoustic models. The TDNN acoustic model gives the best performance as compared to other acoustic models. The best formant modification factor α is 0.1 for linear prediction order 6 for narrowband speech (WER 13.82%), and α is 0.1 for linear prediction order 20 for wideband speech (WER 12.19%) for the TDNN acoustic model. Further, we have also compared the method with vocal tract length normalization (VTLN) and speaking rate adaptation (SRA), and it is found that the proposed method gives a better reduction in WERs as compared to VTLN and SRA.

Keywords: Children's speech recognition · Linear prediction · Formant modification · TDNN

1 Introduction

Speech recognition for children has many potential applications, such as learning a second language, education, entertainment, and games. Recent developments in machine learning methods have led to a major improvement in automatic speech recognition (ASR). ASR for children's speech is still a challenging task because

ⓒ The Author(s), under exclusive license to Springer Nature Switzerland AG 2023
A. Karpov et al. (Eds.): SPECOM 2023, LNAI 14338, pp. 483–493, 2023.
https://doi.org/10.1007/978-3-031-48309-7_39

all publicly available software and tools do not work well for children's speech as compared to adult speech. Neural network models require a large amount of speech data to achieve good performance, whereas for children, a limited amount of speech data is available publicly. To solve this problem, mismatched ASR was proposed [29, 31], where the system was trained on adult speech and tested with children's speech. This kind of mismatched ASR suffers from acoustic and linguistic mismatches between training and testing speech data. So, it is necessary to build an ASR system for children's speech that is robust for various mismatch conditions.

In the last two decades, speech recognition-based applications have been developed [26]. This application is affected by several factors, such as age, accent, gender, speaking rate, pitch, and formant frequencies. To overcome this variability between speakers, the ASR model is trained with a large amount of speech data from different age groups of speakers. In addition, to adapt the variation techniques, like feature-space maximum likelihood linear regression (fMLLR) [6] and vocal tract length normalization (VTLN) [18] are commonly used.

The main acoustic mismatches between children and adult speakers are speaking rate, pitch, and formant frequencies [3, 19, 27]. To overcome the acoustic mismatches between adult and child speech, many studies have been done. In [12, 14, 30, 31, 33] effect of acoustic differences between adult and child speech has been studied, and it has been observed that system performance degrades mainly due to large differences in the acoustic properties of adult and child speech. Prosodic features such as intensity, loudness, and voice probability were studied in [12] and found that combining these features with mel-frequency cepstral coefficients (MFCCs) gave a reduction in WER. Pitch and speaking rate modifications were studied in [1, 10, 13, 29] to overcome the mismatch between adult and child speech. In [7], stochastic feature-based data augmentation was explored to improve the system's performance for children's speech. Formant frequencies change with age, as explored in many studies [8, 19, 27, 34]. When we compared the formant frequencies between children's speech and adult speech outcomes, it showed that children's speech consists higher [19, 27]. The effects of formant frequency modification were explored in [9, 15, 16] and they improved the system performance under mismatch conditions.

In this paper, a role of linear predictive order to modify formant frequencies is proposed to overcome the differences between adults and children's speech and improve the ASR system's performance. The method aims to show the effect of linear prediction in order to overcome the differences in formant frequencies between adults and children's speech. The study was conducted for narrow band (8 kHz) and wide band (16 kHz) speech data. The proposed study shows that the effect of linear prediction order to modify formant frequencies and improve the system performance for narrowband and wideband applications for children's speech under mismatched conditions.

2 Effect of Linear Prediction Order to Modify Formant Location

In this study, we focus on modifying the formant structure of children's speech by applying a technique known as warping to the Linear Prediction (LP) spectrum. The LP spectrum represents the characteristics of the vocal tract resonances, or formants, in speech. By warping the LP spectrum, we can systematically shift the formant frequencies to achieve the desired modifications.

To perform the formant modification, we introduce the concept of the warped LP spectrum, denoted as $S_\alpha(f)$, where α represents the warping factor. The warped LP spectrum is obtained by applying the warping function $w_\alpha(f)$ to the original LP spectrum $S(f)$ computed from children's speech:

$$S_\alpha(f) = S(w_\alpha(f)). \tag{1}$$

In the conventional analysis of LP, the estimation of the current speech sample $s(n)$ is obtained by taking a linear combination of past samples. This estimation, denoted as $\hat{s}(n)$, is computed using the LP coefficients a_k and the past P samples according to Eq. (2).

$$\hat{s}(n) = \sum_{k=1}^{P} a_k s(n - k). \tag{2}$$

By applying the Z-transform to Eq. (2), we can express the prediction spectrum $\hat{S}(z)$ in terms of the LP coefficients a_k and the speech spectrum $S(z)$. The Z-transform equation is given by:

$$\hat{S}(z) = \left(\sum_{k=1}^{P} a_k z^{-k} \right) S(z), \tag{3}$$

where z^{-1} represents the unit delay filter, $\hat{S}(z)$ and $S(z)$ denote the Z-transforms of the prediction and speech signals, respectively.

To introduce the desired formant modifications, we replace the unit delay filters with an all-pass filter denoted as $D(z)$. This filter allows us to warp the frequency scale of the LP spectrum. Specifically, we employ a first-order all-pass filter [17,32] represented by the equation:

$$D(z) = \frac{z^{-1} - \alpha}{1 - \alpha z^{-1}}, \tag{4}$$

where α represents the warping factor, constrained within the range of $-1 < \alpha < 1$. By leveraging the warping function $D(z)$, we can systematically shift the spectral resonances (formants) of the LP spectrum. Notably, positive values of α result in a shift of the formant frequencies towards lower frequencies.

The modified LP coefficients, denoted as a_k', obtained after applying the warping function, can be utilized to filter the residual signal (difference between the original signal $s(n)$ and the predicted signal $\hat{s}(n)$) for speech synthesis [20].

This synthesis process generates the modified speech signal, referred to as the "modified" speech signal in this study. The modified speech signal serves as the input to the Automatic Speech Recognition (ASR) system. The overall steps of the proposed method are visualized in the block diagram shown in Fig. 1.

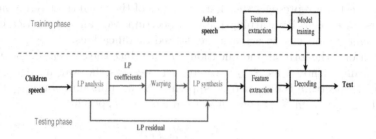

Fig. 1. Block diagram of proposed method.

The effect of linear prediction order to modify the formant frequencies is illustrated in Fig. 2 (narrowband (8 khz) speech) and Fig. 3 (wideband (16 khz) speech) by showing spectra. The red and blue curves were computed from the speech utterances of an adult and a child speaker, respectively. The black, green, and purple curves show the effect of LP order on formant modification. From the figures, it can be noted that the formants of the child speaker are higher compared to those of the adult speaker. So after applying the formant modification method, it reduces the mismatch between child and adult speakers. From the figures, the effect of linear prediction order can also be seen; the best LP order to modify formant frequencies is 6 for narrowband speech and 20 for wideband speech.

3   Database and Experimental Setup

WSJCAM0 [24] for adult speech and PF-STAR [2] for children's speech used for experiments. Both speech databases are from British English corpora. The train set of adult speech from WSJCAM0 has 92 adult (39 female) speakers and a total of 15.5 h of speech data. The age range of adult speech varied from 18 to 60. Testing set of children's speech contain 1.1 h of speech with 60 speakers from PF-STAR. Child speakers age range varies between 4–14 years. Most of the speech processing applications used on mobile phones use narrowband signals. So, in this study, we have explored the effect of the proposed algorithm on narrowband (sampled at 8 kHz) and wideband (sampled at 16 kHz) speech applications.

The kaldi recipe [22] was used to build the ASR system. A 13 dimensional base Mel frequency cepstral coefficient (MFCC) was computed using 20-ms of hamming window with 10-ms of frame shift and a 40-channel Mel-filterbank. Cepstral mean and variance normalization (CMVN) was used for de-correlation.

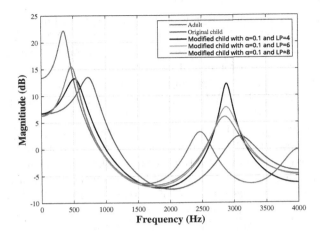

Fig. 2. LP spectra computed from narrowband (8 khz) signal showing variation in formant frequencies. The red and blue curves were computed from speech utterances of an adult and child speaker, respectively. The black, green and purple curves shows the effect of LP order (4, 6 and 8) for formant modification. (Color figure online)

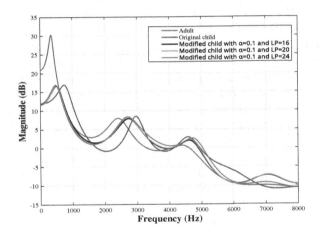

Fig. 3. LP spectra computed from widewband (16 khz) signal showing variation in formant frequencies. The red and blue curves were computed from speech utterances of an adult and child speaker, respectively. The black, green and purple curves shows the effect of LP order (16, 20 and 22) for formant modification. (Color figure online)

Cepstral feature-space maximum likelihood linear regression (fMLLR) was used for normalization [23].

Three types of acoustic models were explored in the study: the Gaussian mixture model (GMM), deep neural network (DNN) and the time delay neural network (TDNN). The hidden Markov model (HMM) was utilized to train the acoustic models. GMM and HMM were used to generate observation probabilities [5]. For training the DNN-HMM-based ASR system, a 5 hidden layer with

1024 hidden nodes for each layer was chosen. The *tanh* function was used to model nonlinearity in the hidden layers. To train the DNN-HMM parameters initially, a 0.015 learning rate was set, which was reduced to 0.002. The minibatch size of 512 selected for neural network training. For decoding children's speech, a domain-specific bigram language model (LM) was used. Transcripts of the speech data of PF-STAR, excluding the test set, were used to train the Bigram LM.

Kaldi setup [21] was used to train the TDNN acoustic model. MFCC features were used to train the TDNN acoustic model with GMM alignment labels. As per recipe, i-vectors [25] were used to perform speaker adaptation. Time warping was used to increase training data by 3-fold. To train the TDNN acoustic model, the initial learning rate was set at 0.0005, further reduced to 0.00005. Two-pass decoding was done, trigram LMs were used in the first pass to generate lattices and were rescored by 4-gram LMs in the second pass.

4   Results and Discussion

The baseline system WERs in % are reported in Table 1 for GMM-HMM, DNN-HMM, and TDNN acoustic models and for both narrowband and wideband speech data. From the Table 1 it can be observed that the baseline performance is poor because of the mismatch conditions between training (adults' speech) and testing (children's speech) data. The best baseline system WERs are achieved for the TDNN acoustic model for both narrowband and wideband speech. To overcome the mismatch factor between training and testing data, the effect of linear prediction order in the proposed formant modification method was explored. The proposed formant modification method has a tunable parameter α that was varied from –0.05 to 0.25 with a step size of 0.05, and the linear prediction order was varied from 2 to 40 with a step size of 2. The effect of linear prediction order with tunable parameter α is shown in Figs. 4 and 5 for both narrowband and wideband speech, respectively, and for the GMM-HMM, DNN-HMM, and TDNN acoustic models. From the Fig. 4 it can be noticed that for narrowband speech, the best tunable parameter α is 0.10 and the best linear prediction order is 6, achieving a 13.82% WER for the TDNN acoustic model. For wideband speech, the best WER of 12.19% is reported in Fig. 5 for the tunable parameter α of 0.10 and the linear prediction order of 20 for the TDNN acoustic model. For the other acoustic models, GMM-HMM and DNN-HMM also improved the system performance as compared to the baseline system for both narrowband and wideband speech.

Further, the effect of linear prediction order on proposed methods is compared with vocal tract length normalization (VTLN) [4, 11, 28] and speaking rate adaptation (SRA) [13, 35]. The proposed method gives the best performance as compared to VTLN and SRA, as reported in Table 2 for GMM-HMM, DNN-HMM, and TDNN acoustic models, and for both narrowband and wideband speech.

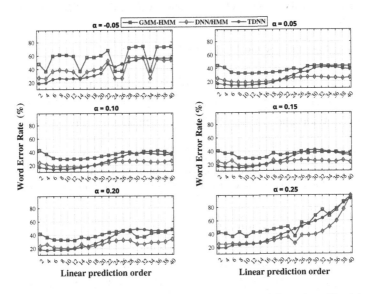

Fig. 4. WERs with respect to linear prediction order varied from 2 to 40 with step size 2, and different formant modification factors α varied from –0.05 to 0.25 for children's narrowband (8 kHz) speech. The analysis is done for the GMM-HMM, DNN-HMM, and TDNN acoustic models.

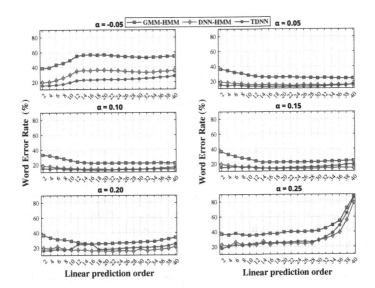

Fig. 5. WERs with respect to linear prediction order varied from 2 to 40 with step size 2, and different formant modification factors α varied from –0.05 to 0.25 for children's wideband (16 kHz) speech. The analysis is done for the GMM-HMM, DNN-HMM, and TDNN acoustic models.

Table 1. Baseline ASR system WERs for the GMM-HMM, DNN-HMM, and TDNN acoustic models.

Speech bandwidth	WER (%)		
	Acoustic model		
	GMM-HMM	DNN-HMM	TDNN
Narrowband	44.65	26.23	15.83
Wideband	32.83	19.58	14.16

Table 2. WERs for the Baseline system, the VTLN and SRA techniques, and the proposed best linear prediction order for the formant modification method. The experiments were conducted using the GMM-HMM, DNN-HMM, and TDNN acoustic models.

Acoustic model	Speech bandwidth	WER (%)			
		Baseline	VTLN	SRA	Proposed
GMM	Narrowband	44.65	35.06	34.23	32.85
	Wideband	32.83	24.30	22.04	20.59
DNN	Narrowband	26.23	23.34	21.98	19.95
	Wideband	19.58	15.17	16.68	14.22
TDNN	Narrowband	15.83	15.19	14.86	13.82
	Wideband	14.16	13.84	13.18	12.19

5 Conclusion

Children's speech recognition using an adult speech trained model degrades the system's performance. This kind of system leads to an acoustic mismatch between training and testing data because of vocal tract length differences between adult and child speech. So, to tackle mismatch, in this paper we have proposed the formant modification method and the effect of linear prediction order. The proposed method was used to modify the testing speech to overcome the acoustic mismatch between training and testing data. From the experiments, we have noticed that the proposed method improves the ASR system's performance as compared to the baseline system for the GMMM-HMM, DNN-HMM, and TDNN acoustic models for narrowband and wideband speech. The TDNN acoustic model gives the best performance as compared to other acoustic models. From the proposed method, it can also be noticed that the best formant modification factor, α is 0.10 with the best linear prediction order of 6, and it achieves 13.82% WER for narrowband speech; for wideband speech, α is 0.10 with the best linear prediction order of 20, and it achieves 12.19% WER for the TDNN acoustic model. Further, we have also compared the proposed method with VTLN and SRA, and it has been noticed that the proposed method is better.

References

1. Ahmad, W., Shahnawazuddin, S., Kathania, H., Pradhan, G., Samaddar, A.: Improving children's speech recognition through explicit pitch scaling based on iterative spectrogram inversion. In: Proceedings of INTERSPEECH 2017, pp. 2391–2395 (2017). https://doi.org/10.21437/INTERSPEECH.2017-302
2. Batliner, A., et al.: The PF_STAR children's speech corpus. In: Proceedings of INTERSPEECH, pp. 2761–2764 (2005)
3. Bhardwaj, V., et al.: Automatic speech recognition (ASR) systems for children: a systematic literature review. Appl. Sci. **12**(9), 4419 (2022)
4. Claes, T., Dologlou, I., ten Bosch, L., van Compernolle, D.: A novel feature transformation for vocal tract length normalization in automatic speech recognition. IEEE Trans. Speech Audio Process. **6**(6), 549–557 (1998)
5. Dahl, G., Yu, D., Deng, L., Acero, A.: Context-dependent pre-trained deep neural networks for large vocabulary speech recognition. IEEE Trans. Speech Audio Process. **20**(1), 30–42 (2012)
6. Digalakis, V., Rtischev, D., Neumeyer, L.: Speaker adaptation using constrained estimation of Gaussian mixtures. IEEE Trans. Speech Audio Process. **3**, 357–366 (1995)
7. Fainberg, J., Bell, P., Lincoln, M., Renals, S.: Improving children's speech recognition through out-of-domain data augmentation. In: INTERSPEECH 2016, pp. 1598–1602 (2016). https://doi.org/10.21437/INTERSPEECH.2016-1348
8. Huber, J., Stathopoulos, E., Curione, G., Ash, T., Johnson, K.: Formants of children, women, and men: the effects of vocal intensity variation. J. Acoust. Soc. Am. **106**, 1532–42 (1999). https://doi.org/10.1121/1.427150
9. Johnson, A., Fan, R., Morris, R., Alwan, A.: LPC augment: an LPC-based ASR data augmentation algorithm for low and zero-resource children's dialects. In: ICASSP 2022–2022 IEEE International Conference on Acoustics, Speech and Signal Processing (ICASSP), pp. 8577–8581 (2022). https://doi.org/10.1109/ICASSP43922.2022.9746281
10. Kathania, H.K., Ahmad, W., Shahnawazuddin, S., Samaddar, A.B.: Explicit pitch mapping for improved children's speech recognition. Circ. Syst. Signal Process. **32**, 2021–2044 (2018)
11. Kathania, H.K., Ghai, S., Sinha, R.: Soft-weighting technique for robust children speech recognition under mismatched condition. In: 2013 Annual IEEE India Conference (INDICON), pp. 1–6 (2013)
12. Kathania, H.K., Shahnawazuddin, S., Adiga, N., Ahmad, W.: Role of prosodic features on children's speech recognition. In: 2018 IEEE International Conference on Acoustics, Speech and Signal Processing (ICASSP), pp. 5519–5523 (2018)
13. Kathania, H.K., Shahnawazuddin, S., Ahmad, W., Adiga, N., Jana, S.K., Samaddar, A.B.: Improving children's speech recognition through time scale modification based speaking rate adaptation. In: 2018 International Conference on Signal Processing and Communications (SPCOM) (2018)
14. Kathania, H.K., Shahnawazuddin, S., Sinha, R.: Exploring HLDA based transformation for reducing acoustic mismatch in context of children speech recognition. In: 2014 International Conference on Signal Processing and Communications (SPCOM), pp. 1–5 (2014)
15. Kathania, H.K., Kadiri, S.R., Alku, P., Kurimo, M.: A formant modification method for improved ASR of children's speech. Speech Commun. **136**, 98–106 (2022)

16. Kumar Kathania, H., Reddy Kadiri, S., Alku, P., Kurimo, M.: Study of formant modification for children ASR. In: ICASSP 2020–2020 IEEE International Conference on Acoustics, Speech and Signal Processing (ICASSP), pp. 7429–7433 (2020). https://doi.org/10.1109/ICASSP40776.2020.9053334
17. Laine, U.K., Karjalainen, M., Altosaar, T.: Warped linear prediction (WLP) in speech and audio processing. In: Proceedings of ICASSP 1994, IEEE International Conference on Acoustics, Speech and Signal Processing, vol. 3, pp. III-349. IEEE (1994)
18. Lee, L., Rose, R.: A frequency warping approach to speaker normalization. IEEE Trans. Speech Audio Process. 6(1), 49–60 (1998)
19. Lee, S., Potamianos, A., Narayanan, S.S.: Acoustics of children's speech: developmental changes of temporal and spectral parameters. J. Acoust. Soci. Am. 105(3), 1455–1468 (1999)
20. Makhoul, J.: Linear prediction: a tutorial review. Proc. IEEE 63(4), 561–580 (1975)
21. Povey, D., et al.: Semi-orthogonal low-rank matrix factorization for deep neural networks. In: Proceedings of INTERSPEECH 2018, ISCA, pp. 3743–3747 (2018)
22. Povey, D., et al.: The Kaldi Speech recognition toolkit. In: Proceedings of ASRU (2011)
23. Rath, S.P., Povey, D., Veselý, K., Černocký, J.: Improved feature processing for deep neural networks. In: Proceedings of INTERSPEECH (2013)
24. Robinson, T., Fransen, J., Pye, D., Foote, J., Renals, S.: WSJCAM0: a British English speech corpus for large vocabulary continuous speech recognition. In: Proceedings of ICASSP, vol. 1, pp. 81–84 (1995)
25. Saon, G., Soltau, H., Nahamoo, D., Picheny, M.: Speaker adaptation of neural network acoustic models using i-vectors. In: 2013 IEEE Workshop on Automatic Speech Recognition and Understanding, Olomouc, Czech Republic, 8–12 December 2013, pp. 55–59. IEEE (2013)
26. Schalkwyk, J., et al.: Your word is my command: google search by voice: a case study. In: Advances in Speech Recognition: Mobile Environments, Call Centers and Clinics, vol. 4, pp. 61–90 (2010)
27. Scukanec, G.P., Petrosino, L., Squibb, K.: Formant frequency characteristics of children, young adult, and aged female speakers. Percept. Mot. Skills 73(1), 203–208 (1991)
28. Serizel, R., Giuliani, D.: Vocal tract length normalisation approaches to DNN-based children's and adults' speech recognition. In: 2014 IEEE Spoken Language Technology Workshop (SLT), pp. 135–140 (2014)
29. Shahnawazuddin, S., Adiga, N., Kathania, H.K.: Effect of prosody modification on children's ASR. IEEE Signal Process. Lett. 24(11), 1749–1753 (2017)
30. Shahnawazuddin, S., Dey, A., Sinha, R.: Pitch-adaptive front-end features for robust children's ASR. In: INTERSPEECH (2016)
31. Shivakumar, P.G., Georgiou, P.: Transfer learning from adult to children for speech recognition: evaluation, analysis and recommendations. Comput. Speech Lang. 63, 101077 (2020). https://doi.org/10.1016/j.csl.2020.101077
32. Strube, H.W.: Linear prediction on a warped frequency scale. J. Acoust. Soc. Am. 68(4), 1071–1076 (1980)
33. Yadav, I.C., Shahnawazuddin, S., Govind, D., Pradhan, G.: Spectral smoothing by variational mode decomposition and its effect on noise and pitch robustness of ASR system. In: 2018 IEEE International Conference on Acoustics, Speech and Signal Processing (ICASSP), pp. 5629–5633 (2018)

34. Yildirim, S., Narayanan, S., Byrd, D., Khurana, S.: Acoustic analysis of preschool children's speech. In: In ICPhS-2015, pp. 949–952 (2003)
35. Zhu, X., Beauregard, G.T., Wyse, L.L.: Real-time signal estimation from modified short-time fourier transform magnitude spectra. IEEE Trans. Audio Speech Lang. Process. **15**(5), 1645–1653 (2007)

Gammatone-Filterbank Based Pitch-Normalized Cepstral Coefficients for Zero-Resource Children's ASR

Syed Shahnawazuddin[1], Ankita[1]($\boxtimes$), Avinash Kumar[2], and Hemant Kumar Kathania[2]

[1] National Institute of Technology Patna, Patna, India
{s.syed,ankita.ph21.ec}@nitp.ac.in
[2] National Institute of Technology Sikkim, Ravangla, India
{avinash_ece,hemant.ece}@nitsikkim.ac.in

Abstract. The work presented in this paper focuses on zero-resource children's speech recognition task. In such tasks, adults' speech data is used for learning the acoustic models. However, this leads to severe acoustic mismatch and hence poor recognition rates. One of the main mismatch factor is that the pitch values are higher in the case of children's speech. In order to mitigate the ill-effects of pitch-induced acoustic mismatch, two front-end speech parameterization techniques are proposed in this study. The proposed approaches employ spectral smoothing based on either pitch-adaptive cepstral truncation or variational mode decomposition. Furthermore, we have used Gamma-tone-filterbank for warping the spectra to the ERB scale. Consequently, the cepstral coefficients exhibit lower variance than those obtained using Mel-filterbank. Therefore, the proposed features are observed to be very effective resulting in a relative reduction in word error rate by nearly 17% over the baseline.

Keywords: Children's ASR · Zero-resource ASR · Spectral smoothing · Gamma-tone-filterbank · VMD

1 Introduction

The automatic speech recognition (ASR) systems available these days are mostly trained on adults' speech and hence, works well for adult speakers. When children's speech is given as an input to such an ASR system, it suffers from degradation in recognition performance. We refer to this scenario as *zero-resource children's ASR* i.e., the task of recognising children's speech using a system trained on speech data from adult speakers. The reason behind the said degradation in the case of zero-resource children's ASR is the fundamental mismatch of acoustic attributes between the adults' and children's speech [3,5,9,13,17,18,22]. Even though, the acoustic correlates of adults' and children's speech are starkly different, it is highly desirable that an ASR should be compatible with both

© The Author(s), under exclusive license to Springer Nature Switzerland AG 2023
A. Karpov et al. (Eds.): SPECOM 2023, LNAI 14338, pp. 494–505, 2023.
https://doi.org/10.1007/978-3-031-48309-7_40

adults' and children's speech. This will lead us towards a more robust speaker-independent ASR system which is primary motive of the work presented in this study. Zero-resource condition needs attention because there is a paucity of freely available data from children. For majority of the languages, there is literally no data at all.

n order to deal with the scarcity of speech data from child speakers, several out-of-domain data augmentation approaches have been reported [19–21]. In a very recent work, the role of formant modification on children's ASR task was studied. Motivated by that study [8], an out-of-domain data augmentation technique based on formant and duration modification was proposed in [7]. The said technique has been employed in this work as well in order to overcome the issues of data scarcity. The primary motive of all the aforementioned data augmentation techniques is to modify the attributes of adults' training speech in a way that it becomes acoustically closer to children's speech. The modified data is then pooled into training in order to better capture the missing targeted attributes. However, data augmentation does not completely alleviate the ill-effects of the acoustic mismatch in the case of zero-resource children's ASR task. Therefore, we explored the efficacy of combining data augmentation with other approaches of reducing the acoustic mismatch as discussed in the following.

It is well known that the pitch for a child speaker is higher than that for adults' speech which leads to severe acoustic mismatch in the case of zero-resource children's ASR. Adding a spectral smoothing module in the front-end speech parameterization process is noted to help in reducing pitch-induced acoustic mismatch [22]. At the same time, the use of Gamma-tone-filterbanks leads to a better modeling of the human pitch perception mechanism [6]. Hence, replacing the standard Mel-filterbank with Gamma-tone-filterbank while computing the front-end acoustic features can enhance the robustness towards speaker-dependent variability. These two facts have motivated us develop front-end parameterization techniques that employ Gamma-tone-filterbank and explicit spectral smoothening to minimize the pitch-induced acoustic mismatch. Employed spectral smoothing is based on either pitch-adaptive cepstral truncation (PACT) [22] or variational mode decomposition (VMD) [4]. An analysis presented in this study shows that the proposed front-end acoustic features exhibit lower variance than those extracted using Mel-filterbank suggesting enhanced robustness. Furthermore, we have combined the proposed front-end acoustic features with a recently reported data augmentation technique [7] to further improve the recognition performance as well as to further boost our confidence in the efficacy of the proposed approaches.

The rest of this paper is organised as follows: In Sect. 2, the proposed front-end speech parameterization techniques is described. The experimental evaluations demonstrating the effectiveness of the proposed approaches are presented in Sect. 3. Finally, the paper is concluded in Sect. 4.

2 Proposed Pitch-Normalized Front-End Acoustic Features

To begin with our exploration, we replaced the triangular Mel-filterbank employed in the conventional Mel-frequency cepstral coefficients (MFCC) feature extraction process with the Gamma-tone-filterbank (GTF). The Mel-filterbanks are designed to model the human pitch perception mechanism [6]. On the other hand, the Gamma-tone functions provide a mathematical model for the auditory response determined experimentally [11,23]. The two types of filterbanks are shown in Fig. 1. In order to understand the effect of filtering the power-spectrum using the Gamma-tone-filterbank, the following analysis was done next. We computed the cepstral coefficients from the Gamma-tone filtered power-spectrum (referred to as GTF-CC in the rest of this paper) using all the short-time frames corresponding to the central region of the vowel /IY/ extracted from children's speech. The variance was then determined and the same is shown in Fig. 2(b) for the 12 coefficients of the GTF-CC features. This analysis was repeated using the PACT-MFCC features [22] (a pitch robust version of MFCC) as well, and the corresponding variance plot is given in Fig. 2(a). As evident from the figures, GTF-CC features have lower variance than PACT-MFCC. Consequently, the GTF-CC are expected to result in better recognition performance due to enhanced robustness towards speaker-dependent variability. This was found to be true when we conducted the experimental evaluations and the results for those are presented later in this paper.

As mentioned earlier, the GTF-CC features were extracted by simply replacing the Mel-filterbank with the Gamma-tone-filterbank in the conventional approach for deriving MFCC features. On the other hand, the PACT-MFCC features employ an spectral smoothing module prior to filtering the power-spectrum using Mel-filterbank. It was argued and demonstrated in [22] that sufficient spectral smoothing can reduce pitch-induced acoustic mismatch in the context of zero-resource children's ASR and thus significantly enhance the recognition performance with respect to child speakers. Motivated by the findings of that work, two different approaches are used in this study for pitch normalization through spectral smoothing in order to enhance the robustness of GTF-CC features towards pitch-induced spectral distortions. Those are pitch adaptive cepstral truncation [22] and variational mode decomposition [4]. The block diagrams of the proposed pitch-normalized front-end feature extraction techniques employing Gamma-tone-filterbank are shown in Fig. 3.

To begin with, speech data is analysed into short-time frames using overlapping Hamming windows. Next, short-time Fourier transform (STFT) is applied to each of the frames in order to obtain the magnitude spectrum. This is followed by the application of inverse discrete Fourier transform (IDFT) on the log-compressed magnitude spectrum to obtain the respective cepstral representation for each of the frames. These steps are essentially linear filtering of the speech signal and hence, preserving the inherited periodicity of the signal waveform. The signal is then subjected to smoothing of it's pitch harmonics. An appropriate low-time lifter is applied for this purpose. The lifter length is deter-

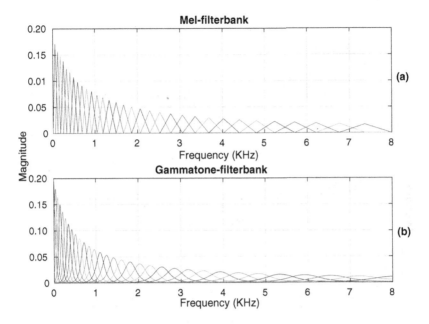

Fig. 1. (a) The triangular Mel-filterbank and (b) The Gamma-tone-filterbank.

mined using the average pitch computed from the input speech signal. To revert back to the spectral domain representation from the cepstrum, discrete Forier transform (DFT) is applied after zero-padding. The resulting smoothed spectrum is passed through the Gamma-tone-filterbank followed by discrete cosine transform (DCT) and low-time liftering once more. The features hence obtained are pitch-normalized features, referred to as PACT-GTF-CC in this paper.

Alternatively, sufficient spectral smoothing can also be achieved through the application of VMD on short-time magnitude spectra. In this case, the magnitude spectrum is broken down into a number of components using VMD. Next, the higher-order modes are discarded and the spectrum is reconstructed from the first two modes only as shown in Fig. 3. The smooth spectrum is then warped to a non-linear scale using Gamma-tone-filterbank. Finally, DCT is applied followed by low-time liftering to obtain the proposed pitch-normalized VMD-GTF-CC feature vectors. As a result of PACT as well as VMD, the ill-effects of pitch-induced spectral distortion are mitigated to a large extent and the variance of the feature vectors is further reduced as evident from Fig. 1(c and d). This, in turn, results in significant improvements in the recognition performance as demonstrated through the experimental studies presented in the following section.

In order to visualize the effects of PACT- or VMD-based spectral smoothing, the following analysis was done. A segment of speech data from a high-pitched child speaker was taken ($F0$ was approximately 400Hz). The magnitude spectrum for a voiced frame extracted from the considered speech segment is shown in Fig. 4(a). The effects of pitch-harmonics are clearly visible. Next, the spec-

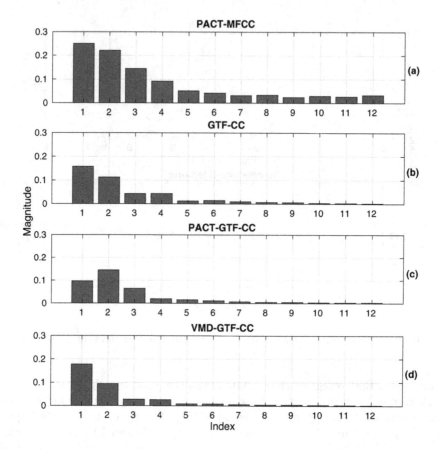

Fig. 2. Variance plots for the different front-end acoustic feature types studied in this work. Variance was computed using all the feature vectors corresponding to the short-time frames extracted from the central region of the vowel /IY/ spoken by high-pitched child speakers. The proposed features show lower variance.

trum was smoothed using the discussed two approaches. The resulting smoothed spectra are also shown in Fig. 4(b and c). The smoothed spectra clearly capture only the envelope of the magnitude spectrum to a large extent. This is highly desirable since the ill-effects of the pitch-harmonics get reduced as a consequence of spectral smoothing. Furthermore, both PACT- as well as VMD-based spectral smoothing approach result in similar looking spectra. However, the VMD-based approach does not require an estimation of average pitch unlike PACT-based spectral smoothing.

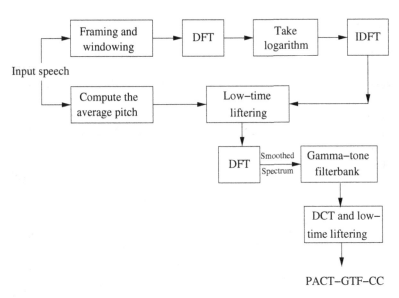

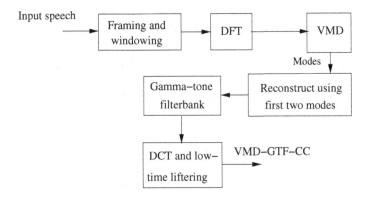

Fig. 3. Block diagram for the proposed front-end acoustic feature extraction approach employing spectral smoothing based on pitch-adaptive cepstral truncaton and variational mode decomposition.

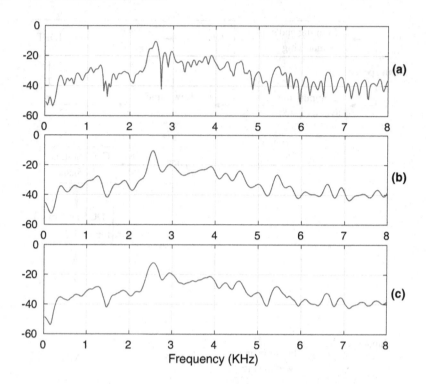

Fig. 4. (a) Short-time magnitude spectra corresponding to a voiced frame of speech from a high-pitch child speaker ($F0$ was approximately 400Hz). (b) and (c) spectrum obtained after smoothing using pitch-adaptive cepstral truncaton and variational mode decomposition, respectively.

3   Experimental Evaluations

3.1   Database and Experimental Specification

Two British English speech corpora, WSJCAM0 [16] and PF_STAR [1], were used for experimental evaluations. Both the WSJCAM0 and the PF_STAR corpora contain read speech. The former consists of adults' speech and it was used in the current study as the training data. The training set of WSJCAM0 had 15.5 h of speech data from 92 adult speakers (39 females). On the other hand, the PF_STAR corpus contains children's speech. The test set of PF_STAR comprised of 1.1 hours of speech data from 60 speakers (28 females). The age of the child speakers in this corpus varies between 4 and 13 years. Furthermore, a development set of children's speech was also derived from the PF_STAR corpus. This set consisted of 2.1 h of speech data from 63 speakers whose age varied between 6 and 14 years. This set was used for determining the optimal values for the tunable parameters.

The Kaldi toolkit was used to perform all the experiments [14]. However, front-end speech parameterization was done using MATLAB. The PACT-MFCC features reported in [22] were used for front-end speech parameterization in the case of baseline ASR system since those are observed to be more suitable than other existing features in the context of children's speech recognition task. Speech data was analyzed in overlapping Hamming-windowed frames of duration 25 ms with a frame-shift of 10 ms to compute the 13-dimensional base feature vectors. A 40-channel log-Mel-filterbank was used during feature computation. The base features were time-spliced with context size of ± 4 frames and then projected to a 40-dimensional subspace and de-correlated using linear discriminant analysis (LDA) and maximum-likelihood linear transform (MLLT). For feature normalization, cepstral mean and variance normalization (CMVN) as well feature-space maximum likelihood linear regression (fMLLR) were used. This helps in imparting robustness towards speaker variations. In the case of the GTF-CC features as well as the proposed PACT-GTF-CC and VMD-GTF-CC features, frame-size and frame-overlap were chosen as 25 ms and 10 ms. The magnitude spectrum was broken down into 8 modes using VMD. The specifications for PACT were the same as those reported in [22]. The Gamma-tone-filterbank consisted of 40 channels. The base features extracted in these cases were also 13-dimensional. LDA, MLLT, CMVN and fMLLR were then applied in succession to obtain 40-dimensional feature vectors.

Hidden Markov models (HMM) were used for acoustic modeling. The observation probabilities for the HMM states were generated using Gaussian mixture

Table 1. WERs and CERs for the children's speech test set with respect to an ASR systems trained on adults' speech as well as another one trained on augmented data.

Data used for training	Front-end features	Evaluation metrics	
		WER (%)	CER (%)
Adults' speech	PACT-MFCC	17.30	12.57
	GTF-CC	15.91	11.84
	PACT-GTF-CC	14.65	10.76
	VMD-GTF-CC	**13.72**	**10.08**
Adults' speech + Adults' (FM-TSM)	PACT-MFCC	10.19	7.45
	GTF-CC	9.65	7.08
	PACT-GTF-CC	8.69	6.16
	VMD-GTF-CC	**8.49**	**5.99**

models (GMM) and time-delay neural network (TDNN) [12,24]. Cross-word triphone models consisting of eight diagonal covariance components per state were used for the GMM-HMM-based ASR system. Furthermore, decision tree-based state tying was performed with the maximum number of tied states (senones) being fixed at 2000. Speaker-adaptive training employing fMLLR transforms was used to optimize the final GMM-HMM system. The time-alignments generated using this GMM-HMM-based ASR system was used for initializing the TDNN-HMM. The lattice-free maximum mutual information (LF-MMI) criterion [15] was used for training TDNN-HMM-based ASR system. The TDNN consisted of 13 hidden layers with 1024 nodes per layer. The initial and final learning rates were set to 0.0005 and 0.00005, respectively. Prior to learning the the TDNN parameters, 100-dimensional i-vectors were extracted and appended to the 13-dimensional acoustic feature vectors. The universal background model employed for extracting i-vectors consisted of 512 Gaussian components.

A domain-specific 1.5k bi-gram language model (LM) was used while decoding the children's speech test set. This LM was trained on the transcripts of the speech data from PF_STAR corpus after excluding the utterances from the test set. The employed LM had an out-of-vocabulary rate of 1.20% and a perplexity of 95.8 for the children's speech test set. The lexicon consisted of 1969 words including pronunciation variations. The metric used for performance evaluation are word error rate (WER) and character error rate (CER).

3.2   Results and Discussions

The WERs and CERs for the children's speech test set with respect to an ASR system trained on adults' speech are given in Table 1. The baseline ASR system is trained using PACT-MFCC features as already stated earlier. Compared to the baseline, a relative reduction of 8% in WER is achieved by the use of GTF-CC features. Similarly, the relative reduction in CER is nearly 6%. These drops in WER annd CER demonstrate that reducing variance of the feature coefficients by the use of Gamma-tone-filterbank enhances the robustness as argued earlier. Further to that, significant reductions in WER as well as CER are obtained when spectral smoothing is applied. A relative reduction of nearly 17% in WER over the baseline is achieved in the case of VMD-GTF-CC features. On the other hand, the relative reduction in CER is nearly 20% over the baseline. The relative gains are somewhat lesser in the case of PACT-MFCC. In order to further boost our confidence in the efficacy of the proposed features as well to obtain a better baseline ASR system, the recently proposed out-of-domain data augmentation approach was also incorporated into our experimental setup [7]. For that purpose, the duration of the adults' speech training set was increased by a factor of 1.4 using the technique reported in [2]. Next, formant frequencies of the time stretched samples were up-scaled by a factor of 0.08. For formant modification, the approach proposed in [8] was used which employed scaling of the linear prediction coefficients [10]. These modifications were motivated by the fact that the speaking-rate is slower in the case of children's speech while the formant frequencies are higher. Hence, time stretching helps in compensating for

Table 2. Age-group specific WERs and CERs for the children's speech test sets with respect to an ASR system trained on augmented data.

Front-end features	WER (%)		CER (%)	
	GR-I	GR-II	GR-I	GR-II
GTF-CC	16.23	7.40	12.68	4.99
PACT-GTF-CC	12.20	6.38	9.16	4.08
VMD-GTF-CC	**11.60**	**6.22**	**8.70**	**4.12**

the acoustic mismatch resulting from the differences in speaking-rates. Similarly, the differences in the formant frequencies is compensated by up-scaling the formant locations. Finally, the modified (referred to as Adults' (FM-TSM) training set) and original adults' speech data-sets are pooled together and another ASR system is trained.

The WERs and CERs with respect to this ASR system are also given in Table 1. Significant reductions over baseline are obtained when the proposed features are used. The relative reductions in WER and CER over the baseline are 17% and 20%, respectively, when the proposed VMD-GTF-CC features are used. Next, we performed another study to determine the age-group-specific analysis. For that purpose, the test set was split into two groups. The first one (GR-I) consisted of speech utterances from speakers in the age-group 4–8 years. The second one (GR-II) comprised of data from speakers in the age-group 9–14 years. The age-group specific WERs and CERs are given in Table 2. The relative reductions obtained through spectral smoothing are more in the case of GR-I. Since the pitch is higher in this age-group, the pitch-induced spectral distortion is also more pronounced. Therefore, pitch-normalization is noted to be more effective.

4 Conclusion

The work presented in this paper deals with task of developing an efficient ASR system for children's speech under zero-resource conditions. In such a scenario, due to absence of domain-specific data, adults' speech is used for training. This leads to severe acoustic mismatch between the training and test sets as a result of the differences in the attributes of adults' and children's speech. In order to deal with the scarcity of domain-specific data, formant frequencies as well as the duration of the adult's speech training data-set was suitably modified and then pooled into training. At the same time, two front-end speech parameterization techniques that are more robust for zero-resource children's ASR task are also proposed. The proposed approaches employ spectral smoothing through pitch-adaptive cepstral truncation and variational mode decomposition, respectively, in order to mitigate the ill-effects of pitch-induced acoustic mismatch. Furthermore, we have replaced the conventional Mel-filterbank with Gammatone-filterbank in our approaches. On combining data augmentation with the proposed front-end acoustic features, we achieved relative reduction in WER close to 17%.

References

1. Batliner, A., et al.: The PF_STAR children's speech corpus. In: Proceedings of INTERSPEECH, pp. 2761–2764 (2005)
2. Damskägg, E.P., Välimäki, V.: Audio time stretching using fuzzy classification of spectral bins. Appl. Sci. **7**(12), 1293 (2017). https://doi.org/10.3390/app7121293
3. D'Arcy, S., Russell, M.: A comparison of human and computer recognition accuracy for children's speech. In: Proceedings of INTERSPEECH, pp. 2197–2200 (2005)
4. Dragomiretskiy, K., Zosso, D.: Variational mode decomposition. IEEE Trans. Signal Process. **62**(3), 531–544 (2013)
5. Gerosa, M., Giuliani, D., Narayanan, S., Potamianos, A.: A review of ASR technologies for children's speech. In: Proceedings of Workshop on Child, Computer and Interaction, pp. 7:1–7:8 (2009). https://doi.org/10.1145/1640377.1640384
6. Gold, B., Morgan, N., Ellis, D., O'Shaughnessy, D.: Speech and audio signal processing: Processing and perception of speech and music, second edition. J. Acoust. Soc. Am. **132**, 1861 (2012). https://doi.org/10.1121/1.4742973
7. Kumar, V., Kumar, A., Shahnawazuddin, S.: Creating robust children's ASR system in zero-resource condition through out-of-domain data augmentation. Circ. Syst. Signal Process. **41**(4), 2205–2220 (2021). https://doi.org/10.1007/s00034-021-01885-5
8. Kumar Kathania, H., Reddy Kadiri, S., Alku, P., Kurimo, M.: Study of formant modification for children ASR. In: ICASSP 2020–2020 IEEE International Conference on Acoustics, Speech and Signal Processing (ICASSP), pp. 7429–7433 (2020). https://doi.org/10.1109/ICASSP40776.2020.9053334
9. Lee, S., Potamianos, A., Narayanan, S.S.: Acoustics of children's speech: developmental changes of temporal and spectral parameters. J. Acoust. Soc. Am. **105**(3), 1455–1468 (1999). https://doi.org/10.1121/1.426686
10. Makhoul, J.: Linear prediction: a tutorial review. Proc. IEEE **63**(4), 561–580 (1975). https://doi.org/10.1109/PROC.1975.9792
11. Patterson, R., Nimmo-Smith, I., Holdsworth, J., Rice, P.: An efficient auditory filterbank based on the gammatone function (1987)
12. Peddinti, V., Povey, D., Khudanpur, S.: A time delay neural network architecture for efficient modeling of long temporal contexts. In: Proceedings of INTERSPEECH (2015)
13. Potaminaos, A., Narayanan, S.: Robust recognition of children speech. IEEE Trans. Speech Audio Process. **11**(6), 603–616 (2003). https://doi.org/10.1109/TSA.2003.818026
14. Povey, D., et al.: The Kaldi Speech recognition toolkit. In: Proceedings of ASRU (2011)
15. Povey, D., et al.: Purely sequence-trained neural networks for ASR based on lattice-free MMI. In: Proceedings of INTERSPEECH, pp. 2751–2755 (2016)

16. Robinson, T., Fransen, J., Pye, D., Foote, J., Renals, S.: WSJCAM0: a British English speech corpus for large vocabulary continuous speech recognition. In: Proceedings of ICASSP, vol. 1, pp. 81–84 (1995). https://doi.org/10.1109/ICASSP. 1995.479278

17. Russell, M., D'Arcy, S.: Challenges for computer recognition of children's speech. In: Proceedings of Speech and Language Technologies in Education (SLaTE) (2007)

18. Serizel, R., Giuliani, D.: Deep-neural network approaches for speech recognition with heterogeneous groups of speakers including children. Nat. Lang. Eng. **23**(3), 325–350 (2017). https://doi.org/10.1017/S135132491600005X

19. Shahnawazuddin, S., Adiga, N., Kathania, H.K., Sai, B.T.: Creating speaker independent ASR system through prosody modification based data augmentation. Pattern Recogn. Lett. **131**, 213–218 (2020). https://doi.org/10.1016/j.patrec.2019.12. 019

20. Shahnawazuddin, S., Adiga, N., Kumar, K., Poddar, A., Ahmad, W.: Voice conversion based data augmentation to improve children's speech recognition in limited data scenario. In: Proceedings of INTERSPEECH, pp. 4382–4386 (2020). https:// doi.org/10.21437/Interspeech.2020-1112

21. Shahnawazuddin, S., Adiga, N., Sai, B.T., Ahmad, W., Kathania, H.K.: Developing speaker independent ASR system using limited data through prosody modification based on fuzzy classification of spectral bins. Digital Signal Process. **93**, 34–42 (2019). https://doi.org/10.1016/j.dsp.2019.06.015

22. Sinha, R., Shahnawazuddin, S.: Assessment of pitch-adaptive front-end signal processing for children's speech recognition. Comput. Speech Lang. **48**, 103–121 (2018). https://doi.org/10.1016/j.csl.2017.10.007

23. Slaney, M., et al.: An efficient implementation of the Patterson-Holdsworth auditory filter bank. Apple Computer, Perception Group, Technical Report, vol. 35, no. 8 (1993)

24. Waibel, A., Hanazawa, T., Hinton, G., Shikano, K., Lang, K.: Phoneme recognition using time-delay neural networks. IEEE Trans. Acoust. Speech Signal Process. **37**(3), 328–339 (1989). https://doi.org/10.1109/29.21701

System Assisted Vocal Response Analysis and Assessment of Autism in Children: A Machine Learning Based Approach

Soma Khan, Tulika Basu, Joyanta Basu$^{(\boxtimes)}$, Madhab Pal, and Rajib Roy

Centre for Development of Advanced Computing, Kolkata, India
{soma.khan,tulika.basu,joyanta.basu,madhab.pal,
rajib.roy}@cdac.in

Abstract. This study focuses on development of a Machine Learning (ML) based framework for software assisted assessment of Autism in children, using automated analysis and recognition of vocal responses following Speech-Language and Communication criteria under Indian Scale for Assessment of Autism. Audio-visual responses from 82 children (with autism) are recorded within a supervised computer based interaction setup showing human acted and avatar based audio-visual stimuli designed with experts' consultation in Hindi, Bengali and English languages. Software recorded interactions are manually diarized, annotated and samples are gathered for seven response classes (Child Speech, Clapping, Echolalia, Non-speech (jargon word), Repetitive Speech, Unusual Noises and Pronoun Reversal). ML models are trained with MFCC, Chroma STFT and Mel-Spectrogram combined features and using five ML classifiers for automated detection of child responses. Detection results indicate that system generated feedbacks (occurrence and duration) on vocal traits will help human assessor to provide correct grading on autism severity under digital or existing assessment protocol.

Keywords: Autism Assessment · Vocal Response Analysis · ISAA · Speech-Language and Communication

1 Introduction

Autism is the world's third most common developmental disability, a neurological illness that usually manifests by the age of three. As per recent study and updates from WHO website, worldwide about 1 in every 100 children is having autism [1]. In India, it has been estimated that more than 2 million people might be affected with Autism Spectrum Disorder (ASD) [2]. As per experts, a quarter of children with autism spectrum condition have a regression in language or social abilities, most commonly between the ages of 18 and 24 months. With these alarming figures of autism in India, diagnosis and intervention of the same at the early years becomes very much necessary. Hence, dependency on the autism assessor side is gradually increasing following any of the standard autism assessment protocols with the traditional pen-paper based assessment procedure. This scenario serves the basic background to work out on ICT based automation framework

A. Karpov et al. (Eds.): SPECOM 2023, LNAI 14338, pp. 506–519, 2023.
https://doi.org/10.1007/978-3-031-48309-7_41

for autism assessment and generating Machine Learning (ML) guided feedbacks that can be accepted or modified by an expert human assessor during the assessment session. Moreover, machine generated second opinion will also help in unbiased diagnosis by psychiatrists working under limited resources, having patients load and within limited timeframe.

We particularly focus here in our work, on Spoken Language, one of the core areas, which particularly are affected and exhibit an undeniable feature in autism diagnosis. Children with autism usually produce very little speech, use non-verbal gestures, peculiar vocal or non-speech sounds and shrill noises, often repetitive in nature. Parents or care givers can spot these speaking behaviors in scattered observations of the child while the early growth years. But the same can only be meaningfully quantified and marked during the autism assessment session by an expert psychologist, special educator or autism therapist under the Speech-Language communication and Social behavior related assessment criteria. All the well-known standard autism measures or assessment scales like CARS (Childhood Autism Rating Scale) [3], INCLEN [4], ADOS (Autism Diagnostic Observation Schedule) [5] etc. and recently Indian Scale for Assessment of Autism (ISAA) [6] in Indian scenario, include specific assessment criteria for analyzing the vocal (or speech) response features to diagnose autism in young children.

2 Speech and Vocal Response Based Autism Assessment

2.1 Review of Literature

In prior studies, researchers have used speech and language related several features to distinguish children with ASD from age-matched typically developed (TD) children using ML based automatic classification techniques [7]. In [8], researchers used pitch features extracted from ADOS based interview of 146 children, including mean and median of F0 values and median absolute deviation from the median (MAD), and trained a Naïve Bayes classifier using leave-one-out cross validation method. Their approach correctly classified voice samples of ASD and TD children around 74% of the time, indicating usefulness of pitch features among others in detecting ASD. In [9], researchers studied prosody features like speech rate, rhythm, voice quality and intonation features in semi-structured voice samples taken from 43 children with ASD and 26 TD controls involved in a story retelling task. Model trained on speech rate and rhythm features performed best, correctly classifying children with ASD and TD approximately 69% of the time. A study [10] investigates the differences between ASD and TD children in acoustic properties of filler sounds and laughter, which are often considered as specific social signals. Using features like signal power and cepstral centroid calculated from Short Time Fourier Transform (STFT), and then Principle Component Analysis (PCA) with HMM based modeling, significant differences were found in the standard deviation of the filler feature and the skewness of the block-wise mean of the laughter feature. Another research work [11] focuses on detecting the vocal stereotypy among (four) ASD children who lack verbal communication. The study uses Orthogonal Least Squares (OLS) based feature selection over frequency band wise signal power and related features and includes subspace learning from the experimental acoustic data applying Orthogonal Subspace matching Pursuit (OSP), that finally worked in distinguishing vocal stimming from environment noise (including verbal communication of other persons in the room) and correctly identifying frustration level in ASD children with relation to the detected vocal stereotypy. The work in [12], describes Language Environment Analysis (LENA) using various developed detector models to recognize child and adult vocalizations with some additional expressions of affect, like fillers, laughter or crying in naturalistic condition.

Thus we found that, overall speech based features are being explored for differentiating children with ASD from TD in most of the prior studies, and very few studies experimented on the acoustic properties of filler sounds and laughter in vocalization of ASD and TD children. But sometimes, only speech based features may not be sufficient to detect autistic traits or may lead to confusing results. As autism is a neuro developmental disorder, verbal children who are on the verge of getting autism or showing autistic features also produce meaningful speech similar to that of the TD children. But then, presence of other specific voice traits (like sudden unusual noises, high pitched vocalization, peculiar non-speech sounds, repetitive behavior in generating jargon sounds or speech etc.) help in detecting the autistic characteristics. Also sometimes, children with ASD tend to produce these types of voice traits more frequently than standard meaningful speech. Thus, we hereby found a gap in previous literature, where all these voice traits need to be tactfully recorded, diarized, labeled, and analyzed properly and trained by ML models with classified data for automatic detection of autistic characteristics from vocal sounds or speech.

2.2 Purpose of the Paper

This paper describes a process of software assisted autism assessment using computer based framework and an indigenously developed software to capture and analyse verbal and non-verbal audio responses of children using ML based methods following ISAA based assessment criteria related to Speech-Language and Communication.

Here, our problem is not to classify among the speech of TD and ASD children. Rather our aim is to detect and recognize different vocal response traits (like clear speech, speaker noises, non-speech and also clapping and silence) wherever found in ASD children response and show their occurrence frequencies and durations as software generated feedbacks that will assist psychiatrists or autism therapists during autism assessment sessions.

Our framework for ML assisted autism assessment is as follows: ISAA criterion based audio-visual stimulus is designed and presented before child (some unusual behavior has been noticed or autism traits has been reported by parents or caregiver) and then vocal or speech response of the child is captured by a software. Therapist can change the type of stimuli as per child's interest, response level or assessment requirements. Captured vocal responses are then manually diarized (to extract child and instructor's speech parts), analyzed, labelled and trained using ML methods. These trained ML models are afterwards used to classify and recognize future vocal responses and auto-generate feedbacks on the observed type of child responses (like, adult speech, child speech, silence, unusual noises, non-speech, clapping etc.) that the human assessor can accept or modify to consolidate and calculate final assessment scores using ISAA. Thus the entire framework assists the assessor in a meaningful way for correct diagnosis of autism, helps in reducing the workload and sole dependency on the human assessor. The framework also serves a substantial number of children for timely assessment and initiation of intervention mechanism.

2.3 ISAA Criteria for Vocal Response Assessment

ISAA includes mainly six sub domains, like, Social Relationship and Reciprocity, Emotional Responsiveness, Speech-Language and communication, Behavior patterns, Sensory Aspects and Cognitive component, constituting a total 40 numbers of assessment criteria. We focused on the following 9 criteria under Speech Language and Communication and Cognitive component and mapped related child responses for data analysis from audio recordings:

Table 1. ISAA criteria for autism assessment and mapped child response.

ISAA criteria no	ISAA criteria of Speech Language assessment	Mapped child response/action taken
16	Has difficulty in using non-verbal language or gestures to communicate	Nonverbal actions, like Child Clapping
17	Engages in stereotyped and repetitive use of language	Repetitive speech
18	Engages in Echolalic Speech (may repeat or echo questions or statements made by other people)	Echolalic speech
19	Produces infantile squeals /unusual noises	Unusual Noise
20	Unable to initiate or sustain conversation with others	Child Speech
21	Uses Jargon or meaningless words	Non Speech
22	Uses Pronoun Reversal (reversed pronouns like "I" for You".)	Pronoun Reversal
23	Unable to grasp pragmatics of communication (real meaning)	Non-verbal actions
38	Shows delay in responding (Cognitive component)	stimuli to child-response duration averaged for all the above criteria

3 Data Collection Methodology

Entire data collection drive have been carried out at National Institute for the Empowerment of Persons with Intellectual Disabilities (NIEPID), Regional Centre (RC) in Kolkata after expert based regular autism assessment sessions. Only mild and moderate category of ASD children within the age range of 3 years to 13 years are included for the computer based data collection in this study. It is worth mentioning here that the children are new comer and have not gone through any intervention therapy before the data collection session. Children having comorbid conditions like moderate to severe Intellectual Disability, Speech and Hearing Impairment, Down syndrome etc. are excluded for this study. Data collection methodology includes following steps:

3.1 Stimulus and Approach Planning

Specific audio-visual stimulus are planned to fetch response for ISAA criteria 16, 20, 22 & 23, as those need special speech commands or interactions to evoke responses from children. As repetitive speech, echolalia, unusual noises are inherent in autism and are found naturally, so no specific stimulus are planned for ISAA criteria 17, 18, 19 & 21 and responses are planned to be captured from the entire session recordings. No specific stimulus is planned for 38 as well, for it can be calculated from averaged time to response after stimuli playing for all the other vocal/speech criteria. For ISAA criteria no. 22 & 23, stimuli is planned, but responses are not assured as per expert, so they are excluded for now from ML based study.

3.2 Design of Stimulus

Two types of audio-visual stimuli are designed and developed to capture audio response from children with autism for training of ML based models. Those are, human acted stimuli videos and avatar based animated flash card stimuli videos. Sample of both types of stimuli videos are presented in Fig. 1 below.

Human Acted Stimuli Videos. Human acted stimulus is important to start initial interactions with the child (with autism) and to make them easy with the computer based data collection setup, where they would feel the urge to speak and not simply watch the computer screen silently, like watching mobile or television at home. For ISAA criteria specific response analysis, a total of 12 human acted stimuli videos were designed in Hindi and Bengali languages after finalizing the content in discussion with eminent autism experts. Those videos were acted and prepared by 2 special educators (served as instructors in this entire study) under guidance of autism assessor from NIEPID Kolkata.

Avatar Based Flash Cards Stimuli Videos. These are designed to enhance the training data for ML based model as responses captured from playing human acted stimuli videos were found to be very less and quite uncertain. These videos are designed to attract children and capture short word specific speech responses in a state forward way.

- Flash Card based digital stimuli are designed in Bengali, Hindi & English languages such that the content includes different types of vowel-consonant combinations and also fits to the socio-cultural background of India
- Total 9 categories of object images are shown as digital Flash cards, like Fruits, Vegetables, Food items, Colours, Shapes, Animals, Household things, Vehicles and child Activity. Each category includes 5 videos; hence total 45 numbers of videos are designed for each language.

Child following stimuli, Clap your hands!   What is THIS?

Fig. 1. Samples of Human acted and Flash card based animated stimuli videos.

Thus, a total $((12*2)*2 + (9*5)*3 =)$ 183 videos were designed by the special educators from NIEPID RC, Kolkata. In one language a child can respond up to $(12 + 45) = 57$ number of videos which is quite sufficient. All the stimuli contents, duration, sequences of playing stimuli etc. were validated as per advice and discussion with eminent autism experts in India.

3.3 Vocal Response Capture Framework

Three types of audio data collection processes are carried out and a web based software framework is developed to include all these three types of processes.

Stimuli Based Response Collection from Child

- Suitable for both verbal & non-verbal children, who are having *medium to high sitting tolerance level* and showing less self-stimulating behavior
- Child needs to be seated in front of the data collection set-up and give responses on seeing the played audio-visual stimuli
- Data collection for ISAA criteria no. 16, 20, 22, 23 are being facilitated

Entire Session Audio/Video Recording

- Essential for Non-verbal children. Suitable specifically for *children with less sitting tolerance level* or showing more self-stimulating behavior
- No stimuli are shown as per ISAA criteria, so process doesn't expect child to sit in-front of the data collection setup and respond accordingly
- Data collection for ISAA. 17, 18, 19, 21 & 38 are being facilitated

Offline Upload of Pre-Recorded Response Audio Files

- No stimuli needed, only natural data to be recorded by parents, caregiver etc. at home or other surroundings
- Outside the lab based data collection set-up like using mobile phone, voice recorder etc. whenever child response is found
- Later those files can be uploaded into the data collection system for processing

3.4   Response Data Collection Software

A software based universal framework has been designed mainly for response capture and storage for post processing of the same. The software includes some unique features like, child wise enrolment with unique registration ID, basic metadata information and parent's consent, browsing, loading and playing of child specific audio-visual digital stimuli, stimulus based audio and also entire session audio-visual child's response capture, date wise, session wise structured storage of captured data. System includes modular integrity to easily integrate processes of response annotation, response analysis and data feeding to backend training of ML modules. Screen shot of the data collection software is presented in Fig. 2.

4   Child Response Annotation, Statistics and Analysis

Before AI-ML based training, preparing an annotated and labelled corpus of different types of verbal and non-verbal responses is necessary. For assessing criteria 16, we have taken only child clapping responses for having an audio counterpart.

Fig. 2. Screenshot of software showing Flash card based animated stimuli and response capture from children.

4.1   Child Response Annotation

Responses are labelled under seven responses categories like Child Clapping, Repetitive Speech, Echolalic speech, Unusual noise, Child Speech, Non-speech, Pronoun Reversal, which are mapped with proper ISAA criteria as shown before in Sect. 2.3, Table 1. Audio recordings were collected from the software and were analyzed in audio data editing software i.e. Praat [13] for criteria specific child response marking, labeling. Then they are programmatically annotated, fetched and saved in label wise respective response folder. Each filename contains children registration id (child name, parent name initials with date-time), content (like potato, bus etc. for speech & jargon or noise or clap for others) and file id in the sample's filename. All overlapped response samples are excluded for now to maintain purity of data in each type of response classes.

4.2   Child Response Statistics

Audio data were collected from total 82 children during regular autism assessment sessions at NIEPID, Regional Centre (RC), Kolkata. Audio data considered for annotation are from 76 children, as no audio response is achieved from 6 children among the 82 children. Data from 76 children were analyzed among four age groups (Group A, B, C and D respectively) with increasing order of age ranges and the same has been shown in Table 2. It can be seen from Table 2, that highest number of children belong to Group A i.e. age ranging from 3 to 6 years and Group D consists least number of child i.e. only one. As this vocal response data is collected to build a software assisted ML guided model for early assessment of Autism in children under computer based setup, and early assessment is always beneficial to start early intervention procedures, hence more number of children in Group A and least number of child in Group D is justified.

Table 2. Distribution of ASD Children ages in four age groups.

Name of the Group	Age Range	Number of Autistic Children belonging to the group
Group A	3 to 6 years	51
Group B	7 to 9 years	17
Group C	10 to 12 years	7
Group D	Above 12 years	1

Data collection in Hindi language is done for 4 children at NIEPID, RC, Kolkata. Amount of data in different response classes and distribution of different responses in number of children is shown in Figs. 3 and 4 respectively.

From the corpus statistics, it is observable that, apart from child's speech, unusual noises, non-speech sounds and echolalia are the most common vocal responses found in most of the children data. Much amount of the meaningful and complete child-speech response data is contributed from children with mild autism features and is found in more numbers as those were evoked from showing flash card based stimuli. Pronoun reversal and Repetitive speech are found to be very rare (within presently collected child response data).

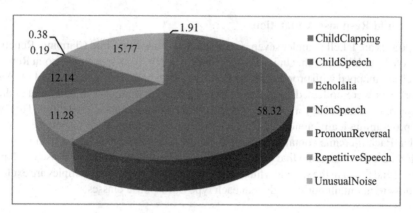

Fig. 3. % Amount of response data in different types of response classes.

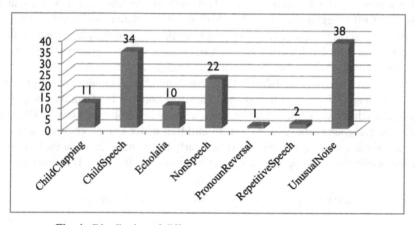

Fig. 4. Distribution of different responses in number of children.

4.3 Observations While Data Collection and Response Analysis

Some interesting observations are sighted from field data collection, response analysis and response statistics generation.

- All the children have shown their interest to computer based data collection set-up. Some of them became more active and treated it as a new toy or exposure.
- Most of them remain attentive during their respective sessions. Some children silently watched the human acted stimuli videos but then responded to the flash card based stimuli.
- Children were excited on seeing their own face, activities and surroundings in the computer screen and got interested to interact with the computer based software.
- Some initial guiding prompts from instructors were found necessary and useful to get verbal responses from child timely (following stimuli) and appropriately. But if insisted, some children with less sitting tolerance however found this irritating and reacted with unusual noises, crying, yelling etc.

- Children who enjoyed the stimuli based data collection session sometimes responded before completion of the stimuli and also produced more Echolalic speech. But those resulted into overlapped response samples and are excluded for ML based study for the time being.

- In some cases, children (with mild to moderate autism) produced incomplete speech, like "ah" for Apple, "bah" for bottle etc. or uttered mispronounced speech data like "onange" for Orange, "gaali" for Gaari (car in Bengali), though TD child of the same age are usually able to pronounce them easily and correctly. These altered pronunciations may have occurred due to inherent difficulties of having autism, but meaningful occurrences of the same within the expected time frame (given for child response capture) are quite satisfactory, which we can consider as positive attitude of the children towards our designed data collection setup.

5 Response Modelling Experiments

In our work, the field collected and annotated audio responses from ASD children along with audio prompts in stimuli and instructor prompts are used to build ML based models. A first level classification has been performed to classify between child's responses and adult speech (in stimuli prompts and instructor's prompts) as child response portions need to be detected first during automated assessment setup. Then the second level classification is performed within child response portions to classify among 4 types of child responses, i.e. Child Clapping, meaningful Child speech, Non-speech and Unusual Noises.

5.1 Experimental Settings

We have used Librosa library [14] of Python to conduct all the experiments.

Selection of Features. We studied a number of features and finally chosen three types of acooustic features for our experiment, these are Mel Frequency Cepstral Coefficient (MFCC) [15], Chroma Short Time Fourier Transform (Chroma STFT) [16] and Mel-spectrogram [17] features. Each frame of the data is represented by a composite feature vector set comprised of 40 dimentional MFCC followed by 12 dimentional Chroma STFT and then 128 dimentional Mel-Spectrogram features. Feature standardisation is applied by subtracting the mean value and dividing by the standard deviation in each frame.

Selection of Classifiers. Librosa package offers experimenting with a number of classifiers to build ML based models. Based on some initial experiments and better classification accuracies on our dataset, we have finally selected five best performing classifier algorithms. These are Decision Tree (DT) [18], Random Forest (RF) [19], Gradient Boosting Machines (GBM) [20], X Gradient Boost (XGB) [21], Light Gradient Boosting Machines (LGB) [22]. Specification of different parameters for the five classifiers are given in Table 3.

Table 3. Specification of different parameters of classifiers.

#	Model	Parameters
1	DT	criterion = "entropy", max_depth = 3
2	RF	n_estimators = 100, criterion: "gini", min_samples_split = 2, min_samples_leaf = 1
3	GBM	loss = 'log_loss', learning_rate = 0.1, n_estimators = 100, criterion = 'friedman_mse', min_samples_split = 2, min_samples_leaf = 1, max_depth = 3
4	XGB	learning_rate = 0.1, n_estimators = 100, max_depth = 3, booster = 'gbtree'
5	LGB	boosting_type = 'gbdt', learning_rate = 0.1, n_estimators = 100, min_child_samples = 20

5.2 Adult Speech vs Child Response Experiment

Data from all types of child responses except Child clapping category are merged together to ASD child response class and on the other side data from audio stimuli prompts and instructor's prompts are merged for the adult speech part for this experiment.

5.3 Child Response Classification Experiment

In this experiment, all the meaningful speech responses in Repetitive speech, Echolalia, Pronoun Reversal are merged together with child speech to form the Child speech category. Here, classification is done among Child Clapping, meaningful Child speech, Non-speech and Unusual Noises.

5.4 Child Response Classification on Merging Speech and Non-Speech

As speech and non-speech classes are found to be very similar from signal perspective, merging these two classes will obviously generate better classification accuracy across these 3 classes i.e. child clapping, unusual noises and child speech & non-speech merged.

Dataset Partition. For each experiment, dataset (including child response dataset and adult prompts) is being partitioned into train, evaluation (eval) and test sets in a ratio of 70: 20:10 with random sample selection method. Distribution of wave files for above three types of classification experiments are given in Table 4.

eval and *test* sets are merged for final experient setup, as the annotated data is not balanced for all the response classes and some response classes have very few samples. We do not address the data imbalance here, as this refelects the true nature of occurances of different instances in ASD child vocalisations.

Classification accuracies in different experiment setup are summarised in Table 5, across five types of ML based classifiers.

Both the GBM and XGB classifiers have performed better with above 96% accuracy during the adult vs child response classification task in experiment 1. In the second experiment, it is observed that the clapping, and child speech data is recognised very

Table 4. Instances per class in train, evaluation and test data partitions.

Classes	Data in train	Data in eval	Data in test
Adult speech	36	10	6
Child response (merged)	431	123	62
Child Clapping	14	4	2
Meaningful speech	513	146	75
Non-speech	88	25	14
Speech- Non-speech merged	602	172	87
Unusual Noises	115	33	17
Total	1799	513	263

Table 5. Accuracies in different experiment setup using the five classifiers.

Experiment	Accuracy in DT	Accuracy in RF	Accuracy in GBM	Acc. in XGB	Accuracy in LGB	Polled accuracy
Adult /Child	0.93233	0.96241	**0.96993**	0.96993	0.96241	0.96992
Child clapping/ speech/Non-speech/Unusual noise	0.7152	0.75633	0.73734	0.75	**0.76899**	0.7595
Child clapping/ speech + nonspeech /Unusual noise	0.87301	0.90794	**0.91111**	0.89206	0.90476	0.91429

precisely, but confusions are found while classifying the child non-speech and unusual noise types of responses as some 30% of the test samples were miss-classified as child speech. Hence, the overall accuracy achieved is around 71% to76% and LGB classifier performs better in this 4 class classification experiment. Merging non-speech with speech samples resulted in better classification accuracy in experiment 3, where GBM classifiers generate best results with around 91% accuracy.

Thus from our initial experiments, we ensure (with 96% accuracies) to isolate and fetch out audio segments with child responses from a recorded computer based assessment session and automatically generate feedbacks (on duration and frequencies) for those. Human assessor can play out, be assured and accept the feedback for decision making. On further recognising the child response classes, assessor may sometimes need to modify system generated output, (i.e. within child clapping, speech/non-speech and unusual noise classes) and relabel the segment with proper child-response type label. Still, assesor can make decisions on playing out those segments only and needs not to listen to the entire recording of the child-assessor interaction. Thus, the framework fulfills present assessment requirements and also serves appropriate labeled data (verified by assesor) for re-training of the ML based models to generate more precise results in future.

6   Conclusion

The present work broadly discussed on an indigenous effort for computer based software assisted assessment of Autism with focus on the Speech–Language and communication related assessment criteria under ISAA. However, large number of acoustic variations found within each response class clearly dictates the immense variability of ASD child responses. After ML based initial processing, still there remains a lot of scope to apply speech recognition (ASR) and text processing techniques to further identify child responses under repetitive speech, echolalia and pronoun reversal categories. We foresee to collect more amounts of data from children at different parts of our country for having diversity in ML models. This is a unique and first of its kind exploration type study with real time field collected audio data and also using indigenously developed data collection framework. The study is also having some interesting observations and experiment results that could be followed in future developments with similar aim of assisting human assessor for autism assessment.

Acknowledgement. We gratefully acknowledge the contribution of our partner institute National Institute for the Empowerment of Persons with Intellectual Disabilities (NIEPID), Regional Centre (RC), Kolkata for their invaluable assistance in data collection from children with autism. We would also like to express our sincere appreciation to the Ministry of Electronics and Information Technology (MeitY), Government of India, for funding this research work. Furthermore, we extend our thanks to NIEPID RC Noida and CDAC Noida for providing feedback and necessary support whenever needed during our activities. We express our sincere gratitude to the special educators and domain experts who generously shared their knowledge and expertise, further enriching our research. Lastly, we are very much thankful to the parents and family members who willingly gave their consent for collecting vocalization data from their child (with autism) and also supported the child during software based data collection. Without the collective efforts of all such individuals and organizations, this work would not have been possible.

References

1. Zeidan, J., Fombonne, E., Scorah, J., et al.: Global prevalence of autism: a systematic review update. Autism Res. **15**, 778–790 (2022). https://doi.org/10.1002/aur.2696
2. Chauhan, A., Sahu, J.K., Jaiswal, N., et al.: Prevalence of autism spectrum disorder in Indian children: a systematic review and meta-analysis. Neurol. India **67**, 100 (2019)
3. Chlebowski, C., Green, J.A., Barton, M.L., Fein, D.: Using the childhood autism rating scale to diagnose autism spectrum disorders. J. Autism Dev. Disord. **40**, 787–799 (2010). https://doi.org/10.1007/s10803-009-0926-x
4. Juneja, M., Mishra, D., Russell, P.S.S., et al.: INCLEN diagnostic tool for autism spectrum disorder (INDT-ASD): development and validation. Indian Pediatr. **51**, 359–365 (2014). https://doi.org/10.1007/s13312-014-0417-9
5. Akshoomoff, N., Corsello, C., Schmidt, H.: The role of the autism diagnostic observation schedule in the assessment of autism spectrum disorders in school and community settings. Calif. Sch. Psychol. **11**, 7–19 (2006). https://doi.org/10.1007/BF03341111
6. National Institute for The Mentally Handicapped: Ministry of Social Justice and Empowerment G of I (2008) Indian Scale for Assessment of Autism-Test Manual

7. Minissi, M.E., Chicchi Giglioli, I.A., Mantovani, F., Alcaniz Raya, M.: Assessment of the autism spectrum disorder based on machine learning and social visual attention: a systematic review. J. Autism Dev. Disord. **52**, 2187–2202 (2022)

8. Kiss, G., Santen, J., Prud'hommeaux, E., Black, L.M.: Quantitative analysis of pitch in speech of children with neurodevelopmental disorders. In: 13th Annual Conference International Speech Communication Association 2012, INTERSPEECH, vol. 2, pp. 1342–1345 (2012)

9. Bone, D., Black, M.P., Ramakrishna, A., et al.: Acoustic-prosodic correlates of awkward prosody in story retellings from adolescents with autism. In: Interspeech, pp. 1616–1620 (2015)

10. Mitsumoto, D., Hori, T., Sagayama, S., et al.: Autism spectrum disorder discrimination based on voice activities related to fillers and laughter. In: 2019 53rd Annual Conference on Information Sciences and Systems (CISS), pp. 1–6. IEEE (2019)

11. Min, C.-H., Fetzner, J.: Vocal stereotypy detection: an initial step to understanding emotions of children with autism spectrum disorder. In: 2018 40th Annual International Conference of the IEEE Engineering in Medicine and Biology Society (EMBC), pp. 3306–3309. IEEE (2018)

12. Pawar, R., Albin, A., Gupta, U., et al.: Automatic analysis of LENA recordings for language assessment in children aged five to fourteen years with application to individuals with autism. In: 2017 IEEE EMBS International Conference on Biomedical & Health Informatics (BHI), pp. 245–248. IEEE (2017)

13. Weenink, D., Boersma, P.: Praat Website (2016). http://www.fon.hum.uva.nl/praat/

14. McFee, B., Raffel, C., Liang, D., et al.: librosa: Audio and music signal analysis in python. In: Proceedings of the 14th Python in Science Conference, pp. 18–25 (2015)

15. Davis, S., Mermelstein, P.: Comparison of parametric representations for monosyllabic word recognition in continuously spoken sentences. IEEE Trans Acoust **28**, 357–366 (1980). https://doi.org/10.1109/TASSP.1980.1163420

16. Bartsch, M.A., Wakefield, G.H.: Audio thumbnailing of popular music using chroma-based representations. IEEE Trans Multimed **7**, 96–104 (2005)

17. Shen, J, Pang, R, Weiss, RJ, et al: Natural TTS Synthesis by Conditioning Wavenet on MEL Spectrogram Predictions. In: 2018 IEEE International Conference on Acoustics, Speech and Signal Processing (ICASSP). IEEE, pp. 4779–4783 (2018)

18. Pal, M., Mather, P.M.: An assessment of the effectiveness of decision tree methods for land cover classification. Remote Sens. Environ. **86**, 554–565 (2003)

19. Belgiu, M., Drăguţ, L.: Random forest in remote sensing: a review of applications and future directions. ISPRS J. Photogramm. Remote Sens. **114**, 24–31 (2016)

20. Natekin, A., Knoll, A.: Gradient boosting machines, a tutorial. Front. Neurorobot. **7**, 21 (2013)

21. Bentéjac, C., Csörgõ, A., Martínez-Muñoz, G.: A comparative analysis of gradient boosting algorithms. Artif. Intell. Rev. **54**, 1937–1967 (2021)

22. Kopitar, L., Kocbek, P., Cilar, L., et al.: Early detection of type 2 diabetes mellitus using machine learning-based prediction models. Sci. Rep. **10**, 11981 (2020)

Addressing Effects of Formant Dispersion and Pitch Sensitivity for the Development of Children's KWS System

Jayant Kumar Rout[(✉)] and Gayadhar Pradhan

Department of Electronics and Communication Engineering, NIT, Patna, Patna,
India
{jayant.ec18,gdp}@nitp.ac.in

Abstract. The accuracy of an automatic keyword spotting (KWS) system is observed to reduce in presence of mismatches such as pitch, speaking rate, formant dispersion, and background noise. To address these mismatches to some extent, this paper proposes a simple and efficient technique through front-end speech parameterization. In the proposed approach, firstly, the formant dispersion is suppressed by temporal averaging of the short-term magnitude spectra (ST-MS) over adjacent frames. Next, the high-frequency oscillations due to pitch harmonics are smoothed out by processing through a low-pass data adaptive single pole filter (DA-SPF), whose pole value changes adaptively for each analysis frame. It provides a non-uniform spectral smoothing for voiced and non-voiced speech frames. The Mel frequency cepstral coefficient (MFCC) extracted from the smoothed spectra is appended with five logarithmically compressed resonant peaks to construct the acoustic feature termed as temporal averaged smoothed spectra (TASS)-MFCC-ARP. The TASS-MFCC-ARP results in a relative improvement of 104.07% compared to baseline MFCC for pitch mismatched test conditions on a deep neural network - hidden Markov model (DNN-HMM) based KWS system. As the bandwidth of filters used for computation of MFCC has a direct impact on pitch harmonics of ST-MS, we have next studied the performance of the proposed feature for varying sizes of Mel-filterbank. A notable performance gain for the KWS system is shown by decreasing the Mel-filterbank size. A further improvement in pitch and speaking rate variations is also achieved by data-augmented training through prosody modification.

Keywords: Keyword Spotting · Pitch-Mismatch · Single-Pole
Filtering · Temporal Averaging · Spectral Smoothing ·
Data-Augmented Training · DNN

1 Introduction

Keyword spotting (KWS) system refers to recognizing the occurrences of the desired set of words or phrases from a continuous speech utterance with the

A. Karpov et al. (Eds.): SPECOM 2023, LNAI 14338, pp. 520–534, 2023.
https://doi.org/10.1007/978-3-031-48309-7_42

help of a machine [16]. KWS system can be used in many user applications such as spoken term detection [17], audio document indexing, searching and retrieval [3], voice-based dialling [6], monitoring of telephone services using target keywords [32], intelligent personal assistants in smart-phones [18] etc. Most of these applications are assessed by both adults and children. According to studies reported in [14], the intra- and interspeaker variability of children's speech is greater than that of adults and tends to decline with age.

For any practical applications of the KWS system, the test speech data differs from the training data mainly due to the environmental noise and speaker-dependent variabilities [4]. In general, KWS systems are trained on adults' speech data and optimized to produce good results for the adult population. A substantial degradation in KWS performance is observed when children's speech is tested against the acoustic models developed from adults' speech [30]. This low performance is due to a large difference in acoustic characteristics between adults' and children's speech [5]. The shorter vocal tract length (VTL) of children speakers leads to formant dispersion [21], and at the same time, the low mass vocal fold leads to higher fundamental frequency or pitch harmonics in the children's speech [22,36]. Furthermore, children speak more slowly overall, and their speaking rates vary more widely than adults [5,21]. Collectively all of these factors contribute to a significant difference in acoustical attributes between adults' and children's speech [9]. Consequently, achieving high detection performance for children's speech on a KWS system developed on adults' speech becomes quite challenging [14,21].

Several works have been reported in the literature to improve the performance of a KWS system by addressing the aforementioned acoustic mismatches. In particular, different promising speaker adaption techniques such as maximum likelihood linear regression (MLLR) [9], maximum a posteriori (MAP) adaption [8], speaker adaptive training (SAT) [1], cluster adaptive training (CAT) [7] and various speaker normalization techniques such as cepstral mean and variance normalization (CMVN) [11], vocal tract length normalization (VTLN) [13], and feature-space maximum likelihood linear regression (fMLLR) [25] have been probed to reduce the speaker-dependent acoustic variations. Despite the employment of these strategies, the KWS system performs much worse under the mismatched test condition than the matched test condition. The model-based adaptation approaches discussed here, employ linear transformations with no assumption about the specific nature of acoustic mismatch being addressed. Since all sources of acoustic mismatch may not be adequately modeled by a linear transformation, it is preferable to compensate them explicitly. Many studies in the literature have shown that explicit normalization of mismatching factors (pitch, formant position, speaking rate, etc.) of test speech, further improves the effectiveness of the adaptation techniques [10,35]. The Mel-frequency cepstral coefficient (MFCC), is a well-known front-end acoustic characteristic for speech parameterization used in several applications of automatic speech recognition (ASR) and KWS. However, its characteristics vary with the variation in pitch, and formant dispersion [29]. Particularly, for signals with higher pitch values, the periodicity of the excitation is not well smoothed down during the liftering operation. A variety of spectral warping [13] and spectral smoothing [20,31,34] approaches have been reported in the literature to deal with the pitch effect on MFCC. However, the majority of approaches provide equal spectral smoothing to the voiced and non-voiced frames, and that may lead to over or under-smooth the spectra.

The slowly varying envelope of the short-term magnitude spectra (ST-MS) carries information about phonemes, stress, and voicing. The variation over a short range of frequencies (high-frequency oscillations) in the ST-MS carries information about the nature of the excitation (pitch and breathiness). The nature of ST-MS also changes from one analysis frame to another depending on the sound units and context of the spoken utterance. So for a better compensation of the pitch sensitivity of MFCC, a simple and effective data-adaptive (DA) low-pass filtering approach using a single pole filter (SPF) was proposed in our previous work [27]. The magnitude of the pole value is crucial in providing considerably more smoothness to voiced frames than non-voiced frames. The MFCC extracted from the obtained smoothed spectra is termed as single-pole smoothed (SPS)-MFCC. The SPS-MFCC is observed to be less sensitive to pitch and environmental variations compared to the baseline MFCC, and other explored features. However, due to formant dispersion and variation in speaking rate, the MFCC obtained from the smoothed spectra for children's speech differed from those of adults' speech. The formant peaks in the ST-MS have a larger magnitude than the neighbouring frequency regions. Thus, by boosting the higher magnitude peaks in ST-MS, formant dispersion can be reduced. In [28], we have proposed an approach by temporal averaging of ST-MS over adjacent frames to reduce the formant dispersion. The MFCC computed from the temporally averaged magnitude spectra (TAS-MFCC) is shown to perform better than other explored features. The DA-SPF [27] provides pitch robustness to the MFCC by suppressing the high-frequency oscillation in ST-MS. Whereas the temporal averaging of ST-MS [28] reduces the impact of formant dispersion on the MFCC. Thus, combination of these two approaches simultaneously handles the impact of pitch sensitivity and formant dispersion on the MFCC features. Motivated by these observations, in this paper, the pitch effect on temporal averaged ST-MS is further suppressed by applying spectral smoothing using DA-SPF. The MFCC extracted from the temporally averaged smoothed spectra (TASS-MFCC) is noted to perform better than the other explored features for the task of KWS in pitch matched and mismatched test conditions. The resonant spectral peaks of temporally averaged ST-MS are unique for different sound units. Thus, to boost the performance of the KWS system even further, five logarithmically compressed spectral peaks at least separated by 400 Hz are appended with TASS-MFCC, referred to as the TASS-MFCC-ARP feature.

The impact of pitch and formant dispersion on the cepstral features also depends on the Mel-filterbank size used in the computation process of MFCC. The decrease in the Mel-filterbank size used for the computation of the MFCC feature increases the bandwidth of the individual filters. Consequently, it provides additional smoothing to the high-frequency pitch variations. Motivated by this, we have next studied the performance of the explored and proposed features for varying sizes of Mel-filterbank. We have also compared the proposed and explored feature with data-augmented training with explicit pitch and duration modification for further validating the merits of the proposed speech parameterization approach.

The remainder of this paper is organized as follows: Sect. 2 describes the proposed approach for acoustic feature extraction. Section 3 presents the experimental setup used to develop the KWS system. The experimental findings and discussions are presented in Sect. 4. Finally, Sect. 5 concludes this study.

2 Proposed Approach for Computation of MFCC by Filtering the Formant Enhanced ST-MS

The sequence of steps adopted for the application of DA-SPF to formant enhanced spectra is shown in Fig. 1. As shown in the figure, the speech signal is processed in the following steps to compute the proposed TASS-MFCC-ARP feature.

i) **Computation of formant enhanced spectra:** The input speech data $(s(n))$ is firstly analyzed using fixed-length Hamming windows of 20 ms with a smaller frameshift of 1 ms. The ST-MS for each windowed frame is computed using the discrete Fourier transform (DFT). Let the ST-MS of the ith analysis frame be $S(i, k)$, where k represents a particular frequency bin. The ST-MS obtained for each analysis frame are then temporally averaged over $2N$ adjacent frames with a shift of N frames to compute the formant enhanced ST-MS $(X(j, k))$.

$$X(j,k) = \frac{1}{2N+1} \sum_{n=-N}^{N} S(i+n,k), \quad N = 10 \tag{1}$$

where $j = 1, 2, ..M$, here M equals to the number of ST-MS obtained by processing input speech data in 20 ms frames with a frameshift of 10 ms. For computing formant enhanced ST-MS for next frame $(X(j+1,k))$, in Eq. 1, i is incremented by N (i.e., $i = i + N$).

ii) **Spectral smoothing of the formant enhanced spectra:** In this stage, the pitch effects on the formant enhanced ST-MS, which vary non-uniformly across an utterance, are smoothed out adaptively by using a DA-SPF. Following the approach presented in [27], firstly, the per utterance normalized data-adaptive pole-magnitude (β_j) for each format enhanced ST-MS $X(j, k)$ corresponding to the (0–2500) Hz is computed by processing it through a cascaded of two SPFs. The transfer function $(H(z))$ of the two cascaded SPFs which mostly capture the spectral dynamics [12] is given by

$$H(z) = \frac{1}{1 - 2z^{-1} + z^{-2}} \tag{2}$$

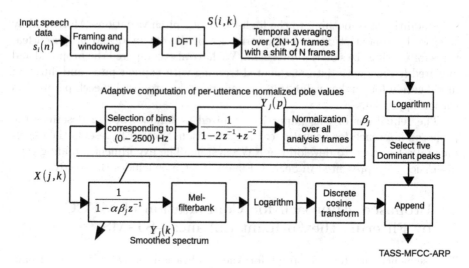

Fig. 1. Block diagram representing the computational of TASS-MFCC-ARP feature from a given speech utterance.

The spectral dynamic for voiced frames is more in the $(0 - 2500)$ Hz frequency band due to the higher magnitude of resonant peaks than the unvoiced frames within this frequency band [12]. Consequently, the cascaded SPFs output has a higher magnitude for voiced frames than non-voiced frames in the selected frequency band. *The only difference lies in the fact that here β_j are computed from formant enhanced ST-MS whereas in [27], β_j are computed from the original ST-MS.* The spectral smoothing of the formant enhanced ST-MS is performed by processing through the DA-SPF, whose pole magnitude $(\alpha\beta_j)$ for each analysis frame varies depending on the value of β_j, where α is a real scalar constant, and $\alpha < 1$. The key reason for multiplying α with β_j is to address the marginal stability problem of DA-SPF, where β_j values equal to one. It also addresses the over-smoothing of the magnitude spectra for the higher values of β_j.

iii) **Computation of the TASS-MFCC-ARP feature**: The TASS-MFCC feature is then computed from the smoothed formant enhanced spectra $Y_j(k)$ following the standard procedure of MFCC feature computation. Next, logarithmically compressed five resonant peaks magnitudes at least separated by 400 Hz are appended to the TASS-MFCC feature. As shown in Fig. 1, these resonant peaks are directly detected from the formant-enhanced spectra. The TASS-MFCC feature appended with resonant peaks is termed TASS-MFCC-ARP.

2.1 Analysis of Proposed Approach for Reducing the Effects of Pitch and Formant Dispersion

To demonstrate the effectiveness of the suggested approach, we compared the smoothed and original ST-MS for a high-pitched speaker. Figure 2(a) shows a 20 ms hamming windowed speech frame taken from the mid-portion of a vowel /a/ of a high-pitched speaker. The corresponding logarithmically compressed ST-MS obtained by direct computation of DFT is shown in Fig. 2(b). The logarithmically compressed formant enhanced ST-MS achieved by employing the temporal averaging method is shown in Fig. 2(c). When this formant enhanced ST-MS is processed through the DA-SPF for the values of α equals to 0.9 the obtained smoothed ST-MS is shown in Fig. 2(d). Figure 2(d) also shows the locations of five resonant peaks in the formant-enhanced smoothed ST-MS. It is evident from the comparison of the original and formant enhanced ST-MS that temporal averaging has sufficiently boosted formant positions in the ST-MS relative to nearby regions. In the temporally averaged ST-MS, the bandwidth of the formant area is also decreased. As a result, it is anticipated that this will lessen the issue of formant dispersion in the case of child speakers. By comparing the magnitude spectrum obtained from the output of DA-SPF (Fig. 2(d)) with the formant-enhanced ST-MS (Fig. 2(c)), it is evident that the DA-SPF suppress the magnitude of the high-frequency variations present in the formant enhanced ST-MS due to pitch. Therefore, it is expected that the MFCC extracted from temporarily averaged smoothed spectra (TASS-MFCC) to be more resistant to pitch variation and formant dispersion.

3 Experimental Setup

In this paper, the KWS system is developed and evaluated using two spoken British English corpora namely WSJCAM0 (Adults' speech corpus) [26] and PF-STAR (Children's speech corpus) [2]. The WSJCAM0 database has 140 adults (male and female) native British English speakers, each of whom spoke approximately 110 utterances. On the other hand, the PF-STAR corpus contains speech data from 158 British children speakers aged 3 to 14 years. In this work, the WSJCAM0 speech corpus is divided into two non-overlapping datasets: *AD_train*, and *AD_test*. The *AD_train* dataset is utilized to train the KWS system for all experimental assessments. It comprises 6812 speech utterances with a duration of 13.3 h collected from 80 male and female adult speakers. The *AD_test* dataset has 2.9 h of speech data from 32 male/female speakers uttering 1336 speech utterances is used for testing the KWS system in the matched condition. The child test (*CH_test*) dataset is taken from the PF-STAR corpus to assess the performance of the KWS systems under pitch-mismatched test conditions. It contains 6.31 h of speech data, consisting of 642 speech utterances collected from 133 child speakers. All the experimental speech data are sampled at a rate of 16 kHz. The performance of the KWS system is evaluated using a set of 10 keywords in pitch mismatched test conditions. We also evaluated the

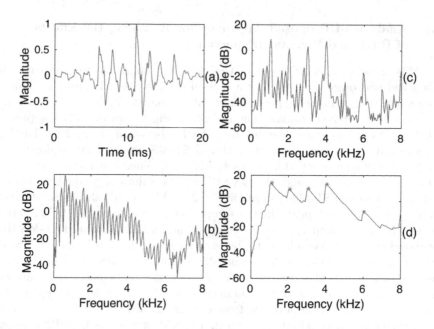

Fig. 2. Figure illustrating the impact of proposed approach on ST-MS. (a) a frame of hamming windowed speech signal taken from the mid-portion of a vowel /a/, (b) corresponding logarithmically compressed ST-MS, (c) logarithmically compressed ST-MS obtained by temporal averaging approach, (d) smoothed spectrum obtained by filtering through DA-SPF of temporal averaged ST-MS along with five resonant peaks.

effectiveness of the KWS system for a set of 20 keywords to further study the proposed and explored features. The list of selected keywords is given in Table 1.

Table 1. List of keywords selected for the *AD_test* and *CH_test* datasets.

keyword set	List of keywords
10	zero, one, two, three, four, five, six, seven, eight, nine
20	zero, one, two, three, four, five, six, seven, eight, nine, ten, they, people, with, bank, there, month, number, point, year

In this study performance of the proposed feature (TASS-MFCC-ARP) is compared with MFCC and MFCC extracted from smoothed spectra obtained using variational mode decomposition (VMD-MFCC) [20], pitch adaptive cepstral truncation (PACT-MFCC) [31] and data-adaptive single pole filtering (SPS-MFCC) [27]. To demonstrate the merit of the proposed approach, we have also evaluated the performance of MFCC computed from only temporal averaged spectra (TAS-MFCC) [28]. The speech data is initially pre-emphasized with a filter coefficient of 0.97 to boost the high-frequency components. Speech frames are then produced using overlapping Hamming window of length 20 ms and a frameshift of 10 ms for all the acoustic features except TAS-MFCC and TASS-MFCC-ARP. For these two features, the initial frameshift is fixed at 1 ms. The 13-dimensional base features are then derived using a 40-channel Mel-filterbank, following the procedure reported in corresponding works. The underlying features are time-spliced with a context size of ±4 frames to add temporal contextual information. Then, to lower the dimension to 40 and decorrelate in feature space, the linear discriminant analysis (LDA) and maximum likelihood linear transformation (MLLT) are employed. In addition, cepstral mean and variance normalization (CMVN) followed by feature-space maximum likelihood linear regression (fMLLR) are applied to normalize the inter-speaker variabilities.

The Kaldi toolkit [23] is used to develop a DNN-HMM-based KWS system employed in this work. The speech recognition module of the KWS system is developed using 3-state left to right HMM. A decision tree-based state tying is used for statistical modeling of context-dependent cross-word triphone models, with the maximum number of tied states (Senones) fixed to 2000. The observation probabilities of the HMM states are generated using the Gaussian mixture model (GMM) and DNN. The context-dependent cross-word triphones in the GMM-HMM system are modeled with 8 diagonal covariance Gaussian components per state. The fMLLR-normalized feature vectors are time-spliced once more with a context size of 9 frames to train the acoustic model parameters of the DNN-HMM system. The DNN-HMM system has a total of 8 hidden layers, each of which contains 1024 hidden nodes with $tanh$ activation function. The initial and final learning rates for the DNN-HMM parameters training are set at 0.015 and 0.002, respectively.

4   Experimental Results and Discussions

The performance of KWS systems is measured using term-weighted value (TWV) [33]. The TWV for a given keyword (kw) is computed as

$$TWV(kw, \alpha) = 1 - P_{miss}(kw, \alpha) - \beta P_{fa}(kw, \alpha) \tag{3}$$

where α is a system dependent threshold and $\beta = 999.9$ is a predefined constant. The TWV of a perfect KWS system will be one [33]. However, the increased in false alarm (P_{fa}) and missed detection (P_{miss}) pushes the TWV towards $-\infty$. The performance improvement of explored and proposed features relative to the baseline MFCC is also evaluated using percentage relative improvement PRI_b as follows:

$$PRI_b = \frac{|(TWV_m - TWV_b)|}{|(TWV_b)|} \times 100 \tag{4}$$

where TWV_m and TWV_b, respectively, indicate the TWV measured for the KWS system using modified MFCC and baseline MFCC.

4.1 Performance of TASS-MFCC-ARP in Pitch-Matched and Mismatched Test Conditions

The TASS-MFCC-ARP feature is derived by incorporating the merits of DA-SPF and formant enhanced methods. Therefore, for a better performance comparison, the $TWVs$ obtained for SPS-MFCC, TAS-MFCC, TAS-MFCC-ARP, and TASS-MFCC-ARP are given in the Table 2. The percentage relative improvement (PRI) obtained for TASS-MFCC-ARP with respect to TAS-MFCC-ARP is also given in the table. For the children's test data, the PRI observed for TASS-MFCC-ARP with respect to the TAS-MFCC-ARP is 6.47% and 3.5% for the 10 and 20 keyword sets, respectively. On the other hand, the performance observed for the adults' test data is very similar. It is worth noting that in TASS-MFCC-ARP and TAS-MFCC-ARP last five feature dimensions are common. Therefore, the performance improvements are mainly due to the removal of pitch variations from the formant-enhanced spectra.

Table 2. The $TWVs$ obtained for both adults' (AD_test) and children's (CH_test) test datasets are given for the 10 and 20 - keyword sets. The PRI obtained for the TASS-MFCC-ARP with respect to TAS-MFCC-ARP is also given.

No. of keywords	Test data	TWV				PRI
		SPS-MFCC	TAS-MFCC	TAS-MFCC-ARP	TASS-MFCC-ARP	
10	AD_test	0.8314	0.8339	0.8394	0.8396	0.02
	CH_test	−0.3078	−0.1235	0.0849	0.0904	6.47
20	AD_test	0.7017	0.7062	0.7083	0.7154	1.00
	CH_test	−0.0718	−0.0633	0.1568	0.1623	3.50

4.2 Impact of Mel-Filterbank Size on the Proposed Feature

The decrease (or increase) in the Mel-filterbank size used for the computation of the MFCC feature increases (or decreases) the bandwidth of the individual triangular filters. The change in Mel-filterbank size also shifts the positioning of the center frequencies of each filters. The increase in bandwidth of the filters provides an additional smoothing to the pitch by averaging over more frequency bins, specifically in the lower frequency band of the ST-MS. The increase in bandwidth and shifting of the center frequencies may also decrease the effect of formant dispersion on the cepstral features. Motivated by this, we have next studied the performance of TASS-MFCC-ARP for varying sizes of Mel-filterbank. This study is performed using 10 keyword set. The KWS system architecture and other experimental setups have remained the same as presented in the previous Section. The KWS performance of the proposed cepstral feature on the AD_test

and CH_test datasets for different sizes of Mel-filterbank are given in Table 3. The TWV is observed to change with the size of the Mel-filterbank and the best TWV is observed when the features are computed using 25 number of Mel-filterbank. Further, reduction in Mel-filterbank size reduces TWV value due to over-smoothing of the ST-MS.

Table 3. The $TWVs$ obtained for the proposed cepstral feature TASS-MFCC-ARP are given for the varying size of Mel-filterbank. The experimental results are given for both adults' (AD_test) and children's (CH_test) test datasets for 10 keywords.

Acoustic feature	Test data	Mel filters					
		45	40	35	30	25	20
TASS-MFCC-ARP	AD_test	0.8150	0.8396	0.8438	0.8513	**0.8577**	0.8166
	CH_test	0.0173	0.0904	0.1145	0.1382	**0.1627**	0.0016

4.3 Performance Comparison of TASS-MFCC-ARP with Other Features for the Modified Size of Mel-Filterbank

The KWS performance employing the explored features may also improve by reducing the Mel-filterbank size. For a fair comparison, we have reevaluated and compared the performances of explored features with the proposed feature for the modified size of Mel-filterbank. For this experimental study, except for the change in Mel-filterbank size, all other parameter settings in the feature computation process remained same. The DNN-HMM-based KWS architecture is also fixed for all kinds of features. For the performance comparison, we have used the following metric. Percentage relative improvement of each feature with respect to Mel-filterbank size (PRI_f).

$$PRI_f = \frac{|(TWV_{mf} - TWV_{of})|}{|(TWV_{of})|} \times 100 \tag{5}$$

where the TWV observed for the KWS system employing cepstral features computed by 40-channel Mel-filterbank (original) and 25-channel Mel-filterbank (modified) is represented by TWV_{of} and TWV_{mf}, respectively.

The TWV observed for the explored and proposed feature computed using 25– and 40– channel Mel-filterbanks are given in Table 4. Expect for the PACT-MFCC, the performance of all the explored features improves by reducing the Mel-filterbank size to 25. The performance reduction in the case of PACT-MFCC may be due to over-smoothing of the spectra reconstructed through cepstral truncation. For all other features, the observed PRI_f is more for the children's speech compared to the adults' speech. As discussed, with the reduction in number of filter the fine variations (pitch) present in the ST-MS is normalized. Consequently, the TWV observed for the KWS system employing the MFCC feature is also improved. By comparing the performance relative improvement of TWV with respect to the baseline (PRI_b) it can be observed that the performance of the proposed feature is also improved compared to the baseline. With the reduced size of Mel-filterbank, the TASS-MFCC-ARP also provides the best performance for the children's as well as adults' speech. It is worth mentioning that the relative performance improvement trained observed for the TASS-MFCC-ARP features remained the same as in the case of the 40 filterbank size. The performance improvement observed in the case of TASS-MFCC-ARP is mainly due to a reduction in pitch effects on TAS-MFCC. Because the magnitude of the resonant peaks is independent of the Mel-filterbank.

Table 4. The TWV obtained for both adults' (AD_test) and children's (CH_test) test datasets are given. The performances are given for all the explored and proposed features using 40 and 25 - channel Mel-filterbank. The PRI_f represents the PRI of a particular feature with respect to change in filterbank size. PRI_b represents the PRI obtained for the modified MFCC with respect to baseline (MFCC) when the features are computed using a 25 - channel Mel-filterbank.

Acoustic features	AD_test				CH_test			
	TWV		PRI_f	PRI_b	TWV		PRI_f	PRI_b
	$40-FB$	$25-FB$			$40-FB$	$25-FB$		
MFCC	0.8064	0.8088	0.29		−2.2189	−0.7626	65.63	
VMD-MFCC	0.8122	0.8123	0.01	0.43	−0.7115	−0.0538	92.43	92.94
PACT-MFCC	0.7891	0.7859	0.40	−2.83	−0.5160	−1.9925	−286.14	−161.27
SPS-MFCC	0.8314	0.8497	1.83	5.05	−0.3078	0.0171	105.55	102.24
TAS-MFCC	0.8339	0.8515	2.11	5.27	−0.1235	0.0912	173.84	111.95
TAS-MFCC-ARP	0.8394	0.8537	1.70	5.55	0.0849	0.1430	68.43	118.75
TASS-MFCC-ARP	0.8396	0.8577	2.15	6.04	0.0904	0.1627	79.97	121.33

4.4 Performance of TASS-MFCC-ARP with Data-Augmented Training

Children's speech has a lower speaking rate and high pitch than that of adults [15,19,27]. Applying appropriate pitch or speaking rate modification to the children's test speech to correspond with the adults' train speech is one method for lowering the discrepancies between the adults' train speech and children's test speech. However, these discrepancies can also be minimized by altering the pitch and speaking rate of the adult training speech, and the acoustic model can be trained by combining the prosody-modified speech with the original adult speech. As reported in [15,27], spectral smoothing combined with data-augmented training via explicit pitch and duration modulation increases the children's KWS system performance. Motivated by this, we also evaluated the effectiveness of proposed approach using data-augmented training. The pitch and duration modifications are performed using the epochs-based approach reported in [24]. The performances of different acoustic features (explored and proposed) in this study for two optimally selected pitch scaling (PS) factors and duration scaling (DS) factors are given in Table 5. For this experimental evaluation, the explored and proposed features are computed by using a 25-channel Mel-filterbank. Similar to the other experimental conditions, the TASS-MFCC-ARP provides better performance compared to the other features. This is mainly due to the proposed data-adaptive compensation of pitch and formant dispersions. All the experimental results presented in this work infer that the adaptive compensation of pitch and formant dispersion is a better choice for suppressing the ill effects of speaker-related mismatches for the development of children's KWS system.

Table 5. Performance of KWS systems is given for data-augmented training. The relative performance improvement of proposed and explored features with respect to the MFCC baseline (PRI_b) is also given. This experimental study is performed by fixing the Mel-filterbank size as 25. In the table, PS and DS refer to pitch scaling and duration scaling, respectively.

Test data	Acoustic features	PS125		PS135		DS065		DS075	
		TWV	PRI_b	TWV	PRI_b	TWV	PRI_b	TWV	PRI_b
AD_test	MFCC	0.8394		0.8296		0.8372		0.8326	
	VMD-MFCC	0.8546	1.81	0.8322	0.31	0.8294	−0.93	0.8297	−0.34
	PACT-MFCC	0.8459	0.77	0.8271	−0.30	0.8305	−0.80	0.8319	−0.08
	SPS-MFCC	0.8602	2.48	0.8517	2.66	0.8916	6.49	0.8700	4.49
	TAS-MFCC	0.8651	3.06	0.8539	2.93	0.8927	6.62	0.8710	4.61
	TAS-MFCC-ARP	0.8697	3.60	0.8591	3.55	0.8992	7.40	0.8764	5.26
	TASS-MFCC-ARP	**0.8705**	3.71	**0.8597**	3.62	**0.8995**	7.44	**0.8782**	5.47
CH_test	MFCC	−0.3584		0.3658		−0.2391		−0.2179	
	VMD-MFCC	0.0273	107.61	0.3719	1.66	−0.0929	61.14	−0.1756	19.41
	PACT-MFCC	0.2041	156.94	0.1072	−70.69	−0.2146	10.24	−0.2095	3.85
	SPS-MFCC	0.2717	175.80	**0.6792**	85.67	0.0255	110.66	0.0038	101.74
	TAS-MFCC	0.2752	176.78	0.3751	2.54	0.2316	196.86	0.1323	160.71
	TAS-MFCC-ARP	0.2763	177.09	0.3796	3.77	0.2381	199.58	0.1752	180.40
	TASS-MFCC-ARP	**0.2788**	177.79	0.4018	9.84	**0.2396**	200.21	**0.1773**	181.36

5 Conclusion

This paper first presents an approach for acoustic feature representation by incorporating the merits of the DA-SPF and temporal averaging of ST-MS to the MFCC feature computation process, here termed as TASS-MFCC-ARP. The TASS-MFCC-ARP feature is observed to be outperformed the acoustic feature derived by applying only spectral smoothing (SPS-MFCC) and temporal averaging of ST-MS (TAS-MFCC) in pitch-matched and mismatched test conditions.

Next, to provide an additional normalization of pitch variations, the bandwidth of the filters is increased by decreasing the size of the Mel-filterbank. On reducing the size of the Mel-filterbank, a significant performance improvement is observed for the KWS systems employing MFCC (baseline) and proposed feature. The KWS performance of explored and proposed features computed with reduced Mel-filterbank size is also compared with data-augmented training. In this situation, too, the TASS-MFCC-ARP outperformed other features. The experimental results present in this work show that adaptive normalization of pitch and formant dispersion present in ST-MS is a better choice for the development of children's KWS system.

References

1. Anastasakos, T., McDonough, J., Schwartz, R., Makhoul, J.: A compact model for speaker-adaptive training. In: Proceedings of International Conference on Spoken Language Processing, vol. 2, pp. 1137–1140 (1996)
2. Batliner, A., et al.: The PF-STAR children's speech corpus. In: Proceedings of INTERSPEECH, pp. 2761–2764 (2005)
3. Burget, L., et al.: Indexing and search methods for spoken documents. In: Proceedings of 9th International Conference on Text, Speech and Dialogue, pp. 351–358 (2006)
4. Byrd, D.: Preliminary results on speaker-dependent variation in the TIMIT database. J. Acoust. Soc. Am. 92(1), 593–596 (1992)
5. Eguchi, S., Hirsh, I.J.: Development of speech sounds in children. Acta Otolaryngol. Suppl. 257, 1–51 (1969)
6. Fraser, N.M.: Voice-based dialogue in the real world. In: Proceedings of Human Comfort and Security of Information Systems, pp. 75–86 (1997)
7. Gales, M.J.F.: Cluster adaptive training of hidden Markov models. IEEE Trans. Speech Audio Process. 8(4), 417–428 (2000)
8. Gauvain, J.L., Lee, C.H.: Maximum a-posteriori estimation for multivariate Gaussian mixture observations of Markov chains. IEEE Trans. Speech Audio Process. 2(2), 291–298 (1994)
9. Gerosa, M., Giuliani, D., Brugnara, F.: Acoustic variability and automatic recognition of children's speech. Speech Commun. 49(10–11), 847–860 (2007)
10. Giuliani, D., Gerosa, M., Brugnara, F.: Improved automatic speech recognition through speaker normalization. Comput. Speech Lang. 20(1), 107–123 (2006)
11. Joshi, V., Prasad, N.V., Umesh, S.: Modified mean and variance normalization: transforming to utterance-specific estimates. Circ. Syst. Signal Process. 35(5), 1593–1609 (2016)
12. Kumar, A., Shahnawazuddin, S., Pradhan, G.: Non-local estimation of speech signal for vowel onset point detection in varied environments. In: Proceedings of INTERSPEECH, pp. 429–433 (2017)
13. Lee, L., Rose, R.: A frequency warping approach to speaker normalization. IEEE Trans. Speech Audio Process. 6(1), 49–60 (1998)
14. Lee, S., Potamianos, A., Narayanan, S.S.: Acoustics of children's speech: developmental changes of temporal and spectral parameters. J. Acoust. Soc. Am. 105(3), 1455–1468 (1999)

15. Maity, K., Pradhan, G., Singh, J.P.: A pitch and noise robust keyword spotting system using SMAC features with prosody modification. Circ. Syst. Signal Process. **40**(4), 1892–1904 (2021)
16. Makhoul, J., et al.: Speech and language technologies for audio indexing and retrieval. Proc. IEEE **88**(8), 1338–1353 (2000)
17. Mamou, J., Ramabhadran, B., Siohan, O.: Vocabulary independent spoken term detection. In: Proceedings of the 30th Annual International Conference on Research and Development in Information Retrieval, pp. 615–622 (2007)
18. Michaely, A.H., Zhang, X., Simko, G., Parada, C., Aleksic, P.: Keyword spotting for google assistant using contextual speech recognition. In: Proceedings of Automatic Speech Recognition and Understanding Workshop, pp. 272–278 (2017)
19. Pattanayak, B., Pradhan, G.: Pitch-robust acoustic feature using single frequency filtering for children's KWS. Pattern Recogn. Lett. **150**, 183–188 (2021)
20. Pattanayak, B., Rout, J.K., Pradhan, G.: Adaptive spectral smoothening for development of robust keyword spotting system. IET Signal Process. **13**(5), 544–550 (2019)
21. Potamianos, A., Narayanan, S.: Robust recognition of children's speech. IEEE Trans. Speech Audio Process. **11**(6), 603–616 (2003)
22. Potamianos, A., Narayanan, S., Lee, S.: Automatic speech recognition for children. In: Eurospeech, vol. 97, pp. 2371–2374 (1997)
23. Povey, D., et al.: The kaldi speech recognition toolkit. In: Proceedings of Workshop on Automatic Speech Recognition and Understanding (2011)
24. Prasanna, S., Govind, D., Rao, K.S., Yegnanarayana, B.: Fast prosody modification using instants of significant excitation. In: Proceedings of Speech Prosody (2010)
25. Rath, S.P., Povey, D., Veselỳ, K., Cernockỳ, J.: Improved feature processing for deep neural networks. In: Proceedings of INTERSPEECH, pp. 109–113 (2013)
26. Robinson, T., Fransen, J., Pye, D., Foote, J., Renals, S.: WSJCAM0: a British English speech corpus for large vocabulary continuous speech recognition. In: Proceedings of International Conference on Acoustics, Speech and Signal Processing, vol. 1, pp. 81–84 (1995)
27. Rout, J.K., Pradhan, G.: Data-adaptive single-pole filtering of magnitude spectra for robust keyword spotting. Circ. Syst. Signal Process. **41**(5), 3023–3039 (2022)
28. Rout, J.K., Pradhan, G.: Enhancement of formant regions in magnitude spectra to develop children's KWS system in zero resource scenario. Speech Commun. **144**, 101–109 (2022)
29. Russell, M., D'Arcy, S.: Challenges for computer recognition of children's speech. In: Proceedings of Workshop on Speech and Language Technology in Education (2007)
30. Shahnawazuddin, S., Maity, K., Pradhan, G.: Improving the performance of keyword spotting system for children's speech through prosody modification. Dig. Signal Process. **86**, 11–18 (2018)
31. Sinha, R., Shahnawazuddin, S.: Assessment of pitch-adaptive front-end signal processing for children's speech recognition. Comput. Speech Lang. **48**, 103–121 (2018)
32. Warren, R.L.: Broadcast speech recognition system for keyword monitoring, US Patent 6332120 (2001)
33. Wegmann, S., Faria, A., Janin, A., Riedhammer, K., Morgan, N.: The tao of ATWV: probing the mysteries of keyword search performance. In: Proceedings of Workshop on Automatic Speech Recognition and Understanding, pp. 192–197 (2013)

34. Yadav, I.C., Kumar, A., Shahnawazuddin, S., Pradhan, G.: Non-uniform spectral smoothing for robust children's speech recognition. In: Proceedings of INTER-SPEECH, pp. 1601–1605 (2018)
35. Yadav, I.C., Pradhan, G.: Significance of pitch-based spectral normalization for children's speech recognition. IEEE Signal Process. Lett. **26**(12), 1822–1826 (2019)
36. Yadav, I.C., Pradhan, G.: Pitch and noise normalized acoustic feature for children's ASR. Dig. Signal Process. **109**, 102–922 (2021)

Emotional State of Children with ASD and Intellectual Disabilities: Perceptual Experiment and Automatic Recognition by Video, Audio and Text Modalities

Elena Lyakso[1]($\boxtimes$) (iD), Olga Frolova[1] (iD), Aleksandr Nikolaev[1] (iD),
Severin Grechanyi[1] (iD), Anton Matveev[1] (iD), Yuri Matveev[1] (iD), Olesia Makhnytkina[2] (iD),
and Ruban Nersisson[3] (iD)

[1] The Child Speech Research Group, St. Petersburg State University, St. Petersburg, Russia
lyakso@gmail.com
[2] ITMO University, St. Petersburg, Russia
[3] School of Electrical Engineering, Vellore Institute of Technology, Vellore, India

Abstract. The paper presents the results of perceptual experiments (by humans) and automatic recognition of the emotional states of children with Autism Spectrum Disorders (ASD) and Intellectual Disabilities (ID) by video, audio and text modalities. The participants of the study were 50 children aged 5 - 15 years: 25 children with ASD, 25 children with ID, and 20 adults - the participants of the perceptual experiment. Automatic analysis of facial expression by video was performed using FaceReader software runs on the Microsoft Azure cloud platform and convolutional neural network. Automatic recognition of the emotional states of children by speech was carried out using a recurrent neural network. This study was conducted in accordance with the design developed in the study of the recognition of the emotional states of children with Down syndrome by facial expression, voice, and text. The results of the perceptual experiment showed a greater accuracy in recognizing the emotional states of children with ASD and ID in comparison with automatic classification. The emotions of children with ASD are more accurately recognized by the video modality, children with ID - by the text modality. The novelty of the research is the comparative results for groups of children with similar and overlapping symptoms of ASD and ID, and in setting tasks related to the analysis of the emotional sphere of children with atypical development.

Keywords: Emotional State · Perceptual and Automatic Recognition · Children with Autism Spectrum Disorders and Intellectual Disabilities · Video · Audio and Text Modalities

1 Introduction

Knowledge about the emotions sphere of children with atypical development and developmental disorders is widely used in medical practice as an additional diagnostic technique, in the field of artificial intelligence to create systems of assistive, alternative communication and in Robotics technology for enhancing education for children. Conversational agents, virtual assistants and educational robots are developed for adults and children with autism spectrum disorders (ASD) [1, 2] and intellectual disabilities (ID) [3]. Educational programs and virtual assistants, as a rule, are based on multimodal interaction, relying primarily on visual and acoustic information in recognizing the emotional states of children [4]. These developments will be widely used in practice with the correct psychological approach to evoke emotional states and their manifestations in the facial expressions, voice and behavior of individuals with ASD and with ID [5, 6]. In the case of developmental disorders and/or atypical development of the child, there may be a discrepancy between the internal state and the external manifestation of emotions [7], a discrepancy in the manifestation of emotions in facial expressions and voice [8].

ASD is characterized by impairments in language and social–emotional cognition. Multiple symptomatology of disorders, combined into an "autistic triad", includes a violation of social behavior and speech, limited forms of behavior, and a tendency to stereotypes. The degree of its expression, the age of manifestation of all characteristic symptoms, the presence of a leading symptom complex are individual for ASD children [9]. The researchers note that the literature on autistic facial expressions remains small, however, with disparate methods and results suggesting a limited understanding of autistic emotions [10].

The children with ID are characterized by a delay in speech development, in cognitive functions, and the specificity of the emotional sphere [11–13]. According to the World Health Organization, 50% of children with ASD are accompanied by ID. The greatest similarity of acoustic features of speech was revealed for children with ASD and ID, which was also shown for linguistic characteristics [14], which does not allow to use only speech as a distinguishing feature of diseases.

Therefore, the study of the emotional sphere of children with ASD and ID on the one hand can give distinctive signs of diseases, on the other hand, data from the reflection of emotions in facial expressions and voice can be used to recognize the emotional states of children. This study was conducted in accordance with the design developed in the study of the recognition of the emotional states of children with Down syndrome (DS) by facial expression, voice, and text [15].

The aim of the study was to reveal the specificity of human recognition of the emotional state of children with ASD and ID by their facial expressions and speech, and to test the possibility of automatic recognition using existing programs and developed algorithms.

2 Methods

2.1 Participants of the Study

The participants of the study were 50 children aged 5 - 15 years: 25 children with ASD and 25 children with ID. The number of children in each age (5–7 years, 8–11 years, 12–14 years, 15 years) was the same for ASD and ID participants. The choice of children was carried out in accordance with the selection criteria for testing by CEDM [16].

20 adults were participated in the study:

1 researcher – selected video and audio fragments from continuous recordings of the child's testing (see below 2.3); 2 experts – annotated fragments. 3 – experts-1 (age – 45.3 ± 17.6 y) with professional experience (16.0 ± 6.9 y) working with atypically developing children. Experts-1 analyzed the testing data and assigned points score for the tasks completed by the children, they did not take part in the perceptual experiment. 14 adults – experts (age 39.3 ± 14.6 y; 7 – male, 7- female) took part in a perceptual study by listening to audio tests and watching video tests.

2.2 Data Collection

Video and audio recordings of emotion expression of children were made in the Medical Center in St. Petersburg, Russia. The children were testing by the Child Emotional Development Method (CEDM) [16, 17]. The duration of testing was from 1 to 2 h, which was determined by the psychoneurological state of children and the characteristics of their behavior. The testing scheme was constant [16], regardless of the group of children - ASD, ID. Children were tested in the presence of their parents.

The recording was carried out in a room measuring $18\,m^2$, there is no noise-absorbing wall, but with soft puzzle mats on the floor.

For video recording of facial expression of children, a SONY HDR-CX560 video camera (maximum resolution 1920 x 1080 at 50 frames per second) was used, which was located at a distance of 1 m from the child's face. To record children's speech, Marantz PMD660 tape recorder with a SENNHEIZER e835S external microphone was used. The microphone was set at a distance of 30–50 cm from the child's face. Audio files were saved in.wav format, 48000 Hz, 16 bits.

The parents of the children participating in the study signed an informed consent approved by the Ethics Committee of St. Petersburg State University.

2.3 Dataset

We used the original dataset containing video and audio fragments of children's emotional states. From the recordings according to the CEDM, the expert selected the video fragments, during which the child demonstrates facial expressions corresponding to one of the four emotional states (neutral, joy, anger, sadness), only those video clips were selected when the child's face and entire head were completely in the frame and were not covered by hands or toys. Original dataset includes 82 video fragments (with audio track) for children with ID and 91 video fragments for ASD children. All video fragments were annotated by two experts in state "joy- neutral (calm) - sadness - anger".

Then, the selected video fragments were viewed by 3 experts. They determined the degree of emotion expression on a 4-point Likert scale [18] "1 = no, 2 = slightly, 3 = moderate, 4 = perfect". The number of fragments for which there was an agreement (Cohen kappa coefficient, k = 1.0, perfect agreement, [19, 20]) between three experts was counted (scores 1, 2, 3, 4). The percentage of selected fragments reflecting each emotional state was calculated in relation to the number of fragments in the dataset for the corresponding emotion for children with ASD and ID. Based on the perfect agreement between the experts on the Likert scale scores, video fragments (S-Fr) that reflect emotions in children with ASD and ID were selected (points 2–4) (Fig. 1).

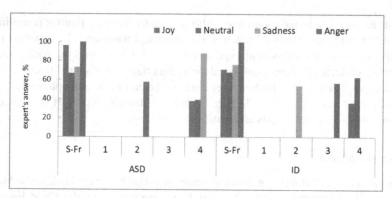

Fig. 1. Agreement between three experts in assessing the emotions expressed in children with ASD and ID on the Likert scale. S-Fr – selected fragments; 1, 2, 3, 4 - Likert scale scores.

According to experts, joy and a neutral state are perfect (4 points) expressed in children with ASD and ID; sadness is perfect expressed in children with ASD (4 points), slightly (2 points) in children with ID; anger state is expressed in children with ASD slightly (2 points), in children with ID - moderately (3 points). Emotions manifestation for children with ASD is brighter vs. ID children.

2.4 Perceptual Study

Video and audio tests were created for the perceptual experiment. 50 video fragments were selected from the dataset of children with ASD and ID. Two video tests (for children with ASD and ID) were created. The video tests did not include video fragments that, according to the agreement between experts, didn't reflect emotion (point 1). The duration of the fragments was from 3 to 30 s. Before each video fragment, the number was inserted. The pause between the fragments was 10 s. Each of the video fragments was included in the test once.

The video test was presented to a group of adults (experts) without sound from a monitor of a personal computer. Watching the test, experts noted the emotional state of the children, choosing one of the four proposed categories: neutral, joy, sadness, anger, and indicated whether the emotion was expressed or not (1 - yes, 0 - no).

The audio test contained children's speech corresponding to video fragments. Each speech signal was repeated once in the test, the pause between speech signals was 5 s. The audio test was presented to experts (the same that watched the video) in an open field. There was no preliminary training of adults. The video and audio tests were used for automatic analysis.

2.5 Automatic Analysis of Facial Expression and Emotional Speech of Children

Analysis of facial expression in FaceReader program. Analysis of facial expression was performed in the FaceReader v.8.0 program (Noldus Information Technology, Netherlands). FaceReader software runs on the Microsoft Azure cloud platform. The program automatically highlights six basic emotions "joy - sadness - anger - surprise - fear - disgust", and a neutral state [21]. Based on the algorithms embedded in the program, the following parameters are determined: the time during which the child demonstrates a certain emotional state in facial expression (as a percentage of the time of the video fragment), arousal, and the valence of the emotions. The data obtained from the automatic analysis of children's facial expression were compared with the results of a perceptual experiment.

Analysis of Facial Expression Using Convolutional Neural Network. For preprocessing, the video records were split into series of frames (static images) with FFmpeg [22], a free and open-source software project consisting of a suite of libraries and programs for handling video, audio, and other multimedia files and streams, and then each frame was processed with Multi-task Cascaded Convolutional Networks (MTCNN) via Deepface [23], a lightweight face recognition and facial attribute analysis framework. Since the video segments with a single child contained only a small number of frames without a detected face, we applied a sliding window to filter out the empty frames, timestamp the segments, and map them to the labels. For the face emotion detection, we used a simple convolutional neural network with five convolutional, three pooling, and two fully-connected layers trained on the Fec2013 dataset from the Kaggle facial expression recognition challenge in 2013 [24].

Analysis of Emotional Speech Using Recurrent Neural Network (RNN). For the audio records, the segments with utterances of a single child were manually clipped via Audacity [25], a free and open-source digital audio editor and mapped to the labels. For the speech emotion detection, we used a simple recurrent neural network with two recurrent and two fully-connected layers with 128 RNN and dense units each trained on a combination of The Ryerson Audio-Visual Database of Emotional Speech and Song (RAVDESS), Toronto Emotional Speech Set (TESS), and Berlin Database of Emotional Speech (EMO-DB) datasets. We did not apply any additional transfer learning or fine-tuning.

Automatic Analysis of the Text of child's Speech. The graphematic text analysis was conducted automatically - the number of sentences, the number of unfinished words, and the average number of tokens were counted in the child's speech. Morphological text analysis was made using the morphological analyzer pymorphy2 [26], and the relative frequencies of the use of different parts of speech for each child were calculated. The assessment of the use of positive and negative words was carried out using the LinisCrowd 2015 tone dictionary [27].

Confusion matrixes for perceptual experiments were prepared. We counted recall, precision, F-1 score for each emotion, Unweighted Average Recall (UAR) - for all emotions [28]. Agreement between experts is assessed using the Cohen kappa statistic (k) [19, 20]. Relative strength of agreement was associated with kappa statistics [29].

3 Results

3.1 Perceptual Experiment

Recognition of the Emotional State by Facial Expression of Children. An analysis of the results of the perceptual experiment showed that by video fragments of children with ASD and ID, experts recognize the joy and neutral state better than sadness and anger (Table 1). The Unweighted Average Recall (UAR) was 0.72 for children with ASD, 0.68 for children with ID. Experts demonstrated perfect agreement in recognizing joy state by facial expressions of ASD children (Cohen's kappa coefficient - 0.829) and substantial agreement – for children with ID (0.764) (see Table 3).

Table 1. Confusion matrix for recognition by experts of the emotional states of children with ASD and ID by video fragments (% of answers).

	joy		neutral		sadness		anger	
	ASD	ID	ASD	ID	ASD	ID	ASD	ID
joy	**88**	**89**	11	10	1	1	0	0
neutral	1	1	**89**	**76**	7	15	3	8
sadness	1	2	40	54	**43**	**38**	16	6
anger	2	4	22	16	9	13	**67**	**67**
Recall	0.88	0.89	0.89	0.76	0.43	0.38	0.67	0.67
Precision	0.96	0.93	0.55	0.49	0.72	0.57	0.78	0.83
F1-score	0.92	0.91	0.68	0.59	0.54	0.46	0.72	0.74
UAR	ASD = **0.72**; ID = **0.68**							

Table 2. Confusion matrix for recognition by experts of emotional states by speech of children with ASD and ID (% of answers).

	joy		neutral		sadness		anger	
	ASD	ID	ASD	ID	ASD	ID	ASD	ID
joy	**58**	**60**	30	39	7	0	5	1
neutral	10	3	**66**	**72**	15	25	9	0
sadness	4	3	29	27	**60**	**65**	7	5
anger	8	9	16	27	9	14	**67**	**50**
Recall	0.58	0.6	0.66	0.72	0.6	0.65	0.67	0.5
Precision	0.73	0.8	0.47	0.44	0.66	0.63	0.76	0.89
F1-score	0.64	0.69	0.55	0.54	0.63	0.64	0.71	0.64
UAR	ASD = **0.63**; ID = **0.62**							

Recognition of the Emotional State of Children by Speech. The experts recognize anger and a neutral state better than sadness and joy by speech of ASD children; neutral and sadness state – for children with ID (Table 2). The UAR was - 0.63 for children with ASD, 0.62 – for ID children.

Maximum agreements between experts were revealed for recognition anger state by speech: moderate for ASD (0.561) and ID children (0.476) & for neutral state: moderate for ID children (0.472) (Table 3).

Experts demonstrate better agreement in recognizing all emotional states by the video and audio of children with ASD (0.579 - video; 0.492 - audio test) than by the video and audio of children with ID (0.530 - video; 0.416 - audio).

Table 3. Agreement between experts when recognizing the emotional state of children with ASD and ID by video and audio (Cohen's kappa coefficient).

Modality	Groups	Emotions	Cohen's kappa coefficient
Video	ASD	joy	**0.829**
		neutral	0.542
		sadness	0.419
		anger	0.522
		all	**0.579**
	ID	joy	**0.764**
		neutral	0.468
		sadness	0.398
		anger	0.512
		all	**0.530**
Audio	ASD	joy	0.482
		neutral	0.470
		sadness	0.488
		anger	**0.561**
		all	**0.492**
	ID	joy	**0.472**
		neutral	0.334
		sadness	0.464
		anger	**0.476**
		all	**0.416**

The second task - determining the intensity of emotion caused great difficulties for the experts. When watching the video test, the experts noted a small number of fragments with expressed manifestation of emotion in facial expression (32% for ASD, 28% for ID). They noted a greater intensity of joy in children with ASD and ID (69% of fragments from the fragments in the test corresponding to the joy) vs. other emotions (Table 4). The maximal experts' agreement was for the state of sadness: moderate (0.416) – for ASD, fair (0.303) – for ID, for which the number of fragments with expressed emotion was small. According to the voice of children with ASD, experts noted maximal number of fragments (46%) and agreement - fair (0.259) for the state of anger; for children with ID, maximal number of fragments (38%) and consistency - fair (0.323) for joy state. Agreement between experts is higher for video than for audio.

Table 4. Analysis of the intensity of children's emotions in video and audio - the answers of experts.

Modality	Groups	Emotions	A. Number of fragments with marked expression (probability 0.5 – 1.0), %	B. Cohen's kappa coefficient
Video	ASD	joy	69	0.314
		neutral	15	0.20
		sadness	27	**0.416**
		anger	15	0.333
		all	32	**0.273**
	ID	joy	69	0.296
		neutral	8	0.172
		sadness	8	**0.303**
		anger	25	0.176
		all	**28**	**0.241**
Audio	ASD	joy	31	0.197
		neutral	0	0.039
		sadness	27	0.244
		anger	**46**	**0.259**
		all	26	**0.209**
	ID	joy	**38**	**0.323**
		neutral	0	0.031
		sadness	25	0.232
		anger	25	0.315
		all	**22**	**0.213**

3.2   Automatic Analysis of Facial Expression

FaceReader Program. Automatic analysis in the FaceReader 8.0 program showed that the facial expressions of children with ASD correspond mainly to a neutral state and joy; for children with ID correspond to a neutral state. The neutral state and joy were recognized better, than sadness and anger (Table 5). The program defines as a neutral, sadness and anger of children with ASD; and the state of joy, sadness and anger of children with ID. The facial expression of children in a state of joy is characterized by positive valence (0.354 – for children with ASD, 0.182 – for children with ID); state of sadness (-0.15/- 0.206 - for ASD/ID children), anger (-0.178/-0.187) and neutral state (-0.082/-0.13) - by negative valence. The highest arousal was revealed for the joy state for children with ASD (0.504); the least arousal – for neutral state for ID children (0.324) & sadness state for ASD children (0.341) facial expressions.

Table 5. Duration of the emotional state manifestation in the facial expression of children, % of the time of the video test (FaceReader 8.0).

	Emotional state	joy	neutral	sadness	anger	fear	surprise	disgust
ASD	joy	**0.434**	0.322	0.045	0.001	0.041	0.033	0.02
	neutral	0.061	**0.578**	0.054	0.083	0.052	0.133	0.013
	sadness	0.063	0.514	**0.118**	0.108	0.055	0.032	0.043
	anger	0.087	0.447	0.117	**0.094**	0.058	0.046	0.131
ID	joy	**0.273**	0.464	0.059	0.012	0.026	0.053	0.021
	neutral	0.021	**0.680**	0.080	0.076	0.037	0.091	0.011
	sadness	0.045	0.589	**0.148**	0.11	0.038	0.062	0.048
	anger	0.043	0.557	0.059	**0.185**	0.051	0.035	0.057

Note: Rows correspond to real emotional states; columns correspond to emotional states highlighted by the FaceReader 8.0 program

Analysis Using Convolutional Neural Network. By the video of ASD and ID children, the joy state was classified better than neutral, anger and sadness state (Table 6). The neutral state was classified better by video of children with ASD, the sadness state – by children with ID. UAR for ASD children were 0.48, for children with ID – 0.47.

3.3 Automatic Analysis of Child Speech

Analysis Using Recurrent Neural Network. For the audio, neutral state was classified better than joy, anger and sad state (Table 7). The performance is lower than for video. By audio of children with ASD, the joy and sadness states were not classified automatic, by audio of children with ID – the anger state.

Analysis of the Text of the Speech. Using GradientBoostingClassifier to predict class labels (emotional states) for children with ID achieved an accuracy of 0.72. For the text, we obtained the weighted-averaged precision of 0.71, the weighted-averaged recall of 0.72, and the weighted-averaged F1-score of 0.71. The performance is above chance.

Table 6. Confusion matrix for automatic classification of emotional state of children by video.

	joy		neutral		sadness		anger	
	ASD	ID	ASD	ID	ASD	ID	ASD	ID
joy	**78**	**74**	14	14	8	12	0	0
neutral	0	0	**58**	**32**	33	5	9	18
sadness	5	4	48	22	**42**	**62**	5	12
anger	23	28	3	21	32	3	**15**	**21**
Recall	0.78	0.74	0.58	0.32	0.42	0.62	0.15	0.21
Precision	0.74	0.7	0.39	0.36	0.37	0.4	0.52	0.41
F1-score	0.74	0.72	0.39	0.34	0.37	0.49	0.52	0.28
UAR	ASD = **0.48**; ID = **0.47**							

Table 7. Confusion matrix for automatic classification of emotional state of children by audio.

	joy		neutral		sadness		anger	
	ASD	ID	ASD	ID	ASD	ID	ASD	ID
joy	**0**	15	92	85	0	0	8	0
neutral	0	0	**85**	**92**	0	8	15	0
sadness	0	0	91	75	**0**	**25**	9	0
anger	8	8	69	75	0	17	**23**	**0**
Recall	00.00	0.15	0.85	0.92	0.00	0.25	0.23	0.00
Precision	0.00	0.67	0.26	0.29	0.00	0.50	0.43	0.00
F1-score	0.00	0.25	0.40	0.44	0.00	0.33	0.30	0.00
UAR	ASD = **0.27**; ID = **0.33**							

For the text, anger was classified better than joy, sadness and especially neutral state. Using AdaBoostClassifier to predict class labels (emotional states) for children with ASD achieved an accuracy of 0.36. For the text, we obtained the weighted-averaged precision of 0.37, the weighted-averaged recall of 0.36, and the weighted-averaged F1-score of 0.32. The performance is above chance. For the text, anger was classified better than joy, neutral state and especially sad state (Table 8).

Table 8. Classification results (text of children's speech).

	joy		neutral		sad		anger	
	ASD	ID	ASD	ID	ASD	ID	ASD	ID
joy	**46**	**69**	8	23	0	0	46	0
neutral	15	54	**15**	**38**	8	8	62	0
sad	18	17	18	25	**9**	**50**	55	8
anger	15	8	8	0	8	0	**69**	**92**
Recall	0.46	0.85	0.15	0.62	0.09	0.50	0.69	0.92
Precision	0.50	0.73	0.33	0.67	0.33	0.67	0.31	0.79
F1-score	0.48	0.79	0.21	0.64	0.14	0.57	0.43	0.85
UAR	ASD = **0.35**; ID = **0.72**							

4 Discussion

Different approaches to the analysis of the recognition of the emotions in children with ASD and ID - a perceptual experiment, automatic classification by facial expression, revealed that the emotions of children with ASD were recognized better. Emotional manifestations of ASD children are more expressive - based on data on the intensity of emotions and the agreement of experts.

The study was conducted to determine possible differences in the manifestation of emotions in children with ASD and ID and to compare the obtained data with the results of the study on emotion recognition in children with DS [15]. For the correct comparison of the results, a unified approach to the collection and analysis of material [16] was used.

An analysis of the results of the perceptual experiment showed that by video fragments of children with ASD and ID experts recognize the joy and neutral state better than sadness and anger, that corresponding data for children with DS. The Unweighted Average Recall was maximum for ASD children.

The experts recognize anger and a neutral state better than sadness and joy by speech of ASD children; the similar result was shown for children with DS. The data on better recognition of the state of anger by the speech of children with ASD and DS in the classification of four emotional states "joy - neutral - sadness - anger" are confirmed by the data of the perceptual experiment and an automatic classification based on GMM model for the recognition of three states "comfort - neutral state - discomfort". This study showed a greater accuracy in recognition of the state of discomfort, compared with other states [30]. The experts recognize neutral and sadness state for children with ID. Automatic classification of emotional states of children with ASD and ID by their facial expression and voice showed low accuracy, which is consistent with the works about difficulties in classifying emotions in individuals with ASD [31, 32] and ID [33, 34]. The approach, which revealed average results in recognizing the emotions of children with DS, showed poor results for children with ASD and ID, which poses the problem of using other approaches.

What could be the reason for this - with the approaches used for automatic classification or with the material, especially for the video modality? The dynamic image of the face is not reduced to the summation of static images. Under conditions of dynamic exposure, weak expressions are recognized more accurately than discrete ones, which is due to the influence of the time factor [35]. The movement of facial features provides additional unique temporal information that contributes to more accurate recognition of emotions [36]. On the other hand, when recognizing a dynamic stimulus, difficulties may be associated with the specifics of the deployment of a complex of emotional manifestations in time and the appearance of additional affective components [37]. Emotional manifestations of children with ASD could be both characteristic of the corresponding emotional states, and manifest themselves in the form of rapidly and abruptly changing grimaces, when facial expression corresponding to a comfortable state is similar to negative manifestations [38]. Therefore, one of the tasks of further research may be the recognition of the facial expression of children by static images - photographs. Physiological study noted that human recognition of negative emotions by voice takes about 400 ms, somewhat longer (up to 500–600 ms) recognition for positive emotions takes [39]. A fast change in the manifestation of emotions in the voice of children with ASD and ID apparently leads to classification errors by human and automatically, due to the allocation of the longest manifested or the most expressed emotion. Automatic analysis of children's texts showed that anger and joy are better recognized by verbal markers, with better recognition of the emotions of children with ID than children with ASD. This may be explained by the frequency of words that reflect the emotions of joy and anger in children of the two groups. Furthermore, children with ASD more often utter vocalizations manifesting emotions than children with ID.

Our study is related to another problem that we posed earlier [38] and that is discussed by other researchers [10]. It is traditional to compare the manifestations of emotions in children with ASD and children with typical development. However, facial expressions of children with ASD are considered unusual, which is represented in the questionnaires used for autism diagnosing [10]. Adults noted that the emotions of children with ASD are more diverse than emotions suggested in the questionnaire of a perceptual experiment, more reminiscent of complex emotional expressions of adults. For example, a calm, neutral state can be described as neglect, misunderstanding, detached state, self-absorption, concentration [38].

Limitation: 1. Small number of audio and video fragments for automatic classification. 2. We used existing software to classify the emotional states of children with ASD and ID for the purpose to compare with the data for children with DS.

Future: 1. Development of a classification of emotional manifestations of children with ASD. 2. Creation of new approaches for automatic classification of emotional state of children with atypical development, taking into account their psychoneurological state.

5   Conclusion

Adults recognize the emotional states of children with ASD and ID by video better than by audio. The accuracy and agreement between experts are maximal when recognizing the state of joy by video and the state of anger by speech of children.

Automatic classification of the emotional states of children by facial expression using the algorithms of the FaceReader program revealed better results for joy and neutral state than for sadness and anger; by convolutional neural network – the joy state was classified better than neutral, anger and sadness state. The neutral state was classified better for video of children with ASD, the sadness state – for children with ID.

Automatic analysis of child speech using recurrent neural network revealed the lower performance than for video. By audio of children with ASD and ID the neutral state was classified automatic better than other states. For children with ASD the joy and sadness state could not be effectively classified with automatic approaches and similarly for ID children – anger state could not be classified. Automatic analysis by the texts of child speech revealed better results for anger and joy state with more accuracy for children with ID.

The novelty of the results obtained lies in comparative data for groups of children with similar and overlapping symptoms - ASD and ID, and in setting tasks related to the analysis of the emotional sphere of children with atypical development.

Acknowledgements. This study is financially supported by the Russian Science Foundation (project 22–45-02007) - for Russian researches, DST/INT/RUS/RSF/P-57/2021 – for Indian researches.

References

1. Schadenberg, B.R., Reidsma, D., Heylen, D.K.J., Evers, V.: Differences in spontaneous interactions of autistic children in an interaction with an adult and humanoid robot. Front. Robot. AI **7**(28), 1–19 (2020)
2. Garg, R., et al.: The last decade of HCI research on children and voice-based conversational agents. In: Proceedings of the 2022 CHI Conference on Human Factors in Computing Systems (CHI 2022), Article 149, pp. 1–19. New York, NY, USA (2022)
3. Scassellati, B., et al.: Improving social skills in children with ASD using a long-term, in-home social robot. Sci. Robot. **3**(21), eaat7544 (2018)
4. Leung, F.Y.N., et al.: Emotion recognition across visual and auditory modalities in autism spectrum disorder: a systematic review and meta-analysis. Dev. Rev. **63**(1), 101000 (2022)
5. Vandevelde, S., et al.: The scale for emotional development-revised (SED-R) for persons with intellectual disabilities and mental health problems: development, description, and reliability. Int. J. Dev. Disabil. **62**(1), 11–23 (2016)
6. Sterkenburg, P.S., et al.: Scale of emotional development–short: reliability and validity in two samples of children with an intellectual disability. Res. Dev. Disabil. **108**, 103821 (2021). https://doi.org/10.1016/j.ridd.2020.103821
7. Fridenson-Hayo, S., et al.: Basic and complex emotion recognition in children with autism: cross-cultural findings. Mol. Autism **7**, 52 (2016)
8. Russell, J.A., Bachorowski, J.-A., Fernández-Dols, J.-M.: Facial and vocal expressions of emotion. Annu. Rev. Psychol. **54**(1), 329–349 (2003). https://doi.org/10.1146/annurev.psych.54.101601.145102
9. Wing, L.: The definition and prevalence of autism: a review. Eur. Child Adolesc. Psychiatry **2**(1), 61–74 (1993)
10. Jacques, C., Courchesne, V., Mineau, S., Dawson, M., Mottron, L.: Positive, negative, neutral or unknown? The perceived valence of emotions expressed by young autistic children in a novel context suited to autism. Autism **26**(7), 1833–1848 (2022)

11. des Portes, V.: Intellectual disability. In: Handbook of Clinical Neurology, vol. 174, pp. 113–126 (2020)
12. Frolova, O., Lyakso, E.: Communication skills of preschool children with mental retardation and developmental disorders. In: Abstract book of 19th European conference on Developmental Psychology. ECDP - 2019, p. 159, Greece, Athens (2019)
13. Frolova, O.V., Lyakso, E.E.: Perceptual features of speech and vocalizations of 5–8 years old children with autism spectrum disorders and intellectual disabilities: recognition of the child's gender, age and state. In: Proceedings of International congress, Neuroscience for Medicine and Psychology, p. 486, Sudak, Russia (2020)
14. Lyakso, E., Frolova, O., Nikolaev, A.: Voice and speech features as diagnostic symptom. In: Pracana, C., Wang, M. (eds.) Psychological Applications and Trends, pp. 259–363. Science Press, Lisboa, Portugal (2021)
15. Lyakso, E., et al.: Recognition of the emotional state of children with down syndrome by video, audio and text modalities: human and automatic. LNAI **13721**, 438–450 (2022)
16. Lyakso, E., Frolova, O., Kleshnev, E., Ruban, N., Mekala, M., Arulalan, K.V.: Approbation of the Child's Emotional Development Method (CEDM). In: Companion Publication of the 2022 International Conference on Multimodal Interaction (ICMI '22 Companion), pp. 201–210. New York, NY, USA (2022)
17. Frolova, O., Kleshnev, E., Grigorev, A., Filatova, Y., Lyakso, E.: Assessment of the emotional sphere of children with typical development and autism spectrum disorders based on an interdisciplinary approach. Hum. Physiol. **49**(3), 216–224 (2023)
18. Likert, R.: A technique for the measurement of attitudes. Arch. Psychol. **22**, 5–55 (1932)
19. Md Juremi, N.R., Zulkifley, M.A., Hussain, A., Zaki, W.M.D.: Inter-rater reliability of actual tagged emotion categories validation using Cohen's Kappa coefficient. J. Theor. Appl. Inf. Technol. **95**, 259–264 (2017)
20. Bobicev, V., Sokolova, M.: Inter-annotator agreement in sentiment analysis: machine learning perspective. In: Recent Advances in Natural Language Processing Meet Deep Learning, pp. 97–102. Varna, Bulgaria (2017)
21. Ekman, P.: Basic emotions. In: Dalgleish, T., Power M.J. (eds.) Handbook of Cognition and Emotion, pp. 45–60. Wiley, Hoboken (1999)
22. FFmpeg. https://ffmpeg.org. Accessed 13 Jul 2023
23. Multi-task Cascaded Convolutional Networks (MTCNN) via Deepface. https://github.com/serengil/deepface. Accessed 13 Jul 2023
24. Kaggle facial expression recognition challenge in 2013. https://www.kaggle.com/c/challenges-in-representation-learning-facial-expression-recognition-challenge. Accessed 13 Jul 2023
25. Audacity. https://www.audacityteam.org. Accessed 13 Jul 2023
26. Korobov, M.: Morphological analyzer and generator for Russian and Ukrainian languages. Anal. Images Soc. Netw. Texts **542**, 320–332 (2015)
27. LinisCrowd 2015 tone dictionary. http://linis-crowd.org/. Accessed 13 Jul 2023
28. Dalianis, H: Evaluation Metrics and Evaluation, pp. 45–53. Springer, Cham (2018).https://doi.org/10.1007/978-3-319-78503-5_6
29. Landis, J.R., Koch, G.G.: The measurement of observer agreement for categorical data. Biometrics **33**(1), 159–174 (1977)
30. Matveev, Y., Lyakso, E., Matveev, A., Frolova, O., Grigorev, A., Nikolaev, A.: Automatic classification of the emotional state of atypically developing children. In: Proceedings of the 24th International Congress of Acoustics, ABS-0338, pp. 1–7. Gyeongju, Korea (2022). https://ica2022korea.org/
31. Marchi, E., et al.: Typicality and emotion in the voice of children with autism spectrum condition: evidence across three languages. In: Interspeech, pp. 115–119. Dresden, Germany (2015)

32. Landowska, A., et al.: Automatic emotion recognition in children with autism: a systematic literature review. Sensors (Basel) **22**(4), 1649 (2022)
33. Wishart, J.G., Cebula, K.R., Willis, D.S., Pitcairn, T.K.: Understanding of facial expressions of emotion by children with intellectual disabilities of differing aetiology. J. Intellect. Disabil. Res. **51**(Pt 7), 551–563 (2007)
34. Hammann, T., et al.: The challenge of emotions — an experimental approach to assess the emotional competence of people with intellectual disabilities. Disabilities **2**, 611–625 (2022)
35. Barabanschikov, V.A., Korolkova, O.A., Lobodinskaya, E.A.: Perception of facial expressions during masking and apparent motion. Exp. Psychol. **8**(1), 7–27 (2015)
36. Ambadar, Z., Schooler, J.W., Cohn, J.F.: Deciphering the enigmatic face: the importance of facial dynamics in interpreting subtle facial expressions. Psychol. Sci. **16**(5), 403–410 (2005)
37. Barabanschikov, V.A., Suvorova, E.V.: Human emotional state assessment based on a video portrayal. Exp. Psychol. **13**(4), 4–24 (2020)
38. Lyakso, E.E., Frolova, O.V., Grigorev, A.S., Sokolova, V.D., Yarotskaya, K.A.: Recognition by adults of emotional state in typically developing children and children with autism spectrum disorders. Neurosci. Behav. Physiol. **47**(9), 1051–1059 (2017)
39. Pell, M.D., Kotz, S.A.: On the time course of vocal emotion recognition. PLoS ONE **6**(11), e27256 (2011)

Linear Frequency Residual Features for Infant Cry Classification

S. Uthiraa, Aastha Kachhi$^{(\boxtimes)}$, and Hemant A. Patil$^{(\boxtimes)}$

Speech Research Lab, DA-IICT, Gandhinagar, Gujarat, India
{uthiraa_s,aastha_k,hemant_patil}@daiict.ac.in

Abstract. Classification of normal *vs.* pathological infant cries is a socially relevant task as crying is the only known mode of infant communication. Due to quasi-periodic sampling of the vocal tract system, the spectrum formed by high pitch-source harmonics results in extremely poor spectral resolution for commonly used features. This paper investigates the effect of excitation source-based features captured using Linear Prediction Residual for classification of normal *vs.* pathological infant cries. The performance of Linear Frequency Residual Cepstral Coefficients (LFRCC) was compared for *matched* conditions (of train and test data) against state-of-the-art feature sets, namely, Mel Frequency Cepstral Coefficients (MFCC) and Linear Frequency Cepstral Coefficients (LFCC) using Gaussian Mixture Model (GMM) and Convolutional Neural Network (CNN) as classifiers. This study also investigated the effect of LFRCC on cross-database (i.e., *mismatched* conditions) and combined database evaluation scenarios. It was observed that LFRCC outperformed MFCC and LFCC by 24.9% and 17.43%, respectively, for mismatched conditions and over 0.27%–1.11% for the combined database. The relatively better performance of LFRCC feature set maybe due to its capability in representing excitation source information, which is very prevalent in infant cry as formant structures are not well developed in the initial period of life.

Keywords: Infant cry classification · Excitation source information · LP residual · Linear frequency residual cepstral coefficients

1 Introduction

Infant cry research is interdisciplinary in nature involving pediatrics, cognition, psychology, engineering, language acquisition, robotics, prosody, and autism spectrum disorders (ASD) [11]. For example, language acquisition research has shown that infants have a remarkable ability to distinguish two different languages (including native *vs.* non-native) within just *four* days of birth and thus, deeper research in language acquisition may help for developing better speech recognition and speech understanding systems, such as in robotics. In addition, cry units of infants, who were later diagnosed with ASD were also found to have

© The Author(s), under exclusive license to Springer Nature Switzerland AG 2023
A. Karpov et al. (Eds.): SPECOM 2023, LNAI 14338, pp. 550–561, 2023.
https://doi.org/10.1007/978-3-031-48309-7_44

higher fundamental frequency (F_0) than controls similar to pathological infant cry, thereby making it challenging to identify acoustic cues of normal, ASD, and pathological infant cry samples.

Around 3 million infants die within the first four months of birth due to various reasons, such as pathology, malnutrition, vaccine-preventable disease, abnormalities in the brain stem controlling breathing function, etc. In this context, infant biometrics using fingerprint and cry signal are developed [11]. In the context of pathologies, birth asphyxia, and related abnormalities, in particular, sudden infant death syndrome (SIDS) are the leading cause of death for infants [14]. Landmark investigations sponsored by the National Institute of Health (NIH), USA, reported evidence of abnormalities in the brainstem (in particular, medulla oblongata) that is known to control breathing functions, for the infants who died of SIDS [4]. Further, clinical diagnosis of asphyxia is logistics-heavy and costly and thus, it is mostly diagnosed late, however, by then, severe neurological damage would have already occurred to the infants [10]. Further, acoustic cues of the deaf infant cry are related to hearing loss, type and duration of rehabilitation, and the age of pathology detection [15]. Moreover, not every infant has the luxury of being taken care of by a Neonatal Intensive Care Unit (NICU) and a team of pediatricians, more so, in the Indian context. To that effect, several attempts to develop assistive technologies, such as baby cry analyzer [1], baby pod [2], and Ubenwa mobile app indicates a genuine need to develop a cost effective and non-invasive cry diagnosis tool as a supplement to well known *Apgar* count (that is a function of baby weight, preterm *vs.* full term, cry being vigorous *vs.* shill, etc.). In this context, this paper investigates a signal processing-based approach for infant cry classification, where asphyxia and deaf are considered pathological cry signals.

Even though research on infant cry analysis started as early as the 1960s and this problem is socially relevant, the progress in this field is slower primarily due to several technological challenges. In particular, ethical issues associated with data collection, higher fundamental or pitch frequency (F_0), and hence, infant cry signal suffers from poor spectral resolution. Original investigations in [20] identified ten distinct cry modes to indicate differences in the manner of modes of vibrations associated with the vocal folds voicing, i.e., F_0 and its harmonics ($kF_0, k \in Z$) via narrowband spectrogram (having window duration less than a pitch period, i.e., $\sim$1–2 ms [16]). However, these investigations were limited to only normal infant cries and later extended to analysis of asthma, Hypoxic Ischemic Encephalopathy (HIE), and larynx abnormalities. These studies exploited narrowband spectrograms due to their capability of reflecting the manner of variations in F_0 and kF_0, where formant structures are difficult to observe due to quasi-periodic sampling of vocal tract spectrum by high pitch-source harmonics (under the assumption of linear time-invariant cry production model). Recently, Mel Frequency Cepstral Coefficients (MFCC) features modeled using a statistical classifier, namely, Gaussian Mixture Model (GMM) are used for this task [3]. Recent study in [12] shows the effectiveness of Linear Prediction (LP) in detection of genuine *vs.* spoofed speech. To that effect, this paper investigates the excitation source-based features based on the classic concept of Linear Prediction (LP) for infant cry analysis. Since, cries, in general, are very difficult to distinguish for the human ear, excitation source-based features, which capture the characteristics of glottal airflow, in particular, the presence or absence of voicing needed for sound (cry) production proved to be effective.

The rest of the paper is organized as follows: Sects. 2 and 3 present details of LP and proposed LFRCC features, respectively. Section 4 gives the details of the experimental setup used for this study. Section 5 presents the analysis of the results, and Sect. 6 concludes the paper along with future research directions.

2   Linear Prediction (LP) Residual

From the system identification and control literature, the Linear Prediction (LP) approach has been traditionally employed, primarily in the context of speech coding applications [5,13]. This approach has found extensive use in various speech-related applications due to the inherent dependencies that speech signals exhibit in the sequential information of their samples. In LP analysis, each speech sample is represented as a linearly weighted combination of the previous 'p' speech samples, where 'p' represents the order of the linear predictor. The weights in this combination are commonly referred to as Linear Prediction Coefficients (LPCs) [13]. If 's(n)' denotes the current speech sample at the 'n^{th}' instant, then the predicted sample can be expressed as follows:

$$\hat{s}(n) = -\sum_{k=1}^{p} a_k s(n-k), \tag{1}$$

In Eq. (1), where a_k represents the Linear Prediction Coefficients (LPCs), it is evident that the LP approach is employed to model $s(n)$ with the aim of capturing linear dependencies within the sequence of signal samples $s(n)$. However, it's important to acknowledge that within this sequence of samples, there might exist non-linear relationships that the LP model does not account for or represent. The disparity between the actual speech sample 's(n)' and the predicted samples $\hat{s}(n)$ is commonly referred to as the LP residual or error, denoted as $r(n)$, and is defined as follows:

$$r(n) = s(n) - \hat{s}(n) = s(n) + \sum_{k=1}^{p} a_k s(n-k). \tag{2}$$

Specifically, if we apply an all-pole inverse filtering technique to the speech signal based on the LP analysis described above, we obtain the following result:

$$A(z) = 1 + \sum_{k=1}^{p} a_k z^{-k}, \tag{3}$$

$$H(z) = \frac{G}{1 + \sum_{k=1}^{p} a_k z^{-k}}, \tag{4}$$

In this context, G represents the *gain* term within the LP model, while A(z) denotes an inverse filter that corresponds to an all-pole LP filter H(z). This filter H(z) encapsulates the characteristics of the vocal tract-based system. Importantly, excitation source information is integrated with the system information within the cepstral domain. The LP residual inherently contains this excitation source information, and further processing is conducted in the cepstral domain. This processing involves using a filterbank to represent the spectral envelope of the excitation source signal across various subbands, thereby allowing the extraction of this critical information.

3 Linear Frequency Residual Cepstral Coefficients (LFRCC)

Figure 1 illustrates the functional block diagram of the proposed LFRCC feature set. To ensure a balanced representation of both lower and higher frequency components, the input cry signal undergoes pre-emphasis filtering [19]. Subsequently, the signal is processed through the Linear Prediction (LP) block, resulting in the LP residual signal denoted as r(n). Frame blocking and windowing techniques are applied to the LP residual waveform, using a 30 ms frame duration with a 15 ms frame shift. Following this, a filterbank consisting of 40 linearly spaced triangular subband filters is employed, with power spectrum estimation carried out for each frame of the LP residual. The final step involves applying the Discrete Cosine Transform (DCT) to achieve feature dimensionality reduction, feature decorrelation, and energy compaction, resulting in the LFRCC feature set. Cepstral Mean Normalization (CMN) is applied to minimize distortion and ensure consistent feature scaling across the dataset.

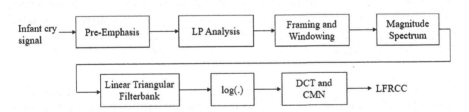

Fig. 1. Functional block diagram of LFRCC feature extraction. After [19].

4 Experimental Setup

4.1 Dataset Used

Baby Chillanto database used for this work was originally developed by the recordings conducted by medical doctors, which is a property of NIAOE-CONACYT, Mexico [17,18]. Table 1 shows the statistics of the Baby Chilanto database with a total of 1049 healthy cries and 1219 pathological cries. Another database used was the DA-IICT infant cry database. It was collected by [7,8]. Table 1 shows the statistics of the DA-IICT infant cry database with a total of studies reported in 793 healthy cries and 416 pathological cries. For a fair comparison, each cry segment from both corpora was resampled at a uniform sampling frequency of 16 kHz.

Table 1. Number of Cry Recordings in Baby Chilanto and DA-IICT Corpora. After [7,8,17], and [18].

Class	Category	Baby Chilanto	DA-IICT
Healthy	Normal	507	793
	Hunger	350	-
	Pain	192	-
Pathology	Asphyxia	340	215
	Deaf	879	-
	Asthma	-	182

4.2   Classifiers Used

Experiments were performed using the *10*-fold cross-validation method

Convolutional Neural Network (CNN): It was trained using the sigmoid activation function. It employes 5 convolutional layers, each with output 16, 64, 64, 16, and 16, respectively, with kernel size of 3 × 3. Each convolutional layer was followed by max-pooling of 2 and ReLU function. 2 fully-connected layers were employed with a dropout of 0.25. The details are shown in Table 2.

Gaussian Mixture Model (GMM): This paper employs a conventional classifier, the Gaussian Mixture Model (GMM), in its methodology. To train the Baby Chilanto dataset, 512 Gaussian mixtures were utilized, while the DA-IICT infant cry dataset, having a smaller dataset size, used 128 Gaussian mixtures. A Gaussian Mixture Model comprises a combination of Gaussian probability density functions (*pdf*) characterized by sets of mean vectors, covariance matrices, and mixture weights for each constituent Gaussian component. When describing a random vector, denoted as y_n, represented by N Gaussian components with mean vectors μ_g and covariance matrices Σ_g, where $g = 1, 2, ..., P$ denotes the component indices, the *pdf* of y_n is expressed as [6]:

$$f(y_n|\alpha) = \sum_{g=1}^{P} \pi_g N(y_n|\mu_g, \Sigma_g),$$

(5)

Table 2. CNN Architecture.

Output Size	Description
(39,893,16)	LFCC
(19,446,16)	convolution layer, 16 filters, BN, relu
(19,446,16)	max-pooling, (2,2), dropout (0.25)
(19,446,32)	convolution layer, 32 filters, BN, relu
(9,223,32)	max-pooling, (2,2), dropout (0.25)
(9,223,64)	convolution layer, 64 filters, BN, relu
(4,111,64)	max-pooling, (2,2), dropout (0.25)
(4,111,16)	convolution layer, 16 filters, BN, relu
(4,111,16)	dropout (0.25)
(4,111,16)	convolution layer, 16 filters, BN, relu
(4,111,16)	dropout (0.25), followed by flattening
128	dense layer, relu
64	dense layer, relu
64	dropout (0.25)
1	dense, sigmoid

Here, π_g represents the weight of the gth mixture component. We define the Gaussian Mixture Model as $\alpha = (\pi_g, \mu_g, \Sigma_g | g = 1...P)$. To calculate the likelihood of a feature vector given this GMM, we can utilize Eq. (5). In the speech literature, it is a common assumption that acoustic feature vectors are *statistically-independent* [16]. Consequently, for a sequence of feature vectors denoted as $Y = (y_n | n \in 1, ..., Z)$, the probability of observing these features given the GMM can be approximated as described in [6]:

$$p(Y|\alpha) = \prod_{n=1}^{Z} p(y_n|\alpha). \qquad (6)$$

Typically, GMM training involves the Expectation Maximization (EM) algorithm [9], which is an iterative process aimed at improving the likelihood of the data with respect to the model.

4.3 Baseline Used

The performance of the proposed LFRCC feature set was compared with state-of-the-art feature sets, namely, MFCC and LFCC. 39-D MFCC and 39-D LFCC features were extracted using a window length of 30 ms and window overlap of 15 ms. Each containing 13-D static + 13-Δ + 13-$\Delta\Delta$ features.

5   Experimental Results

In this subSection, we discuss the results and analysis obtained by the effect of
LP order, mismatched *vs.* matched conditions.

5.1   Spectrographic Analysis

Figure 2(a) shows the narrowband spectrogram of normal infant cry, whereas
Fig. 2(b) shows the normal spectrogram of corresponding LP residual. Figure 3
presents similar analysis for pathological infant cry. It can be clearly observed
that LP residual captures the voicing information (i.e., presence and absence
of glottal vibrations or glottal activity) because the spectrogram of LP residual
follows the pitch source harmonics of spectrogram of any signal, implying LP
residual signal will have impulse-like excitation pulses whenever glottis closes
suddenly, because it is the sudden closure of glottis that excites the real physical
system (i.e., vocal tract system). For particular, LP residual becomes maximum
at the instant of glottal closure as the LP model is capable to predict cry signal
as time series unless and until excitation pulse travel in vocal tract system.

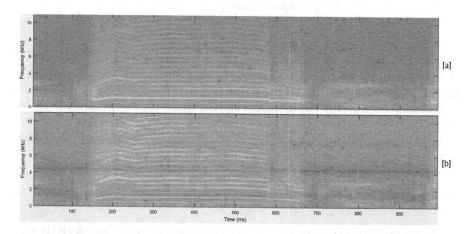

Fig. 2. Spectrogram of [a] original healthy infant cry, and [b] spectrogram of LP residual
of healthy infant cry sound.

5.2   Effect of LP Order

In this sub-section, we present the results obtained by varying LP order during LFRCC feature extraction. Figure 4 shows the effect of LP order on both
datasets. It can be observed from Fig. 4 that % classification accuracy decreases
as we increase the LP order. The results at LP orders 2 and 3 were less and

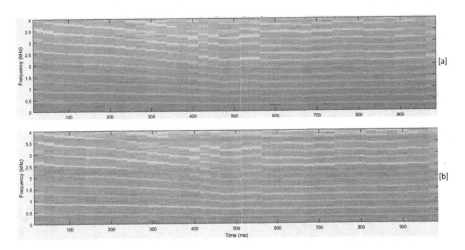

Fig. 3. Spectrogram of [a] original pathology infant cry, and [b] spectrogram of LP residual of pathology infant cry sound.

then the accuracy increased at LP order 4 and decreased after that. The optimal results are obtained keeping LP order 4, where we get 99.03% and 91.50% accuracy on Baby Chilanto and DA-IICT datasets, respectively. Thus, excitation source modeling is not working for higher LP order as the vocal tract system for babies is very small as compared to adults and has less mass of the vocal folds. Hence, for infants, the glottal cycle (i.e., it consists of closed phase, open phase, and return phase) is of relatively lesser duration ($\sim$1–2 ms) as compared to adults and the contextual information is not needed for infant cry analysis and the higher order predictor memory might confuse the model. Further, may be due to the fact for lesser LP order, LP filter (i.e., H(z)) captures less information and hence, more information remains in the LP residual resulting in better classification for lower LP orders. Further, due to the much lesser length of the vocal tract (around 5 cm), lesser predictor memory is required to model it [5].

5.3   Results for Matched Conditions

Table 3 shows the classification accuracy of proposed LFRCC features on GMM and CNN classifiers. From Table 3, it can be inferred that LFRCC gives comparable results with baseline MFCC and LFCC (99.21% and 91.83% for Baby Chillato and DA-IICT corpus, respectively). LFRCC outperforms MFCC and LFCC by 0.78% and 0.27%, respectively. This is because LFRCC, being excitation source-based features, it is able to identify the difference in characteristics of glottal airflow used for cry production for different pathologies. The increase in number of training and testing samples also help in classifying cries better.

Table 3 shows that the results from deep neural network-based CNN classifier, where the proposed LFRCC feature set outperforms MFCC and LFCC by 0.77% and 4.12%, respectively, for DA-IICT corpus. Infant cries have high pitched

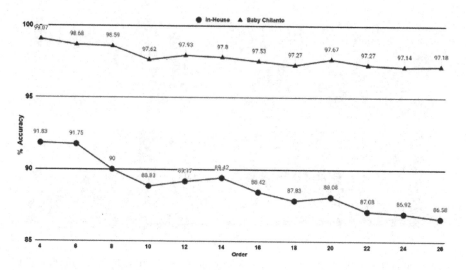

Fig. 4. Effect of LP order for LFRCC using GMM classifier on both Baby Chilanto, and In-house DA-IICT corpora.

cries, which results in greater spectral-roll of factor [16]. This results in the rich discriminative acoustic cues in the lower frequency regions. MFCC having better spectral resolution in lower frequency regions than LFCC, resulting in better performance of MFCC than LFCC. These results indicate that the excitation source-based features help in binary classification of infant cry because the glottal airflow needed for different cry category is of different characteristics, and thus, indicating its potential for this study.

Table 3. Classification Accuracy (%) of MFCC, LFCC, and LFRCC on GMM and CNN Classifier Structures.

DataSet	Classifier	MFCC	LFCC	LFRCC
Baby Chillanto	**GMM**	99.47	99.25	**99.21**
	CNN	98.59	97.88	**97.02**
DA-IICT	**GMM**	95.75	94.75	**91.83**
	CNN	87.91	84.56	**88.08**
Combined	**GMM**	96.43	96.96	**97.23**
	CNN	97.12	97.56	**98.23**

5.4   Results for Mismatched Database

Table 4 highlights the classification accuracy for cross-database (CD) or mismatched conditions. Here, CD1 implies training with Baby Chilanto dataset and testing on DA-IICT dataset. In CD2, training is done on DA-IICT dataset, and testing on Baby Chilanto database. It can be observed from Table 4 that the proposed LFRCC features work well for cross-database classification. For CD1, LFRCC gave the best performance as all the categories of cries on testing were present in training (normal, asphyxia, and asthma), which helps in classification as the proposed features captured the breathing and in turn, the sound production (cry) better for all the classes. The classification accuracy drops to 56.34% in LFRCC because, the proposed feature is capable of extracting the excitation source-based information and the categories of cries used in testing (hunger, pain, deaf) are different than that used in training. MFCC does not perform well as it is based on human sound perception and the cries used have minimal difference when heard thus, making it difficult to differentiate. These observations prove that LFRCC features can be used for real-life infant cry analysis as in real-life setup, it is highly likely that the training and testing samples will be different.

Table 4. Classification Accuracy (%) of MFCC, LFCC, and LFRCC using GMM Classifier.

Database	MFCC	LFCC	LFRCC
CD1	31.08	39.67	**60.50**
CD2	35.95	59.74	56.34

CD1: Train = Baby Chillanto, Test = DA-IICT CD2: Train = DA-IICT, Test = Baby Chillanto

6   Summary and Conclusion

In this study, LFRCC, a feature based on the excitation source, was employed for infant cry classification. For performance comparison, vocal tract-based cepstral features, namely, MFCC and LFCC were also used. The objective was to utilize the complementary information obtained from excitation source-based features to enhance infant cry classification. The results demonstrated comparable performance with traditional state-of-the-art (MFCC and LFCC) features. LFRCC proved particularly valuable for cross-database classification due to its focus on the source (glottal airflow) required for sound (cry) production. Its ability to distinguish cries that are generally difficult for humans and auditory-based spectral features to differentiate, and thus, served as the motivation for this study. Future research will explore score-level, classifier-level, and feature-level data fusion strategies to investigate the potential complementary information captured by LFRCC beyond MFCC or LFCC alone. However, to best of our knowledge, the Baby Chilanto database remains the only available corpus with pathological infant cries for infant cry classification research. Hence, evaluating the performance in cross-database scenarios, as conducted in our study, becomes crucial and more so, practically relevant. This evaluation highlights the need and importance of developing a new In-House corpus dedicated to infant cry research. More so, the development of Application Programming Interfaces (APIs) for infant cry classification systems, as well as real-time data acquisition, presents open research questions. Creating efficient and user-friendly APIs is crucial to enable the seamless integration of infant cry classification technology into various applications and platforms. Further one of the limitations of this work could be LFRCC applies only the linear relations in the sequence of samples which may not completely characterize the chaotic characteristics of pathological infant cries. For this, our future research efforts will be directed toward exploring the significance of number prediction using the Volterra-Weiner, polynomial to capture possible hidden nonlinear relations that may help in infant cry classification.

Acknowledgements. The authors would like to express their heartfelt gratitude to several entities for their invaluable contributions to this research. First and foremost, we extend our thanks to the National Institute of Astrophysics and Optical Electronics and CONACYT Mexico for graciously providing access to the Baby Chilanto database, which played a pivotal role in our statistical analyses. We are also deeply appreciative of the Ministry of Electronics and Information Technology (MeitY), New Delhi, Government of India, for their generous sponsorship of the consortium project titled 'BHASHINI,' with the subtitle 'Building Assistive Speech Technologies for the Challenged' (Grant ID: 11(1)2022-HCC (TDIL)).

Furthermore, we would like to acknowledge the leadership of Prof. Hema A. Murthy and Prof. S. Umesh from IIT Madras, who spearheaded the consortium project. Their guidance and expertise have been instrumental in shaping this research endeavor. Lastly, we extend our gratitude to the authorities at DA-IICT Gandhinagar, India, for their unwavering support and collaboration throughout the course of this study.

References

1. Baby Crying Analyzer. http://www.showeryourbaby.com/whycrbacran1.html/. Accessed 25 Nov 2022
2. Baby Pod. https://babypod.net/en/babypod-device/. Accessed 25 Nov 2022
3. Alaie, H.F., Abou-Abbas, L., Tadj, C.: Cry-based infant pathology classification using GMMs. Speech Commun. **77**, 28–52 (2016)
4. Armbrüster, L., Mende, W., Gelbrich, G., Wermke, P., Götz, R., Wermke, K.: Musical intervals in infants' spontaneous crying over the first 4 months of life. Folia Phoniatr. Logop. **73**(5), 401–412 (2021)
5. Atal, B.S., Hanauer, S.L.: Speech analysis and synthesis by linear prediction of the speech wave. J. Acoust. Soc. Am. (JASA) **50**(2B), 637–655 (1971)
6. Bishop, C.M.: Pattern Recognition and Machine Learning. Information Science and Statistics (ISS). Springer, New York (2006)
7. Buddha, N., Patil, H.A.: Corpora for analysis of infant cry. In: Oriental COCOSDA, Vietnam (2007)
8. Chittora, A., Patil, H.A.: Data collection of infant cries for research and analysis. J. Voice **31**(2), 252.e15–252.e26 (2017)

9. Dempster, A.P., Laird, N.M., Rubin, D.B.: Maximum likelihood from incomplete data via the EM algorithm. J. Roy. Stat. Soc. Ser. B (Methodol.) **39**(1), 1–22 (1977)

10. Engelsma, J.J., Deb, D., Cao, K., Bhatnagar, A., Sudhish, P.S., Jain, A.K.: Infant-ID: fingerprints for global good. IEEE Trans. Pattern Anal. Mach. Intell. **44**(7), 3543–3559 (2021)

11. Esposito, G., Venuti, P.: Understanding early communication signals in autism: a study of the perception of infants' cry. J. Intellect. Disabil. Res. **54**(3), 216–223 (2010)

12. Gupta, P., Patil, H.A.: Linear frequency residual cepstral features for replay spoof detection on ASVSpoof 2019. In: 2022 30th European Signal Processing Conference (EUSIPCO), pp. 349–353. IEEE (2022)

13. Makhoul, J.: Linear prediction: a tutorial review. Proc. IEEE **63**(4), 561–580 (1975)

14. Mehler, J., Jusczyk, P., Lambertz, G., Halsted, N., Bertoncini, J., Amiel-Tison, C.: A precursor of language acquisition in young infants. Cognition **29**(2), 143–178 (1988)

15. Onu, C.C., et al.: Ubenwa: cry-based diagnosis of birth asphyxia. In: 31st Conference on Neural Information Processing Systems (NIPS), Long Beach, CA (2017)

16. Quatieri, T.F.: Discrete-Time Speech Signal Processing: Principles and Practice, 1st edn. Pearson Education India (2015)

17. Reyes-Galaviz, O.F., Cano-Ortiz, S.D., Reyes-García, C.A.: Evolutionary-neural system to classify infant cry units for pathologies identification in recently born babies. In: 2008 Seventh Mexican International Conference on Artificial Intelligence, 27–31 October 2008, Atizapan De Zaragoza, Mexico, pp. 330–335. IEEE (2008)

18. Reyes-Galaviz, O.F., Cano-Ortiz, S.D., Reyes-García, C.A.: Validation of the cry unit as primary element for cry analysis using an evolutionary-neural approach. In: 2008 Mexican International Conference on Computer Science, pp. 261–267 (2008)

19. Tak, H., Patil, H.A.: Novel linear frequency residual cepstral features for replay attack detection. In: INTERSPEECH, Hyderabad, India, September 2018, pp. 726–730 (2018)

20. Xie, Q., Ward, R.K., Laszlo, C.A.: Automatic assessment of infants' levels-of-distress from the cry signals. IEEE Trans. Speech Audio Process. **4**(4), 253–265 (1996)

Speech Processing for Medicine

Identification of Voice Disorders: A Comparative Study of Machine Learning Algorithms

Sharal Coelho$^{(\boxtimes)}$ and Hosahalli Lakshmaiah Shashirekha

Mangalore University, Mangalore, India
sharalmucs@gmail.com, hlsrekha@mangaloreuniversity.ac.in

Abstract. A voice disorder is a state that influences the quality, loudness, or pitch of a person's voice. Classifying voice disorders automatically by non-invasive methods can help doctors to diagnose voice disorders quickly and more effectively. Machine Learning (ML) algorithms play a role of non-invasive methods to automatically classify the voice disorders using voice samples. This study compares different ML algorithms trained with spectral features for the classification of voice samples as healthy or pathological. The experiments are conducted using the sustained samples of the vowel /a/ of healthy and disordered voice, selected from Saarbruecken Voice Database (SVD). As the selected subset is imbalanced, various resampling methods are explored to balance the dataset. The performance of the classifiers are evaluated in terms of accuracy, precision, recall, and F1-score. Among the proposed models, Random Forest (RF) and Extreme Gradient Boosting (XGBoost) algorithms resampled with SMOTE-ENN have shown very promising accuracies of 0.902 and 0.906, respectively.

Keywords: Machine Learning · Non-Invasive Approach · Voice Disorders · Spectral Features · Imbalance Data

1 Introduction

Voice pathology also known as voice disorder is a medical condition that arises due to the paralysis of vocal cords, swelling, drug addiction, or inappropriate use of voice [6]. This results in unstable pitch, loudness, and inappropriate quality of voice generated by the larynx, which affects the way one speaks. Individuals and professionals such as lawyers, singers, and teachers, who use their voice regularly and at a higher volume than average run the danger of developing pathological vocal issues. People who struggle with voice disorders will have a hard time in clearly expressing their views, opinions, or feelings with others. As a result, such people may experience insecurity, anxiety, and sadness, leading to serious problems.

Traditionally, the diagnosis of voice disorders is carried out by invasive procedures (laryngeal endoscopy and stroboscopy) as advised by doctors [29]. These

A. Karpov et al. (Eds.): SPECOM 2023, LNAI 14338, pp. 565–578, 2023.
https://doi.org/10.1007/978-3-031-48309-7_45

procedures necessitate the use of skilled clinicians and specialized equipment which are expensive. Added to this, the results of the personal inspection process of an individual may vary depending upon the interpretation of the findings by the doctors. This has led to the development of non-invasive approaches that help in diagnosing the voice pathologies based on the voice samples of an individual. Non-invasive approaches are beneficial to individuals as they do not come in contact directly with an individual as opposed to invasive approaches and also minimize the healthcare cost and waiting time for the clinical results. Hence, these approaches can act as an assistive tool for doctors to speed up the diagnosis of voice pathologies more effectively.

Sustained vowel samples, audio recordings of reading standardized texts, speech utterances, and conversational speech samples of individuals are the resources used as voice samples for the identification of voice pathologies. While sustained vowel sample is a sound of the vowel /a/, /i/, or /u/ in a single deep breath by an individual in a certain pitch, speech utterance is a spoken expression of a word or phrase produced by an individual. Samples at various pitch levels aid in comprehending the pitch variations associated with voice disorders. Both sustained vowel samples and speech utterances are used for speech assessments and speech therapy sessions. Compared to speech utterances, sustained vowel recordings are more stable and require fewer articulatory movements, making the analysis of acoustic features simpler. Also, speech utterances can vary significantly in length, making it difficult to compare with other recordings. Sustained vowels are typically recorded for a fixed duration ensuring that the data collected is consistent across samples. The samples with different pitches represent different fundamental frequency distributions. When a voice has a low pitch, the vocal fold vibrations are deep or have a low frequency. On the other hand, a voice with a high pitch has comparatively high vocal fold vibrational frequencies. Low-high-low pitch potentially refers to a voice that modulates between low, high, and low pitches. Normal pitch voice falls within the regular pitch range.

Voice features provide a unique representation of the speech signals, capturing different aspects of the signal such as voice quality, intonation, spectral features, spectrogram, prosody, etc. These features which act as the characteristic features of the voice samples can be used for the identification of voice pathologies. The spectral properties (amplitude, bandwidth, fundamental frequency, and frequency range) illustrate how signal information is distributed across different frequencies and provide useful insights into the nature of the signal. Spectral features are numerical representations derived from deviations in the spectral properties of speech signals and they include spectral centroid, Mel-frequency Cepstral Coefficients (MFCCs), Zero Crossing Rate (ZCR), Root-Mean-Square (RMS), spectral flatness, spectral bandwidth, etc.

ML approaches play the role of non-invasive approaches in addressing the challenges of identifying voice pathologies using voice samples. The ML framework for the identification of voice pathologies using voice samples include preprocessing the voice samples, and extracting the voice features to train the ML models. The trained models are then used to identify whether the given voice sample is pathological or not.

The goal of this study is to distinguish between healthy and pathological voice samples by extracting the spectral features (MFCCs, ZCR, spectral roll-off, spectral centroid, spectral contrast, mel spectrogram, and chroma) from sustained samples of the vowel /a/, to train the ML models (AdaBoost, Bagging classifier, Gradient Boosting (GBoosting), Multi-layer Perceptron (MLP), k-Nearest Neighbors (kNN), Logistic Regression (LR), Decision Tree (DT), RF, and XGBoost). The experiments are carried out on the subset of SVD [4] created by selecting the voice samples of vowel /a/ at normal, low, high, and low-high-low pitches of healthy and few voice disorders (Psychogene Dysphonie, Hyperfunktionelle Dysphonie, Laryngitis, Reinke Ödem, Dysarthrophonie). The distinctive characteristics of the voice samples of these disorders help to distinguish between healthy and pathological voice disorders.

The subset of the SVD dataset created consists of more pathological samples than healthy samples making the dataset imbalanced and imbalanced data may affect the performance of the classifier. Hence, the data imbalance problem is addressed by resampling techniques (Synthetic Minority Oversampling Technique (SMOTE), Borderline-SMOTE, Adaptive Synthetic Sampling (ADASYN), and SMOTE-Edited Nearest Neighbor (SMOTE-ENN)).

The rest of the paper is organized as follows: Information in Sect. 2 relates to earlier research works while Sect. 3 describes the methodology followed by the experiments and results in Sect. 4. The paper ends with a conclusion in Sect. 5.

2 Related Work

The use of ML algorithms to identify voice disorders has increased significantly [17]. Researchers have explored several datasets (SVD, Massachusetts Eye and Ear Infirmary (MEEI) [2], and Arabic Voice Pathology Database (AVPD) [20]), several voice features (spectral roll-off, spectral centroid [16], spectral contrast, chroma, MFCCs [18], and ZCR) and several classifiers (RF [27], kNN [7], Support Vector Machine (SVM) [21], and Gaussian Mixture Models (GMM) [26]) for identifying the voice pathologies. Most of the voice pathology identification systems make use of sustained voice samples (vowel sounds of /a/, /i/, and /u/). A brief description of the works that are relevant to this study is given below:

Al-Nasheri et al. [3] used only sustained samples of vowel /a/ produced at a normal pitch corresponding to three voice pathologies (vocal fold cysts, vocal fold polyps, and unilateral vocal fold paralysis) from MEEI, SVD, and AVPD datasets. By implementing autocorrelation and entropy approaches to extract informative features to train the SVM classifier to classify the pathological voice samples, they obtained classification accuracies of 99.54%, 99.53%, and 96.02% for MEEI, SVD, and AVPD, respectively. Online Sequential Extreme Learning Machine (OSELM) algorithm proposed by AL-Dhief et al., [1] for detecting voice pathologies using MFCC features extracted from 600 samples of vowel /a/ belonging to SVD, obtained accuracy, sensitivity, and specificity of 85%,

87%, and 87%, respectively. The findings imply that the OSELM algorithm offer promising results for detecting voice pathology.

Gupta [11] employed 33 features corresponding to MFCC, spectral contrast, spectral centroid, and chroma features, to train Long Short Term Memory (LSTM) model and obtained sensitivity, specificity, and average recall of 22%, 97%, and 56% respectively. They used a private dataset consisting of sustained vowel sound recordings of both healthy and pathological individuals provided by the Far Eastern Memorial Hospital (FEMH) voice disorder database. Syed et al. [23] performed a comparative analysis of two Neural Network (NN) architectures - Convolutional NN (CNN) and Recurrent NN (RNN), on pathological samples corresponding to Balbuties, Dysphonie, Funktionelle Dysphonie, and Spasmodische Dysphonie disorders. From these samples, they extracted MFCC, pitch, ZCR, energy entropy, spectral flux, roll-off, spectral centroid, and energy, to train NN models. Using 10-fold cross-validation, they obtained accuracies of 87.11% and 86.52%, for CNN and RNN respectively. In another study, Syed et al. [22] used ML algorithms for identifying voice pathologies (Laryngitis, Cyst, Non-fluency syndrome, and Dysphonia) using speech samples from the SVD. For four ML classifiers: SVM, Naïve Bayes (NB), DT, and ensemble, they obtained accuracies of 93.18%, 99.45%, 100%, and 51% respectively.

From the audio and EGG signals in the SVD, Omeroglu et al. [21] extracted hand-crafted features (MFCC, Linear Predictive Coefficients (LPC), F0 (pitch), spectral slope) and using CNN they extracted deep features to identify the voice disorders. By using InfoGainAttributeEval they obtained a subset of the features extracted and used them to train SVM model. This arrangement helped them to obtain an accuracy of 90.10%. Fan et al. [9] has addressed the class imbalance problem of speech samples in the MEEI database using SMOTE, Borderline-SMOTE, and ADASYN. Fuzzy Clustering (FC)-SMOTE algorithm proposed by Fan et al. [10] to handle imbalanced dataset of different types of pathological voices, outperformed SMOTE, Borderline-SMOTE, and ADASYN, and the RF model for classification of voice samples obtained recall and specificity of 1.00 and 1.00 respectively.

The related work illustrates that, many ML algorithms are used for the identification of voice pathologies. However, different studies use different voice disorders and different features. This gives scope to explore different features and different classifiers to identify the voice disorders.

3   Methodology

The proposed methodology for the identification of voice disorders using sustained samples of vowel /a/ includes: i) Preprocessing, ii) Feature Extraction, and iii) Model Building. The framework of the ML approach is shown in Fig. 1 and a description of the steps are given below:

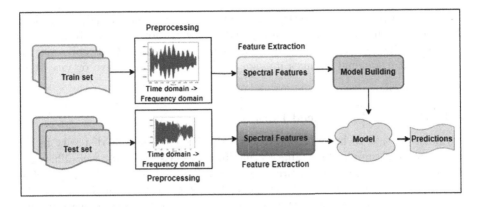

Fig. 1. Framework of Machine Learning approach

3.1 Preprocessing

The sustained vowel samples are converted from time domain to frequency domain as speech signals in the frequency domain provide frequency distribution of the speech signals which is important for examining the frequency components to detect voice disorders. If the audio samples have higher sample rate, they are resampled to a lower sample rate as lowering the sample rate decreases the amount of data that is required to be processed and analyzed.

3.2 Feature Extraction

One of the most important steps in the ML framework is feature extraction [15] which extracts the features from the given data. The pathological voice samples are characterized by more irregular spectral properties as compared to healthy voice samples and these irregularities can be captured by the spectral features. Spectral roll-off, spectral centroid, spectral contrast, mel spectrogram, chroma, MFCCs, and ZCR features are the spectral features extracted from the given voice signals. MFCC is a spectral feature that captures irregularities or variations in the spectral properties of the voice signals from voice signals even if the voice samples consist of noise. Due to this MFCCs are widely used in speech and audio signal processing [25].

Pathological voice samples are characterized by pitch breaks, fluctuation, or pitch range limitations due to disturbances or irregularities in the vocal production process. Such pitch information of the speech signals affected by the voice pathologies can be identified by chroma feature [28]. They provide the pitch deviations of speech signal, aiding in the identification of abnormalities. Spectral centroid captures the changes in an abnormal voice by providing the single value of the center of mass of the speech signal's spectrum [22]. Spectral roll-off focuses on the distribution of energy in the frequency domain. Spectral contrast is useful for detecting spectral changes in speech signal and is often used for classifying voice disorders [11]. Hoarseness and roughness are common conditions of pathological voices caused by polyps or other laryngeal disorders. These conditions can cause irregular vocal fold vibrations, leading to increased changes in the speech signal, resulting in higher ZCR values. ZCR represents the rate at which a signal changes its sign from positive to negative or vice versa over time.

3.3 Handling Imbalanced Data

A dataset is said to be imbalanced when there is considerable disparity in the distribution of samples belonging to the different classes in a dataset. This data imbalance may affect the performance of classifiers favoring the majority class and hence, the imbalanced dataset has to be balanced. The imbalanced data is balanced either by increasing the samples of the minority class by oversampling techniques or by decreasing the samples of the majority class by undersampling techniques. These techniques together are referred as resampling techniques. SMOTE, Borderline-SMOTE, ADASYN, and SMOTE-ENN are the common resampling techniques used to balance the imbalanced data. SMOTE enhances the random oversampling to decrease the possibility of overfitting, but sometimes leads to overgeneralization [5]. Borderline-SMOTE is an extension of SMOTE that concentrates on the borderline samples of the minority class [13]. Near the decision boundary, borderline samples are more likely to be incorrectly identified by a classifier. For minority class, ADASYN generates synthetic samples with a focus on the samples that are challenging to categorize properly. For those instances of the minority class that are situated in regions of the feature space where the class overlap with the majority class is substantial, it adaptively creates more synthetic samples [14]. By emphasizing these areas, ADASYN makes it easier for the classifier to distinguish between the two classes. The SMOTE-ENN method combines the ability of SMOTE to generate synthetic examples for the minority class and the ability of ENN to remove some observations from both classes that are identified as having different classes between the observation's class and its kNN majority class.

The dataset created from the SVD is imbalanced. Hence, experiments are conducted with SMOTE, Borderline-SMOTE, ADASYN, and SMOTE-ENN, to balance the dataset and the balanced data is used to train the ML models for identification of voice disorders.

3.4 Model Building

The model performance is strongly influenced by the dataset [21], the features, and the classifiers used. AdaBoost, Bagging classifier, GBoosting, DT, MLP, kNN, LR, RF, and XGBoost models are explored for the identification of voice disorders. A brief description of these classifiers is given below:

AdaBoost is an ensemble ML algorithm that is used to classify the given data by converging multiple base learners into strong learners. Bagging classifier[1] also uses an ensemble approach to increase the predictive accuracy by

---

[1] https://www.geeksforgeeks.org/ml-bagging-classifier/.

training numerous base learners (e.g., DT) on different subsets of the train set and then combining their predictions to create a final classification. DT consists of decision nodes to make the decisions for classification based on the features of the given dataset. kNN[2] is a simple ML classifier that stores the training set and categorizes new data based on similarity. MLP is a model consisting of multiple layers and the nodes of the layers are neurons with nonlinear activation functions. There may be one or more nonlinear hidden layers between the input and the output layer. LR model provides a simple approach for predicting the probability of given input belonging to a certain class.

XGBoost is an ML algorithm that belongs to the category of GBoosting algorithms. Due to its exceptional performance and adaptability, it is frequently used for classification tasks. It is an ensemble learning technique that iteratively aggregates the predictions of various weak learners. RF is the most used ML classifier that employs a modified tree learning algorithm and examines a random subset of the features at each learning split.

4   Experiments and Results

4.1   Dataset Description

SVD is a collection of speech and EGG samples of more than 2000 speakers (healthy and voice pathological individuals) consisting of the recordings of the sentence "Guten Morgen, wie geht es Ihnen?" ("Good morning, how are you?") and sustained vowel samples of /a/, /i/, and /u/ recorded at normal, high, low, and low-high-low pitches.

Table 1. Statistics of the dataset before and after balancing

	Imbalanced Data	Balanced Data
Healthy samples	868	1299
Pathological samples	1299	1299
Total	2167	2598

In this work, speech signals of only sustained vowel /a/ with normal, low, low-high-low, and high pitches, for healthy and selected voice disorder (Psychogene Dysphonie, Hyperfunktionelle Dysphonie, Laryngitis, Reinke Ödem, Dysarthrophonie) samples available in SVD are used. Psychogene Dysphonie disorder (Psychogenic Dysphonia) [19] causes hoarseness or difficulty in speaking without any observable physical or structural abnormalities in the vocal cords. Hyperfunktionelle Dysphonie disorder (Hyperfunctional Dysphonia) [12] is the one in which the vocal apparatus is not used properly during speech production resulting in extreme muscle strain. Laryngitis disorder [8] is characterised by swelling and

---

[2] https://www.javatpoint.com/k-nearest-neighbor-algorithm-for-machine-learning.

inflammation of the vocal cords. Due to the vocal cords' reduced capacity to efficiently vibrate and produce sound, it frequently causes hoarseness or complete voice loss. Reinke-Ödem disorder (Reinke's Edema) [24] is a particular kind of condition of the vocal cords that is characterized by swelling and fluid buildup in Reinke's space, a gelatinous layer of the vocal cords. Dysarthrophonie (Dysarthrophonia) is a voice disorder due to poor muscle control and coordination of the speech-producing muscles. Figure 2 and 3 illustrate waveforms of the speech signals of healthy and pathological samples respectively at four pitches.

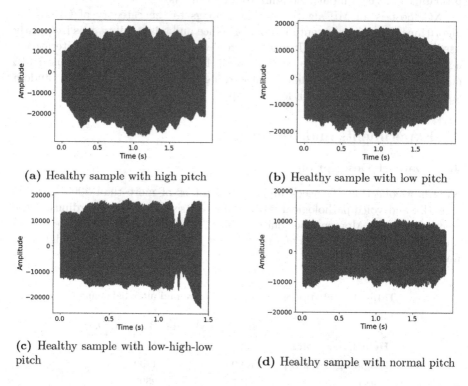

(a) Healthy sample with high pitch

(b) Healthy sample with low pitch

(c) Healthy sample with low-high-low pitch

(d) Healthy sample with normal pitch

Fig. 2. Waveforms of healthy voice samples at different pitches

Spectral features of the speech signals are extracted using Librosa[3] library and to balance the dataset, imbalanced-learn library[4] is used. To oversample the minority class (healthy class), the sampling strategy parameter is set to 'auto' while instantiating the oversampling algorithm (SMOTE) and the random state parameter which sets a seed value to control the randomness is set to 42, allowing consistent results which is crucial for comparisons and debugging. Table 1 gives the statistics of the dataset before and after applying the resampling techniques.

---

[3] https://librosa.org/doc/main/index.html.
[4] https://imbalanced-learn.org/stable/.

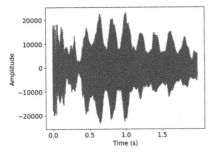

(a) Pathological sample with high pitch

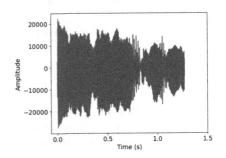

(b) Pathological sample with low pitch

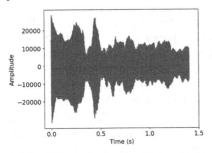

(c) Pathological sample with low-high-low pitch

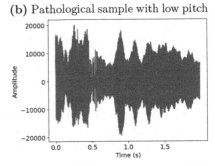

(d) Pathological sample with normal pitch

Fig. 3. Waveforms of pathological voice samples at different pitches

4.2 Results

The performances of the ML models with and without resampling techniques, measured in terms of accuracies are shown in Fig. 4. The results clearly indicate that the accuracies of all the classifiers has not crossed 76% for imbalanced data as the models failed to classify the minority class samples, leading to a high number of false negatives. After applying the resampling techniques to balance the class distribution, the accuracies of the models have improved significantly, reaching upto 90%.

As RF and XGBoost models have performed better than other ML models, fine-tuning the hyperparameters is applied only for these two models to improve the performance further. n_estimator is a hyperparameter used in ensemble learning methods, like RF and XGBoost, to limit the number of DTs constructed by the ensemble model. Experiments are conducted by setting the n_estimators of RF model to 50, 100, and 150 and that of XGBoost model to 100, 150, 200, and 300.

Table 2. The parameters of fine-tuned ML models used in the proposed work

Classifier	Parameters
RF	{'bootstrap': True, 'class_weight': None, 'criterion': 'gini', 'max_depth': None, 'max_features': 'sqrt', 'n_estimators': 100}
XGBoost	{'objective': 'binary:logistic', 'learning_rate': 0.1, 'n_estimators': 200, 'random_state': 42,'tree_method': None}

The parameters and the values of the parameters used in RF and XGBoost models are shown in Table 2. For all the other parameters, the default values are used. The comparison of the performances of fine-tuned RF and XGBoost models with and without resampling techniques measured in terms of accuracies are shown in Fig. 5 and 6, respectively. The results obtained by XGBoost and RF models, with and without resampling techniques (SMOTE, ADASYN, Borderline-SMOTE, and SMOTE-ENN) are shown in Table 3. The results clearly indicates that SMOTE-ENN has performed better for balancing the data, with accuracies of 0.902 and 0.906 for XGBoost and RF models respectively.

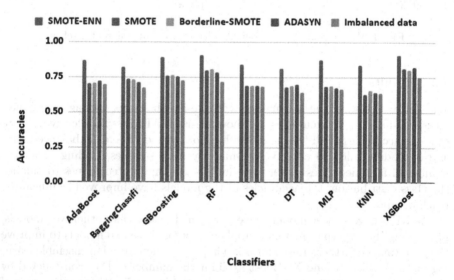

Fig. 4. Comparison of the performances of ML models with and without resampling techniques

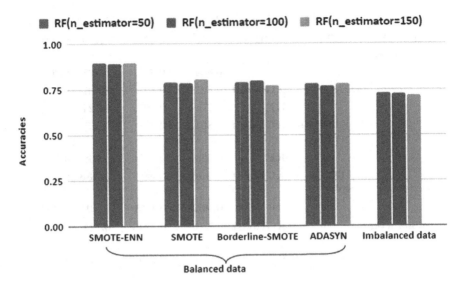

Fig. 5. Comparison of the performances of fine-tuned RF models with and without resampling techniques

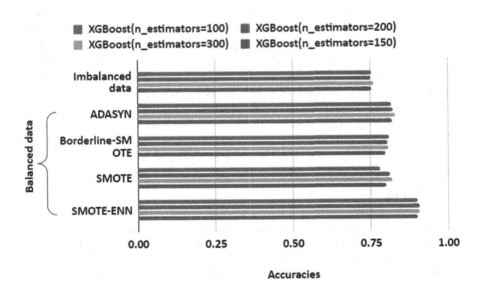

Fig. 6. Comparison of the performances of fine-tuned XGBoost models with and without resampling techniques

Table 3. Results of the XGBoost and RF models with resampling techniques

Data		Model	Accuracy	Precision	Recall	F1-score
Balanced data	SMOTE	XGBoost	0.810	0.831	0.789	0.809
		RF	0.804	0.829	0.777	0.802
	ADASYN	XGBoost	0.821	0.831	0.807	0.819
		RF	0.774	0.807	0.724	0.763
	Borderline-SMOTE	XGBoost	0.804	0.838	0.765	0.8
		RF	0.798	0.825	0.768	0.795
	SMOTE-ENN	XGBoost	**0.906**	**0.89**	**0.888**	**0.885**
		RF	**0.902**	**0.873**	**0.891**	**0.882**
Imbalanced data		XGBoost	0.750	0.773	0.824	0.798
		RF	0.726	0.740	0.836	0.785

5   Conclusion

This paper gives the comparative study of ML classifiers (AdaBoost, Bagging classifier, GBoosting, DT, MLP, kNN, LR, RF, and XGBoost) for the identification of voice samples as healthy or pathological and the resampling techniques (SMOTE, ADASYN, Borderline-SMOTE, and SMOTE-ENN) for balancing the imbalance data. The spectral features (MFCCs, ZCR, spectral roll-off, spectral centroid, spectral contrast, mel spectrogram, and chroma) are used to train the ML models and the algorithms are evaluated on the subset of SVD by considering sustained samples of vowel /a/ of healthy and selected voice disorders (Psychogene Dysphonie, Hyperfunktionelle Dysphonie, Laryngitis, Reinke Ödem, Dysarthrophonie). Among all the classifiers, RF and XGBoost model using SMOTE-ENN obtained accuracies of 0.906 and 0.902 respectively. Other voice features will be explored further by considering a larger dataset.

References

1. Al-Dhief, F.T., et al.: Voice pathology detection using machine learning technique. In: IEEE 5th International Symposium on Telecommunication Technologies (ISTT), pp. 99–104. IEEE (2020)
2. Al-Nasheri, A., et al.: An investigation of multidimensional voice program parameters in three different databases for voice pathology detection and classification. J. Voice **31**(1), 113.e9–113.e18 (2017)
3. Al-Nasheri, A., et al.: Voice pathology detection and classification using autocorrelation and entropy features in different frequency regions. IEEE Access **6**, 6961–6974 (2017)

4. Barry, W., Putzer, M.: Saarbrucken Voice Database. Institute of Phonetics, University of Saarland (2007)
5. Blagus, R., Lusa, L.: Smote for high-dimensional class-imbalanced data. BMC Bioinform. **14**, 1–16 (2013)
6. Cordeiro, H., Meneses, C., Fonseca, J.: Continuous speech classification systems for voice pathologies identification. In: Camarinha-Matos, L.M., Baldissera, T.A., Di Orio, G., Marques, F. (eds.) DoCEIS 2015. IAICT, vol. 450, pp. 217–224. Springer, Cham (2015). https://doi.org/10.1007/978-3-319-16766-4_23
7. Dahmani, M., Guerti, M.: Glottal signal parameters as features set for neurological voice disorders diagnosis using k-nearest neighbors (KNN). In: 2nd International Conference on Natural Language and Speech Processing (ICNLSP), pp. 1–5. IEEE (2018)
8. Dworkin, J.P.: Laryngitis: types, causes, and treatments. Otolaryngol. Clin. North Am. **41**(2), 419–436 (2008)
9. Fan, Z., Qian, J., Sun, B., Wu, D., Xu, Y., Tao, Z.: Modeling voice pathology detection using imbalanced learning. In: International Conference on Sensing, Measurement & Data Analytics in the Era of Artificial Intelligence (ICSMD), pp. 330–334. IEEE (2020)
10. Fan, Z., Wu, Y., Zhou, C., Zhang, X., Tao, Z.: Class-imbalanced voice pathology detection and classification using fuzzy cluster oversampling method. Appl. Sci. **11**(8), 3450 (2021)
11. Gupta, V.: Voice disorder detection using long short term memory (LSTM) model. arXiv preprint arXiv:1812.01779 (2018)
12. Guzman, M., Castro, C., Testart, A., Muñoz, D., Gerhard, J.: Laryngeal and pharyngeal activity during semioccluded vocal tract postures in subjects diagnosed with hyperfunctional dysphonia. J. Voice **27**(6), 709–716 (2013)
13. Han, H., Wang, W.-Y., Mao, B.-H.: Borderline-SMOTE: a new over-sampling method in imbalanced data sets learning. In: Huang, D.-S., Zhang, X.-P., Huang, G.-B. (eds.) ICIC 2005. LNCS, vol. 3644, pp. 878–887. Springer, Heidelberg (2005). https://doi.org/10.1007/11538059_91
14. He, H., Bai, Y., Garcia, E.A., Li, S.: ADASYN: adaptive synthetic sampling approach for imbalanced learning. In: IEEE International Joint Conference on Neural Networks (IEEE World Congress on Computational Intelligence), pp. 1322–1328. IEEE (2008)
15. Hegde, S., Shetty, S., Rai, S., Dodderi, T.: A survey on machine learning approaches for automatic detection of voice disorders. J. Voice **33**(6), 947.e11–947.e33 (2019)
16. Islam, R., Abdel-Raheem, E., Tarique, M.: A study of using cough sounds and deep neural networks for the early detection of COVID-19. Biomed. Eng. Adv. **3**, 100025 (2022)
17. Islam, R., Tarique, M., Abdel-Raheem, E.: A survey on signal processing based pathological voice detection techniques. IEEE Access **8**, 66749–66776 (2020)
18. Lee, J.N., Lee, J.Y.: An efficient SMOTE-based deep learning model for voice pathology detection. Appl. Sci. **13**(6), 3571 (2023)
19. Martins, R.H.G., Tavares, E.L.M., Ranalli, P.F., Branco, A., Pessin, A.B.B.: Psychogenic dysphonia: diversity of clinical and vocal manifestations in a case series. Braz. J. Otorhinolaryngol. **80**(6), 497–502 (2014)
20. Mesallam, T.A., et al.: Development of the Arabic voice pathology database and its evaluation by using speech features and machine learning algorithms. J. Healthc. Eng. **2017**, 1–13 (2017)

21. Omeroglu, A.N., Mohammed, H.M., Oral, E.A.: Multi-modal voice pathology detection architecture based on deep and handcrafted feature fusion. Eng. Sci. Technol. Int. J. **36**, 101148 (2022)
22. Syed, S., Rashid, M., Hussain, S., Imtiaz, A., Abid, H., Zahid, H.: Inter classifier comparison to detect voice pathologies. Math. Biosci. Eng. **18**(3), 2258–2273 (2021)
23. Syed, S.A., Rashid, M., Hussain, S., Zahid, H.: Comparative analysis of CNN and RNN for voice pathology detection. Biomed. Res. Int. **2021**, 1–8 (2021)
24. Tavaluc, R., Tan-Geller, M.: Reinke's edema. Otolaryngol. Clin. North Am. **52**(4), 627–635 (2019)
25. Tirronen, S., Kadiri, S.R., Alku, P.: Hierarchical multi-class classification of voice disorders using self-supervised models and glottal features. IEEE Open J. Sig. Process. **4**, 80–88 (2023)
26. Verde, L., De Pietro, G., Sannino, G.: Voice disorder identification by using machine learning techniques. IEEE Access **6**, 16246–16255 (2018)
27. Wu, Y., Zhou, C., Fan, Z., Wu, D., Zhang, X., Tao, Z.: Investigation and evaluation of glottal flow waveform for voice pathology detection. IEEE Access **9**, 30–44 (2020)
28. Zakariah, M., Ajmi Alotaibi, Y., Guo, Y., Tran-Trung, K., Elahi, M.M., et al.: An analytical study of speech pathology detection based on MFCC and deep neural networks. Comput. Math. Meth. Med. **2022**, 7814952 (2022)
29. Żurek, M., Jasak, K., Niemczyk, K., Rzepakowska, A.: Artificial intelligence in laryngeal endoscopy: systematic review and meta-analysis. J. Clin. Med. **11**(10), 2752 (2022)

Transfer Learning Using Whisper for Dysarthric Automatic Speech Recognition

Siddharth Rathod$^{(\boxtimes)}$ ⓓ, Monil Charola ⓓ, and Hemant A. Patil ⓓ

Dhirubhai Ambani Institute of Information and Communication Technology,
Gandhinagar, India
{siddharth_rathod,monil_charola,hemant_patil}@daiict.ac.in

Abstract. Dysarthria is a motor speech disorder that affects an individual's ability to articulate words, making speech recognition a challenging task. Automatic Speech Recognition (ASR) technologies have the potential to greatly benefit individuals with dysarthria by providing them with a means of communication through computing and portable digital devices. These technologies can serve as an interaction medium, enabling dysarthric patients to communicate with others and computers. In this paper, we propose a transfer learning approach using the Whisper model to develop a dysarthric ASR system. Whisper, Web-scale Supervised Pretraining for Speech Recognition, is a multi-tasking model trained on various speech-related tasks, such as speech transcription on various languages, speech translation, voice activity detection, language identification, etc. on a wide scale of 680,000 h of labeled audio data. Using the proposed Whisper-based approach, we have obtained an word recognition average accuracy of 59.78% using 155 words of UA-Speech Corpus, using the Bi-LSTM classifier model.

Keywords: Dysarthria · Encoder-decoder transformer · WSPSR (Whisper) · Automatic speech recognition (ASR)

1 Introduction

Dysarthria is a prevalent speech disorder characterized by impairment in the dynamic movements of the articulators and upper respiratory system, leading to difficulties in producing intelligible speech. The disorder arises from various neurological conditions, including cerebral palsy, muscular dystrophy, stroke, brain infection, brain injury, facial paralysis, tongue or throat muscular weakness, and nervous system disorders. These conditions result in a lack of coordination between the brain and the muscles involved in natural speech production mechanism, which makes it difficult for dysarthric patients to produce intelligible speech and hence, causing a range of speech disorders, including dysarthria, stuttering, apraxia, and dysprosody [5].

© The Author(s), under exclusive license to Springer Nature Switzerland AG 2023
A. Karpov et al. (Eds.): SPECOM 2023, LNAI 14338, pp. 579–589, 2023.
https://doi.org/10.1007/978-3-031-48309-7_46

Individuals with dysarthria often exhibit physical limitations that restrict their movements, resulting in challenges not only in interpersonal communication but also in accessing and interacting with various technological interfaces, such as keyboards, mouse, and smartphones. Consequently, the development of effective assistive technology solutions for individuals with dysarthria is critical to enhance their communication abilities and quality of life. Automatic Speech Recognition (ASR) is an innovative technology that has the potential to serve as an interface for dysarthric patients, for other individuals as well as technological devices [15]. ASR technology offers numerous benefits, such as enhanced accessibility, increased efficiency, and improved communication. By utilizing ASR, individuals with dysarthria can interact more easily with various technological interfaces and devices. Moreover, the integration of ASR technology into Internet of Things (IoT) devices can lead to a more seamless experience for dysarthric individuals with debilitated physical conditions and thus brings individuals with dysarthria into mainstreamed society.

ASR tasks can be classified into three main categories based on the speaker's characteristics. The first category is the Speaker Independent (SI) system, which is a general system capable of recognizing any speech input without considering the speaker's identity. The second category is the Speaker Dependent (SD) system, which is designed to cater to specific dysarthric individuals, and the models are trained accordingly. Finally, the third category is the Speaker Adaptive (SA) system, which involves fine-tuning the SI system to work effectively for specific individuals or a specific set of individuals [10]. In [10], a novel approach was proposed for SI automatic speech recognition (ASR) systems that utilizes a hybrid speaker adaptation, based on maximum a posteriori (MAP) estimation and maximum likelihood linear regression (MLLR) technique, to enhance the traditional Hidden Markov Model (HMM) in the baseline ASR using Mel Frequency Cepstral Coefficients (MFCC) features along with Δ and $\Delta\Delta$ features. However, HMM-based approach for dysarthric ASR often yields poor performance. This is attributed to the significant variability present in dysarthric speech and the inadequacy of available data to train the ASR system effectively, and thus it poses a great technological challenge.

Recently, some end-to-end deep learning models have been employed, incorporating data augmentation and synthetic data generation techniques. For instance, in [11], an isolated speech dysarthric ASR was developed by leveraging visual features of words through a 2-dimensional Spatial Convolutional Neural Network (S-CNN). In this study, we propose a transfer learning approach utilizing the pre-trained Whisper model, an open source transformer encoder-decoder-based speech recognition model trained on a vast labeled speech data amounting to 680,000 h. As the whisper model is trained on very large amount of audio data, authors believe that better performance of proposed Whisper-based ASR system is due to capabilities to capture characteristics of natural *vs.* dysarthric speech.

The rest of the paper is organised as follows: Section 2 presents details of Whisper model and technical details of the proposed Whisper-based methodology. Section 3 gives details of the experimental setup used for this study, whereas Sect. 4 presents the analysis of results and related discussions. Finally Sect. 5 concludes the paper along with future research directions.

2 Proposed Work

This section provides background information on the open-source, pre-trained Whisper Model, a multilingual deep-learning model. This section also explores the various Whisper Model variations, classified according to their size. Furthermore, the employed pipeline used for this work is explained.

2.1 Introduction to Whisper

Whisper is an open-source, pre-trained model that utilizes sequence-to-sequence transformer encoder-decoder model similar to the one stated in [13], as its architectural foundation. It was recently released in September 2022, at https:// github.com/openai/whisper. Primarily, it is developed for multilingual and multitask ASR. Unlike its predecessors like *wav2vec 2.0* [3], which is pre-trained on unlabelled audio data, Whisper has been trained on vast amount of labelled audio transcription data. The name Whisper is derived from the acronym **WSPSR**, which represents **W**eb-scale **S**upervised **P**retraining for **S**peech **R**ecognition [8]. It essentially signifies the fact that training on a large and diverse dataset and focusing on zero-shot transfer helps minimizing performance degradation and increasing generalizability in actual cross-dataset validation scenarios in comparison to models trained on single datasets.

2.2 Weakly Supervised Training of Whisper

Whisper is a multilingual and multitasking model that has been trained to perform various tasks, such as transcription, voice activity detection, alignment, translation, and language identification on audio samples. A dataset containing $680,000$ h of labelled audio data, of which $117,000$ h comprising multilingual audio samples, and $125,000$ h comprising of foreign language to English translational data, was created by scraping transcribed audio data from the Internet [8].

As a result, the dataset is diverse, comprising a wide range of sounds from various environments, recording setups, speakers, and languages. The large volume and wide range of audio quality definitely assists in training the model that can generalize to unseen data high performance, and robustness.

2.3 Whisper Models

Whisper comprises five different models with increasing sizes, namely, tiny, base, small, medium, and large. The models vary in terms of their number of trainable parameters and the number of transformer encoder-decoder layers they use, as summarized in Table 1. The encoder features of Whisper are fixed-dimensional vectors that are obtained at the end of the encoder module, with sizes of 1 × 1500 × 384, 1 × 1500 × 512, 1 × 1500 × 768, 1 × 1500 × 1024, and 1 × 1500 × 1280 for the tiny, base, small, medium, and large models, respectively. The second dimension of the fixed vector remains constant for all models, as it captures the temporal information of the input audio signal.

Table 1. Whisper Models. After [8].

Whisper Model	Layers	Width	Heads	Parameters
Tiny	4	384	6	39M
Base	6	512	8	74M
Small	12	768	12	244M
Medium	24	1024	16	769M
Large	32	1280	20	1550M

2.4   Proposed Transfer Learning Methodology

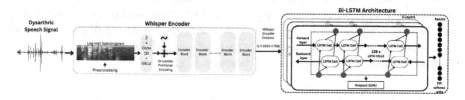

Fig. 1. Functional Block Diagram of Proposed Whisper Encoder Transfer Learning Pipeline in Tandem with Bi-LSTM Classifier.

Transfer learning has proved its effectiveness in many natural language processing and speech recognition tasks. Transfer learning is a type of machine learning approach that involves utilizing pre-existing knowledge gained from a related task to improve learning for a new task. This is achieved by taking an already trained model, and retraining it using a new dataset. During retraining, certain trainable hyperparameters and neurons are frozen to preserve the information learned from the original dataset [12]. The goal of transfer learning is to leverage the knowledge gained from the related task to improve the model's performance, and reduce the amount of data needed to train the new model.

This study introduces a transfer learning method to recognise dysarthric words, where the pre-trained Whisper model's Transformer Encoder module is utilized to extract relevant information for this task. Utilizing the pre-trained Whisper encoder allows us to take advantage of its capability to extract high-level features from the audio data. This study tests the hypothesis that the

Whisper encoder captures all the necessary information of the speech signal into a fixed-dimensional vector representation at end of the Whisper encoder's last layer. We refer these vector representations as Whisper encoder features.

We selected this particular approach as the dataset used for training had significant variability, which makes the model more robust and appropriate for our problem. This transfer learning method enables us to leverage the model's ability to generalize to unseen data. We have then, utilized these Whisper encoder features in tandem with DNN classifiers as shown in Fig. 1 for dysarthric ASR.

2.5   Working of the Employed Pipeline

Figure 1 illustrates the proposed pipeline used in this study. In the first step, the speech signal undergoes preprocessing to prepare it for input into the Whisper encoder module. The preprocessing involves resampling giving the input audio signal to 16 kHz and padding it to a length of 30 s for uniformity. An 80-channel Log-Mel spectrogram is computed using a window length of 25 ms and a stride of 10 ms, and the resulting coefficients are normalized to values between -1 and 1. Two convolution layers with a kernel size of 3 and GELU activation function are then applied to these values. In addition, sinusoidal embeddings are used to aid the Whisper encoder in learning the relative positions within the input, as described in [8]. The processed signal is then passed through the Whisper encoder block, which generates a fixed-dimensional vector as output in its final hidden state. This output is then fed into a deep neural network (DNN) classifier, which classifies the cry signal into its respective classes.

During the training phase, the Whisper encoder module is kept frozen, and only the weights of the DNN classifier are updated through back-propagation of errors. To ensure that the features generated by the Whisper encoder are not biased towards a particular DNN architecture, the experiments are conducted using both a Convolutional Neural Network (CNN), and a Bidirectional Long Short Term Memory (Bi-LSTM) Network as classifiers, as described in [7].

3   Experimental Setup

This section includes a detailed description of our experimental setup, including important information about the dataset used, the classifiers incorporated into our employed pipelines, and the main objective of our study, the identification of isolated Dysarthric Speech.

3.1   Dataset Used

In this work, we have used standard and statistically meaningful Universal Access Dysarthric Speech (UA-Speech) corpus [4]. UA-Speech corpus consists of data from 15 dysarthric (mostly spastic dysarthria type) speakers with cerebral palsy and 13 normal speakers. In total, there are 765 isolated words collected in three blocks, out of which 455 are distinct words. Each block has 10 digits, 26 international radio alphabets, 19 computer commands, and 100 common words. This adds up to a total of 155 common words. Moreover, each block contains 100 uncommon words. The details of the dysarthric speakers are shown in Table 2. We have used block B1 and B3 for training purposes, and block B2 for testing [10].

Table 2. Patient Wise Details of UA-Corpus Dataset. After [4].

Speaker	Gender	Dysarthric Severity-Level
M04	Male	High
F03	Female	
M12	Male	
M01	Male	
M07	Male	Medium
F02	Female	
M16	Male	
M05	Male	Low
M11	Male	
F04	Female	
M09	Male	Very Low
M14	Male	
M10	Male	
M08	Male	
F05	Female	

3.2 Classification of Isolated Dysarthric Speech

In this study, we propose a transfer learning-based end-to-end speech recognition system using the Whisper encoder in tandem with a BiLSTM classifier, which classifies the speech into 155 classes, each for one word. The functional block diagram of the training for our ASR system is shown in Fig. 1.

Whisper Encoder. The Whisper Models are openly accessible on GitHub in various sizes, as detailed in Table 1. In this study, we have imported the publicly available model, and made modifications to utilize solely its Encoder blocks. We have also appended a Bi-LSTM classifier, at the end of Whisper Encoder output, which further acts as a classifier. The Whisper encoder blocks are built upon the well established transformer structure, first introduced in [13]. The transformer encoder is widely regarded as a powerful and state-of-the-art architecture, particularly in the field of natural language processing, due to its capacity to selectively attend to various segments of the input sequence, and capture intricate relationships between them.

The Whisper encoder utilized in our experiments has been trained on a diverse range of datasets, as outlined in Sect. 2. This extensive training enables the Whisper encoder to effectively capture the variations commonly observed in dysarthric speech, thereby achieving high performance without the need for additional data augmentation or synthetic data generation techniques.

Convoluitonal Neural Network (CNN). A Convolutional Neural Network (CNN) was employed as one of the classifiers in this study. CNNs mimic the way the human brain perceives images and are therefore effective for image classification tasks [2]. The CNN model used in this study consists of three convolutional layers, each with a kernel size of 3×3 and strides of 2. Each convolutional layer is followed by a max-pooling layer of size 2×2, along with spatial 2D dropout layers with dropout probabilities of 0.1. Two Fully-Connected (FC) layers were then used, with ReLU and Softmax activation functions, respectively [1]. The Adaptive Moment Estimation (Adam) optimizer was employed with a learning rate of 0.001, and the categorical-cross-entropy loss function was used for training the model [14].

Bidirectional Long Short Term Memory Network (Bi-LSTM). Bidirectional Long Short-Term Memory (Bi-LSTM) is a type of Recurrent Neural Network (RNN) that is commonly used in sequence modeling tasks, such as natural language processing and speech recognition. Bi-LSTM is an extension of the conventional LSTM architecture and performs both forward and backward processing of the input sequence, allowing it to gather information from both previous and future time steps [9]. For this study, three Bi-LSTM layers were used, each consisting of 128 units, with a dropout of 10% at the end of each layer. Finally, a dense layer with 155 units, and a softmax activation function was used as the output layer for classification.

4   Experimental Results

The present study involved the development of ASR systems. One of these systems was designed to operate on the entire UA-Speech dataset, regardless of the severity-level of the dysarthric condition. Additionally, four distinct ASR systems were devised for each dysarthric severity-level, as outlined in Table 2. To further investigate the efficacy of the ASR models, we conducted five repetitions of the aforementioned experiments, substituting a CNN classifier for the Bi-LSTM classifier, as depicted in Fig. 1.

4.1   Severity-Level Independent ASR System

In our initial research study, we have developed an Automatic Speech Recognition (ASR) system that is capable of recognizing speech from individuals with varying dysarthric severity-levels. To train our model, we utilized a dataset pre-pared according to the methodology described in Sect. 3.1, where Blocks B1 and B3 were used for training while keeping the whisper encoder portion frozen in the block diagram illustrated in Fig. 1. Block B2 was then employed for testing the model.

Our results show that the CNN classifier pipeline yielded an average word accuracy of 58.69%, while the Bi-LSTM classifier achieved an average word accuracy of 59.2%, as illustrated in Fig. 2.

4.2   Severity-Level Dependent ASR System

Given the sub-optimal performance of our initial ASR system on speakers with varying dysarthric severity-levels, we sought to investigate alternative approaches. In particular, we explored a speaker-adaptive strategy, whereby we developed ASR systems that are tailored to dysarthric severity levels.

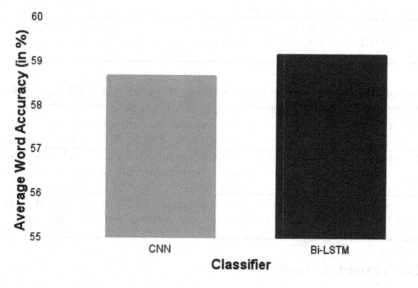

Fig. 2. Performance Analysis of Severity-Level Independent ASR System.

Through this approach, we were able to design ASR systems that are specif-ically optimized for each severity-level of dysarthria. Our results, as shown in Fig. 3 indicate that this speaker-adaptive approach using the Bi-LSTM classifier outperforms the initial ASR system, achieving higher average word accuracy of 59.78%. These findings suggest that a tailored approach may be more effective for recognizing speech from individuals with varying degrees of dysarthria.

The results illustrated in Fig. 3 reveal that the proposed pipeline, which uti-lizes a Bi-LSTM classifier, outperforms the CNN classifier. This can be attributed to the fact that the whisper model used in our pipeline is a transformer encoder-decoder model, which is specifically designed for processing sequential information processing. As such, the Bi-LSTM classifier, which is capable of effectively capturing and processing sequential information, performs better than the CNN classifier in our proposed pipeline.

It is worth highlighting that the issue of data scarcity is a pervasive challenge in the field of dysarthric speech recognition, which has also affected previous deep learning-based end-to-end models. To address this challenge, several authors, such as those in [6,11], have employed data augmentation or synthetic data generation techniques to artificially increase the size of their datasets.

Therefore, it would be unfair to compare the performance of our proposed methodology with those of prior studies that utilized data augmentation or synthetic data generation techniques. However, our experimental results demonstrate promising potential in the proposed methodology to outperform existing systems, highlighting the effectiveness of our approach in recognizing speech from individuals with varying severity of dysarthria.

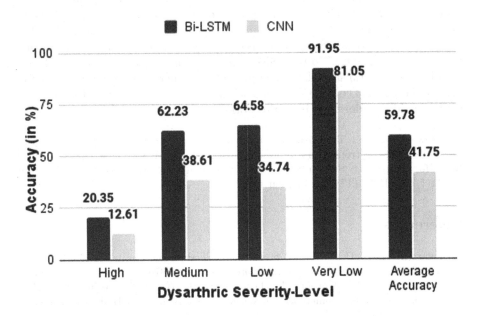

Fig. 3. Performance Analysis of Severity-Level Dependent ASR system

5   Summary and Conclusions

This research study aimed to investigate the potential of the recently proposed Whisper transformer encoder-decoder-based speech recognition system for dysarthric ASR, a crucial assistive speech technology for socially relevant research problem. In order to fully explore the significance of the Whisper-based approach, we chose not to employ data augmentation techniques, as has been done in recent studies in the literature. Despite this, our proposed method was able to achieve comparable performance to those methods that utilized data augmentation, despite having significantly less training data. These findings suggest that the Whisper-based approach is indeed a promising solution for dysarthric ASR.

Looking ahead, our future research will focus on combining various data augmentation and synthetic data generation techniques with the Whisper-based system for ASR. Additionally, we plan to extend this study to other dysarthric speech datasets, such as the TORGO corpus, to further evaluate the effectiveness of the proposed method. Further, the two standard speech corpora, namely, UA_Speech and TORGO contains mostly spastic type of dysarthria and hence, extending this work on other type of dysarthria, such as Flaccid, Ataxic, Hypokinetic, Hyperkinetic and mixed type of dysarthria would be our focus. The authors also plan to study other deep learning models such as the wave2vec 2.0, and compare their performances with the Whisper Model. Further developments would also focus on the development of Application Programming Interfaces (APIs) along with practical real-time speech recordings for dysarthric patients. In addition, dysarthric speech being medical data, maintaining its privacy is another technological challenge. To that effect, exploiting recent developments of federated learning to transmit the model parameter rather than the actual sensitive private data from the edge devices, such as mobile, sensors, etc., to the cloud server would be prioritised in future works.

Acknowledgments. The authors would like to express their sincere appreciation to the Ministry of Electronics and Information Technology (MeitY), New Delhi, Govt. of India, for the project 'Speech Technologies in Indian Languages BHASHINI', (Grant ID: 11(1)2022-HCC (TDIL)) for their support.

References

1. Agarap, A.F.: Deep learning using rectified linear units (ReLU). CoRR abs/1803.08375 (2018). http://arxiv.org/abs/1803.08375. Accessed 6 Feb 2023
2. Bock, S., Weiß, M.: A proof of local convergence for the ADAM optimizer. In: 2019 International Joint Conference on Neural Networks, IJCNN, Budapest, Hungary, pp. 1–8 (2019)
3. Iwamoto, Y., Shinozaki, T.: Unsupervised spoken term discovery using Wav2Vec 2.0. In: 2021 Asia-Pacific Signal and Information Processing Association Annual Summit and Conference (APSIPA ASC), Tokyo, Japan, pp. 1082–1086 (2021)
4. Kim, H., et al.: Dysarthric speech database for universal access research. In: INTERSPEECH, Brisbane, Australia, pp. 1741–1744 (2008)
5. Lieberman, P.: Primate vocalizations and human linguistic ability. J. Acoust. Soc. Am. (JASA) **44**(6), 1574–1584 (1968)
6. Lin, Y.Y., et al.: A speech command control-based recognition system for dysarthric patients based on deep learning technology. Appl. Sci. **11**(6), 2477 (2021)

7. O'Shea, K., Nash, R.: An introduction to convolutional neural networks. arXiv preprint arXiv:1511.08458 (2015). Accessed 25 Feb 2023
8. Radford, A., Kim, J.W., Xu, T., Brockman, G., McLeavey, C., Sutskever, I.: Robust speech recognition via large-scale weak supervision. arXiv preprint arXiv:2212.04356 (2022). Accessed 6 Mar 2023
9. Schuster, M., Paliwal, K.K.: Bidirectional recurrent neural networks. IEEE Trans. Signal Process. **45**(11), 2673–2681 (1997)
10. Sehgal, S., Cunningham, S.: Model adaptation and adaptive training for the recognition of dysarthric speech. In: Proceedings of SLPAT 2015: 6th Workshop on Speech and Language Processing for Assistive Technologies, Dresden, Germany, pp. 65–71 (2015)
11. Shahamiri, S.R.: Speech vision: an end-to-end deep learning-based dysarthric automatic speech recognition system. IEEE Trans. Neural Syst. Rehabil. Eng. **29**, 852–861 (2021). https://doi.org/10.1109/TNSRE.2021.3076778
12. Torrey, L., Shavlik, J.: Transfer learning. In: Handbook of Research on Machine Learning Applications and Trends: Algorithms, Methods, and Techniques, pp. 242–264. IGI Global (2010)
13. Vaswani, A., et al.: Attention is all you need. In: Advances in Neural Information Processing Systems (NIPS), vol. 30, Long Beach, USA (2017)
14. Zhang, Z., Sabuncu, M.: Generalized cross entropy loss for training deep neural networks with noisy labels. In: Advances in NIPS, vol. 31, Montreal, Canada (2018)
15. Zhao, Y., Kuruvilla-Dugdale, M., Song, M.: Voice conversion for persons with amyotrophic lateral sclerosis. IEEE J. Biomed. Health Inform. **24**(10), 2942–2949 (2019)

Significance of Duration Modification in Reducing Listening Effort of Slurred Speech from Patients with Traumatic Brain Injury

Oindrila Banerjee[1], D. Govind[1(✉)], Suryakanth V. Gangashetty[1],
Akhilesh Kumar Dubey[1], Rajeev Aravindakshan[2], Sasikumar Panicker[3],
and K. Reshma[3]

[1] Department of Computer Science and Engineering, Koneru Lakshmaiah Education
Foundation, Greenfields, Vaddeswaram 500302, Andhra Pradesh, India
{2102030002,d_govind,svg.in,dubey18oct}@kluniversity.in
[2] All India Institute of Medical Sciences (AIIMS) Mangalagiri, Vaddeswaram 500302,
Andhra Pradesh, India
rajeev.a@aiimsmangalagiri.edu.in
[3] Kumar Centre for Stroke and Neuro Rehabilitation, Vaduthala, Kochi 682023, India

Abstract. The objective of the work presented in the paper is to check
the significance of duration modification for improving the speech intelligibility of the patients having slurred speech disorder due to traumatic
brain injury (TBI). A slow speaking rate has been observed in the speech
utterances of a patient having diffuse axonal injury, a type of TBI. To
compensate the slow speaking rate, the utterances are subjected to duration modification for various scaling factors. Subjective listening tests are
then conducted for assessing the effort required to understand the spoken utterances among a group of medical and non-medical listeners. The
improved mean opinion scores (MOS) confirmed that the duration modification is indeed reduce the listening effort while perceiving the slurred
speech utterances. From the listening tests, a speaker dependent duration modification factor of 0.75 has provided the best enhancement of
the slurred speech with improved intelligibility.

Keywords: Speech disorder · TBI · Slurred speech · Duration
modification

1 Introduction

Human speech is produced as a result of coordinated nuero-muscular activities
involving cognitive areas of brain and voice articulators [1,27]. Impairments in
any of these areas adversely affect the produced speech in terms of reduced
intelligibility and poor naturalness. Listeners have to put more effort to understand a spoken utterance with reduced intelligibility and naturalness [22]. In

A. Karpov et al. (Eds.): SPECOM 2023, LNAI 14338, pp. 590–600, 2023.
https://doi.org/10.1007/978-3-031-48309-7_47

the context of speech based health care, these voice disorders are generally termed as dysarthria [2,13]. In the present work, studies on the dysarthric speech with slurred speech characteristics of patients affected by traumatic brain injury (TBI) are presented.

In general, to develop robust speech based systems, large corpora consisting of speech recording of healthy speakers recorded in various conditions are used. Compared to healthy speech recordings, collecting the dysarthric speech is difficult for the following reasons: (1) the data has to be collected from clinical environments from patients, (2) less number of speakers affected with voice impairments as compared to healthy speakers, and (3) unable to record longer sessions of speech recordings from patients with voice disorders. For the task of analysis of specific type of dysarthric conditions, it is hard to record data from patients affected by that specific voice impairment [25]. To develop AI based systems for speakers with voice impairments, Google has started Euephonia project [11,28]. The long term objective of this project was to make the speech recognition to work for speech with various voice disorders. The Euephonia team aimed to improve the speech recognition performance for voice disorders by creating platform for recording the disordered speech [5]. Alternatively, there have been attempts to improve the recognition accuracy by transforming the disordered speech to normal [26]. There are works reported in the literature which aim at improving the robustness for the children speech and speech recorded in adverse scenarios such as severe noisy conditions [8]. In all those cases, the approach was to transform the speech parameters such as source and vocaltract parameters of the original speech so that speech recognition can be improved. In the present work, we use the voice transformation approach to improve the intelligibility of the disordered speech to have a robust processing of the disordered speech by the existing AI based systems.

A patient who has acquired a slurred speech dysarthric condition due to a traumatic brain injury (TBI) is the subject considered for the study presented in this paper. The patient is undergoing a speech therapy for correcting the slurred speech in a neuro rehabilitation centre. The natural interactions in the languages, Malayalam language (L1 of the speaker) and English (L2 of the speaker) are recorded from the patient for the analysis of the slurred speech. Among the type of TBIs, in particular, the patient has a condition known as diffuse axonal injury (DAI) [12]. According to the theory of cognitive speech processing, major areas in cerebrum that take part during the speech production are: (1) Broca's Area and (2) Wernecke's Area. To utter a word which is heard, the primary auditory cortex sends instructions to Wernecke's area of the cerebrum. As Wernecke's area is responsible for comprehension and language related skills, it directs Broca's area to send commands to primary motor cortex [18,29]. It is the function of primary motor cortex that configures speech articulators for producing the voice using neuro-muscular commands. A person with impairments in the Broca's or motor cortex looses control over the speech production. As a result, the person loses intelligibility or naturalness in the spoken utterances which in-turn affects his/her natural communication with other people.

Based on the preliminary inspection of the speech by listening a slow speech rate was evidently observed. The neurological tests such as Montreal Congnitive Assessment (MOCA) and Rancho Los Amigos (RLA) scale tests for the diagnostics of the cognitive activities, rated the patient with mild cognitive impairment [3,16]. The neurologists further confirmed the condition of mild cognitive impairment from the patient's MRI data. However, as diagnosed by the neurologists, the slurred speech characteristics was evidently perceivable by listening. According to the speech quality metric, the speech rate is one of the important prosodic parameters which influences the intelligibility of speech. Therefore, in this paper a time scale modification (Duration modification) is attempted to compensate for the slow speaking rate and thereby improving the intelligibility of the slurred speech words in the utterances. Based on the works carried out in the paper, the proposed novelties of the paper are the following:

- Does the duration modification really help in improving the intelligibility of the spoken utterances?
- If the duration modification improves the intelligibility of spoken utterances then what should be the duration scaling factor which provides the best enhancement?

The paper is organized in the following way: Section 2 provides preliminary analysis of the slurred speech characteristics of the patient. Section 3 provides epoch based duration modification used for time scaling the slurred speech by preserving the perceptual quality. The details of the perceptual studies conducted are provided in Sect. 4. Section 5 summarizes the work with suggestions for future work.

2   Analysis of Slurred Speech

2.1 F_0 Analysis

A preliminary analysis has been carried out by analyzing the F_0 contours and speaking rate. Figure 1 compares the waveform segments and F_0 contours obtained from the conversation of the patient with TBI and a healthy speaker. Comparative analysis of subplots ((c) and (d)) in Fig. 1 shows a flat F_0 characteristics of a voice segment as compared to the healthy speaker. Due to the slurred speech impairments, there is reduced dynamic variations in the pitch as compared to the F_0 contour of the healthy speaker even for the same sound unit.

2.2   Speaking Rate

Speaking rate is computed as the average number of words or syllables spoken by the speaker per second. As the syllable marking has not been carried out, the speaking rate is computed based on the number words spoken per second. The Table 1 shows the comparison of speaking rates of TBI patient and healthy speaker. The speaking rate has been computed by manually counting the number

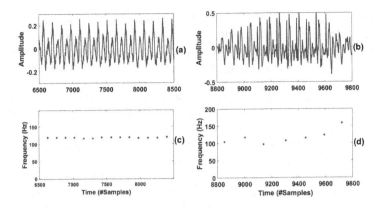

Fig. 1. Analysis of F_0 contour. The voiced waveform segments of a (a) patient with DAI, (b) healthy speaker. ((c) and (d)) are the corresponding F_0 contours. The waveform segments belong to the same word occurred in the natural conversation between patient and healthy speaker (moderator).

of words spoken by a particular speaker in the conversation. The average count of words per second is then used as a measure of speaking rate. From the Table 1 it has to be noted that there is a significant difference in speaking rates of the slurred speech patient when compared to the healthy speaker. Even though speaking rates vary according to the sentences spoken, it was observed that slurred speech of the patient's speaking rate was consistently low in all the 4 conversations in both L1 (Malayalam) and L2 (English) as compared to the healthy speaker.

3   Epoch Based Duration Modification of Speech

Table 1. Comparison of speaking rates. Average count of words spoken per second across five conversations in L1 and L2 of the patient. Healthy speaker was involved in the facilitating the conversation.

Speaker	Speaking Rate of L1 (Malayalam)	Speaking Rate L2 (English)
DAI Patient	0.8 words/s	0.9 words/s
Healthy Speaker	3 words/s	1.2 words/s

Duration modification is the process of altering the duration of a given signal without changing the characteristics related to the speaker [6,14,19,21]. There are mainly two stages in prosody modification. First stage is the estimation of the analysis pitch marks from the speech. In the second stage, waveform is generated according to the time-scale factor by copying the samples of the pitch cycles to the synthesis pitch marks. Essentially, in duration modification, the pitch cycles of the original speech utterance are either repeated (increasing duration) or dropped (reducing duration). In the case of epoch based duration modification, glottal closure instants (also known as epochs in speech) estimated accurately from speech waveform is used as the analysis pitch marks for duration modification. To ensure the naturalness of duration modified speech, perceptually relevant speech samples around epochs in a pitch cycle are copied to the synthesis pitch marks during the waveform modification [23,24]. The perceptual relevance of speech samples around the epochs are utilized for the speech enhancement applications where the epochal regions are least affected by the noise [9,10,20]. There are various algorithms developed to estimate the epochs from speech signals [4,15,17]. For the current study, zero frequency filtering based method has been used for estimating epochs as the analysis pitch marks for duration modification [15].

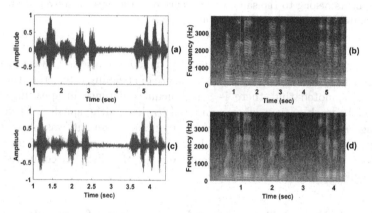

Fig. 2. Original (a) waveform and (b) wide-band spectrogram of an utterances from the DAI patient. (c) and (d) plot the respective waveform and spectrogram of duration modified speech with a duration modification scaling factor as $\beta = 0.75$

Figure 2 plots the duration modified slurred speech waveform and wide band spectrogram of an utterance recorded from the DAI patient. An arbitrary modification scaling factor, $\beta = 0.75$, is used for the time scale modification for generating the plots. The wideband spectrogram plot is used to analyze the harmonic structure of the original speech and duration modified speech. In the example shown in Fig. 2, since the duration of the original utterance is scaled down by a factor of 0.75, 1/4 of the total number of pitch cycles are dropped to achieve duration modification. Therefore, a reduction in the total energy of utterance can be observed from the spectrogram. As there are considerable difference in the harmonic structure of duration modified speech as compared to the spectrogram of the original utterance, perceptual quality is preserved by the epoch based duration modification algorithm. However, for the healthcare applications speech recordings are expected to be recorded from non-studio environments, minimal perceptual distortions may be present due to noises introduced during the speech recording.

Table 2. Description of the scores used for assessing the listening effort of the duration modified speech.

Score	Descriptive Justification	Perceptual Quality
5	No effort in listening and understanding and sounds similar to the voice of a healthy speaker	Excellent
4	Very less listening effort but the files sounds slightly different from a healthy speaker	Very good
3	Moderate level of effort required to understand the words spoken	Good
2	Higher level of effort required to understand the voice in the files	Fare
1	Extremely hard to understand	Poor

Table 3. Mean opinion scores obtained for different duration modification factors on Malayalam and English language utterances.

MOS group	Dur. Mod. Fact. (Malayalam)				
	0.25	0.5	0.75	0.9	1
Medical	2.56	3.16	3.34	3.06	2.84
Non-Medical	2.38	3.71	3.79	3.71	3.08
Average	2.47	3.43	3.57	3.39	2.96
	Dur. Mod Fact. (English)				
	0.25	0.5	0.75	0.9	1
Medical	1.94	2.75	2.99	2.68	2.49
Non-Medical	2	2.96	3.56	3.35	2.52
Average	1.97	2.85	3.28	3.02	2.49

Table 4. Mean opinion scores provided by Malayalam (L1) Listeners for different duration modification factors of English utterances.

MOS group	Dur. Mod. Fact.				
	0.25	0.5	0.75	0.9	1
Medical	2.5	2.88	3.10	2.93	2.56
Non-Medical	2.08	3.42	3.92	3.58	2.08
Average	2.29	3.14	3.51	3.26	2.32

4 Perceptual Evaluations and Results

4.1 Data for Perceptual Evaluations

Natural interactions with a patient in the age group of 35–40, who has suffered a DAI due to an accident, are recorded using an audio recorder. Data was collected from Kumar center for stroke and neuro rehabilitation, Kochi, Kerala, India, where the subject is undergoing a treatment for the speech therapy for correcting the slurred speech. Speech data recording sessions were started after obtaining the ethical and privacy preservation clearance from the center where the patient was being treated. The interactions were recorded in Indian languages such as Malayalam (L1, Subject's mother tongue) and English (L2). Speech was recorded approximately for 2 to 3 min. The speech data has been recorded at a sampling rate of 48 kHz and 16 bits per sample resolution. For generating the stimuli for the listening test, the utterances were downsampled to 8 kHz.

4.2 Neurological Diagnosis of the Patients's Cognitive Impairment

In addition to the routine CT scan based diagnosis, the patient was subjected to the neurological tests like MOCA [16] and RLA scale test [3] to assess the affect of impairments on the cognitive activities. After suffering from multiple bone injuries, the CT scan revealed extra axial bleed along the fronto-temporo-parietal convexity and right temporal convexity which confirmed the DAI. A few tiny parenchymal contusions in the left frontal and temporal lobes are also noted from CT scans of the patient. The cognitive impairment test showed a score of 28/30 at the time of data collection from the patient. Rancho scale test is a common test carried out on the patients with brain injury for assessing the progression of recovery. Based on the Rancho neurological scale test, the patient was rated at level 7 which was "Automatic-appropriate minimal assistance for daily living skills". The descriptions of the scales are reported in [3,7]. The results showed the patient has mild cognitive impairment which has affected in the form of slurred speech characteristics.

4.3 Perceptual Evaluation for Assessing Listening Effort

Speech utterances in 4 different sentences are used for conducting listening tests in each language. Duration of each sentences has been scaled down using to 4 scaling factors such as 0.9, 0.75, 0.5, 0.25 and 1. For instance, the duration scaling factor of 0.9 corresponds to a down scaling of 0.9 times the original duration of the speech utterance. The modification factor of 1 indicates no modification performed by the time scaling algorithm. The speech utterances with duration modification factor of 1 were generated for keeping the level of minimum perceptual distortions introduced by algorithm consistent across all the files used in the perceptual evaluation and to avoid biasing of the listeners while rating the files. The methodology used for the perceptual evaluation was motivated by the assessment conducted based on the listening effort for oesophageal disordered speech synthesis by Raman et al. [22].

For the subjective listening test, the listeners were given instructions to assess based on the effort required to understand the words in each utterance. A pilot study was carried out where the listeners were demonstrated that how scores had to be given. The utterances used for pilot study were not included in the files used for the listening test. To avoid the bias of the listeners in providing the scores towards a particular method, the filenames of all the files have been encoded. All listeners were asked to rate with an opinion score in a five point scale. The Table 2 shows the significance of each score used for listening.

Participants of the listening tests were further divided into group of subjects who work in technology related areas (non-medical) and a group of medical doctors. The group of 10 medical doctors who participated in the listening test include two neurologists of Kumar center for stroke and neuro-rehabilitation and remaining doctors from departments of ENT, community medicine and physiology of All India Institute of Medical Sciences (AIIMS) Mangalagiri. Opinion scores obtained from the participants are segregated into these medical and non-medical groups and mean opinion score (MOS) ratings are computed for each group. Table 3, shows the MOS ratings obtained for the languages by the two groups of participants. At the gross level of analysis, the trend in the MOS scores are the same. By looking at the table for both the language utterances, participants of both the groups provided lower scores for the files which were not time scaled. Relatively lower MOS (around 2.5) shows that listening effort is involved in understanding the utterances spoken by the patient. For the utterances spoken in Malayalam language, which is the $L1$ of the speaker, obtained highest MOS for the duration modification factor of 0.75. The listeners whose $L1$ and $L2$ are Malayalam and English respectively, rated the Malayalam utterances with high MOS ratings. Reason for this could be attributed to the ease in articulating the $L1$ utterances by the patient.

Table 4 provides the MOS ratings obtained for time scaled English language utterances in various duration scale factors provided by listeners whose $L1$ is Malayalam. 5 listeners having $L1$ as Malayalam are selected from both medical and non-medical group for the analysis of their ratings which they provided for English utterances. Compared to average MOS ratings computed for all listeners of medical group, $L1$ Malayalam listeners from the medical group provided relatively higher MOS ratings. This indicates the influence of the $L1$ of the listeners while rating the L2 utterances in a listening test. Based on the analysis of Malayalam and English language utterances, listeners provided a highest MOS for the time scale modification factor of 0.75. The results are found to be consistent with the groups of medical and non-medical listeners. Therefore, the optimal value of the duration modification that can be selected based on MOS ratings obtained for both the languages is 0.75 which provides the best least listening effort in understanding the utterances. Table 4 further confirms the enhancement of duration scaling by 0.9, 0.75 and 0.5 times the duration of the given original utterances. Among various duration scaled utterances, the duration modification factor of 0.75 (time scaling for keeping 75% of the original length of the utterances) provided the highest MOS. Similarly, listeners of the non-medical group also rated the utterances with higher opinion scores compared to the medical group. Compared to MOS ratings obtained from all listeners for the English utterances, the non-medical listener group provided higher MOS. The scale factor of 0.75 received the higher MOS ratings reinforces the MOS analysis carried out from the Table 3.

5 Summary and Conclusion

The work presented in the paper studies the effect of duration modification on the intelligibility of the slurred speech characteristics recorded from a TBI patient. Slow speaking rate was evidently perceptible by the first level analysis of the voice recordings collected from the patient. From the listening tests, low speaking rate was observed to be less intelligible with more listening effort required by the listeners to understand the sentences spoken by the patient. Therefore, a time scale modification was proposed to compensate the slow speaking rate to reduce the listening effort and thereby improving the intelligibility of the slurred speech. To preserve the perceptual quality of during the duration modification, epoch based duration modification is used as the tool for time scaling the speech utterances. A listening tests carried on the groups of medical and non-medical group of participants confirmed the effectiveness of the duration modification in enhancing the intelligibility of the duration modified slurred speech utterances. Additionally, a duration scaling by 0.75 times the original utterance duration was confirmed to show reduced listening effort in understanding the sentences.

Based on the slurred speech analysis, it was also observed that occurrences of flat F_0 contours with lack of natural dynamic variations in the F_0 values. The future work may consider incorporating the natural variations in F_0 values by pitch modification without changing the speaker characteristics. Further, the duration analysis has to be extended to syllable or phoneme levels to identify the class of sounds units which are affected by the mild cognitive motor impairments.

Acknowledgements. Authors would like to convey our sincere gratitude towards all the people who participated in the listening test. The paper would not have been possible without the time spent by the doctors of All India Institute of Medical Sciences (AIIMS) Mangalagiri who have prior experience interacting with stroke and TBI patients. Further, authors would like to appreciate the hospital management of Kumar center for stroke and neuro rehabilitation for helping us to collection the data and providing the ethical clearance for using the data for the academic research.

The funding for this paper is from the National Language Translation Mission (NLTM) sub consortium of the project titled "Speech Technologies in Indian Languages", MEITY, Govt. of India.

References

1. Adank, P., McGettigan, C., Kotz, S.A.E.: The Cognitive and Neural Organisation of Speech Processing. Frontiers Media, Lausanne (2016)
2. Celin, T.A.M., Vijayalakshmi, P., Nagarajan, T.: Data augmentation techniques for transfer learning-based continuous dysarthric speech recognition. Circuits Syst. Sig. Process. **42**, 601–623 (2023)
3. Dowling, G.A.: Levels of cognitive fnctioning: evaluation of interrater reliability. J. Neuro Surg. Nurs. **17**(2), 129–134 (1985)
4. Drugman, T., Thomas, M., Gudnason, J., Naylor, P., Dutoit, T.: Detection of glottal closure instants from speech signals: a quantitative review. IEEE Trans. Audio Speech Lang. Process. **20**, 994–1006 (2012)

5. Gale, R., Chen, L., Dolata, J., van Santen, J., Asgari, M.: Improving ASR systems for children with autism and language impairment using domain focused DNN transfer techniques. In: Proceedings Interspeech (2019)

6. Govind, D., Prasanna, S.R.M., Yegnanarayana, B.: Neutral to target emotion conversion using source and suprasegmental information. In: Proceedings Interspeech 2011, August 2011

7. Hartmann, A., Kegelmeyer, D., Kloos, A.: Use of an errorless learning approach in a person with concomitant traumatic spinal cord injury and brain injury: a case report. J. Neurol. Phys. Ther. **42**(2), 102–109 (2018)

8. Kathania, H.K., Kadiri, S.R., Alku, P., Kurimo, M.: A formant modification method for improved ASR for children speech. Speech Commun. **136**, 98–106 (2022)

9. Krishnamoorthy, P., Prasanna, S.R.M.: Reverberant speech enhancement by temporal and spectral processing. IEEE Trans. Audio Speech Lang. Process. **17**(2), 253–266 (2009)

10. Krishnamoorthy, P., Prasanna, S.R.M.: Enhancement of noisy speech by temporal and spectral processing. Speech Commun. **53**(2), 154–174 (2011)

11. MacDonald, R.L., et al.: Disordered speech data collection: lessons learned at 1 million utterances from project euphonia. In: Proceedings Interspeech (2021)

12. Mesfin, F., Gupta, N., Hays, A.S., et al.: Diffuse Axonal Injury. Treasure Island (FL). StatPearls Publishing (2022). https://www.ncbi.nlm.nih.gov/books/NBK448102

13. Mitchell, C., Bowen, A., Tyson, S., Butterfint, Z., Conroy, P.: Interventions for dysarthria due to stroke and other adult-acquired, non-progressive brain injury. Cochrane Database Syst. Rev. **25**(1) (2017)

14. Moulines, E., Charpentier, F.: Pitch-synchronous waveform processing techniques for text-to-speech synthesis using diphones. Speech Commun. **9**, 452–467 (1990)

15. Murty, K.S.R., Yegnanarayana, B.: Epoch extraction from speech signals. IEEE Trans. Audio Speech Lang. Process. **16**(8), 1602–1614 (2008)

16. Nasreddine, Z.S., et al.: The montreal cognitive assessment, MoCa: a brief screening tool for mild cognitive impairment. J. Am. Geriatr. Soc. **63**(4), 695–704 (2005)

17. Naylor, P.A., Kounoudes, A., Gudnason, J., Brookes, M.: Estimation of glottal closure instants in voiced speech using DYPSA algorithm. IEEE Trans. Audio Speech Lang. Process. **15**(1), 34–43 (2007)

18. Nicolas-Alonso, L.F., Gomez-Gil, J.: Brain computer interfaces- a review. Sensors **12**(2), 1211–1279 (2012)

19. Prasanna, S.R.M., Govind, D., Rao, K.S., Yenanarayana, B.: Fast prosody modification using instants of significant excitation. In: Proceedings Speech Prosody, May 2010

20. Prasanna, S.R.M., Yegnanarayana, B.: Extraction of pitch in adverse conditions. In: Proceedings ICASSP, Montreal, Canada, May 2004

21. Quatieri, T.F., McAulay, R.J.: Shape invariant time scale and pitch modification of speech. IEEE Trans. Sig. Process. **40**(3), 497–510 (1992)

22. Raman, S., Serrano, L., Winneke, A., Navas, E., Hernaez, I.: Intelligibility and listening effort of Spanish oesophageal speech. Appl. Sci. **9**(16), 3233 (2019)

23. Rao, K.S., Yegnanarayana, B.: Prosody modification using instants of significant excitation. IEEE Trans. Audio Speech Lang. Process. **14**, 972–980 (2006)

24. Rao, K.S., Yegananarayana, B.: Duration modification using glottal closure instants and vowel onset points. Speech Commun. **51**(12), 1263–1269 (2009)

25. Row, H.P., Gutz, S.E., Maffei, M.F., Green, K.T.J.R.: Characterizing dysarthria diversity for automatic speech recognition: a tutorial from the clinical perspective. Frontiers Comput. Sci. **19** (2022)
26. Rudzicz, F.: Acoustic transformations to improve the intelligibility of dysarthric speech. In: Proceedings Second Workshop on Speech and Language Processing for Assistive Technologies (2011)
27. Schultz, T., Wand, M., Hueber, T., Krsienski, D.J., Herff, C., Brumberg, J.S.: Biosignal-based spoken communication: a survey. IEEE Trans. Audio Speech Lang. Process. (2015)
28. Shor, J., et al.: Personalizing ASR for dysarthric and accented speech with limited data. In: Proceedings Interspeech, pp. 784–788 (2019)
29. Tremblay, P., Dick, A.S.: Broca and Wernicke are dead or moving past the classic model of language neurobiology. Brain Lang. **162**, 60–71 (2016)

Speech Signal Segmentation into Silence, Unvoiced and Vocalized Sections in Speech Rehabilitation

Dariya Novokhrestova[1]([✉]) [iD], Evgeny Kostyuchenko[1] [iD], Ilya Krivoshein[1] [iD], and Lidiya Balatskaya[1,2] [iD]

[1] Tomsk State University of Control, Systems and Radioelectronics, Lenina Str. 40, 634050 Tomsk, Russia
ndi@fb.tusur.ru
[2] Tomsk Cancer Research Institute, Kooperativniy Av. 5, 634050 Tomsk, Russia
nii@oncology.tomsk.ru
http://www.tusur.ru, http://www.oncology.tomsk.ru/

Abstract. The article considers an algorithm for segmenting a speech signal into sections of silence and voiced and unvoiced segments. The use of the segmentation algorithm will make it possible to assess the quality of speech based on the comparison of two different implementations of the same phoneme separately, not as part of a whole syllable. The algorithm under study is based on the classification of individual signal frames into classes of silence, unvoiced or voiced section and the selection of segments by combining adjacent frames of the same classes. Testing showed the efficiency of the algorithm both on normal (undistorted) speech and on distorted speech of patients undergoing speech rehabilitation. An algorithm was investigated with class definition parameters proposed by the authors of the algorithm. Also, new classification parameters were proposed, selected using methods for optimizing the values of the exposed segment boundaries based on the analysis of a dataset from normal and distorted speech. The use of optimally selected parameters made it possible to reduce the segmentation error by an average of 60%. The applicability of the considered segmentation algorithm for solving the problem of dividing syllables into phonemes is shown.

Keywords: Speech Assessment · Speech Signal Segmentation · Speech Rehabilitation · Phoneme Pronunciation Quality Assessment

1 Introduction

The statistics of oncological diseases of the organs of the vocal tract shows that speech rehabilitation, and, accordingly, algorithms for assessing speech in rehabilitation are an important area of research [1, 2]. Evaluation of speech in speech rehabilitation after surgery on the organs of the vocal tract allows you to quantify the quality of speech in two areas: general speech intelligibility [3] and the quality of pronunciation of individual speech elements (for example, syllables or phonemes) [4]. Algorithms for calculating such estimates were proposed and introduced into the rehabilitation process

A. Karpov et al. (Eds.): SPECOM 2023, LNAI 14338, pp. 601–610, 2023.
https://doi.org/10.1007/978-3-031-48309-7_48

carried out based on Tomsk Cancer Research Institute (Russia) [4]. However, the actual problem remains the development of algorithms that will allow to separate individual speech elements from the recorded speech of patients for further processing. In particular, this applies to algorithms for segmenting syllables into phonemes, since the process of recording the phonemes of the Russian language separately is difficult, especially when working with patients in the process of speech rehabilitation. Also, the presence of such segmentation algorithms will make it possible to apply a more individual approach to the rehabilitation process itself, namely, to single out problematic phonemes for each patient separately and compose sets of exercises aimed at restoring these problematic phonemes.

The speech of patients after the surgical intervention changes for the worse. Accordingly, the segmentation algorithm should work adequately both for normal (undistorted, pre-operational) speech and for distorted speech. The previously implemented segmentation algorithm [5] made it possible to determine only certain classes of phonemes, while the following features and disadvantages were highlighted:

- low accuracy of the segmentation algorithm into minimal speech units (for example, with a deviation from manual boundaries within 10 ms accuracy is 43.3% and 33.3% for phonemes at the beginning and end of a syllable, respectively);
- the presence of so-called 'extra' boundaries, especially in vowel phonemes;
- testing was carried out only on normal (undistorted) speech.

This paper proposes the use of segmentation algorithms that allow you to determine the intervals of voiced and unvoiced sections. This approach is possible due to the presence of a pre-known structure of syllables in data sets, while this structure is an alternation of silence, unvoiced and voiced sections.

2 Experiment and Results

2.1 The Segmentation Algorithm

For the task of segmentation into voiced and unvoiced sections, a sufficiently large number of algorithms have been described, which are based on the calculation of signal parameters and/or its sections. In [6], Cai proposed an analysis of the average energy frequency distribution based on wavelet transforms and combining this measure with ZCR (zero-crossing rate) and STE (short-term signal energy). Atal and Rabiner [7] used ZCR, STE, inter-neighbor correlation, linear coding analysis (LPC), LPC error. Ijitona and others in [8] described a method based on the variance of the linear prediction error (LPEV), as well as the calculation of STE and ZCR.

This paper proposes the use of an algorithm based on the work of Warule et al. [9]. The algorithm is based on dividing the signal into frames and calculating the short term signal energy (STE) for each frame. By comparing the calculated value with some thresholds value, the frames are classified into three classes: silence, unvoiced section, or voiced section. Based on the classification results, parcel boundaries are defined as boundaries between frames of different classes. The algorithm block diagram is shown in Fig. 1.

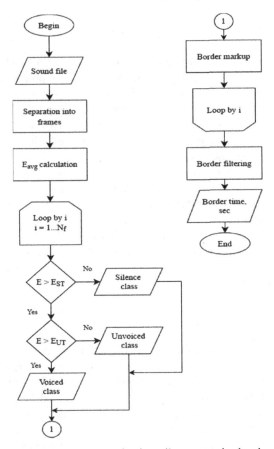

Fig. 1. Algorithm for signal segmentation into silence, unvoiced and voiced sections.

First, the audio signal is divided into frames lasting 20 ms with an overlap of 10 ms. Next, the STE values are calculated for each frame (for example, frame k):

$$E_k = \sum\nolimits_{n=1}^{N} s_k^2(n) \tag{1}$$

where N is number of samples per frame.

The average signal energy is calculated as the average of the frame energies:

$$E_{avg} = \frac{1}{K} \sum\nolimits_{k=1}^{K} E_k \tag{2}$$

where K is number of frames is audio signal.

Next, thresholds are calculated for the boundary between the silent and unvoiced segment (E_{ST}) and for the boundary between the unvoiced and voiced segments (E_{UT}). They are calculated as follows:

$$E_{ST} = \alpha * E_{avg} \tag{3}$$

$$E_{UT} = \beta * E_{avg} \qquad (4)$$

where α and β are predefined constant values. Based on the results of the analysis carried out by Warule and others [9], optimal threshold values were proposed at $\alpha = 0.02$ and $\beta = 0.12$. Thus, the value of E_{ST} is $0.02 * E_{avg}$ and the value of E_{UT} is $0.12 * E_{avg}$.

Classification is carried out according to the following principle: if the STE of the current frame is greater than E_{UT}, the frame is considered a voiced section. If the STE is between E_{ST} and E_{UT}, the frame is considered unvoiced. Finally, when STE is less than E_{ST}, the frame is defined as silence.

To draw boundaries between sections, firstly, the classes of each frame are determined. Then adjacent frames are found, the classes of which differ. Finally, at the beginning of a frame with a class different from the previous one, a segment boundary is placed. The resulting array of time values in seconds, which determine where the border will be placed, is filtered by a threshold of 30 ms in order to reduce the number of so-called 'extra' borders. «Extra» boundaries mean those boundaries that are set during the execution of the algorithm, but which are not present in the case of manual analysis carried out by an expert.

2.2 The Data Set

The data set contains 180 audio files in wav format, a sampling rate of 12 kHz, 16-bit encoding, one channel (mono). The files were divided into 2 folders: 90 files in each. Each file contains a recording of the pronunciation of a syllable by a patient or a healthy speaker. The first folder contains sound recordings recorded by people with normal functioning of the speech-forming apparatus (healthy speaker). In the second folder, the recordings with distorted pronunciation, these recordings were made by people undergoing speech rehabilitation (patient). In this case, speech rehabilitation was carried out after hemiglossectomy, the diagnosed disease is tongue cancer. Such a data set is justified by the need to check the performance and applicability of the algorithm both in normal speech and in distorted speech.

Each of the folders contains sets of sound recordings for each problematic phoneme. The set of problematic phonemes was determined jointly with the specialists of Tomsk Cancer Research Institute as the most frequently distorted phonemes after surgical intervention in the organs of the vocal tract. The set is containing 6 different phonemes of the Russian language: [k], [k'], [s], [s'], [t], [t']. 15 recordings for each phoneme: 5 recordings of syllables, which contain phoneme at the beginning of syllable, 5 recordings of syllables, which contain phoneme at the middle of syllable, 5 recordings of syllables, which contain phoneme at the end of syllable.

2.3 The Result of the Algorithm with Initial Constant Values

The algorithm was implemented in the MATLAB programming environment version R2023a [10]. A demonstration of the results of the algorithm on normal (undistorted) speech is shown in Fig. 2. It should be noted that the boundaries of the green segments are determined manually based on the spectrogram from the Wavesurfer program [11], the red boundaries are the result of the algorithm. Class 'S' corresponds to the silence segment, class 'UV' corresponds to the unvoiced segment, class 'V' corresponds to the voiced segment. A demonstration of the result of the algorithm on distorted speech is shown in Fig. 3.

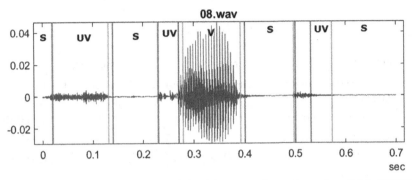

Fig. 2. Demonstration of the results of the algorithm on undistorted speech, syllable 'СКАТ' (in Russian) [sk'at].

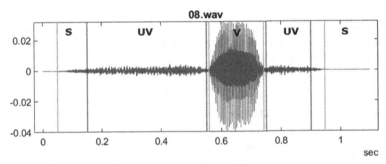

Fig. 3. Demonstration of the results of the algorithm on distorted speech, syllable 'СКАТ' (in Russian) [sk'at].

According to the results of a visual evaluation of the algorithm's operation on the original parameters (constant values), it was found that some boundaries are set too far from the reference ones. No 'extra' boundaries were found, in contrast to the previously used algorithm.

2.4 The Algorithm Improvement Based on Minimization of the Number of Classification Errors

A hypothesis was formulated that when using individually selected parameters instead of standard ones, the classification error would decrease. Classification error refers to the number of incorrectly classified frames.

Initially, in order to improve the algorithm, it was decided to try to manually calculate new thresholds α and β based on the STE in each of the manually selected segments of the audio file for all 90 files in the folder in question, as well as the average STE value in each audio file.

The resulting minimum, average, and maximum STE values for undistorted and distorted speech, summarized across segment types and all files, are shown in Table 1 (S is silence segment, UV is unvoiced segment, V is voiced segment).

Table 1. STE values in segments.

	min STE		average STE		max STE	
	Undistored speech	Distored speech	Undistored speech	Distored speech	Undistored speech	Distored speech
S	$2.608*10^{-8}$	$2.608*10^{-8}$	$3.475*10^{-5}$	$5.901*10^{-6}$	$1.088*10^{-2}$	$1.143*10^{-3}$
UV	$8.196*10^{-8}$	$6.147*10^{-8}$	$9.849*10^{-4}$	$2.270*10^{-4}$	$2.649*10^{-2}$	$7.957*10^{-3}$
V	$3.092*10^{-7}$	$8.568*10^{-8}$	$6.453*10^{-3}$	$5.521*10^{-3}$	$1.190*10^{-1}$	$6.499*10^{-2}$

As a result of the analysis of the STE values, it was found that there are no clear boundaries between the energy values of the segments, since the intervals intersect with each other. Thus, it turned out to be impossible to choose the optimal parameters based on the analysis of the minimum, average, and maximum energy values in the segments.

It was decided to present the thresholds α and β as independent variables for a function of the following form:

$$f(\alpha, \beta) = C_{err} \tag{5}$$

where C_{err} is the number of classification errors for segments as unvoiced, voiced and silence.

In order to determine the number of classification errors, an additional script was developed that compares the energy values in each of the frames with the reference energy values of each class in the entire data set. In this case, the reference values were calculated in the same way as at the classification stage (formulas 3, 4):

$$E(S) \in [0; E_{ST}) \tag{6}$$

$$E(UV) \in [E_{ST}, E_{UT}] \tag{7}$$

$$E(V) \in (E_{UT}; +\infty) \tag{8}$$

where $E(S)$, $E(UV)$, $E(V)$ are frame energies for silence, unvoiced and voiced speech, respectively.

To minimize the number of C_{err} errors, the Nelder-Mead method [12] was applied with a starting point (0.02; 0.12). The solution was found in 48 iterations. The obtained new threshold values α and β, as well as the results of the algorithm before and after the optimization, are presented in Table 2, where N_E is the total number of energy values in 180 files (16905).

Table 2. Optimization results and obtained parameter values.

	α	β	C_{err}	$C_{err}/N_E, \%$
Initial parameters	0.02	0.12	6060	35.847
Parameters after optimization	0.0017	0.8482	3849	22.768

The results of the algorithm with new values of the parameters and, accordingly, the thresholds for undistorted and distorted speech are presented in Fig. 5 and 6, respectively. The results of working with the original parameters are shown earlier in Figs. 2 and 3.

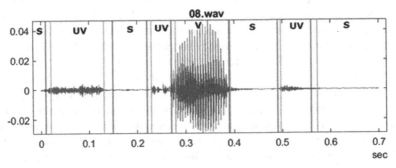

Fig. 4. The results of the algorithm with new threshold values, undistorted speech, syllable 'СКАТ' (in Russian) [sk'at].

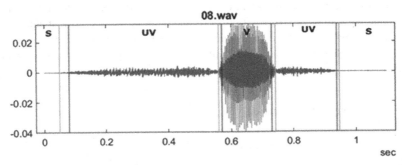

Fig. 5. The results of the algorithm with new threshold values, distorted speech, syllable 'СКАТ' (in Russian) [sk'at].

2.5 The Algorithm Improvement Based on Minimizing the Distance to Manual Boundaries

As an alternative, an algorithm was proposed to minimize the magnitude of errors, which is the total distance between manually set and automatic boundaries in milliseconds (D_{err}). Minimization was carried out using cross-validation. Several principles were formulated for dividing the data set into training and test samples to check the obtained parameter values:

inclusion of 9 files with normal speech and 9 files with distorted speech in each test sample, ten-fold cross-validation (principle 1);
inclusion of 18 files with numbers in steps of 10 (files with numbers 1, 11, 21 and so on) in each test set, ten-fold cross-validation (principle 2);
inclusion of 36 files with numbers in steps of 5 (files with numbers 1, 6, 11 and so on) in each test set, five-fold cross-validation (principle 3);
inclusion of 18 random files in each test set, ten-fold cross-validation (principle 2).

In principles 1, 2, and 4, the size of the test sample was 10%, and that of the training sample was 90%. In principle 3 the dimensions were 20% and 80% respectively. Test samples necessarily included an equal ratio of audio files with normal and distorted speech. Principle 2 also considered the need for the test sample to have syllable recordings with each possible position of problematic phonemes in syllables. The training samples contained the rest of the audio recordings from the data set.

At each of the cross-validation iterations, thresholds α and β were selected using the training data, then the error value was calculated on the test data. The following restrictions were imposed on the values of α and β: α and β are non-negative, β is greater than α. Considering the requirements for minimization conditions, an algorithm based on the interior point method using the confidence region method [13] was applied.

The results of the optimization algorithm, the obtained values of the parameters and the values of the distance errors (D_{err}) are presented in Table 3. Based on the obtained results, when using optimally selected parameters, the error value decreased by an average of 60%.

A statistical test was applied to the error values obtained on each of the 10 test samples to compare the groups of errors with the original parameters and those obtained during the minimization. Since the data are dependent (the same set of audio recordings for calculations, with a change only in the value of the parameters), the Wilcoxon criterion was chosen [14].

Table 3. The parameters values and the values of the distance errors.

α	β	D_{err}	Note
0.02	0.12	46230	Initial parameters
1.0734	1.2348	16038	Application of the parameters obtained in the first variant of the algorithm improvement (minimization of classification errors)
0.8597	1.2198	18632	Principle 1
0.9665	1.2273	16985	Principle 2
0.6460	1.2050	20286	Principle 3
0.8597	1.2198	20063	Principle 4

The null hypothesis H0 was put forward that there are no statistical differences between the error sample on the original parameters and the error sample on the parameters obtained during the minimization. Accordingly, the H1 hypothesis is formulated as 'there are statistically significant differences between the samples with errors'.

The results of applying the test with the α parameter equal to 0.05, as well as a 95% confidence interval, are presented in Table 4. Principle 3 was not used due to the small amount of data in the compared samples.

Table 4. Results of applying the Wilcoxon test.

The principle of forming a test sample	Significance level (p-value)	Accepted hypothesis
Principle 1	0.005	H1
Principle 2	0.007	H1
Principle 4	0.005	H1

Thus, in all cases, significant differences in distance errors were established between the use of the original and those found using the parameter minimization algorithm.

3 Conclusion

The algorithm for automated segmentation of speech signals into unvoiced and voiced sections was implemented and improved. The resulting algorithm was tested on audio recordings of syllables with normal (correct) and distorted pronunciation of problematic phonemes (taking into account the speech characteristics of postoperative patients). The analysis of the results of the algorithm was carried out with the subsequent modification of the algorithm. After the modification of the algorithm, a reanalysis of the results of its work was carried out.

Based on the results of re-studying the results of the algorithm, it was found that the distance error values for new (optimally selected) parameters are less than the error values for the original parameters by an average of 60%. This allows us to conclude that it is possible to individually select parameters for the recordings under study to improve the segmentation accuracy. The next stage of the research will be the collection and labeling of a larger data set (increasing the number of both healthy speakers and patients) and comparison of the proposed algorithm with analogues when working with distorted speech. The specific values of the algorithm parameters to be used in the final version, or the method for calculating them, will be determined after study on an expanded data set.

Acknowledgments. Acknowledgments. This research was funded by the Ministry of Science and Higher Education of the Russian Federation within the framework of scientific projects carried out by teams of research laboratories of educational institutions of higher education subordinate to the Ministry of Science and Higher Education of the Russian Federation, project number FEWM-2020–0042.

References

1. Kaprin, A.D., Starinskiy, V.V., Shahzadova, A.O.: Malignancies in Russia in 2021 (Morbidity and mortality), 252 p. MNIOI name of P.A. Herzen, Moscow (2022)
2. Kaprin, A.D., Starinskiy, V.V., Shahzadova, A.O.: The state of oncological care for the population of Russia in 2021, 239 p. MNIOI name of P.A. Herzen, Moscow (2022)
3. Kostuchenko, E., et al.: The Evaluation Process Automation of Phrase and Word Intelligibility Using Speech Recognition Systems. In: Albert Ali Salah, Alexey Karpov, Rodmonga Potapova, (ed.) Speech and Computer: 21st International Conference, SPECOM 2019, Istanbul, Turkey, August 20–25, 2019, Proceedings, pp. 237–246. Springer International Publishing, Cham (2019). https://doi.org/10.1007/978-3-030-26061-3_25
4. Novokhrestova D. I., Kostyuchenko E. Yu., Hodashinsky I. A. Algorithm and method of quantitative assessment of the similarity of speech signals // Proceedings of TUSUR University. - 2022. - V. 25, No. 3. - P. 45–51 (In Russian). DOI: https://doi.org/10.21293/1818-0442-2022-25-3-45-51
5. Kharchenko, S.S., Novokhrestova, D.I., Kostyuchenko, E.: The problem of segmentation into phonemes in assessing the quality of pronunciation of syllables in the framework of speech rehabilitation. Mater. Int. Sci. Conf. Electron. Devices Control Syst. 1–1, 223–226 (2018). (In Russian)
6. Cai, R.: A modified multi-feature voiced/unvoiced speech classification method. In: 2010 Asia-Pacific Conference on Power Electronics and Design. IEEE, pp. 68–71 (2010)
7. Atal, B., Rabiner, L.: A pattern recognition approach to voiced-unvoiced-silence classification with applications to speech recognition. IEEE Trans. Acoust. Speech Signal Process. 24(3), 201–212 (1976)
8. Ijitona, T., Yue, H., Soraghan, J., Lowit, A.: Improved silence-unvoiced-voiced (SUV) segmentation for dysarthric speech signals using linear prediction error variance. In: 2020 5th International Conference on Computer and Communication Systems (ICCCS). IEEE, 2020, pp. 685–690 (2020)
9. Warule, P., Mishra, S.P., Deb, S.: Significance of voiced and unvoiced speech segments for the detection of common cold. Signal, Image and Video Process. 17(5), 1785–1792 (2023). https://doi.org/10.1007/s11760-022-02389-8
10. MATLAB R2023a, https://www.mathworks.com/products/matlab.html, Accessed 5 May 2023
11. Wavesurfer, https://sourceforge.net/projects/wavesurfer/, Accessed 5 May 2023
12. Lagarias, J., Reeds, J., Wright, M., Wright, P.: Convergence properties of the nelder-mead simplex method in low dimensions. SIAM J. Optim. 9(1), 112–147 (1998)
13. Byrd, R., Gilbert, J., Nocedal, J.: A trust region method based on interior point techniques for nonlinear programming. Math. Program. 89(1), 149–185 (2000)
14. Wilcoxon, F.: Individual comparisons by ranking methods. Biometrics Bulletin, № 1 (6), 12, pp. 80–83 (1945)

Respiratory Sickness Detection from Audio Recordings Using CLIP Models

Bhuma Chandra Mohan[(⊠)] [ID]

Bapatla Engineering College, Bapatla, India
chandrabhuma@gmail.com

Abstract. In this work, a deep learning algorithm is proposed to detect whether the cough belongs to a healthy one or sick one. The objective of this work is to propose an improved deep learning algorithm for accurately classifying the cough recordings into two classes i.e., sick and healthy. Features are extracted from the pre-trained Contrastive Language Image Pre-training (CLIP) models. CLIP models are trained on very large image text pairs. Hence, rich and diversified features can be extracted from these CLIP models. The cough audio recordings are converted to Mel Spectrograms, Tempograms, and Chromagrams. These spectral distributions are converted into images. The images are sent through CLIP models and the features are extracted from the CLIP models by using transfer learning approach. Pool of feature arrays are formulated from the three types of spectral distribution images and various CLIP models. Features extracted from these models are fused by using several approaches i.e., Concatenation, Max fusion, Min fusion, and feature interleaving. With appropriate choosing of a classifier and feature selection, strategy the balanced classification accuracy is computed. The proposed algorithm is tested on a database consisting of sick and not sick audio recordings. Feature vector size is reduced by using Particle Swarm Optimization. With the proposed approach, the balanced classification accuracy is well above 85%. Various other classification metrics i.e., precision, recall, and F1 score are also evaluated with cross validation and robustness of the proposed approach is justified with extensive simulations. Further, improved classification metrics are reported on Virufy dataset also.

Keywords: CLIP Models · Cough Classification · Pre-Trained CNN

1 Introduction

Respiratory diseases like asthma, Chronic obstructive pulmonary disease (COPD), and bronchitis are increasing amongst the urban population globally due to increase in the pollution levels caused by industries, urbanization and usage of unscientific methods of wastage disposal. One common symptom that persists in many respiratory diseases is cough. There is some unique pattern in cough sounds that enables professional physician to identify the sickness of the patient. In recent times, sickness detection from cough sounds using machine learning and deep learning techniques were addressed by many researchers [1]. As the technology in Artificial Intelligence is progressing at a rapid

© The Author(s), under exclusive license to Springer Nature Switzerland AG 2023
A. Karpov et al. (Eds.): SPECOM 2023, LNAI 14338, pp. 611–625, 2023.
https://doi.org/10.1007/978-3-031-48309-7_49

rate, health care system is trying to adopt the modern techniques in identification of diseases. This assists the doctors for better diagnosis and cost-effective solutions. The world has seen the spread of COVID-19 virus and the damage it caused to the mankind globally. Shortage of qualified, experienced doctors and hospitals further complicated the problem in the diagnosis and treatment [2]. Accurate and cost effective solutions are essential scenario. AI plays an important role in the disease prediction and detection [3].

For detecting asthma diseases, several neural network based algorithm were available and were discussed in Amrulloh et al. [4]. A comprehensive survey on the usage of artificial intelligence techniques for COVID-19 analysis by various modalities was proposed by Shuja et al. [5]. This work highlighted the usage of both image (CT and X-ray) and audio recordings (cough sounds) in the detection of COVID-19. They highlighted the importance of both the modalities and they have proposed a dataset also. Audio analysis was carried for the detection of COVID-19 and several techniques were reviewed by Deshpande and Schuller [6].

Spectral recordings were used for identification of COVID-19 [7]. Mel Frequency Cepstral Coeffcients (MFCC) were used as the features and Support Vector Machine (SVM) was used as a classifier. An accuracy of 95.86% was reported on Virufy Dataset [8] which has 121 audio samples. On same dataset, by using MFCC coefficients a deep neural network was trained [9] and an accuracy of 97.5%, and an F1 score of 0.974 was reported.

By using both temporal and spectral features i.e., spectral energy, instantaneous frequency, instantaneous frequency peak and spectral information presence of COVID-19 from the cough audio recordings was detected in the work of [10]. Results were reported on a combination of Virufy and Coswara datasets [11] with Random Forests classifier. An accuracy of 80%, Sensitivity of 93.81%, and F1 score of 0.921 was obtained. By using a crowd sourced dataset comprising 5634 recordings [12], a convolution neural network was trained using RMS energy, spectral centroid, roll-off frequencies, zero-crossing, MFCC, duration, and tempo onsets. An accuracy of 80% was obtained. In addition to accuracy metric, precision and recall were also evaluated. By using MFCC features, COVID-19 detection was done by training a convolution neural network on MIT Open-source dataset which has 5320 audio recordings [13]. Accuracies in excess of 97% and 98% sensitivity and 94% specificity was obtained. By using 1927 cough sound samples [14], and MFCC features, COVID-19 was detected using Recurrence dynamics and variable Markov model.

A recent work on Virufy dataset using Multi Layer Perceptron (MLP), Recurrent Neural Network (RNN), Convolution Neural Network (CNN) with Long Short Term Memory networks (LSTM) was reported [15] with 5 fold data augmentation and transfer learning approach. The performance of MLP outperformed CNN and LSTM by a fair margin. An accuracy, average precision, and average recall of MLP were 96.8, 91, and 89.5%. Features are extracted from the last pooling layer of VGG-19 network, and these features are applied to an SVM classifier. A meagre accuracy of 81% was obtained. The precision value is 72% for presence of COVID-19 and 89% for Non COVID case.

In this work, a dataset of 2542 sick and 4045 not sick audio recordings were considered [16]. The aim is to identify whether the cough recording belongs to a healthy person or sick person. The dataset has train, validation and test folders with varying number of images in each folder. In this work, all the samples are combined as a whole and various train test splits are used to test the robustness of the proposed model. This dataset is a compiled one from ESC-50 [17] and AudioSet [18] datasets by using BMAT annotation tool. Further, the proposed algorithm is tested on Virufy dataset also.

The paper is organized as follows. Section 2 illustrates the CLIP models used in the work, Sect. 3 presents the details of the dataset used and in Sect. 4, proposed algorithm is described. The simulations are given in Sect. 5. Concluding remarks are given in Sect. 6.

2   CLIP Models

Contrastive Language-Image Pretraining (CLIP) model [19] is primary a foundation vision model and it is basically a transform based model. A combination of a text transformer and a vision transformer is contained in CLIP. Both text embeddings and image embeddings are used in CLIP. Similar images and text are aligned in vector space. Image-text pairs are taken and their output vectors are pushed closer where as non-pairs are made apart. There are no explicit class labels to be available while training CLIP reducing the burden of manual labelling which is quite expensive and laborious. The first CLIP was trained on 400 Million image text pairs. All the image-text pairs were collected from internet in an automatic manner without any manual intervention. It is the contrastive loss that is used in CLIP rather than cross entropy loss which is used in classification tasks. As CLIP is trained on large datasets it is trained on more diversified and discriminative features of the images. This led to excellent zero shot classification of CLIP models on popular benchmark datasets. CLIP models are trained on a combination of sentences and their relevant images. In contrary to classification approaches, where the models are trained class labels, here CLIP models are trained on text sentences. Hence, the CLIP can learn a lot and can correlate the text with the images. There are many CLIP models trained on various datasets as shown in Table 2. Most of the models in Table 2 are trained on Large-scale Artificial Intelligence Open Network (LAION) dataset. Large scale datasets comprising image-text pairs are provided by Large-scale Artificial Intelligence Open Network (LAION) organization. LAION-5B [20] comprises 5.85 billion multilingual image-text pairs filtered by CLIP, LAION-2B consists of 2.32 billion English image-text pairs, LAION-400M has 400 million English image-text pairs. Yahoo-Flickr Creative Commons (YFCC-15M) [21] contains 15 million image-text pairs and Conceptual Captions (CC-12M) [22] contains 12 million image-text pairs. Compared to conventional pre-trained models, these models are superior in terms of capturing the diversified features from the images. These CLIP models are particularly suitable for zero shot classification tasks. In zero shot classification, there is no training as such as the model has already learnt the nature of the images from the text captions. It can be easily adapted to down stream tasks of classification. They can also be used as feature extractors for the images. They are known as image embeddings. In this work, all the CLIP models are used as feature extractors only. Each CLIP model has its own constraints of image size, and normalization requirements. It depends on the chosen architecture i.e., ResNet50, ViT-B-32 or any other model specified in Table 2.

3 Dataset Description

The dataset comprises a total of 6587 audio recordings with a class distribution of 2542 sick and 4045 not_sick category. There are two classes i.e., sick and not_sick. Under train folder, there are 1435 wav files in sick and 2283 wav files in not_sick category. 468 wav files of sick and 753 of not sick are available in validation folder. For testing, 642 and 1012 files of sick and not_sick are present. In addition to wav files, spectrograms, Mel spectrograms and continuous wavelet transforms of the wav files are also available. Sick and not_sick audio recordings are shown in Fig. 1. For the present work, all the wav files under train, validation and test folders are combined and kept into sick and not_sick folders only. This is to ensure that the model is a more general one and robust. Mel spectrograms, Chromagrams, Constant Q Power Spectrum and Tempograms for the sick and not_sick classes are computed and are shown in Fig. 1. In this work, for computing features, Mel spectrum, Chromagram and Tempogram are only considered. The dataset was compiled from ESC-50 and AudioSet using BMAT Annotation Tool.

For building a database of cough sounds to identify the presence of COVID-19, an organization called Virufy was formed. Virufy dataset is basically a crowd sourced dataset obtained from diversified people from various countries. The pre-processed data consists of 121 segmented cough audio recordings obtained from 16 patients and is labelled with PCR test status. Background noise and silence periods were removed from the audio recordings. There are 73 negative samples (having no COVID-19) and 48 positive samples (presence of COVID-19). It is also an imbalanced dataset. For this dataset also, Mel spectrograms, Chromagrams, and Tempograms are computed and they are converted into images. Resolution of the images is selected as 950x636.

4 Proposed Algorithm

Variation of a certain quantity over time is called a signal. In case of audio signal, the variation is the pressure. For getting digital audio, the audio recording is usually sampled at a rate of 44.1 kHz. The information from the audio recording can be extracted from the time domain waveform or frequency domain representation. Human auditory perception of frequencies doesn't follow linear scale. Differences in lower frequencies are more distinguishable than the higher frequencies. In mel scale, equal distances in pitch are perceived equally from an auditory perspective. When the frequencies of a spectrogram are converted into mel scale, we get Mel spectrogram. Intensity of each pitch is displayed for each pitch in Chromagram [23]. Harmonic and melody characteristics of music are well captured in Chromagram. Rate of the musical beat is measured in Beats Per Minute(BPM). In Tempogram, [24] the mid level representation of tempo information is displayed. All the audio recordings are at first converted into Mel spectrograms, Chromograms and Tempograms.

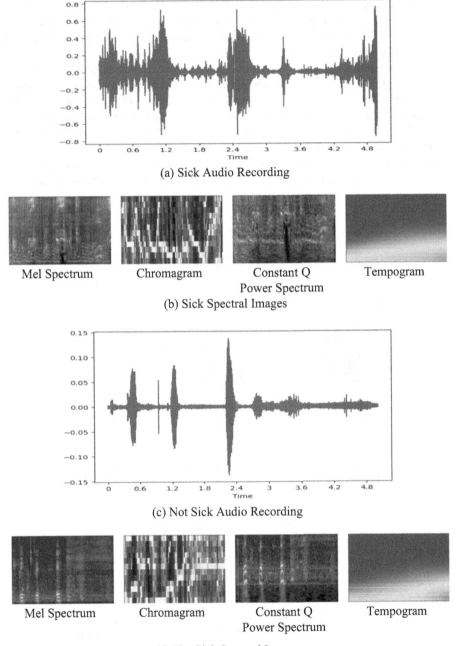

(a) Sick Audio Recording

Mel Spectrum   Chromagram   Constant Q   Tempogram
                                          Power Spectrum
(b) Sick Spectral Images

(c) Not Sick Audio Recording

Mel Spectrum   Chromagram   Constant Q   Tempogram
                                          Power Spectrum
(d) Not Sick Spectral Images

Fig. 1. Illustration of audio recordings and various spectra.

Mel spectrograms, chromograms and Tempograms are converted into images. All the images are resized and preprocessed as per the chosen CLIP model. Features are extracted from the CLIP models by passing the mel spectrograms, Chromagrams and Tempograms. A pool of feature arrays are prepared. From the pool, each feature array is tested with appropriate cross validation and classifier. The best feature array offering highest balanced accuracy is identified. The best single feature array is fused with rest of the feature arrays for improving the classification accuracy. For feature fusion, various fusion methods i.e., concatenation, interleaving, max fusion, min fusion, parallel fusion, weighed fusion, augmented fusion and average fusion [25] are used and the relevant expressions are given in Table 1. Let X and Y be two feature spaces, ζ be the pattern sample space and φ is a random sample in ζ. α and β, are the feature vectors of φ, where $\alpha \in X \ and \ \beta \in Y$. If the feature dimensions of α is $l1$ and β is $l2$ then the concatenated feature vector η has a size of $l1 + l2$.

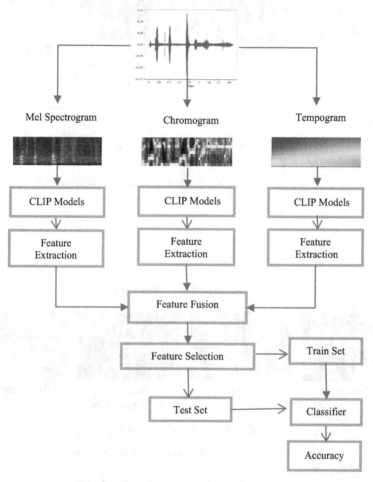

Fig. 2. Block diagram of the proposed work.

Not all the features are relevant for a classification task. Hence, some features which are redundant may removed. There are many feature selection algorithms available in the literature. In this work, a meta-heuristic based feature selection algorithm using Particle Swarm Optimization (PSO) [26] is selected for reducing the size of the feature vector. Removal of redundant features not only reduces the training time, but also improves classification accuracy in general. PSO is a bio-inspired algorithm. It has very less number of hyperparameters and an optimal solution is obtained from the search space. Only the objective function is required and there is no need to have differential form of the objective function. A school of fish or a flock of birds can benefit from the other fishes or birds. If a bird or fish searches for food at random, the experience of the other birds or fishes in the group can help to find the best search. The solution offered by PSO is not the best global but it is very closer to it. When multiple particles are manipulated, each particle can be updated in parallel. Updating can be done once in an iteration by collecting all the individual modifications (Fig. 2).

The best fusion method is chosen. If the fusion method is either concatenation or interleaving, the feature vector size increases.

Table 1. Feature fusion methods.

Types of Feature Fusion	Analytical Expression
Feature Concatenation	$\alpha \oplus \beta$
Feature Interleaving	$m = Min(size(\alpha), size(\beta))$ $\alpha_m \otimes \beta_m$
Parallel Feature Fusion	$\sqrt{\alpha^2 + \beta^2}$
Maximum Fusion	$Max(\alpha, \beta)$
Minimum Fusion	$Min(\alpha, \beta)$
Average Fusion	$\frac{\alpha+\beta}{2}$
Weighed Fusion	$w_1\alpha + w_2\beta$
Augment Fusion	$m = Min(size(\alpha), size(\beta))$ $\alpha_m \oplus \beta_m$

5 Simulations and Results

Simulations are carried using PyTorch deep learning frame work under Google Colab pro environment with A100 GPU. Mel Spectrograms, Chromagrams, and Tempograms are computed using Librosa [27]. Various CLIP models trained on different datasets used in this work are listed below in Table 2. There are 176 feature arrays comprising the features obtained by passing Mel spectrograms, Chromagrams, and Tempograms through the models listed in Table 2. Initially, all the 176 models were tested with

Table 2. CLIP models used in the work.

Name of the Model	Trained Dataset
RN50	Openai,YFCC15M,CC12M
RN50-quickgelu	Openai,YFCC15M,CC12M
RN101,RN101-quickgelu	Openai,YFCC15M
RN50x4, RN50x16, RN50x64	Openai
ViT-B-32	Laion2B_e16,Laion2B_s34b_b79k,datacomp_m_s128m_b4k,commonpool_m_clip_s128m_b4k,commonpool_m_Laion_s128m_b4k,commonpool_m_image_s128m_b4k,commonpool_m_text_s128m_b4k,commonpool_m_basic_s128m_b4k,commonpool_m_s128m_b4k,datacomp_s_s13m_b4k,commonpool_s_clip_s13m_b4k,commonpool_s_Laion_s13m_b4k,commonpool_s_image_s13m_b4k,comonpool_s_text_s13m_b4k,commonpool_s_basic_s13m_b4k,commonpool_s_s13m_b4k
ViT-B-32-quickgelu	Openai, Laion400m_e31, Laion400m_e32
ViT-B-16	Laion400m_e31,Laion400m_e32,Laion2B_s34b_b88k,datacomp_l_s1b_b8k,commonpool_l_clip_s1b_b8k,commonpool_l_Laion_s1b_b8k,commonpool_l_image_s1b_b8k,commonpool_l_text_s1b_b8k,commonpool_l_basic_s1b_b8k,commonpool_l_s1b_b8k
ViT-B-16-plus-240	Laion400m_e31,_e32
ViT-L-14	Openai,Laion400m_e31,Laion400m_e32 Laion2B_s32B_b82k,datacomp_xl_s13b_b90k,comonpool_xl_clip_s13b_b90k,commonpool_xl_Laion_s13b_b90k,commonpool_xl_s13b_b90k
ViT-L-14-336	Openai
ViT-H-14	Laion2B_s32B_b79k
ViT-g-14	Laion2B_s12B_b42k
ViT-g-14	Laion2B_s34b_b88k
ViT-bigG-14	Laion2B_s39b_b160k
Roberta-ViT-B-32	Laion2B_s12B_b32k
ConvNeXt_base	Laion400m_s13b_b51k
ConvNeXt_base_w	Laion2B_s13b_b82k
ConvNeXt_base_w	Laion2B_s13b_b82k_augreg
ConvNeXt_base_w	Laion_aesthetic_s13b_b82k
ConvNeXt_base_w_320	Laion_aesthetic_s13b_b82k
ConvNeXt_base_w_320	Laion_aesthetic_s13b_b82k_augreg
ConvNeXt_large_d	Laion2B_s26b_b102k_augreg
ConvNeXt_large_d_320	Laion2B_s29b_b131k_ft
ConvNeXt_large_d_320	Laion2B_s29b_b131k_ft_soup
ConvNeXt_xxlarge	Laion2B_s34b_b82k_augreg
ConvNeXt_xxlarge	Laion2B_s34b_b82k_augreg_rewind
ConvNeXt_xxlarge	Laion2B_s34b_b82k_augreg_soup
Coca_ViT-B-32	Laion2B_s13b_b90k
Coca_ViT-B-32	Mscoco_finetuned_Laion2B_s13b_b90k
Coca_ViT-L-14	Laion2B_s13b_b90k
Coca_ViT-L-14	Mscoco_finetuned_Laion2B_s13b_b90k
EVA01-g-14	Laion400m_s11b_b41k
EVA01-g-14-plus	Merged2B_s11b_b114k
EVA02-B-16	Merged2B_s8b_b131k
EVA02-L-14	Merged2B_s4b_b131k
EVA02-L-14-336	Merged2B_s6b_b61k
EVA02-E-14	Laion2B_s4b_b115k
EVA02-E-14-plus	Laion2B_s9b_b144k

a stratified 10 fold cross validation by using RidgeClassifierCV and the performance metric chosen is balanced accuracy. As the selected dataset is an imbalanced one, the suitable metric is balanced accuracy. Most of the models classification accuracy varies between 70% and 80% with a peak value of 82.5% obtained for the model number 102. This is shown in Fig. 3. The model is EVA01-g-14Laion400m_s11b_b41k and it is obtained from mel spectrogram with a feature vector size of 1024. This models features are fused with rest of the models features by using various feature fusion techniques and are illustrated in Fig. 4. Fused Models and the best accuracy obtained is given in Table 3. In Table 3, first column specifies the models used for fusion with EVA01-g-14Laion400m_s11b_b41k and type of the spectrogram used along with its feature vector size. Second column specifies the type of feature fusion used for getting the best accuracy. As the highest classification accuracy is obtained for average feature fusion. Its feature vector size is reduced by using Particle Swarm Optimization (PSO) and the feature vector size is reduced to 510 with an average classification accuracy of 83.79% and the minimization of fitness function with iterations is shown in Fig. 5. The variation of the classification accuracy for various folds is shown in Fig. 6.

Simulations are also carried on Virufy dataset. The summary of the simulations is given in Table 4. Various other classification metrics for both the datasets are given in Table 5. Minimization of fitness function with iterations for Virufy dataset is given in Fig. 7. In order to compare with the existing works, the data is split into 70% train and 30% test split and it is repeated ten times to ensure the robustness of the approach. The balanced accuracy obtained is 89%. A comparison with the existing work is given in Table 6 (Fig. 8).

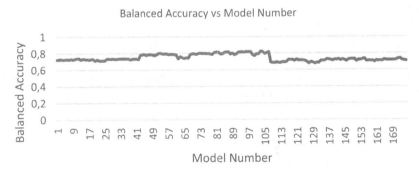

Fig. 3. 10 fold stratified cross validation (balanced accuracy) of various models.

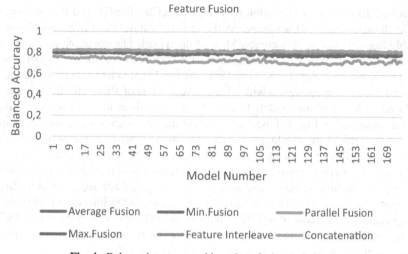

Fig. 4. Balanced accuracy with various fusion techniques.

Table 3. Feature fusion methods and best accuracies obtained.

Models	Feature Fusion Type	Best Accuracy
ConvNextxxlargeLaion2b_s34b_b82k_augreg-rewind Feature vector size:1024, Mel Spectrogram	Average Feature Fusion	82.85%
EVA01-g-14Laion400m_s11b_b41k Feature vector size:1024, Mel Spectrogram	Min. Feature Fusion	82.5%
EVA01-g-14Laion400m_s11b_b41k Feature vector size:1024, Mel Spectrogram	Max. Feature Fusion	82.5%
ConvNextlarge_d_320Laion2b_s29b_b131k-ft Feature vector size:768, Mel Spectrogram	Feature Interleave	82.79%
ViT-L-14Laion400m_e32 Feature vector size:768, Tempogram	Parallel Feature Fusion	76.39%
ConvNextlarge_d_320Laion2B_s26b_b102k_augreg Feature vector size:768, Mel Spectrogram	Concatenation	82.7%

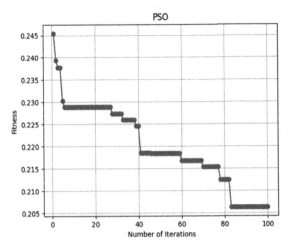

Fig. 5. Fitness function minimization in PSO (sick dataset).

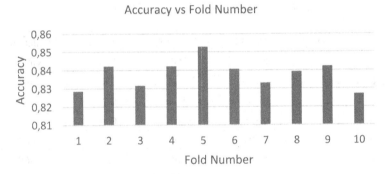

Fig. 6. Accuracy vs folds.

Table 4. Virufy dataset simulation parameters.

Number of Models used	186
Models Used	ViT-B-32commonpool_m_basic_s128m_b4k ViT-B-32commonpool_s_text_s13m_b4k RN101yfcc15m
Type of Spectrograms	Mel Spectrograms
Feature Fusion Type	Concatenation
Feature Vector Size	1536 (3x512)
Reduced Feature Vector Size	683
Classifier	Linear SVC

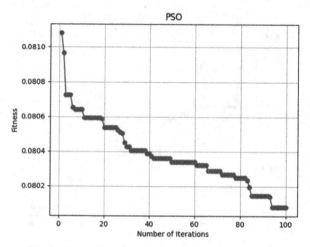

Fig. 7. Fitness function minimization (Virufy dataset).

Table 5. Performance metrics of sick and Virufy datasets.

Performance Metrics	10 fold Cross Validation		5 fold Cross Validation	
	Sick	Virufy	Sick	Virufy
Balanced Accuracy	0.829	0.892	0.824	0.890
F1 Score	0.789	0.858	0.784	0.858
Average Precision	0.868	0.961	0.864	0.961
Average Recall	0.782	1.000	0.775	1.000
F1_Micro	0.839	0.868	0.835	0.868
F1_Macro	0.830	0.867	0.825	0.867
F1_Weighted	0.839	0.869	0.835	0.869
Jaccard Score	0.653	0.752	0.645	0.752
ROC_AUC	0.911	0.974	0.909	0.974

Accuracy vs Folds (Virufy)

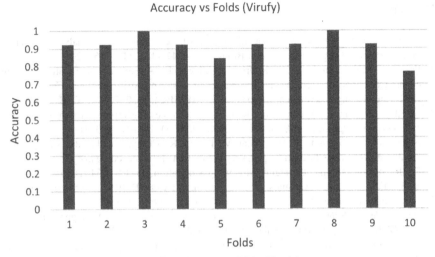

Fig. 8. Accuracy vs folds (Virufy).

Table 6. Comparison of proposed work with existing works.

Works of	Performance Metrics
Kapoor et al. [15]	Transfer Learning approach: VGG-19 Accuracy: 81% Train-Test Split: 70–30%
Proposed	Transfer Learning approach: CLIP Models Balanced Accuracy: 89.0% (70–30% split repeated 10 times)

6 Conclusions

In this work, an algorithm is presented for detecting sickness from the cough audio recordings using CLIP models and spectrograms. Mel spectrograms, Chromagrams, and Tempograms are computed for the audio recordings of the dataset. Features of these spectrograms are computed by using CLIP models. Pool of features arrays are prepared and the best combination of the features for feature fusion is identified. Size of the feature vector is reduced by using a meta-heuristic algorithm PSO. For sick dataset, the average feature fusion is able to give a classification accuracy of 82.9%. For Virufy dataset, feature concatenation resulted in a 89.2% average balanced accuracy for a 10 fold stratified cross validation. It is observed that after feature selection by PSO, the average classification accuracy increased to 83.79% for sick and 91.53% for Virufy dataset. Mere usage of train test split cannot ensure the robustness of the model, hence proper cross validations are to be carried which is done in this work compared to the work of [15].

References

1. Abeyratne, U.R., Swarnkar, V., Setyati, A., Triasih, R.: Cough sound analysis can rapidly diagnose childhood pneumonia. Ann. Biomed. Eng. **41**(11), 2448–2462 (2013)
2. Pramono, R.X.A., Imtiaz, S.A., Rodriguez-Villegas, E.: Automatic identification of cough events from acoustic signals. In: Proceedings of 41st Annual International Conference on IEEE Engineering and Medical Biology Society (EMBC), pp. 217–220. IEEE (2019)
3. Al-Khassaweneh, M., Abdelrahman, R.B.: A signal processing approach for the diagnosis of asthma from cough sounds. J. Med. Eng. Technol. **37**(3), 165–171 (2013)
4. Amrulloh, Y., Abeyratne, U., Swarnkar, V., Triasih, R.: Cough sound analysis for pneumonia and asthma classification in pediatric population. In: Proceedings of 6th International Conference on Intelligent Systems, Modelling Simulation, pp. 127–131 (2015)
5. Shuja, J., Alanazi, E., Alasmary, W., Alashaikh, A.: COVID-19 open source data sets: a comprehensive survey. Int. J. Speech Technol. **51**(3), 1296–1325 (2021)
6. Deshpande, G., Schuller, B.: An overview on audio, signal, speech, & language processing for COVID-19. https://arxiv.org/abs/2005.08579. Accessed 2 Feb 2023
7. Manshouri, N.M.: Identifying COVID-19 by using spectral analysis of cough recordings: a distinctive classification study. Cogn. Neurodyn. **16**, 239–253 (2021)
8. Khanzadam, A., Wilson, T.: Home page Github Dataset. Virufy COVID-19 Open Cough Dataset. https://github.com/virufy/virufy-data. Accessed 06 May 2023
9. Islam, R., Abdel-Raheem, E., Tarique, M.: A study of using cough sounds and deep neural networks for the early detection of Covid- 19. Biomed. Eng. Adv. **3**, 100025 (2022)
10. Tena, A., Clariá, F., Solsona, F.: Automated detection of COVID-19 cough. Biomed. Signal Process. Control **71**, 103175 (2022)
11. Sharma, N., et al.: Coswara–a database of breathing, cough, and voice sounds for COVID-19 diagnosis. arXiv preprint arXiv:2005.10548 (2020)
12. Brown, C., et al: Exploring automatic diagnosis of Covid-19 from crowdsourced respiratory sound data. In: Proceedings of the 26th ACM SIGKDD International Conference on Knowledge Discovery and Data Mining, pp. 3474–3484. ACM(2020)
13. Laguarta, J., Hueto, F., Subirana, B.: COVID-19 artificial intelligence diagnosis using only cough recordings. IEEE Open J. Eng. Med. Biol. **1**, 275–281 (2020). https://doi.org/10.1109/OJEMB.2020.3026928
14. Mouawad, P., Dubnov, T., Dubnov, S.: Robust detection of COVID-19 in cough sounds. SN Comput. Sci. **2**(1), 1–13 (2021)
15. Kapoor, T., Pandhi, T., Gupta, B.: Cough audio analysis for COVID-19 diagnosis. SN Comput. Sci. **4**(2), 125 (2023)
16. OSF Home. https://osf.io/tmkud/wiki/home/. Accessed 21 Sept 2023
17. Piczak, K.J.: ESC: dataset for environmental sound classification. In: Proceedings of the 23rd Annual ACM Conference on Multimedia, Brisbane, Australia (2015)
18. https://research.google.com/audioset/index.html. Accessed 21 Sept 2023
19. Radford, A., et al.: Learning transferable visual models from natural language Supervision. CoRR arXiv:2103.00020 (2021)
20. Schumann, C., et al.: LAION-5B: An open large-scale dataset for training next generation image-text models (2022). arXiv:2210.08402. https://doi.org/10.48550/arXiv.2210.08402
21. Thomee, B., et al.: YFCC100M: the new data in multimedia research. Commun. ACM **59**(2), 64–73 (2016)
22. Sharma, P., Ding, N., Goodman, S., Soricut, R.: Conceptual captions: a cleaned, hypernymed, image alt-text dataset for automatic image captioning. In: Proceedings of ACL, pp. 2556–2565 (2018)

23. Daniel, P.W.E.: Chroma feature analysis and synthesis. https://www.ee.columbia.edu/~dpwe/resources/matlab/chroma-ansy. Accessed 9 Sept 2023
24. Grosche, P., Müller, M., Kurth, F.: Cyclic tempogram - a mid-level tempo representation for music signals. In: IEEE International Conference on Acoustics, Speech and Signal Processing, Dallas, TX, USA, pp. 5522–5525 (2010). https://doi.org/10.1109/ICASSP.2010.5495219
25. Yang, F., Ma, Z., Xie, M.: Image classification with superpixels and feature fusion method. J. Electron. Sci. Technol. **19**(1), 100096 (2021)
26. Eberhart, R., Kennedy, J.: A new optimizer using particle swarm theory. In: MHS 1995, Proceedings of the Sixth International Symposium on Micro Machine and Human Science, pp. 39–43. IEEE (1995)
27. McFee, B., et al.:. librosa/librosa: 0.10.0.post2 (0.10.0.post2). Zenodo (2023). https://doi.org/10.5281/zenodo.7746972

Investigating the Effect of Data Impurity on the Detection Performances of Mental Disorders Through Spoken Dialogues

Rohan Kumar Gupta$^{(\boxtimes)}$ ⓘ and Rohit Sinha ⓘ

Indian Institute of Technology Guwahati, Guwahati 781039, India
peeroff@iitg.ac.in
https://www.iitg.ac.in

Abstract. The automatic detection of mental disorders has been mainly performed through binary classifiers trained on the behavioral data collected through an interview setup. Such classifiers are usually trained by keeping the data from the participants having the disorder of interest in the positive class while the data from all other participants are kept in the negative class. In practice, it is well known that some mental disorders have common symptoms. Thus, the behavioral data may carry a mixed bag of attributes related to multiple disorders. As a result, the negative class may carry attributes related to the mental disorder of interest. This data impurity may lead to sub-optimal training of the classifier for a mental disorder of interest. In this study, we investigate this hypothesis in the context of major depressive disorder (MDD) and post-traumatic stress disorder detection (PTSD). The results show that upon removal of such data impurity, the MDD detection performances are significantly improved. However, such improvement is not observed consistently for PTSD detection, which may attribute to PTSD being a subtype of MDD.

Keywords: Human-computer interaction · Audio modality · Correlated mental disorders · Hybrid deep learning models

1 Introduction

Recently, the research on the automatic detection of mental disorders has increased exponentially [18]. For the development of a mental disorder detector, the behavioural data from the participants is collected through an interview conducted by a human interviewer/computer agent. The interview is mainly conducted through a set of questions that are related to the mental disorder of interest. The participants' behavioural data is collected in distinct modalities, such as audio [6,14,15,21], video [6,14,21], and physiological signals [5,22]. Several studies have been reported on such modalities targeting the detection of a mental disorder of interest [5,12,20]. In those studies, the ground truth is obtained mainly based on the participant's responses to a self-reported questionnaire for that mental disorder. The criteria followed by these self-reported questionnaires are mentioned in the diagnostic and statistical manual of mental disorders (DSM) [1]. And it refers to having the least number of symptoms out of a predefined set of symptoms for diagnosing a mental disorder. In the DSM, it can be observed that some mental disorders share a few symptoms. Due to this, during a clinical interview, a participant suffering from the mental disorder of interest may provide similar behavioral data, to some extent, to the participants having a related mental disorder(s). Among the reported studies, the detector for a mental disorder is mainly developed using a binary classifier comprising data from participants with and without that particular disorder forms positive and negative classes, respectively. The presence of data from the participants, who are not suffering from the mental disorder of interest but have related mental disorder(s), in the negative class may lead to increase misclassification rates.

Major depressive disorder (MDD) is the most widely investigated mental disorder. On the other hand, post-traumatic stress disorder (PTSD) is another commonly occurring mental disorder, though relatively less studied. In the 5th version of DSM [1], the sets of symptoms characterizing MDD and PTSD have four common symptoms. The authors in [23] have conducted a genetic analysis to investigate the relation between MDD and PTSD. It is found that PTSD is the subtype of MDD. Based on the correlation analysis of the responses to the self-reported questionnaires, it is reported that MDD and PTSD are highly correlated [16]. Thus, these reported findings indicate that the characteristics of MDD and PTSD are somewhat similar. The Distress Analysis Interview Corpus Wizard-of-Oz (DAIC-WOZ) [6] is one of the most widely referred publicly available audio-video datasets. In DAIC-WOZ, each participant's data is labeled for both presence and absence of MDD and PTSD. The majority of the reported research works performed the detection of MDD without referring to the labels of PTSD [7,8,12,20]. Upon analyzing the labels of the DAIC-WOZ dataset, we found that the data from a few non-depressed participants are labeled for PTSD. Similarly, the data from a few participants who are not labeled for PTSD but for MDD. Since MDD and PTSD are highly correlated and share some symptoms, it is possible that some acoustic and visual markers are shared between the MDD- and PTSD-diagnosed populations in the DAIC-WOZ dataset. As a result of that a binary classifier trained for MDD detection may lead to increase misclassification rates if the data from PTSD-diagnosed participants is included in the negative class. Degradation may be observed for PTSD detection performance if the data from MDD-diagnosed participants is included in the negative class.

In this study, we aim to analyze the effect of existing instances of a related mental disorder in the negative class on the binary classification performance for the detection of a mental disorder of interest. For the same, we utilized the DAIC-WOZ dataset which is labeled for MDD and PTSD. Both disorders are assigned as the primary and related mental disorders interchangeably. The rest of the paper is organized as follows. Section 2 provides the experimental details.

The experimental results are presented in Sect. 3. The summary of the study and inferences of the obtained results are provided in Sect. 4. The final remarks are provided in Sect. 5.

2   Experimental Details

In the following, we provided details of the dataset, methodology, and model architectures employed in this study.

2.1   Dataset

This study utilized the DAIC-WOZ dataset [6]. It comprises 189 recorded interactions in audio-video format between a virtual interviewer and the participants. Labeling the audio-video data is based on participants' responses to self-reported questionnaires. The Patient Health Questionnaire (PHQ-8) [11] and PTSD Checklist – Civilian version (PCL-C) [2] questionnaires were utilized to obtain labels for the detection of MDD and PTSD, respectively. A participant is diagnosed with the disorders if their score on the questionnaires exceeds a predefined threshold which is 10 and 45 for PHQ-8 and PCL-C questionnaires, respectively.

The dataset is further divided into training, development, and test partition comprising data from 107, 35, and 47 participants, respectively. Figure 1 shows the distribution of the participants in the training, development, and test partitions, respectively, among 'healthy control' and 'non-healthy control' groups. The healthy control refers to the group comprising data from participants neither diagnosed with MDD nor PTSD. In contrast, the non-healthy control group comprises data from participants diagnosed with MDD or PTSD, or both. For MDD detection, a binary classifier has been utilized that includes classes consisting of data from participants with or without MDD. Upon analyzing the partitions of the DAIC-WOZ dataset, we found that the negative class of the MDD classifier comprises the data from 9, 1, and 4 participants with PTSD in the training, development, and test partitions, respectively, along with data from the healthy control group participants. The same can also be deduced from Fig. 1. Similarly, for PTSD detection, the negative comprises data from 7, 4, and 5 participants with MDD in the training, development, and test partitions, respectively, along with data from the healthy control group participants.

2.2   Methodology

This study is performed to analyze the impact on the detection performance of a mental disorder of interest due to the existence of another related mental disorder in the targeted population. The experiments are performed for MDD as being the primary disorder and PTSD as a related disorder, and vice-versa. For this study, we propose a modification that involves the removal of data of the participants with a related mental disorder from the negative class of a binary

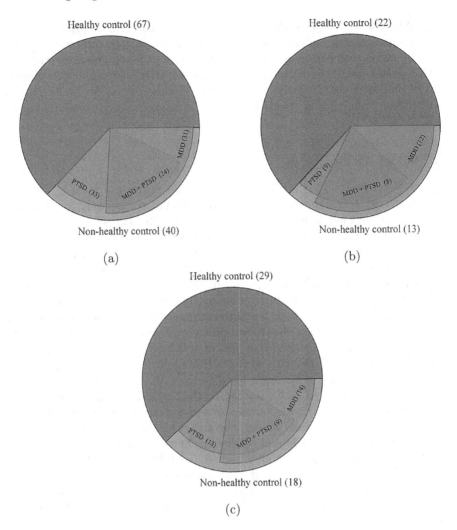

Fig. 1. Distribution of the participants in the (a) training, (b) development, and (c) test partitions in the DAIC-WOZ dataset. The number in the brackets indicates the population of the participants in a particular group.

classifier trained to detect the primary mental disorder. When MDD is selected as the primary disorder, the data of the participants diagnosed with PTSD in the negative class is removed. Similarly, when PTSD is selected as the primary disorder, the data of the participants diagnosed with MDD in the negative class is removed. For both cases, the removal of the participants' data is performed either on the training partition or on both training and development partitions, which are used in separate experiments. The test partition is unaltered in all experiments. For MDD as the primary mental disorder, the resultant training and development partitions comprise data from 98 and 34 participants, respectively. Whereas, for PTSD as the primary mental disorder, the resultant training and development sets comprise data from 100 and 31 participants, respectively. It can be noted that the change in the distribution of development partition is relatively more for PTSD detection compared to MDD detection after applying the proposed modification. The baseline of these detection performances is created by training and developing the models on the original partitions of DAIC-WOZ.

2.3 Model Architectures

This study utilizes two hybrid deep learning architectures proposed in [12] and [3], and referred to as 'DepAudioNet' and 'Raw Audio', respectively. We used the source code of the models developed by the authors in [3]. The schematic diagram of the models is depicted in Fig. 2. The models are excited either by raw audio input or by low-level descriptors (LLDs) of the raw audio input. The raw audio is first pre-processed based on the methods outlined in [12]. The pre-processing step comprises the removal of long pauses in each audio file by utilizing the onset and offset time specified in the corresponding transcript file. The remaining portions are then concatenated together in the original sequence. The audio input is a non-overlapping segment of 61440 samples, corresponding to 3.84 sec. For the DepAudioNet model, a feature extraction step is referred to that outputs mel-filter bank features as LLDs, with 40 banks being selected. The Hanning window length used for creating LLDs is set to 64 msec, with a corresponding hop size of 32 msec. The extracted LLDs are fed to the one-dimensional convolutional neural network (1D-CNN) with kernel size 3 and stride 1 of the DepAudioNet. In contrast, for the raw audio model, the audio segment is directly fed to the 1D-CNN with kernel size 1024 and stride 512. The raw audio model used either 1 or 2 convolutional layers. In which, the second 1D-CNN layer has kernel size 3 and stride 1. The 1D-CNN layer is used to capture the local variation among the low-level descriptors. All other layers in both models are kept identical. The convolutional layer(s) is followed by batch normalization, rectified linear unit activation, max pooling (kernel 3, stride 3), and dropout (0.05). These layers are not shown in Fig. 2a and Fig. 2b for brevity. Subsequently, two unidirectional long short-term memory (LSTM) layers are employed, having 128 hidden nodes. The LSTM layers are used for capturing the long-term dependencies. The outputs of the LSTM layers are transformed to the probability of an input segment belonging to the positive class using a fully-connected layer that comprises sigmoid non-linearity. The final prediction for a participant is made based on the majority voting rule over all segments of that participant. The rate of decay of the learning rate (λ), a hyperparameter, is set to either 1 or 2. In both models, the binary cross-entropy loss function is utilized. The models are trained using Adam optimizer.

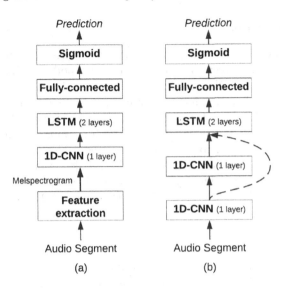

Fig. 2. The schematic diagram of the model architecture of (a) 'DepAudioNet', (b) 'Raw Audio' in which the dotted line shows the alternative architecture with one less CNN layer.

3   Results

In the following, we present the detection performances of the experiments mentioned in Sect. 2.2. At first, we presented the MDD detection performances of the models trained on the modified training partition under two cases corresponding to development partition being modified and unmodified. These cases are also investigated for PTSD detection, and their performances are given in the subsequent subsection. The detection performances on the original partitions are also given for contrast purposes. To further establish the efficacy of the proposed approach, we compared its detection performances with the other approaches reported in the literature which happen to utilize the considered model (DepAudioNet). In this study, for each experiment, we have trained each model five times on randomly generated training subsets, and the final outcome is obtained by averaging the probabilities predicted by those. The performances of the detectors are evaluated in terms of the F1-score of positive and negative classes along with their average on the test partition of the DAIC-WOZ dataset. The hyperparameters of the models are kept identical for all experiments unless specified. All the experiments are conducted on audio data only. The deep learning models are realized using Pytorch modules running on NVIDIA RTX A6000 GPU.

3.1 MDD Detection

Table 1 shows MDD detection performances for considered models. In which *Baseline* refers to the detection performance of the models trained using original partitions. For DepAudioNet model, with the reported macro-averaging F1-score of 0.382 in [13], the Baseline has yield a competitive score of 0.401. The detection performances listed under *Case-1* and *Case-2* correspond to the proposed modification done only on the training and both training and development partitions, respectively. It can be observed from the table that across all models, except one, Case-1 provided significantly better detection performances compared to that of Baseline. The increment in the detection performance in terms of macro-averaging F1-score (Avg.) lies in the range of 2.09–15.21%. A similar trend is observed upon comparing the detection performances of Case-2 with the Baseline.

Table 1. MDD detection Performances on the test partition of the DAIC-WOZ dataset in terms of F1-score. λ: rate of decay of the learning rate, C: number of convolutional layers, PC: positive class, NC: negative class, Case-1: modified training partition, Case-2: modified training and development partitions.

Model	λ	C	Baseline			Case-1			Case-2		
			PC	NC	Avg.	PC	NC	Avg.	PC	NC	Avg.
DepAudioNet	2	1	0.235	0.567	0.401	0.250	0.613	**0.432**	0.250	0.613	**0.432**
DepAudioNet	3	1	0.235	0.567	0.401	0.267	0.656	**0.462**	0.267	0.656	**0.462**
Raw Audio	2	1	0.267	0.656	0.462	0.240	0.725	**0.482**	0.240	0.725	**0.482**
Raw Audio	3	1	0.375	0.677	0.526	0.320	0.754	**0.537**	0.320	0.754	**0.537**
Raw Audio	2	2	0.167	0.714	**0.441**	0.242	0.590	0.416	0.242	0.590	0.416
Raw Audio	3	2	0.160	0.696	0.428	0.294	0.600	0.447	0.313	0.645	**0.479**

3.2 PTSD Detection

Table 2 shows the PTSD detection performances for the Baseline, Case-1, and Case-2. To the best of our knowledge, PTSD detection on the test partition of the DAIC-WOZ dataset is yet to be reported. It can be observed from the table that the detection performances have not improved for the majority of models upon applying the proposed modification on the training partition (Case-1) compared to the Baseline. On the other hand, no definitive trend is observed upon comparing the detection performances of Case-2 with the Baseline.

Table 2. PTSD detection Performances on the test partition of the DAIC-WOZ dataset in terms of F1-score. λ: rate of decay of the learning rate, C: number of convolutional layers, PC: positive class, NC: negative class, Case-1: modified training partition, Case-2: modified training and development partitions.

Model	λ	C	Baseline			Case-1			Case-2		
			PC	NC	Avg.	PC	NC	Avg.	PC	NC	Avg.
DepAudioNet	2	1	0.320	0.754	**0.537**	0.345	0.708	0.526	0.323	0.667	0.495
DepAudioNet	3	1	0.276	0.677	0.476	0.345	0.708	0.526	0.357	0.727	**0.542**
Raw Audio	2	1	0.160	0.696	0.428	0.087	0.704	0.396	0.214	0.667	**0.441**
Raw Audio	3	1	0.250	0.743	**0.496**	0.174	0.732	0.453	0.160	0.696	0.428
Raw Audio	2	2	0.276	0.677	**0.476**	0.182	0.750	0.466	0.256	0.473	0.365
Raw Audio	3	2	0.167	0.714	0.441	0.222	0.687	**0.454**	0.174	0.732	0.453

Table 3. Evaluating the efficacy of the proposed approach for MDD detection with respect to the reported ones on the test partition of the DAIC-WOZ dataset in terms of macro-averaging F1 score (Macro-F1).

System attribute	Approach	Macro-F1
Data augmentation [13]	Noise augmentation	0.477
	VTLP	0.462
	Speed perturbation	0.431
	Pitch perturbation	0.431
	FrAUG	0.479
Proposed	Case-1	**0.510**
	Case-2	0.479

3.3 Comparison with Similar Works Involving Data Modification

We performed a literature survey to benchmark the detection performances of the proposed approach for the considered models (DepAudioNet and raw audio). In our survey, we found a recent study [13] that reported MDD detection performances for the DepAudioNet model only. We have not found any work for PTSD detection. The authors in [13] has proposed a data augmentation strategy for MDD detection and compared its effectiveness with other state-of-the-art data augmentation strategies. The proposed strategy, named FrAUG, employs a different combination of frame length and shift for the extraction of the mel-spectrogram. The other employed strategies are noise augmentation [17], vocal tract length perturbation (VTLP) [9], speed and pitch perturbation [10]. Each strategy has been applied only on the training partition of the DAIC-WOZ dataset while keeping the development and test partition intact. The detection is performed at speaker level and the utilized source code of the DepAudioNet model from the same repository [3] used by us. Thus, the reported detection performances for various data augmentation strategies can be compared with our proposed data modification approach. To obtain the optimal detection performance for the proposed approach, we fine-tuned hyper-parameters of the model on the development partition. The tuned hyper-parameters are batch size, learning rate, and learning rate decay factor.

Table 3 shows the MDD detection performance for the proposed approach, in terms of macro-averaging F1-score, along with the reported detection performance on the test partition in [13]. It can be observed that the proposed approach (Case-1) outperformed all refereed data augmentation approaches. The increment in the detection performance with respect to the best data augmentation approach (FrAUG) is found to be 6.47%.

4   Summary and Discussion

This study analyzed the existing data impurity in the DAIC-WOZ dataset and showed its impact on the detection performance of a mental disorder of interest. The dataset comprises audio-video data of participants labeled for MDD and PTSD detection. Upon analyzing the dataset, we found that a few participants not having MDD are suffering from PTSD and vice-versa. The reported studies suggest that there may exist some similarities between the population of patients with MDD and PTSD. Thus, the detection performance of MDD/PTSD for a binary classifier may get affected if the negative class comprises data from the patient with PTSD/MDD. To analyze this hypothesis, we proposed a modification to be applied to the existing partitions of the dataset. The proposed modification involves the removal of the data of the participants with PTSD in the negative class for MDD detection. Similarly, for PTSD detection, the data of the participants with MDD in the negative class are discarded. Separate binary classifiers are created on the modified training or both training and development partitions of the DAIC-WOZ dataset for MDD/PTSD detection. The performances obtained for the original partitions of the DAIC-WOZ create the baseline.

Results show that the proposed modification applied only on the training partition and on both training and development partitions of the DAIC-WOZ dataset leads to a substantial improvement in the detection performance of MDD over the created baseline. It implies that data from participants with PTSD in the negative class of the binary classifier for MDD detection increases misclassification rates. On the other hand, such improvement is not observed consistently for PTSD detection. This is attributed to the finding in [23] that state that PTSD is a sub-type of MDD. Thus, the information provided by the MDD-diagnosed participant in the negative class may contribute to improving the detection of PTSD.

To further validate the efficacy of the proposed approach, we compare its MDD detection performances with the reported ones in [13] on the test partition of the DAIC-WOZ for the DepAudioNet model. Our proposed approach provides identical or better detection performance compared to the best detection performance reported in [13]. The increment is found to be 6.47%.

The presented analysis in this study may significantly affect many state-of-the-art performances, which are mainly performed on the binary classifier to detect a mental disorder. This study also highlights the problem with the data collection protocol. In contrast to many textual corpora in which text data are labeled for multiple mental disorders [4,19], the existing audio datasets are labeled for a limited number of mental disorders [6,14,15] and, in some cases, for only one [21]. This limits further analyzing the data in the negative class. Thus, to mitigate this issue, the data collection protocol needs to obtain labels for multiple mental disorders.

We acknowledge the limitations inherent in this study, which is exclusively conducted within the audio modality. This study can be extended to other modalities as well. Furthermore, utilizing limited deep learning models would be another limitation. This study is performed for only two correlated mental disorders. It would be interesting to explore various other correlated mental disorders.

5   Conclusions

This study investigates the effect of existing data impurity in a dataset on the detection performances of a mental disorder of interest. For the same, a publicly available audio-video dataset labeled for MDD and PTSD detection is utilized. The experimental results on audio data show that the MDD detection performances on the test partition are improved substantially upon removing the data impurity from the training partition and both the training and development partitions of the dataset. However, such improvement is not observed consistently for PTSD detection, which may attribute to PTSD being a subtype of MDD. Further validation of the proposed approach is done by comparing its efficacy with the strategies reported for enhancing the detection performance on the identical model. The proposed approach is found to be better than the reported one. The future direction would involve replicating the study on other modalities as well as on different state-of-the-art models. Exploring other mental disorders would be another future direction.

References

1. Diagnostic and statistical manual of mental disorders: DSM-5, 5th edn. American Psychiatric Association (2013)
2. Andrykowski, M., Cordova, M., Studts, J., Miller, T.: Posttraumatic stress disorder after treatment for breast cancer: Prevalence of diagnosis and use of the PTSD checklist - civilian version (PCL-C) as a screening instrument. J. Consult. Clin. Psychol. **66**(3), 586–90 (1998)
3. Bailey, A., Plumbley, M.D.: Gender bias in depression detection using audio features. arXiv:2010.15120 [cs.SD] (2021)
4. Benton, A., Mitchell, M., Hovy, D.: Multitask learning for mental health conditions with limited social media data. In: Proceedings of the 15th Conference of the European Chapter of the Association for Computational Linguistics, pp. 152–162 (2017)

5. Garcia-Ceja, E., Riegler, M., Nordgreen, T., Jakobsen, P., Oedegaard, K.J., Tørresen, J.: Mental health monitoring with multimodal sensing and machine learning: a survey. Perv. Mob. Comput. **51**, 1–26 (2018)
6. Gratch, J., et al.: The distress analysis interview corpus of human and computer interviews. In: Proceedings of the International Conference on Language Resources and Evaluation, pp. 3123–3128 (2014)
7. Huang, Z., Epps, J., Joachim, D.: Exploiting vocal tract coordination using dilated CNNs for depression detection in naturalistic environments. In: Proceedings of the IEEE International Conference on Acoustics, Speech and Signal Processing (ICASSP), pp. 6549–6553 (2020)
8. Huang, Z., Epps, J., Joachim, D., Stasak, B., Williamson, J., Quatieri, T.: Domain adaptation for enhancing speech-based depression detection in natural environmental conditions using dilated CNNs. In: Proceedings of the Annual Conference of the International Speech Communication Association (INTERSPEECH) (2020)
9. Jaitly, N., Hinton, E.: Vocal tract length perturbation (VTLP) improves speech recognition. In: Proceedings of the ICML Workshop on Deep Learning for Audio, Speech and Language, vol. 117, p. 21 (2013)
10. Ko, T., Peddinti, V., Povey, D., Khudanpur, S.: Audio augmentation for speech recognition. In: Proceedings of the Annual Conference of the International Speech Communication Association (INTERSPEECH) (2015)
11. Kroenke, K., Strine, T.W., Spitzer, R.L., Williams, J.B.W., Berry, J.T., Mokdad, A.H.: The PHQ-8 as a measure of current depression in the general population. J. Affect. Disord. **114**(1–3), 163–173 (2009)
12. Ma, X., Yang, H., Chen, Q., Huang, D., Wang, Y.: DepAudioNet: an efficient deep model for audio based depression classification. In: Proceedings of the 6th International Workshop on Audio/Visual Emotion Challenge, pp. 35–42 (2016)
13. Ravi, V., Wang, J., Flint, J., Alwan, A.: FrAUG: a frame rate based data augmentation method for depression detection from speech signals. In: Proceedings of the IEEE International Conference on Acoustics, Speech and Signal Processing (ICASSP), pp. 6267–6271 (2022)
14. Scherer, S., et al.: Automatic behavior descriptors for psychological disorder analysis. In: Proceedings of the 10th IEEE International Conference and Workshops on Automatic Face and Gesture Recognition (FG), pp. 1–8 (2013)
15. Schultebraucks, K., Yadav, V., Shalev, A., Bonanno, G., Galatzer-Levy, I.: Deep learning-based classification of posttraumatic stress disorder and depression following trauma utilizing visual and auditory markers of arousal and mood. Psychol. Med. **52**(5), 957–967 (2020)
16. Smoller, J.: The genetics of stress-related disorders: PTSD, depression and anxiety disorders. Neuropsychopharmacol. Off. Publ. Am. Coll. Neuropsychopharmacol. **41**(1), 297–319 (2016)
17. Snyder, D., Garcia-Romero, D., Sell, G., Povey, D., Khudanpur, S.: X-vectors: robust DNN embeddings for speaker recognition. In: 2018 IEEE International Conference on Acoustics, Speech and Signal Processing (ICASSP), pp. 5329–5333 (2018)
18. Thieme, A., Belgrave, D., Doherty, G.: Machine learning in mental health: a systematic review of the HCI literature to support the development of effective and implementable ML systems. ACM Trans. Comput.-Hum. Interact. **27**(5) (2020)
19. Tran, T., Kavuluru, R.: Predicting mental conditions based on "history of present illness" in psychiatric notes with deep neural networks. J. Biomed. Inf. **75**(2), S138–S148 (2017)

20. Valstar, M., Gratch, J., Schuller, B., Ringeval, F., Cowie, R., Pantic, M.: AVEC 2016: depression, mood, and emotion recognition workshop and challenge. In: Proceedings of the 6th International Workshop on Audio/Visual Emotion Challenge, pp. 1483–1484 (2016)
21. Victor, E., Aghajan, Z.M., Sewart, A., Christian, R.: Detecting depression using a framework combining deep multimodal neural networks with a purpose-built automated evaluation. Psychol. Assess. 31(8), 1019 (2019)
22. Wijsman, J., Grundlehner, B., Liu, H., Hermens, H., Penders, J.: Towards mental stress detection using wearable physiological sensors. In: Proceedings of the Annual International Conference of the IEEE Engineering in Medicine and Biology Society, pp. 1798–1801 (2011)
23. Zhang, F., et al.: Genetic evidence suggests posttraumatic stress disorder as a subtype of major depressive disorder. J. Clin. Invest. 132(3), e145942 (2021)

Author Index

A

Acharya, Rajul II-335
Agafonova, Olga I-350
Agarwal, Ayush I-142, II-539
Agrawal, Saurabh II-490
Aitawade, Aniket I-258
Akhter, Md. Tousin I-233
Akhtyamova, Svetlana I-430
Akulov, Artem I-159
Alam, Jahangir II-18, II-307, II-446, II-550
Alam, Md Shahidul II-307
Anand, Konjengbam II-127
Ananthanarayanan, Gayathri II-513
Angra, Ananya II-461
Ankita I-494, II-140
Apanasovich, Kirill I-391
Aravindakshan, Rajeev I-590
Arya, Lalaram I-222, II-258
Ashish Khuraishi, K. S. II-173
Axyonov, Alexandr I-18
Aziz, Shahid II-380, II-395

B

Badiger, Sandhya II-164, II-173
Baghel, Shikha I-189
Balatskaya, Lidiya I-601
Bandekar, Jesuraja II-164, II-173
Banerjee, Oindrila I-590
Banerjee, Padmanabha I-233
Bannulmath, Prashant II-195
Basavaraju, Satisha II-182
Basu, Joyanta I-506, II-114
Basu, Tulika I-364, I-506, II-114
Basumatary, Karnalius II-173
Bharati, Puja I-245, I-258, II-529
Bhattacharjee, Mrinmoy I-189, II-437
Blake, John II-59
Blinova, Olga V. I-455
Bogach, Natalia II-59
Bogdanova-Beglarian, Natalia I-322, I-455
Boulianne, Gilles II-73
Boyina, Prasanth Sai II-322

Brahma, Aditya Kiran II-46
Bukreeva, Liudmila I-68, II-357

C

Chandra Mohan, Bhuma I-611
Chandra, Sabyasachi I-245, I-258, II-529
Chanu, Yamben Jina II-114
Charola, Monil I-579, II-421
Chowdhury, Amartya Roy I-32, II-127, II-195
Coelho, Sharal I-565

D

Das Mandal, Shyamal Kumar I-245, I-258
Dasare, Ashwini II-127, II-182
Date, Gauri II-173
Deekshitha, G. II-164, II-173
Deepak, K. T. II-127, II-182, II-195
Deshpande, Gauri II-3
Deshpande, Pallavi II-3
Dhar, Sandipan I-233
Dihingia, Leena II-195
Dileep, A. D. II-461, II-475
Dolgushin, Mikhail I-68, II-357
Dubey, Akhilesh Kumar I-590
Dwivedi, Priyanka II-114

E

Evdokimova, Vera I-68, II-357

F

Fadte, Swapnil II-231
Fathan, Abderrahim II-307, II-446, II-550
Frolova, Olga I-469, I-535

G

Gafiaytova, Elzara I-430
Ganesh, Mirishkar Sai I-130
Gangashetty, Suryakanth V. I-590
Ganji, Sreeram II-367
Garera, Nikesh II-151
Ghosh, Krishnendu I-415

A. Karpov et al. (Eds.): SPECOM 2023, LNAI 14338, pp. 639–642, 2023.
https://doi.org/10.1007/978-3-031-48309-7

Ghosh, Prasanta Kumar I-339, II-164, II-173, II-208
Ghosh, Subhayu I-233
Gogoi, Parismita I-94
Gohil, Raj II-490
Gorbyleva, Anastasia I-380
Goswami, Urvashi II-475
Gosztolya, Gábor I-79
Gothi, Raj I-57
Govind, D. I-590
Grave, Platon I-469
Grechanyi, Severin I-535
Gupta, Bhaskar I-364
Gupta, Ishika II-243
Gupta, Priyanka II-335
Gupta, Rohan Kumar I-626
Gupta, Shivang II-503
Gupta, Vishwa II-73
Guseva, Daria I-68, II-357

H
H., Muralikrishna II-461
Hora, Baveet Singh I-116

I
Ilyas, Abylay I-469
Iriskhanova, Olga I-350
Iskhakova, Anastasia I-271
Ivanko, Denis I-18

J
Jain, Shelly I-339
Jaiswal, Rahul II-271
Jana, Nanda Dulal I-233
Jayakumar, Anjali II-164
Joshi, Anuradha Rajiv II-3
Joshi, Raviraj II-151

K
Kachhi, Aastha I-550, II-407
Kagirov, Ildar II-87
Kamble, Madhu R. II-490
Karpov, Alexey I-18
Karthika, P. II-173
Karuna, Kasturi II-46
Kashevnik, Alexey I-18
Kathania, Hemant Kumar I-483, I-494
Kaur, Navneet II-208
Kaustubh, Kumar I-94

Khadse, Parth Sanjay I-258
Khan, Soma I-506
Khaustov, Victor II-59
Khaustova, Veronica II-59
Khmelev, Nikita I-159
Khokhlova, Maria V. I-455
Kiose, Maria I-350
Kipyatkova, Irina II-87
Kleshnev, Egor I-469
Kochetkova, Uliana I-301
Kolobov, Rostislav I-43
Komalova, Liliya I-402
Kopparapu, Sunil Kumar I-210, II-32
Kostyuchenko, Evgeny I-107, I-601
Koushik, A. Sai Chandra II-182
Krivoshein, Ilya I-601
Kumar, Avinash I-494
Kumar, Devesh I-142
Kumar, Hitesh II-164
Kumar, Ravi II-503
Kumar, Saurabh II-164, II-173
Kumar, Udara Laxman I-483
Kumar, Vuppala Anil I-130
Kuriakose, Punnoose I-169
Kurimo, Mikko I-483
Kuryanova, Irina I-287

L
Lalhminghlui, Wendy I-314
Laptev, Pavel I-107
Lavrentyeva, Galina I-159
Leonteva, Anna I-350
Litovkin, Sergey I-107
Lokhandwala, Seema II-367
Lyakso, Elena I-469, I-535

M
Mahanta, Shakuntala II-222
Makhnytkina, Olesia I-391, I-469, I-535
Mallela, Jhansi II-322
Manche, Pavanitha II-513
Mandal, Sandipan I-415
Mandal, Shyamal Kumar Das II-529
Mary Mekala, A. I-469
Matveev, Anton I-535
Matveev, Yuri I-391, I-535
Mehta, Arjun Singh II-173
Menon, Aditya Srinivas II-127
Meshcheryakov, Roman I-271

Mikhaylovskiy, Nikolay   I-43
Mirishkar, Sai Ganesh   II-503
Mishra, Jagabandhu   I-142, II-100, II-437,
   II-513
Misra, Hemant   II-46
Monteiro, Sean   II-461
Mora, Sai Praneeth Reddy   II-173
Motepalli, Kowshik Siva Sai   II-503
Mukherjee, Sougata   II-100
Muralikrishna, H.   II-475
Murthy, Hema A.   II-243

N

Nanavati, Jai   II-173
Nanavati, Raoul   II-173
Nandakishor, Salam   II-344
Nanduri, Sai Kalyan   I-442
Nandyala, Sahaja   II-513
Narasinga, Vamsi   II-503
Nersisson, Ruban   I-469, I-535
Nikolaev, Aleksandr   I-469, I-535
Novokhrestova, Dariya   I-601
Novoselov, Sergey   I-159

O

Obotnina, Vasilisa   I-68, II-357
Odetti, Nanci   I-3
Oza, S. K.   II-3

P

Pai, Priyanka   II-173
Pailla, Balakrishna   II-367
Pal, Madhab   I-506
Pal, Priyanshi   I-339
Pandharipande, Meghna   I-210
Panicker, Sasikumar   I-590
Patel, Anuj   I-245
Patel, Sachin   II-3
Pati, Debadatta   II-344
Patil, Ankur T.   II-335
Patil, Hemant A.   I-116, I-550, I-579, II-283,
   II-295, II-335, II-407, II-421
Pawar, Jyoti D.   II-231
Peralta, Ivan   I-3
Petrov, Andrey   I-350
Phatnani, Kirtana Sunil   II-283
Pipariya, Kishan   II-529
Potapov, Vsevolod   I-287
Potapova, Rodmonga   I-287

Pradhan, Gayadhar   I-520
Pramanik, Debolina   I-258, II-529
Prasad, G. Satya   I-245, I-258
Prasanna, S. R. Mahadeva   I-32, I-94, I-142,
   I-189, I-222, II-100, II-127, II-195,
   II-258, II-437, II-513, II-539
Prashanthi, V.   II-173
Priya, Anu   II-271
Pushp, Shivesh   II-395
Pusuluri, Aditya   II-407
Pyshkin, Evgeny   II-59

R

Raghavan, Srinivasa   II-173
Raj, B. Sai   II-182
Rajan, Padmanabhan   I-177
Rajasekhar, Gnana Praveen   II-18
Rajesh, Krishna K. S   II-490
Rajkhowa, Tonmoy   I-32
Rangappa, Pradeep   II-46
Ranjan, Snehal   I-442
Rao, Preeti   I-57
Rathod, Siddharth   I-579, II-421
Reddy, B. Lohith   II-182
Redkar, Hanumant   II-231
Reshma, K.   I-590
Rohith, V. Krishna Sai   II-182
Rout, Jayant Kumar   I-520
Roy Chowdhury, Amartya   II-258
Roy, Nilay   I-415
Roy, Rajib   I-506, II-114
Rufiner, Hugo L.   I-3
Ryumin, Dmitry   I-18
Ryumina, Elena   I-18

S

Sabu, Kamini   I-200, II-490
Sadashiv T. N., Rishith   I-142, II-539
Saha, Arup   I-364
Saikia, Krisangi   II-222
Sarkar, Achintya Kr.   II-114
Sarmah, Priyankoo   I-314
Schuller, Björn W.   II-3
Shahnawazuddin, Syed   I-494, II-140,
   II-380, II-395
Shaik, M.   I-200
Shaik, M. Ali Basha   II-490
Shambhavi   II-140
Sharma, Mukesh   I-200

Sharma, Neeraj Kumar I-314
Shashirekha, Hosahalli Lakshmaiah I-565
Sheikh, Tehreem II-195
Sherstinova, Tatiana I-43, I-455
Simha, Narasinga Vamshi Raghu I-130
Singh, Abhayjeet II-164, II-173
Sinha, Rohit I-626, II-367
Skrelin, Pavel I-301
Solnyshkina, Marina I-430
Solovyev, Valery I-430
Stoika, Daria I-322
Sun, Xiaoli I-322

T
Thenkanidiyoor, Veena II-461, II-475
Tiwari, Nitya I-200
Tongbram, Michael II-114
Turovsky, Yaroslav I-271
Tyagi, Akansha I-177
Tzudir, Moakala I-142, II-539

U
Udupa, Sathvik II-164, II-173
Uthiraa, S. I-116, I-550, II-295

W
Wolf, Daniyar I-271

V
Vahrusheva, Alexandra I-430
Varalakshmi, M. I-469
Vasileva, Polina I-301
Vayyavuru, Venkatesh II-46
Vaz Fernandes, Edna II-231
Vetráb, Mercedes I-79
Vikram, C. M. II-490
Virdi, Prakul I-442
Viswanathan, Ramya II-490
Volkova, Marina I-159
Volokhov, Vladimir I-159
Vupalla, Anil Kumar I-339
Vuppala, Anil Kumar II-503

Y
Yadav, Rishi II-46
Yarra, Chiranjeevi I-339, I-442, II-322

Z
Zaides, Kristina I-322
Zhu, Xiaolin II-446

Printed in the United States
by Baker & Taylor Publisher Services